Intersubjective Communication and Emotion in Early Ontogeny

The concept of 'intersubjectivity', explicit or implicit, has emerged as a common denominator in approaches to interpersonal engagements in early infancy and children's understanding of others' thought and emotion. This book brings together for the first time some of the most senior international figures in psychology, psychopathology, sociology, primatology and neuroethology to address the key question of the role of intersubjectivity in early ontogeny. Together, they offer a new understanding of child development, learning and communication and important comparisons with processes in autism and in infant ape development. Theory and findings are integrated in the following domains: intersubjective attunement in human infancy; companionship and emotional responsiveness in early childhood; imitation, emotion and understanding in primate communication; and intersubjective attunement and emotion in language learning and language use. The book is an invaluable resource for researchers in emotion and communication across the social and behavioural sciences.

Stein Bråten is Professor of Sociology at the University of Oslo and Chairman of the Theory Forum on the Foundations of Intersubjective Communication, Centre for Advanced Study at the Norwegian Academy of Science and Letters.

STUDIES IN EMOTION AND SOCIAL INTERACTION
Second Series

This series is jointly published by the Cambridge University Press and the Editions de la Maison des Sciences de l'Homme, as part of the joint publishing agreement established in 1977 between the Fondation de la Maison des Sciences de l'Homme and the Syndics of the Cambridge University Press.

Cette collection est publiée co-édition par Cambridge University Press et les Editions de la Maison des Sciences de l'Homme. Elle s'intègre dans le programme de co-édition établi en 1977 par la Fondation de la Maison des Sciences de l'Homme et les Syndics de Cambridge University Press.

Titles published in the Second Series:

The Psychology of Facial Expression
0 521 49667 5 Hardback and 0 521 58796 4 Paperback
Edited by James A. Russell and José Miguel Fernández-Dols

Emotions, the Social Bond, and Human Reality: Part/Whole Analysis
0 521 58491 4 Hardback and 0 521 58545 7 Paperback
Thomas J. Scheff

For a list of titles in the First Series in Emotion and Social Interaction, see the page following the index.

Intersubjective Communication and Emotion in Early Ontogeny

Edited by

Stein Bråten

CAMBRIDGE
UNIVERSITY PRESS

Editions de la Maison des Sciences de l'Homme
Paris

CAMBRIDGE UNIVERSITY PRESS
Cambridge, New York, Melbourne, Madrid, Cape Town, Singapore, São Paulo

With Editions de la Maison des Sciences de l'Homme
54 Boulevard Raspail, 75270 Paris Cedex 06, France

Cambridge University Press
The Edinburgh Building, Cambridge CB2 2RU, UK

Published in the United States of America by Cambridge University Press, New York

www.cambridge.org
Information on this title: www.cambridge.org/9780521622578

First published 1998
This digitally printed first paperback version 2006

A catalogue record for this publication is available from the British Library

Library of Congress Cataloguing in Publication data

Intersubjective communication and emotion in early ontogeny / edited
by Stein Bråten.
p. cm. – (Studies in emotion and social interaction. Second
series)
Includes bibliographical references and indexes.
ISBN 0 521 62257 3 (hardcover)
1. Interpersonal communication in infants. 2. Interpersonal
communication in children. 3. Emotions in infants. 4. Emotions in
children. 5. Autism in children. 6. Psychology, comparative.
I. Bråten, Stein. II. Series.
BF720.C65I92 1998
155.4'18–dc21 97–47525 CIP

ISBN-13 978-0-521-62257-8 hardback
ISBN-10 0-521-62257-3 hardback

ISBN-13 978-0-521-02989-6 paperback
ISBN-10 0-521-02989-9 paperback

Contents

Figures

Tables

Contributors

Nameera Akhtar, University of California, Santa Cruz, Psychology Department

Kim A. Bard, Emory University, Yerkes Regional Primate Research Center

Patrick Bateson, University of Cambridge, Sub-Department of Animal Behaviour

Julie D. Brown, University of Kent at Canterbury, The Tizard Centre

Stein Bråten, University of Oslo, Department of Sociology and Human Geography

Richard W. Byrne, University of St Andrews, Scottish Primate Research Group, School of Psychology

Judy Dunn, University of London, Institute of Psychiatry

Carolyn Pope Edwards, University of Nebraska, Department of Family Studies

Juan Carlos Gómez, University of St Andrews, Scottish Primate Research Group, School of Psychology

Paul L. Harris, University of Oxford, Department of Experimental Psychology

Mikael Heimann, University of Gothenburg, Department of Psychology and Department of Special Education

R. Peter Hobson, The Tavistock Clinic, Developmental Psychopathology Research Unit

Giannis Kugiumutzakis, University of Crete, Department of Psychology

Patricia K. Kuhl, University of Washington, Department of Speech and Hearing Sciences

Andrew N. Meltzoff, University of Washington, Department of Psychology

M. Keith Moore, University of Washington, Department of Psychology

Lynne Murray, University of Reading, Department of Psychology

Ragnar Rommetveit, University of Oslo, Department of Psychology

Ross A. Thompson, University of Nebraska, Department of Psychology

Michael Tomasello, Emory University, Department of Psychology

Colwyn Trevarthen, University of Edinburgh, Department of Psychology

Andrew Whiten, University of St Andrews, Scottish Primate Research Group, School of Psychology

Preface

This is a source book in virtue of two characteristics. First, the authors are themselves sources of findings and conceptions challenging traditional theories of child development and certain comparative distinctions. Second, taking stock of their findings from complementary positions and proposing testable explanatory principles attuned to these new empirical grounds, they invite new directions for research and theoretical studies for which this book can serve as a cross-disciplinary source of references.

Thanks to the authors' unfailing support of this project from the very beginning, this book can now be offered as a foundation and framework for further research on intersubjective attunement and understanding in early child development and pertinent comparative domains. The project crystallized when some of us (Patrick Bateson, Judy Dunn, Andrew Meltzoff, Andrew Whiten and I) were invited to a King's College Research Centre Workshop on the Perception of Subjects and Objects, in Cambridge, September 1992. There, they asked Andrew Meltzoff and me to open by dialogue the general discussion on intersubjectivity. I realized then that the time was ripe for a source book integrating theory and findings from complementary perspectives.

The invited authors met – many of them for the first time – in August 1994, in a preparatory symposium in the Norwegian Academy of Science and Letters, Oslo. Some of them (Carolyn Edwards, Mikael Heimann, Ragnar Rommetveit and Colwyn Trevarthen) followed up by joining my group in the Academy's Centre for Advanced Study in the academic year 1996–7, and some others (Paul Harris, Patricia Kuhl and Andrew Meltzoff) by joining us for workshops or a briefer stay in that period.

Among the authors, I owe special thanks to Colwyn Trevarthen for many lively conversations and disputes. We first met in August 1987 at a workshop on Intersubjective Communication, Department of Cognitive Psychology, University of Bergen, which I organized (with Tordis Dallan Evans) upon my arrival there as invited professor of cognitive science. We were both delighted, I think, to discover the fit between his findings on infant intersubjectivity and my dialogical systems postulate of an inborn virtual other. Only much later did we realize our disagreement on whether or not there is a higher-order level of mental simulation of other minds, which I had proposed in the seventies. Our fruitful disputes in this respect have sharpened my intention with this book: to invite dialogue between conflicting positions, examining whether in the end they may reveal themselves to be complementary. That pertains, for example, to the gap between the social-emotional *communicative* perspective and the social-cognitive *mindreading* perspective. This book purports to bridge some of that gap by providing for the first time a comprehensive examination from *both* these perspectives of the nature, nurture and perturbation of intersubjective attunement and understanding in early child development and pertinent comparative domains.

Through all the stages of preparation and finalizing of this book I have had unfailing support, including finance, from these institutions with which I am associated: the Department of Sociology and Human Geography, and the Faculty of Social Sciences, University of Oslo; the Norwegian Academy of Science and Letters, and its Centre for Advanced Study, Oslo. In addition, I gratefully acknowledge financial support of the preparatory symposium from the Norwegian Research Council Program for Youth Research (UNGFORSK). In organizing that meeting I would also like to thank my colleagues at the University of Oslo and fellow members of the Theory Forum network's organizing and reference group: Jon Roar Björkvold, Rolv Blakar, Dagfinn Föllesdal, Signe Howell, Karsten Hundeide, Inge Lönning and Ragnar Rommetveit.

I am also grateful to Susan Powers, University of Oslo, for her dedicated efforts in administrative help and in language polishing and printing preparation of the symposium pre-proceedings, and to Rune Engebretsen who, while at the Centre for Advanced Study, found time to assist me in the language polishing of chapter 5 of this book, teaching me in the process to appreciate the music in the English language. I would like to thank the Cambridge University Press commissioning editor, Catherine Max, as well as the publisher's series editors and evaluators, for valuable advice, including desiderata on volume size, which has been a challenge in view of the rich source material contained herein. I also thank my research assistant, Anders Nöklestad, for dedicating himself – between our efforts at connectionist explorations of egocentric and altercentric perception – to splendid assistance in the preparation of the book in electronic form.

Stein Bråten
Centre for Advanced Study, Oslo, August 1997

Introduction

Stein Bråten

In recent decades the concept of *intersubjectivity* has emerged – explicit or implicit – as a common denominator of approaches to interpersonal engagements in early infancy and children's understanding of thought and emotion in others. In this source book, seminal authors of new conceptions and empirical findings in conflict with traditional theories of child development and certain comparative distinctions in psychopathology and primatology examine and define the foundations of intersubjective attunement and understanding in early ontogeny. In their examination, at least three meanings of intersubjectivity may be distinguished.

First, there is the immediate, albeit unconventional, sense of *interpersonal communion* (Buber, 1958; Marcel, 1950; Stern, 1985) within and between persons who mutually attend and attune to one another's emotive states and expressions. Trevarthen (1979a), for example, has found 'primary intersubjectivity' in this embodied sense of motivated subject–subject connectivity to characterize dyadic protoconversation in early infancy.

Second, there is the more conventional sense of *joint attention* to objects of reference in a shared domain of extra-linguistic or linguistic conversation (Habermas, 1970; Stout, 1903/1915), for example found by Tomasello (1988) to play a critical role in early language development. This is intersubjectivity in the triangular sense of subject–subject–object *relatedness and aboutness* (Hobson, 1993a) in a shared world of object reference and manipulation.

Third, there is the first- and second-person *reflective and recursive* intersubjectivity in the sense of communicative understanding mediated by (meta)representations, including symbolic references to actual and fictional worlds of imagination or joint pretence, for example by the 2-year-old's declaring 'I a Daddy' (Dunn and Dale, 1984). The capability to draw inferences about intentions, beliefs and feelings in others (Gopnik and Meltzoff, 1997) – probably evoked when communicative understanding is perturbed, and certainly in attempting or discerning deception – indicates a second-order mode involving imagining, simulating or reading the mental states or processes in others (Astington, Harris and Olson, 1988; Bråten, 1974; Humphrey, 1984; Whiten, 1991).

From their different positions and foci, the contributors to this volume examine the nature, nurture and perturbation of intersubjectivity in the above meanings.

Examples of findings by the source book authors inviting a new understanding

These authors are sources of experimental, ethological and cross-cultural findings and models inviting a new understanding of the foundations of intersubjective communication and emotion in child development and in the comparative domains of psychopathology, neuroethology and animal communication. They take stock of their experimental, ethological and cross-cultural findings and propose reconceptualizations and testable and tested explanatory principles attuned to the empirical grounds that have emerged in the recent decades from their research. That comprises *inter alia* studies of infants' attunement to the movements, sounds and emotive expressions of others, studies of children's understanding of others' minds and emotions, studies of autism, and neuroethological and systems modelling of learning in infants and non-human primates.

For example, neonatal imitation has been uncovered by experimental procedures (Kugiumutzakis, 1985b, 1993; Meltzoff and Moore, 1977, 1989; Heimann and Schaller, 1985). Sensitive person-oriented procedures have revealed imitation of sounds and movements even in the first hour after birth (Kugiumutzakis, 1985a; this volume). In the first weeks of life, the reciprocal nature of parent–child interplay, exhibiting mutually attuned emotional expressions and synchronized rhythmic movements, has been documented (Murray, 1980; Murray and Trevarthen, 1985; Trevarthen, 1974a, b). Comparative studies of speech perception in 6-month-old infants reveal them to be culture-sensitive in disregarding distinctions that make no sense in their familiar culture (Kuhl *et al.*, 1992; Kuhl, this volume). These findings have brought into focus the precursory and nurturing role of early intersubjective attunement for sociocognitive development and learning later in infancy (cf. Parts I, II and IV in this volume).

In view of such experimental evidence, traditional questions about young infants' responsiveness have been replaced by questions about the impact of limited responsiveness by caregivers, for example when suffering from postnatal depression, or as studied in perturbed infant–parent communication (Murray, 1980, 1991; this volume). The shaping and differentiating role of early companionship and social-emotional relationships has been highlighted, and studied across families and cultures. For example, empathy and prosocial behaviours have been found in toddlers and shown to decline in some cultures and contexts with age as a function of parental influence (Whiting and Edwards, 1988). Even where prosocial behaviour is rare between siblings, Dunn (1988) has found the second-born 18-month-old to be as likely as a 4-year-old to attempt to comfort a sibling in distress (cf. Part II in this volume).

When children's emotional and social responsiveness to imitate, learn and participate in communicative and pretend activities is compared to subjects with autism, or to non-human primates exhibiting tactical deception, some of the results evoke a re-examination of earlier comparative distinctions (Byrne and Whiten, 1988, 1991; Gómez *et al.*, 1993a; Hobson, 1993; Tomasello *et al.*, 1993). For example, Bard (this volume) reports emotional and imitational responsiveness to foster parents by newborn chimpanzees, while Byrne and Byrne (1993) have found that young wild mountain gorillas learn complex feeding skills from their elders, inviting a redefinition of levels in imitative learning (cf. Part III in this volume).

As for the human species-specific capacities for cultural learning, speech and dialogue, laboratory studies in the first six months of infancy have uncovered prespeech efforts, as well as attentive and discriminative attunement to speech patterns in the familiar linguistic culture (Kuhl *et al.*, 1992; Kuhl and Meltzoff, 1982; Trevarthen, 1990b). Children's acquisition of emotional word meanings (Rommetveit, 1968; Rommetveit and Hundeide, 1967), beginning in the second year to predicate (Akhtar and Tomasello, this volume) and to participate in joint pretence (Dunn and Dale, 1984; Harris, 1994b), indicates an intersubjective basis for the development of symbolic and dialogical thought, retaining an emotive accompaniment even in adult fiction and discourse (cf. Part IV in this volume).

Authors of such pertinent findings join in this book with proponents of models and comparative distinctions from pathology and primate studies to take stock of results, to examine potential mechanisms and ontogenetic implications from their different positions, and to propose reconceptualizations attuned to the emerging empirical landscape which they have helped to reshape.

Organization of the book

The volume's organization reflects to some degree the circular or spiral structure of interaction between natural, nurtural and cultural factors in communicative development and intersubjective understanding. Maintaining a sequential progression, consistent with the subject of development, the chapters are grouped in four parts according to domains and levels of development. In accordance with the interlaced nature of intersubjective communication and emotion, there are also interconnections across the four parts. Thus, the beginning of Part I connects to the beginning of Part II. The last two chapters in Part III connect to Part I, and Part IV recursively closes the circular connection to Part I

Part I recounts and offers explanations of infant attunement to caregiver or experimenter – from neonatal imitation and protoconversation to imitational learning and realization of target intentions from exposure to unrealized acts. Ontogenetic implications are spelt out and possible underlying mechanisms are indicated. The motivational or emotional nature of such early intersubjective attunement is emphasized, as are results that demonstrate the communicative and identity-probing role of imitation in human infancy, and infants' capacity for participation in others, compared to subjects with autism.

Part II focuses on the development of empathy and emotional understanding in children, and on the role that companionship and local cultural conditions play in the nurturing and hampering of prosocial tendencies and caring behaviours towards others in need. The reciprocal nature of early mother–child interplay is demonstrated. The possible impact of lack of responsiveness by the caregiver, caused by postnatal maternal depression, is studied. Here is further examined how differences of interpersonal relationships make an individual difference in children's understanding of others.

Part III examines communication, imitation and the development of understanding in normal children, in children with autism, and in non-human primates. Perspectives are brought to bear from neuroethological modelling and from concepts of mindreading or theory of mind. Domains for such concepts of children's social-cognitive understanding of others are partly distinguished from the social-emotional domains of infant intersubjectivity. Studies of emotional responsiveness to learn in young chimpanzees are reported, and implications are spelt out for learning by imitation entailed by the discovery of complex feeding skills in mountain gorillas.

Part IV examines the intersubjective foundations of thought and linguistic attunement, including early speech perception and emotional response to fiction. Here are reported findings of early intersubjective attunement to human speech patterns, from subsequent studies in the quest for underlying operational mechanisms, and from the use of new methods to elicit joint attention and intersubjective understanding in early language learning. The emphasis on dialogicity and intersubjective attunement in adult language usage and discourse returns to the levels of intersubjectivity, introduced in Part I, supporting operation at higher levels (cf. the concluding chapter).

From the history of ideas and findings

When considered together, the various parts of this volume offer a corrective to traditional theories of child development advanced earlier in this century, and reactivate certain pertinent questions raised at the end of the last century.

For example, in *The expression of emotion in man and animals*, Darwin (1872), who approaches emotional expression as a form of communication, finds similarities across human cultures, and raises the possibility of some common innate basis for emotional communication in children. Reporting, for example, how his 6-month-old son once immediately reproduced his nurse's sad expression, Darwin speculates about the possibility of an innate basis for the imitation of facial gestures. About 100 years later, laboratory results on neonatal imitation confirm his speculations (cf. Part I in this volume), and comparative and cross-cultural studies revive this concern with emotional responsiveness and communication (cf. Parts II and III).

Baldwin (1895) reformulates and reduces in terms of motor attitudes Darwin's principles of emotional expressions. Searching for a common denominator for ontogeny and phylogeny that would allow the principle of natural selection to be supplemented by mechanisms of communication and adjustment, Baldwin arrives at the concept of the self-repeating *circular reaction* (which Piaget adopts and adapts). Motions that are felt to be pleasant are reinforced through fine-tuning and repetition. Baldwin proposes that the infant's consciousness is infused with emotion, and that infants are able to feel what others are feeling by imitating their movements. Discarding a report (from Preyer) about imitation in 3-month-olds, he presents his model of manual gestural imitation in one of a series of articles in *Science*.

The discovery of neonatal imitation

Eighty-six years later, experimental results on neonatal imitation of manual and facial gestures were reported in the same journal. The Meltzoff-Moore results on neonatal imitation were at first met with scepticism – and with outright rejection by those who failed to replicate their findings. But gradually, replicative evidence began to accumulate from a number of laboratories around the world, including Kugiumutzakis' records of imitation in 30-minute-olds. Meltzoff and Moore expanded their studies, for example by modelling novel movements to neonates as young as 42 minutes and by studying imitative learning throughout infancy. With their demonstration of how innate releasing mechanisms fail to account for the results, and their proposal of a representational space that enables *active intermodal matching*, the quest for explanatory mechanisms had begun. The role of imitation in children's learning and communicative development again came into focus (cf. Parts I and III in this volume).

Baldwin's point about imitation as a confusion between own and others' activities is taken up by Piaget (1926/1959) in his seminal book *The language and the thought of the child*. Here Piaget is also influenced by the Freudian attribution of an autistic-like autonomy to newborn infants (cf. Freud's (1911) metaphor of a bird's egg and his use of Bleuler's term). This attribution of 'normal autism', which Freud later abandoned, and which was falsified by Anna Freud's studies of young wartime children, came to be retained in some versions of Object Relations Theory. But a breakaway was signalled by Winnicott's (1953) discovery of infants' creative re-enactment of emotional communication by means of 'transitional objects'. In his theory, Piaget assumes an 'ego-centric' attitude and 'autistic thinking' as points of departure for higher-order stages. He thereby implies that the ontogenetic path towards intersubjectivity can only come by way of *decentration*.

Intersubjectivity and the discovery of protoconversation

Piaget's auto-centric point of departure was contested by Vygotsky (1934) who insisted, like G. H. Mead (1934/1986), upon the primacy of the interpersonal in the ontogeny of thought and language. For Vygotsky, occurrences of so-called 'ego-centric speech' are merely outward manifestations of the internal dialogue that characterizes thinking in problem-solving contexts. Mead points to the phylogenetic path from 'conversation by gestures' among animals and to children's ontogenetic path from inter-play to symbolic understanding of others by means of a developed generalized other. This is partly reflected in Rommetveit's (1968, 1974, 1990) approach to speech acts in terms of an intersubjective architecture that also opens for emotional aspects in the learning of word meanings. Neither Vygotsky nor Mead, however, addressed the theoretical issue of how the nurtured acquisition of such higher-order means for mediational intersubjectivity would require a primary socioemotional capacity to participate affectively in others and learn from them in some unmediated mode of felt immediacy (Bråten, 1986, 1988a, 1989, 1993).

Such a primary capacity was to be documented in Mary Catherine Bateson's (1975) analyses of what she termed 'protoconversation' and in Trevarthen's (1974a, 1977, 1979a) descriptive analyses of infant–adult communication in terms of *infant intersubjectivity.* Informed by his brain research and on the basis of his micro-analyses of protoconversations with 2-month-olds, Trevarthen (1974a, 1980) assumes the infant to be endowed with a cerebral system that enables direct alteroception and responsive attunement in delicate, emotionally regulated engagements with supportive others. This innate capacity for early subject–subject engagements he terms 'primary intersubjectivity'. Here again, as befits science, we have a case of initial scepticism and rejection of an attribution which breaks radically with the auto- and ego-centric assumptions in Freudian and Piagetian traditions. Guided by philosophers' use of the term 'intersubjectivity', many infant researchers found it difficult to apply Trevarthen's term to early engagements before the infant could share in joint attention to some object besides the other subject, which Trevarthen and Hubley (1978) term 'secondary intersubjectivity'. For example, Tomasello *et al.* (1993) point to joint attention as the critical criterion, and Stern (1985), demonstrating the critical role of 'affect attunement' in early mother–child communion, reserves the term 'intersubjective relatedness' for 7 to 9 months of age. The pivotal point of infant intersubjectivity theory, however, is that the mutual subject–subject attunement in earlier infant–adult engagements, attending one another's states, has that same motivational and emotionally regulated character of shared understanding of the other's intentional states as when, later in infancy, they can jointly turn to states of affairs in their surroundings.

The advance of theories of children's theory or simulation of other minds

The above focus on emotionally regulated intersubjective attunement contrasts with the cognitive focus of approaches to the understanding and deception of others in terms of children's theory of mind or their ability to imagine or simulate mental states in others. In its various versions, some of which employ computational metaphors, the focus here is on social-cognitive abilities to imagine or simulate others' minds and emotions (the simulation version of the 'theory of mind'), or to draw inferences from a theory of other minds (the theory version of the 'theory of mind'). Thus, the understanding of others' cognitive and emotional states is assumed to be mediated by a model or theory of other minds, or in virtue of imaginative or simulation processes

(Astington *et al.*, 1988; Brown and Dunn, 1991; Butterworth *et al.*, 1991; Dunn, 1988; Harris, 1989). Two different versions of this family of theories have been voiced. According to the theory version, children develop and employ a folk-psychological theory which they use for inferences, prediction and explanation of other people's minds (Gopnik and Wellman, 1995). Proponents differ with regard to learning and maturation. Leslie (1988:41), for example, speaks of the 'innate basis of theory of mind', while Gopnik and Meltzoff (1993) point to infant imitation as a 'theory-of-mind' tutorial. According to the mental simulation version (Goldman, 1989; Gordon, 1986; Harris, 1991) children imagine or simulate other's thoughts or emotions, putting themselves, as it were, in the shoes of the other.

In the social semantics of speech acts, similar ideas have been proposed by Grice (1975) and in Bråten's (1973, 1974) cybernetic model of mental 'co-actor simulation', influenced by G. H. Mead (1934) and explored in computer simulations and laboratory studies of perturbed dialogues in which interlocutors falsely believe they share the same definition of the task situation. While this seemed to evoke mental simulation of understanding from the other's perspective as a late or last resort, such a mode appeared to be insufficient for resolving such perturbed situations.

Another matter is that of employing such a mode in deception, one of the key empirical issues for the concept of 'theory of mind'. The concept came independently into prominence when applied to young children's understanding, and to the comparative domains of autism and primate behaviour (Baron-Cohen *et al.*, 1993; Leslie, 1988; Premack and Woodruff, 1978). This has evoked extensive debates, reflected *inter alia* by the distinction of fundamental issues by Whiten and Perner (1991) in terms of 'mindreading'. Harris (1991), for example, argues that children's mindreading should be seen in analogue with the biographer's imagination rather than the cognitive scientist's psychological theory. According to Harris (1989, 1994b) the child can understand emotions in others by mental simulation of their feeling states, and can understand pretend actions without needing a 'theory of mind'. Harris and Gross (1988) explain the ability of 6-year-olds to distinguish between feeling states and emotional expressions in terms of the same kinds of recursive processes that are involved in deception. Byrne and Whiten (1991) do not hesitate to talk of computation and mindreading in tactical deception by non-human primates.

The question 'Does the chimpanzee have a "theory of mind"?' was later echoed in the same format with regard to autism and answered in the negative (Baron-Cohen *et al.*, 1993). As stated by Leslie, should it turn out that the logical machinery for pretence is fundamentally impaired, this will suggest a serious neurodevelopmental problem in autism – 'one that tragically strikes at the innate basis of theory of mind' (Leslie, 1988:41).

Two controversial issues inviting continuing dialogue

Between social-emotive and theory-of-mind positions

To this theory-of-mind position Hobson (1991a, 1993c) has strongly objected. In his theory, deficits in autism stem not from any logical deficiency but rather from an impairment in the innate capacity to interact emotionally with others. Arguing against the view that children develop a 'theory' about other people's minds, Hobson emphasizes that their understanding of other persons is grounded in their capacity for personal relatedness, partly constituted by innately determined perceptual-affective sensibilities towards the bodily appearance and behaviour of others. Hobson's position is congenial to how Trevarthen (1986) specifies in terms of 'alteroception' the innate motivational ground for intersubjective attunement in early infancy, consistent with Bråten's (1986) independent postulate of an innate 'virtual other' that complements the bodily self and enables (proto)-dialogic closure and 'altercentric participation' in the mode of felt immediacy – as distinct from higher-order mediation by mental simulation.

The nature and nurture of intersubjectivity is one of the fundamental issues with regard to which the contributors to this volume have taken different stands. Some have voiced positions (*P*) emphasizing the social-emotional nature of intersubjective attunement. Others have leaned towards (*Q*) positions emphasizing social-cognitive intersubjective understanding in virtue of mindreading, mental simulation or a 'theory of mind'. Yet others have rather reflected a complementary *R*(*P*,*Q*) position, pointing to a dialogical path of complementary capabilities in ontogeny, in which early bodily attunement and social-emotional communication is a precursory or enduring basis for higher-order capabilities. These different positions, being partly in the process of being transcended in this book, are reflected in Table 0.1.

By providing an intersubjective space in which these different perspectives are given room to be articulated in relation to one another, this book invites a dialogue – in the authors and the readers – to examine whether one can bridge or transcend the gap prevailing between the *communicative* (*P*) perspective, with its focus on social-emotional connectivity, and the *mindreading* (*Q*) perspective, with its

Table 0.1 *Some of the present authors' past foci and views on the nature and nurture of intersubjectivity*

(P) Social-emotive focus on a primary motivational and affective communicative basis	*(Q) Cognitive-oriented focus on perspective-taking, mindreading, mental simulation or theory of mind*	*R(P,Q) Dialogue-oriented foci on complementary (P) and (Q) relations in development*
Trevarthen (1974a, 1979a, 1992) postulates an innate motivational ground for infant intersubjectivity, defining levels of communication in culture in contradistinction to theory-of-mind notions.	Meltzoff and Gopnik (1993) point to a tutorial path from infant imitation (body similarity) to theory of mind (mental similarity), questioning whether others' emotions are directly perceived.	Rommetveit (1968, 1974) defines an intersubjective architecture of speech act understanding, specifying emotional activity as a part process in the act of symbolic reference.
Kugiumutzakis (1988, 1993) emphasizes the emotional nature of the neonatal imitation of gestures and sounds that he has recorded in the first hour after birth.	Dunn (1994) emphasizes how individual differences, reflected *inter alia* by the child's relationships, will make for individual differences in children's collaborative pretence and understanding of other minds.	Harris (1989, 1994a) explains children's emotional understanding by their imagining others' feelings, and how children can engage in pretence without any need of a theory of mind.
Murray (1980) studies with her replay design the socio-emotional sensitivities and expressive capacities of 2-month-old babies in communication with their mothers.	Byrne and Whiten (1988, 1991) report on deliberate tactical deception in non-human primates; Whiten and Perner (1991) define basic issues in theory-of-mind approaches in terms of mindreading.	Gómez (1993) examines the sensitivities of infants and anthropoid apes to conspecifics' expression of emotion, and points to a socio-emotional precursory to children's understanding of mind.
Hobson (1991a) argues against the theory of children's theory of mind from his emphasis on the affective grounds for interpersonal understanding.	Tomasello *et al.* (1993) distinguish levels of cultural learning in terms of simple perspective-taking in imitative learning in infants, representative theory of mind in 4-year-olds, and a mental state language in 6-year-olds.	Bråten (1988a, 1996a) distinguishes the primary mode of engaging with others in felt immediacy from the higher-order mode of mental simulation of processes in the other, evoked upon perturbation of conversation (Bråten, 1973, 1974).

focus on social-cognitive understanding. For example, Kugiumutzakis (this volume) suggests that there are two kinds of processes in harmonious operation already in neonatal imitation, one of conscious deliberation and one of spontaneous emotive connectivity, operating outside the conscious level of volition. Here is a precursory parallel to distinctions made by Bechara *et al.* (1997) and Damasio (1994) in their comparison of adult decision-makers with patients with prefrontal damage and decision-making defects (cf. Bråten, chapter 5, this volume). And in Parts III and IV, Gómez, Hobson, Harris, Rommetveit and Bråten indicate in various ways an ontogenetic path involving *R*(*P*,*Q*) complementarity at higher levels of thought, fiction and discourse, for which underlying modes of felt immediacy and affective relatedness continue to be operative. We are still far from understanding, however, the qualitative jump from early intersubjective attunement in a dyadic and triangular sense to children's higher-order understanding of others' minds and emotions.

Innateness

Another fundamental issue that remains unresolved, inviting rethinking in terms of connectionist perspectives (Elman *et al.*, 1996) and inter-connectionist simulations, concerns innateness. The authors reflect different stands in the nature–nurture controversy, or transcend it by emphasizing mutual influences from the outset.

This issue is raised, for example, by Edwards (this volume) in her discussion about whether children's nurturing behaviour towards other children, exhibited across cultures, arises from innate releasing mechanisms, or is complemented by cultural learning. The question of innate factors in cultural learning was highlighted in a discussion in *Behavioral and Brain Sciences* in which seven of the contributors to this book participated. The authors of the target article, Tomasello *et al.* (1993), prefer to bracket natal factors in the nature–nurture–culture equation of cultural learning. Trying to avoid nativist assumptions, they would like to attribute all novel human behaviours to cultural learning. Quite apart from the human innately overriding predispositions for cultural learning implied by such an attribution, commentators objected: Gopnik and Meltzoff (1993c), for example, point to the apparent innate capacity for connecting the perceived movements of others to one's own internal kinaesthetic sensations that underpins the path from imitation to higher-order connectivity. Trevarthen (1993) emphasizes innate predispositions for reciprocal intersubjective attunement that nurture higher-order abilities, and Bråten (1993) suggests that the innate, not constructed, nature of the learner's virtual other enables from the outset learning by socioemotional participation in actual others.

Bateson (1991) cautions, however, against unqualified attribution of innateness, and demonstrates the variety and complexity of influences and outcomes in the complex developmental behavioural matrix (cf. Fig. 10.1, this volume). This keynote warning from one who has brought neuroethology to maturity, pertains to the quest for possible mechanisms that underlie many of the phenomena uncovered by the contributions to this book. Bateson (1991, this volume) emphasizes the interaction between natural and nurtural factors all the way down to the neurological levels.

The triple helix of nature, nurture and culture in communicative development may never be fully charted, and the interplay of social-emotional and social-cognitive factors in intersubjective attunement and cultural learning may never come to be fully comprehended. Contributing, however, to redefining the landscapes by integrating theory and empirical findings, the authors in this source book point to new paths for further cross-disciplinary studies, and some of them offer falsifiable propositions that invite (dis)confirmation.

PART I

Intersubjective attunement in human infancy and impairment in autism

CHAPTER 1

The concept and foundations of infant intersubjectivity

Colwyn Trevarthen

Introduction

Film observations made around 1970 showed that very young infants sought engagement of expressions with a sympathetic human partner. This finding prompted a search for a satisfying theory of the infant mind.

The concept of intersubjectivity had a natural place in certain philosophical debates on the social context of human consciousness of reality, and concerning moral and religious impulses, shared meaning, and self-consciousness (Jopling, 1993). It related to the unconscious emotional forces in relationships, including relationships of therapy, that psychoanalysts had defined (Kohut, 1977; Stolerow *et al.*, 1983; Sullivan, 1953), and to the feminist challenge to Freudian theory that valued the quest for personal relationships, as opposed to separation or individuation (Benjamin, 1988; Gilligan, 1982). Intersubjectivity is implied in theories of the intended social and cooperative functions of adult speaking (Habermas, 1970; Rommetveit, 1968; Searle, 1969), and it finds application in studies concerned with the 'pragmatic social context' in which language and thought of a young child acquire meaning (Ryan, 1974).

The innate intersubjectivity of infants

All of the above positions are strengthened by realization that the newborn infant already has an effective interpersonal intelligence. Nevertheless, it has been generally assumed, somewhat paradoxically, that human sympathetic consciousness is not a set goal in development, but an acquired skill. The new evidence from infancy was incompatible with this belief. The innateness of the behaviours observed was apparent from the way communication was taken up in direct face-to-face exchanges by an infant a few weeks after birth, and from the emission of effectively coordinated vocal, oral and gestural expression.

On the basis of these observations, the theory of innate intersubjectivity was proposed (Trevarthen, 1974a, 1979a). The claim made, while not questioning that development involves learning or that infants depend on care, underlined that a child is born with motives to find and use the motives of other persons in 'conversational' negotiation of purposes, emotions, experiences and meaning. The efficiency of sympathetic engagement between persons signals the ability of each to 'model' or 'mirror' the motivations and purposes of companions, immediately. It requires a 'virtual other' representation of the kind that Bråten (1988a, 1992) has described. Infants evidently have this.

Advances in cognitive psychology focused experimental psychologists' attention on the physically defined *input* of mental life. The coherent central patterning of a subject's purposeful *output* in attending and intending, the strivings (conations), regulated by emotion, that generate 'experience' (knowledge 'from trying'), were neglected. Infants certainly possess investigative curiosity. When only a few months old, they take part in experiments that measure development of binocular acuity, selective attention, awareness of categories of object that persist in time, remembering of contexts for object recognition, grasp of 'physical' laws of objects with mass that are in motion through a three-dimensional space with holes, barriers, surfaces, etc., discrimination of face patterns and musical and phonological parameters of sounds, and so on, all reported in the infancy literature of the past three decades. Infants instinctively look, feel, listen and learn, and they apply a practical logic in their learning. But this individual knowing and learning is readily prompted and supported from the outset by impulses borrowed from other persons, intersubjectively. This required explaining.

The 'classical' view, and towards a psychology of mutually sensitive minds

The modern scientific concept of the infant has reflected the approach of medical doctors who take responsibility for the delivery and care of the biological immaturity of newborns. But the image of the biological newborn needing 'socialization' to become a person does not apply when attention turns to evidence for complex psychological expressions in the responses of contented healthy newborns to people who take them as persons with intentions and feelings of companionship, and who feel pleasure when an infant responds. Much follows from the more accurate account of what the newborn can do with appropriate human support. We can construct a different psychology of the interpersonal relationships between individuals of all ages, seeing their expressed purposes, interests and feelings as having important meaning and uses of their own – referring directly to the inner subjective personal life, not only to the problematic context of objective reality.

Instead of asking what developing cognition gives to human purposes, we can ask what effect innate human communicative competence has on learning, recognizing and thinking. Instead of asking how language develops from immature utterances by imitation, or instinctive growth of a 'language acquisition device', we can ask in what ways language enriches the infant's already competent non-verbal, presemantic expressions of alert purposiveness and human-sensing emotion, and why the adult finds this rewarding. We can begin to understand what it is that gives our actions moral value, and our words metaphorical meanings with infinite future significance and narrative power. We can even develop a theory of how natural human motives for cooperation in gaining sense of the world and performing cooperative tasks can lead to the scientific, technical and economic activities in our elaborately organized and institutionalized adult society, with its politics and laws (Barnes, 1995).

The idea of infant intersubjectivity is no less than a theory of how human minds, in human bodies, can recognize one another's impulses, intuitively, with or without cognitive or symbolic elaborations (Trevarthen, 1987a).

How research on infants' intersubjective intentions began: theory and observations

The theory of infant intersubjectivity developed by the following steps:

1. The foundation was a recognition of the *coherent intentionality and active consciousness of the infant at birth.* Neonatal experience-seeking motor patterns of looking and visual tracking showed whole-body integration by rhythmic coordination of eyes and head. Newborns were found to couple their hands with head and eyes in 'prereaching' movements, as well as exhibiting hand-to-mouth coordination. They have a cerebral representation of a unified body-centred space/time of eye-hand-mouth behaviours.

2. *One-month-old infants emitted different patterns of behaviour to persons and to objects.* They were observed to listen to and look at persons, directing expressions to them. Two 'volitional states' were defined, one sensitive to reafference induced by the *physical properties of objects*, the other able to detect and interact with *expressed motives or feelings in other persons. 'Doing' with objects*, to 'use' them, and *'communicating' with persons* were neither simply reflections of levels of physiological arousal, nor 'innate release mechanisms' triggered by

'sign stimuli'. Infants appeared sensitive to *dynamic motive patterns* in persons through many modalities, and aware of others' attention directed towards themselves.

3. *In the first six months, communicating with persons develops conversational proficiency or expressive reciprocity before the infants can perform effective manipulation of objects.* 'Protoconversational' motives effectively regulate development and learning before any 'object concept' represents the affordances of physical things for manipulative use or for intellectual contemplation.

4. The *subtle timing and complementary emotional expressions in protoconversations by 2- and 3-month-olds were perceived to be preparatory to linguistic communication,* but to achieve their meaning and their effects in development by exercise of non-linguistic forms of facial, vocal and gestural expression in interaction with partners who offered complementary sympathetic human responses. Rudiments of speech and sign gestures emerge in the early expressive phases.

5. Follow-up through the second 6 months, to the threshold of protolinguistic behaviour, proved that *the different intentions of infants towards persons and objects undergo systematic age-related integrations leading to joint interest in purposes towards objects and events in the shared environment.* After a significant developmental change at 9 months, cooperative task performance becomes both possible and attractive for the infant, who now shows 'person–person–object awareness'.

6. Observations of games generated spontaneously between infants and familiar persons around the middle of the infant's first year indicated that *the playfulness of the infant was guiding family partners into systematic rituals of body expression and vocalization, first in 'person–person games', involving humorous joking and gentle teasing in 'narrative-like' episodes, to animation of toys in 'person–person–object games' in which emotional gestures and sounds were linked with 'serious' attempts to master the objects' affordances for use.* Games with things, by drawing the baby into regulated changes of intention and emotion, evidently prepare for voluntary acceptance of joint interests and purposes in cooperation, and negotiation of new purposes. While, at this age, infants, in familiar company, show 'prestance' or self–other-consciousness and pride in ritualized performances, unfamiliar persons stimulate expressions of anxiety and mistrust.

7. Experiments were initiated to test the emotional responses of infants to perturbation of communication. We became interested in *emotions as regulators of interpersonal contact and relationships,* not just 'state-regulators' of the infant's 'self'. Two-month-old infants were sensitive to the mother's emotions and seeking both sympathetic reciprocity of dynamic motives and appropriate matching of their

feelings by supportive or cooperative reactions. The infants' coordinated positive and negative expressions were comprehended by their mothers as expressions of purposes and feelings.

Steps 1, 2 and 3 were completed at the Center for Cognitive Studies, Harvard, in 1967 and 1968. Subsequent steps were made at Edinburgh after 1971.

Supported by Jerome Bruner's 'Research Program on Intellectual Development' at Harvard University, Martin Richards and I analysed films of sixteen infants from the day after birth to 3 months, and conceived the theory of two purposeful modes: 'doing' with objects and 'communicating' with persons (Fig. 1.1). In August 1967, the new theory was summarized in a statement including the following points:

The two states 'are not arousal states, but more like the "central excitatory" or "integrative" states of the English neurophysiologists' (Sherrington, 1906). 'State adjustment [is] patterning of motions.' Communication involves 'transfer of states of activity between brains . . . the outgoing signal is carried by specific activity patterns' (gestures and vocalizations), each partner 'orienting to and following the messages from the other individual'. In contrast, 'being busy with things, "brain–thing" behaviour, is exploratory and manipulative, following changes provoked by the object'. Later I described the internal regulatory states as 'motives' for individual exploration and cooperative learning (Trevarthen, 1978, 1980, 1982b, 1984a, 1992, 1998a).

With T. Berry Brazelton, Richards and I set up a Two Behaviors Study of three girls and two boys who came for weekly ciné recordings between January and July 1968, from 1 or 2 weeks after birth until they were 6 months of age. We focused on communicative reactions to mothers' expressions, and responses to the presentation of small attractive objects. A mirror behind the infant obtained near full-face pictures of the mother and the infant on each frame (Fig. 1.2). Thus we could see exactly how the interactions progressed – what expressions were made, and how they were timed. Black-and-white silent 16mm films at 16 frames/second were viewed frame by frame. Sound was recorded separately on tape.

We examined the attentive and expressive behaviours of the infant, identifying behaviours for 'doing' and 'communicating'. A third type of motive, inward or self-directed, which we called 'contemplation', received but passing attention. 'Doing' increased after 3 months, as the infants began efficient tracking of objects and attempted reaching to grasp them. It was, we felt, highly significant that a desire for conversation-like communication, as distinct from responding to caregiving and 'state-control', developed before these attempts to

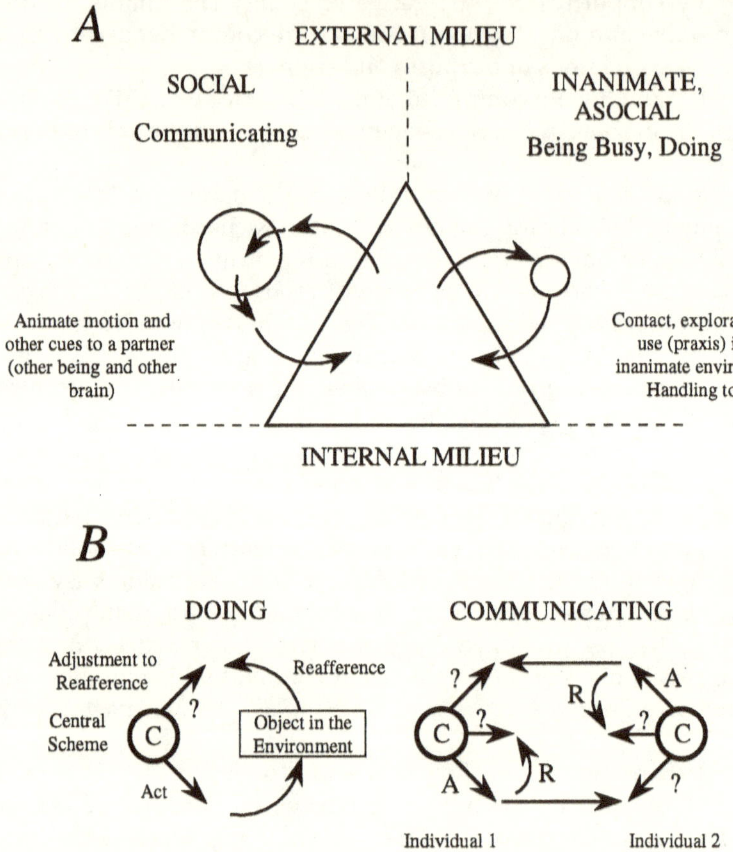

Fig. 1.1 *A*: The formulation of August 1967, representing two modes of 'central excitatory state' by which the subject deals with the external world: *communicating* and *doing*. In communicating, the other subject's central excitations are taken into account. The self-regulations of the subject have three facets: two addressing the external milieu; one facing the internal milieu of the body. *B*: A diagram, also from 1967, of adjustments (?) to reafference (R) generated prospectively with the form of an act (A) by the central motivating scheme (C) in 'doing' and in 'communicating'. In the latter, interactions occur between messages from the other subject's body movements and reafference (R) from the self.

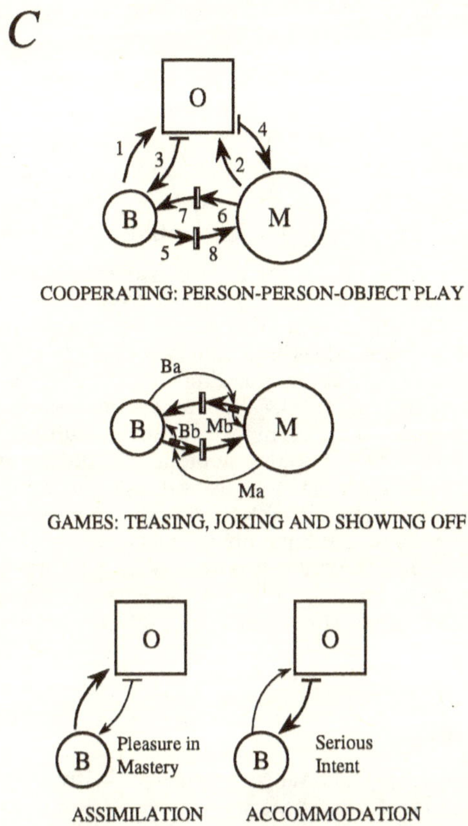

Fig. 1.1 (cont.) *C*: Explanation of how intersubjective regulations and subject–object regulations combine in cooperation (secondary intersubjectivity) between infant (B) and mother (M) (Trevarthen, 1979a; Trevarthen and Hubley, 1978). The infant's experience of an object (1 → 3) and the mother's experience of the same object (2 → 4) are integrated with their communications (5 → 8 + 6 →7). In a co-operative interaction, actions and experiences circulate round the triangle in any order. In teasing and 'showing off' games, the mother may act (Ma) on the baby's expressive or other actions to cause awareness of them to be a goal (Bb). Conversely, the baby may make play (Ba) with the mother's actions and expressions (Mb) (Trevarthen, 1990b). Piaget (1945/1962) noted that 'assimilation' of experience to a strong cognitive scheme, in *play*, is accompanied by expression of 'pleasure in mastery'; 'accommodation', or tracking of an object by a weak scheme, in *imitation*, is performed with expression of 'serious intent'. This distinguishes two phases of voluntary (prospect-controlled) action by their emotional accompaniments, or signals of regulation.

master objects. We knew of no evidence that this behaviour had been studied in infants so young.

Ben Sylvester-Bradley informs me that our idea was certainly not new. G. F. Stout (1903/1915:170) said, in discussing the growth of intersubjective intercourse, that 'from the first there is a marked difference between the child's relations to persons and his relations to inanimate things'. Stout notes that the baby gets a very different response from the two classes of phenomena, continuing:

> The child must interpret the behaviour of others as expressive of a subjective experience like his own . . . As he finds and seeks and learns to count on social cooperation, he not only becomes aware of others as having perceptions, ideas and interests like his own; he becomes aware of them as perceiving, thinking about, and interested in the things which he perceives, thinks about and is interested in . . . He becomes aware of them as concerning themselves with his own wants and requirements, and cooperating with him, for their satisfaction . . . Thus the primitive tendency to regard external things as having an inner being which is the counterpart of our own subjective life, finds in social intercourse a unique field for its development . . . [but] . . . Intersubjective intercourse can only exist in a rudimentary stage before the growth of imitation and language as the vehicle of ideal construction and ideal communication. (Stout, 1903/1915: 172–3)

Intentional contexts for experience

The two *modes of behaviour* (Fig. 1.1) were identified with *intrinsic central activity states*, conceived as entities, 'formed in the nervous system, simultaneously shaping motor output and processing sensory input', integrating 'an *internal context of behaviour*' within the CNS. Each act and each percept is part of such a context.

Studies I made in 1967 of neonatal eye movement, visual tracking and prereaching showed that the infant is born with a 'spatial frame coordinating all acts and experiences in a behavioural space', and 'description of infant behaviour enables one to distinguish separate systems or contexts', defined by the infant's central motive states.

The first public mention of Richards' and my hypothesis of two kinds of behaviour was made by Bruner in his Heinz Werner Lecture at Clark University in 1968. Bruner (1968:56–7) discussed the 'innate predisposition to expect reciprocation [in] specific gestures' (of eye-to-eye contact, smiling, crying and vocalisation), and he described studies of the effects of a non-responding face, including one with Hanus Papousek, on the reactions of young infants to unpredictable disappearance of the mother.

My orientation, encouraged by Bruner's interest in infants'

voluntary actions, was based on experience with Roger Sperry's motor theory of perception (Sperry, 1952), and on his model of 'corollary discharge from efference' (Sperry, 1950), and von Holst's 'Reafferenzprinzip' (von Holst and Mittelstaedt, 1950), the motor physiology of Paillard (1960), and Bernstein's *The coordination and regulation of movements* (1967). I later restated the theory in terms of intersubjective motor control by rhythmic expression, assuming the infant's innate sensitivity to kinematic, energetic and physiognomic parameters of others' movements in *alteroception* (Trevarthen, 1986a).

Discovering protoconversation and the intentions of primary intersubjectivity

Protoconversation, the spontaneous face-to-face interaction between an infant of 2 to 3 months and the mother, by means of patterned vocal, facial and gestural expressions, was discovered in Cambridge, MA by M. C. Bateson. In 1969–72, beginning shortly after giving birth, Bateson studied mother–infant vocal exchanges from films made by Margaret Bullowa, which she analysed in the Research Laboratory of Electronics at MIT (Bateson, 1971, 1975, 1979). She summarized her findings with an infant 7–15 weeks of age, as follows: 'the mother and infant were collaborating in a pattern of more or less alternating, non-overlapping vocalisation, the mother speaking brief sentences and the infant responding with coos and murmurs, together producing a brief joint performance similar to conversation, which I called "protoconversation"' (Bateson, 1979:65). With a background in anthropology and linguistics, and interest in ritual healing and second language learning, Bateson interpreted the infant's behaviour as an innate emotive foundation for language and learning of culture, and for the making of emotionally-regulated, and emotional health-regulating, social bonds.

In 1972, at a meeting on language development organized by Eric Lenneberg, I showed microanalyses of films demonstrating that newborns were coherent in their behaviour, and that expressive movements of the mouth, hands and eyes exhibited matching and coupled rhythms (Trevarthen, 1974b). I suggested that intrinsic rhythmicity was essential to the intercoordination observed in protoconversations. Lenneberg, of course, had long been interested in the time-patterns of animal action and communication (Lenneberg, 1967).

In 1971 Daniel Stern reported a film study he had made in New York of game play at home between $3\frac{1}{2}$-month-old twins and their mother. He emphasized the rhythmic coordination of a multi-channelled expressiveness in both infants and adults. Subsequently,

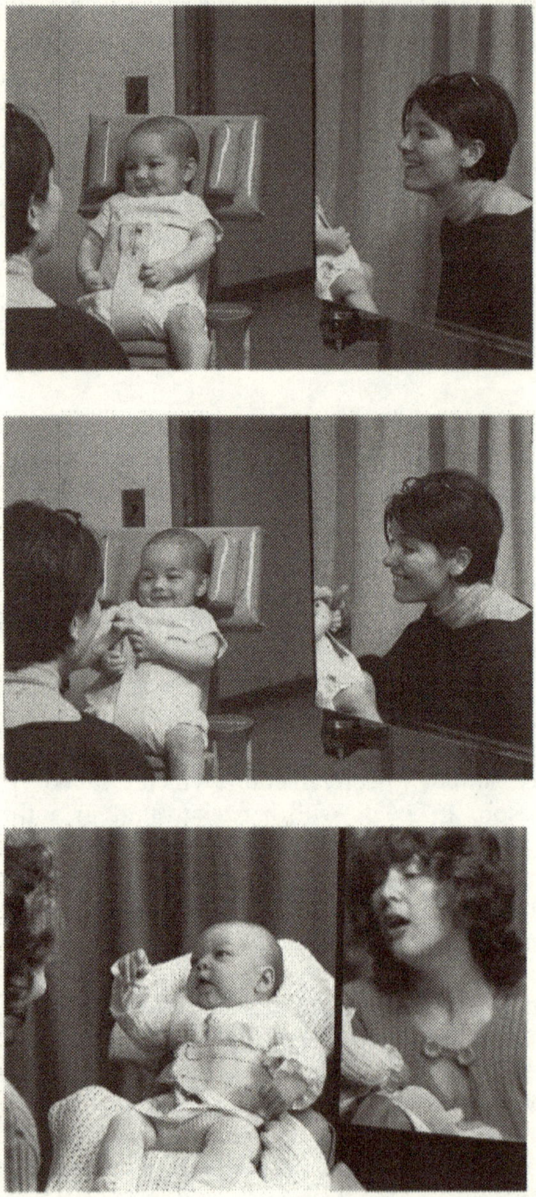

Fig. 1.2 Mother–infant protoconversations and early games. *Top and centre:* Boy JC, 10 weeks, Harvard, 1968. *Bottom*: Girl LP, 6 weeks, Edinburgh, 1979.

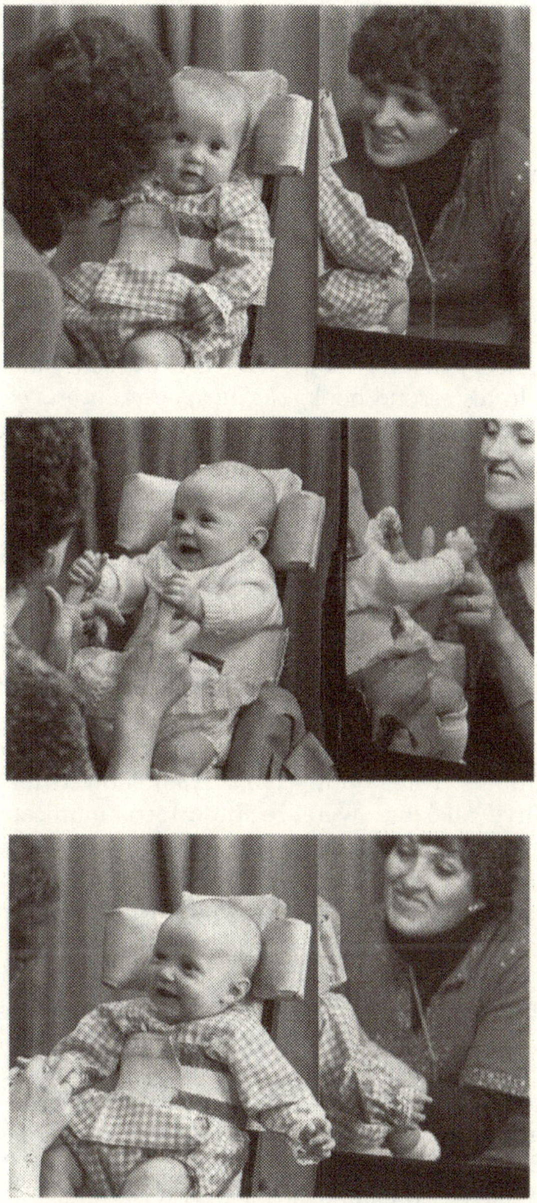

Fig. 1.2 (cont.) Girl LO, looking at her reflection in the mirror surface of the camera window (20 weeks); responding with pleasure to her mother's rhythmic bouncing of her hands (16 weeks); avidly anticipating the ritual of the song with hand tickling, 'Round and round the garden, like a teddy bear'.

with Jaffe, Beebe and others, he confirmed the communicative skills of infants, and, conversant with techniques applied in adult 'conversational analysis', they stressed the importance of *timing* (Beebe *et al.*, 1979, 1985; Jaffe *et al.*, 1973; Stern and Gibbon, 1980; Stern *et al.*, 1975, 1977). Condon, with Sander (1974), showed that newborns could synchronize hand movements to syllables of adult speech in any language. However, this important observation was described as an 'entrainment', suggesting a passive infant, led by the adult.

Stern later studied intonation in mothers' speech to infants (Stern *et al.*, 1982), and used his understanding of early interactions and the 'affect attunements' of the mother (Stern *et al.*, 1985) to challenge the psychoanalytic theory that the infant was born with an undefined and ineffectual self. In his second book, *The interpersonal world of the infant* (1985), Stern precipitated new dialogue between the clinical disciplines and developmental psychology, and marked a major advance in clinical perception of the infant as a person, also aided by sensitive observations of mothers greeting their newborns by Klaus and Kennel (1982). However, Stern then described the neonate's Emergent Self as purely emotional, and did not allow the infant an Intersubjective Self before 7 or 8 months.

Mutual gaze and smiling were known to be features of protoconversation, and to regulate the interpersonal contact (Fig. 1.2). It became increasingly apparent that the infant was not producing single reflex responses, nor was smiling or looking triggered by any identifiable simple sign stimulus. Peter Wolff (1963, 1968) showed that smiling and 'non-nutritive sucking' were reciprocal communicative behaviours from birth. Papousek (1967) recorded that when infants were working in an operant procedure, they made emotional expressions that communicated their cognitive effort and feelings about results 'in a human way'.

The new evidence on social and communicative behaviour of infants was brought out by three books in the late seventies (Bullowa, 1979; Lock, 1978; Schaffer, 1977). In *Before speech* Margaret Bullowa gives a very complete picture of the discoveries of the preceding decade, saying: 'I believe that one of the things which has delayed the study of the earliest human communication is our habit of thinking of communication as consisting mainly of language. Students of language acquisition are just now coming to recognize that to understand child language requires a great deal of attention to pragmatics – to the contexts in which it is used.' This includes, Bullowa (1979:11) says, not only the situation but also all extra-verbal communication. And, on the communicative state, she makes this point: 'For an infant to enter into the sharing of meaning he has to be in communication, which may be another way of saying sharing rhythm' (Bullowa, 1979:15).

In Bullowa's book I described a 'specifically human system for person-to-person communication' appearing long before the infant can speak, but with 'rudiments of speech activity as well' (Trevarthen, 1979a:321). *Prespeech* – i.e. lip and tongue movements resembling adult articulation movements and coupled with expressive head movements, eye movements and hand gestures – was illustrated with pictures of a girl 7 weeks old. I called the expression of individual consciousness and intentionality *subjectivity*, and concluded that, 'In order to communicate, infants must also be able to adapt or fit this subjective control to the subjectivity of others: they must also demonstrate *intersubjectivity*' (p. 322). Details of the infant's protoconversational behaviours in interaction with the mother (Fig. 1.2) were also reported in Schaffer's book (Trevarthen, 1977).

Lock's *Action, gesture and symbol* (1978) brought presentations of a new approach to social pragmatics in infancy. The editor's orientation was in the tradition of social learning theory (Mead, 1934), and sociohistorical explanations (Vygotsky, 1934/1986), adults being given the role of intelligent interpreters of the child's naive reaching out and vocalizing 'as if' these acts were linguistic, transforming 'actions' into 'gestures', and then into 'symbols'. This approach was strongly represented in the work of Newson and Shotter at Nottingham, where important early work was done on imitations and on the role of intersubjectivity in the development of significant gestures (Newson, 1977, 1979; Pawlby, 1977; Shotter, 1974).

The intended imitations and 'provocations' of newborns

Experiments on neonatal imitation reported by Maratos (1973, 1982) proved the sensitivity of infants to the configuration or physiognomy of human expressions. Earlier observations by Zazzo (1957) of young infants imitating were confounded by deference to Piaget's theoretical rejection of all imitation before the 'object concept' around the end of the first year, when infants imitate acts directed to objects. Uzgiris (1981) observed that young infants imitated familiar expressions of communication, and proposed that imitation serves both cognitive and interpersonal functions.

Meltzoff and Moore (1977) substantiated and elaborated Maratos' findings. They offered a theory of 'intermodal equivalence' allied to Bower's interpretations of neonates' awareness of one environment informed by vision, touch and hearing (Bower, 1974). Kugiumutzakis (1983, 1985, 1993) confirmed that neonates, including prematurely

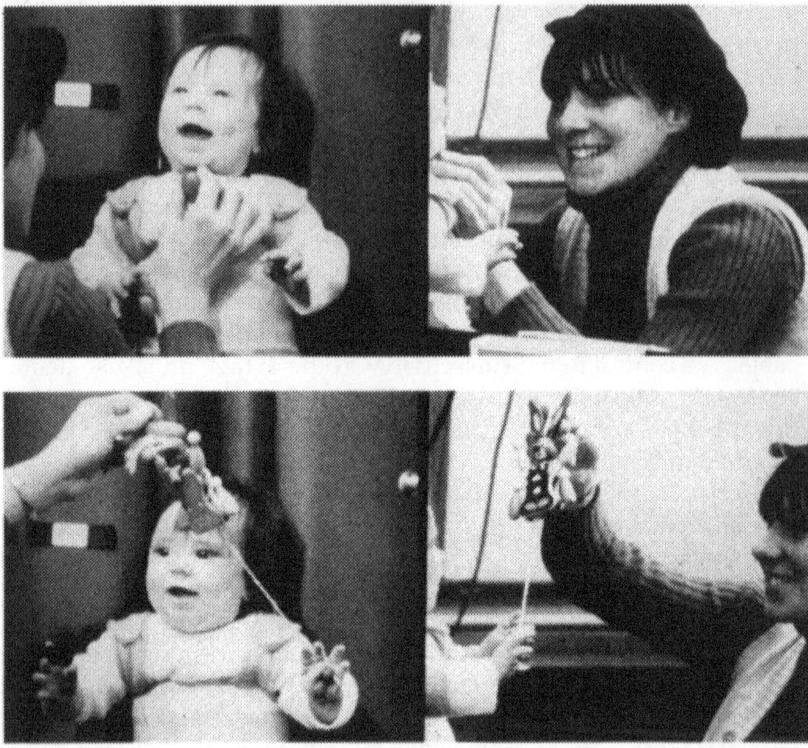

Fig. 1.3 Getting in touch: 'person–person games'. *Left*: Girl TR, Edinburgh, 1974, climax of a teasing ritual in which the mother zooms an object TR wants to grasp, then hits her under the chin. TR watches her mother while pulling the string to make the puppet move. (Trevarthen and Hubley, 1978)

born ones, could imitate actively and intentionally in communication, and he supported Maratos' and Uzgiris' evidence for age-related changes in imitation. Field (Field *et al.*, 1982) and Heimann (Heimann, 1989; Heimann and Schaller, 1985; Heimann *et al.*, 1989) have added to our understanding of the range, variability and development of early imitations.

In protoconversations, it is typical for the mother to imitate more than the infant. I suggested that the process of matching in 'magnetic' imitation by neonates, 'does not necessarily depend on body sensations caused by movement of the limbs or face, or comparison of seen and felt movements, but some kind of adjustment of the "image" of a movement to be made to that of a movement seen must be taking place in the brain. In order to imitate, the infant must have a cerebral

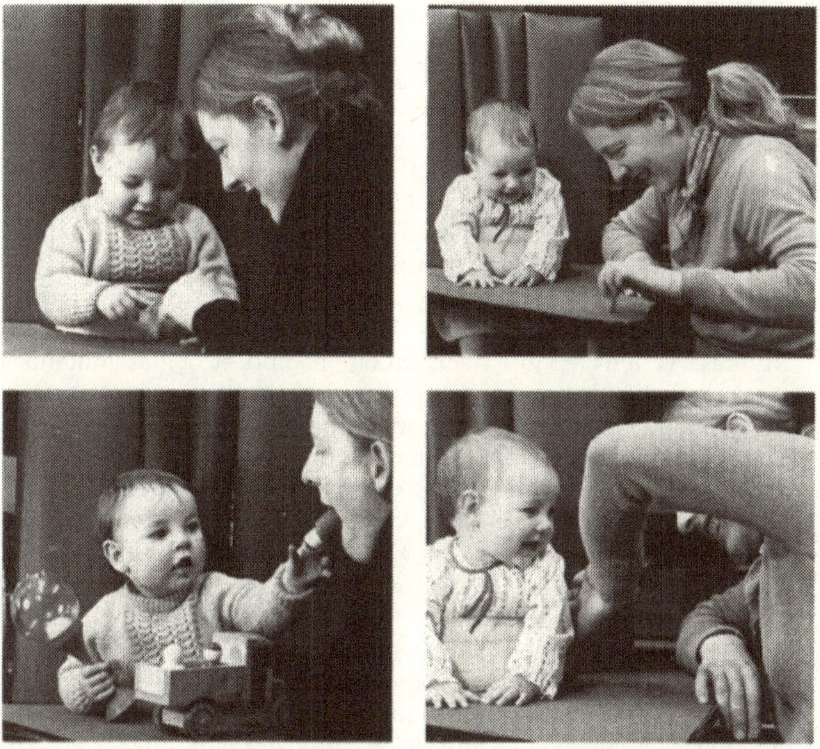

Fig. 1.3 (cont.) *Left*: Girl, 50 weeks, touches fingertips with her mother, and joins in game of putting a toy in her mother's mouth. *Right*: Girl, 8 months, enjoys a variant of 'Round and round the garden' in which her mother creeps towards her over the table, then tickles her under the arm. (Photos, Penelope Hubley; Hubley and Trevarthen, 1979)

representation of persons' (Trevarthen, 1979a:331). Now I would say that the cerebral 'representation' of the 'other' is rooted in a 'motor image' (Di Pelligrino *et al.*, 1992; Jeannerod, 1994; Sperry, 1952) sensitive to both the body-related form and the timing of the movement imitated, and in these respects indifferent to the sensory modality by which the movement is apprehended. A formal theory of how intrinsic pacemakers coordinate body part with body part prospectively by reference to any or all forms of proprioceptive information when a subject is moving without reference to external goals has been developed by Lee *et al.* (1998), and this may offer a key, also, to the problem of what information is critical in intersubjective coordination.

More deliberate 'discretionary' imitations by older infants (Uzgiris, 1981; Trevarthen, 1979a:332), who imitate social expressions in communication games as well as others' actions on objects, watching for the effect on playmates, are more obviously 'studied' and varied to test their communicative effects (Fig. 1.5). The interpretation that even newborns imitate in direct response to other people's motives, perceived in their expressions, is confirmed by Kugiumutzakis' observations on the conditions that favour their imitative responses. Data collected by Kokkinaki in Greece and Scotland amplify this functional explanation, and show how imitative responses to fathers and mothers may differ, how families differ, and how parents' imitations change under the influence of infants' development (Trevarthen, Kokkinaki and Fiamenghi, 1998).

My reservations about 'deliberation' behind neonatal imitations must be qualified by demonstrations of intention in newborns' communication. DeCasper, using instrumental responses, has shown that newborns will work with attentive purposiveness to elicit vocal responses from an audio recording of human speaking, showing preference for their mother's voice, which must have been learned *in utero* (DeCasper and Carstens, 1981; DeCasper and Spence, 1986). Even more remarkable are demonstrations by Nagy and Molnár (1994, 1997) that newborns a few hours old not only may readily imitate tongue protrusion, mouth opening, lip protrusion, smiles, a surprise expression, head movements and finger movements, but that if the expressive partner waits patiently while looking at the baby after eliciting tongue protrusion, the baby will, after even 2 or 3 minutes, deliberately poke out the tongue to 'provoke' another response from the attentive adult. Nagy has further shown that whereas imitation is accompanied by heart rate acceleration, provocation is coupled to heart deceleration, symptomatic of an 'anticipating' state. This proves that the newborns are reciprocating in intending and attending with the partner. Meltzoff and Moore (1994) found that at 6 weeks an infant can remember an imitation and use the same act the next day, to 'test' the 'identity' of a stranger, or possibly as an attempt at communication with an acquired convention.

Collaborative learning and innate emotions as regulators of contacts and relationships

After moving to Edinburgh in 1971, I continued recording communication and object manipulation in infancy. With Penelope Hubley I traced the evolution of game-playing, finding increasingly complex metacommunicative patterns. The infant took increasing initiative, and Hubley discovered, in July 1974, the change in a 10-month-old girl's behaviour that identified 'secondary intersubjectivity' – the systematic combining of purposes directed to objects with those that invoked interest and interaction from a companion (Trevarthen and Hubley, 1978) (Fig. 1.4). We diagrammed steps in the differentiation and mutual assimilation of the infant's two rival classes of motives, and defined the process by which cooperative awareness developed. The following year Hubley published her thesis study of five female infants, confirming a highly significant change around 9 months (Hubley and Trevarthen, 1979). In collaboration with Professor A. C. Mundy-Castle of the University of Lagos we charted these developments in one population of infants from three socioeconomic groups in Scotland and in another group, with an equal number of traditional urban mothers with infants in Lagos, Nigeria. Using similar recording studios we confirmed, though there were differences, that the essential phases of protoconversation, games and 'cooperative awareness' in the first year were independent of racial, cultural and sub-cultural differences (Trevarthen, 1988).

Lynne Murray began PhD research in 1974 on the emotional regulations of Primary Intersubjectivity. Following an MA project by John Tatam, who observed that 2-month-old infants became distressed if the mother, while facing her infant, spoke as to an adult and non-contingently (Tatam, 1974), Murray (1980; Murray and Trevarthen, 1985) showed that a 'blank-faced' mother caused an infant to emit integrated expressions of agitation and distress, and to look away from the mother's face except for brief 'paranoid' glances. A study by Tronick found the same disruptive effect of a 'still face' on the infant's emotional engagement in protoconversation (Brazelton *et al.*, 1975; Tronick *et al.*, 1978). This led to a series of important contributions by Tronick on the emotional regulations of interactions with infants, and phases of maternal emotional support in interaction (Cohn and Tronick, 1983; Tronick, 1989; Tronick *et al.*, 1980; Weinberg and Tronick, 1994, 1996).

In 1975 Murray visited the Papouseks in Munich, where she built a film prototype of the Double Television Intercom experiment. Hanus and Mechtilde Papousek were building procedures to test infants' awareness of their mirror images in real time, or with a delay, and the effects of interrupting or distorting the mother's 'intuitive parenting' behaviours (Papousek and Papousek, 1977, 1987). Murray's TV replay test showed that a 2-month-old becomes distressed and avoidant if the mother's behaviour, however friendly and expressive, is inappropriate in timing and unreactive to what the baby is doing (Murray, 1980; Murray and Trevarthen, 1985; Trevarthen, 1985a). A reciprocal experiment showed that a mother is

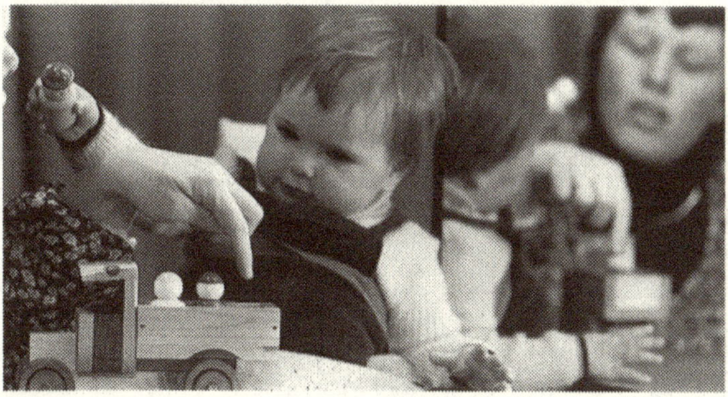

Fig. 1.4 Girl BM, Edinburgh, 1979. Cooperating in a task; taking initiative; and applying cultural knowledge in joint attention. *Left*: BM accepts the doll after the mother has asked her to 'put it in the truck', puts it in, and looks up with satisfaction to receive her mother's praise. *Top right*: BM insists, repeatedly, that her mother put the doll in, while the mother points to the truck saying, with emphasis, 'you're meant to put it in'. *Bottom right*: BM asks for the *National Geographic*, which she knows well, and turns the pages, while her mother assists.

equally sensitive, at a subconscious level, to non-contingent expressions in a replayed recording of the infant's positive intersubjective communication (Murray and Trevarthen, 1986). The conclusion is that normal, happy, protoconversational games need mutual awareness and purposeful replies, with both parties in immediate sympathetic contact (Trevarthen, 1984b). Research by Beebe (1982; Beebe and Lachmann, 1988), Field (1992), and Tronick and Weinberg (Tronick and Field, 1986; Tronick and Cohn, 1989; Tronick and Weinberg, 1997; Weinberg and Tronick, 1994, 1996) has demonstrated the refined emotional sensitivity that supports mutual awareness between a mother and her infant, and the effects of disregulation of this system by lack of normal response in either mother or infant. Lynne Murray has continued her research into examination of the immediate effects of maternal postnatal depression on infant behaviour, and on psychological development in infancy and early childhood. There is evidence that the course of development depends on contributions from both mother and infant, as well as from their family environment (Murray, 1988, 1992; Murray *et al.*, 1993; Murray and Cooper, 1997).

In 1981, we summarized our conclusions in Davis and Dobbing's *Scientific foundations of paediatrics*, with a critical review of prevailing theories of infant perception, movement, learning and emotion (Trevarthen *et al.*, 1981). We emphasized the primacy of motor coordinations and endogenous rhythms in the epigenesis of sucking, neonatal looking, prereaching, 'prespeech' and primary gestures. We related infants' perceiving to their acting according to the ecological perception theory of Gibson, and to the known chronology of developments in oculomotor coordination, visual acuity and object prehension. We rejected the idea of emotions as expressions of the induction and reduction of physiological drives, and the concept of interpersonal emotions developing from a continuum of arousal states between boredom and panic in response to the degree of 'discrepancy' of stimuli. The reductive arousal theory was replaced by a theory of 'motives that determine temporo-spatial limits to the organisation of goals in experience and action' (Trevarthen *et al.*, 1981:237). Emotions were described both as regulators of motivational harmony or conflict within the intentional subject, and as expressions of human feeling that regulate contacts and relationships with others (Trevarthen, 1984b).

We recorded developments of 'person–person games' in the middle of the first year, in which mothers and infants made fun of their own communications, teasing one another, and mothers stimulated babies with rhythmic body play, and much facial and vocal expression (Figs.

1.2, Right; 1.3, Right). These games gradually incorporated toys as babies gained skill in looking, listening, reaching and manipulating, becoming 'person–person–object games' (Fig. 1.3). These we perceived to be preparatory to the advances of joint attention, shared interest and cooperative task performance of Secondary Intersubjectivity.

Innate human intersubjectivity as the foundation for language

At the time infants' protoconversational abilities were described, Joanna Ryan (1974) made an influential review of evidence from diary studies of early language development. Children enter language by communicating states of mind and shared interests with familiar persons in familiar circumstances. Ryan made a critique of linguistic analysis, explaining how the philosophy of language led to the conclusion that adults use language within social awareness, a 'communicative competence' that is more fundamental than language itself. She proposed that a combination of Speech Act Theory and a European phenomenological and psychoanalytic philosophy of language, which seeks to define the intersubjective functions of speech (Habermas, 1970), could explain how mothers succeed in questioning, prohibiting, informing, encouraging or rejecting their infants before the latter can speak. Ryan said:

> Habermas (1970) argues that verbal communication cannot be understood only as an application of linguistic competence, limited by prevailing empirical conditions, but instead that the 'structure of intersubjectivity' that makes such application possible has to be explained. Intersubjectivity between any speakers capable of mutual understanding is made possible by what he calls 'dialogue constituent universals', and communicative competence is defined as mastery of these. Such universals allow for the interlacing of perspectives between speakers, for the relating of speakers to the referents of conversation, and for other pragmatic aspects of the speech situation . . . Whilst one might query the explicitly linguistic nature of Habermas' dialogue universals, his emphasis on the structure of intersubjectivity presupposed by successful speech is extremely important. (Ryan, 1974:187)

Speech Act Theory became popular in studies of mother–infant communication (Bates, 1979; Bruner, 1976; Dore, 1983). Bruner (1983) analysed the intentions of communicative precursors of language that embody linguistic rules. According to Halliday's (1975, 1979) sociosemiotic theory, the child is not just cognitive system, but a human agent, achieving understanding by cooperating with others. He charted his son's systematic progress through 'protolanguage' to speech with lexico-grammar, motivated by intentions to express vocally what he wanted to share.

These considerations of how children learn to speak give new meaning to the view in John Macmurray's Gifford Lectures (1953–4) on *The Form of the personal*, that human society is not just a collection of individual agents, but a community of 'persons in relation'. This is the title Macmurray gave to the second of two volumes on his lectures (1961), which was influential in bringing together developmental linguists persuaded by Ryan's arguments and social psychologists who were attracted to the ideas of Mead (1934) and Vygotsky (1934/1986). Macmurray's ideas on intuitive sympathy can, like Stout's, be traced to Hutcheson (1755) and Smith (1759), philosophers of the Scottish Enlightenment, and even more directly to Martin Buber's theology (Buber, 1958). Macmurray, however, takes as specially human the fundamental helplessness of the infant in a mother's care. In this he echoes the British psychoanalysts, notably Winnicott (1960), in a position that has limited comprehension of the infant's active and discriminating contribution to the interpersonal relationship (Trevarthen, 1998b).

Recognition of the relevance to language acquisition of all human intersubjective expressions is still withheld by those seeking an innate mental mechanism for language, and only language. Thus, for example, Pinker (1994:40), in *The language instinct*, ignores protoconversation and is dismissive of research into 'motherese', denying that there is any point in talking to infants. Locke (1993), in *The child's path to spoken language*, has a different understanding. He traces the emergence of speech from infant 'talking', an approach more in tune with Bullowa's perspective, or the sociolinguistic theory of Halliday's 'protolanguage' in *Learning how to mean* (Halliday, 1975).

Musicality in mother–infant play: mimesis, rhythm and sympathy in cultural learning

Reciprocity in *rhythmic timing* and *somatic equivalence* of movements (mimetic sympathy), which characterize adult and infant when they act together in protoconversation, and the *phrasing of utterances* that promotes turn-taking, require organized and coherent motives on both sides (Trevarthen, 1986b). Sensitivity to what Stern (1993) calls the 'dynamic emotional envelopes' generated by the movements and vocalizations of an affectionate and sympathetic parent animated by joy (Stern, 1990) becomes vividly evident in rhythms and melodies of musical/dancing interactive play with infants older than 3 months. The infant 'shadows' the partner's actions by immediate sympathetic identification with expressive forms and their emotional qualities. Soon the infant learns the rules of participation in game rituals (Bruner and Sherwood, 1975).

I have, with the aid of my research students Theano Kokkinaki and Geraldo Fiamenghi, and my musician colleague, Stephen Malloch (Malloch *et al.*, 1997), elaborated on intersubjectivity theory to explain how (and why) neonates imitate at certain points in the negotiation of expressive and receptive initiatives with adults, or in interaction with infants of the same age as themselves, and how imitations develop (Trevarthen *et al.*, 1997). I cannot see how the cooperative patterns of *assertion* and *acceptance* can be explained in terms of 'co-regulation' in a 'non-linear dynamic system' of separately generated behaviours (Fogel and Thelen, 1987), because this does not specify, or allow a place for, intrinsic motive 'constraints' exhibited by both partners. The l'apouseks' theory of the infant's role in early communication and the support of cognitive development by 'intuitive parenting' (Papousek and Papousek, 1989, 1997), and Tronick's theory of co-regulation of 1dyadic states of consciousness' (Tronick and Weinberg, 19967) both explicitly accept that the infant is born with intersubjective capacities that actively regulate 'didactic interactions' (Papousek and Bornstein, 1992).

Research on song and dance in play between parents and infants in the familiar intimacy of the home now leads us to search, in longer melodies and rhythmic phrases, for the foundations of the human sense of dramatic narrative, and brings us to the same conclusion as the anthropologist Victor Turner (1982), concerning the emotive role of ritual and theatre in generating and sustaining 'communitas', as distinct from the physical coexistence of 'societas'. Turner writes of 'the human seriousness of play'. The significance of intersubjective universals in what Donald (1991) refers to as 'mimesis', the use of displays of body expression and gesture to convey meanings and messages without language, is taken up by Bruner in his latest book on *The culture of education* (1996), in which he advocates creation of 'communities of learners', and suggests that the future of educational theory is in the direction of a search for understanding of human learning in anecdotal intersubjectivity, rather than just cognitive argument and the practice of skills.

There is an affinity between the expressive forms of music and the dynamic texture of emotions in speech, and motherese universally has striking musicality (Fernald, 1989; Fernald *et al.*, 1989; Grieser and Kuhl, 1988; Papousek *et al.*, 1991). The study of infant semiosis shows that meanings are learned in emotionally regulated social life (Trevarthen, 1987, 1990b, 1994; Trevarthen and Logotheti, 1987). Recently attention has been drawn to the fact that infants have a rich sensitivity for musical play (Papousek, 1994; Stern, 1993; Stern *et al.*, 1982, 1985). Tests of infants' musicality show that 6-month-olds discriminate features of tempo, rhythm, melody and key in the structure of both song and instrumental sound, and that they can isolate one musical invariant in spite of changes in other features (Trehub, 1990; Trehub *et al.*, 1993). This awareness unites an extraordinary perceptiveness for phonatory and articulatory features of the human voice with sensitivity for timing and phrasing of sounds and expressive movements of all kinds.

'Meta-communicative' teasing games: friendly rivalry of initiatives, negotiating topics to share

Rapid developments that transform infants' vision and touch, stability of posture, head support and control of reaching by 4 months give new power over the environment. At the same time, encounters with partners become increasingly lively and comical as interactive and emotional possibilities are explored (Figs. 1.2, Right; 1.3; 1.5).

Comedians and magicians know the importance of timing. Older infants play with the fun and deceit of making their actions coincide with or collide against those of indulgent partners in teasing games (Nakano, 1994; Nakano and Kanaya, 1993; Reddy, 1991; Reddy *et al.*, 1997). When they play with reactive mobiles, this seems not simply a response to contingency of physical motion, as Watson (1972) believed: rather is it an imaginative variant of the capacity for intersubjective negotiation, as Papousek (1967) demonstrated. In fact, play is richer with a partner who is not merely moving contingently, but also qualifying the moves of self and other with 'mock' expressions of surprise, anxiety, joy, etc.

Stern's 'dynamic emotions' describe the continuum of states that synchronize and alternate, match and contrast, in the flow of play (Stern, 1993). They give sense to the discrete 'categorical affects' shown in photographs of the climax facial expressions of anger, joy, sadness, disgust, fear, surprise. These visible forms punctuate a more music-like expression of interpersonal feelings in the voice, and in the 'dance' of body movement and hand gestures. The analysis of double video recordings clarifies this point (Trevarthen, 1993b). Alternations of address and reply, of asserting and attending, between the infant and an adult in a conversation game are animated by continuously changing expressions of mixed emotions – smiles and laughter signalling joy in sharing, bold and mock angry threats as self-expression, looks away and frowns of impatience with intrusions, fear of strange and startling events, pouts and cries of anger with fatigue or when actions are frustrated, tears of sadness with loneliness or hurt, and so on (Trevarthen, 1993a).

Mutual 'attunement' of dynamic feelings and imitation of actions and expressions allow subtle regulation of sharing, or of rejection. The infant can ignore a partner or show decisive avoidance. Indeed a mother's play often seems designed to challenge the assertive independence of the baby. Mothers asked 'Who leads?' say 'We both do', or 'The baby is boss'. Parental teasing games, common in good relationships, are highly informative about this negotiation. Infants also tease their companions, especially after 3 months, which, with demonstrations of 'coyness', proves that infants already have a subtle interest in the motives of the mother. Reddy (Reddy *et al.*, 1997) describes it as evidence of 'other-awareness'.

Self-consciousness or other-consciousness? Acting for others' appraisal

Infants react to others' attention with self-sensing mannerisms, creating a socially conscious 'bearing'. Wallon (1928) called this 'prestance': a presenting of oneself to others by assuming a ceremonial posture or manner, acknowledging a 'public' and their formal or intuitive appreciation. Six-month-olds often 'show off', making odd postures or grimaces, or displaying imitated 'trick' behaviours, such as head shaking, bouncing, hand-clapping, 'silly' faces, shouting, theatrically coughing or squealing, repeating these to amuse themselves or familiar companions who appreciate teasing and joking (Trevarthen, 1990b; Reddy, 1991). Infants also turn these display behaviours to face a mirror and examine themselves with amusement, which proves a kind of self-consciousness that is part of awareness of others (Fiamenghi, 1997; Reddy *et al.*, 1997; Trevarthen *et al.*, 1997). Siblings, and adults, take advantage of the developing sense of fun to make the infant laugh with mock attacks. Infants also develop, at about 7 or 8 months, both stronger attachment to the mother and increased stranger fear (Fig. 1.5).

I regard these developments as elaborations of motives that prepare for cooperative learning of conventional behaviours and symbolic meanings. First meanings make sense only in the restricted culture of the family, and may be misunderstood by unfamiliar persons. In the last months of the first year they are readily incorporated in delayed imitative reproductions (Meltzoff, 1995; Trevarthen, 1990b), which proves their role in development of symbolic representations (Akhtar and Tomasello, 1996; Piaget, 1945, 1962).

The games parents play with 6-month-olds increasingly involve

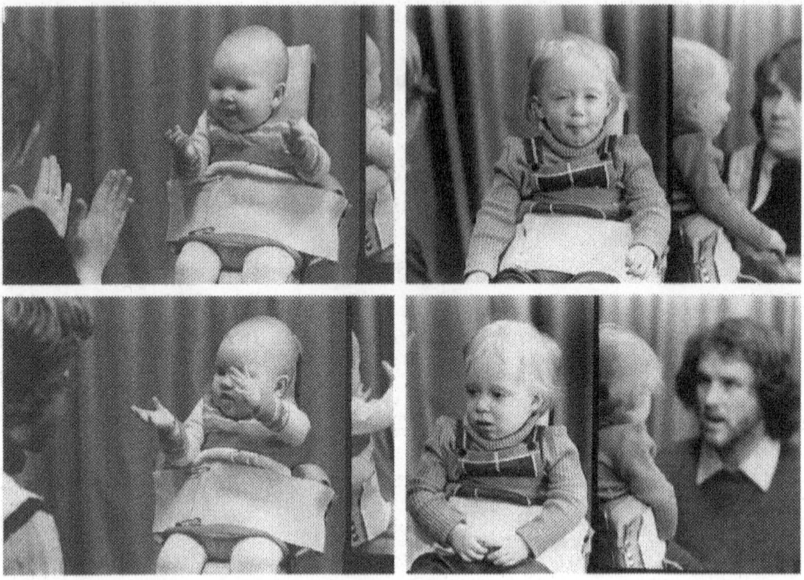

Fig. 1.5 Self-and-other consciousness, Edinburgh, 1979. Enjoying tricks and jokes with mother, or with the mirror; showing boldness or anxiety with strangers: *Left to right*: Girl EB, 28 weeks, shows clapping to the mother's request, happily; bravely shows clapping to an uncomprehending stranger, trying to 'break the ice'. Boy AS, 53 weeks, makes a silly face to his reflection to amuse himself while his mother is sitting 'blank-faced', and looks sadly at a stranger, followed shortly by crying; Girl EM, 40 weeks, favourite 'wrinkle nose' joke with her mother. *Top right*: Boy AS chases a ping-pong ball that his mother makes hard to catch – a 'person–person–object' game. *Bottom right*: Boy AF pokes tongue out to the mirror after his mother has invited him to imitate.

objects (Hubley and Trevarthen, 1979; Trevarthen and Hubley, 1978). The increasing complexity of communication brings more and more opportunities for joining interest in the private knowledge of things with the shared experiences of being an actor. Imbalance in the complex of motives emerging at this time in a disordered brain mechanism of intersubjectivity may be the principal factor precipitating autism (Hobson, 1993a; Trevarthen, Aitken, Papoudi and Robarts, 1998). Other 'empathic disorders' (Gillberg, 1991) may be due to faulty intersubjective differentiation at another stage (Trevarthen and Aitken, 1994). Autism usually becomes evident in the second year. It cannot take on the appearance of a disorder in a verbalizable 'theory of mind' until many months have passed.

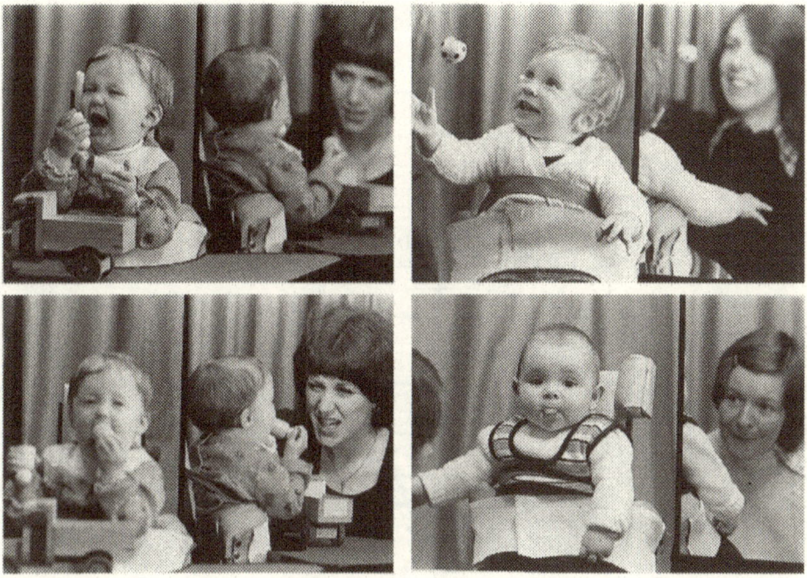

Integrating motives for self, objects and others

We can see, from the way infants' motives develop, that, at the start, human nature is neither entirely dependent on external regulation of self-state by attachment to the mother, nor merely imitative, remarkable as the neonate's ability to imitate and take initiative in imitative exchanges certainly is. The active and curious infant is not concerned only with mastering concepts of objects through exploratory investigation and manipulative use. Protoconversation is an adaptation to *cultural learning in companionship* (Bateson, 1975, 1979; Trevarthen, 1988, 1992). The infant is seeking others to share expressions of motives, understandings and purposes, in self–other regulation (Aitken and Trevarthen, 1997).

The ways that the fundamental three facets of motives and emotions (to one's own body, to objects, to other persons) become integrated to generate the emergence of cooperation, with assistance from a responsive and affectionate human environment, can be represented as in Figure 1.6. Developmental changes seem to follow something like a spiral course, the mind of the infant and young child being at times more preoccupied with intrinsic problems of self-regulation and autopoesis, or cognitively directed to investigate objects and operations on them, or hoping to find friendship and sharing of meaning in conscious companionship with other persons. The way is not always

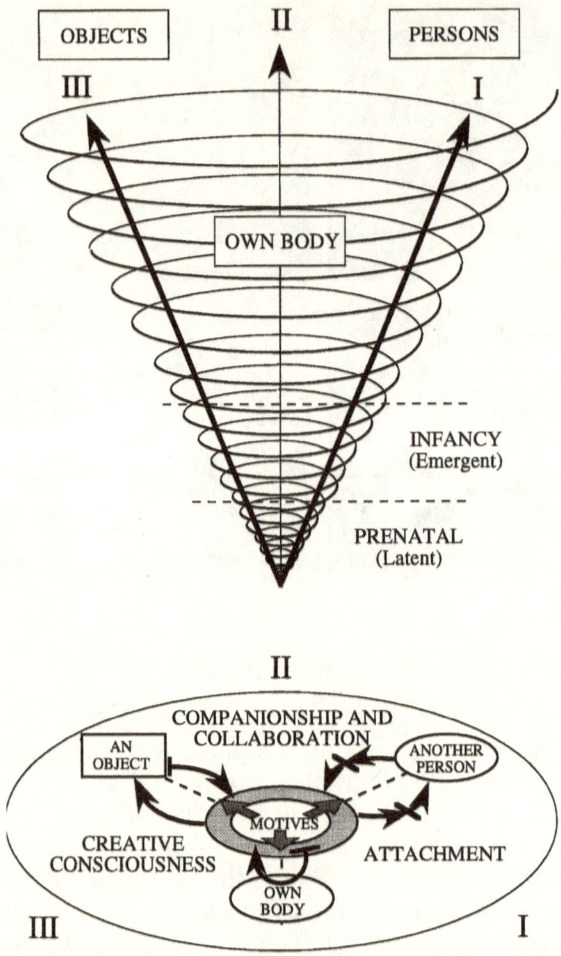

Fig. 1.6 Acquired forms of human behaviour develop their applications through combinations of object-related, intersubjective and body-regulating motives, associated respectively with 'aesthetic', 'moral' and 'nurturant (somatic and visceral)' emotions (Trevarthen, 1993a). Functions of I: 'attachment and caring', II: 'cognitive objectivity and creative work', and III: 'collaborative companionship' develop as the three-part fabric of cultural life. All three domains of mental function are present in latent form at birth, and they undergo age-related differentiations, under constraints that emerge from the developing brain while actively gained experience is assimilated in proliferating networks (Trevarthen, 1990a). Developments are particularly spectacular in early childhood, but they continue throughout the life cycle, and with a high intensity, again, at adolescence.

smooth and motive transitions are often preceded by 'difficult periods' (Rijt-Plooij and Plooij, 1993). How, in detail, human bodies and brains accomplish this development guided by intersubjective sensibilities may be a mystery, but that they do so is clear.

Appendix: On infant intersubjectivity and the brain

The brain of any animal develops as a congregation of cells and their interconnections that carries many images of the body in which it has formed. Genes that map the body also map the cell systems of the brain. Body and brain have the same symmetry and polarity, the body and brain together being adapted to seeking transactions with the environment, choosing places and objects by guiding locomotion, orienting prospectively with special receptors (especially eyes, ears and hands), making various acts of commitment that take in objects selected for their usefulness or which defend against life threatening events (Trevarthen, 1985b). Different mid- and fore-brain regions carry magnified maps of the fields of experience of these receptors, linked to motor systems that move them in concert to sustain the subject's intelligence. The balance of inner metabolic functions, protection against stress and injury and activities of reproduction has to be regulated in relationship to this behaviour.

The emotional brain acts as the supreme integrator of this body-in-world activity (Holstege *et al.*, 1997). It has three parts related to three groups of effectors: the proximal or axial somatic muscles move the skeleton and surface tissues, regulating whole body posture and locomotion; distal muscles make fine movements of the appendages, including the adjustments of reception by eyes, hands, mouth, ears; the visceral and sympathetic motor system is directed to the muscles of internal organs, including the heart, lungs and gut. It works in association with the neuroendocrine regulations mediated through the hypothalamus. These major functions of the 'greater limbic system' (MacLean, 1970; Nieuwenhuys, 1996) are already represented in the anatomical and physiological patterns and relationships of the human embryo brain, in ways that compare with homologous systems of other species, but with important additions (O'Rahilly and Müller, 1994). From this early stage they influence the formation of cortical tissues that will be essential for thinking, intelligent learning and skilled actions, the integration of emotion with cognition being a fundamental principle of both prenatal brain formation and postnatal cognitive growth and function (Damasio, 1994; Trevarthen and Aitken, 1994).

The human brain is born already able to coordinate movements of the trunk and limbs and with special receptors capable of aiming pickup of detailed information about objects both separately and in coordination. All these movements, including those preformed in adaptation to future walking, talking, gesturing, and reaching and grasping for objects and bringing them to the mouth, are played out in one frame of time, or intersynchronized (Pöppel, 1994), which proves that the 'pacemakers' of various motor systems are already coupled by integrated motive mechanism. This time-coupling is manifest in a hierarchy of motor rhythms with specified rates. Furthermore, a healthy newborn has effective emotional reactions and 'state regulations', demonstrating that cerebral systems also integrate autonomic and endocrine processes, linking visceral and somatic activities. Foetuses hear and can sense the fluids and surfaces that touch their body, and they can move with coordinated grace (Cioni and Castellaci, 1990; Lecanuet *et al.*, 1995). Newborns can see within minutes of birth, in spite of the immaturity of the neocortical visual system. The subcortical brain is capable of assimilating these informations and learning, and integrating them with subcortical mechanisms of emotional expression (Ploog, 1992).

Neonatal imitations and protoconversation prove that the human brain is formed to integrate expressive body movements, of eyes, face, mouth, vocal apparatus, hands, and postural attitudes with emotions and state regulation (Trevarthen, 1996, 1997a). Moreover, these intricate expressions of central motives by distal musculature are sensitive to corresponding expressions in a conversational partner. Clearly there have to be temporal and morphological markers or goals in the perceived human that the infant can identify and assimilate into his or her motives and actions. While an infant's autonomic and endocrine state can be affected by stimuli from touching the mother's body, from hearing her voice, from taking her milk, and these are vital in formation of a beneficial attachment and self-regulation (Kraemer, 1997; Schore, 1994), it is also the case that the infant is seeking a different level of integration with the mother's dynamic emotions and conversational rhythms. This communication has potential for developing into a way of learning about other person's motives, ideas, beliefs, purposes, and so on, i.e. for companionship, mimetic narrative and cultural learning. It is associated with elaboration of uniquely intricate facial and vocal expressive systems and sensitivity to visible and audible signals from other humans. The remarkable expressiveness of human hand gestures and their appearance in young infants as both emissions and imitations, demonstrates another way in which the human emotional motor system with its perceptual regulations has advanced beyond that of apes. Donald (1991) hypothesizes that

Homo erectus employed a rich vocal-gestural mimesis for narrative communication before language. Such communication becomes highly effective in infants and toddlers and acts as a foundation for language. Language mechanisms in the brain are clearly integrated with a wide range of cortical and subcortical systems, including components of the emotional brain (Ross, 1996; Trevarthen, 1997b). The poly-rhythmic motor coordinations that are fundamental to mimesis (and its manifestations in drama, poetry and music: Turner and Pöppel, 1983) would appear to involve integration of association and pre-limbic cortices with several subcortical afferent and efferent centres, most important among which are evidently the pulvinar, medio-dorsal thalamic nucleus, ventral striatum and cerebellum, the latter integrated with intrinsic pacemakers of the medulla and mid-brain. The peri-insular parietal cortex and the prefrontal cortex are in close anatomical linkage with these subcortical systems, which presumably have a key role in regulating perception and motor control in both subjective narrative thought ('executive functioning') and intersubjective narrative messages (Saper, 1996; Groenewegen *et al.*, 1996).

The brain mechanisms involved in such coordination must be extensive and coherent, with an intrinsic unity and systematic patterning. The intrinsic motive apparatus with which the infant is born must be open to interaction and coordination with the motive activities of the other person (Trevarthen and Aitken, 1994). The mapping of the infant's body into the infant's brain must also be able to reflect the form and activity of the other person's body outside. The mechanisms that do this, like the mechanisms of emotional and linguistic communication and cultural praxis in the adult brain, are asymmetric (Trevarthen, 1996; Tucker, 1992), apparently as an evolutionary elaboration of ancient asymmetries in brain stem regulators of autonomic and endocrine functions.

While the amygdala appears to be a nodal structure in the communication of cognitive intelligence with the hypothalamus and brain-stem emotional system (Aggleton, 1992; Allman and Brothers, 1994; LeDoux, 1993), feeding back in memorizing of emotionally charged experiences (especially those related to fear and anger), and the septal nuclei are involved in linking subcortical reward systems with the cortex, the orbital and prefrontal cortices are positioned to be essential in integration of feelings with expressions, and for the perception of expressive actions of others (Price *et al.*, 1996), especially, perhaps, expressions involving the hand and mouth, which may be 'seen' in dorso-lateral prefrontal cortex (Di Pelligrino *et al.*, 1992). There are input processing systems for recognition of eyes and facial expressions in the superior temporal cortex. These feed on to the rostral temporal cortex and amygdala (Damasio, 1994; Ross, 1996), which are undoubtedly active in infants when they interact face-to-face with their mothers (Schore, 1994).

The brain mechanisms that represent the human body of the single subject in all its intelligent and emotional activities and states are at the same time very extensive, of ancient lineage, and greatly elaborated. The mirror system that enables the expressions of other individuals' bodies to play a part in regulating emotion and rational activity and learning intersubjectively, the 'virtual other' mechanism (Bråten, 1988a, 1994a, b, this volume), must be similarly extensive. It is interwoven with self-consciousness, and unconscious embodiment of motives, at every level. A very substantial part of its processes is active and effective in communication from early infancy, and is ready to be transformed, but not replaced, by extensive post-natal brain developments.

CHAPTER 2

Infant intersubjectivity: broadening the dialogue to include imitation, identity and intention

Andrew N. Meltzoff and M. Keith Moore

What is the problem of intersubjectivity and why does it intrigue us so? The problem stems from the fact that persons are more than physical objects. When we describe a person's height, weight, eyes, etc., we do not exhaust our description of that person. We have left off their psychological makeup. If a self-mobile, human-looking body were devoid of psychological characteristics it would not be a person at all, but a robot or, to use a philosopher's favourite, a zombie. A fundamental issue is how we come to know others as persons like ourselves.

Each one of us has the phenomenological experience that he or she is not alone in the world, in particular that we are not the unique bearer of psychological properties. We know that we think, feel, have intentions; we also find ourselves believing that others have similar psychological states, despite the fact that we do not experience others' states in the same way that we experience ours. Reflection on this gulf between ourselves and others intrigues us and can raise questions about our understanding of other persons. A computer with voice synthesis could be made to cry out, but we would not think it felt pain. A robot might be programmed to wrinkle its elastic 'face' when an internal chip detected sobbing, but we would not ascribe empathy to it. Why, then, do we ascribe psychological states to other humans?

Philosophers seek to justify the inference that the moving sacks of skin that we see are animated by psychological states just like our own. They contemplate whether this way of thinking might be a fiction and criteria for knowing whether it is or is not. Developmental psychologists ask different questions. They inquire how such a view takes hold among humans. Is it present at birth? Does it develop through social interaction? Does the nature of intersubjectivity change with age?

The philosophical questions about intersubjectivity remain unsettled, but every day people continue to talk, act and write in the (often vain) hope of changing the minds and hearts of others. Regarding the developmentalist's questions, there have been wide swings of the interpretive pendulum. At the apogee in one direction is Piaget (1936/1977, 1954) who famously argued that the infant is born a 'solipsist'. Piaget's infant was not an intersubjective infant, still less was his newborn. At the apogee in the other direction is Trevarthen (1979a, 1983; Trevarthen and Hubley, 1978; also Bråten, 1988a), who argued for an innate intersubjectivity wired into the human brain at birth.

Recent debates about early intersubjectivity often cite literature on three phenomena: the mutual timing and turn-taking aspects of adult–infant interactions (Bråten, 1988a; Brazelton *et al.*, 1974; Brazelton and Tronick, 1980; Stern, 1985; Trevarthen, 1979a), joint attention (e.g., Bruner, 1975, 1983; Butterworth and Cochran, 1980; Butterworth and Jarret, 1991; Moore and Dunham, 1995) and social referencing (e.g., Campos and Stenberg, 1981; Sorce *et al.*, 1985). These are thought to be important clues to non-verbal intersubjectivity, because they indicate a certain attitude, a 'taking into account' of the other by the infant.

The logical prerequisite for inferring intersubjectivity, however, is that the infant take into account the *psychological* aspects of the other, not solely the physics of the other. If a baby climbs on the shoulders of another simply as a footstool, this involves an other but not intersubjectivity, because it is not the other's mind that was taken into account. Thus not all interactions between social agents necessarily entail intersubjectivity.

A conservative reading of the oft-cited phenomena can shake one's confidence in them as direct measures of intersubjectivity (Baldwin and Moses, 1994; Hobson, 1994a; Meltzoff and Gopnik, 1993; Tomasello, 1995b; Tomasello *et al.*, 1993; Whiten, 1994). Some faith-shaking questions are the following. Does sensitivity to timing actually entail that the infant attributes psychological properties to the other? What if joint attention is accomplished solely through perceptual geometry, the extension of a line in space from the adult's pupil? How do we know that in the classic social referencing set-up, the adult's reaction to the novel toy (their fright face) does not itself frighten the infant without necessitating any understanding of the adult mental state? Moreover, both joint attention and social referencing have onsets late in infancy, and therefore do not uniquely support a nativist thesis; nor do they fall out of a Piagetian analysis. Far from being the foundation for intersubjectivity, they have developmental roots that need to be explained.[1]

What was once settled ground in Piaget's time, and was resettled by Trevarthen and colleagues, is now again open for reconceptualization. In this window of opportunity, we need to re-examine what we mean by intersubjectivity and the kind of evidence developmental psychologists can bring to bear on its origins and development.

In this chapter we will argue that newborns are not isolated from others at birth, but on the other hand do not yet understand the internal feelings and mental states of others in the way a 2-year-old does (Gopnik and Meltzoff, 1997). A developmental view is needed. The promise of a developmental view is obvious, but it requires evidence and a cogent argument to be taken seriously. One goal of this essay is to provide the needed detail about the development of intersubjectivity in the preverbal period. We will propose that the imitation of human actions is the first bridge between the infant and others, and that imitation serves the dual functions of differentiating the broad class of 'others' into individuals and providing an early means of communication with them. It is through mutually imitative games, we argue, that infants progress from conceptions of others as entities with whom one can share actions to persons with whom one can share goals and intentions.

Overview of a developmental account

The bedrock on which intersubjective development is built is recognition of the 'like-me-ness' of others. This provides a basis for connection between the infant and other. Imitation is perhaps the first observable act demonstrating this connection. In newborn facial imitation, there is an apparent gulf to be bridged. The self can be felt, but cannot be seen. The other's face can be seen, but cannot be felt. Yet self and other somehow connect. The other can be understood as like me, at least in the sense that we can do the same acts.

True intersubjectivity requires not only connection but also differentiation. It involves more than a feeling of communion with an undifferentiated class of 'other'. It also entails relations with particular others who are valued as individuals. This in turn raises the question of how to determine their identity. A complete theory of early intersubjectivity must account for infants' ability to distinguish individuals from one another and reidentify a person as the same one again. We show that young infants deploy imitation as one means of sorting out the identity of individual people. Young infants are sometimes unsure about whether someone is the self-same person who has changed appearance or a new person who looks like the old one. They use imitation to help make these determinations. They do so by treating the distinctive games people play as shared memories or at least shared experiences by which the other can be reidentified. They treat distinctive games as if they are invisible marks that can be rendered visible through interaction. This further illustrates the intersubjective significance of early imitative behaviour, for it is one of the earliest means by which infants solicit and recreate the distinctive acts of particular others.

The imitation game is a bidirectional experience through which infants explore relations between self and other. The parent can propose and the infant answer, or the infant propose and the adult answer. Parents spend hours playing reciprocal imitation games with their children, banging when they bang, shaking when they shake. We suggest that these games provide an engine for development. Such episodes provide infants with evidence that self and other are commensurate bearers of genuinely psychological properties like goals and intentions. This delimits the class of entities to which the infant ascribes psychological properties. Infants should construe people (but not things) as intentional beings, because people can be imitated, are like them, and engage in reciprocal games.

A fuller understanding of others as 'subjects' is that they can intend something different from what they actually achieve. In the adult ontology, 'subjects' are entities for which there is a differentiation between intention and behaviour. We found that 18-month-olds can recognize the intention of another even when the adult accidentally fails to fulfil this end. At least by this age they make a differentiation between the surface behaviour of people (what they actually do or say) and another deeper level involving goals and intentions. This differentiation in turn underlies linguistic communication (Grice, 1957) and arguably sows the seeds for ascribing more complex mental states to others (e.g. beliefs), which have been studied under the label of 'theory of mind' research (Astington and Gopnik, 1991; Flavell, 1988; Gopnik, 1993; Harris, 1989; Perner, 1991; Wellman, 1990).

Intention reading in infancy

In investigating the origins of intersubjectivity one is immediately confronted with the question of how to 'ask' infants whether they read below surface behaviour into the minds and hearts of others. This seems a difficult question to pose without language, because all we can do is show the infant behaviour and measure their behavioural (or physiological) responses. How can we test whether infants treat another as some*one* who has a psychology and not some*thing* that is completely described by physics?

To address this question, a new procedure was developed, which was dubbed the behavioural re-enactment paradigm. The procedure capitalizes on the fact that human infants are highly imitative. However, it uses this proclivity in a new way, by testing if infants can read below the literal surface behaviour to something like a psychological state.

The study involved showing infants an unsuccessful act. For example, the adult tried to perform a behaviour, but his hand slipped. Thus the goal-state was not achieved. Alternatively, the adult accidentally under- or overshot his target. To an adult, it was easy to read the actor's intention though he was not able to fulfil it. The experimental question was whether infants also read through the surface behaviour to the underlying goal or intention of the actor. The measure of how they interpreted the event was what they chose to re-enact, in particular whether they chose to produce the intended act despite the fact that it was never present to the senses.

Using this paradigm, Meltzoff (1995) tested four groups of 18-month-old infants. The Demonstration(target) group saw the adult successfully fulfil his intentions and perform a series of target acts on five different objects. The Demonstration(intention) group saw accidental failures for five different events. With each object, the adult strove to reach the goal but did not successfully carry out his intention. The Control(baseline) group simply omitted any adult demonstrations. The Control(adult activity) group saw the adult perform control actions on the objects for the same length of time as in the two Demonstration groups, but the adult showed neither the target acts nor the intention to achieve them. The control acts were carefully designed so as to control for the possibility that spatial proximity of the adult's hands to the target, or proximity of two objects with each other, might 'suggest' the target behaviour (see Meltzoff, 1995 for details).

The results were very clear cut. Infants in the control groups did not tend to produce the target acts spontaneously or by chance. However, infants in the two Demonstration groups produced more than 75% of the target acts. They reproduced the targets after observing the adult do so, which is straightforward imitation. The important, new finding is that they also produced the targets in the intention condition. Indeed infants were just as good at duplicating the target after seeing the adult trying but failing as they were when the target was actually achieved.

We next inquired how infants would respond to a mechanical device that mimicked the same movements as the actor in the failed-attempt condition. One stimulus used was the effort to pull apart a

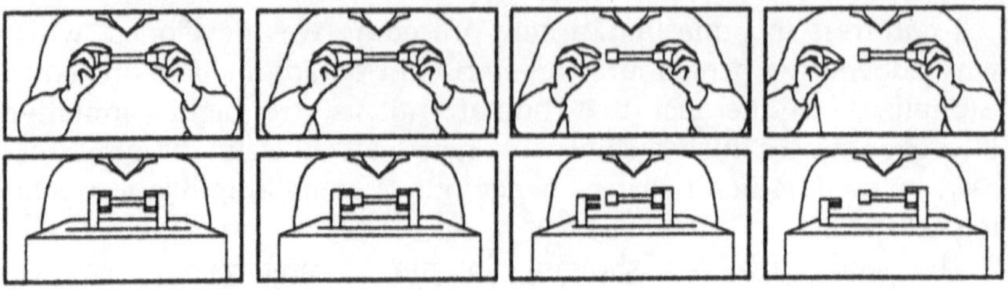

Fig. 2.1 Human demonstrator (*top panel*) and mechanical device performing the movements (*bottom panel*) (from Meltzoff, 1995)

dumbbell-shaped object, which failed because the adult's hand accidentally slipped off. An inanimate device was constructed that had poles for arms and mechanical pincers for hands. It did not look human but it could move very similarly to the human (Fig. 2.1). For the test, the pincers 'grasped' the dumbbell at the two ends just as the human hands did. One mechanical arm was then moved outwards, just as in the human case, and its pincer slipped off the end of the dumbbell just as the human hand did. The movement patterns of machine and man were closely matched from a purely spatiotemporal description of movements in space.

The results showed that infants did not attribute a goal or intention to the movements of the inanimate device. Although they looked at the device as long as at the human display, they simply did not see the sequence of actions as implying a goal. Infants were six times more likely to pull apart the dumbbell after seeing the human failed attempt than after the 'failed attempt' of the inanimate device.

This research helps to codify a distinction that was made earlier and is important for scientists gathering data on intersubjectivity. It is essential for our research to distinguish between construing the behaviours of others in purely physical versus psychological terms. To help keep this distinction clear we call the former *movements* or *motions* and the latter *human acts*. The behaviour of another person can be described using either physics or psychology. We can say 'Kate's hand contacted the cup, the cup fell over' or 'Kate was trying to pick up the cup.' Behaviourists try to stick to the former description precisely because they eschew appealing to invisible psychological states. Evidently, infants are not behaviourists. They construe the behaviour of others not simply as 'hold the dumbbell and then remove one hand quickly' but rather as an effort at pulling. Moreover, the new work shows that infants have a differentiation in the kinds of attributions they make to people versus things. In this sense infants have adopted an intersubjective stance; they construe people, but not things, as 'subjects' with whom they might have an intersubjective relation.

The imitation game

We propose that imitative games lead to growth of intersubjectivity. Parent–infant games are often reciprocally imitative in nature. First, the infant begins banging a tabletop. The parent seizes the opportunity for making a communicative connection and bangs in return. Next the child repeats the same. . .then the parent. . .and so on in a kind of non-verbal exchange game. Many theorists have focused on the temporal patterning, the turn-taking aspect, of the interaction, and much has been made of this (e.g., Bråten, 1988a, 1992; Brazelton *et al.*, 1974; Bruner, 1975, 1983; Stern, 1985; Trevarthen, 1979a).

We see additional value in such interactions in the congruence between self and other in the bodily activities performed and the intentions underlying them. Physical objects may come under temporal control, but only people, indeed only people who are paying attention to you and acting intentionally, can imitate your behaviour in a generative fashion. We will make much of this.

If congruence is important, one needs to demonstrate that infants are sensitive to it. It is not addressed by the (quite fascinating) perturbation studies in which a mother stops responding to her infant, and the infant's affect is monitored (Muir and Hains, 1993; Murray and Trevarthen, 1985; Tronick *et al.*, 1978). Such an arrangement disrupts the timing of the interaction, and infants may find this change disturbing without any recognition of the fundamental similarity between oneself and another human being.

The issue in question is difficult to examine in natural interaction. However, we can arrange a structured interaction that focuses on the problem. In our laboratory interactions, 14-month-old infants sat across a table from two adults who sat side by side (Meltzoff, 1990). One adult imitated everything the infant did and the other did not imitate. Let I = infant; I′ = imitating adult; NI = non-imitating adult. We wanted NI not only to be active, but to do 'baby-like' things with the toys so that no preference for I′ could be based solely on a differentiation of adult versus infantile actions. A yoked-control procedure was used in which the adult interactants viewed TV monitors that were behind the infants. One monitor displayed the actions of the current infant, live; the other the immediately preceding infant. Each adult copied one of the infants, so each acted like perfect babies. Could the infants distinguish which adult was acting just like the self (gaze, affect, etc. were controlled)?

The results showed that they could. They looked longer at I′; smiled more at I′; and directed testing behaviour at I′. By 'testing' we mean that infants often modulated their acts by performing sudden and unexpected movements to check if I′ was following what they did. The Marx brothers are famous for substituting see-though glass with a confederate on the other side for a mirror. The actor in such a situation self-consciously varies his acts to see if the other is still in congruence. Infants acted in this same way.

These results suggest that being imitated is attention-getting and pleasing at this age. Given a choice between an adult who was or was not imitating them, infants looked longer and smiled more at the imitating adult. This is a laboratory demonstration that reciprocal imitation focuses the infant's attention and is emotionally stirring.

How did the babies detect the imitative relationship? Two kinds of information are available: temporal contingency and structural congruence. It is relevant to theories of intersubjectivity to distinguish between these two bases. The former only requires that infants are sensitive to contingency information, but the latter implies that they are processing the relationship between self and other at least at the level of human acts.

A new study was designed in which the temporal aspects were equated by having both experimenters act at the same time. Both experimenters sat with neutral expressions until the infant performed a target act from a predetermined list. If and only if the infant exhibited one of these target actions, both experimenters began to act in unison. I′ performed the infant's act; NI performed a different behaviour from the list. What differentiated the two interactions is not timing, but the structure of their actions *vis-à-vis* the subject.

The results showed that the infants looked, smiled and directed more testing at the adult who acted just like them. Evidently infants do not just recognize that another moves *when* they move (temporal synchrony), but recognize that another moves in the same *manner* as they do (structural congruence). We can infer that infants recognize a similarity between themselves and other people, something exceeding shared timing and based on a more fundamental commonality. Only people can act 'like me' across a wide range of behaviours and interactions.

Further research revealed that even infants younger than 2 months of age are attentive to being imitated. However, we found an important difference between the younger and the older infants. Although younger infants increase the particular gesture being imitated, they do not switch to mismatching gestures to see if they will be copied. For example, if infant mouth opening is being copied, young infants' attention is attracted and they increase the like behaviour; but they do not switch to tongue protrusion to test this relationship. Younger infants seem to interpret being copied within a causal framework, as though their act causes the adult's act. The older infants go beyond this interpretation and treat the interaction as a matching game that is being shared.

By saying that the older infant appreciates the matching game *per se*, we mean that the relationship is being abstractly considered – the notion is that 'you will do what I do' where the particular behaviours are infinitely substitutable. It is not the notion that mouth opening causes mouth opening (a mapping at the level of a particular behaviour), but the more abstract notion that the other is doing 'the same as' I do. By 14 months, infants undoubtedly know that adults are not under their total control, and part of the joy of this exchange is the realization that although the infant does not actually control the other (the neonate's illusion), nonetheless the other is choosing to do just what I do. Together these two factors may help to explain why older infants will joyfully engage in the imitation game for 20 minutes or more – much longer and with greater glee than watching themselves in a mirror.

Newborn imitation and intersubjectivity

We have argued that the infant is sensitive not only to the timing of interactions but to the structural congruence between his own acts and those of other people. A developmentalist is immediately drawn to the question of origins. If one is interested in origins, the study of 14-month-olds or even 2-month-olds will not do. The place to look is the newborn.

The response of newborns to human faces is doubly interesting. On the one hand, it involves their reaction to a conspecific, one half of the intersubjective duet. On the other hand, we know with complete assurance that they have never seen their own face. At first blush it would seem out of the question that newborns could know anything about the fundamental similarity between their own face and that of the faces they see.

First impressions can be wrong. Research indicates that newborns are especially sensitive to human faces (Boysson-Bardies *et al.*, 1993; Morton and Johnson, 1991). More importantly for intersubjectivity, infants are not just visually attracted to faces, they are motivated to perform actions that match those they see. This is shown by the studies of neonatal imitation which have been replicated in more than twenty studies from a dozen independent laboratories (e.g. Abravanel and Sigafoos, 1984; Field *et al.*, 1982; Fontaine, 1984; Heimann, 1989; Heimann and Schaller, 1985; Heimann *et al.*, 1989; Jacobson, 1979; Kaitz *et al.*, 1988; Kugiumutzakis, 1985b; Legerstee, 1991; Maratos, 1982; Meltzoff and Moore, 1977, 1983a, 1989, 1992, 1994; Reissland, 1988; Vinter, 1986). In Meltzoff and Moore (1983a, 1989) literal newborns were tested. The oldest infant was 72 hours old, and the youngest was 42 minutes old. One cannot trace a human's response to other humans much farther back than this. This is the initial state.

We suggest that early imitation has deep intersubjective and communicative significance. This argument is a delicate one and takes some patience to get through. It is not so much that newborns imitate, but *how* they do so that is critical. If imitation were automatic, rote and reflexive it would have less far-reaching consequences. In fact, early imitation is non-reflexive, volitional and intentional.

Non-reflexive nature of imitation

If imitation were a simple reflex, it might fall to chance if a delay and intervening activity were inserted between eliciting stimulus and the motor response. In one study, a pacifier was put in infants' mouths as they watched the display (Meltzoff and Moore, 1977). Infants engaged in competing motor activity (sucking on the pacifier) during the presentation. The adult then stopped gesturing, assumed a neutral face pose, and only then removed the pacifier. The results showed that infants were able to imitate. Meltzoff and Moore (1994) pushed the delay further. Infants saw gestures on one day and were sent home. When they returned the next day the same adult sat before them with a neutral face. The infants stared at the adult and produced the particular gesture they saw the day before. These studies suggested that imitation can be mediated by a representation of the now-absent acts.

It had originally been supposed, without much empirical evidence, that neonatal imitation existed but then 'dropped out' of the infant's repertoire in the first 2–3 months of life. This was seized on as supportive of the reflexive account. Such 'drop out' was disproved when both Kugiumutzakis (1985b) and Field *et al.* (1986) found evidence for imitation in the so-called drop out period. Meltzoff and Moore (1992) also conducted a relevant test and likewise did not find drop out. Indeed, we were able to show how the 'drop out' misconception got started. We showed that the same infants who did not imitate under one test paradigm nonetheless responded with imitation when tested in a different way. It turned out that the capacity for imitation never disappeared; instead infants' interest at 2–3 months shifted to other types of social games and greeting (smiling, cooing).

Imitation could be robustly elicited if the social situation was arranged to focus on imitation rather than the more common games of this age period. Although imitative drop out is still found in textbook and chapter summaries, it can be explained by performance or motivation factors that can easily be reversed.

Volitional nature of early imitation

The volitional nature of imitation is shown by the fact that infants may choose to perform a different gesture than the one they are being shown. In particular, they may imitate a gesture that they have in memory rather than the one that is in the perceptual field. Infants demonstrate this in two ways: (a) they imitate the gesture shown the day before when the same person returns and shows a neutral face (Meltzoff and Moore, 1994); (b) when confronted with two adults in succession, they may imitate person-1's gesture when viewing person-2's (Meltzoff and Moore, 1992). This pattern suggests the nonautomatic nature of imitation. It is not solely driven by the information presented to the senses but appears to be under voluntary control. As shown by the findings discussed in the following section (pp. 58–60), infants deploy imitation according to their interpretation of the social interaction rather than having it triggered by the physical stimulus.

Intentional nature of early imitation

Early imitation is an intentional activity. In one experiment, 6-week-old infants were shown a novel oral movement, a large tongue protrusion to the side. For most babies the initial response was not an exact copy of the adult. Instead they made mistakes. A microanalysis of the response profile documented that infants corrected these initial attempts over successive efforts (Meltzoff and Moore, 1994). This pattern over time suggests that young infants can imitate novel motor patterns by monitoring and modifying their own acts to bring them into congruence with others'. The infant's goal seems to be to match the adult's act. Other research showed that infants commit rule-governed errors in their efforts to match the adult (Meltzoff and Moore, 1997), which further supports the notion that early imitation is goal-directed, intentional activity.

Intersubjective significance

The new empirical evidence supports the inference that early imitation is non-reflexive, volitional and intentional. We have developed a detailed model of the psychological mechanism mediating such early imitation (Meltzoff and Moore, 1997). In the model, the perception and production of human acts can be represented within a common supramodal framework. The model depicts infant imitation as a cross-modal matching-to-target process. The goal or behavioural target is specified visually. Infants' self-produced movements provide proprioceptive information that is compared to the visually specified target.

Our notion of a supramodal framework has implications for foundations of intersubjectivity, because it means that infants have a code for interpreting that the other is 'like me' right from the earliest phases of infancy. Self and other can be related because their bodily actions can be compared in commensurate terms: 'I can act like the other does and the other can act like me.' An early instance of intersubjectivity may be the 'state of being' experienced while intentionally imitating. This would encompass feelings about: the self (one's proprioceptive awareness and affective tone within the context of striving to match), the other (the other's acts felt/understood from the inside, having been carried out oneself), and the relationship (the infant is not alone, but is like the person who is seen, thus conferring a sense of identity or belonging).

Identity of individuals as a prerequisite for intersubjective relations

Intersubjectivity is not an oceanic feeling of connectedness between oneself and the universe of others. Our adult intuition is that 'subjective' experience is, at bottom, personal experience. Adult intersubjectivity arises from one's relation to specific others, each of whom is valued in their individuality.

A theory of the development of intersubjectivity must be concerned with how and when infants develop a notion of individual others. This raises an identity problem: How does an infant distinguish one person from another and reidentify a person as the 'same one' again, as someone with whom I have this relationship?

In thinking about this issue it is important to be clear about two meanings of 'identity' or 'sameness'. One meaning of 'the same' concerns the notion of an object being the self-same individual over different encounters in space and time. No two objects are 'the same' in this sense. A different meaning concerns appearances, in the sense that the features of this object are 'the same' or 'identical to' the features of that object. Many objects may be 'the same' in this sense. We refer to the first as 'unique identity' and the second as 'featural identity'.[2]

Unique identity is crucial to the adult notion of intersubjectivity. For example, one loves a person despite a change in hair style or wardrobe; one loves a specific person, not her twin, etc. The intersubjective relation goes between oneself and a particular other, where the unique identity of the other is essential.

One immediately becomes interested in whether infants are sensitive to the unique identity of persons. This matters because infants' intersubjective world would be very different from ours if they loved humanity but did not love individuals, or if an intersubjective relationship was not maintained whenever the surface features of the other were altered. To the degree that infants' notion of 'subject', or even their notion of individual, differs from our own, then the type of intersubjectivity this supports must be correspondingly different.

We conducted several studies in an effort to explore whether young infants paid any heed to unique identity at all, or whether their world of people was limited solely to a featural analysis.[3] In one study we showed 6-week-olds a gesture on one day and brought them back after a 24-hour delay when they were shown the same person sitting with a neutral face (Meltzoff and Moore, 1994). The results showed that infants remembered and imitated the particular gesture the adult did the day before. This suggested to us that infants were probing whether this person was 'the same one as' was seen the day before, despite the fact that the person's surface behaviour was clearly different. It is as if the infants were asking, 'Didn't we play this?' 'Aren't you the one who does this?'

The previous study concerned infants' use of gestures to reidentify people. We also explored their ability to differentiate individuals from each other. We presented 6-week-old infants with people who came and went in front of them, as would happen in real world interaction (Meltzoff and Moore, 1992). The mother appeared and showed one gesture (say, mouth opening); then she exited and was replaced by a stranger who showed a different gesture (say, tongue protrusion). When infants visually tracked these exchanges they could switch their actions to play two different gestural games, mouth opening with one person and tongue protrusion with the other. This finding, taken together with the previous one, suggests that young infants are showing a sensitivity to the individuality of the other. Thus, we think early interactive behaviour is directed toward *human individuals* and meets one minimal criterion for being treated as an intersubjective relation.

We also observed an interesting error infants made in the two-person experiment. We found that if the mother and stranger changed places without the infant visually tracking the exchange, they paused to inspect the new person, and then performed a burst of the actions shown by the previous person. This behaviour, as odd as it seems, is quite revealing. Recall that in the same test situation, when infants visually tracked the exchange, they smoothly switched gestures. It appears that if infants see the exit of one person and entrance of the second, they appropriately construe it as two individuals. However, in the absence of clear evidence that there are two people, in the absence of spatiotemporal evidence of twoness, very young infants were confused: Is it the same person who looks different, or a new person in the old place?

These questions are consistent with studies investigating the criteria infants use for maintaining the identity of a physical object. They show that very young infants predominantly rely on spatiotemporal information, such as places and trajectories, rather than featural appearances to determine unique identity (Bower, 1982; Moore *et al.*, 1978; Moore and Meltzoff, 1978; Meltzoff and Moore, 1995, 1998; Xu and Carey, 1996).

Our research goes beyond this previous work, because we made people, not inanimate things, disappear and reappear before the infant. Infants deployed imitative reactions to sort out their questions about the identity of people. This suggests that infants use *functional criteria* to complement other criteria for identity, at least for people. It is not only how a person looks, but the distinctive games he or she plays that helps to verify their unique identity. Distinctive games are functional properites that can be elicited through interaction. Infants deploy imitative behaviours as a tool for probing the identity of the other, as if the earlier interaction is a marker particular to that person.

That infants use imitation in this way suggests that they remember individual others and their own interactions with them. Instead of being limited to generalized reactions, such as smiling, cooing and greeting of 'humans in general', the specialness of particular relationships is born. Others become individuals whose relations with the infant are differentiated from each other. Because adult-like intersubjectivity depends on having individualized others with whom to relate, the deployment of imitation as a non-verbal criterion of identity gives it special relevance to the origins of intersubjectivity and communication.

Origins and development of infant intersubjectivity

We are now in a position to examine the innate structure infants bring to their first encounters and how this starting state is transformed through interpersonal interaction.

Human acts are the currency of early intersubjectivity

Let's start at the beginning, with newborns. What we are calling the *human act* may be the most elementary parsing of the world into things that bear on self–other relations and those that do not. Human acts are especially relevant to infants because they look like the infant feels himself to be, and because they are things infants can intend. When a human act is shown to a newborn baby, it may provide a primordial 'aha' experience. 'Something interpretable! That (seen) event is like this (felt) event.' It is not simply the features of the adults – the eyes, the lips, the hair – that are special for infants but the way the body moves and its relation to the self. The fact that infants can recreate the act allows them to give it special meaning.

On this view, the initial cut infants impose on the world is not any one of the usual suspects found in textbooks. It is not animate versus inanimate (because armadillos are only of passing interest), not self-mobile versus moved-by-a-seen force (because swinging clock pendulums are not viewed as special), nor even people (as adults know them) versus things. The most elementary distinction may be something closer to human acts versus other events.

Infants' tendency to see behaviour in terms of human acts that can be imitated has interesting implications: (a) the world of physical bodies is then divisible into those that perform human acts (people) and those that do not (things): (b) having made the division in the external world, new meanings are possible. Because human acts are seen in others and performed by the self, the infant can represent the other as 'like me': I can act like the other and reciprocally the other can act like me. Thus the newborn is not a social isolate and is provided with a bridge connecting self and other right from the beginning of infancy.

From shared acts to shared minds

Although we are postulating powerful innate tools for exploring self–other correspondences, experience with reciprocal imitation games provides a host of information for enriching this understanding. Such interaction carries at least the following information: (a) the adult's behaviour matches the infant's, (b) it is not a random congruence, (c) the specific behaviours do not matter, because the invariant of the game is to match, (d) from the infant's viewpoint, the infant's own novel behaviours were intended acts, (e) either the infant can propose and the adult respond or vice versa, and (f) either can withhold the reciprocal act. This provides grounds for an important realization by the infant: 'I intend to produce these acts, the adult performs these same acts, they are not chance events, therefore the adult intends his acts.' In other words, the similarity transcends the surface behaviour. This is a matching of intended acts.

There are dual implications from considering these interactions at the level of mutually intended acts, instead of only shared behaviours. Going in one direction, the infant now knows more about the other. The adult is an intending other. Going in the other direction, since the other is also like me, the infant could reconceptualize the intentional aspects of self. We have already shown that very young infants have intentions; but having intentions is different from being aware that one has intentions. The conception of self as one-who-intends and is like an intending-other would mark a considerable advance in intersubjectivity.

Infants begin life with a rich innate structure, which changes as their understanding of persons – themselves and others – is transformed through interpersonal exchanges. By the end of infancy they appreciate that they are psychological beings among other psychological beings, different from others, yet neither alone nor unique in the world.

Acknowledgements
Preparation of this chapter was supported by a grant from NIH (HD-22514). We thank Craig Harris and Calle Fisher for assistance on the research, and are deeply grateful for many helpful discussions on intersubjectivity with Pat Kuhl and Alison Gopnik. Special thanks go to Stein Bråten, our editor, without whose patience and quiet wisdom this essay would not have been completed. Correspondence concerning this chapter should be sent to Andrew N. Meltzoff, Department of Psychology, University of Washington (Box 357920), Seattle, WA 98195–7920.

Notes

1 A word about what this chapter is not. It is not our goal to reject previous discoveries about non-verbal intersubjectivity (mutual timing, joint attention and social referencing). Instead we hope to show how new work and theorizing complement these discoveries to provide a more comprehensive and developmental view.

2 With reference to the adult mind, philosophers refer to the former as 'numerical' or 'particular' identity (Strawson, 1959). We believe infants are engaged by this aspect of identity, but that the criteria they use to determine numerical identity are different from the adults'.

3 Previous work had shown that very young infants at least process the visual features of people. They can visually discriminate between a familiar facial pattern versus a novel one (e.g. Bushnell *et al.*, 1989; Field, Cohen, Garcia and Greenberg, 1984; Walton *et al.*, 1992). This does not inform us about their grasp of the unique identity of persons (Meltzoff and Moore, 1992, 1995).

CHAPTER 3

Neonatal imitation in the intersubjective companion space

Giannis Kugiumutzakis

Introduction

In this chapter I will describe four experimental studies undertaken to investigate the possibility that imitation could be observed with neonates less than 45 minutes old (Kugiumutzakis, 1985a).

In interpreting my observations I will discuss several hypotheses, old and new, which indicate that the first function served by human imitation is one of intersubjective communication (Trevarthen, 1977, 1993a). I will propose, first, that neonatal imitation involves concrete kinds of shared experience between the two partners; second, that it is motivated by two kinds of emotion or motive; third, that it takes place in a 'companion space' signifying the social and dialogical nature of the newborn mind (Bråten, 1986, 1988a, b, 1992, 1993, 1994a, b); and fourth, that it involves the harmonious function of processes at a conscious level and at an unconscious level. Finally, I will make the point that neonatal imitation in *experimental* semi-natural conditions may release some neonatal capacities and block others. In an appendix on mimesis in ancient Greek thought I shall succinctly review how imitation, and relations between cognition and emotion, were regarded by these philosophers: the Pythagoreans, Heraclitus, Democritus, Plato and Artistotle.

In dialogue with the past

Initial 'adualism' or 'dualism'?

Aristotle's notion that humans imitate by their nature has been confirmed by developmental research of the last thirty years (see Heimann, this volume; Meltzoff and Moore, this volume). Were one, however, to ask Aristotle if this innate nature of imitation could be manifest at birth, I would expect his answer to be negative, not just because innate potentialities are perfected by habit, but because the Aristotelian neonate would have no positive emotions to express to a parent, and no capacity to discriminate his or her self from the other (*Nicomachean ethics*, 1161b). The latter claim has been made explicit at the beginning of our century. According to Baldwin (1892), Freud (1911), Piaget (1932/1977:158; 1936/1977:80; 1968:12), and Vygotsky (Luria and Vygotsky, 1992:91, 95), the neonate lacks the necessary perceptual ability to observe the other's behaviour as a model. The assumed state of an initial 'adualism' excludes, by definition, imitation at birth.

About 200 years after Aristotle, however, this conflicting claim was made by the Stoic Hierocles: upon birth, all animals, man included, perceive their own limbs and organs and are 'conscious' of their proper functions, not derived from experience or rational inference (Inwood, 1984; Long and Sedley, 1987, I:313–14, 347; II:310–12, 344–5). For Hierocles, all animals have innately 'not just . . . a perception of themselves, but also of themselves *in relation to other animals*' (Inwood, 1984:161, emphasis added). Hierocles' observation of the initial dualism was ignored for more than 2000 years. Now it appears to be supported by relevant developmental research of recent decades (Baillargeon *et al*., 1985; Ball and Vurpillot, 1981; Butterworth, 1981, 1991; Kugiumutzakis, 1985a, 1988, 1993; Neisser, 1993; Stern, 1985; Trevarthen, 1977, 1986a). Inasmuch as the neonate is able to discriminate and reproduce a modelled behaviour, this directly disproves the notion of an initial adualism. By logical and psychological necessity, initial dualism is a precondition for human imitation at birth (Kugiumutzakis, 1992a).

'Uncontrolled' observations on neonatal and early imitation

During the last hundred years, neonatal and early infant imitation of the following models has been observed: (a) mouth opening at 15 days by Valentine (1930); (b) tongue protrusion at 17 weeks by Preyer (1887, in Guillaume, 1925/1971), at 15 weeks by McDougall (1908, in Miller and Dollard, 1941), at 11 weeks by Scupin (1907, in Guillaume, 1971), at 6 weeks by Gardner and Gardner (1970) and between the 7th and 25th day by Zazzo (1957); (c) lip protrusion at 15 weeks by Preyer (1887, in Guillaume, 1971); and (d) vocal models at 9 weeks by Brazelton and Young (1964), and during the neonatal period by Sully (1896, in Cressini, 1987).

Prandtl (1910, in Guillaume, 1971) asked this question: 'Why does the infant imitate the acts of a person, but not the movements of a curtain?' According to Maratos (1973), Lewis (1936) observed that infants preferentially imitate the human voice rather than non-human sounds. Bain (1855, in Miller and Dollard, 1941) had reported that the imitative behaviour of infants frequently 'disappears', and that, during early infancy, parents imitate infants much more than infants imitate parents.

All these 'uncontrolled', but accurate, observations have been confirmed in the last thirty years (see Kugiumutzakis, 1993). Under the influence of the Piagetian, behaviouristic, psychoanalytical and ethological theories, however, they were disregarded or dismissed as nothing more than manifestations of simple automatic reflexes.

Experimental studies on neonatal imitation

Learning to imitate, or imitating by nature?

The view that men imitate by nature was supported by Baldwin (1895), Darwin (1871, 1872) and Itard (1800, in Lane, 1977). The contrary view was entertained by the behaviourists (Bain, 1855, in Guillaume, 1971; Bandura, 1977; Miller and Dollard, 1941; Skinner, 1953), albeit failing to determine the exact kind of learning involved in the genesis of imitation. Piaget (1935, 1945/1962) proposed that humans learn to imitate and that neonatal imitation is impossible.

However, Maratos' (1973, 1982, 1996) experimental study indicated that 4-week-olds were able to imitate the facial models of tongue protrusion and mouth opening. In two, more controlled, experimental studies Meltzoff and Moore (1977) reported neonatal imitation of these and other movements in 12- to 21-day-old infants. In 1974, Trevarthen observed similar phenomena in neonates (Trevarthen, 1977), and other researchers reported imitation of facial gestures even by 1- to 2-day-olds (Field *et al.*, 1982). Partial failure to replicate the Meltzoff-Moore findings raised the possibility that neonatal imitation was not a fact, but an 'artifact' or, in the best case, an unimportant reflex-like phenomenon controlled by innate releasing mechanisms (Eibl-Eibesfeldt, 1989; Hayes and Watson, 1981; Jacobson, 1979; Kaitz *et al.*, 1988; Koepke *et al.*, 1983; McKenzie and Over, 1983).

With the neonate's permission

If it could be shown, however, that infants imitate right after birth, this would eliminate all explanations of imitation based on learning and would also force us to rethink our current conceptions of the social, cognitive, emotional and communicative abilities of the newborn. So, in the early eighties, under the influence of Maratos' study and Trevarthen's new theoretical proposals and research data, I tried to investigate the possibility that imitation can occur immediately after childbirth.

The first pilot study (N = 18, 2- to 8-month-old infants) took place in Athens and the second (N = 40 neonates, less than 45 minutes old) in Crete, while the four main studies took place in a maternity hospital in Heraklion, Crete (Kugiumutzakis, 1985a).

With the permission of the doctors and the parents-to-be, I was present at the births by vaginal deliveries and caesarian sections of all infants who took part in the studies. In a period of 13 months (March 1983 to April 1984) I attended 452 births (40 for the second pilot study and 412 for the main studies). In the delivery room I asked the mother's and the pediatrician's permission to test the baby. I noted the time of birth and the Apgar scores, and I attended the baby's first paediatric examination and her/his first bath, made by the midwife. About 10–15 minutes after the birth, the infant met her/his father, grandparents and other relatives in a room close to the lying-in room. There, with the help of the clinic's staff, I asked the permission of the father and grandparents to test the baby. This granted, the father, or more often he and the grandmother(s), took the newborn to the laboratory and placed her/him gently on the baby bed. In the case of preterm babies (see below) the paediatrician also came to the laboratory and remained present during the test. Relatives and the paediatrician observed the testing on a soundless TV screen located at the corner of the room and behind a black screen out of sight of the baby.

The laboratory was an isolated and warm room, where the sound of other crying babies was out of earshot. There was a baby bed set at about 10 degrees to the horizontal. Behind and above the bed a large vertical front-face mirror reflected my face and hands. Beside the bed there was a dimmer control, with which I regulated the lighting when the baby's visual system could not adapt to the room's lighting (see below). The bed, the mirror, a small table and my seat were surrounded by a black screen ensuring that my face would be the brightest object in the baby's visual field. For the same reason, I wore a black shirt during the test. A camera with high sensitivity to low lighting, located behind of the black screen, was directed to the baby's face and the mirror, recording simultaneously in the same image the movements of myself and the baby (Kugiumutzakis, 1985a, 1988).

In violation of standard criteria

In those years (1983–4), several experimental designs were advocated (Jacobson, 1979; Maratos, 1973; Meltzoff and Moore, 1977). But my experience in the lying-in room and the second pilot study led me to adopt my own more flexible design adapted to the neonates' age (less than 45 minutes old), systems, needs, wishes, individual differences and levels of communicative readiness at the moment of the test. My procedure 'violated' intentionally four of the standard criteria used in preceding studies of infant imitation, as follows:

First, it has been proposed that the infant subjects in such studies should be born at full term without complications, by mothers who received no medication during pregnancy, labour and delivery. Given that the cause–effect relation between these factors and the suspected consequence is 'often taken for granted on the basis of insufficient evidence' (Prechtl, 1982:23; Prechtl and O'Brien, 1982), I decided to test *no risk, alert* full-term and preterm neonates born vaginally or by caesarian section, the selection being based on the findings of the first paediatric examination and the Apgar scores.

Second, it has been suggested that the posture of *all* babies has to remain the same during the test period. This criterion disregards the relation between the baby's posture and her/his calmness, the latter being a necessary condition for the presentation of the facial models. In the delivery room I observed that a change of the posture of a whimpering baby often stimulated a calm state. It was natural for the midwives to change the baby's posture in an effort to calm her/him in the delivery room, a practice also adopted intuitively by parents during the neonatal period (see also Ronnqvist, 1993; Stratton, 1982). I decided to present the facial models with the baby either lying down on the baby bed or, if she/he did not *like* this posture (as judged from whimpering or a facial expression of uneasiness), I should hold the baby upright with the head in one hand and torso in the other. Thus the procedure was adapted to the neonates' postural needs at the moment of the test.

Third, it has also been proposed that the lighting of the experimental room should remain constant during the test. But, such a criterion disregards the difficulties of many babies for visual adaptation to the lighting of the new environment immediately after the birth, and also rapid adaptation of vision that a neonate may show when a sensitive adult either lowers or turns off the light, puts the hands around the baby's face or puts his or her body between the neonate's eyes and the source of the light. When helped in one of the above ways, the neonates in the delivery room were observed to open their eyes in less than 40 seconds. Thus, it was decided that if the eyes of the baby were closed when he/she entered the laboratory, I should lower or turn off the light with the dimmer control in an effort to help the infant's visual adaptation. Again the design was adapted to the baby's visual functioning and responsivity at the moment of the test (see Attkinson and Braddick, 1982; Prechtl, 1982; Prechtl and O'Brien, 1982; Stratton, 1982; Trevarthen, 1986a).

Fourth and finally, it has been proposed that responses of the newborn occurring during presentation of the standard model must be ignored, because the experimenter's behaviour may be influenced by the baby's behaviour, that is, the experimenter might imitate the baby (Masters, 1979). In the pilot study I presented each model five times and then I waited for the baby's response. The majority of the babies (77%) reacted after the fifth presentation of the model. The rest reacted (imitatively or not) after either the first, second, third or fourth model presentation. Masters' advice was not followed in the present studies for three reasons: (a) each model was presented as soon as the baby was entirely motionless and silent, (b) the digital time presented on the video screen makes it easy to decide who influences whom, and (c) this criterion ignores entirely the individual differences in communicative readiness of neonates in early interactions, and for this reason it is unrealistic and restrictive, sacrificing a recording of the complexity of the early imitative phenomena in the name of *the* ideal experimental design.

It was clear that I had to choose a maximum number of presentations of the models (say five times), but it was equally clear that some babies did not need all five model presentations – some needed four, and some only one. Thus, it was decided that when the baby started reproducing the model (for instance tongue protrusion) or emitted other scored responses (mouth opening, blinking, etc.), I stopped presenting the models regardless of the number of presentations already made. In natural mother–infant interactions co-actions are the exception rather than the rule. Again, the design was suited to the babies' communicative readiness at the moment of the test.

The above four modifications were introduced, on the one hand, to eliminate unnecessarily restrictive criteria and, on the other hand, to 'ask the baby's permission' for this semi-natural interaction. For instance, I sometimes observed clear avoidance movements during the presentation of the facial models, and in those cases stopped presenting the models out of respect for the infant.

Subjects and models

These were the criteria for admission to the studies: (a) the neonates should be no-risk babies, (b) they should be less than 45 minutes old, and (c) in each study, each baby would be exposed (if she/he 'liked to') to all models once, i.e. to either two models (Studies 1, 2, 3) or six models (Study 4) (See Table 3.1).

Following my observations at the 412 deliveries of the neonates who were recruited to take part in the main studies, twenty-six were excluded from attendance in the laboratory by criterion (a) (respiratory problems, etc.). Two caregivers refused to permit the testing of their babies. A further 214 of the 384 remaining neonates who came to the laboratory were excluded from data analysis by criterion (c) (eighty-two babies because of crying, sixty-four because of drowsiness, and sixty-eight because of diffuse motor activities and/or active, observable avoidance movements during the presentation of the models). In these cases the test either never started or was stopped. If the baby was crying, she/he was calmed by the experimenter and taken by the caregivers to a room where they waited for the mother. Thus 170 neonates finally met all three admission criteria.

In Study 1 took part fifty girls and forty-eight boys of mean birth weight 3435g; 1-min. Apgar $\bar{x}$ = 7, range 6–9; 5-min. Apgar $\bar{x}$ = 9.5, range 8–10. In Study 2 took part six girls and five boys of mean birth weight 3600g; 1-min. Apgar $\bar{x}$ = 6.6, range 6–8; 5-min. Apgar $\bar{x}$ = 9.2, range 8–10. In Study 3 took part four girls and eight boys of mean birth weight 2750g; range 2400–3320g; 1-min. Apgar $\bar{x}$ = 7.3, range 7–9; 5-min. Apgar $\bar{x}$ = 9.5, range 9–10. These babies were born either vaginally (three girls, one boy) or by caesarian section (one girl, seven boys). Estimation of the gestational age, made by the obstetricians, was based upon the date of the last menstrual period. Finally, in Study 4 took part twenty-two girls and twenty-seven boys of mean birth weight 3420g; 1-min. Apgar $\bar{x}$ = 7.1, range 6–9; 5-min. Apgar $\bar{x}$ = 9.5, range 8–10. Details of the subject groups are summarized in Table 3.1.

Procedure

Testing began with an adaptation period of 40 to 100 seconds with the baby alone on the baby bed and the experimenter out of sight. Until this moment the baby had no opportunity to observe my face. This adaptation period was introduced (a) to help the babies to adapt their visual system to the room's lighting, or to adapt the room's lighting with the dimmer control to the baby's visual system (the latter was required in 48% of the cases analysed), and (b) to judge if the facial models could be presented with the baby lying down on the baby bed; if not, I held the baby upright with the head supported in one hand and torso in the other (54%).

At the end of this period and as soon as the newborn was entirely calm (that is, in State 3 with open eyes, regular respiration and lack of gross movements and vocalization, see Prechtl and O'Brien, 1982), the first model was presented. The models were presented in a random

Table 3.1 *Number, gestational age, age and kinds of models presented in each study*

Study	Number of Infants	Gestational Age (weeks)	Mean Age at Recording (minutes)	Models for Imitation*
1	98 Vaginal full-term	39.5	27.0 (Range: 10–45)	TP and MO
2	11 Caesarian full-term	39.3	27.2 (Range: 15–40)	TP and MO
3	12 Preterm	36 (Range: 35–36)	26.0 (Range: 13–35)	TP and MO
4	49 Vaginal full-term	39.4	25.0 (Range: 14–42)	TP; MO; EM Sounds /a/, /m/, /ang/

* TP = tongue protrusion; MO = mouth opening; EM = eye movements

order with a different order for each infant. The facial models were presented at a distance of 20–23 cm from the baby's face, and the vocal models were presented with the baby lying down on the bed. The presentation time of the facial models depended on when the baby watched my face and on individual variation between the infants ($\bar{x}$ = 10 sec., range 3–19 sec.). If needed, I emitted four or five tongue clicks before each facial model presentation to elicit baby's visual fixation on my face. I presented each model five times (see above) and the presentation period was followed by a 10 sec. response interval, during which I presented a calm face. The next model was presented according to the same procedure.

Scoring and analysing the data

Three judges scored each videotape recording twice. Six kinds of responses were scored on the basis of standard descriptions, and the intra- and inter-scorer reliabilities were high. Six categories of responses were scored as follows: TP = the tongue must be seen to leave the mouth with a clear forward thrust beyond the lips, and then to re-enter the buccal cavity. MO = the lips must be widely separated and form an O. Yawnings were not scored. EM = the two eyelids must be seen to close and open in a clear blink. Sounds /m/, /a/ and /ang/: any vocal response containing clearly the respective sound.

The experimenter first analysed the data twice using 100% of the data. His intra-scorer assessment was conducted twenty days after the data had been analysed for the first time. His intra-scorer reliabilities across the scored categories ranged from .88 to .96. Second, a judge blind to the purpose of the study and unaware of the presented models coded 33% of the facial responses. This scorer could only see the baby's image on the screen, the experimenter's face being hidden by a black cloth. The intra-scorer assessment for this judge was conducted from a repeated analysis of the 33% of the data a week later. Intra-scorer reliabilities across the scored categories ranged from .97 to .98. A third scorer analysed 100% of the vocal responses by ear. Her assessment was repeated one week after the material had been scored the first time, using 100% of the data. Intra-scorer reliabilities across the scored sounds ranged from .87 to .91. To assess inter-scorer reliabilities the °-correlation was computed between the scores of each pair of judges. These correlations were 1.0 in all cases.

Because the scored responses may occur spontaneously, some of the responses counted as imitative may well be instances of spontaneous responses. True imitation can be said to occur only if the babies produce significantly more TP-responses after the presentation of the TP-model than after the presentation of the other models (MO and EM). For each study and response a t-test was then used to compare the probability of a response after the presentation of the corresponding model with the base rate (BR). If the above probability was reliably higher than BR, then a study was considered to yield evidence of imitation (Kugiumutzakis, 1985a, 1988).

Results

The results demonstrate that imitative responses, although present in spontaneous neonatal behaviour, are given significantly more often in the presence of the corresponding model than in its absence. On this criterion, neonates, less than 45 minutes old, imitated the facial models in the four studies, regardless of whether they were born naturally or by caesarian section and regardless of whether they were full-terms or preterms. In Study 4 the babies imitated (or more accurately, they clearly tried to imitate) the sound /a/, but not the sounds /m/ and /ang/. Table 3.2 indicates t values, BRs and the probabilities of each response in each study after the presentation of the corresponding model, p(R/M)s.

Further analysis of the imitators' behaviour indicated that they used two strategies of attention and three forms of reproductive behaviour. These behaviours are not typical either of automatic reflexes or of fixed action patterns. During the presentation of the facial models and

Table 3.2 *Comparison of BRs* and p(R/M)s* during the experimental conditions for each response and each study*

Responses	Study	BR	p(R/M)	t	p
Tongue protrusion (TP)	1	0.38	0.63	−3.57	0.0005
	2	0.30	0.67	−1.88	0.05
	3	0.33	0.71	−2.02	0.05
	4	0.28	0.53	−2.36	0.025
Mouth opening (MO)	1	0.37	0.61	−3.43	0.0005
	2	0.33	0.69	−1.82	0.05
	3	0.29	0.66	−1.96	0.05
	4	0.24	0.53	−2.81	0.005
Eye movement (EM)	4	0.21	0.48	−2.67	0.01
Sound /m/	4	0.26	0.27	−0.11	NS
Sound /a/	4	0.41	0.60	−1.91	0.05
Sound /ang/	4	0.25	0.26	−0.11	NS

* BR = base rate = probability of a response after the presentation of a different model(s); p(R/M) = probability of a response after the presentation of the corresponding model

the sound /a/ the neonates used two strategies of attention: (a) The majority of the neonates try – with a real, observable effort – to direct their attention to the moving part of the experimenter's face. The attention intensifies from a relatively fixed gaze to selective visual exploration. The baby inspects the moving part of my face with *clear interest while frowning*. According to Darwin, 'the frown shows that the mind is intent on one object' (Darwin, 1938, in N Notebook, obs. 58, cited in Gruber, 1974, p. 341). Premature neonates have to invest much energy during active perception, partly because of their low muscle tone and low toleration of respiratory loads, and partly because the moving human face affords much 'stimulus information'. Their visual exploration and frowning are longer than those of the full-term infants. The mean and range of the attention time of the full-term babies were $\bar{x}$ = 10 sec., range 3–19 sec. while for the preterm infants they were $\bar{x}$ = 15.2 sec. and range 12–19 sec. During the presentation of the sound /a/ model, I observed in the majority of the imitators a gradual localization of the sound by head turning, eye widening while the brows were held high – the latter movement occurs in attention listening (Rinn, 1984). (b) The second strategy of attention was observed in only a minority of full-term neonates. In the case of the facial models, the infant looks at the movement hastily, and as far as one can see from the video recordings played back in slow motion, it is as if the baby observes only the first presentation. She/he then starts reproducing the model immediately ($\bar{x}$ = 3.6 sec., range 3–4 sec.). A minority of full-term neonates responded immediately after the first or the second presentation of the sound /a/. Examining the recordings in slow motion, I observed eye widening only during the model presentation time ($\bar{x}$ = 7.6 sec., range 6–9 sec.). It was observed, furthermore, that the imitators attended somewhat longer to the EM model (range 8–19 sec.) than to the TP and MO models (range 3–19 sec.).

Three forms of reproductive behaviour were observed in imitation of the facial models:

(a) *Immediate or direct imitation:* the neonates reproduce the models once and the similarity of their reaction to the model's action is precise. The EM model was reproduced by the majority of the imitators once.
(b) *Successive, improving imitation:* the newborns reproduce the model a number of times, and in every additional effort they converge towards a more precise matching. This observation confirms findings reported by Maratos (1973) and Meltzoff and Moore (1977, 1983a). The babies follow this pattern mostly when imitating TP and MO models. Sometimes their efforts start with preparatory movements of the tongue inside the buccal cavity.
(c) *Successive deteriorating imitation:* the first imitative effort is a satisfactory reproduction of the model, and as they continue, neonates do not produce better results. In every additional 'effort' they depart more and more from the result of their first successful effort. It is as if they lose interest in imitation (Kugiumutzakis, 1985a).

The babies imitated the TP model more often and more easily than the MO model. Also they imitated the oral models more frequently than the EM model. The frequency of EM imitative responses during the reaction time was low (1–2 responses), and it seemed difficult for the babies to achieve the target of closing their eyes; they made crude and coarse movements of the eyelids. The imitative responses to the sound /a/ were strained. The baby tried hard to emit the sound, the result was usually an intense explosion of a prolonged and unstructured /a/ sound. The response was accompanied by stretching hand movements and closed eyes. Neurophysiological data suggest an explanation of why the babies imitated the oral models more easily than the EM model, and why they tried to imitate the /a/ sound but not the /m/ and /ang/ sounds. The oral region is controlled by many agile, small muscles that permit movement in many directions while the upper part of the face is controlled by fewer less differentiated muscles that do not permit movement in many directions. In addition, the muscles that move the mouth and especially the tongue have more proprioceptive receptors than the muscles that move the eyes. Moreover, there are differences in how different parts of the face are represented in the so-called topographic map of the body's muscles, located in the anterior lip of the central sulcus of the cerebral cortex. The size of the representation of each face part reflects the corresponding fine motor control. On that map the representation of the oral area is much longer than that of the upper face area. Also, in the brainstem there is a column of cell bodies making up the facial nerve nucleus. Specific cell groups in this nucleus map specific peripheral parts of the facial nerve. Those cell groups that innervate the muscles of the mouth are larger than the ones that innervate the upper face (Rinn, 1984). These data suggest that the control of the oral region develops earlier, which may explain why the baby is able to imitate oral models so much better, and why the neonates follow the 'immediate or direct imitation' (see above) when they reproduce the EM model. The neonates imitated (or better, tried to imitate) the sound /a/, but not the sounds /m/ and /ang/. According to Ferguson (1978:278–9), the progression of the myelinization in the primary motor cortex goes from the back of the mouth to the front. The emission of the sound /m/ requires neuromuscular control of the front part of the mouth and the neonate's vocal system is less mature for such an achievement. The vocal model of /ang/ may, likewise, be too difficult for imitation by babies less than 45 minutes old. The emission of the sound /a/, which is a non-front vowel (see Kugiumutzakis, 1985a), is evidently easier for them; the sound appears in crying (B. Brehmer, personal communication) and in other vocal emissions observed during the first hour of life. Two months later the babies are able to imitate all three sounds much better, as we have found in two longitudinal studies (see Kugiumutzakis, 1985a: Study 5, 1993, in press).

It was also found that 75% of the imitators reproduced the models (for instance mouth opening response to mouth opening model) in the *first* imitative effort, while the remaining 25% of the babies began by producing one to two tongue movements inside the buccal cavity, then they went on to open and close their mouth several times. No significant differences were found between imitation and sex.

As far as I know, all comparable studies of neonatal and early imitation have found babies, as I did, who do not imitate the models. For example, in Study 1, eighteen out of ninety-eight neonates did not imitate the MO model. Three out of the eighteen babies responded by TP to the MO model, two babies responded by blinking, one baby by hand movements, one baby with avoidance responses and eleven neonates did nothing. These eleven babies looked at the model carefully, and after the presentation of the model, they continued looking at my face, as if they expected the repetition of an interesting event. It was also observed that the same baby, in the same session, may imitate the TP model, but not the MO model (see Kugiumutzakis, 1985a, 1988).

Discussion

The above results confirmed those of Maratos (1973), Meltzoff and Moore (1977, 1983a, b), Dunkeld (1978) and Field *et al.* (1982). The same year Heimann and Schaller (1985) found evidence of neonatal imitation of the TP model. During the ensuing years, additional positive evidence has appeared that confirms the *fact* of neonatal imitation (Heimann, 1989; Heimann *et al.*, 1989; Legerstee, 1991; Kugiumutzakis, 1985a: Study 5, 1993; Meltzoff and Moore, 1989, 1992; Reissland, 1988; Vinter, 1986; Wolff, 1987) (see also Heimann, this volume; Meltzoff and Moore, this volume).

In my four studies, I observed two forms of attention during the presentation of the models, three kinds of reproductive behaviour, individual differences in communicative readiness for imitation, active participation of the imitator's whole body, alert neonates who did not imitate some or all of the models. In two other studies (Kugiumutzakis, 1985a: Study 5, 1993, in press), I found that selective imitation never disappears during the first six months. This polymorphic emergence and developmental picture of neonatal and early human imitation undermines directly the comparative ethological interpretations proposed by Eibl-Eibesfeldt (1989) and Jacobson (1979) (see also Maratos 1973, 1982; Meltzoff and Moore, 1977, 1983a, b, 1989, 1992; Trevarthen, 1977, 1986a).

The complexity of the phenomenon of neonatal imitation has led to a *richesse* of interesting theoretical explanations that stress, in different degrees, the perceptual, motor, cognitive, social, emotional and communicative aspects, the problem of the individual differences, the type of motivation (cognitive vs. emotional), and generally the course of development of imitation during infancy and early childhood (Bråten, 1984, 1992, this volume; Eckerman, 1993; Field *et al.*, 1982; Heimann, 1989, this volume; Heimann and Schaller, 1985; Kugiumutzakis, 1985a, 1988, 1993; Maratos, 1973, 1982, 1996; Meltzoff and Moore, 1977, 1983a, b, 1989, 1992, this volume; Nadel, 1980; Nadel and Pezé, 1993; Papousek and Papousek, 1977, 1989; Trevarthen, 1977, 1986a, this volume; Uzgiris, 1981).

The comparative studies of Bard (1994a, b, this volume) open a new way to consider the differences (the easy aspect) and the similarities (Darwin's purpose) of the same behaviour in two species and its different functions between them; and, why not, the challenging question of interspecies intersubjectivity.

Hypotheses and theory propositions

My hypotheses concerning the essentially social nature of neonatal imitation have been developed gradually under the influence of similar old and recent works (Kugiumutzakis, 1983) and my research experience (Kugiumutzakis, 1985a, 1988, 1993) and especially of Maratos' study, Trevarthen's research and theoretical works, and Bråten's thesis of the 'virtual other'. Below I summarize the basic features of my hypotheses.

I assume that before the first correct imitative response the neonate simultaneously has to (a) perceive clearly the models, (b) discriminate the self and the other as two separate interacting persons, (c) recognize the face isomorphism, (d) detect the experimenter's motivation, and (e) feel some motivation to imitate the models. After these perceptual, behavioural, cognitive and emotional experiences, the newborn infant can start reproducing the model. These five points will now be specified.

(a) The neonate has to perceive clearly the models, seeing clearly the facial models or hearing distinctly the vocal models, otherwise she/he has no chance to reproduce them. To do so the neonate has to *try*. This is evidenced by the neonates' real, observable efforts to direct their attention to the moving part of the experimenter's face. Their attention intensifies from a relatively fixed gaze to selective visual exploration. They inspect the moving face with *clear interest* and many of them *frowned* during this effort. In the case of presentation of the sound /a/ model, I observed gradual localization of the sound by head turning, eye widening while the brows were held high (see above). I consider these observable efforts as a *conscious* neonatal activity seeking and regulating experience.

(b) The neonate has to discriminate the self and the other as two separate persons co-existing in the same 3D space, both involved within an *interacting unit*. Without this discrimination neonatal imitation is impossible. Neonatal *dualism*, not only in the level of perception (see above) but in the level of action, is evidenced by the fact that 79% of the neonates in the present studies reacted *after* the fifth presentation of the models, although they had the opportunity to interrupt the experimenter's action. This ability to know when to take turns (a core, dialogical characteristic of innate intersubjectivity) means, in adultomorphic, declarative terms: '*I* know when *you* have stopped *your* action and when *I* have to start *my own*.' Contrary to the notion of an initial perceptual, cognitive and behavioural chaos, human neonates have not only a knowledge of themselves, but also a knowledge of themselves in relation to others, as has been claimed independently, at different times and through different studies, by Hierocles and Trevarthen, the latter's research leading to a new look at human development from its beginnings.

(c) The newborn has to re-cognize that her/his unseen, unmoving mouth corresponds to the other's moving mouth that she/he sees before her/him. Namely, the neonate has to re-cognize the model as something known. But how does it happen? Maratos (1982) has assumed that the neonate possesses 'a certain notion of his body schema' (p. 97). Trevarthen has assumed that the newborn infant has 'a discriminating image of the visible and audible movements' of the other's face (1979, p. 539). Meltzoff and Moore (1977, 1983a, b, 1989) have proposed that through an 'active intermodal matching/mapping', the baby can, 'at some level of processing', apprehend the face equivalences (1983a:708; 1989:961). I have hypothesized that the neonate has a relative 'memory engram' (Kugiumutzakis, 1985), while Butterworth assumes that there exists an 'equivalence-class detecting device', which authorizes the match between the visual input and proprioceptive output (Butterworth, 1993, personal communication). In the present studies 75% of the imitators reproduced the models correctly in their first imitative effort. This means that the crucial recognition has happened *before* the start of the reproductive movements, otherwise one cannot explain the correctness of the first imitative movement in the majority of imitators who made a mouth opening response to the mouth opening model from the start. Whatever the name of the mechanism, I think that the re-cognition of the face isomorphism is a precondition, not, as Meltzoff and Moore seem to assume, a result of the 'active intermodal *matching*', unless they mean by 'at some level of processing', an event occurring *before* the baby's first imitative effort. The ability to recognize the face isomorphism supports the notion of a non-reflex intermodal coordination functioning at birth. The neonates do not have to learn to recognize that others have body parts that are like their own, and how to relate with others (for instance how to take turns), if such feats were possible.

(d) The neonate has to detect the experimenter's intention and motivation for communication through imitation, when the model is being presented. Given that the models are movements and sounds, do these movements and sounds specify to the baby the other's intention and motivation to invite imitation? I have proposed that the neonate detects the defining invariants of the experimenter's motivation for communication, which lie behind the kinematic and acoustical surface of the models, before the first imitative reaction (Kugiumutzakis, 1985a). It has been found that human movement specifies to a human observer the factors responsible for its generation, and that intention, motivation and emotions are some of the psychological factors perceived (Frykholm, 1983a, b; Runeson, 1977, 1983; Runeson and Frykholm, 1981, 1983; Trevarthen, 1986a; Vedeler, 1991). Although the critical invariants over the kinematic and acoustical patterns of the models presented for imitation are so far unknown, we have to assume that the experimenter's motivation in the imitation test is detected. But the question is this: by what kind of psychological invariants? Is it possible that the neonate detects that the modelled movements and sounds are incomplete (Kugiumutzakis, 1994) and that it is the baby's turn and task to act and feel in a complementary way in the form of an imitation (see Michotte, 1946/1963; Trevarthen, 1986a)? The baby appears to perceive directly the motivation attached in the model movements and sounds (Gibson, 1979) and to return them with the same actions by which they were perceived.

(e) When awake, persons – newborns included – usually perceive, think, act and feel at once. Is neonatal imitation an emotional phenomenon? I have suggested that emotions involved in neonatal imitation can be either 'negative' or 'positive' (Kugiumutzakis, 1993, 1994). When neonates imitate other newborns' cries they appear to attempt empathic communication (Martin and Clark, 1982; Sagi and Hoffman, 1976). Although more research is needed in this crucial field, detection of the other's sorrow, specified in the acoustical and visual invariants, cannot be excluded. As for the positive emotions, I do not think that each of the facial models (tongue protrusion, blinking, mouth opening) has a specific emotion behind its surface. I assume that neonates can experience sadness, happiness and surprise, but not that they experience the actual emotions when imitating an actress's exaggerated expressions of such emotions, as studied by Field (1982) and her co-workers (see, however, Kraut, 1982; Strack *et al.*, 1988; Tomkins, 1962, 1980). I propose that the neonate, before, during and after the imitative episode, feels two interacting emotions: enjoyment and interest. Both interest and pleasure motivate the intersubjective, imitative game (Kugiumutzakis, 1993, 1994).

Relative studies have shown that interest and enjoyment are functional at birth of full-term and preterm infants, both are positively related, and behaviour motivated by their interaction leads to the successful completion of a task and subsequent enjoyment and interest (Dienstbier, 1979; Izard, 1979, 1992; Izard and Buechler, 1980; Malatesta *et al.*, 1986; Panksepp, 1992; Sullivan *et al.*, 1992; Tomkins, 1979, 1980; Trevarthen, 1977, 1982a, 1984b, 1993a; Tronick, 1989; Zajonc, 1980, 1984).

I propose that the emotion of enjoyment may be evoked by the potential sharing in the occurrence of a desired encounter. The recognition of the other as an actual other in the baby's companion space (Bråten, 1986, 1988a, b, 1992, 1993, 1994a, b) may evoke the enjoyment or pleasure of being-together. The model invites the baby's gaze, ears and mind, and serves 'as a goal in an alteroceptive or intersubjective space' (Trevarthen, 1986a:237) where the playful sharing, as an inborn disposition, takes place. The adult's invitation has been recognized and accepted, the intersubjective expectation has been confirmed, the space of the virtual other has been filled by a friendly, actual and similar being, the game of potential sharing has started and it has to be completed. Furthermore, the recognition of the modelled movements and sounds as *incomplete, imitable, known* tools of communication and as novel and changing stimuli may evoke the emotion of interest – the basic emotion, which elicits, focuses and maintains attention to the modelled movements and sounds and motivates the complementary, social, imitative activity, engaging the neonate, immediately after the birth, into the social world. The other's dynamic personal presence, emotions and motivation are directly felt in presentational immediacy. They are felt as an invitation for interaction inside the nest of the emotions of the intersubjective companion space. I think that enjoyment and interest are, at least immediately after the childbirth and during early infancy, causes and regulators of the perception, action and cognition involved in neonatal imitation. Kokkinaki's (1998) innovative, longitudinal, intercultural, naturalistic study of early infant–father and infant–mother imitations indicates interest and enjoyment to be the prevailing emotions of parents and infants.

If it is true that vowel sounds carry the affective values important for interpersonal exchanges, the findings in the present Study 4, that the neonates tried to imitate only the /a/ sound, and those of another naturalistic study (Kugiumutzakis, 1993) that 76% of the mother–infant vocal imitations were vowel sounds, indicate that neonatal and early infant imitation are not emotionless phenomena. Although more studies are needed in the area of the emotional dimensions of the neonatal imitation, the study of the latter offers us the opportunity to investigate cases of the unconflicting co-operation of emotions, cognition, perception and action in two interacting persons, instead of being forced to consider the stable primacy of either cognition or emotions. Meltzoff and Moore (1989, 1992) have suggested that neonatal imitation is motivated by the baby's detection of a mismatch or conflict between the adult's passive face following the presentation of the model and the stored representation of the model. I rather assume that the baby's imitation is the result of a drive for intermental and behavioural matching, originated in a neonatal exploratory motive system that is seeking another emotional being with whom to play together a cooperative, complementary, intersubjective game.

Over ten years ago, I tried to explain the mechanism of the imitative reproduction itself in terms only of the intermodal aspects (Kugiumutzakis, 1985a). I had disregarded the existence in the neonate of the coordinative structures and the plurimodal control of movement. From a consideration of the temporal rhythms of interaction, it has been proposed that neonates share with adults 'matching oscillators'. As Trevarthen (1986a) proposes, the rhythmic intercoordination of the two partners' motivation and emotions may lead to the intercoordination of their matching oscillators, and this gives rise to the neonatal imitative response, exciting parallel sensory effects in the proprioceptive, exproprioceptive and alteroceptive modalities. The selection of the correct motor schema may not be the most difficult step in this prereflecting process, because the neonate possesses neuromotor systems representing the modelled movements as events in time and space.

I have noted these difficult steps in imitative interaction: first, the observable efforts the newborns make to perceive the models clearly (see above), and second, the difficulty they have in the execution of the reproductive behaviour itself. The difficulty of the latter step may depend on the infant's gestational age (full-term vs. preterm), on the relative maturation of different neuromuscular systems, and on the differences of control for the musculature of upper and lower parts of the face (see above).

Some steps are probably difficult, requiring manifest effort on the part of the neonate (to perceive and reproduce the models), while other steps may occur in a pre-reflective, effortless manner (self–other discrimination, detection of the face isomorphism and the experimenter's motivation, feelings of transient emotions, and selection of the appropriate motor schema). If this distinction is correct, then – in addition to assuming the dual cerebral representation of self and other in various states of motivation – one can hypothesize that the mind of the newborn infant, when interacting with the actual other, is functioning at *two intercoordinated* levels: (1) one *unconscious*, intuitive and probably conceptless level, in which the baby perceives, recognizes and communicates with the core of the other's mind, and (2) another *conscious* and effortful level, in which the neonate strives to perceive clearly and tries to imitate the models in a satisfying way. Thus, I propose two kinds of processes functioning in harmony, respectively, one operating outside of conscious awareness at the interpersonal, intersubjective level, and another operating under volitional control at the intramental and behavioural level. Neonatal imitation may indicate that these two hypothetical processing systems are simultaneously functional and cooperative at birth. Both cortico-amygdala and thalamo-amygdala projections (LeDoux, 1986, 1989) may be involved in neonatal imitation.

Conclusion

Neonatal imitation is an intersubjective phenomenon which offers us the opportunity to study what, consciously and intuitively, the two partners share. They appear to share the same three-dimensional space, and the same intersubjective companion space. They share the tendency to act and interact in turns, and the capacity for self–other discrimination and face and voice isomorphism. They share the same code of communication, and the ability to read each other's motives and intentions, the same transient emotions. They demonstrate the ability to imitate each other's actions – in the beginning, imitation could be defined 'operationally' as the sharing of the same action. Neonatal imitation in experimental conditions, however, is a semi-natural kind of interaction that may release some neonatal capacities and block others. The adult (psychologist) is less intuitive and more conscious than the infant and her/his parents are when they are playing spontaneous imitative games. In spite of their differing in many other respects and abilities, however, what they do share suffices for the first emotional contacts, indicating them to be 'other-seekers', minds ready to extend beyond the skin to meet the other intermentally and co-behaviourally.

Appendix: On mimesis, reason and emotion in ancient Greek philosophy

During the last 200 years, psychological theories of human imitation have, I believe, over-stressed the cognitive aspect and under-estimated the emotional, as if imitation occurs within emotionless contexts and between emotionless persons. Piaget's (1962) theory of early imitation is typical of the cognitivist tradition. Does this tradition have some progenitors in ancient Greek philosophy? To answer this question, I shall succinctly describe how the concept of mimesis (imitation) has been used there, and ask whether emotions and cognition are involved in imitative phenomena as described by the Pythagoreans, Heraclitus, Democritus, Plato and Aristotle. Here one finds imitation regarded as a fundamental process at intercosmic, interspecies and intrahuman levels.

The Pythagoreans: Intercosmic and intrahuman imitation

The Pythagoreans regarded imitation as a metaphysical mechanism of cosmic re-creation and, at the same time, as a human kind of learning by imitation. In the 'beginning' there was an original point, the womb of the macrocosm, identified with the number One. Its self-division created the harmonious macrocosm of the spherical earth, planets and sun, which revolve round the One. The microcosm of humans, animals and objects is regarded as an imitative re-creation of the macrocosm, though we are not informed about the imitator's nature. Both cosms are numerable, both are Numbers and have limited structures with correct quantitative relations between opposite qualities – the harmony of the opposites. Macrocosm is divine while the microcosm is mortal. The human body is the mortal prison of the immortal soul, which is a little fragment of the divine, universal Soul. The salvation of the human soul is by soul-training through imitation of three kinds of models: first, the best model, the life of the philosophers and mathematicians who study and know the order and beauty seen in the starry sky; second, the life of the politicians, who aim at social recognition; and third, the life of the 'appetitive' men, who try to satisfy only their own needs (Bagionas, 1992; Beardsley, 1982; Copleston, 1962; Guthrie, 1967; Veikos, 1988).

In the Pythagorean theory of imitation, the cognitive element is of paramount significance (all are Numbers, quantitative relations of the opposites, etc.) – a tradition continued by Plato. Negative emotions are to be controlled ('people are bad') and positive emotions (friendship) to be promoted, like the harmony in terms of numbers in the centre of this old philosophical school. Even Alcmaeon of Croto (about 500 BC), who made anatomical studies and asssumed sensation and thought to occur in the brain, did not estimate emotions (Hunt, 1993; Kirk *et al.*, 1983; Leahey, 1987; Zeller and Nestle, 1883/1980).

Heraclitus: Man imitates the One-in-many

In Heraclitus' (544–483 BC) theory, nature is the unity and conflict of opposites – all are One and Fire. Nature is the unity in difference and the identity in diversity – the One-in-many. Change is the only lawful constant in the 'hidden attunement' of Nature. Nature loves to hide. The divine Mind taught men to imitate (Axelos, 1974:235). Through their imitative arts (fine arts and vocations) men try to reproduce the tension, conflict and unity of the opposites. As imitators, men may know what they are doing, for example, in the mixing of opposite colours. But their imitative efforts do not lead to deeper truths, because they cannot perceive the model as part of the One; the unity and the conflict of the opposites are sometimes sensible and sometimes not. Being embodied in the One, men can sometimes reproduce some aspects and moments of the opposites, and imitative arts could sometimes become creative (Axelos, 1974; Copleston, 1962).

In Heraclitus' theory of imitation, the primacy of reason (*logos*) is again clear. Emotions have either to be unsatisfied or to be controlled by reason – the unity, but most of all the conflict of the opposites. Located in the breast, emotions are the opposite of reason. And this is exactly the human drama, because man has to fight with herself/himself: 'It is difficult to make war on your heart . . .' (Frag. 85 in Axelos, 1974:216–17).

Democritus: Man imitates animals

Democritus (460–370 BC) promoted a thesis about the evolution of culture, in which imitation plays an important role. Human culture was regarded as the product of need. The first social bonds and social groups were created as a defence against the attacks of the wild animals. Language arose from the need to communicate and understand. Vocations and fine arts developed gradually and they were based upon man's ability to imitate natural things, especially animals: 'In most of our important achievements we have been students and imitators of the animals: in the arts of weaving and sewing we have been imitators of the spider; in the art of building houses we have been imitators of the swallow, and in the art of song we have been imitators of songbirds, swans and nightgales' (Frag. 154 in Papadopoulos 1979:177).

In this theory, imitation leads not only to new, useful products and achievements, but to a better understanding of the model: know the model by imitating it. Imitation is not a faithful and simple copy of the model, but an intentional and creative activity of reproduction, supplementation and perfection of the model, in order to meet basic and aesthetic human needs. It is an inventive re-creation of a new human product (e.g. a house), the model of which can be found in nature (a swallow's nest) (Copleston, 1962; Papadopoulos, 1979).

In Democritus' theory of interspecies imitation (see Bard 1994b), cognition plays the basic role, while emotions are more or less ignored, albeit attributed a minor role in moral dilemmas (Papadopoulos 1979:270–1).

Plato: On the re-creation and imitation of shadows, and why the head has a body

Plato's (429–347 BC) theory is probably the first ancient theory in which we can find clear relations between imitation, emotions and cognition. Imitation is considered to be both a metaphysical process and a human activity, playing a crucial role pertaining to these three hierarchically organized levels of reality: first, the level of ideal Forms; second, the level of sensible objects; and, third, the level of artistic works. Despite the unclear meanings of the imitation concept in Plato's complex philosophical system, imitation is attributed to 'solve' various difficult problems, such as the origin and nature of the cosms, species, virtues, arts, etc. For Plato, time imitates eternity; sounds are imitations of the divine harmony; words are imitations of things; laws imitate truth; human governments are imitations of the True Government; moral men try to imitate their gods; sensible objects are imitations of the Forms; artistic works are imitations of the sensible objects (Plato, *The Republic*, 596A-597E; *Laws*, 713E; *Kratylos*, 423E-424B, 432B-D; *Kritias*, 107B-C; *Phaedros*, 252C-D, 253B; *Politikos*, 293E, 297C, 300C; *Timaios*, 38A, 47B-C, 50C, 80B).

According to Plato, some 'God' (the Good, the Reason, the One) created the macrocosm of Forms, and 're-created' by imitation the microcosm of humans, animals and objects. Forms are considered incorporeal, uncompounded, changeless, timeless, spaceless, inaccessible to the highly imperfect human senses and apprehensible only by abstract thought ('philosophical dialectics') and mathematical reason.

Inasmuch as the Forms (the first level of reality) are Real, and the sensible objects (the second level) are imperfect imitations of the Forms, then artists who try to imitate the sensible objects in painting, music and poetry, do nothing more than to reproduce a shadowy reality (the third level). A painter, for example, merely imitates an imperfect imitation. The product of this effort stands at three removes from truth. The hierarchical structure of reality does not permit direct manifestation of the first level at the second and third levels. This pertains even to artists guided by the Muse, who wants them to come up with expressions reflecting the first level of reality. Being in ecstatic 'divine' madness – a moment of contact of the first two realities, of the divine God with the mortal man – the artists are not able to catch clearly the ideal message – their relative representations are confused.

Returning to sanity, the artists try to translate, re-present, reproduce, imitate the message. Imitation is the basis of arts, says Plato, and yet does not lead the artists to true imitative products.

Entailing the absence of pure reason, the imitative arts are addressed to the emotional 'part' of human nature. The emotions aroused by the arts are usually deleterious and encourage weakness rather than self-control. In his utopian State, with a few interesting exceptions, Plato rejected arts as capable of revealing truth, of offering moral models, or helping with emotional temperance. Reason has to control both imitation and emotions after deciding (through the Guardians of the Law and the Minister of Education) what art is to be excluded and what is to be admitted in the ideal State (Plato's *Republic, Phaidon, Sophistis, Laws, Kratylos, Kritias, Phaidros, Politikos, Timaios*).

Although in the last years of his life Plato had a somewhat more favourable opinion about the imitative arts and was more pessimistic about the power of cognitive control over the emotions, he did not alter his thesis about the primacy of reason. The emotional part of soul (located in the breast), unless corrupted, is (has to be) under the control, as an obedient horse, of the rational part (located in the head). The head as the container of reason is spherical, in imitation of the cosmic whole, and Plato explains *why the head has a body*: 'In order, accordingly, that it should not roll about on the ground, which has all kinds of hills and hollows, and be puzzled to know how to climb over the one and out of the other, they [the Gods] gave it the body as a carriage and means of movement' (*Timaios*, 44E). Emotion cannot be a source of Real knowledge. The rational part thinks best when neither senses, desires nor emotions trouble it (*Phaidon*, 65C). In Plato's thesis about the primacy of reason, when one has to maximize pleasures one has to balance immediate pleasures against future pains and immediate pains against future pleasures. Something like a 'hedonist calculus' is needed, and this only reason can offer (Adkins, 1970:132).

For Plato, emotions appear at birth and the solution to the problem of their conflict with reason is to make the rational and irrational (emotions and desires) coincide from an early age by some kind of conditioning (*Republic*, 441A; see also Adkins, 1970). In the *Odyssey*, as a poetic re-presentation of the human life, Odysseus is controlling his emotions. That is why Plato prefers him as a good model for people (De Romily, 1992).

Aristotle: Man imitates man

In Aristotle's (384–322 BC) theory, imitation is considered as an innate human capacity/potentiality, made perfect by habit. 'Imitating is natural to human beings from childhood onwards: man differs from other animals in being extremely imitative; his first steps in learning are made through imitation, and all people get pleasure from imitation . . . Imitating, melody and rhythm are natural to us' ('Poetics', 1448B; see also *Nicomachean ethics*, 1102–3). Vocal imitation is regarded as the most precise form of imitation, because the vocal organs are the most accurately reproductive of all parts of the body (*Rhetoric*, 1140A).

For Aristotle, arts imitate and complete nature. Artists are able to imitate or re-present an event or object by using their infallible perception and fallible thinking. Poetry involves the creative intervention of the imitator: observation, discovery, selection, formation, purging and penetrating of the modelled elements offered by the empiric, historic and mythical world. The poet does not see reality as it is, full of particular and accidental events, but he searches the regularity of the parts and re-presents the general, universal truths. Poetry is based upon imitation and nurtured by the pleasure of imitation. Natural in all men is a tendency to get pleasure in observing imitations performed by others. While we find it painful, for example, to see dead men, we enjoy looking at perfect imitation of them in theatre. This pleasure is for cognitive reasons (Sykoutris 1936:80), not just from the perception of the actor's behaviour, but in virtue of the onlookers being led to reasoning, step by step, towards a realization by 'syllogismos' how each thing is. Especially in tragedy, where happiness and unhappiness are re-presented, there is another emotional phenomenon involved: tragedy leads to the 'purification' (catharsis) of the emotions. 'By means of pity and fear, it [tragedy] contrives to purify the emotions of pity and fear' in the onlookers (*Poetics*, 1449B).

For Aristotle, the human body and soul are inseparable and mortal. The human soul includes the qualities of the plant souls (reproduction and nutrition), and the animal souls (senses, desires to move, to seek pleasure, and to avoid pain; memory, imagination and emotions). One part of the soul, called Active Mind, is not united with the body and is pure thought, stable, identical in all men, survives death and leads to the rational knowledge of the universals. Mind is always right (*De anima*).

Human emotions are innate, appear at birth, are felt 'without choice' by soul and body. Indeed, emotions are 'embedded in the matter' of the body (*Nicomachean ethics*, 1105B, 1148B; *De anima*, 403A; *Logic*, Book 8). Emotions are defined as to 'change people so as to alter their judgements and are accompanied by pain and pleasure – for example, anger, pity, fear and their opposites' (*Rhetorics*, 1378A).

Emotions are subdivided by these two basic features: pain and pleasure. In *Rhetorics* Aristotle analyses these emotions: feeling angry, feeling mildly, friendly feelings, hatred, feeling afraid, feeling confident in the face of danger, the feeling of being disgraced, kindly feelings, pity, righteous indignation, envy, feeling of eagerness to match the accomplishments of others (see Cooper, 1993:183–4). Children and young people are swept away by their emotions. Emotions are intrusive feelings that '*occupy the mind and absorb and direct attention*' (*ibid.*:191), thus altering men's judgements. Emotions are more evident during the early years leading more to action than to knowledge. Emotions 'without reason . . . are evidently hurtful' notes Aristotle (*Nicomachean ethics*, 1144B, see also 1094B, 1128B). Emotions are twofold: one part of them ('the plant element') in no way shares in reason, while the other (the appetitive, concerned with desires) partakes of reason in so far as it listens and obeys it (*ibid.*:1102B).

Aristotle claims that man is by nature a social animal. Society cannot function, however, when the irrational emotions prevail. People have to avoid the excesses and defects of their emotions and actions – they have to seek and choose the intermediate, the Mean, and to learn to control their emotions. For that reason people educate young children by steering them with the aid of pain and pleasure, and at the level of the State the legislators make citizens good by forming habits in them. But the irrational passions (emotions) are not easily controlled. Therefore men have to be satisfactorily habituated, because their emotions do not yield to reason but to force: 'We shall need laws for this [the control of the emotions] as well, and generally speaking to cover the whole life' (*Nicomachean ethics*, 1180A). In everyday life and art, men have to seek the Mean, determined by the rational principles.

If you control the way children play . . .

In the philosophical theories reviewed above, except in Plato's theory, imitation serves mostly learning, ethics and aesthetic needs. Imitation is regarded (a) as a metaphysical, intercosmic process of creation and re-creation of the macro- and microcosm (the Pythagoreans, Plato), (b) as an interspecies learning by inventive imitation of animal behaviour, resulting in new human achievements and better understanding of the model (Democritus), (c) as a specific kind of learning by imitation either of the hidden natural attunement, ending usually in imperfect artistic works (Heraclitus), of the Forms and their shadowy sensible objects, resulting always in imperfect artistic reproductions and very limited true knowledge (Plato), or of the real, historical and mythical models, ending, through creative intervention, in satisfactory art products and knowledge of the universals (Aristotle), and (d) as the usual intrahuman kind of learning by imitation of the basic human skills – man imitates by nature (Aristotle).

Cognition was regarded as an ever-present prior element of imitation, while emotions were either ignored and underestimated (the Pythagoreans, Democritus), present but evil and requiring to be controlled by reason (Plato, Heraclitus), or present and accepted because of their cognitive origin (Aristotle). Although Aristotle discriminated between the positive and negative emotions and had hopes about the virtual power of friendship (*Nicomachean ethics*, 1172A), he also stressed the irrational nature of emotions (the 'plant' element). And Plato advocates his canon of control: 'If you control the way children play, and the same children always play the same games under the same rules and in the same conditions, and get pleasure from the same toys, you'll find that the conventions of adult life too are left in peace without alterations . . . Change . . . is extremely dangerous' (Plato, *Laws*, 797A).

The ancient philosophical and the current psychological theories on human imitation are in the same tradition with regard to these aspects: first, asserting the primacy of reason; second, in focusing on learning as one out of the many functions of imitation; and third, entertaining the notion that emotions and cognition are more or less opposites. Despite the stress of the ancient theories on the need to control emotions by reason, however, the theories of Plato and Aristotle indicate that imitation does *not* occur within emotionless contexts and between emotionless persons.

Acknowledgements

I am indebted to Berndt Brehmer (Uppsala University) and to Colwyn Trevarthen (University of Edinburgh) for valuable comments throughout the preparation of this work.

CHAPTER 4

Imitation in neonates, in older infants and in children with autism: feedback to theory

Mikael Heimann

The neonate's capacity to imitate has been an issue among infancy researchers for more than two decades. The debate was initially motivated by the systematic observations reported during the 1970s by Maratos (1973) and Meltzoff and Moore (1977), observations that indicated an imitative ability among almost newborn infants. Both Meltzoff and Moore, and Maratos reported that infants less than one month old were able to imitate facial gestures, findings that contrasted sharply with Piaget's (1945/1962) theory of the early development of imitation. The scientific community reacted partly with surprise and disbelief to these findings and, as a consequence, most studies to date have primarily investigated whether the phenomenon is real or should be regarded as an artifact. However, a clear majority of these studies have been able to support the early findings by Maratos as well as by Meltzoff and Moore (e.g. Abravanel and DeYong, 1991; Abravanel and Sigafoos, 1984; Dunkeld, 1978; Field *et al.*, 1983; Fontaine, 1984; Heimann, 1992; Heimann and Schaller, 1985; Heimann *et al.*, 1989; Kaitz *et al.*, 1988; Kugiumutzakis, 1985a; Legerstee, 1991; Meltzoff and Moore, 1983a, 1989; Reissland, 1988; Vinter, 1986; Wolff, 1987). Thus, neonatal imitation must be considered a robust phenomenon that can be observed directly at birth,[1] although its role and significance for the early development of the infant remain to be formulated.

It has been suggested, and this is further supported through observations by Kugiumutzakis (1993), Legerstee (1991), Meltzoff and Moore (1992, 1994) and Holmlund (1995), that the newborn baby can be described as already knowing something about his/her body and that this 'knowledge' makes it possible for the infant to differentiate between the inside and the outside world (see also Trevarthen and Aitken, 1994). For the purpose of this chapter, the basic assumption is that newborn infants are able to imitate facial gestures and that this capacity probably is based on the infant's sensitivity to facial configurations (Johnson and Morton, 1991), on the existence of innate social motives (Trevarthen, 1993a, this volume; Trevarthen *et al.*, 1997) and on an innate dialogical organization of the infant's mind (Bråten, 1988a). Together, these three prerequisites 'propel' the child to increased attention and motivation for interaction when, for instance, being held in a face-to-face position.

More specifically, this chapter aims at discussing two questions about which we still lack conclusive evidence. (1) Is neonatal imitation in any way directly related to imitation observed later during the first year of life? (2) Could we expect children with autism to show an ability to imitate at birth? Some preliminary answers will be provided through a review of published and unpublished studies carried out by me and my colleagues in Göteborg, Sweden. After a brief outline of a theoretical starting point, the chapter goes on to present some of our Swedish findings. First, observations on imitation during the neonatal period are presented: this is followed by observations on imitation beyond the neonatal period. Thereafter, possible connections between neonatal imitation among children with autism will be discussed. The chapter ends with a brief summary aimed at integrating the reported findings.

A possible starting point

Although the scientific support presented above for the human neonate's imitative capacity may seem impressive, it is worth reminding the reader of the fact that neonatal imitation has been defined almost exclusively on a purely behavioural basis: *Neonatal imitation (NI) = A selective increase in frequency of the behaviour that has been modelled compared with observed frequency after the presentation of alternative gestures.*

Thus, reported imitation within the neonatal period simply tells us that we can observe an increase of a certain behaviour (e.g. mouth opening) after modelling of that behaviour as compared with the observed frequency when an alternative gesture is modelled (e.g. tongue protrusion). As defined, the concept by itself does not imply any specific inner psychological process: the phenomenon is based purely on behavioural observations and statistics based on frequency counting. Note also that the definition says nothing about the number of presentations needed, rate of presentation, the response window allowed, the infant's state or physical aspects (e.g. illumination or humidity) – all factors that differ across studies and that, most probably, explain a large part of the controversy that arose among various researchers in the late 1970s and early 1980s.[2]

Meltzoff and Moore (1977, 1983a) proposed that the infant, at birth, already possesses a representational system which makes it possible to imitate a behaviour that the infant cannot see itself perform (e.g. tongue protrusion). Later, Vinter (1986) suggested, in accordance with Goldman-Rakic (1985), that NI is based on representation mediated through subcortical processes, whereas imitation developing at later ages is based on cortical processes. This view is supported by findings on multimodal individual neurons and multisensory maps in subcortical areas (e.g. the superior colliculus: Stein and Meredith, 1993) as well as by observations indicating that face preference at birth is subcortically mediated (Simion *et al.*, 1996). In conjunction, these findings indicate a possible neuropsychological basis for neonatal imitation.

Uzgiris (1981) has pointed out that imitation serves different functions within the cognitive and the social domains and that we may not be able fully to understand neonatal imitation as long as we focus only on imitation as a cognitive skill (as in the Piagetian tradition). Over the years, this view has come to be adopted by most researchers interested in the early imitative capacities of the infant, and several authors have concluded that NI must be interpreted within a social framework (e.g. Heimann, 1989; Kugiumutzakis, 1985a; Maratos, 1982; Meltzoff and Moore, 1992). This view is also supported by Holmlund (1995) who states that 'from birth, communication is a directed and intentional process for the purpose of prolonging pleasing feelings' (p. 45). Holmlund submits that imitation is congenital and should be considered as an important part of the early social and communicative interactions taking place between the child and his/her parents. Her own observations indicate that this rudimentary communicative pattern forms a specific sequence: the infant (1) turns his or her attention towards the parent for 20 to 30 seconds, (2) displays eye blinking, (3) shows an increase in motor reactions, (4) averts gaze briefly, and (5) engages in prespeech behaviour. Holmlund points out that this is a very fragile pattern not always clearly visible during the neonatal period, but that it might be vital for parents and researchers to be aware of the long initial orientation period often displayed by the young infant. Otherwise one might easily miss responses or reactions, and might misinterpret the dynamics of an interaction that is slowly taking off.

A related, but more radical, theoretical perspective has been proposed by Bråten (1988a, 1994b, this volume) who submits that the basic organization of the mind is both dialogical and intersubjective, and that the infant has 'an innate capacity. . .to take part in an immediate dialogic "dance" with the actual other' (Bråten 1988a:195; see Figure 4.1[3]). The mother and the infant are seen as one unit of dialogic closure

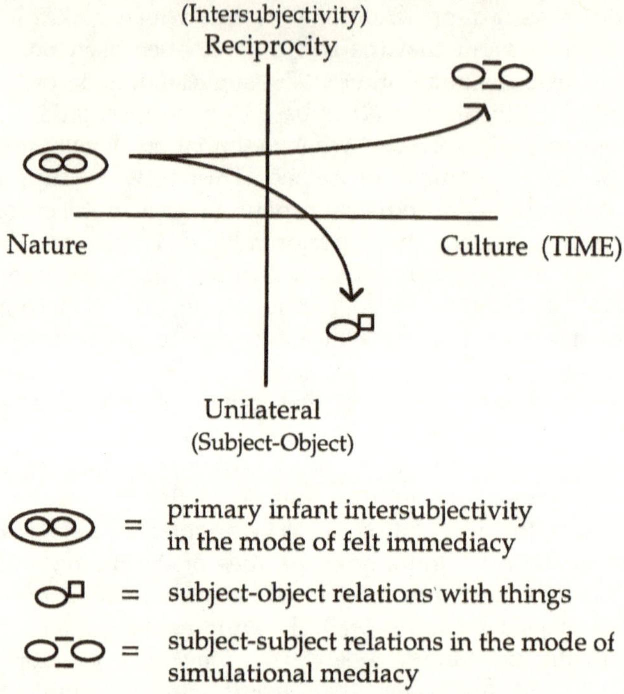

Fig. 4.1 Child development in the new infant research perspective proposed by Bråten (1996c) in contradistinction to Freudian and Piagetian theories with autocentric points of departure in the lower left field

that is organized in a dyadic form already from birth (described as 'subject–subject reciprocity in the mode of felt immediacy' in Figure 4.1), which makes it possible to observe protoconversations already during the first month of life. The infant has the ability to act in a complementary way and the participants step into each other's dialogic circle. This further implies that any behaviour emitted by the infant is best understood if analysed within this relational context. Finally, Figure 4.1 also illustrates different developmental paths for relations with people as compared with relations with objects.

Taken together, observations to date suggest that there are good grounds for accepting NI as one example of the infant's innate socio-emotional competence. However, we cannot with any certainty state that NI has any bearing on the child's psychological development beyond the infancy period. Hopefully, the observations presented throughout this chapter will add essential information and take us a small step closer to a more complete understanding of the relationship between NI and imitation at later ages.

Immediate effects: imitation during the neonatal period

We explored the willingness of thirty-two[4] children to imitate mouth opening (MO) and tongue protrusion (TP) at 3 days, 3 weeks and 3 months of age (Heimann *et al.*, 1989). Our procedure started with a baseline period followed by counterbalanced presentations of the three target gestures. Each gesture was modelled for a period of 30 to 40 seconds followed by a 60-second response period. In short, we found clear evidence of imitation of TP at 3 days and 3 weeks when analysing responses emitted during the *response period*.[5] More than two thirds of the infants imitated TP during the first month while only about 45% displayed imitation of MO. Recently, we have also observed NI of both MO and TP in a new sample of 2-day-old infants (Heimann, 1997).

In addition, we also assessed if imitation at 3 days was related to imitation observed at 3 weeks. Three imitation indexes were constructed (see Heimann *et al.*, 1989 for details) and the analysis revealed a short-term stability in imitative behaviour over the first 3 weeks of life. Four out of fourteen correlations between imitation index scores at 3 days and 3 weeks of age came out significant (range of $r = .49 - .68$; $p < .05$), and one came very close to being significant ($r = .44$; $p < .06$). Three of these correlations were related to MO, a finding that suggests 'real' imitation of MO in spite of the fact that only a minority of the children actually imitated this gesture.

However, the story of NI was not as uncomplicated as we had expected. When we analysed responses from only the *presentation period*,[6] a different pattern emerged. We now found[7] that our subjects imitated MO at 3 months, but not when 3 days or 3 weeks old. For TP, responses emitted during the presentation period revealed low levels of imitation at all ages. Thus, it seems that NI is only observed for responses during the response period while imitation at a later age (e.g. MO at 3 months) might be a faster and more controlled response. This developmental change in imitation is probably a result of several parallel processes: biological maturation (e.g. more cortical involvement, fewer direct multimodal sensory processes, better-controlled motivational processes) and social development (face-to-face interaction, playfulness).

In our attempt to find out more about necessary conditions for observing NI we also investigated the optimal response time needed for a newborn infant to imitate (Heimann *et al.*, 1989). First, we divided the 1-minute response period into two parts (each 30 seconds), which revealed identical results regardless of whether we used the first or the last 30 seconds of the response period. Second, we experimented with even longer response periods (90, 120 or 150 seconds) which made the imitation effect vanish. We could no longer detect any selectivity among the infants' responses. Thus, a 60 seconds response period is sufficient for observing neonatal imitation. Using a longer period only increases the risk of not being able to detect any imitation.

Observations on imitation beyond the neonatal period

NI and imitation at three months of life

In his study from 1985, Kugiumutzakis reported different developmental trends for imitation of different behaviours over the first six months, and his conclusion was that the tendency to imitate is unchanged over the first six months of life, but that 'what will be imitated and will not be imitated changes' (Kugiumutzakis, 1985b:7), a conclusion supported by observations made within our longitudinal project, findings that indicate different imitative trends for different behaviours (Heimann *et al.*, 1989; Heimann, 1991). Imitation of TP during the *response period* showed a decline over the first 3 months (only 29% imitated at 3 months) while imitation of MO seemed to be more stable (45% imitated).

As for the observations presented in the previous section regarding immediate stability, we also investigated possible relationships in imitative responses over the first 3 months. Imitation at 3 days and at 3 weeks was compared with imitation at 3 months. For both comparisons, only one correlation out of fourteen reached significance, which is almost what could be expected by chance. Thus we initially concluded that there seems to be no evidence for stability in the infant's imitative response pattern beyond the first month of life – a conclusion that might have to be reconsidered since further exploratory analyses revealed a possible link between children being judged as high imitators at day 3 and imitation at 3 months (Heimann, 1994). This was investigated by categorizing each individual child as either high or low on imitation depending on the type of the response emitted (strong, weak or medium) and the number of gestures actually imitated at each observation. It was found that children judged to be low imitators at 3 days also tended to be judged as low at 3 months. Thus, this analysis shows that imitation at birth is related to the child's imitative tendency 3 months later.

NI and imitation at 12 months

A question that has been unanswered to date relates to the possible long-term effects of the imitative competence that has been observed among neonates. It is, from a strict empirical view, uncertain whether NI has its primary function during the early months of life, or if this neonatal ability can be viewed as an early precursor of a more mature imitative capacity that emerges later during the first year of life.

In spite of the difficulty of the task, we added a 12-months observation to our longitudinal study (Heimann, 1991; Heimann *et al.*, 1989), as a first attempt to explore possible links between imitation observed early in life and later emerging imitative skills towards the end of the first year. This observation included several imitation tasks within different domains (object manipulation, social gestures, vocal tasks and facial imitation) as well as observations of free play, spontaneous verbal imitation, temperament and language. We followed the suggestion made by Field, Goldstein, Vega-Lahr and Porter (1986) and included as broad a range of tasks as possible in order to make it more likely for us to detect any long-term relationships (if any existed). All in all, sixteen imitation tasks (see Table 4.1) were presented in a playful manner to the thirty participating children and each presentation was carried out twice unless the child imitated after the first presentation.

In addition, the 12-month visit included measures of spontaneous vocal imitation, vocabulary and temperament. Data on vocal imitation were collected from twenty-five children observed in a 4-minute play session with their mother. Furthermore, we used the parents' estimation of their child's vocabulary as a global measure of early language development and the child's temperament was assessed with the Toddler Behavior Questionnaire (TBQ; Hagekull, 1985; Hagekull *et al.*, 1980; Hagekull, 1985).[8]

At 12 months we observed relatively high levels of object imitation and vocal imitation (see Table 4.2) while imitation of social and facial gestures was more difficult to elicit. Only a minority of the children imitated any of the social (e.g. eye blink and sniffing on flower) or facial (TP and MO) gestures. We found no indication of any direct correlation between imitation of facial gestures during the first weeks of life and our measures of imitation at 12 months. This also held for correlations between early imitation and other domains of development (e.g. temperament or vocabulary) when the child was 1 year old. Thus, no direct link between NI and imitation at 1 year was detected.

In contrast, our analysis of imitation at 3 months and at 12 months revealed two significant correlations. Imitation of TP at 3 months was positively related to vocal imitation at 12 months ($r = .42$; $p < .05$) and imitation of MO at 3 months correlated with object imitation at 12 months ($r = .38$; $p < .05$). None of the other comparisons made for imitation and measures within related domains (e.g. spontaneous imitation, temperament or language) came out as significant.

Table 4.1 *Imitation tasks presented at the 12-month follow-up*

Task		Act modelled by the experimenter (E)[a]
Object manipulation	1	A small wooden block was slowly moved towards E's mouth.
	2	A small, coloured, wooden block was manipulated, while held in mid-air.
	3	A block was dropped on the floor.
	4	Stirring with a spoon in a cup.
	5	E held a playphone receiver as if talking.
	6	E brushed her hair with a soft brush.
	7	E pretended to drink from a cup.
	8	Building a stack of two blocks.
Social gestures	9	Hand clapping.
	10	Eye blinking.
	11	Head shaking.
	12	Sniffing a flower.
Facial gestures[b]	13	Tongue protrusion.
	14	Mouth opening.
Vocal imitation	15	A hand doll drops a small wooden block and says 'Oy!' as if surprised.
	16	A hand doll pretends to drink from a cup and then says 'Aaah!'

Notes:

[a] Two identical sets of toys were used, one for the experimenter and one for the child.

[b] Each gesture was presented one to five times depending on the child's attention.

NI and mother–infant interaction

In an attempt to investigate possible connections between early dyadic interaction and NI, a face-to-face observation was included at the 3 months observation (Heimann, 1989). Twenty-four mother–infant dyads were videotaped and the first two minutes were subsequently analysed using categories adopted from an early version of the Infant Monadic Phases (Tronick *et al.*, 1980). The analysis revealed very few significant correlations between observed imitation and our interactional categories. Out of ninety correlations, seven reached statistical significance; this is only a few more than can be expected by chance alone. However, four of these correlations did relate to brief gaze aversion (= averting gaze less than 3 seconds) which displayed several significant negative correlations to imitation at 3 months,

Table 4.2 *Mean imitation index score at 12 months of age*

Imitation task	Imitation Index Score[a]		
	n	Mean	SD
Object imitation (8 tasks)	29	1.25	.28
Social gestures (4 tasks)	29	.51	.44
Facial gestures (2 tasks)	25	.68	.69
Vocal imitation (2 tasks)	29	.85	.68
All 16 tasks		.86	.25

[a] 0 = no imitation, 1 = partial imitation, and 2 = full imitation.

3 weeks and 3 days of age. More than half of all significant correlations observed were related to the negative pattern obtained for the relationship between brief gaze aversion and imitation.

These observations indicate that children displaying a high level of imitation show fewer instances of brief gaze aversion when observed in spontaneous interaction with their mothers. Gaze aversion reflects eye-to-eye contact which, in turn, might be indicative of the quality of the emerging mother–infant relationship (Field, 1977; Greenspan, 1982; Keller and Gauda, 1987). The brief gaze aversion measure used in our study can be conceived of as a brief pause in the ongoing interaction, a pause that might be used by the child to modulate the intensity of the interaction. Thus, a possible interpretation of our finding is that infants displaying imitation easily and often need fewer brief pauses than children imitating to a lesser degree. Imitation might help the child to be more attuned to his or her mother as suggested by Stern (1985). In other words, NI can function as one important early building block which helps the infant to play an active part within the co-regulative interactive process already taking place between mother and child from the first day of life (Fogel, 1993). In addition, recent observations (Fiamenghi, 1996) suggest that imitation also plays an important role within early infant–infant interactions.

Finally, we also explored possible links between mother–infant interaction at 3 months and imitation at 12 months. These analyses revealed that brief gaze aversion at 3 months correlated negatively with vocal imitation at 12 months ($r = -.45$; $p < .05$). Since we had already detected a negative correlation between concurrent

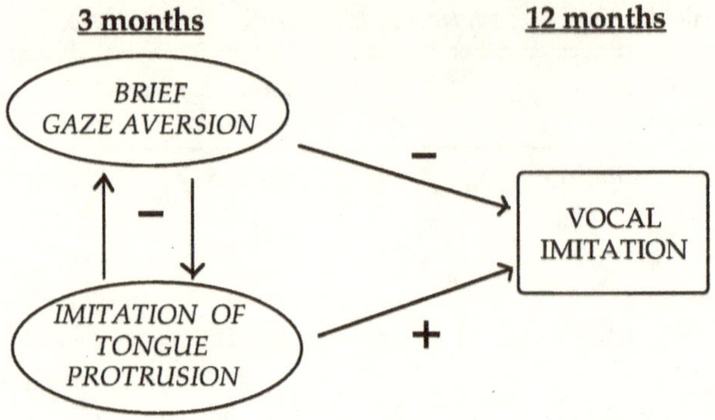

Fig. 4.2 Significant correlations between imitation and gaze aversion at 3 months and vocal imitation observed at 12 months

observations on imitation of TP and levels of infant gaze aversion in a face-to-face situation at 3 months (see above) as well as a positive correlation between imitation of TP at 3 months and vocal imitation at 12 months (see previous section), these findings indicate that a special pattern may exist for children imitating TP at 3 months (see Figure 4.2). Children imitating TP at 3 months might be more easily motivated by social encounters and thus become more often engaged in emotionally rewarding interactions. This, in turn, might increase the chances of the child participating in mutual imitative-like games with the caregiver. A further effect could be that these children develop a higher sensitivity to changes within an ongoing interaction and also a more socially oriented interactive style: a style that motivates them to display vocal imitation more easily at 12 months (but, needless to say, this is a very speculative conclusion).

On the question of early imitation in autism: a brief comment

The role of imitation among children with autism has been of interest to researchers since shortly after Kanner's (1943) seminal paper (e.g. Ritvo and Provence, 1953). Over the years, a large number of investigators and clinicians have noted that, on the one hand, children with autism often imitate to a lesser degree than other children, while on the other hand they tend to show pathological imitation of both sounds (echolalia) and gestures (echopraxia). This view has also been supported by parents when they retrospectively describe the early development of their children (e.g. Dahlgren and Gillberg, 1989). However, to date, the research carried out on imitation and children with autism has failed to provide a clear picture of the role of this deficit for diagnosis or of its developmental significance and this inconclusiveness did put imitation out of fashion for some time. In contrast, many teachers and therapists continued to focus a substantial part of various psychoeducational programmes on training imitation skills.

Research since the 1980s (e.g. the growing interest in early cognitive capacities of the neonate as well as in theory of mind issues) has, to some extent, put imitation back on the agenda for investigators focusing on children with autism. Maybe early imitation is important for later skills like theory of mind, and if so, then a lack of imitation within the newborn period may be an early sign that something is wrong with a child's ability to relate to the outside world. This view has been most explicitly formulated by Rogers and Pennington (1991) in their attempt to describe possible deficits very early in life that may lead to autism and an inability to understand theory of mind problems. In short, they argue that NI is an important social competence, and that this ability will be missing in newborn children who later develop autism. Also Hobson (1993a) suggests that imitation might be of special importance for understanding the developmental processes leading up to full-blown autism in a child aged 2–4 years. According to Hobson, 'abnormalities in . . . interpersonal-affective co-ordination are basic to most if not all cases of autism' (pp. 78–9) and an imitation deficit reflects one of the possible roots of this abnormality.

A basic problem with all theories assuming an early imitation deficit in autism is that there exist no studies on imitation among children with autism younger than 1 year, although studies on somewhat older subjects indicate that children with autism do have severe problems with imitation (e.g. Charman and Baron-Cohen, 1994; DeMyer *et al.*, 1972; Heimann *et al.*, 1992; Heimann and Ullstadius, 1997; Sigman and Ungerer, 1984; Smith and Bryson, 1994). On the other hand, the observations presented in previous sections of this chapter indicate possible important roles for imitation early in life for typically developing children. Neonatal imitation is related to the child's interactional behaviour while in face-to-face interaction with his or her mother and some early imitation and later imitation are positively correlated. Thus, preliminary support does exist for the positions taken by Hobson (1993a) and Rogers and Pennington (1991) regarding the role of NI in normal development. Recent findings have also found evidence of imitation of facial gestures among 1-month-old children with Down's syndrome (Heimann *et al.*, 1997), observations that extend the possibly important role of neonatal imitation also to atypically developing children.

The picture is less clear, however, if we continue to focus on children with autism. Children with autism are mostly diagnosed late,

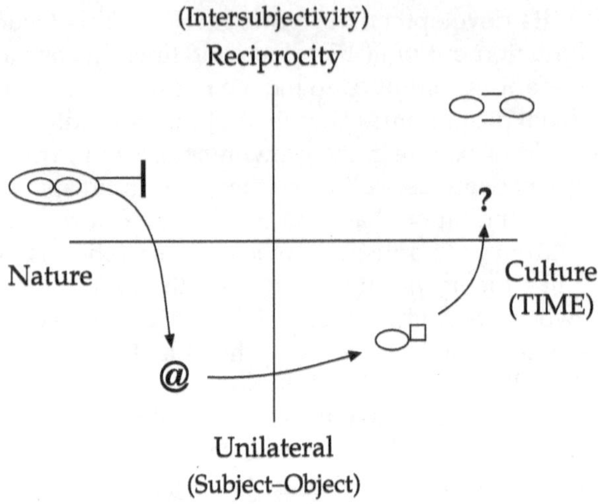

Conventions (*see also Fig. 4.1*)

@ = autocentric; closed off from social reality

? = possible but uncertain route of development

○□ = subject–object relations with things and human beings

Fig. 4.3 Route to autism 1: an initially normal development is biologically arrested by brain pathology leading to autistic behaviour

which makes it almost impossible to gather prospective data, and some children seem to develop autism without any previous signs of abnormality (Osterling and Dawson, 1994). A theory of the role of imitation in autism must be able to incorporate children with a late onset of autism. Thus, since there is probably more than one kind of autism, there should also be more than one role given to an early imitation deficit. For children with autism, imitation within the newborn period is probably only affected if the part of the brain responsible for primary intersubjectivity (Trevarthen and Aitken, 1994) is damaged, and this should also include the basic dialogical organization of the mind (Bråten, 1988a).

The model presented by Bråten (1996b,c; Fig. 4.1) can be used to illustrate the fact that, from a psychological perspective, there must be at least two main routes to disorders within the autististic spectrum. The first alternative (see Fig. 4.3) indicates that the child is born with a dialogical mind which enables him or her to display neonatal imitation, to engage in an immediate dialogical 'dance' and to show primary intersubjectivity. Thus, it is not possible to distinguish this child – who

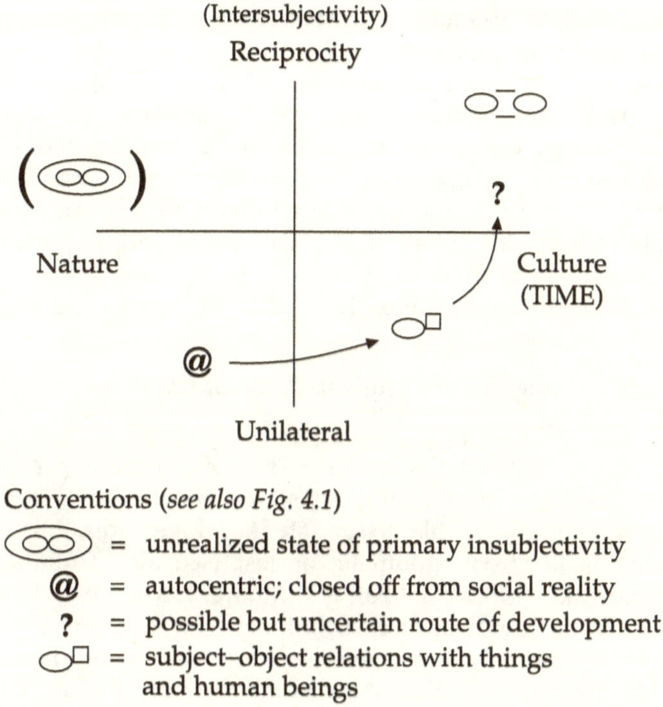

Fig. 4.4 Route to autism 2: development deviates from normality already at birth

will later develop autism – from a typically developing child during these first weeks or months of life. However, owing to a faulty development of the nervous system (e.g. genetic or perinatal factors) some paths of normal brain development are arrested and a deviant route is taken (illustrated by the thick bar in Figure 4.3). From this point in time, the child will show an increasingly pathological development. As stated elsewhere (Heimann and Ullstadius, 1997) a child who develops autism according to this scenario will probably not start to display deviant imitation until he or she is close to reaching the level of secondary intersubjectivity (somewhere around 7 to 9 months).

The second possible path to autism is illustrated in Fig. 4.4. Here, the child is born with a central nervous system that, already from birth, is different. This is the hypothesis suggested by Rogers and Pennington (1991). The child is not able to enter into reciprocal interactions or to display neonatal imitation. Thus, according to this scenario, a lack of imitative responsiveness at birth is a possible marker of later autism.

Hopefully, this very brief comment on NI and children with autism has made it clear (1) that deviant and/or delayed imitation is often observed among children with autism, but (2) that a lack of NI should not automatically be considered a possible marker for autism. It will be up to future studies to provide observations that can disentangle the role of neonatal imitation in both normal and atypical development. Based on current knowledge, it is my view that we need to operate with both possibilities depicted in Figures 4.3 and 4.4.

Towards an integration: a motivated, dialogical and multimodal infant

The studies reviewed (Heimann, 1989, 1992; Heimann *et al.*, 1989) suggest, in accordance with most studies in the field to date, that newborn babies are able to imitate facial gestures, but that this imitation is far from automatic or fast (see also Holmlund 1995; Kugiumutzakis, 1985a; Meltzoff and Moore, 1983a, 1994). In addition, our observations indicate a clear link between imitation displayed in the newborn period and at 3 weeks, as well as between imitation at 3 and 12 months, and also show some support for an association between NI and imitation at 3 months. Thus, several relationships across time exist for imitation observed during the newborn period although no direct link was found between NI and imitation at 12 months. We also failed to detect a clear trend indicating less imitation over the first 3 months of life which supports Kugiumutzakis' (1985a) claim that imitation overall stays the same although imitation of specific behaviours may change. This conclusion is also supported by Meltzoff and Moore (1992), who found that infants between 2 and 3 months do imitate if the procedure is adjusted so that they become motivated to participate in imitation games. Furthermore, related findings have demonstrated that the infant stepping reflex, thought to disappear early in life, actually reappears when conditions are changed (see Thelen and Smith, 1994).

One might ask why the children in our study (Heimann *et al.*, 1989) did imitate *after* presentation of the gesture during the first month of life, but *during* the presentation period at 3 months. In my opinion, this question may in part be answered by changes in processing capabilities during the first months of life. A newborn child needs more time in order to 'take in' what is going on and to organize his or her response, while a 3-month-old baby reacts faster. This is supported by Holmlund (1995) who found that it takes 20 to 30 seconds for a newborn infant to respond, but only a few seconds when the child is 2 or 3 months old (see also Meltzoff and Moore, 1994; Kugiumutzakis, 1985a). It is my suspicion that the way the immature brain handles information from different senses in part explains this time lag observed in newborns. The starting point is a mind with multimodally organized sensory systems that – from the child's point of view – give rise to an immediate amodal experience. Thus, the initial problem is probably not one of supramodal representation (Meltzoff and Kuhl, 1994) since sensations within one 'modality' can be evoked directly by a stimulus from another (Maurer and Maurer, 1988; Stein and Meredith, 1993; Stein *et al.*, 1994). According to this view it is possible that infants are born 'synesthetic, although most gradually grow out of it' (Stein and Meredith, 1993:12). Imitation occurs as a result of a direct process at a subcortical level where visual, auditory and somatosensory information share the same neural maps or even the same multimodal neurons. According to Stein and Meredith, 'the superior colliculus is one of the sites in the central nervous system in which' (p. 14) such convergence occurs, and they continue: 'physiological studies have shown that multisensory neurons become functional quite early in postnatal life and are retained throughout adulthood' (pp. 14–15). Furthermore, these multimodal processes are probably part of the innate motive formation that Trevarthen (this volume; Trevarthen *et al.*, 1997; Aitken and Trevarthen, 1997) postulates as an emerging 'generator of motives and emotions by which human contacts and relationships are regulated'. In addition, they might also help to trigger prewired motor patterns operating during the first days or weeks of life for the control of facial movements (Blass, personal communication). A possible site for such programmes would be the median forebrain bundle.

Already at birth the infant experiences similarity between self and other movements. This provides the starting point for a 'theory' that eventually will give the infant the knowledge that 'I am like the other person', but this knowledge does not exist at birth (cf. Gopnik and Meltzoff, 1997). Instead, this self-knowledge develops as part of a process, as a result of recurrent experiences and interactions with an 'other'. Initially, the infant mind is organized in such a way that this pattern of development has a higher probability of occurring. Usually, this primary road to self-awareness is easily found by most infants since several attractors (e.g. face recognition, the basic dialogic structure of mind, innate social motives and prewired motor patterns) act as excellent road signs.

The capacity of the newborn infant makes intersubjective encounters possible, but at birth this is a fragile system. The infant does not succeed at all times in creating such encounters; the dialogical mind of the infant may not operate in all interactions. Thus, it is my view that NI is a possible social response with an innate base. It is also my view that this early capacity is regulated by a motivational system (Trevarthen, this volume) as well as being based on a dialogical organization of the emerging mind (Bråten, 1988a, this volume). The formation of an imitative response is, however, a difficult task for the infant and it is in no way automatic or reflex-like. It takes time for the infant both to process the sensory information and to put together a coherent response that is picked up by the adult partner. Several biological, psychological and social factors have to act in concert in order for imitation to occur. There is no specific imitation module located anywhere within the brain.

Acknowledgements
The research presented in this chapter has been supported by grants from the Bank of Sweden Tercentenary Foundation (89/313), from the First of May Flower Annual Campaign for Children's Health, Göteborg, Sweden, and from Claes Groschinsky's Foundation, Stockholm, Sweden. The writing of this chapter was made possible through generous support from the Centre for Advanced Study, the Norwegian Academy of Science and Letters, Oslo, Norway. Special thanks are also due to all babies and families who participated in the studies.

Notes

1 Both Kugiumutzakis (1985a) and Meltzoff and Moore (1983a) observed imitation in newborns less than 1 hour old. In addition, the author also (informally and non-scientifically) observed imitation in a baby girl only 40 minutes old in 1986. This girl was extremely alert at birth – she was looking at the people in the delivery room before she was even completely outside her mother! She continued to be calm and visually attentive for the next hour, showing almost no mouth movements. No tongue protrusion was seen until her father stuck out his tongue when she was 40 minutes old. She then waited for a brief period of time after which she made a couple of clear tongue protrusions. Although not evidence in a scientific way, her behaviour was definitely perceived as imitation by her parents.

2 The methodological variations between studies that have found evidence of NI also provide additional support for the robustness of NI. Furthermore, they also indicate that NI is not a reflex-like response since it is not elicited in exactly the same way across studies.

3 This figure is based on an original illustration by Bråten (1996c:175).

4 The actual number of children included varied somewhat across observations, depending on the infant's state while being observed or on distracting factors (as judged by independent observers).

5 Response period = the experimenter has ceased modelling and is passive. It is now up to the infant to react. This phase was 60 seconds long.

6 Presentation period = the initial phase when the experimenter is modelling the gesture. This phase took between 30 and 40 seconds.

7 Previously unpublished observations.

8 TBQ is made up of six different subscales: Approach/Withdrawal, Intensity/Activity, Regularity, Sensory Sensitivity, Attentiveness and Manageability. (A full description of the TBQ can be obtained from the author.)

CHAPTER 5

Infant learning by altercentric participation: the reverse of egocentric observation in autism

Stein Bråten

Introduction

In the previous chapters in this volume, accounts have been offered of social-emotional communion and intersubjective attunement in human infancy. In this chapter, I shall follow up with these questions:

(Q1) First, what kinds of connectivity and remembering are involved in infants who exhibit deferred imitation (Meltzoff, 1988; Piaget, 1946/1962) or learn to reciprocate spoon-feeding before their first birthday (Bråten, 1996b, in press)?

(Q2) Second, when 18-month-olds realize a novel target act from watching the adult's failing, for example, in trying to pull a dumbbell apart (Meltzoff and Moore, this volume), how may that be explained?

(Q3) Third, why is it that subjects with autism who comply with the model's invitation to 'Do as I do' (as in the situations reported by Whiten and Brown, this volume) may be expected to exhibit imitation errors as in grasping the thumb or rotating the hand?

The replies to be offered to these questions derive from a systems postulate about an inherent self–other connectivity that enables infants unwittingly to feel a virtual moving with the movements of others, affording an 'e-motional' memory (in the double sense of emotional and motional). Such virtual co-enactment with the author of the performance, evoking mental simulation of its successful closure even when the model fails, entails a predispositional participatory perception of the model's movements from the model's stance. Hence, subjects with deficits in this capacity, confined as they are to viewing the facing model from an outside egocentric stance, are expected to exhibit gestural imitation errors. In the discussion will be indicated how the theory of bodily communion and learning by virtue of this capacity which I only recently have uncovered and called 'altercentric' yields falsifiable implications also in the neurological domain. I shall refer to some partly pertinent animal studies which indicate that networks can be sensitized to allocentric viewing (O'Keefe, 1992), and that premotor units can be activated by the sight of another's target movements (Di Pellegrino *et al.*, 1992).

From accounts of neonatal imitation and protoconversation

Neither prenatal experience nor innate releasing mechanisms can account for the finely tuned inter-coordination and matching of movements in early face-to-face encounters that have been documented by the authors of the previous chapters. Meltzoff and Moore (1989) account for neonatal imitation in terms of active equivalence mapping in virtue of a supramodal body scheme. Kugiumutzakis (this volume) and Heimann (this volume) point to the social-emotional and communicative nature of newborns' imitation even in the first hours of life. In his theory of infant intersubjectivity, Trevarthen (1986a, 1989) proposes that the infant's anticipatory cerebral system is prepared for 'alter-oception' of the variety of sounds, gestures and movements that humans afford.

Independently, from simulation and systems studies of adult conversation in perturbed and imperturbed task conditions, I have postulated a 'virtual other' complement to the bodily self that offers a participant (companion) space in which others may be included in felt immediacy (Bråten, 1986). In terms of this 'innate readiness to envelop the actual other' in dialogic closure, the mutual dancing movements in protoconversation, as uncovered by M. C. Bateson (1975), Trevarthen (1974a) and others, could thus be accounted for: infant and adult complement each other's movements and follow them up as processes interlaced in the specific networks of circular processes generated by the operationally closed dyadic system that they jointly constitute (Bråten, 1988a).

In none of the above accounts, which the present account will follow up and partly integrate, has the issue been raised about how infant re-enactment of gesture- and sound-producing movements in face-to-face situations depends on perceptual reversal of the model's movements (Bråten, 1994a, b, 1996a). They evoke, I propose, sensory-motor perception in a participatory sense, involving virtual co-enactment of the model's movements *as if* the infant were the co-author of the model's movements and moved with the model's movements in the same direction. This I term 'altercentric participation'.

Re-enactment from e-motional memory of co-enacted movements (Q1)

Moving with the mother's bodily movements

Prenatal experiences of moving in rhythmic concert with the mother's bodily movements may prepare for some aspects of such participatory perception but not for the perceptual reversal required in face-to-face interplay. Our culture, in which much interplay between infant and caregiver occurs face-to-face, may be contrasted to other cultures, for example that of the Gusii in which infants are carried on the backs of their older siblings. Eye contact with the mother is rare. Even adults in intimate conversation sit side-by-side with faces in parallel (LeVine and LeVine, 1988).

The frequent face-to-face interplay between infant and adult in our culture may also be contrasted to other primate species, like gorillas and chimpanzees. They carry their offspring, when old enough, on their backs. Riding on the mother's back, the offspring moves with the mother's movements, and experiences the world and others in it from the mother's position. There can be joint attention and e-motional memory from an egocentric perspective, without transcending or reversing the mother's perspective.

The same kind of opportunity to move with the mother's movement is illustrated in Fig. 5.1 (*top left*). Here the Balinese boy Karba (between 11 and 12 months) is being taught to pick food by his mother. Being hand-guided and facing in the same direction as her, he is afforded the e-motional experience of participating in her enactment in an actual manner of co-enactment.

The situation is different in the dancing lesson with his father (Fig. 5.1, *bottom left*). Here Karba follows up his father's right-arm gesture from a complementary position. Karba is raising his right-arm, apparently re-enacting his father's gesture in a semblant manner. Were he, however, to copy his father's gesture as seen from an egocentric stance, one might have expected – disregarding normal hand preference – that Karba's left arm would be raised with the inside of his hand inwards. (I shall return to this point in the section on gestural imitation errors in autism.)

When infants reciprocate feeding

Parents and caretakers sometimes experience how infants, of not more than 10 to 12 months, reciprocate feeding by offering food by hand to the caregiver's mouth and opening their own mouths in the process.

Fig. 5.1 Infants (10–12 months) in interaction with caregivers. *Left*: The Balinese boy Karba in lesson with parent (drawing from photos by G. Bateson, 1955). *Right*: The Norwegian boy Thomas reciprocating his sister's spoon feeding (drawing from video records by S. Bråten).

Eibl-Eibesfeldt (1979:15) records, for example, a Yanomami baby who, being held by her sister, extends a morsel to her sister's mouth and – naturally – opens her own mouth as the morsel approaches her sister's mouth. In my own observations of face-to-face interplays in home environment, I have recorded infants (around $11\frac{3}{4}$ months) who, after some weeks of having been spoon-fed, can reciprocate the caretaker's spoon-feeding when allowed to take the spoon with the food in his own hand (Bråten 1996b, 1997a, b, 1998).

Consider the everyday situation pictured in Fig. 5.1 (*top right*): the young infant is being spoon-fed by the caregiver. Such a situation, when viewed from the stance of an outside observer, appears to be a unilateral give-and-take situation: the caregiver feeds, the baby is being fed. Much more is at play here, however, as revealed by the video recordings. We see evidence of mutually attuned companion movements that complement and fulfil one another in bodily communion, for example by the way the caregiver unwittingly opens her mouth when feeding a spoonful into the baby's mouth and the baby adjusting his posture to the caregiver's movements. And when the baby is allowed to take in his own hand the spoon with food, he reciprocates by offering the spoon with food to his caregiver's mouth in a semblant manner (Fig. 5.1, *bottom*). As he somewhat clumsily reaches out the spoon with food towards his sister's mouth, he unwittingly opens his own mouth.

Circular re-enactment from e-motional memory

Such reciprocating by the baby boy indicates that his feeders' movements have somehow afforded the non-conscious experience of co-enacting the food-giving movements, even though his caregivers were the authors of those movements. The enacting actual other who complements the infant's bodily self evokes in the infant processes that differ from responses to expressive cues and from conceptually ordered perception. First, these processes differ from expressive emotions in terms of discrete categories (such as 'joy', 'surprise', 'disgust', 'rage'); feelings of bodily life form are elicited rather in the affective sense of what Stern (1985: 54–7) terms 'vitality affects'. Second, these processes differ from perception of others in conceptual re-presentational mediacy (like G. H. Mead's 'generalized other'); the actual other's movements are instead unwittingly felt to be co-enacted in a participatory sense of felt immediacy. That is why I use the composite term '*e-motional*' (combining the root sense of 'out of motion' and the folk sense of 'being moved by') to qualify the affective experience of bodily communion and the non-conscious remembrance of virtually moving with the other's movements (Bråten, 1994a, b, 1996a, in press).

Assuming that deferred imitation does not necessarily require the intervention of conceptual representations, but that some sort of representative or pre-representative element must be at play, Piaget (1962:63, 69) gives this example of re-enactment by a 16-month-old girl:

> At 1;4(3) J. had a visit from a little boy of 1;6 whom she used to see from time to time, and who, in the course of the afternoon got into a terrible temper. He screamed as he tried to get out of the play-pen and pushed it backwards, stamping his feet. J. stood watching him in amazement, never having witnessed such a scene before. The next day, she herself screamed in the play-pen and tried to move it, stamping her foot lightly several times in succession. (Piaget, 1946/1962:63)

Given the e-motional capacity for participatory perception, this interpretation may be offered: watching the boy, the girl unwittingly participates in the boy's movements and his accompanying emotions in the way that Stern (1985) terms 'affect attunement'. Her virtual participation in what the boy was doing, as if she had been doing the screaming, pushing and stamping with him, informs and motivates her subsequent re-enactment.

The account above derives from my postulate (Bråten, 1988a, b) about the virtual other complement of the bodily self-feeling that offers a companion space for

(i) e-motional involvement in others who complement the bodily self in the space of the virtual other, re-creating the format of
(ii) self-involvement (with the virtual other) re-creating the format of (i).

Thus, circular re-enactment, including the kind of self-imitation that Baldwin (1891) and Piaget (1946/1962) term 'circular reaction', is here qualified to evoke circuits that involve the other – actual or virtual. Baldwin proposes that infants, once they are able to imitate, can feel what others are feeling by imitating their movements. That proposal is here turned around: by virtue of their capacity unwittingly to move with the gestural- and sound-producing movements of others, even neonates should be capable of re-enacting simple novel movements. Meltzoff and Moore (1989) report, for example, clockwise head-rotation being imitated in a clockwise, and hence inverted, direction by some newborns while the model pauses for 20 seconds to control for 'perceptual tethering' (which is a term for actually moving with the perceived other).

Deferred re-enactment by 9-month-olds

Meltzoff (1988) documents imitation by 9-month-olds deferred by 24 hours after having been exposed to a novel model enactment on an object out of their reach, for example, producing a beeping sound by pushing a submerged button (Fig. 5.2). The infants simply watch the model's enactment. Not until the next day are they allowed access to the object enacted upon. When they now re-enact, I suggest, they re-enact from e-motional memory of unwittingly participating in the co-enacting of the model's movements. In this theory, then, deferred imitation entails successful completion (closure) of the two self-organizing circuits of self–other connectivity depicted in Fig. 5.2 (*bottom*). In the first circuit (i) the infant's perceptual participation in the model's movements affords e-motional experience of moving with

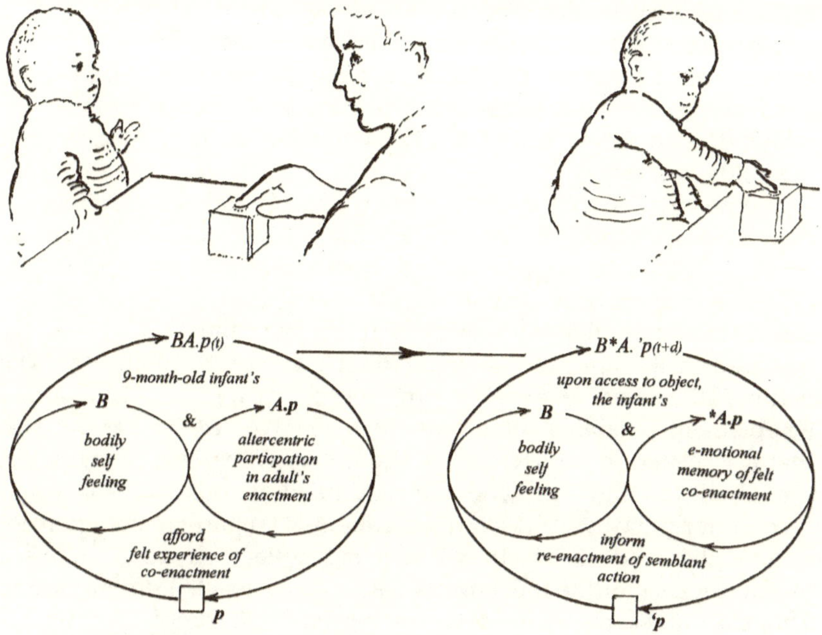

Fig. 5.2 Deferred imitation by 9-month-old: situation and state transition diagram (from Bråten, in press).

the author of those movements. The second circuit (ii), re-creating the operational format of (i), involves the infant's self-concentrated effort to re-enact from the e-motional memory of his unwitting virtual co-enactment in (i). In short, what the infant has jointly felt to do with his actual other, the infant will now attempt to do with his virtual other.

Face-to-face exposure requires inverted alteroception of the model's movements

In this way, infant learners can re-enact from the e-motional memory of moving with the model, even though the facing model has been the author of the movements, just as in the case of Thomas who learned to reciprocate spoon-feeding (Fig. 5.1, *right*). In spite of sitting in this way on his baby stool, face-to-face with his caregivers, he must have experienced their enactments in an appropriating manner so as to allow for reciprocal re-enactment. In contrast to an observer who views the feeding situation from the outside and perceives how the feeder's spoon reaches his mouth, Thomas must have been able to participate in the feeder's movements from the feeder's stance, evoking a *perceptual (mirror-like) reversal* in the infant – the very reverse of what is seen from an outside, egocentric stance in such a face-to-face situation. This is the radical entailment of the e-motional capacity for altercentric participation posited here: face-to-face situations evoke inverted alteroception of the movements afforded by others (Bråten, 1994a, b, 1997a, b). An explanation may be offered in the following terms.

In both circuits, (i) and (ii), the infant's bodily self is complemented by the other – actual or virtual. The way in which the infant's virtual other is posited to complement the bodily self with the operational efficiency (*virtus*) of an actual other, allowing itself to be replaced by actual others in felt immediacy, implies that there is asymmetry involved in the operational circuits that give rise to (i) and (ii). The bodily-self feeling (evoked in proprioception) and its virtual-other complement (enabling alteroception) may give rise to perspectives that are related in an asymmetrically reversed manner, perhaps like the format in which left hand and right hand are related. That would account for the way in which re-enactment from participatory perception of the model's enactment in a face-to-face situation entails a virtual reversal of the movements felt to be co-enacted. In the case of Thomas, for example, in virtue of his feeders' complementing his bodily self (in the same asymmetric manner as it is otherwise complemented by his virtual other) the actual other's movements are unwittingly felt to be co-enacted by the baby, as if being hand-guided and facing the same direction as the feeder.

The same would apply, though reciprocity is not involved, to the 9-month-olds in Meltzoff's (1988) deferred imitation experiments (Fig. 5.2). Sitting on the parent's lap, they are placed face-to-face with the model in order to keep the object enacted upon out of their reach. From having watched the model's enactment, virtually moving with the model's movements, they are able to re-enact on the next day.

Successful closure from altercentric participation in a failing model's effort (Q2)

Now, from a Gibsonian view of direct perception (with which in many respects I concur) there is a natural objection. The infants in the above experiments do not need to participate in the model's movements; they just re-enact from having seen the object affordance demonstrated, for example how a submerged button invites to be pushed or how a dumbbell invites to be pulled apart. That interpretation is ruled out by the control demonstration reported by Meltzoff and Moore (this volume). They show that while exposure to *human* effort to pull the dumbbell apart elicits re-enactment by 18-month-olds, exposure to a *mechanical* model's pulling the dumbbell apart (Fig. 2.1, this volume) does not result in re-enactment. Even when the human model fails in his demonstrated effort to pull it apart, the toddlers follow up by pulling it apart. To this I shall now turn, proposing that they do so from their participatory perception of the model's effort, virtually moving with and completing in their companion space his target-oriented movements.

This capacity of moving with the movements of others in sympathy with their efforts was noted by Adam Smith (1759). He used the example of spectators watching a French line dancer. As the dancer moves on the slack line, the spectators are moving with him. In the above terms, they perceptually participate in the dancer's efforts from the dancer's stance and even try to adjust for his position, when he appears to lose his balance, in their shared virtual effort to co-enact the dancing.

In the same vein, we may regard the 18-month-olds in Meltzoff's (1995) behavioural re-enactment design who successfully realize and enact a novel target act from watching a model failure (Meltzoff and Moore, this volume). It concerns the question (Q2) of how they can realize an unrealized target from merely watching someone aiming for the target. To this I shall now turn.

Mental simulation circuits evoked by altercentric participation

Now, these toddlers appear not to realize that the model's actual intent is to pretend a failure. If they had, they might have shared in the model's pretence and, perhaps, re-enacted the target failure. Instead, they show off, sometimes with a satisfied smile, managing to do what the model failed to do. Thus, they appear to invite an account in terms other than a theory-of-mind capability in the theory-version sense. Even if some of the toddlers should have been able to discern that the model's intention in pretending a failure was to invite a successful target enactment, they realize the behavioural target direction in a way that permits an account in terms of imagining or mental simulation, in the sense of Gordon (1986) and Harris (1991). Two somewhat pertinent proposals about simulation have been made, one by myself (Bråten, 1973, 1974), concerning intrapersonal monitoring of speech acts, and another by Berthoz (1996), concerning neural support of planning movements.

In my social-semantic approach, influenced by Naess (1953) and informed by my object-oriented simulations of interpersonal communication, I have proposed that when an adult interlocutor tries to correct for failure to understand, circuits of mental simulation of the co-actor's reverse coding are evoked in the production and processing of a speech act (Bråten, 1973, 1974). Even if inefficient and prone to errors – as mental simulation always is – it entails, for example, a virtual co-enactment of the co-actor's encoding in order to adjust one's own decoding. At a precursory, lower-order level, an analogue may be considered in the case of the 18-month-olds: virtual co-enactment of the model's target movement evokes mental simulation of its completion and realization in an adjusted format.

The second pertinent proposal has been made by Berthoz (1996:97). He regards motor imagery as the manifestation of the internal simulation that normally accompanies the planning and execution of movements. Suggesting that the same central neural networks could be involved in both imagined and executed movements, Berthoz raises the question of whether the same or different types of neurons are activated in simulated and executed movements and expects it to be settled by experimental results on monkey neurons. In the discussion below, I shall refer to an experiment by Di Pellegrino *et al.* (1992) that indicates the activation of premotor neurons not only while in the act of grasping a piece of food but even at the sight of another doing the grasping. That result pertains, I think, to his question and to questions (to be raised below) about whether there could be feasible neural support of mechanisms that would realize these processes in the toddler watching the failing model performer: *Altercentric participation in the model's target-oriented movements, affording e-motional experience of the failing movements, evokes a virtual completion of those movements brought to successful closure in the toddler's companion space.* This mental simulation of the corrected target act motivates and informs the actual enactment of the target act (Fig. 5.3).

The static depiction in Fig. 5.3 of the virtual and actual realization of the target act conforms to the format portraying the 9-month-old in Fig. 5.2. In both cases there is actual (re-)enactment from virtual co-enactment, e-motionally experienced in virtue of altercentric participation in the model's movements. The difference is the enhanced, higher-order capability in the older infant to imagine those movements brought to a successful closure from alteroception of the model's behavioural direction.

Manual and gestural imitation errors from egocentric perception in autism (Q3)

In the experimental situations discussed above, the infants, like Thomas in the home situation, have been face-to-face with the model.

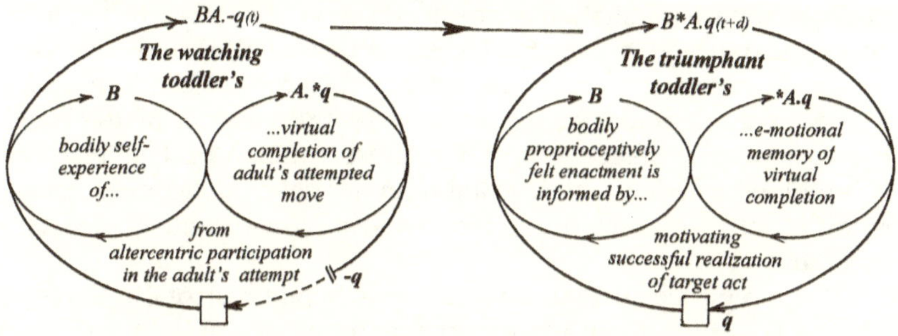

Fig. 5.3 A model of the processes in the 18-month-old realizing an unrealized target act in the behavioural re-enactment design described by Meltzoff and Moore (this volume).

Yet they act and re-enact as if they have been facing the same direction as the model. The learner and the model need not face the same direction, unless the novel movements are very complex, or the child has learning problems that require hand-guidance or use of a mirror in teaching skills that require reciprocal and complementary movements. Being or not being in a face-to-face situation makes little or no difference *if* you have the capacity of moving with the actual other's movements, reversed in virtue of the putative bodily-self/virtual-other asymmetry, whereas it makes a crucial difference if you are deprived of or impaired in the capacity to engage in such felt immediacy in facing others.

In subjects with autism, internal auto-enclosed cycles may be operative without the social-emotional nurture of others' perspectives as felt in inside participating (Bråten 1993:515). Examining her own autism, Grandin (1995), for example, emphasizes her inability to be a participant and to pick up emotional cues: 'All my life I have been an observer, and I have always felt like someone who watches from the outside' (Grandin, 1995:132). Unlike the infants in the above examples who appear capable of participating in the model's movements from the model's stance, evoking alteroceptive reversal and binding, subjects with autism should at best be expected to re-enact the model's enactment as seen and related to their own egocentric position. Hence, given deficits in the e-motional capacity for altercentric perception of others, they are 'expected to have difficulties in imitating body movements in face-to-face situations' (Bråten, 1994a:16).

This theoretically derived prediction is supported by reports on certain asymmetric manual imitation errors in autism by Brown (1996), Ohta (1987) and Smith (1995). Ohta reports experimental findings of partial imitation errors in subjects with autism trying to re-enact gestural and bi-manual tasks. Smith replicates with the same result: children with autism, as compared to control children, manifested errors in imitating gestures, including rotation of the hand. Brown reports imitation errors like 'grasp thumb' (cf. Fig. 14.4, this volume) which defy interpretation in terms of deficits in 'mind-reading' (cf. the concluding comments in Whiten and Brown, this volume).

All the reported manual and gestural imitation errors, referred to above, occur from face-to-face exposure to rather simple manual and gestural demonstrations that involve asymmetry and invite reversal. Inferred in this theory to stem from impairment of the e-motional participatory system, difficulties in autism in imitating asymmetric manual movements should thus be most acute in such face-to-face situations. The above account implies that manual imitation errors, requiring alteroceptive reversal and binding, are to be expected of a child with autism, revealed by comparisons with a normal child when both are placed in a face-to-face situation, perhaps as simplified as in the caricature (Fig. 5.4).

While normal children in virtue of altercentric perception can do what the other is doing (Fig. 5.4, *left*) when invited to do so, children with autism who comply with the invitation are expected to have problems in virtue of seeing the other only from an egocentric position. Observing the model from the outside, the subject is seeing, but not feeling from the inside, what the model is doing. Seeing the resemblance between the inside of the model's hands and the insides of his own, and being incapable of a virtual reversal of the model's movements as felt, the child with autism can only do what is being seen from the child's stance and is thus expected to raise hands with inside inwards (Fig. 5.4, *right*).

Discussion and questions about partial neural support

Subjects with autism fail in spite of understanding the model's intention to 'Do as I do!'

In an empirical review of imitation in autism, Smith and Bryson (1994:264) refer to 'the intriguing possibility that these errors represent attempts of the children with autism to reproduce the gesture so that their view of their own hands matches the view of the model'. This formulation concurs with the above caricature in Fig. 5.4 and has been proposed by Barresi and Moore (1996:120). They suspect that the problem arises from a failure to integrate representation of matched

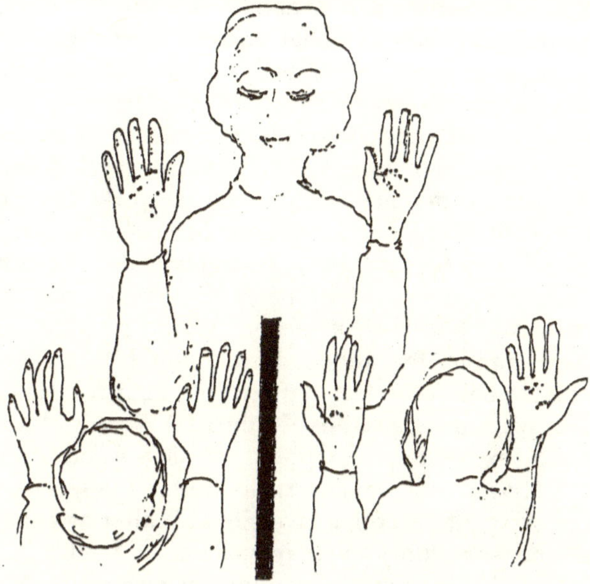

Figure 5.4 *Left*: When invited to do as the adult model does in a face-to-face situation, the model's gesture is correctly imitated by the infant to the left. That is, virtual reversal of the other's gesture as felt being done, and not merely as seen from the outside. In virtue of altercentric participation the normal child is expected to do what the model is doing (with the inside of the raised hands facing outwards), and not what is merely seen with ego-centric eyes (the inside of her raised hands).

Right: Children with autism who understand the invitation to do as the model does are expected to have difficulties. Observing the model from the outside, the subject is seeing, but not feeling from the inside, what the model is doing. Seeing the resemblance between the inside of the model's hands and the insides of his own, and being incapable of a virtual reversal of the model's movements as felt, the child can only do what is being seen from own position, and will raise hands with inside inwards.

first- and third-person information. While they consider a normal 9-month-old to be capable of integrating a first-person perspective and a third-person perspective in virtue of an 'intentional schema', as they term it, subjects with autism appear capable only of first-person perspective. True, but that does not prevent the subjects with autism in the experiments from complying with the second person's invitation. They do understand the model's intention to have them 'Do as I do' (cf. Whiten and Brown, this volume). They are just unable to re-enact in the appropriate asymmetric manual format. Their failure to integrate representation of matched own and other person information, as proposed by Barresi and Moore, should be specified to involve an impaired social-emotional capacity to engage in an I–You format, in the sense of Buber (1958), as distinct from the I–It format.

In normal children, the perspectival relation between the child's bodily self and virtual other, permitting replacement by the actual other in the same format, has been defined above to entail asymmetry, perhaps arising from interlaced neural cell networks that support a relation between first- and second-person perspectives that is *chiral*-like (from Greek for 'handedness'), resembling the peculiar mirror asymmetry of the left and right hand to which Kant drew our attention. Impairment of such a relation would prevent perceptual reversal. (For example, the autistic model for the film *Rainman* is reported to find it painful to face himself in the mirror. He closes his eyes while shaving himself in front of a mirror.) What is critical here is that face-to-face exposure, as opposed to side-by-side, reveals an impaired capacity for e-motional participation in the second person's movements evoking alteroceptive inversion. Children with autism can follow, echo and sometimes even re-enact in a semblant, peculiar manner another (third) person's handling of objects (cf. Nadel and Pezé, 1993) as long as they face or march in the same direction as the model is doing. What appears to be beyond their capacity is the interconnective social-emotional engagement in a dialogically closed first-and-second-person format, which for example Karba and Thomas demonstrate (Fig. 5.1).

Virtuous and vicious circles of re-enactment in ontogeny

This e-motional capacity for altercentric participation has been posited to arise from an architecturally constrained and e-motionally nurtured intersubjective companion space involving an inborn bodily-self/virtual-other asymmetry. This differs from the functionally highly specific 'innate companion schemata' applied in ethology by Uexkull and Lorenz. Eating food from the mother's hand can be accounted for by innate releasing mechanisms and by what Lorenz (1971) terms 'a mother companion schema', but not when the baby in return offers some of the food to the caregiver's mouth in a semblant manner, for example as shown by the Yanomami girl, in Eibl-Eibesfeldt's (1979:15) recording, who offers a morsel to her sister's mouth, and by the Norwegian boy in my own recording (Fig. 5.1) who reciprocates spoon-feeding. Such frequent occurrences invite, as I have attempted to show here and elsewhere, an account in terms of nature-nurture-culture interplay: in virtue of their innate capacity to learn by altercentric participation in the caregivers' movements, the infants reciprocate by re-enacting from their e-motional memory of having unwittingly participated in the movements of their caregivers. This may also explain why toddlers can offer care to another child in need or distress. Previous experience of caregiving provides a basis for circular re-enactment towards others. Altercentric participation in the other child's crying for help or comfort evokes e-motional memory of caregiving experienced in such a state, inviting and informing semblant caring efforts towards the other child (Bråten, 1996a, 1997a).

This implies that not only virtuous circles but also vicious circles of re-enactment may be nurtured in ontogeny. As caring behaviour invites re-enactment, so does abusive behaviour invite circular re-enactment in virtue of the same innate capacity to learn unwittingly by altercentric participation (Bråten, 1996a, 1997a, b; cf. also the discussion by Edwards, this volume). Toddlers, and sometimes adults who have been victims of child abuse, may thus come to re-enact from their non-conscious e-motional memory of having participated in their abuser's enactment.

Such virtual co-enactment of the model's enactment motivates circular re-enactment, and may even evoke simulated closure of incomplete model movements, as the toddlers described by Meltzoff and Moore (this volume) appear capable of. Unless blocked or impaired (cf. Heimann, this volume; Hobson, this volume), this e-motional capacity for bodily communion and virtual participation may nurture the development from simulating others' bodily movements to participating in and simulating others' thoughts and emotions, including fictional absorption (cf. Harris, this volume; Bråten, chapter 20, this volume).

On the unwitting nature of emotional memory and e-motional remembering

I have proposed that infant learners re-enact from a predispositional kind of memory of unwitting participation in the model's movements, a memory that deserves a composite label which combines the root sense of emotion (*'out of'–'motion'*) with the participatory sense of moving with the model's 'motion'. Such virtual participation in the other's movements would afford a sort of remembering that is neither declarative nor conceptual, but e-motional (Bråten, 1994; compare also Frijda's (1986) definition of feeling as involving virtual action tendencies, actualized in evoked emotions). In these terms, deferred re-enactment has been specified to come 'out' of virtual co-enactment of the model's movements in the sense of unwittingly feeling to move with the model's movements affording an e-motional remembering that is non-conscious and yet can subserve in a predispositional manner to inform re-enactment. This probably involves and affects sub-cortical networks in emotional or motivational circuits interlaced with those that are evoked in dispositions for and proprioception of one's own movements. In order for movements of others to be perceived in a participatory sense (for example, with the efficiency exhibited by animals in a hunter–prey dyad), a collateral activation may be required of the neural representations which give rise to its virtual-other complement of the bodily self-feeling and subserve alteroception of the actual other's movements in the operationally closed circuits of a dyadic system.

May one conceive of neural support of such processes? I shall now refer to some neurological studies which may be taken to pertain to some partial aspects of this theory, inasmuch as they indicate, first, the unwitting nature of emotional memory; second, that premotor cells can be activated by the sight of another's target movements; and third, the occurrence of allocentric cells.

First, the term 'emotional memory' is used by LeDoux (1993) as distinct from higher cognitive processes entertained by cortical systems. On the basis of his studies of fear conditioning in rats, he suggests that emotional memories, maintained by subcortical circuits, play a role in integrating diverse sensory inputs and affect behaviours without conscious awareness. Bechara *et al.* (1997) offer evidence in humans of non-conscious dispositional knowledge related to previous emotional experience. Comparing patients with prefrontal damage and decision-making defects to normal individuals in game situations that require decision making, they detect in the normal player autonomic responses that they take as evidence for a complex process of non-conscious signalling. Such signals, acting as covert biases on the circuits that support processes of cognitive evaluation and reasoning, appear to reflect access to records of previous individual experience shaped by reward, punishment, and the emotional state that attends them. Such non-conscious dispositional knowledge from previous emotional experience is apparently held by neural systems other than those that support declarative knowledge and informs actual moves before conscious declarative knowledge plays its part (Bechara *et al.*, 1997:1294; cf. also Damasio, 1994). This should also apply to the kind of unwitting e-motional remembering attributed to the infant learners as discussed above.

When the sight of another's motor activity evokes premotor units

It is one thing to hold a non-conscious emotional memory of one's own previous moves that have turned out to be bad or good. It is quite another to be afforded such cues from merely watching another making good or bad moves. This aspect has not been pursued in the above experiments.

There are, however, some other experimental results, mentioned in the account of the successful enactment of target actions by the 18-month-old toddlers, which may pertain to questions about the kind of architectural constraints on neural support that could subserve processes of virtual co-enactment evoked by the sight of the model's actual, but missing, target-oriented movements. On the basis of their study of functional organization of the macaque monkey brain, Rizzolati *et al.* (1988) suggest that premotor neurons are activated in anticipation of a purposive movement, for example, grasping a piece of food. Now, could such premotor neurons be activated merely by the sight of another's grasping of the food out of one's own reach? De Pellegrino *et al.* (1992) have designed an experimental situation pertaining to that question (Fig. 5.5).

In the first situation the monkey watches the experimenter grasping a piece of food on a plate out of reach of the monkey. In the next situation a plate with a piece of food is offered to the monkey who reaches for food. Premotor cell activation in the monkey is recorded in both situations: first, by the sight of the grasping movements of the experimenter; second, by the animal's own grasping movements.

This could indicate that the sight of the experimenter grasping the piece of food evokes virtual grasping in the monkey, activating the same kinds of networks that combine with others to subserve the monkey's own grasping. It may not be taken to indicate, however, that the monkey necessarily perceptually participates in the experimenter's grasping. Again, in Gibson's term of affordance, an attended piece of food invites to be grasped and eaten: the sight of the piece of food, even though out of reach when the experimenter by his movement draws attention to it, might activate, independently of the sight of grasping, premotor units in preparation of the monkey's grasping. Thanks, however, to the ingenious control experiment with the mechanical dumbbell demonstration, failing to elicit target movements in the watching toddlers (Meltzoff and Moore, this volume, Fig. 2.1), we can discard this possibility in the cases of the infant learners. The premotor cell activation with rather semblant firing profiles in both situations depicted in Fig. 5.5 (to which Fuster (1995:185) drew my attention) may thus retain its relevance.

In conjunction with the results of Meltzoff's behavioural re-enactment design, the above studies, by Di Pellegrino and others, may indicate that it should be possible to conceive of an architecture that may constrain virtual (simulated) and actual (executed) enactment

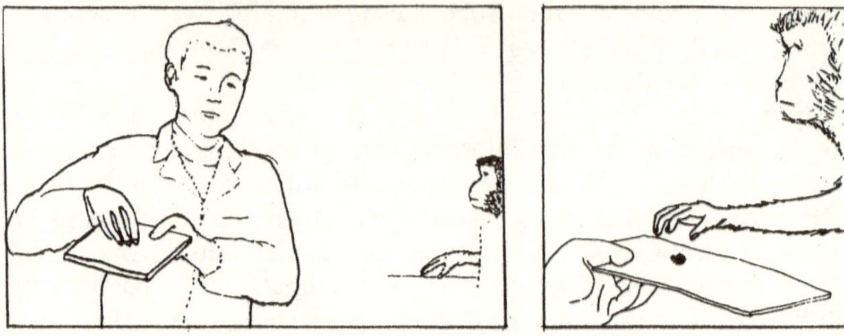

Fig. 5.5 In both these situations, by the monkey's observing a piece of food-grasping movement by the experimenter and by its grasping a piece of food, there is premotor cell activition in the monkey. (Adapted from Di Pellegrino *et al.*, 1992, who also picture the activation profiles of a premotor cell in these two situations.)

of a target movement to be supported by the same premotor units, activated by the sight of another's enactment of that target movement.

On altercentric perception: neurosociological predictions and questions for the future

The key notion here is that such a sight evokes virtual participation in the model's movements, which entails altercentric perception – the reverse of viewing the model from an egocentric perspective. In a Cambridge workshop at King's College, in 1992, where we discussed perception of subjects and objects *inter alia* in infant imitation, John O'Keefe (1992) spoke of an allocentric map you can entertain of the landscape in front of you independent of your position in that landscape, and as distinct from seeing the landscape from an egocentric perspective. For example, in a study of a monkey moved to different places in a spatial environment, O'Keefe (1985) found evidence of *place* cells, dependent upon the place where the monkey was, and different from *view* cells, defined primarily by the view of the environment, and not by the place where the monkey was (cf. also Rolls, 1992). Here are grounds for assuming that differentiated neural systems may be sensitized to allocentric aspects, different from aspects viewed from an egocentric perspective.

Now, if by way of experimental procedures the neural basis supporting egocentric perception and the neural basis sensitized to support allocentric perception are uncovered in humans, then I would expect that neural systems, perhaps even neurons, sensitized to realize altercentric perception will be uncovered in experiments designed to test and disconfirm this expectation.

Weaker and less reductionistic is this prediction. If neurons sensitized to allocentric perception are found in humans, then I expect that more comprehensive neural systems and pathways will be found to support the capacity for altercentric participation by modifying allocentric inputs and competing with egocentric inputs, realizing perceptual reversal in face-to-face situations.

Thus, yielding implications not just at the inter- and intrapersonal level, the theory presented in this chapter opens for falsification attempts and invites questions for the future also from a connectionist or neuroethological perspective, for instance, as reflected by Bateson (1991; this volume) and by Elman *et al.* (1996), while demanding a dyadic systems frame of reference. For example, how may we more specifically conceive of an architecture that could realize in a perceiver a virtual co-enactment of a target movement evoked merely by the sight of another's enactment, and what kinds of neural mechanisms and units could be envisaged to subserve perceptual reversal of that enactment in order to realize feeling and remembering in an appropriating 'e-motional' sense? Such questions await more proper formulations, aided by the kind of neurological studies referred to above and perhaps by some crude connectionist simulations in progress to explore some fragmentary implications. Needless to say, competing networks trained from complementary perspectives (Bråten, in press; Bråten and Espelid, 1990; Wallis and Rolls, 1965) are crucial in such interconnectionist modelling.

Conclusion

The replies offered to the three questions (Q1–Q3) in the beginning of this chapter may now be summarized.

First, when human infants learn from a facing model, for example to reciprocate spoon-feeding (Fig. 5.1) or to produce a beeping sound by pushing a submerged button (Fig. 5.2), they re-enact, I have proposed, from e-motional memory of having felt to co-enact the model's performance in virtue of their capacity for altercentric participation in the facing model's movements.

Second, when toddlers realize a novel target act from watching an adult's failing – irrespective of whether or not they read the model's true intention of actually failing in order to invite a successful performance on their part – their altercentric participation in his target-oriented movements evokes a virtual completion of those movements brought to successful closure that motivates and informs the actual completion of the target act (Fig. 5.3).

Third, when subjects with autism who understand the facing model's invitation to 'Do as I do!' exhibit gestural imitation errors in face-to-face situations, for example, raising hands (Fig. 5.4) or grasp a thumb (Fig. 14.4, this volume), such results have been predicted and explained by impairment of the e-motional capacity for alteroceptive reversal and binding. Confined to observing the facing model from an outside egocentric stance, they fail to achieve what infant learners are capable of: participatory perception from an inside altercentric stance.

There may be a natural, nurtural and tutorial path from infant re-enactment to higher-order levels of intersubjective understanding, as suggested *inter alia* by Meltzoff and Moore (this volume). Rather than in the theory-of-mind direction, I would qualify such a path as being in the mental simulation direction (cf. Harris, 1992; this volume). Children do not have to be like scientists, observing others from the outside and attempting to construct a theory of mind, as Grandin (1995) reports to have been doing in her autistic life. Such a theory construction would at any rate be inefficient, unless nurtured by e-motional memory of altercentric participation, which makes it unnecessary in the first place.

PART II

Companionship and emotional responsiveness in early childhood

CHAPTER 6

Contributions of experimental and clinical perturbations of mother–infant communication to the understanding of infant intersubjectivity

Lynne Murray

Early infant capacities for interpersonal engagement

Over the past two decades a large body of experimental and observational evidence has accumulated concerning the interpersonal capacities of the human infant. The demonstration of neonatal imitation of facial movements and expressions (Maratos, 1973, 1982; Meltzoff and Moore, 1977, 1983; Kugiumutzakis, 1985a, b, 1993), the selective responsiveness to human stimuli (Fantz, 1963; Goren *et al.*, 1975; Friedlander, 1970; Eisenberg, 1975; Leslie, 1984), and the rapid development of preferences for the particular characteristics of the persons involved in infant care (Field, 1985; De Casper and Fifer, 1980; McFarlane, 1975; Bushnell *et al.*, 1989; Cernoch and Porter, 1985; Hepper *et al.*, 1993) together attest to a preadaptation in the human newborn to an environment of consistent interpersonal engagements. Film and video technology has been exploited to serve the microanalytic study of mother–infant contacts in the first postnatal weeks, observations typically being made of face-to-face engagements occurring in standardized conditions when the infant is in a state of quiet alertness (Brazelton *et al.*, 1974; Stern, 1974; Trevarthen, 1979a; Tronick *et al.*, 1979). This research has documented, in infants less than two months old, the capacity to engage in encounters with others in which complex, well-organized repertoires of action and facial expression are displayed that appear responsive to the form and timing of adult communication. On the basis of such evidence, Trevarthen (1979a) proposed an innate capacity of intersubjectivity, or ability both to express and directly to apprehend in others rudimentary intentions and affects.

Since this initial formulation, which principally concerned an infant competence, the notion of infant intersubjectivity has undergone considerable development. In particular, more comprehensive accounts of the role of the adult in mother–infant communication have been elaborated, for example by Stern (1985) and, working within cognitive systems theory, by Bråten (1988a). Bråten argues that the prerequisite for intersubjectivity is the inherently dyadic organization of the individual subject. He proposes that, within the central nervous system of the newborn, there are circuits that specify the immediate co-presence of a complementary participant, or 'virtual other', in place of which the actual other may step. The virtual other is not only the operational prerequisite for intersubjectivity, but a 'felt perspective', an as yet unrealized otherness that is realized by the actual other taking its place in the dialogic circle. The infant and mother thus combine to form one operationally closed system. Hence, the patterns of perfect timing and turn-taking that have been documented in early mother–infant face-to-face interactions are conceived as natural patterns of one, albeit asymmetric, dialogic organization completing its own operationally defined circuits, and not as the outcome of two monologic organizations attempting to be in concert.

Accounts within developmental psychology of early intersubjective relations, and particularly those of Trevarthen and Stern, along with their development within systems theory emphasize the consistency of fit between the characteristics of the environment which the infant seeks out, and the nature of the human contact that the infant ordinarily encounters. Thus Stern argues from experimental evidence of the infant's capacity to experience an equivalence between different sensory modalities (e.g. to equate the proprioceptive experience of a particular surface with its visual counterpart (Meltzoff and Borton, 1979)) that there is a readiness to encounter environmental events that are cross-modal matches of infant actions. When, in the course of face-to-face exchanges, maternal imitative or mirroring responses correspond to these infant expectations, they convey a sense of *déjà vu*, or affirmation. Bråten similarly argues that the complementary nature of adult responses plays a central role in infant psychological development. In particular, he proposes that the repeated experience of the infant's subjectivity being realized in the maternal response provides the basis for the infant's capacity for mental representation, in which self and other come to be perceived as distinct.

These accounts of the significance of interpersonal contacts in the development of representation find close parallels in Object Relations Theory, and particularly in the work of Winnicott and Bion. According to Winnicott a state of Primary Maternal Preoccupation develops in late pregnancy that enables the mother to identify with her infant's experience and provide care that anticipates the infant's needs (Winnicott, 1956). The infant's experience of this quality of engagement, in which incipient intentions are realized in maternal contacts, helps to promote the development of a coherent representation of self and other, where 'the infant changes from a relationship to a subjectively conceived object to an object objectively perceived' (Winnicott, 1960/1985:45). Bion provides a very similar account of the role of maternal responsiveness or '*rêverie*', proposing that infant conceptual development, and in particular the recognition of a distinction between subject and object, is related to the emotional experience of satisfaction, and the linking of infant preconceptions or nascent expectations with their realization in maternal care: 'when the pre-conception is brought into contact with a realisation that approximates to it, the mental outcome is a conception' (Bion, 1962).

Immediate consequences of intersubjective breakdown: perturbation experiments

In the course of normal interactions it can be difficult to identify those features of maternal behaviour that contribute to their harmonious quality, and to estimate the significance of the nature of maternal responsiveness for the infant. However, formal investigation, through experimental studies, of infant responses to contrived episodes of disrupted or perturbed maternal behaviour has been particularly fruitful in elucidating infant sensitivity to the quality of adult communication and their regulatory capacities in face-to-face interaction (Brazelton *et al.*, 1975; Cohn and Tronick, 1989; Papousek and Papousek, 1975; Tronick *et al.*, 1978). In one such study (Murray, 1980; Murray and Trevarthen, 1985) the responses to a variety of disruptions in maternal behaviour were examined in 6- to 12-week-old infants. In this series, the first perturbation presented to the infant comprised an 'Interruption' condition in which a natural alteration in maternal behaviour was effected: following a period of normal communication with the infant, the mother was interrupted by a researcher entering the room and engaging the mother in conversation; during this time the mother turned away from the infant and her style of interaction ceased to show the adaptations characteristic of adult communication with infants (e.g. *en face* presentation, elaborated expressions, raised pitch of voice). The second perturbation again required the mother to cease communicating with her infant, but in this case the disruption was unnatural, and the commonly adopted strategy of the 'Blank Face' presentation was used. Here, the mother, after some period of normal communication with her infant, was signalled to adopt a

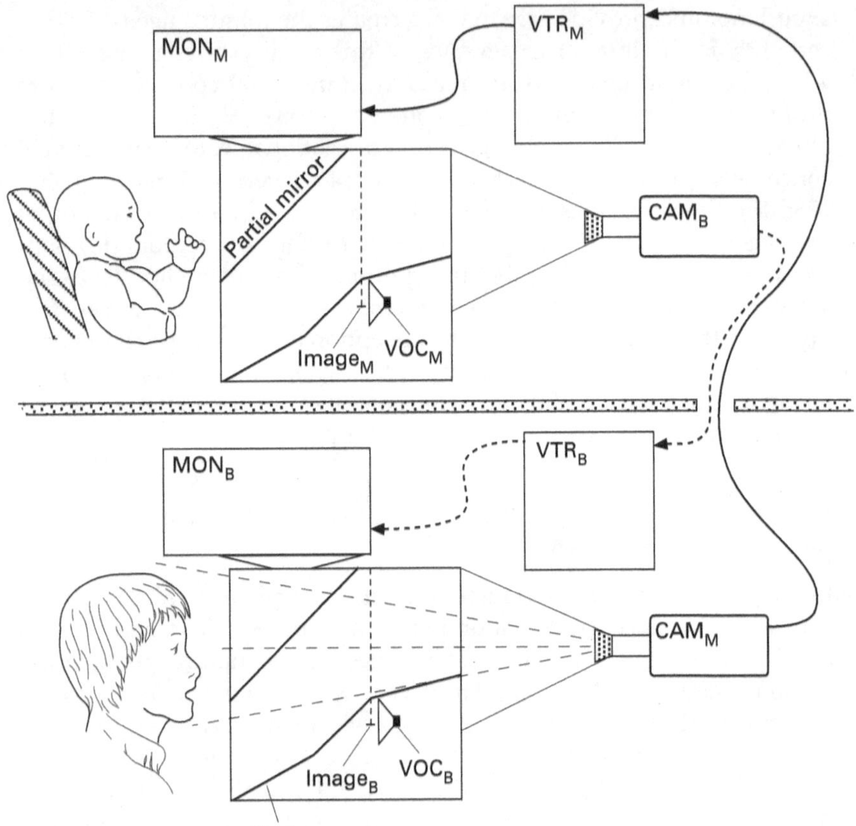

Fig 6.1 The Double Video Technique: mother and infant communicate via a linked video system that permits either live, real-time communication or else a delayed, replayed version to be presented. MON = monitor; VTR = video tape recorder; CAM = camera; VOC = loudspeaker conveying voice of mother or baby.

'Blank Face', and remain immobile and expressionless while continuing to look at the infant. Finally, infants were presented with maternal communication that retained its usual form, but lost its relationship in time to infant behaviour. This was achieved by means of a closed-circuit television system (see Fig. 6.1) in which mother and infant, seated in separate rooms, each viewed a full-face, life-sized video image of the other partner immediately before them, perfect eye-to-eye contact being possible. The images were first relayed in real or 'live' time when the two were able to interact in a normal, mutually responsive fashion. Some minutes after this period of 'live' communication the mother's image was replayed to the infant, so causing the interaction to become perturbed: the infant could see and hear the same maternal behaviours that occurred in the previous live sequence, but in the replay sequence the mother's communication was, of course, unrelated to her infant's current behaviour.

Analyses of infant behaviour during each of these sequences revealed distinctive and, moreover, intuitively appropriate forms of response to the different patterns of adult communication. During the periods of normal interaction the infant's gaze was directed to the mother's face almost all the time, and the infant smiled, made active gestures and 'prespeech' tonguing movements and wide shapings of the mouth. During the Interruption condition, when the researcher distracted the mother, the infant's communicative behaviour subsided and signs of positive excitement were reduced. Nevertheless, there was no indication that the infant experienced the Interruption as distressing – there was no increase in signs of negative affect or in the incidence of displacement behaviours such as fingering the clothes, or sucking the fist. Although the infant gazed less to the mother this seemed not to be a function of active avoidance of her, but rather reflected the infant's interest in the researcher. In contrast to this profile of quietened interest, when the mother presented a Blank Face the infant very quickly appeared disturbed. As has been described by several research groups (e.g. Brazelton *et al.*, 1975; Tronick *et al.*, 1978), an initial form of response frequently occurred that suggested protest; rather than falling off, as in the Interruption condition, active prespeech movements were at first sustained, if not intensified, and frowning increased, and these behaviours occurred while the infant looked at the mother. This phase of apparent protest was typically followed first by signs of distress, such as grimacing, or displacement activities of the hands, and subsequently by withdrawal, with the infant's gaze being averted from the mother's face and the head drooping.

In the closed-circuit television experiment, during live communication sequences the infant's behaviour was very similar to that shown in normal face-to-face interactions. Eye-to-eye contact was sustained in long continuous bouts and the infant gestured and made active 'prespeech' movements of lips and tongue. When confronted with the replay sequence there was a rapid change in behaviour that in some respects resembled the response to the Blank Face perturbation. Gaze was largely averted from the mother and was interspersed with short, darting glances to her, and there were also signs of distress such as frowning and grimacing, and fingering of the clothes and face.

However, unlike the response to the Blank Face disruption, 'pre-speech' tonguing and wide open mouthing occurred less often, and the impression was not so much one of protest, but rather one of puzzlement or confusion. This impression was reinforced by analysis of the simultaneous occurrence of emotional expressions and communicative behaviour with the direction of gaze: this revealed a strong association between frowning and looking away from the mother in the replay condition – the converse of the relationship between these measures in the Blank Face perturbation.

In a final phase of this work the closed circuit television system was used to investigate the impact of infant responsiveness on maternal communication (Murray, 1980; Murray and Trevarthen, 1986). In this experiment, as in the previous study, mother and infant initially communicated in real, live time. Subsequently, the mother was presented with a replay of her infant's behaviour during the live sequence, but she was informed that this was a second live interaction. In this situation the infant's behaviour was identical to that presented earlier, but it was not responsive to the ongoing maternal communication. Although the mothers had no knowledge of the experimental manipulation, several spontaneously remarked that they felt something was odd, and that they could not 'get through' to their infant. When maternal speech to the infant during live and replay sequences was compared on structural and semantic dimensions a number of differences were found. During the live sequence maternal speech showed the usual characteristics of 'motherese': utterances were short, simple and repetitive, and they were predominantly focused on the infant's experience. In the replay condition, by contrast, speech became more complex, more focused on the mother's own experience, and more directive, controlling and critical.

A number of conclusions regarding infant interpersonal capacities follow from this line of work. First, it is clear from the studies of perturbations to maternal behaviour that 2- to 3-month-old infants are indeed remarkably sensitive to the quality of adult communication with them, and in a way that does not seem to be reducible to the detection of changes in simple physical properties. Thus, the distinctive forms of response to the different perturbations – the quiet interest during the Interruption, the protest, distress and withdrawal at the Blank Face, and puzzlement and confusion in the replay sequence of the closed circuit television system – defy explanation in terms of a simple response to the disruption of contingency, or to discrepancy from some acquired schema. Both these elements were present in the Interruption, and yet no distress arose. Although the infant undoubtedly is sensitive to the timing or contingency of the mother's acts, as evidenced in the response to the replay sequence, as well as to the form of her presentation, the infant seems to coordinate such dimensions into higher-order constructs that specify interpersonal states. In addition to an awareness of different interpersonal forms, it is also apparent from this analysis of infant responses to breakdown in maternal communication, and particularly the protest and distress shown in Blank Face condition, that the infant is strongly affected by the quality of adult responsiveness and reveals a motivation to achieve particular forms of interpersonal engagement.

Finally, these experimental studies demonstrate the mutuality of influence, with infant behaviour as well as being responsive to that of the adult also serving to regulate maternal communication.

This was evident in maternal reactions to the perturbation of infant communication in the final closed circuit television experiment, where the normal empathic adjustments to the infant could not be sustained in the face of the infant's unresponsiveness, and it was also apparent in maternal responses to infant behaviour during the Blank Face perturbation. Here, on seeing the infant's withdrawn and sad appearance, the mother was generally moved to become concerned and, upon reunion, was particularly solicitous and attentive.

Depressed mothers and their infants

The findings from perturbation experiments of infant sensitivity to the quality of their interpersonal environment, together with the theoretical predictions outlined above concerning the role of the caretaker's responsiveness in promoting the development of infant mental representations, raise the issue of the possible longer-term consequences for infant functioning of prolonged exposure to an interpersonal environment that is consistently perturbed. Not only is the question raised of the development of cognitive capacities for the representation of objective events, but disturbances in interpersonal contacts may also entail strong affective components with rather different consequences for developmental progress. For example, where a woman comes to motherhood with a legacy of unsatisfied needs and distortions in her childhood relationships, and receives inadequate care and support from those around her, the quality of interpersonal engagement required by the newborn infant, and particularly his dependency and distress, may provoke overwhelming feelings of desperation, anxiety and depression. In such cases the mother may feel the need to switch off from the infant, and is likely to be drawn instead to focus on her own experience. If this is not possible, as may be the case in the face of the infant's persistent demands, the mother may be unable to distinguish the infant's requirements and perspective from the impact his state makes on her, in which case she may experience the infant as trying to tyrannize her, and may respond with hostility.

Just as the cognitive sequel of parental failure to meet infant expressions of intention has been specified within Object Relations Theory, so too has there been a concern with more affectively charged psychological processes, and particularly those to do with a 'sense of self' or the coherence of experience. Thus, it is suggested that if infant experience is not accommodated by the mother, but instead causes her emotional disarray, the infant may be left, not with distress that is made tolerable by maternal care, but with a sense of misunderstanding that gives rise to the sense of 'falling forever', 'unthinkable anxiety' or 'going to pieces' (Winnicott, 1962/1985), or 'nameless dread' (Bion, 1962).

The remainder of this chapter addresses this issue of the possible longer-term consequences of sustained disturbances in maternal responsiveness, and presents results from a study of the children of postnatally depressed and well mothers who were observed in the early postpartum months, and followed up to five years. Features of depressive disorder include anxiety, irritability, and feelings of guilt and hopelessness, in addition to the pervasive low mood; these symptoms normally exert a profound effect on interpersonal relationships and it is likely that these difficulties will extend to the relationship the mother establishes with her infant. By studying the interactions between depressed mothers and their infants and comparing them to those occurring in a well population and relating them to the child's later development it was hoped that it might be possible to assess the relevance for later child functioning of different kinds of early intersubjective contact. In this study face-to-face interactions between mother and infant at 2 to 4 months postpartum were analysed from video recordings. The quality of these interactions was then considered in relation to the children's performance on standardized measures of cognitive development at 18 months and 5 years, and also in a play situation designed to elicit the child's self-constructions.

Mothers taking part in the study were drawn from a community sample of primiparous women who had delivered healthy, full-term infants at the maternity hospital in Cambridge, England. At 6 weeks postpartum, fifty-eight women were identified who had experienced an episode of depression (meeting DSM-III R criteria) since delivery. These women, together with forty-two randomly selected psychiatrically well controls from the same postnatal population were recruited, of whom half were regularly seen for observations of face-to-face interactions (see Murray, 1992 for details of sample). At 18 months, ninety-eight of the hundred mother–infant pairs recruited were followed up, and at 5 years all but three of these were seen again.

Disturbances in intersubjective contacts

Assessments were conducted at 2 months postpartum in a research play room. Typically the mother would feed and change the infant, and then, when the infant appeared alert and contented, interactions were video recorded for a 5 minute period when the mother played with the infant without the use of toys. Given the evidence for the active influence of infant factors on the quality of maternal communication from the closed circuit television experiment, the infant was also filmed in interaction with a female researcher. By using the researcher as a standard adult partner for the infant at this early age, before motivational states such as fear of strangers might be expected to swamp responses to the novel adult, we aimed to gain a measure of individual infant capacities for sustained attention and engagement in interactions, independent of communication with the mother. Maternal and infant behaviour during the interactions was scored using ratings similar to those used for coding behaviour during the perturbation experiments (Murray *et al.*, 1996). Maternal behaviour was rated on a dimension of sensitivity (including assessment of responsiveness, acceptance and warmth, as well as sensitivity itself), and on a scale assessing the extent to which the mother was either remote or was actively engaged with the infant. Infant ratings comprised the degree of positive active engagement (including ratings of attention to the mother, vocalizations, 'prespeech' movements and the quality of affect), and also behaviour on a dimension from distressed to inert. In addition, a number of discrete events were scored on a 1 second time base. For the mother these comprised affirmations, where the mother empathically either imitated or complemented infant behaviour and expressions, and negations, where there was some rejecting or emotionally discordant response to the infant. For the infant, expressions of positive and negative affect were scored, as were episodes of disrupted behaviour; these were moments when the infant, previously actively engaged with the mother, would suddenly arrest his activity and become sober and still.

In addition to these behavioural ratings, transcripts of maternal speech to the infant were analysed on both syntactic and semantic dimensions. These included the extent to which utterances were focused on the infant's experience and the degree of negative affect.

A number of differences were evident in the communication of mother–infant pairs in the two groups (Murray *et al.*, 1993; Murray, Fiori-Cowley *et al.*, 1996). Compared to the interactions of well women, those who were depressed were rated overall as less sensitive, and with regard to individual behaviours, they expressed fewer affirmations of their infants' behaviour and more negations. The analysis of maternal speech gave results that were consistent with these behavioural characteristics; for example, compared to rates in the control group, higher levels of critical and hostile comments to the infant were apparent in the depressed women. In addition, the measure of the extent to which the mother's speech during play had been focused on the infant's experience varied both according to maternal mental state and to infant gender. Thus, depressed mothers' speech to their sons was particularly lacking in infant-focused utterances, whereas speech to female infants was generally high in infant focus and did not differ between the two maternal groups. In spite of the relatively insensitive communication of depressed mothers, especially with their sons, the two groups of women did not differ in the extent to which they were either behaviourally intrusive or withdrawn from their infants. Similarly, the structural properties of maternal speech did not vary as a function of maternal mental state, both groups of mothers talking in the repetitive, simplified manner that is characteristic of 'motherese'.

The quality of infant communication in the face-to-face interaction was highly correlated with that of the mother: the more sensitive the mother, the more actively the infant was engaged with her. Nevertheless, in spite of the significant differences in the communication of the two groups of mothers, infants of depressed and well women in this study showed broadly similar profiles of interactive behaviour. Thus, there were no differences in the extent to which the two groups of infants attempted to engage actively with the mother or showed expressions of positive or negative affect, or in the extent of either flat and inert or else fretful and distressed behaviour. The only difference was in the rate of disrupted behaviour. This was observed in only one of the control group infants compared to fourteen of the infants of depressed women. In order to understand more clearly the nature of these mother–infant interactions, and in particular the extent of infant sensitivity to the quality of maternal communication and the degree of mutual regulation, an examination was made of the relationships between particular maternal and infant behaviours. To this end the immediate precursors of behaviours that had differed between the two groups were identified, i.e. behaviours occurring in the 1 second time interval before maternal affirmations and negations, and before

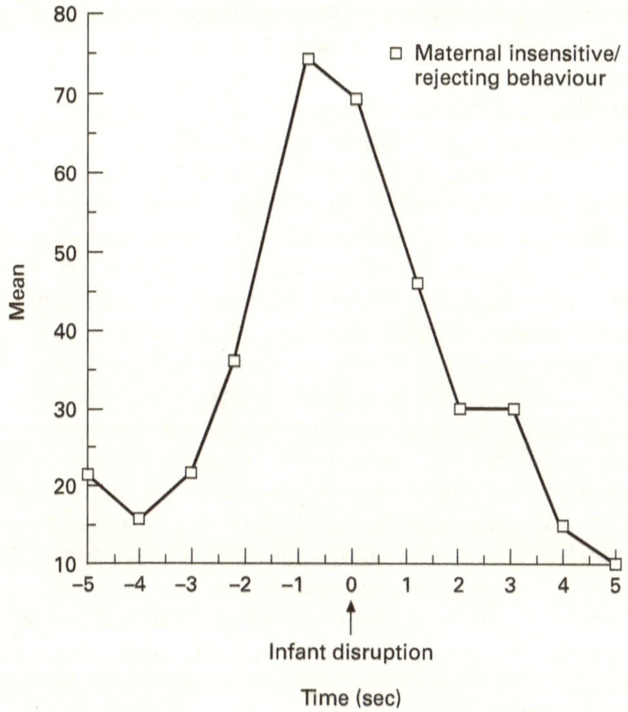

Fig. 6.2 The proportion of 1-second time intervals preceding and following disruptions in infant attention and engagement in which insensitive/rejecting maternal behaviour occurs

infant disruptions. The rate of occurrence of these 'precursor events' at such points in time was then compared to their base rate. These analyses revealed considerable structure in the interaction: thus, episodes where the mother affirmed the infant's behaviour were likely to occur in the context of positive infant affect, whereas negations, in which the mother's response to the infant was discordant and lacking in sympathy, were precipitated by signs of infant distress. Given that levels of distress were equivalent in the two groups of infants, and yet maternal negating occurred almost exclusively in the depressed mothers, this finding suggests that the depressed women were especially sensitive to their infant's negative affect. On the infant's part, analysis of maternal communication immediately preceding infant disruptions showed that these episodes of breakdown in infant engagement were precipitated by maternal negations (see Fig. 6.2). It seemed, therefore, as though the depressed mothers and their infants were becoming locked into cycles of mutually responsive negativity that would culminate in the infant's cutting off for a period before once more resuming attempts at more normal engagement.

The fact that systematic differences were evident in the communication of the two groups of mothers, while infant behaviour differed rather little according to maternal psychiatric state, may seem to suggest that there is a relative insensitivity on the part of the infant to the nature of maternal engagement, a conclusion that is clearly at variance with that drawn from the results of the perturbation experiments. However, a number of lines of evidence argue against such an interpretation, and suggest that any such inconsistency is more apparent than real. First, it is clear that while depressed women's attunement to their infants was less sensitive and empathic than that of well women, their communication nevertheless retained many of the characteristics of normal engagement: their utterances were simple, brief and repetitive, there were high rates of responsiveness (albeit frequently of a more negative kind), and they were neither intrusive nor withdrawn. Thus, unlike maternal behaviour during experimental perturbations, where sustained and somewhat uniform disruptions were effected, it is likely that the behaviour of the depressed mothers approximated sufficiently to infant specifications of an expectable interpersonal environment, or 'virtual other' (Bråten, 1988a; this volume), to elicit the infants' potential for active engagement. Nevertheless, at particular moments of maternal misattunement, where, for example, the mother would negate her infant's experience of distress, the infant would reveal a finely tuned sensitivity to the quality of maternal behaviour, and would show a marked disruption in the flow of activity, before reverting to the previous level of engagement.

Further evidence of infant sensitivity to the quality of the partner's communication in this study was provided by consideration of infant behaviour with the researcher, and its relationship to the nature of mother–infant interactions. As noted previously, the degree to which the infant became actively engaged in communication with the mother was strongly related to the extent of maternal sensitivity. Had this association not reflected an adaptation on the infant's part to the quality of maternal communication, but rather maternal adjustment to infant characteristics, two findings should have followed: first, one would have expected the quality of the infant's behaviour with the mother and that shown with the researcher to be highly correlated. In addition, if maternal behaviour had been principally driven by infant characteristics it should have been possible to predict the quality of the mother's behaviour in the interaction from the nature of infant communication with the stranger. Neither of these predictions was

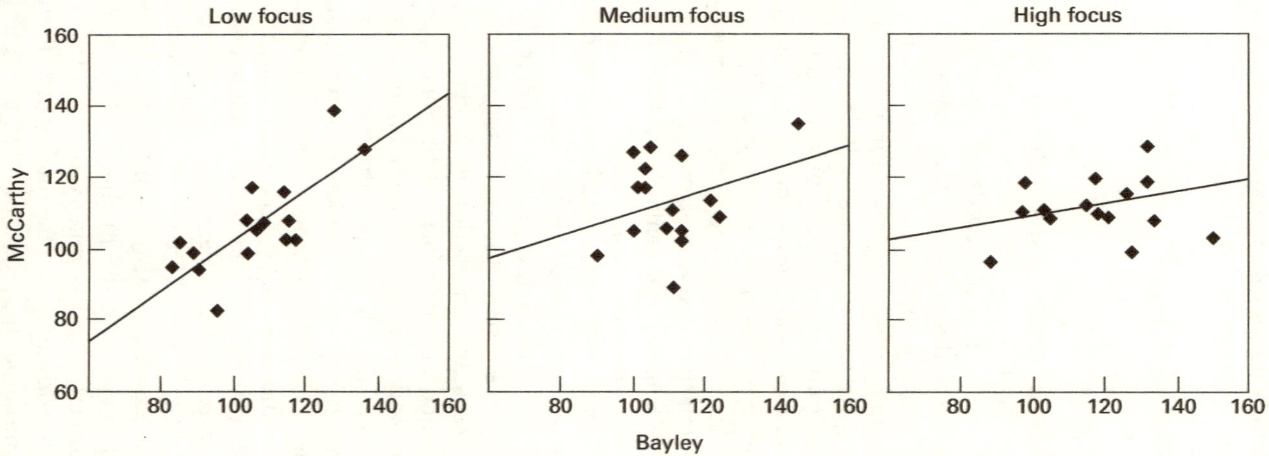

Fig. 6.3 Plots of McCarthy General Cognitive Index at 5 years against Bayley Mental Development Index at 18 months, with children divided into three equally sized groups on the basis of the degree to which their mothers' speech at 2 months was infant-focused. The regression line calculated within each of these groups is also shown. (Permission for reproduction of figure given by the Association for Child Psychology and Psychiatry. First published in Murray *et al.*, 1996.)

borne out: there was only a modest association between the extent of active infant engagement in the two sets of interaction, and the nature of maternal interactions was quite unrelated to the infant's communication with the stranger (Murray and Cooper, 1997).

Implications for later development

(a) Cognitive functioning. In order to explore the possible effects of the infant's early interpersonal experience on later cognitive functioning the infants were assessed on a standardized measure of cognitive development, the Bayley Scales of Mental Development (Bayley 1969) when they were 18 months old (Fig. 6.3). At this time the great majority of women who had been depressed in the postnatal months had recovered (most episodes had remitted within 6 months of onset). Nevertheless, infant cognitive functioning was found to be associated with the occurrence of postnatal depression, as well as the gender of the child: boys of depressed women performed significantly worse than boys of well women, while the girls of depressed women performed rather better than control group girls. This pattern of variation in infant performance was remarkably similar to that occurring in maternal speech to the infant at 2 months postpartum, where depressed mothers' speech to their sons had been particularly lacking in infant-focused utterances. Indeed, when infant cognitive performance was analysed in relation to the quality of maternal communication, and particularly the extent to which the mother had been actively engaged in sensitive interaction with her infant, and had shown a high proportion of infant-focused utterances, the effects of maternal depression and infant gender on infant outcome disappeared. These results clearly suggest that the quality of the mother's communication with the infant played a key role in influencing infant cognitive functioning. However, in order to ensure that performance on the Bayley Scales did not really reflect the influence of infant factors, the quality of the infant's behaviour in interaction with both the mother and the researcher was examined in relation to cognitive outcome. These analyses showed that although 18-month performance on the Bayley Scales was also predicted by the extent of the infant's active engagement with the mother in the 2-month interaction, it was quite unrelated to the quality of the infant's behaviour with the researcher. In addition, once the quality of maternal communication was taken into account, the association between the infant's behaviour with the mother and cognitive outcome disappeared, indicating that the mother's contribution to 18-month infant functioning was the more important.

At 5 years the children were once more assessed on a standardized measure of general cognitive development, the McCarthy Scales of Children's Development (Murray, Hipwell, Hooper, Stein and Cooper, 1996). It was again the case that infant behaviour with the mother in the 2-month interaction, but not that with the researcher, was a significant predictor of cognitive functioning. This influence of the infant's experience of maternal engagement appeared to have been effected by late infancy, for, once the infant's score at 18 months on the Bayley Scales was taken into account, the association between the quality of the early engagement with the mother and 5-year functioning no longer held. Further examination of the patterns of continuity between 18-month performance and that at 5 years indicated that the effects of the early environment were especially strong where the infant had experienced particularly insensitive maternal communication (i.e. where there was a low level of infant-focused speech in the 2-month interaction). In these cases not only was performance at 18 months relatively poor, but the subsequent trajectory of infant cognitive development seemed to become narrowly channelled along a path of less optimal functioning. For infants whose initial maternal environment was more optimal, by contrast, the developmental trajectory appeared far more flexible. These different patterns of development are illustrated in Fig. 6.3, where the continuity between performance at 18 months and 5 years is indicated according to the quality of the early maternal interactions (grouped in three categories of low, medium and high infant-focused speech).

Much discussion concerning the prediction of cognitive development from factors measured in infancy has concerned the role of infant capacities to regulate attention and respond to novel information (see review by Slater, 1995). Generally, these are viewed as intrinsic characteristics of the individual child. Nevertheless, it has long been recognized from observational studies that the characteristic features of parental adjustment in face-to-face interaction, such as the attunement to infant affective expressions and their repetitive elaboration in multi-modal displays, serve to sustain infant attention and positive engagement (Stern *et al.*, 1974; Stern, 1985). In addition, evidence from studies of infant learning indicate that the quality of the infant's interpersonal engagements, and particularly the extent to which infant attention is sustained by contingent responsiveness in the adult, becomes generalized to infant performance in non-social instrumental learning tasks (Dunham *et al.*, 1989). Such findings, together with those from the current study of infant development in the context of maternal depression, indicate that the motivational and attentional processes relevant to cognitive operations are deeply embedded in the infant's experience of interpersonal engagements.

(b) The organization of the child's experience of self. In addition to the assessment of cognitive functioning at 5 years, the children of the postnatally depressed and well mothers were also observed in a situation designed to elicit the way in which they represented the nature of their experience in their families (Murray, 1994). This was achieved using a dolls house play scenario in which the child was invited to choose doll figures to represent the people in their home, and were then asked to play out what happened in a range of family situations. Minimal probes were given by the researcher in order to maximize the spontaneous and self-generated nature of the children's accounts. Transcripts were made of the children's play narratives, and these were then scored using a system (a case grammar analysis) designed to describe the way in which the children constructed and organized their experience; this scheme includes an assessment of the extent to which children perceive themselves as agents who are able to influence events, in contrast to feeling that events are out of their control. Comparison of the accounts of the children of postnatally depressed and well women indicated that the index group children experienced themselves as more helpless and less agentful (Barnard *et al.*, 1997); that is, they already exhibited cognitive styles related to the development of depressive disorder (Abramson *et al.*, 1978). When the way in which the children constructed their accounts of family experience was examined in relation to the quality of early mother–infant relations a strong association was found, but one that was rather different from that pertaining to cognitive functioning. In this case it was the extent of the mother's hostility and criticism in the interactions that was best predictive of a lack of a sense of agency.

General conclusions regarding the role of interpersonal relationships in child development

A number of conclusions may be drawn from the research described in this chapter. First, the evidence from the perturbation studies indicates that infants are remarkably sensitive to the quality of communication in an adult partner, and appear to apprehend the personal significance of different forms of engagement. Moreover, their responses to the various disruptions in maternal communication appear to form complementary adaptations that play a regulatory role in both their own experience and that of their partner.

The second series of studies, involving the long-term follow up infants who are subjected to prolonged periods of forms of engagement that depart in various ways from those normally encountered, serves to elucidate how certain facets of the infant's interpersonal environment become incorporated into the child's experience, causing development to unfold along particular pathways: thus, the capacity for functioning well on the cognitive tasks incorporated into general measures of intelligence appears to be shaped in part by the experience of interactions in which the adult partner succeeds in enlisting the infant's engagement in sustained, reciprocal communication. By contrast, disturbances in the child's sense of self-coherence and sense of agency show a specific association with the experience of a hostile and critical personal environment in which the infant's initiatives and communication are rejected. Such specificity of effect is becoming increasingly evident in research in developmental psychology, and strikingly so in the work of Dunn (1993; and this volume) in which remarkably tight relationships obtain between various forms of family functioning and children's capacities to handle different kinds of interpersonal task.

Together these findings illustrate something of the process whereby the young infant and child's apprehension of the personal and affective significance of others' responses in interpersonal contacts becomes incorporated into the way in which experience of the world and of the self is subsequently organized. On a general level, and in a largely positive frame, this process provides the basis for achieving the shared understandings that reside within different cultures; more particularly, however, it is likely to be a central aspect of the process whereby individual differences, including clinical conditions, arise out of different patterns of interpersonal relationships.

CHAPTER 7

Empathy and its origins in early development

Ross A. Thompson

Empathy is, in many respects, the quintessential intersubjective experience: the vicarious sharing of another's emotion. To students of prosocial motivation, empathy is one basis for moral action: empathy for another's distress is often a motivator of helping and altruism. To scholars concerned with culture and society, empathy is part of the emotional connection between people that fosters mutual sensitivity and reduces selfish concern. To developmental psychologists, the growth of empathy reveals a young child's capacity to respond to another's emotional experience, which is a foundation for social and emotional understanding. Each perspective to empathy reflects its intersubjective quality.

These alternative perspectives to empathy have provoked considerable theoretical and empirical work on empathy and its motivational correlates. At times, however, they have also threatened to obscure a thoughtful appreciation of the complexity and multidimensionality of empathic experience. Empathy is not only a basis for sympathetic understanding, for example, but also for anger or guilt in the presence of a distressed individual. Thus empathy might provoke altruism, but in other situations aggression (towards the perpetrator, or even the victim), self-deprecation or withdrawal. The development of empathy is likewise multifaceted, related to the growth of socioemotional understanding in young children, their interpretation of others' emotional signals, and their increasing comprehension that others' emotional cues are personally relevant, as well as indicators of another's experience. Empathy is thus built upon, but different from, other experiences of emotional sharing that also reflect intersubjectivity. Taken together, although empathy is an intuitively well-defined concept, it is easy to neglect its diverse roles in human motivation, and its multidimensional origins in development.

This chapter is devoted to an appraisal of empathy in early development. In summarizing theoretical and definitional issues and offering a developmental portrayal of empathy, I underscore that empathy is a crucial feature of the growth of intersubjectivity in early childhood. Moreover, recent thinking in allied areas of developmental inquiry – ranging from the emergence of functionalist theories of emotion to studies of young children's 'theory of mind' – makes the current climate of developmental study especially promising for renewed attention to the growth of empathy in the early years.

Theoretical perspectives on the early growth of empathy

During most of this century, the early development of empathy has been discussed in the context of two theoretical perspectives that offer distinctly different, and contrary, views about its emergence.

On one hand, some psychoanalytic and neo-analytic (especially object relations) writers have argued that empathy exists early in the context of the emotional closeness of mother and infant (Burlingham, 1967; Spitz, 1965). From this perspective, the infant is highly sensitive to the mother's immediate feelings, as well as to her more enduring moods, because of the emotional intimacy they share, the baby's dependence on the mother, and the lack of clear self–other differentiation in the infant's psychological growth. However, this early empathic connection also renders the baby vulnerable to maternal feelings and affects, such as anxiety or anger, with which the infant is unprepared to cope without the supportive assistance of the caregiver, and this can sometimes pose a formidable challenge to healthy emotional growth. To many neo-analytic theorists, the child's capacity for empathy increases significantly in sophistication and scope with the growth of object relations and the development of psychological individuation in the second year (Kaplan, 1977; Mahler, Pine and Bergman, 1975). In general, while the analytic view remains heuristically powerful, and is consistent with arguments concerning an innate intersubjective capacity in young infants, it has failed to generate considerable research interest. One reason is that it offers a portrayal of the sophistication of early psychological functioning that is inconsistent with the simpler conceptual structures commonly assumed to exist in early infancy. In addition, this view portrays the infant primarily as the recipient of maternal influences rather than as a truly interactive partner in intersubjective sharing.

On the other hand, most cognitive-developmental theorists, stimulated by Piaget's seminal insights, have assumed that true empathy is beyond the capacities of the infant, whose egocentrism and lack of role-taking ability make it impossible for the infant or young child to appraise sensitively another's emotional state (Deutsch and Madle, 1975; Shantz, 1975). In this view, empathy is instead an achievement of middle childhood when, with the growth of decentred thought and concrete operations, the child can distinguish another's emotional condition from his or her own, appropriately interpret the reasons for another's emotional arousal, and respond appropriately. Consequently, the pre-eminence of cognitive-developmental thinking in research of the 1970s and 1980s tended to direct attention away from the study of empathy in infancy and instead focused on empathy in middle childhood.

In the 1980s and 1990s, however, a third perspective to socio-emotional development has emerged that provides new perspectives on early empathy that are different from those of psychoanalytic and cognitive-developmental views (Thompson, 1993). Functionalist emotions theory proposes that young children are fundamentally social beings for whom emotions, and emotional communication, are significant motivational and organizational catalysts (e.g. Barrett and Campos, 1987; Campos *et al.*, 1989; Frijda, 1986). In the functionalist view, emotional experience arises from the goal structure of the organism's actions, with the success or failure of goal attainment and appraisals concerning its causes underlying differentiated forms of emotional arousal. Emotional expressions, furthermore, serve not only as manifestations of one's underlying arousal but also as potent social signals to others. These emotional signals can, for example, influence the appraisal processes by which others evaluate their current conditions and their goals within them, provoking new emotional reactions in a phenomenon called 'social referencing'. The functionalist view thus emphasizes the social bases of emotional experience, and the salience and importance of emotional signals to developing individuals from an early age.

Consistent with this view, there is now considerable evidence that, rather than being fundamentally egocentric, young children have a very non-egocentric interest in others' feelings and moods because of the importance of others' emotional experiences to their well-being (Bretherton *et al.*, 1981; Dunn, 1993; Harris, 1989, 1994a; Thompson, in press). Young children's queries and utterances reveal a clear differentiation of self and other that is also revealed in early perspective-taking and role-taking skills. Thus a capacity for rudimentary emotional understanding emerges earlier than cognitive-developmental views have long assumed. However, it is also apparent that the growth of emotional understanding, on which empathy is based, is a slow, painstaking process as young children learn about others' emotional expressions as internal, mental states that must be carefully interpreted in light of situational demands and knowledge about others' goals and intentions (Harris, 1994a; Saarni and Harris, 1989; Wellman, 1990). In short, from the view of functionalist emotions theory, a capacity for empathy is not limited by egocentrism but is fostered by the child's early interest in others' emotions and the progressive growth of emotional understanding. This suggests that new directions in the developmental study of early empathy might be usefully built upon research on the early growth of emotional understanding and on children's developing 'theory of mind' and other aspects of their comprehension of others' internal experiences.

Definitional concerns

To be sure, charting the developmental course of empathy depends, in part, on how empathy is defined. If empathy is regarded primarily as a primitive experience of affective sharing, then it probably has early origins in the playful exchanges shared by mother and baby. If empathy is instead defined with reference to the child's cognitive grasp of another's emotional perspective, true empathy might have a very late developmental emergence coincident with the growth of sophisticated role-taking skills. Although empathy clearly entails both affective and cognitive components, theorists vary in the relative emphasis they place on each (Thompson, 1987). Likewise, researchers differ in the extent to which they require an empathic response to match directly the emotion of the target person (e.g. requiring vicarious fear in the presence of a fearful individual) rather than to resemble the target's emotion in its general valence (e.g. vicarious distress in the presence of a fearful individual).

Without striving to resolve these definitional quandaries in this short chapter, the following definition of empathy will be used: *empathy is a vicarious emotional response to another's emotional experience.* Like all definitions, this one has both inclusive and exclusive features. Included within this definition are vicarious emotional responses that do not directly match the emotion of the target individual, but which share the same general emotional tone. Feeling distressed in the company of another person who is fearful, angry or anxious, for example, would be regarded as empathic as long as the distress is truly vicarious rather than self-concerned (such as worry about being the target of another's anger, or afraid of the same event provoking fear in another).

On the other hand, this definition requires that vicarious emotion is a response to another's emotional experience, not merely his or her emotional expressions. For true empathy to occur, in other words, the perceiver must have some rudimentary appreciation of the bases for another's feelings. This means that, in some circumstances, one may empathize with another person without direct perception of his/her emotional expressions, such as when someone is deeply moved by a tragic account. This also means that not all experiences of emotional sharing are empathic in quality. The young infant's capacity to engage in protodialogic emotional give-and-take with a responsive partner (cf. Bråten, 1992) or, in the view of object relations theorists, to engage in projective identification with the mother as a realistic, rather than defensive, phenomenon (Murray, 1991) may each entail the rich sharing of emotion, but are not empathic experiences because they do not derive from the infant's even rudimentary appreciation of the partner's emotional experience. In these, and related, situations we might speak of emotional resonance with another, rather than empathy.

One other definitional concern merits attention. The association of empathy with prosocial behaviour has a long theoretical tradition because of the belief that empathy motivates altruism and helping (Hoffman, 1977). However, because empathy serves many masters – underlying not only prosocial initiatives but also guilt, and sometimes even aggression (when the aggressor is aroused by the victim's distress, either as a protector or a bully) – it is crucial that empathy is measured in terms of its emotional quality, not in terms of the prosocial response it is presumed to motivate. This is especially important in developmental study because young children may be vicariously aroused by another's emotional experience, yet they do not act prosocially but instead seek to be comforted personally, leave the situation, or merely look sad. Sometimes such responses are deemed 'egocentric', yet such children are clearly empathizing with another, and their apparent egocentrism may instead derive from uncertainty about how to assist the other person, competing motives, or their temperamental qualities (such as inhibition or shyness). In short, although empathy may sometimes motivate prosocial initiatives, it is unwise to operationalize empathy in terms of prosocial behaviour because it confounds two very different processes that are influenced in various ways, and researchers may underestimate the presence of empathy in young children when they focus on children's prosocial actions instead.

The distinction between empathy and prosocial behaviour has implications also for theoretical arguments that empathy may be a deeply rooted, biologically based feature of human motivation (e.g. Hoffman, 1981). Empathy can have diverse functions in human motivation: it can provide a basis for caregiving of offspring, marital fidelity, group cohesion, and moral compliance as well as prosocial behaviour. Each of these possible functions has different biological inclusive fitness considerations (depending, in part, on whether empathy motivates assistance to biological kin as well as whether empathy-based actions are likely to be reciprocated by the recipient) and different implications for the ontogenesis of empathic capacities. In general, although an empathic capacity might arise from natural selection, a global, generalized empathic response to human distress is probably an oversimplification of its role in human adaptation. Rather, a biologically based empathic capacity might be specific to particular individuals, in the context of specific relationships, at different life stages. What is still required, then, is a thoughtful analysis of the possible biological bases for empathic responses to particular individuals (who vary in their biological relatedness to the empathizer), and in specific circumstances (that vary in their relevance to the empathizer's reproductive success), and consideration of the implications of this analysis for whether empathy is likely to be an early- or later-developing capacity.

A developmental outline

As functionalist emotions theory proposes, another's emotional arousal is a compelling but motivationally complex experience for a young child. It is likely to provoke concern for oneself as well as interest in what emotional expressions reveal about another's circumstances and internal experience. The child's response is likely to be further complicated by his or her involvement in the conditions yielding another's emotional arousal – as a perpetrator or bystander, for example – and the child's relationship to the person who is aroused. All of these considerations are relevant to the development of empathy, and underscore why charting the growth of an empathic capacity in infants and young children is a formidable task. Nevertheless, the following condensed review of pertinent research yields at least three conclusions (see Thompson, 1987, for an earlier, and more extended, treatment of this literature). First, there is remarkable progress in infants' perception and interpretation of the emotional signals of others, especially in their understanding of the emotional meaning of facial and vocal expressions, and that another's emotional expressions are sometimes referential communications with personal relevance. By the end of the first year they begin to appreciate, in other words, that another's emotions are provoked by certain events that may also affect themselves, and that another's emotional expressions may convey meaningful information relevant to the self. This is especially true when emotional expressions are multimodal – that is, combine facial and vocal expressions – because of the infant's early sensitivity to emotional meaning in the voice (Fernald, 1992). Second, infants' emotions are directly affected by their perception of others' emotional expressions in complex ways, beginning in the early months of life. Although these earliest responses to another's emotions are non-empathic but rather emotionally resonant in quality (since they do not derive from an understanding of another's emotional experience), they may provide important precursors to the later development of empathy. Third, a capacity for true empathy begins to emerge in the second half of the second year of life in toddlers' expressions of 'concerned attention' to expressions of distress and anger they observe in others, especially as these expressions are combined with prosocial initiatives and other behaviours reflecting their vicarious arousal.

Reactive crying in newborns

Several researchers have noted that newborn infants cry in response to the distress cries of other newborns (Martin and Clark, 1982; Sagi and Hoffman, 1976; Simner, 1971). A newborn's cry is more effective in eliciting reactive crying, in fact, than is the cry of an older infant, or a computer-synthesized cry. Although this kind of neonatal reactive crying has been described as 'a rudimentary empathic distress reaction at birth' (Sagi and Hoffman, 1976), it is certainly not true empathy but instead, perhaps, a conditioned distress response to auditory cues resembling the infant's own cry, or an example of what Piaget would have called 'reproductive assimilation'. These interpretations of the newborn's resonant emotional response are supported by the fact that it is another neonatal cry, rather than the cry of an older infant, that provokes reactive distress, since true empathy would presumably not be so limited to a cry that sounds so much like the baby's own.

Affective synchrony and attunement in mother–infant interaction

Another arena of shared emotion in early life is constituted by episodes of parent–infant play when exuberant positive expressions of the adult are matched by the baby's bright smiles and cooing. Apart from their importance to the development of social skills and expectations, these episodes also offer opportunities for emotional sharing and mutuality. The emotional dynamics of mother–infant play have been studied insightfully by Malatesta and her colleagues (Malatesta *et al.*, 1989; Malatesta and Haviland, 1982), who have shown that affective synchrony is largely a result of the mother's sustained matching of infant expressions of enjoyment and interest (as if to prolong such positive expressions), as well as briefly imitating infant expressions of surprise, sadness and anger before quickly changing to a smile (as if to modify the baby's mood in this manner). As a consequence of this kind of maternal contingency, positive synchrony is established in a manner similar to the affective attunement emphasized by other students of mother–infant play (Stern, 1985). The mother's interactive behaviours have a potent effect on the baby, initially as salient elicitors and enhancements of positive emotion, and over time as the basis for the infant's expectation of a positive maternal response to the baby's play initiatives. The importance of these expectations is revealed especially in studies of perturbations in normal face-to-face interaction, when mothers are instructed to interrupt their normal play behaviour by adopting a still face and expressionless demeanour. When they do so, infants typically become sober and withdrawn, and a few become distressed (Cohn and Tronick, 1983).

To be sure, episodes of affective mutuality in mother–infant play are infrequent: they occur less than 30% of the time in face-to-face interaction (Tronick, 1989). Much more of the time, mothers and infants are dyssynchronous because of the baby's, or the mother's, distraction, or lack of interest in or responsiveness to the partner. Moreover, face-to-face play is a limited developmental phenomenon: once infants become mobile, parents and their offspring begin to socialize in other ways. However, even though the goal of creating and maintaining a mutually positive emotional state is infrequently achieved in the context of mother–infant play, it is a goal that characterizes much of their interaction together throughout the first year of life. In other words, mutually positive emotional arousal is a goal of parent–infant interaction that transcends face-to-face play and extends to many other interactive situations. Moreover, when these states of mutuality are achieved, and when mothers are striving to attain them, infants are watching a salient constellation of mature emotional cues in the face, voice and posture that channels and mirrors, at times, the infant's own emotion, and these cues may enhance the infant's awareness of emotional arousal and contribute to the socialization of expressive behaviour through the reflective and reactive behaviour of a significant partner. The emotional resonance that results from their synchronous exchanges, albeit infrequently, is clearly not empathic in quality (it is, after all, the infant's response to carefully structured maternal initiatives), but the baby's resonant emotional response is also more sophisticated than the reactive crying of the newborn. It entails, in other words, rudimentary expectations for the positive behaviour of a familiar partner, and an emotional response that is provoked, channelled and enhanced partly as these expectations are confirmed.

Social referencing

Others' emotional expressions are compelling events to infants, but it is not until mid-way through the first year that emotional expressions in the face and voice, taken alone, become interpreted as emotionally meaningful (when combined cues from face and voice are present, perception of emotion appears to emerge a month or two earlier) (Bornstein and Lamb, 1992). Once emotional expressions are imbued with emotional meaning, infants may incorporate such signals into their assessment of uncertain circumstances in a phenomenon called 'social referencing' (Campos and Stenberg, 1981; Klinnert *et al.*, 1983). At times, infants who encounter ambiguous or unusual events visually 'check back' to the mother, although referencing often occurs as the fortuitous byproduct of affective sharing, secure-base behaviour, and other attachment processes (Baldwin and Moses, 1996). Depending on whether the caregiver's emotional demeanour is positive or negative, infants will either approach or withdraw from the uncertain event (see Thompson, in press).

Why do the adult's emotional expressions have such an effect? There is some evidence that in addition to the information provided by these expressions (i.e. that an adult perceives the ambiguous stimulus as either benign or frightening), their efficacy may also derive from the arousal of resonant emotion within the child (Thompson, 1998). In other words, an adult's display of negative emotion may arouse wariness towards the event that is the focus of the adult's gaze, which fosters behavioural inhibition towards that object. Conversely, an adult's expressions of positive emotion probably produce resonant feelings of assurance towards the object that facilitate approach and exploration. Although the research evidence is equivocal, it suggests that shortly after emotional expressions have become imbued with emotional meaning, they can serve as referential communications to the baby about events of common interest, in which the adult's emotion is part of the message. By the end of the first year, infants exploit these emotional signals as meaningful cues about how to interpret uncertain situations.

Social referencing is an early instance in which infants can use an association between an event, another's emotional response to that event, and personal appraisal of the event to guide behaviour. Moreover, since the typical targets of social referencing are the infant's attachment figures, that adult's emotional expressions have central relevance to the child's sense of security – or perception of threat or danger – in uncertain situations, when reliance on an attachment figure's socioemotional cues is most likely. This heightens the salience, and emotional impact, of the signals the adult provides. Although it is difficult to label the child's resonant emotional response as truly empathic, because social referencing is enlisted as an appraisal of one's current circumstances rather than of another's emotional condition, it is likely that social referencing provides an important avenue to truly empathic responding in the second year. As 1-year-olds begin to enlist others' emotions into their assessment of events, concern with another's emotional experience for its own sake may also occur, especially in circumstances when the infant's self-concern is not so strong.

'Concerned attention' and helping

There is evidence that during the second year toddlers begin to attend to, and interpret, others' emotional expressions in more complex ways. Much of this evidence comes from an ambitious cross-sequential home-observational and experimental investigation by Radke-Yarrow, Zahn-Waxler and their colleagues (see Zahn-Waxler and Radke-Yarrow, 1990, for a review; see also Zahn-Waxler, Radke-Yarrow, Wagner, and Chapman, 1992). Using two cohorts of young children ranging in ages from 9 to 25 months, and studied for as long as a year, these researchers enlisted mothers as informants concerning the reactions of their offspring when witnessing naturally occurring instances of another's distress at home. The maternal reports were supplemented by quasi-experimental simulations of distress performed by an experimenter at the home, during which the child's responses were also carefully scrutinized.

Both maternal reports and experimental simulations yielded striking accounts of young children's concern for the distress of another. In the youngest children, an adult's distress typically elicited orienting and, in many toddlers, distress crying which was labelled 'self distress' by the researchers because of its apparent self-concern (cf. Zahn-Waxler and Radke-Yarrow, 1982). With increasing age, however, 'self distress' responses declined, and there was an increase in expressions of 'concerned attention' (e.g. attention with knit eyebrows), often combined with simple helping initiatives towards the victim, such as seeking another adult's assistance. These reactions were accompanied by other responses reflecting interest and concern for the person's distress. For example, children during the second year increasingly imitated the distress cues of the adult, as if 'trying on' their emotional expressions to comprehend them better, and they also asked other witnesses about the adult's distress, and sometimes visually searched for the cause of that person's upset (e.g., inspecting a stove that had just caused a burn). Thus the second year marks a significant developmental transition from a global, self-oriented distress reaction in the presence of another's distress to greater concerned attention and instrumental aid later that year.

These responses seem to be genuinely empathic in quality. To be sure, these accounts do not provide unequivocal evidence for the emergence of empathy. Toddlers' reactions may have reflected their efforts to comprehend an adult's salient emotional display, or their own surprise at witnessing an adult's sudden distress, without revealing true empathy. In addition, many toddlers simply ignored the other's emotional display in these studies, and helping initiatives were relatively rare. Furthermore, assisting the victim was not the only instrumental response of young children to witnessing another's distress. Toddlers also responded aggressively to the victim, or showed positive emotion, especially when they were the perpetrator. The diversity of these reactions reveals how compelling, but emotionally and motivationally complex, is the experience of witnessing another's distress to very young children. Even so, their expressions of 'concerned attention', which seem to reflect empathic arousal, and the prosocial initiatives of some of the children who witnessed distress, suggest that an empathic capacity emerges during the second year.

Other evidence confirms this conclusion. An extensive series of home-observational and experimental investigations by Cummings and his colleagues has shown that young children are sensitive to expressions of anger that they witness in others (see Cummings and Davies, 1994, and Davies and Cummings, 1994, for reviews of this research). When toddlers during the second year saw adults during angry confrontations at home or in a lab, they often 'froze' during the confrontation, and afterward appeared worried and anxious, seeking reassurance from their mothers. More important, children who witnessed anger also tended to respond angrily themselves, either to one of the adults who were arguing or to another child who was also an uninvolved bystander. Their reactions did not merely imitate the angry behaviour they witnessed, but appeared to reflect a sharing of the angry mood that they observed in adults nearby. Other studies by this research group indicate that the manner in which the angry confrontation was resolved, as well as the child's prior history of witnessing marital conflict between parents at home, affected the extent of older children's vicarious responding to the adult arguments they witnessed.

Taken together, this evidence points to the second year as a pivotal time when a capacity for true empathy begins to emerge. Although there are striking individual differences in the extent of toddlers' 'concerned attention' and helping initiatives (which are associated with temperamental individuality and maternal child-rearing practices; see Zahn-Waxler and Radke-Yarrow, 1990, and Zahn-Waxler, Robinson, and Emde, 1992), the frequency of these responses indicates a normative capacity for empathically responding to another's negative emotions in children of this age. Moreover, when toddlers were themselves responsible for another's distress, their reactions were motivationally more complex – including aggression towards the victim, as well as self-punitive actions – which suggests the possibility of an empathy-based guilt emerging in children this young (Hoffman, 1982; Kochanska and Thompson, 1997). This is consistent with evidence from other studies of young children suggesting that the child of a depressed mother may become empathically overinvolved with the parent's distress and experience too many feelings of guilt and responsibility for the adult's emotional well-being (Zahn-Waxler and Kochanska, 1990).

In some respects, the emergence of empathy in the second year should be unsurprising (Thompson, 1998). This is a period of flourishing self-recognition, self-awareness and linguistic self-reference that is accompanied by a rudimentary but growing awareness of subjective states in oneself and others. It is a period when self-evaluative emotions like pride and shame as well as guilt begin to appear, when embarrassment becomes apparent in certain situations, and when children begin to apply external standards to their own actions and the evaluation of external events. It is also a period of growing emotional understanding as young children begin to connect specific emotions with subjective antecedents associated with a person's goals, beliefs and desires, reflecting an early emergence of cognitions related to 'theory of mind'. The growth of linguistic capacities fosters a young child's emerging grasp of the associations between external events, emotional expressions and subjectivity (Thompson, 1998). Neuropsychologically, the maturation of frontal and prefrontal areas of the cerebral cortex also permits greater integration of the interpretive capacities of cerebral functions with more primitive emotional responses (Thompson, 1998). The second year of life is, in short, a period in which subjectivity reaches a new level of sophistication in the toddler's psychological awareness, and thus in which intersubjective experiences, such as empathy, become more complex and multifaceted.

Sibling relationships

A final arena for the refinement of empathy is the sibling relationship, in which common experiences, perspectives and relationships contribute to shared emotional understanding, and the possibility of mutually empathic responding (see Dunn, this volume). Suggestive evidence that this is so comes from an extensive longitudinal study of early sibling relationships by Dunn and Kendrick (1982), who found that a younger baby brother or sister was the object of considerable interest to their 2- to 3-year-old siblings, who often responded sympathetically to the younger child with expressions of 'concerned attention' and simple assistance (e.g. offering food and toys). In another study with an independent sample, Brown and Dunn (1992) found that siblings commented more frequently to each other about their feelings with increasing age, as well as conversing more about feelings with their mothers. These family conversations about emotion provide rich insights to young children into the meaning of emotion, the causes of emotion, and the consequences of emotion in themselves and others (Dunn, 1993; Dunn, Brown and Beardsall, 1991; Dunn, Brown, Slomkowski, Tesla and Youngblade, 1991) – insights that can ultimately contribute to more acute kinds of empathic responding. As these researchers found, for example, more frequent family (including sibling) discussions about emotion were associated with preschoolers' enhanced emotional understanding in independent tests. At the same time, it is important to note that enhanced emotional understanding not only contributes to potentially enhanced empathic sensitivity, but also to more effective teasing, provocation and rivalry that are also part of many sibling relationships.

Summary and conclusion

As an intersubjective experience, empathy is a crucial but painstakingly achieved emotional capacity in the early years of life. Although newborn infants exhibit an ability to resonate emotionally with the salient distress expressions of other newborns, it is not until they can appropriately interpret the subjective experiences giving rise to emotion in others that true empathy begins to appear. This emerges during the second year in response to others' expressions of distress and anger, when information concerning why a person is so aroused is likely to be apparent and easily interpretable to a toddler. Not surprisingly, this achievement occurs in the context of allied advances in self-understanding, emotional understanding and the rudimentary awareness of subjectivity in others that makes empathy part of a constellation of advances in developing intersubjectivity. It is clear that empathic experiences become more complex, subtle and differentiated with increasing age as young children achieve greater access to others' emotional lives through language (which explains, in part, the importance of family conversations about feelings to the growth of emotional understanding and empathy in the preschool years) and as children acquire greater insight into others' internal, subjective experiences with the growth of theory of mind. From this perspective, the onset of social referencing at the end of the first year provides a valuable avenue to the emergence of true empathy. As infants begin to apprehend the emotional expressions of others as the basis for situational appraisals, in other words, they are likely to begin to attend to the subjective meaning of those emotions in the person conveying salient feelings.

This analysis also reveals that empathy is a motivationally complex vicarious emotion, underlying prosocial initiatives from its earliest appearance but also associated with feelings of guilt and aggressive behaviour. As one part of the burgeoning intersubjectivity of the early years, empathy is a double-edged sword: it makes young children susceptible to the most noble, and most troubling, of human impulses.

CHAPTER 8

Siblings, emotion and the development of understanding

Judy Dunn

The growth of children's understanding of the emotions, desires, beliefs, thoughts and intentions of others is clearly a crucial feature of human development, and it is currently a topic of major interest to developmental psychologists. In the wealth of recent research on the development of this understanding, attention has been chiefly paid to the course of normative development, and the cognitive changes implicated in the developments documented in experimental studies of understanding other minds (Astington *et al.*, 1988; Perner, 1991; Wellman, 1990). This research has transformed our picture of the nature of children's understanding, and of the particular limitations of young preschoolers' grasp of others' inner states. While there is lively dispute about the timing and nature of the conceptual changes underlying the growth of understanding other minds, there is general agreement that during the fourth year of life there are major achievements in this understanding, and that by 4 years old most children have considerable understanding of the mental states and emotions of others.

However, two aspects of these developments have been relatively neglected. One is the issue of what experiences influence the development of individual differences in such social understanding, and the second, what implications such individual differences have for children's social relationships and their later development. It is with these two issues that this chapter is concerned. Our particular focus is on the relations of children's experience with other children – central to the arguments of Bråten (this volume) and Pope-Edwards (this volume) – to the growth of understanding of others' emotions and other minds.

Individual differences in understanding others

Young children differ markedly in their understanding of emotion, and in their ability to 'read' other minds. These differences are evident whether our focus is on performance in standardized assessments (e.g. Denham, 1986) or on children's behaviour in interaction with others – such as their response to others' emotions, their ability to 'read' other minds in social pretend play, or their ability to take account of others' intentions and needs in disputes.

What social experiences or individual characteristics are linked to the development of such differences? In relation to the development of understanding other minds, there has been remarkably little systematic research into individual differences (see however the special issue of *Cognition and Emotion*, 1995). In contrast there has been more attention to the development of individual differences in *understanding emotions*, and a range of different variables have been cited as important. These include the quality of children's attachment to their mothers, parental socialization techniques, the emotional expressiveness of parents (Cassidy *et al.*, 1992), parent–child discourse about feelings (Dunn, Brown and Beardsall, 1991), children's experiences with peers (Denham *et al.*, 1990), and their cognitive ability (Rothenberg, 1970) or temperament (Murphy, 1937).

The relative importance of these various factors can only be assessed with research that includes measures of social relationships, of discourse and of children's characteristics. We carried out such an examination with a longitudinal study, in which we investigated the antecedent correlates of differences in very young children's understanding of others' emotions and mental states, and followed the children for the next five years (the Pennsylvania Study of Social Understanding). The study is described in detail in a number of publications (see, for example, Dunn, Brown, Slomkowski, Tesla and Youngblade, 1991 for the antecedents of early understanding; Dunn, 1995 for a summary of the sequelae; Brown and Dunn, 1996 for analyses of continuities in emotion understanding; Brown *et al.*, 1996 for analysis of the significance of discourse about mental states). In this chapter, key findings relevant to the issue of individual differences in communication and emotion understanding will be summarized, and publications giving full details of each topic will be referenced at the appropriate place.

In brief, fifty children were initially studied as 2-year-olds, at home with their mothers and older siblings, using naturalistic observations of the family interactions as the children played and argued at home. The children were then followed over the next five years, with home observations and a variety of interview assessment procedures, and observations of each child with a close friend (see Table 8.1 for an outline of the study).

At 40 months, the children's understanding of emotions was

Table 8.1 *Outline of time points and selected procedures in the Pennsylvania Study of Social Understanding*

	Preschool			School	
Age (months)	33	40	47	68	75
Home observations					
Mother/sibling	x	x	x		
Friend			x	x	
Assessments					
Emotion understanding		x			x
Mindreading		x	x		
Perception of school				x	x
Response to teacher criticisms					x
Moral sensibility					x

assessed using Denham's puppet procedures (Denham, 1986), and their ability to explain others' behaviour in terms of false belief, with Bartsch and Wellman's (1989) procedures. In the emotion understanding assessments, we found substantial variability in the extent to which the children correctly inferred the relations between situations and the basic emotions assessed (happiness, anger, fear, sadness), and similar differences have been reported in other studies (Denham, 1986; Howe and Ross, 1990). In the false belief tests, too, the children differed considerably in their ability to explain the actions of a puppet premised on mistaken beliefs.

Three aspects of earlier family experiences stood out from our analyses of the antecedents of these individual differences (see Dunn *et al.*, 1991). First, the children who had as 2-year-olds participated in relatively frequent family discourse about feelings and the causes of behaviour showed greater social understanding seven months later on the standard assessments of understanding others. These correlations were not explained by the children's verbal fluency, nor by the amount of talk in the family. We should not of course draw causal conclusions from these correlational data. On the one hand, the findings do fit with the view that the children's understanding of emotions and other minds, reflected in the tasks, may have been fostered through their conversations about inner states; however it is also possible that children's participation in such conversations about causality and feelings and their later success on social cognition tasks both reflect some common underlying ability rather than a direct causal link.

Second, these abilities were related to their earlier engagement in cooperative interactions with their siblings, including their participation in joint pretend play. Interestingly, the detailed examination of the children's pretend play showed that it was the children's engagement in *role enactment* that was linked to later ability to explain others' actions in terms of beliefs (Youngblade and Dunn, 1995). Here too it would be inappropriate to draw conclusions about directional cause–effect links. It could be that through cooperation and play with a sibling children gain insights into the thoughts, actions and feelings of the other child – who is of course closer in interests and feelings to those of the child than a parent would be. This view would be compatible with the arguments that peer interaction plays a special role in the development of social understanding (Piaget, 1932/1977; Hartup, 1983). Moreover, the emotional intensity, frequency of interaction and intimacy of siblings' interaction make this interaction a context in which understanding of the other is likely to be fostered.

But it is also possible that with greater powers of understanding others, children are able to cooperate and play more effectively with others – including their siblings. Thus the pattern of findings could be seen as reflecting a continuity in individual differences between children. In common sense terms it seems likely that both processes may operate.

The third set of links found between the family observations at 33 months and the children's performance on the social cognitive assessments at 40 months concerned interactions between the children's mothers and their siblings. Children who grew up in families in which their mothers engaged in relatively frequent controlling behaviour with their older siblings were more likely to be able to give appropriate explanations in the false belief task; they also tended to be better at affective labelling and perspective taking if their mothers had been highly responsive to their siblings than the children whose mothers and siblings were not frequently involved in this way. The findings show us that a variety of social processes may be implicated in the development of social understanding. They also remind us that children grow up as family members, and that the salient influences on their development include more than the behaviour directed specifically to them: they are very interested in what happened between their parents and siblings, and monitor very closely both the talk (Dunn and Shatz, 1989) and the emotions expressed by the other family members (Dunn and Kendrick, 1982; Dunn and Munn, 1985). Clearly it is highly adaptive for children born into the social group of the family to pay attention to and make sense of the interactions between others within the family early in their own development.

Sequelae and implications of early individual differences in understanding

What are the implications of these early differences in children's understanding of emotions and other minds for children's later development? Three issues raised by the findings of the follow-up study are of particular developmental interest and will be discussed here. The first concerns the significance of child–sibling and child–friend interaction over the next years, in relation to understanding others' inner states. The second concerns the patterns of continuity to middle childhood, and specifically the *differences* in the sequelae of early understanding of emotions and of other minds. The third concerns the issue of the extent to which understanding others can be considered an 'emergent property' of relationships, rather than a 'within-child' characteristic.

Child–sibling and child–friend talk about inner states

We have seen that the children's interactions with their siblings as 2-year-olds – especially their experience of joint pretend play – were associated with greater understanding of others' emotions and inner states seven months later (Youngblade and Dunn, 1995). The significance of child–child interaction continues to be highlighted in the results of the follow-up of the children as they grew into middle childhood. As an example, consider the findings on their participation in talk about feelings, and about mental states.

The ability to talk about feelings – to share what one finds funny, to communicate about one's distress, to ask questions about other people's inner states – is clearly a development that has key implications for children's relationships. While studies have documented the importance of mother–child talk about emotions, the question of how children talk with other children about their own and others' feelings has rarely been studied. Yet this is likely to be a particularly interesting context in which children's understanding of emotion may be fostered. As we have noted, theoretical discussions of sociocognitive development have stressed the significance of interactions between children and their peers. The equal status and the reciprocal nature of child–peer interactions have been emphasized in these accounts as key to the growth of understanding the other; such features are also characteristic of sibling interaction. And the familiarity, intimacy and emotional nature of sibling interaction also suggest that this may be an important context for the growth of understanding others.

In following the children over the next few years we were interested in two possibilities. The first was that child–sibling interaction, and specifically their discussion of feelings and mental states, would increase in prominence relative to children's discussion of inner states with their mothers, as the children became more competent companions in play and in argument with their siblings. We also wanted to examine the possibility that the children's conversations about inner states with their siblings differed in nature, content and context from those with their parents. Mothers most often talk about feelings in didactic or controlling contexts (Brown and Dunn, 1991). Do siblings – in contrast – talk about feelings in contexts that offer children opportunities for reciprocal interaction – for example by drawing attention to their own interests and needs? And are siblings more emotionally expressive than mothers? If so, their uninhibited expression of emotion may well challenge children to respond to another's emotional experience in a way that parent–child interaction does not.

The second possibility we examined was that children who had scored highly on the social understanding assessments at 40 months would be engaged in more frequent and elaborate talk about mental states and feelings with their siblings and friends at the later visits than the children who had been less successful on these assessments.

The evidence of the study supported both sets of ideas. In relation to the first possibility, talk about feelings with siblings quadrupled in frequency between 33 and 47 months (mean child speaker turns about feeling states increased from 1.8 to 4.5 per hour), while such talk to mothers declined in frequency over the same period (means 3.6 to 1.8 respectively). The data on talk about mental states told a similar story. By 47 months, conversations about mental states were strikingly more frequent with siblings and with friends than with mothers (Brown *et al.*, 1996). And the detailed analysis of the feeling state conversations with both partners showed how the siblings' conversations about feelings contrasted with those of the mothers and children: the siblings focused more on their own interests, their status was more equal, and emotions (both positive and negative) were far more frequently expressed. All these features, we suggest, are likely to increase the developmental significance of these exchanges.

More generally the striking increase in child–child conversation that took place over this relatively short period (by the 47-months visits, siblings were far more likely to talk to their younger siblings than they had been at the 33-months visits) reflects the rapid growth of children's capacity to interact with a partner who, unlike the mother, does not make the 'allowances' of an adult motivated to understand and respond sensitively to their needs. Reciprocity in a relationship can encompass far more than friendly cooperation.

The second possibility that we explored concerned individual differences. Here we were interested in whether the differences in children's performance on the standard false belief assessments at 40 months would be related to the children's talk about mental states in their real-life interaction with their siblings and friends. The results showed that, indeed, children who had been more successful on the assessments used mental state terms more frequently with their siblings and their friends. Of particular interest was the finding that frequent use of mental state terms by both partners was related to cooperative interaction in both child–friend and child–sibling dyads. Children in dyads whose interaction was marked by positive cooperative play were more likely to refer frequently to their own and each other's thoughts and ideas as they played together. Among the child–friend pairs, not only the quality of their play but the length of their friendship and the frequency of their interaction were positively related to explicit reference to mental processes. It is notable that pretend play emerged as an important context in which mental state terms were used in conversation, particularly for preschool friends. The cognitive features of pretend play have been repeatedly emphasized in relation to children's developing theories of mind (Harris and Kavanaugh, 1993; Leslie, 1987). But the findings of this study remind us that children begin to entertain 'multiple hypothetical realities' (Perner, 1991) and to 'decouple' reality from fantasy (Leslie, 1987) *in social interactions in which these cognitive states are shared*, not as solitary cognitive exercises. Other children, both siblings and friends, are likely to be of particular significance as the partners with whom these cognitive developments are shared.

Continuities to middle childhood

The research described so far has shown that individual differences in preschool children's understanding of emotions and other minds are related to earlier experiences of cooperative interactions with their siblings as well as family discourse about feeling states, and that these individual differences are linked to later differences in discourse about inner states. Little is known, however, about the continuity of these differences through middle childhood. One of the key features of emotional understanding in middle childhood is the appreciation of the experience of mixed or ambivalent emotions (Fischer *et al.*, 1990; Harris, 1989). It is not until the early school years that children begin to acknowledge that their own and others' experiences may provoke a mix of both positive and negative emotions. This understanding is central to other aspects of children's understanding of themselves and their social world (Harter, 1986), and a large body of research has focused on the normative development of this appreciation of the complex nature of emotions (e.g., Harter and Buddin, 1987; Peng *et al.*, 1992). However the extent of individual differences in these developments and their links with earlier understanding or experiences have rarely been studied. Are the children who are precocious in interpreting others' emotional experience at 3 years especially sensitive to the situations which provoke ambivalent emotions in middle childhood? And do the experiences which are linked to the early understanding of emotions also relate to the appreciation of feelings in middle childhood?

We examined these questions by assessing the children's understanding of mixed emotions at the end of their kindergarten year, when they were on average 75 months old (SD 2.7 months), using a story-telling interview based on that developed by Gordis *et al.* (1989). This part of the research is described in detail in Brown and Dunn (1996).

Three key points were established by the analyses. First, there was significant stability in individual differences in emotion understanding over the 3-year period from 40 months to 79 months of age. Second, the antecedents to emotion understanding at 3 years continued to be significantly related to children's understanding at 6 years: participation in family discourse about feelings and causality, positive interaction with older siblings and language ability as 2-year-olds were significantly correlated with the children's appreciation of ambivalent emotions as 6-year-olds. These links held even when language ability was controlled for. These patterns over time could of course reflect continuity in processes of socialization over the years, *or* continuity in characteristics of the children. Young children who are curious about emotions – their own and those of others – may well initiate more family talk about feelings. We know that even 2-year-olds ask questions about others' feelings (for examples, see Dunn, 1988).

Those children who had been especially successful in the social understanding tasks as 40-month-olds were particularly articulate about the complexity of their emotional experiences with their siblings and at school as 6- to 7-year-olds. Moreover there were connections between the early measures and a range of other aspects of their social understanding and actions in middle childhood: their moral sophistication (Dunn *et al.*, 1995), their positive reports on their peer relations (Brown and Dunn, 1996) and their response to teacher criticism (Dunn, 1995). Most intriguing, there was evidence that while both the early sophistication in understanding emotions and in understanding other minds were correlated with aspects of later understanding, these sequelae were *different* (Dunn, 1995). These topics are beyond the scope of this chapter, but it should be emphasized that they highlight the significance of early understanding of others' emotions and mental states for a broad range of aspects of children's development in middle childhood.

Understanding emotions: a 'within-child' characteristic?

The final issue to be discussed here concerns the question of whether it is appropriate to consider the understanding of others that children show in their real-life interactions as a set of competencies or skills that is characteristic of each individual. Much of the attention to social understanding that is currently shown by developmental researchers is premised on the view that such understanding is indeed a 'within-child' characteristic, and that it acts to mediate the connections between a child's different relationships. For instance, it has been proposed that individual capacities in reading emotions, and in translating this understanding to action, develop in the context of early parent–child relationships, and these capacities then influence the 'competence' children show in their other relationships outside the family. Thus children's difficulties in peer relations have been held to be the result of sociocognitive 'deficits', such as problems in reading the intentions of others, which, it is presumed, have their origins in early parent–child relationships.

How well do these ideas fit the recent evidence on young children's social understanding, such as our observations of the same child in the context of his or her relationship with mother, with sibling and with friend? The research on very young children shows that even in the second year, children possess considerable powers of recognizing the feelings of others and of acting to ameliorate or worsen others' emotional states. With familiar others, they appear to recognize some at least of the connections between others' beliefs and actions remarkably early (see for instance the evidence on teasing and deceit, Newton, 1994). This sophistication means either that they can be supportive, humorous and caring towards others – or that they can be manipulative, teasing and deliberately upsetting towards others. A key point, then, is that the same child could put these capacities of understanding others *to different use in different relationships*, depending on the quality of that relationship. How does this possibility fit with the notion of social understanding as a 'within-child' characteristic?

Two lessons stand out from our analyses of the same children in different relationships. The first is that there was evidence for connections between individual differences in understanding as assessed formally in the test situations, and aspects of the children's interactive behaviour in *each* of their close relationships. Thus children's performance on the false belief tasks was related to children's management of conflict with either their mothers or their siblings (Slomkowski and Dunn, 1992), and with connectedness in their interactions with a close friend.

However the second point is that there was also evidence that the children used their powers of social understanding quite differently in their different relationships, depending on the quality of the relationship. There was for instance no significant correlation between the likelihood that a child in conflict would use her understanding to resolve the conflict through negotiation or compromise with both mother and sibling. The same child who with a sibling was likely to negotiate and take account of the sibling's wishes and needs rarely did so with her mother; others reasoned and negotiated with their mothers but rarely did so with their siblings. The evidence from the observations of the children with their friends underlined the same point. There were no significant correlations between how the children handled conflict, discussed feelings and mental states, or engaged in sophisticated pretend play with their friends and their siblings. The point to be emphasized is that the quality of the relationship between two individuals depends on both partners; it is unlikely to be attributable simply to the sociocognitive skills of either partner. In a sense, the nature of the social understanding that children show within their real-life relationships can be considered an 'emergent property' of that relationship, one that depends on both partners, rather than as a 'within-child' characteristic.

Conclusion

Individual differences in very young children's understanding of others' emotions and inner states are marked. These differences not only show considerable stability from early in the preschool period to the school years, but are related to a wide range of other developmental outcomes, including moral sensibility, perception of others' reactions and of self-competence, and adjustment to school.

These individual differences show clear connections to the experiences children have with their siblings in earlier years, and to their interactions with both siblings and friends in later years. It appears that the experience of affectionate interaction with a sibling or friend may play a special role in the development of this key aspect of human development. There is a parallel here with Bråten's arguments for the significance of children's nurturance shown to other children (1996a, this volume). Our study shows that experience of joint pretend in which a child takes on the role of another may be of particular significance in these developments. The relatively equal status, emotional quality, frequency and intimacy of children's friendly interactions with sibling and friend are good candidates for fostering the development of human understanding. Parallels here with the focus on cooperation of Trevarthen (this volume) and on the 'company they keep' of Edwards (this volume) are evident. An exclusive focus on parent–child – and particularly mother–child – relationships as the forum for developmental advance would misrepresent the significance of what happens between children when they play, argue and talk together.

CHAPTER 9

The company children keep: suggestive evidence from cultural studies

Carolyn Pope Edwards

Introduction

Young children are born into the world well equipped to interact immediately with other human beings and to form significant and meaningful relationships with them. To describe and understand these early relationships, one important domain of research has been that of attachment (Thompson, this volume), which provides a theory of how infants establish primary relationships with one or at most a few caregiving adults who can provide them with a sense of comfort and security as a safe base from which to explore. Yet, other relational motivations of children also emerge very early – for example, for a holding environment, mutuality, eye-to-eye validation, identification, libidinal satisfaction, embeddedness, and to give care to others, to use the integrative framework of Josselson (1996). The scientific study of attachment thus addresses only one aspect of early social relationships, but a more general term, such as 'partnership' or 'companionship', may be a more general and useful entry point into a widened theory of the developing capacity to enter into meaningful, reciprocal, communicative relationships with social partners in dyadic and small-group contexts.

As Bråten (this volume) and Trevarthen (this volume) make amply clear, the understanding of companionship is still in its infancy, from both a methodological and a conceptual standpoint. Yet, there is every reason to believe that the subject matter is a rich and important one, requiring multiple lines of attack and interdisciplinary theory-building. Trevarthen argues that companionship and collaboration concern issues of relationship that are theoretically distinct from issues of attachment. Research on the growth of primary and secondary intersubjectivity and companion space (Bråten, 1996a; Trevarthen, 1988) provide additional needed ways to understand the intra- and interpersonal aspects of infant companionship. A broadened theory of companionship, I would claim, needs to describe the most significant contexts of companionship for children, analyse the processes by which children develop and learn through them, and seek to understand the developmental and evolutionary functions of the various kinds of relationships and social networks of children.

Ethnographic and cross-cultural research must be an essential part of this endeavour, in order to provide the descriptive foundation to ensure that in studying early social development we are covering the whole human domain, not just that part most accessible and convenient to us because of where we live on the earth at one time in history. Indeed, such comparative approaches have already demonstrated that at every stage of child development, distinctively different normative styles of companionship emerge and are influenced by the surrounding context. Beatrice and John Whiting, in founding the contemporary field of comparative child development, coined the term, *cultural learning environment*, to refer to all of the dimensions (macro and micro) of everyday life which set the stage for child development and socialization (Whiting and Whiting, 1975). Thomas Weisner has advanced this basic perspective using the idea of the *ecocultural niche* (Weisner, 1984), or *activity setting* (Gallimore *et al.*, 1993), to retain the functionalist assumption that cultural learning environments evolve continuously over time to promote adaptation to constraints imposed by external factors, changes in the subsistence base, climatic changes, and the political economies of the region. Super and Harkness (1986), focusing on the child as a developing as well as learning organism, have coined the term, *developmental niche*, defined in terms of three key features: (1) the particular physical and social settings in which the child lives and grows; (2) the culturally regulated routines of childcare and child-training used by caregivers; and (3) the culturally based belief-systems and developmental folk-theories ('parental ethnotheories') that caregivers bring to their interaction with children.

Cultural styles of companionship with infants

What has been learned so far about the ecological and cultural dimensions of companionship and collaboration for very young children? At this point we know much more about what children's social contexts look like – what kinds of experiences they appear to provide – than about what actually happens within the children as a result of these culturally varying experiences. Comparative researchers with several different kinds of disciplinary training have described the ecological and cultural dimensions of infant childrearing. For example, comparative psychologists (such as the contributors to the 1991 Bornstein collection) have typically studied variables that are most visible and observable and directly proximate in social interaction. Comparative anthropologists (for example, contributors to the 1977 collection of Leiderman *et al.*) typically have been more concerned with larger ecological and contextual variables that may not be directly observable in the interaction but nonetheless indirectly influence it.

One dimension of mother–infant companionship style that has been most studied by psychologists relates to face-to-face engagement. In some cultural contexts, for example the contemporary settings of North America and Western Europe most familiar to Western researchers, the prototype of mother–child interaction is an intimate, dyadic exchange in the *en face* position, with resulting reciprocity of facial and vocal gestures and turn-taking. In contrast, in communities where exclusive dyadic interaction between mother and infant is less frequent, different patterns more natural in settings of group engagement are the norm. For example, in many African, Asian and South American communities where mothers and babies are usually present with other adults or children, the baby is rarely held *en face* by the mother or other caregiver. Among Marquesas and Fais families, the baby may be more typically held on someone's lap facing outward and encouraged to watch others and interact with everyone present (Martini and Kirkpatrick, 1981; Sostek *et al.*, 1981). Among the Efe of Zaire, the infant is regularly passed from one adult to another and even nursed by the mother's kinswomen (Tronick *et al.*, 1987). Among Mayan families of Guatemala, the infant can expect to be given attention and help from the mother while she simultaneously attends to other tasks or listens and talks with others (Rogoff *et al.*, 1993). Among the agricultural Gusii of western Kenya, an extreme avoidance of the *en face* position between adults and babies has been observed (LeVine *et al.*, 1994). Gusii mothers rarely engage babies in mutual eye contact or exciting, face-to-face conversation, for several reasons. They consider too much attention to be over-stimulating to the baby and an inappropriate form of social relations between elder (high-status) and junior (low-status) persons. Furthermore, they believe that such public focus on the baby could invite malevolence or jealousy in the form of sorcery or the 'evil eye'. Finally, too much mutual eye contact can be felt by the Gusii to be an intrusive, or aggressive, or sexualized style of relating, inappropriate for a public situation where others are present.

Yet, while cultural style differences in use of the *en face* position are clearly seen, their implications for infant development are not yet known. Questions raised are many, however. Does the Gusii avoidance of face-to-face interaction prevent the child from receiving adequate opportunity to engage in protolanguage and intersubjective relationship? Does the Fais and Marquesas Islands cultural preference for the face-outward versus *en face* pattern of infant holding lead in later years to a more diffuse group identification (collectivist values) rather than individualistic values? Does one pattern versus another affect the primitive memories which infants are believed to lay down in their earliest attachment relationships and carry forward into later attachments with peers or sexual partners? We do not yet know, though speculations have been put forward.

Another dimension of infant care which has been of great current interest to psychologists is infant feeding, closely linked to child health and morbidity. In some cultural communities, for example, 'underfeeding' appears to be an expectable outcome of culturally based beliefs about the hierarchy of food entitlement, especially with regard to high-prestige foods like meat and under conditions of food scarcity (Zeitlin, 1996). Underfeeding of sick and weak babies has also been found to be related to cultural beliefs about whether mothers should seek to feed babies who are not actively crying and seeking it (e.g. Engle *et al.*, 1996).

Other variables first identified by anthropologists have also become of interest to developmental psychologists because of how they affect infant and child experience. For example, household sleeping arrangements determine where the baby sleeps, with whom, and for how long, and thus how much physical contact the child experiences and how night-time distress is managed. Climate is a background factor here: in temperate climates, infants typically are wrapped in their own blankets and lie in separate cradles or cribs by themselves, while in tropical climates, they lie in skin-to-skin contact in their mothers' beds (Whiting, 1981). Studies of contemporary societies have suggested that some samples in such countries as Japan and Italy, where there are strong values favouring interdependency between generations, are more likely to allow children to fall asleep next to a parent's body and to come into parents' beds at night. In contrast, cultural groups that explicitly favour independence between generations (e.g. mainstream white Americans, in contrast to eastern Kentuckian rural whites and some African American families) expect infants and young children to fall asleep in their own beds and stay there all night (Abbott, 1992; Wolf *et al.*, 1996). Dutch parents in Leiden, Holland, manage their infants' arousal differently from American parents in Cambridge, Massachusetts; and Dutch babies sleep longer and are less frequently over-stimulated than American babies (Super *et al.*, 1996).

Village versus camp residence affects the experience of children in foraging groups like the Efe of Zaire because it dramatically influences fathers' participation in child-care: men are much more supportive and active in the isolated camp than in the settled village (Morelli and Tronick, 1991). The variables of family size, household density and maternal workloads work together as a constellation to affect infant care. Family size and household density affect how many adult women are available to pick up a crying baby: dense households with many women have more caregivers available (Leiderman and Leiderman, 1977; Munroe and Munroe, 1971). When mothers are extremely busy and involved in subsistence, they feel less available for constant responsive interaction with their infants (Chisolm, 1981, 1989), and desire to involve others in child-care and training (Weisner, 1984, 1987; Whiting and Whiting, 1975).

A focus on companionship itself

In seeking to understand the interface between macro- and micro-dimensions of child development in cultural context, Beatrice Whiting and I have found it most fruitful to question how the *who* of companionship – the gender/age/kinship identities of children's familiar partners – influences the growth of relationship by setting the stage for the emergence and rehearsal of different profiles of interpersonal behaviour. Cultural patterns of companionship are readily observable, and they turn out to be strongly predictive of categories of seeking, offering, and being sociable, and dominant/aggressive categories of social interaction. Indeed, distinctive general profiles of interaction appear to be elicited by each gender/age/kinship category of partner or companion. These are important, we hypothesize, because those forms which are more frequent and are being practised might be expected to develop into enduring and preferred styles of relating to others. We call this the *company-they-keep hypothesis*: the notion that social partners in dyadic interaction shape young children's developing propensities for specific types of social behaviour (Whiting, 1980; also see Edwards, 1992, 1993; Edwards and Whiting, 1993; Whiting and Edwards, 1988).

The significance of the company-they-keep hypothesis for socialization theory lies in finding that, around the world, communities vary greatly in their typical age, sex and kinship opportunities for child companionship (Whiting and Edwards, 1988; Whiting and Whiting, 1975). Children have strikingly different opportunities to interact with infants and toddlers, younger and older siblings, extended family members and in-laws of varied ages and degrees of closeness, child peers not related by kinship, and non-family adults. These opportunities, in turn, are strongly associated with cultural ideologies and macro-cultural features, such as settlement and residential patterns, household and family structures, subsistence strategies and the sexual division of labour, the way in which schooling is organized, and social networks for work, child-care, exchange of goods, and leisure. Thus, around the world, children are offered varying opportunities to form sustained relationships with the major categories of social partners, and they may, as a result, develop differing interpersonal expectations and preferences – expectations, motives, habits and skills that may transfer to other contexts and be carried forward into the future. Gallimore *et al.* state this idea as follows:

> Everyday activities provide opportunities to learn and develop through modeling, joint production, apprenticeship, and other forms of mediated social learning that are embedded in goal-directed interactions . . . Through participation in cultural activities that require cognitive and communicative functions, children are drawn into the use of these functions in ways that nurture and develop them. (1993:538)

These socialization effects of companionship may be ancient in origin, and even apply to the non-human primates. In their extensive reviews of literature on behavioural ontogeny of juvenile primates (prosimians, Old World monkeys, New World monkeys, and apes), Fairbanks and Pereira (Fairbanks, 1993; Fairbanks and Pereira, 1993) have concluded that, in every study measuring spatial relationships, juvenile primates are found to associate selectively with other group members, and that the patterns are remarkably consistent across species. Young juveniles tend to spend much of their time near their mothers; and when the social system allows, they also associate with adult male group members who are most likely to be their fathers. As the juveniles mature, they spend less time near their mothers and instead more near same-sex adults. The young females then gain opportunities to hold and touch the infants of any adult females who will let them come near, while the young males get more opportunities to observe the agonistic, dominance and sexual behaviours of adult males. Likewise, when it comes to practising and perfecting the skills involved in physical and rough-and-tumble play, juvenile primates appear to place themselves in appropriate contexts for learning species-typical and sex-typical behaviours (Pereira and Fairbanks, 1993:365). Pereira (1988) concludes that the juvenile period is critical to non-human primate development: 'Animals are predisposed to learn particular types of behavior, and behavioral ontogeny functions, in part, to *facilitate this selective learning and ensure that certain early social experiences are virtually inevitable*' (my italics) (p. 201).

The Children of Different Worlds Study

The company-they-keep hypothesis thus relates to a larger goal of discovering how socialization goals and values are actualized by the ways in which caregivers decide about the activities in which children shall participate and with whom (Whiting, 1980). The findings on child caretaking to be described come from our study, *Children of different worlds: the formation of social behavior* (Whiting and Edwards, 1988). The book is based on data from six communities studied in 1965–75 by ten collaborators and ourselves,[1] and on re-analysed data from six communities originally studied in 1954–6 by teams under the leadership of John and Beatrice Whiting (Whiting and Whiting, 1975). The sample communities were located in Kenya (five), India (two), and Liberia, Okinawa, the Philippines, Mexico and the United States (one community each), as shown in Table 9.1. In each of these, a sample of between 16 and 104 children aged 2- to 10-years-old was selected for observation.

Nine of these communities (those in Africa, Mexico and the Pacific) were traditionally tribal groups whose subsistence was based on horticulture or pastoralism. Such 'middle level societies' normally make greatest use of children as caregivers and companions of infants and toddlers. At the time of study, these nine sample communities had developed rural peasant economies, and most families had become involved in some cash cropping or wage work to buy products of the industrial world. Contrasting to the first nine communities, the other three (in India and the United States) were part of complex, stratified societies, with economies based on intensive cultivation and/or industry. In these communities, men worked as wage-earners, entrepreneurs or professionals.

Across the whole study, women's workloads varied greatly, with the heaviest in rural Kenya, where mothers desired many children and also performed heavy farm and household work. Settlement patterns of the communities also varied, ranging from large farms, to hamlets, villages, towns and parts of cities. Average household size was smallest in the United States community of Orchard Town, New England, with three children per family, and largest in the Kenyan and north Indian samples, where seven to ten children were usual. Kin availability was greatest in the rural polygynous Kenyan households, which included as many as eight separate dwelling units. Kin availability was also high in many other samples, where relatives lived on contiguous or nearby land. Most isolated from kinfolk were the apartment dwellers of Kariobangi (the housing estate in Nairobi, Kenya), and the Americans in suburban Orchard Town.

Table 9.1 *Communities where children's social interaction was observed*

Location	National affiliation	Linguistic affiliation	Type of settlement	Population
New Samples				
Kien-taa	Liberia	Kpelle, Mende	Section of a town	200
Kokwet Western Province	Kenya	Kipsigis, Nilo-Hamitic	Farm homesteads	447
Kisa Western Province	Kenya	Abaluyia	Farm homesteads	3,000
Kariobangi, Nairobi Central Province	Kenya	Abaluyia	Housing estate in city	13,000
Ngeca Central Province	Kenya	Kikuyu, Bantu	Village surrounded by farm homesteads	6,000
Bhubaneswar Orissa	India	Oriya	City	50,000
Six Culture Samples				
Nyansongo Western Province	Kenya	Gusii, Bantu	Farm homesteads	208
Juxtlahuaca Oaxaca	Mexico	Mixtecan	Barrio, Indian section of a town	600
Tarong, Luzon	Philippines	Iloco	Scattered hamlets	259
Taira	Okinawa	Hokan and Japanese	Village	700
Khalapur Uttar Pradesh	India	Hindu	Town, clustered	5,000
Orchard Town New England	USA	English	Part of a town	5,000

The method of child observation involved timed-observation using Focal-Animal Sampling (cf. Altmann, 1974). Behaviour was recorded as written running records by trained members of the children's culture. In recording the focal child's social acts (event sampling), the observer followed the eyes of the focal child, identifying whenever possible not only the child's social interacts but also the event that invoked it and any response by a social partner. The records were taken in consecutive English sentences, for later coding. Behaviour coding involved judgement of the apparent intention, which often could be made only when the entire sequence of events was known. Before an observation was started, the date, time of day, exact location, people present and activities in progress were recorded. Time records were maintained along the left-hand margin of the paper, with notes as to when people entered or left the interactional space. With the exception of Bhubaneswar, India, observations were limited to the daylight hours and were distributed over four or five periods of the day. In the Six Culture Study, each record was 5 minutes in length; in the New Samples, they were 15 minutes to one hour in length, depending on the community. Methods of training observers and achieving inter-observer reliability were roughly the same across communities.

In coding social events, we categorized each interact as a type of *mand*, defined as an attempt on the part of an individual to change the behaviour of the social partner (Whiting, 1980). We used six major categories of mands, each with sub-categories: *ego-dependent* (seeking comfort, physical contact, help, information, approval, food, other material goods or permission); *ego-dominant* (seeking to injure, annoy, insult, dominate, compete or escape); *nurturant* (offering comfort, physical contact, help, information, approval, food, other material goods or permission); *prosocial* (commanding an economic, household, or child-care chore, commanding hygiene or etiquette, reprimanding another's behaviour); *sociable* (seeking or offering friendly response, including social play, laughing together, talking together, verbal or physical teasing, or horseplay); and *teaching* (offering general information, abstract knowledge, or information about skills necessary for a chore). After coding the interacts, the frequency totals were converted into proportion scores (proportion of all coded social acts by an actor or category of actors).

The most striking finding is that it is far easier to describe gender, age and cultural differences in children's typical companions and activities than to find differences in their social behaviour (relative proportions of nurturance, dominance, dependence and sociability) after controlling for companions and activities. The following generalizations about companionship and activities hold true across communities: (1) from age 3 onward, girls spend more of their day doing responsible or productive work, such as child-care, housework and gardening, while boys spend relatively more of their time in undirected activity or play; (2) gender segregation is the grand rule of social interaction during middle childhood (age 6–10); boys and girls segregate into same-gender peer groups whenever there are enough children available, and especially do so when they have already divided themselves into age-homogeneous groupings (this finding is discussed extensively in Maccoby, 1988); (3) during middle childhood, boys reduce contact and interaction with their mothers and other

Table 9.2 *Percentage of nurturance (as a proportion of all social acts) by children of different ages*

	Percentage of nurturance by children aged 2–10 years				
Community (New Samples)[a]	To lap-children (0–18 months)	To children more than 3 years younger	To near-age children (±2 years)	To children more than 3 years older	To mothers
Kien-taa	36	14	7	8	2
Kokwet	31	15	8	2	3
Kisa	37	13	3	3	3
Kariobangi	38	17	6	4	4
Ngeca	33	13	6	3	2

	Percentage of nurturance by children aged 3–10 years			
Community (Six Cultures)[b]	To lap-child sibling (0–18 months)	To younger children	To older children	To mothers
Nyansongo	48	9	6	8
Juxtlahuaca	50	13	15	7
Tarong	49	11	5	8

[a] Nurturance in the New Samples includes only initiated nurturance. In the Six Culture Samples it includes both initiated and responsive nurturance.
[b] Only the communities where the age of the lap-child could be identified are included in this table.

adult females, and are observed at greater distances from home than are girls; and (4) girls have more contact and interaction with, and responsibility for, infants than do boys.

To give an example of the way in which the social partner shapes the child's interpersonal behaviour, findings for nurturance to various ages are provided in Table 9.2 (from Whiting and Edwards, 1988:162). Children are relatively most nurturant in interacting with children more than 3 years younger than themselves, especially infants under 18 months of age.

In interpreting these data, we claim that each type of companion tends to model and teach specific behaviours to children, and to elicit specific behaviours from them. For example, mothers as companions of young children tend to model nurturing behaviour and to elicit dependent behaviour, while infants (with their small size, round heads, distinctive facial and bodily proportions, and attractive and appealing clinging, smiling and social responsiveness) elicit nurturance. On the basis of field experience and deep reading of the behavioural observations, we are struck by the evident eliciting properties of each type of dyadic interaction. One can speak of 'scripts for partnership', and speculate about *generic* or *prepared responses* to acknowledge their possible source in biobehavioural systems related to human evolution.

These 'scripts for partnership', or generic responses, surface whenever certain kinds of social partners interact. For example, looking at the age relationship between the child and his or her social partner, it is found that *physical* and *verbal dependency* are highest in the child's behaviour towards and with an adult. *Nurturance* and *sociable responsiveness* are highest when the child interacts with an infant. *Prosocial responsibility* and *egoistic dominance* are highest when the child interacts with another child younger than himself or herself (but not an infant), while imitation and *seeking of help and attention* are highest when the child interacts with a child who is older than himself or herself. *Affiliation, conflict* and *challenge* are highest with agemates.

The generic responses appear to be readily learned, more from trial and error and by what works and is satisfying than by explicit parental instruction or parental reward and punishment. Moreover, once learned, the generic responses seem difficult to extinguish, though they can be channelled, modulated, attenuated or amplified by the styles and modalities of how children are handled and raised. For instance, the practices common in our East African communities of prolonged infant-carrying and sleeping with the mother, resulting in months of close and constant physical care, foster a style of toddler dependency with less vocal calling for mothers but more physical proximity-seeking. (This finding is also reported and discussed by LeVine *et al.* (1994) and Richman *et al.* (1988).) The common custom of East African mothers to assign supervision responsibilities to their older children (and then validate these children's emerging authority and dominance) results in a style of sibling–sibling interaction where there is an obvious pecking order and status hierarchy by age, as opposed to the custom in Orchard Town, New England, where parents frequently intervene in children's disputes and undermine any emerging system of dominance or authority by age.

The company-they-keep hypothesis, however, adds a further postulate: that children acquire generalized and enduring preferences (or long-term expectations) for the patternings of nurturing they know best, and that they then bring them to bear in new contexts, such as when interacting with companions who are not infants.

While the data in Whiting and Edwards (1988) do not permit a long-term (longitudinal) test of this prediction, it is possible to perform a statistical test for one predicted type of short-term (cross-sectional) effect. The social relations with peers were compared for children aged 6–10 years, according to whether these children experienced at the same time relatively high versus low interaction with infants. The prediction was that, if experience with infants helps children to develop nurturant social styles, then children who interact most with infants will be relatively more nurturant to same-sex peers (their preferred social partners and companions during the 6–10-year-old age period).

The twelve subgroups of boys and girls aged 6–10 from the six communities in the Six Culture Study provided the data for this test (Table 9.3, from Whiting and Edwards, 1988:264). 'Peers' were defined as children of the same 6–10 age grade as the focal children, but not siblings. We compared the rank ordering of the twelve subgroups ordered from highest to lowest in terms of the percentage of all their observed social acts which were directed to infants under 24 months, with the rank ordering of the same twelve subgroups ordered from highest to lowest in terms of all of their acts to same-sex peers which were coded as *nurturant* in apparent intent (including offers of comfort, physical contact, help, approval, food, other material goods, information and permission). The hypothesized positive correlation was found (Spearman rank correlation, *rho* = .61, $p < .05$, two-tailed; see Whiting and Edwards, 1988:264), supporting the hypothesis of transfer of nurturance from infant to peer contexts for both boys and girls.

Further supporting evidence for this transfer of nurturance has been provided by our colleagues. Weisner (1987) analysed 168 timed observations on sixty-three Abaluyia children aged 2 to 6 living in two Kenyan communities, Kisa and Kariobangi. Mothers made more requests and instructions regarding child-caretaking to girls than to boys. Girls, in turn, were more nurturant and prosocially commanding to other girls (age unspecified), than boys were to boys. Finally, Munroe, Munroe *et al.* (1984) compared boys' and girls' workloads in four societies to their modes of social behaviour when not working. The children lived in four communities with heavy subsistence workloads: Logoli of Kenya; Garifuna of Belize; Newars of Nepal; and American Samoans. In each community, forty-eight children aged 3 to 9 were studied by means of spot observations (thirty per child) and, on separate occasions, timed observations of social behaviour. For both girls and boys, significant positive correlations were found between caretaking levels and nurturance scores when not caretaking, strongly supporting the hypothesis of transfer of nurturance from the infant-caregiving setting to behaviour with other partners.

Table 9.3. *Interaction of 6– to 10-year-old girls and boys with lap children (0–24 months) and proportion of nurturance to same-sex peers*

Interaction with lap-children		Proportion of nurturance to same-sex peers	
Group	Percentage	Group	Percentage
Nyansongo girls	37	Tarong girls	26
Juxtlahuaca girls	34	Nyansongo girls	20
Tarong boys	28	Juxtlahuaca girls	17
Juxtlahuaca boys	26	Tarong boys	13
Khalapur girls	20	Nyansongo boys	11
Tarong girls	18	Juxtlahuaca boys	10
Taira girls	7	Khalapur boys	10
Khalapur boys	6	Orchard Town girls	9
Nyansongo boys	6	OrchardTown boys	9
Orchard Town girls	5	Khalapur girls	8
Taira boys	4	Taira boys	8
Orchard Town boys	0	Taira girls	5
Mean	16		12

Conclusion and discussion

Stein Bråten (1992, 1996a, and this volume) has reinterpreted the findings on children's nurturance to infants in a different way from our explanation in terms of elicitation of generic or prepared responses by stimuli that might be termed 'natural categories of social partners', or 'innate companion schemata'. Instead, Bråten argues that children's emerging nurturance to infants (as in Table 9.2) illustrates the prosocial expressions and caring gestures – the ability to recognize and *feel for* another's perspective – that children who were once themselves cared for nurturantly can demonstrate to others who invite such care. In Bråten's theoretic terms, the prosocial, nurturing behaviours illustrate the circular process of the children re-enacting affective experiences from the e-motional remembrance of moving with the other's motions.

> If others in need or distress reactivate in the child feelings semblant of the form of bodily self-feelings evoked in situations in which the infant has experienced caregiving, then they invite caring efforts resembling the caring afforded by others earlier in infancy by virtue of having partaken in such caring in the reciprocal mode of felt immediacy. (Bråten, 1996a:456)

Contrariwise, he expects the mirror image of these feelings and behaviours for young children who have experienced parental neglect or physical abuse. For them, indifferent, fearful or aggressive behaviours would be predicted when they encounter peers in distress in day care, and this is in fact what has been observed by George and Main (1979), Main and George (1985) and Klimes-Dogan and Kistner (1990). Bråten considers that these developing patterns of toddler behaviour towards peers – whether prosocial or antisocial – are both parts of the same picture affecting the child in enduring ways even later in ontogeny.

Are these two theoretic descriptions, the company-they-keep hypothesis versus the companion space hypothesis, compatible or incompatible? Indeed, they are not logically incompatible or contradictory. That is to say, there is no reason why young children could not be affected both by natural categories which elicit stable and predictable behaviours, and by processes affecting their inborn companion space, enabling learning by reciprocal participation. The two processes, in fact, could be predicted to reinforce each other, because they suggest both that young children would acquire generalized and enduring behaviours and expectations from the patterns of adult care they have directly experienced, and that they then bring these forward in time and to new contexts, such as when interacting with companions who are not family members. It is true that Bråten does not consider how caregivers other than parents, such as child nurses, may affect the child's development, but such a line of reasoning could be added to his formulations without difficulty. An infant or toddler cared for by a devoted, sensitive and giving child nurse, versus a harsh and rejecting one, would be expected to re-enact very different patterns when at another time or in another place finding himself in the presence of a young child in a state of distress or need, and who evokes emotional and motor memories.

Although the two explanations are not incompatible, nevertheless they are not equivalent either. They lead to some overlapping and some non-overlapping predictions. For example, the company-they-keep hypothesis, unlike the companion space theory, does not predict negative behaviour to other young children by abused youngsters; the mechanism involved would not lead to the expectation that small-child partners are a different kind of eliciting stimulus for abused versus non-abused children. Such behaviour by abused children is not necessarily disconfirming to the company-they-keep hypothesis, however; rather, it could simply be that its mechanism is overridden in certain specific situations. That seems reasonable.

The company-they-keep hypothesis does predict that, over time, children's behaviour to infants and toddlers will be shaped by the response their caretaking efforts receive. That is, the theory suggests that infants and toddlers, by virtue of their appealing faces, bodies and gestures, elicit positive behaviour from older children, such as attention and affection. The attention and affection, in turn, make the babies smile, laugh and play – reinforcing the older children, and eliciting further positive caretaking. The elicited behaviours become part of a positive cycle which could be expected to show individual differences between particular dyads of children. Dunn (this volume) also posits the emergence of just these kinds of positive (feedback) cycles between pairs of young siblings, probably both drawing from and contributing to individual differences in understanding of others' minds and emotions and in competencies for cooperative play. In contrast, the companion space theory does not predict this kind of feedback cycle, but instead a circular re-enactment of caretaking behaviours previously experienced. Which is correct? Or are both correct, in different situations? We are still at the initial stages of understanding young children's behaviour with other children in their families and peer networks, and hopefully much more will be learned about the many kinds of underlying individual and relational processes that explain behaviour in this rich domain.

Acknowledgement
I thank Beatrice Whiting for comments on the first draft of this paper.

Notes

1 The research reported in Whiting and Edwards (1988) involved the collaboration of Carol Ember, Gerald Erchak, Sara Harkness, Robert Munroe, Ruth Munroe, Sara Nerlove, Susan Seymour, Charles Super, Thomas Weisner and Martha Wenger. The study was funded by grants from the National Institute of Mental Health (to Beatrice Whiting) and the Carnegie Foundation (to the Child Development Research Unit).

PART III

Imitation, emotion and understanding in primate communication

CHAPTER 10

Ontogeny, communication and parent–offspring relationships

Patrick Bateson

By the mid-1970s a broad consensus had been reached among the biologists studying the development of behaviour. The old dichotomy into learned and unlearned behaviour was regarded as unhelpful and the emphasis was placed squarely on the interplay between the developing individual and his or her environment. The sociobiological revolution changed all that. The marriage of the study of behaviour with population biology, which was E. O. Wilson's (1975) striking achievement, had a major cost. The population biologists were accustomed to thinking of evolution in terms of gene frequencies and development was an irrelevance for them. When challenged on this point, Wilson (1976) wrote that, for the time being, developmental pathways were modules that should be de-coupled while other matters were being sorted out. Implicitly, the development of the individual was regarded as a complex process by which genes are decoded. This was not the same as believing that behaviour patterns could be divided into two groups on the basis of whether or not they were learned. Nevertheless, the effect on thought was equally regressive.

The major achievement of the developmental psychologists and the ethologists up to that period had been the winning of acceptance that development is not an additive process. This was nonchalantly tossed out of the window. Recently, sociobiologists and behavioural ecologists have started to take an interest in the origins of behaviour and the developmentalists have found that they are being listened to again (Bateson and Gomendio, 1992).

A swing first one way and then the other, similar to what has happened in the thinking about behavioural development, has also occurred in studies of communication. The classical ethologists looked on an act of communication as expressing the genuine internal state of the individual sending the signal. They also thought of communication as helpful to both parties. By contrast, in the heyday of sociobiology, which started in the mid-1970s, the emphasis was placed almost exclusively on the manipulative aspects of such exchanges and virtually no regard was given to the informative or sharing aspects of communication. Now the pendulum has started to swing back again with a much greater emphasis on the reliability of signals.

The work on behavioural development in animals is relevant to the current work on the interplay between the human child and his or her parents because it challenges us to look at the dynamics of the developmental process. The modern position on communication is helpful in as much as it buttresses the view that the exchanges may, as often as not, be as cooperative as they are manipulative. In this chapter I consider where developmental thinking has got to among biologists, considering the underpinnings that have come from links to computational approaches and from the neurosciences. Next I review changes in thought about communication. Finally, I take a fresh look at the biological approach to parent–offspring relationships. I have reviewed all three of these topics at greater length elsewhere (Bateson, 1990, 1994, 1995).

Interplay rather than addition

The modern debates about instinct are usually about the sorts of confusion that arise when a great many different dimensions are collapsed into one. The word 'innate' has at least seven separate meanings attached to it: present at birth; a behavioural difference caused by a genetic difference; adapted over the course of evolution; unchanging throughout development; shared by all members of a species; present in the behavioural repertoire before it is functional; and not learned. 'Instinct', when it is used, is deployed in similar ways to innate. A further and special meaning is also attached to instinct, namely a distinctly organized system of behaviour, developmentally regulated and driven from within (see Berridge, 1994). Does it follow that one of the meanings of innate or instinctive necessarily applies to a given activity when the justification for using another meaning has been demonstrated? Consider the following questions which might be applied to any pattern of behaviour:

(a) Does the activity appear at a particular stage in development?
(b) Are individual differences in the activity due to genetic differences?
(c) Was the activity adapted to its present function by the Darwinian process of evolution?
(d) Is the activity shared by all members of the species?
(e) Once present, are the frequency and form of the activity unchanged by experience?

(f) Does the behaviour develop before it is of use to the individual?
(g) Does the activity develop without previous opportunities for learning?
(h) Does the activity have the characteristics of an organized and developmentally regulated behavioural system?

An unqualified 'Yes' or 'No' to any one of the above questions is liable to trigger an academic dispute. The practical difficulties in demonstrating, for instance, that a piece of behaviour is not learned are immense. To take another example, evidence that genetic relatives resemble each other behaviourally is open to the non-trivial objection that they are liable to share common experiences.

Leaving empirical matters on one side, what would be implied if one of the answers to those questions was unequivocally 'Yes'? Would we be compelled to suppose that the answers to all the others would be in the affirmative? It does not take much thought to realize that we would not. For instance, if a behaviour pattern develops without obvious practice or example, the activity may subsequently be modified by learning. A blind human baby may start to smile in the same way as a normal baby. But that does not mean that later on in their lives, sighted people will not modify their smiles to expressions that are characteristic of their own culture.

The major conclusion to draw from the debate about the use of the i-words is that clarity is never a fault. Say what you mean (even if it uses a bit more space) rather than unintentionally confuse your reader by employing a word that means so many different things to so many different people. That plea having been made, it is not difficult to find cases where many of the answers to the questions given above would be 'Yes'. The emotional and communicative systems involved when a human baby interacts with his or her mother are highly organized. They are also characteristic of our species, are likely to be adapted to their present function by the Darwinian process of evolution, and appear at a particular stage of development.

Many examples of animal communication are like the human smile. For instance, birds and mammals may have alarm calls that are given to objects that other members of the species have indicated are frightening. Blackbirds will mob owls, producing a high-intensity pinking call. When a stuffed owl is presented to experienced blackbirds living in aviaries, they start mobbing the mounted bird. Vieth *et al.* (1980) showed that when a naïve blackbird saw a species it had never seen before, it would rapidly associate this species with the mobbing calls made by an experienced bird that was mobbing an owl which the naïve bird could not see. The novel species was an

Australian bird, the Noisy Friar Bird, which previous generations of European blackbird were not likely to have seen. It is specialized for taking honey from wild bees nests and has no feathers on its head. The strangeness and oddity of the stuffed Australian bird were enhanced by painting its head blue. The naïve blackbirds, seeing it as they heard the mobbing calls of experienced adults, soon learned to treat this bird as though it were potentially dangerous and mobbed it themselves in the absence of other blackbirds. In later experiments a brightly coloured plastic bottle was used and the blackbirds even learned to mob this object, although it was not so effective as a novel stuffed bird. Evidently blackbirds respond with alarm to some features more strongly than they do to others. In many ways this is like our own fear of snakes. Humans have a predisposition to avoid them, but this fear can be enormously enhanced by the alarm of others.

We are genuinely better informed about developmental processes underlying behaviour than we used to be. Numerous factors affect their outcome. Dispositions to respond strongly to some features of the environment often develop without direct experience of those features and stereotyped motor patterns often develop without obvious opportunities for practice. But these aspects of a behavioural repertoire, once developed, may then be modified by experience. Similarly, learning processes are also rule-governed and have an organization that may develop without obvious practice but may also change with experience. The plain fact is that several different developmental processes may lead to the adaptive complexity of behaviour, but any given behaviour pattern may be affected by all or several of them.

The chances are that the various influences do not add together and, when that is the case, small changes in certain factors may sometimes make big differences to the outcome. Conversely, large changes in others have no effect whatsoever. Such features are characteristic of inanimate dynamical systems just as they are of animate ones. The idea of behaviour coming from the genes being distinct from behaviour derived from experience evaporates in the face of such knowledge. The issues become even more obvious if the variety of influences and outcomes are drawn out as is shown in Fig. 10.1.

The influences on behaviour may operate in a variety of different ways (enabling, initiating, facilitating, maintaining); they may also have radically different outcomes, some specific and some general. Developmental processes may be remarkably well buffered against fluctuations in the environment. Moreover, if an individual is prevented from developing in one way, the same behaviour pattern may

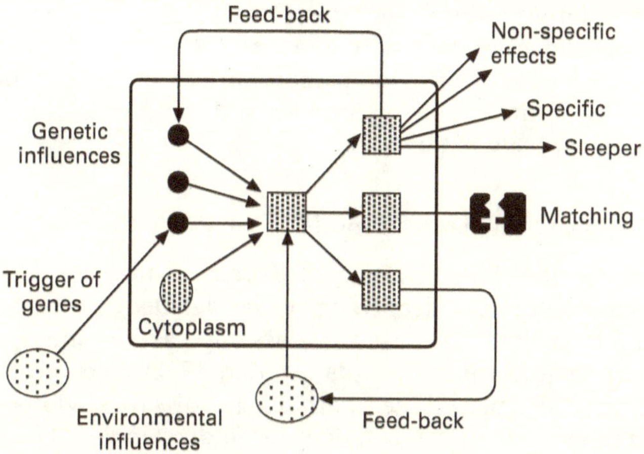

Fig. 10.1 A schematic flow diagram of some of the events occurring during development. The neural structures required for the expression of behaviour depend on genes, cytoplasmic factors and environmental conditions, some of which trigger the expression of particular genes. Feed-back onto genes to stop their expression may occur internally or be mediated through the environment. Some consequences of developmental processes are specific, some are general and some feed forward to later stages in development and, in that sense, are 'sleepers'. Finally, some processes actively match the environment to the individual's characteristics.

sometimes develop in another way. Given their predispositions and proclivities, individuals may choose environments to which their characteristics are well adapted – 'niche-picking' as Scarr and McCartney (1983) called it. Even so, individuals are also equipped with conditional rules so that their behavioural development is directed down one of several different routes, depending on the prevailing conditions.

An important aspect of the developmental processes studied intensively in animals is the active role played by the animal itself. It explores its environment, which helps it to find those features that are of biological importance to it in that context. The recently hatched chick will learn to press a pedal to present itself with an instance of the type of object that is highly effective as an imprinting stimulus and, having done so, will learn to recognize that object and form an attachment to it (Bateson and Reese, 1969). A separate but equally important issue is the effect of a social companion on what else is learned in a given context. The song birds that learn many aspects of their songs will copy more readily in early life those details that they produce later when they have an opportunity to interact socially with the individual who sings them (ten Cate, 1994). These matters of the active engagement of the environment and the emotional state generated by the presence of a companion are obvious points of contact between the studies of young animals and those of the human child reported extensively in this book.

Neural nets and the neurosciences

Advances in the understanding of development have come at the behavioural level with deepening of the detailed knowledge of the various factors that influence processes such as imprinting (Bolhuis, 1991) and song-learning in birds (Marler, 1991). Theory and neural analysis have also played their part. It is not always obvious just what formalization of empirical data does for understanding. However, the mathematicians' approaches to dynamical systems have been an eye-opener to biologists. Great complexity may be generated by simple equations. The same is true of neural nets equipped with the most elementary algorithms for changing connectivity. Some of the simulations of behaviour, readily labelled as 'cognitive', hold out considerable promise for aiding understanding of developmental processes just because they are based on neurally plausible rules for changing connections between components of the network. In collaboration with Gabriel Horn, I have worked on one of these models in order to provide a basis for both linking and taking forward our neural and behavioural work on imprinting.

Imprinting is involved in a process by which animals form exclusive attachments to a caregiver or future sexual partner. This is a learning process, but before learning takes place, the animal has clear preferences for the type of stimuli which it will learn about. It also has in place a suite of responses that it will direct towards those stimuli. Learning takes place at a biologically appropriate time in the life-cycle and few would doubt that the whole process has been adapted during evolution for the kin-recognition function which it currently serves.

In precocial birds, like domestic chicks, filial imprinting occurs shortly after hatching and may simply require exposure to a conspicuous object. Even in very young chicks, transfer of training occurs; animals that have been imprinted may be influenced by this experience when they are given a rewarded discrimination. The nature of the transfer depends on how they have been imprinted and what they are required to discriminate between. If they are asked to discriminate between two objects with which they have been imprinted, then they will benefit from imprinting if the exposure was separated in time. However, their performance will be impaired if exposure to the two objects was close together in time (Chantrey, 1974; Honey *et al.*, 1993). The advantages of using the same information in a variety of contexts can be great. The mother is an ever-present figure in the young animal's life. Her actions may prove extremely important in predicting where it can find crucial resources for itself. While the mother gives signals such as the food call which the chicks respond to without learning, all the chicks hear this and they are in competition with each other. So the smartness involved in transfer of training will pay the individual possessing such attributes.

In one set of experiments, chicks were trained with a flashing, rotating light or with a rotating stuffed jungle fowl and then given a choice between them (Horn and McCabe, 1984; Bolhuis *et al.*, 1985). The artificial and naturalistic stimuli were matched for their effectiveness in eliciting approach from day-old domestic chicks by varying the rate of rotation of the object. Despite the matching, the stuffed jungle fowl became more attractive than the box in untrained birds by the second day after hatching. The shift towards a stronger fowl bias was also apparent in birds that had been imprinted with either a fowl or a box. Features of the jungle fowl that make it especially attractive as the predisposition emerges are located around the head. However, they are not specific to jungle fowl since a stuffed rotating gadwall duck and a polecat were equally attractive (Johnson and Horn, 1988).

Using a neural net helps us to bring together the predispositions of animals that imprint with the effects of experience on their preferences (Bateson and Horn, 1994). The first step in the model involves detection of features in a stimulus presented to a young bird. Aspects of the stimulus which the bird is predisposed to find attractive are thought to be picked out by analysis. The second step involves comparison between what has already been experienced and the current input. Of course, before imprinting has taken place, no comparison is involved. Once it has occurred, recognition of what is familiar and what is novel is crucial. Finally, the third stage involves control of the various motor patterns involved in executing filial behaviour. This model is given the acronym ARE for analysis, recognition and execution.

It is important that the postulated subprocesses are as plausible in neural terms as current knowledge allows and that the whole system has the behavioural structure of an intact animal (Bateson and Horn, 1994). The model exhibits a well-known feature of behavioural development seen in animals, tending to settle into familiar habits, while also able to build with increasing elaboration on the basis of previous perceptual experience. The model simulates the closure of the sensitive period in development, which is known to be dependent on experience, at least in part. The greater the activating value of the features in the experienced stimuli, the more quickly the sensitive period comes to an end. Above all, the various influences on behaviour do not add together.

At the empirical level, an array of different neurobiological techniques have implicated the intermediate and medial part of the hyperstriatum ventrale (IMHV) on both sides of the brain as being sites of a neural representation of the imprinting object (Horn, 1985, 1991). When evidence is open to a variety of interpretations, greater confidence in a particular explanation may be achieved by tackling the problem from a number of different angles. Each piece of evidence obtained by the different approaches may be ambiguous, but the ambiguities are different in each case. When the whole body of evidence is considered, therefore, much greater confidence may be placed on a particular meaning. An analogy is trying to locate on a map the position of a visible mountain top. One compass bearing is usually not enough. Two bearings from different angles provide a much better fix and three bearings give the most reliable position for the top. It was this approach that led to the conclusion that IMHV is a site of the neural representation of the imprinting object and corresponds to the changed weights in the connection within the hypothetical recognition system of the neural net model.

Chicks that have had both left and right IMHV removed surgically are unable to imprint, and if bilateral lesions are placed immediately after imprinting, the birds show no recognition of the imprinting object (see Horn, 1985). However, it is possible for chicks to learn a rewarded discrimination after bilateral removal of IMHV. They will also learn to press a pedal rewarded by the view of an imprinting stimulus even though they do not go on to learn the characteristics of that stimulus (Johnson and Horn, 1986). So it is possible to dissociate the neural mechanisms involved in imprinting from those involved in learning when an external reward is required. Nevertheless, transfer of training means that the two processes are connected in the intact animal.

Lesion studies suggest that another representation (known as S′) is formed in another region of the brain about 6 hours after imprinting (see Horn, 1985). This representation can be prevented by placing a lesion in the right IMHV soon after imprinting. The second store could provide the point of contact between imprinting and rewarded learning. We performed a behavioural experiment showing that when transfer of training is given immediately after imprinting, the rate of learning the discrimination is unaffected by imprinting. However, if discrimination learning was delayed by 6 hours then the type of pre-exposure did affect the rate of learning, with those imprinted with two objects close together in time learning significantly more slowly than the ones that were imprinted with two objects separated in time. In contrast, all birds showed a strong preference for the imprinting object immediately after imprinting. This experiment suggested that, while the memory required for recognition is formed quickly, the memory system sustaining transfer of training is not.

We showed that the functional characteristics of the two mechanisms differ (Honey *et al.*, 1995). Although both left IMHV and S′ supported imprinting preferences, only in the chicks with S′ did the memories formed during imprinting influence the acquisition of a heat-reinforced discrimination in which two imprinted objects served as stimuli. This work is ongoing, but it illustrates how knowledge is advanced by moving backwards and forwards between the behavioural and the neural levels. As this happens, our understanding of the dynamics involved in development continues to improve (cf. also Elman *et al.*, 1996).

Communication, competition and cooperation

Dawkins (1976) played a major role in the change in thought on communication from the era of classical ethology to that of sociobiology. He argued that individual organisms do not survive from one generation to the next, while on the whole their genes do; therefore, Darwinian evolution is primarily about changes in the genes. Dawkins' approach to evolution was presented in characteristically entertaining form when he suggested that the organism is 'a robot vehicle blindly programmed to preserve its selfish genes'. His approach has undoubtedly helped a lot of people to understand the complexities of biological evolution.

While Dawkins certainly cannot be blamed for it, enthusiasm in the 1980s for the 'enterprise society' and 'feeling good about greed' may explain why his parable of selfish genes has commonly been elided with the selfish intentions of individuals. Be that as it may, the general style of thinking about evolution has been applied to the study of animal communication in ways that suggest that all activities directed by one individual towards another are manipulative (Dawkins and Krebs, 1979a). Sometimes this view is clearly correct. We see it in its most obvious form in the interactions between species when one species manages to control the behaviour of another as if it were a puppet. A striking example is the European cuckoo. The mother cuckoo lays each egg in the nest of another species such as the reed warbler. The egg very closely resembles the egg of the host.

The young cuckoo hatches before the reed warblers and ejects the competition from the nest. Then the young cuckoo successfully persuades the unfortunate warbler parents to feed it, even when it is twice their size. By looking like a super-offspring, the cuckoo successfully exploits the normal pattern of interaction that exists between parent and young.

While Dawkins and Krebs (1979a) were eager to extend their manipulation view to as many instances as possible, they also recognized some limitations (Dawkins and Krebs, 1979b). The essentially competitive process of Darwinian evolution does not necessarily imply a competitive outcome. On the contrary, a great deal of communication is to do with signals that carry real information and with cooperation in which all the participants benefit by working with each other. Even though Darwinian evolution is represented as a competitive process, the outcome has often been that animals ended up working with each other. One explanation for cooperation is that, at least in the past, the aided individuals were relatives; cooperation is like parental care and has evolved for similar reasons. Another is that cooperating individuals jointly benefited even though they were not related; the co-operative behaviour has evolved because those who did it were more likely to survive as individuals and reproduce than those that did not. Once again the force of this particular argument can be seen most clearly in communication between different species.

Some small fish, that are conspicuously marked but highly suitable as a morsel of food, clean the teeth of great big predator fish. Before they do their job, the cleaner fish do a characteristic waggling swim in front of the monster. This inhibits the normal feeding response and the great predator opens its mouth, allowing the little fish in. When the big fish needs to eat other little fish, it signals it is switching back into normal hunting mode by jerking its jaw in a particular way. The little cleaner fish scuttle for cover and the symbiotic arrangement is preserved. Both parties benefit by this arrangement.

In cooperating animals of the same species, the mutual benefits of working together can be greatly enhanced if information about the state of the external world can be transmitted from one individual to another. One of the most extraordinary and well analysed examples of such transmission is provided by the so-called dance language of honey bees described so beautifully by von Frisch (1967). The characteristics of the waggle dance performed in the hive provide the crucial information about where the returning bee has successfully foraged. The duration of the dance circuit is strongly correlated with the distance from the hive to the food. In a darkened hive the angle of orientation of the central segment of the dance with respect to the vertical is strongly correlated with the angle between the food source and the sun's position.

Reliable signals in conflict?

The most interesting test-bed of evolutionary thinking about communication is provided by those situations in which individuals compete with each other over resources. The advocates of manipulation urge that a trustworthy mode of communication is always open to cheating (Dawkins and Krebs, 1979a, b). The cheat uses the information provided by its opponent and gives nothing away about itself. As a consequence, it is much more likely to win the resource. And, as a result of that, it is likely to reproduce faster. Before long, it is argued, cheating will have evolved to become the dominant mode of behaviour.

It sounds convincing, but most people who know a particular species well quickly develop a good intuitive sense of whether an animal is likely to attack or escape from its body and facial postures. After the initial location of the opponent, several levels of escalation may precede an actual fight, involving easily recognized and increasingly energetic displays. Neither party will benefit from getting hurt and in the great majority of cases the disputes are settled without serious damage on either side. The encounter can break off at any stage in the process of escalation. The contests are usually won by the larger individual, but if the contestants are of equal size, they are usually won by the holder of the resource. The behaviour of each individual at each stage of escalation indicates how serious it is about continuing.

From a large number of quantitative studies, it is clear that escape *is* very well predicted by certain patterns of behaviour. We can see some sense in this. If one animal suddenly turns tail, it is liable to be attacked and might get injured. The advantage to the loser of not being misunderstood and of expressing the animal equivalent of a white flag are obvious. The winner's benefit from responding appropriately to such a signal is that it does not risk injury by escalating the conflict into a real fight when it need not have done so. The argument is, therefore, that a form of behaviour which effectively negotiates the end of a conflict can be evolutionarily stable.

Attack is predicted by other postures only about half as well as escape (Caryl, 1979). This may arise because of the dynamics of an aggressive encounter; the ability to predict who will win from a given exchange becomes less and less reliable, the longer the encounter has to run after that exchange. Therefore, the empirical evidence suggesting that reliable signals of each actor's state are not seen in the course of animal conflicts may have been misinterpreted.

While most biologists were placing great emphasis on dissimulation, one took a very different line. Zahavi (1975) consistently argued that signalling that carried a handicap to the signaller was honest. Zahavi was treated as an eccentric since the initial attempts to model his ideas about handicaps formally failed to lend substance to them. More recently, however, theoreticians such as Grafen (1990) have been able to satisfy nearly everybody else that if a signal carries a cost, it may also be reliable in the sense of carrying accurate information. Honest signalling is now the rage, although arguments continue about whether honest signals must carry some cost (see Maynard Smith, 1994).

It was perhaps always a little odd that the manipulative theory of communication seemed so persuasive when, in so many contexts, both signaller and receiver had an interest in the successful transmission of reliable information. Even in conflicts over resources there were quite separate grounds from those proposed by Zahavi for supposing that signals do provide reliable guides to the signaller's state and probable course of action.

The crucial question is where the balance is struck between signalling real information about internal state and signalling misinformation (Bond, 1989). Consider analogies with the human game of poker. On the one hand, if we can get away with bluff, we make a lot of money. On the other, if we bluff against an opponent who has a really good hand we may end up very much worse off than if we had decided to throw in our bad hand before we had raised the bet too far. So we might well expect something equivalent to negotiation, as Hinde (1981) has argued. For each individual the optimal outcome of such negotiation should represent a balance between the costs of escalating the conflict to likely injury and the benefits of winning the resource easily. An individual that escalates without assessment is in danger of finding itself in a fight with a much stronger individual.

The evolutionary pressure for some exaggeration of fighting ability is present and many species puff themselves up in various ways, thereby making themselves look more fearsome than they really are. Even so, honest advertisement of strength, providing cues that cannot be faked, may count most in the long run. One example may be the male red deer which competes vigorously with other males for opportunities to mate. Fights occur, of course, but conflicts are most often settled by bouts of roaring at each other. The rate of roaring is increased by each individual as the contest proceeds until one individual gives up. The roaring is extremely exhausting for the animals and the one that can keep it up for longest is also likely to be the strongest. In the roaring contests, both individuals increase the rate of roaring until one seems to recognize it is outclassed and retreats. Clutton-Brock and Albon (1979) played tape-recordings of red deer roars to a real stag. Unlike the stag, the tape-recorder did not get tired and when the tape-recorder roared at a high rate, the stag roared less. It seemed as though the stag had been forced into accepting that it was dealing with a much more powerful opponent. While fake characteristics may gain short-term successes, those individuals that ignore such cues and focus on reliable sources of evidence about their opponents may eventually emerge in the course of evolution.

Parent–offspring relationships

Evolutionary theories about parent–offspring relationships have undergone a similar transformation to those in the heartland of communication. The prediction used to be that young will demand food and care from their parents at weaning when the parents' interests are best served by reserving their efforts for future offspring. Trivers (1974) revolutionized the study of parent–offspring relationships when he pointed out that the long-term interests of the parent are not identical with those of their offspring. A parent may increase its reproductive success by weaning its young earlier than is best for them, because it saves itself from becoming too exhausted and is thus able to have a larger number of offspring than would otherwise have been the case. As a consequence, aggression between parents and offspring was expected, particularly at the time of weaning, and the communication between them was not thought to be reliable.

Trivers' stimulating contribution has been responsible for a large theoretical literature (Mock and Forbes, 1992). However, the insights derived from evolutionary theory have been questioned recently, partly because of changes in theoretical stance about the benefits of reliable signals (Godfray, 1991). More seriously, perhaps, the evolutionary argument had led to an unjustified expectation that conflict of evolutionary interest necessarily implies behavioural conflict. Mock and Forbes wisely suggested that behavioural aggression between parent and offspring should be referred to as 'squabbling', thus avoiding the punning use of 'conflict'. Trivers had undoubtedly intended the pun, basing it on his own observations of tantrums in young baboons and 2-year-old children. Indeed, the linkage between evolutionary theory and behaviour rapidly became established as one of the jewels in the crown of sociobiology. For all that, the behavioural evidence does not fit the theory especially well.

Two-year-old tantrums in humans are now interpreted in precisely the opposite sense from Trivers. When they occur, tantrums seem to be concerned with the difficult process of establishing some autonomy from the parent. Well-attached children do not show them, using their parents as a secure base from which to explore the world (Pettit and Bates, 1989). Rhesus monkey mothers may actively reject their offspring around the time of weaning, while their offspring play an increasingly prominent role in initiating contact with their mother as they grow older (Hinde, 1977). Nevertheless, Gomendio (1991) concluded that squabbles did not arise in this species as a result of mothers' reduction in suckling when they conceived their next offspring. Nor did she find that mothers that failed to conceive had more demanding infants as would have been predicted from the theory of parent–offspring conflict. Occasionally, weaning squabbles between mother and young do occur, particularly if the mother is already pregnant again. However, on the basis of her field studies of baboons, Altmann (1980) observed that conflicts of interest did not invariably lead to such squabbles. Evidence from a variety of mammals suggests that maternal aggression often does not occur at all and, if it does, it is seen at quite different stages in development from the one at which the process of weaning occurs.

In addition to these embarrassments, the classical application of game theory, which has provided much of the logical underpinning for the theory of parent–offspring conflict, is clumsy when it reduces variation in the mother's availability and the offspring's demand to the expression of alternative genotypes. This is because the length of maternal care frequently depends on environmental conditions (Lee *et al.*, 1991). In some species, such as white-tailed deer, mothers extend the period of lactation in a bad year, whereas in others, such as the polar bear, mothers curtail lactation. In yet others, such as vervet monkeys, both effects have been reported.

Perhaps the most damaging falsification of the early manipulative predictions derived from parent–offspring conflict theory was provided by the evidence that mothers both monitor and respond to the progress of their current offspring. Mothers may actively compensate for the slow development of their young or delay conception of the subsequent offspring if the present one is progressing slowly (Simpson *et al.*, 1981). Rat mothers continue to lactate for much longer than would otherwise have been the case when they are given pups younger (Nicoll and Meites, 1959) than the ones they had been suckling, again suggesting that the mother is not necessarily driving the weaning process without due regard for her offspring's condition.

From the offspring's standpoint, young laboratory rats seem to wean themselves spontaneously; a stage is reached in development when they actively choose solid food in preference to milk when tested (Thiels *et al.*, 1988). As the offspring's metabolic costs go up as they get older and larger, they may be forced to wean themselves because they simply do not get enough calories from their mother's milk to survive to the next feed. In domestic cats, the rate of growth starts to slow down around 20 days after birth, particularly in kittens of nutritionally stressed mothers, and then suddenly speeds up again around 30 days as they start to process solid food efficiently (Deag *et al.*, 1987). The discontinuity occurs at different ages in different animals (and is lost, as a consequence, in averaged data). The slowing down of growth before the discontinuity is much more pronounced in larger litters which impose greater energetic demands on their mothers. The eventual inadequacy of the mother to provide for all the nutritional needs of the young is particularly striking in fur seals, in which the mother disappears for several days while she stokes up for the next bout of lactation (Trillmich, 1990). Eventually what she can provide is less than what her pup needs.

The empirical study of behaviour has forced a reappraisal of the optimal route to maximum reproductive success in mothers and the optimal route to highest probability of survival in their offspring. The evolutionary arguments needed to be looked at again, not simply from the standpoint of honest signalling but also bearing in mind how an individual's state might affect the optimal weaning time both from the standpoint of the mother and from that of the offspring (see Bateson, 1994). In species that can breed more than once a year, the mother has a reasonable chance of successfully raising more than one offspring. The current offspring will only survive to independence after a certain minimum amount of care has been given to it. Even when the mother is well fed, the longer she cares for the current offspring, the worse her state may become – such is the heavy depletion of energy resulting from lactation. As a consequence, the costs in terms of the diminished probability of rearing more young may soon outweigh the marginal benefits of giving more milk to the current young.

If the mother's nutritional state is only moderately satisfactory and her current offspring develops more slowly than it would do under ideal conditions, she may increase her reproductive success if she continues to lactate for longer than under ideal conditions. Despite the correspondingly severe knock-on effects for subsequent young, the optimum time to rear the current offspring moves to a later age than for the mothers in good condition. However, if her nutritional state is so poor that her current young are unlikely to survive and conditions are sufficiently variable that she might be expected to recover before she has another, then her best strategy is to abandon the current young.

The probability of having another offspring ought to influence the extent of time and energy devoted to the current one. For example, the mother may have to face a winter in which she cannot breed and which she might not survive. Furthermore, matters may be made worse if finding a mate takes time. With a relatively low probability of breeding again, her life-time reproductive success may be maximized if she gives higher priority to the current offspring than to those that are as yet unborn. Conversely, if she has mated immediately after the birth of the current young and is pregnant while she lactates, as is possible in species such as the cat and the rat, she may give lower priority to the one she is currently looking after than if she were not pregnant. Under most environmental conditions, the optimum weaning time should be earlier than for non-pregnant mothers. Pregnancy arising from matings during a postpartum oestrus is only one of several ways in which the mother might have an enhanced expectation of breeding again. In temperate latitudes she might expect to have a higher chance of breeding again if her current young were born at the beginning of the summer and other young may be reared successfully before the next winter.

Two main conclusions arise from looking at the problems faced by a mother in a variable environment. First, the relation between mother's nutritional state deriving from environmental conditions and time of weaning of the current young may not be linear, explaining what is observed in such species as the vervet monkey. The second general conclusion is that if the mother's probability of breeding again is high, then she should wean the current young earlier.

The reactions of an offspring to its mother's conditional responses to the environment should also be conditional. In many species, the relation between the effect of its behaviour on its probability of surviving before weaning and its probability of surviving after weaning must both be taken into account. This is because offspring survival does not simply depend on getting as much milk as possible from the mother while she is able to provide it. Benefits, such as the protection which it might have derived from her in the post-weaning period, would be lost if it were so demanding in the pre-weaning period that it seriously damaged her health. In the early stages of lactation, the offspring's survival depends utterly on its receiving immediate maternal attention. Moreover, since meeting its needs is relatively easy for the mother because of the offspring's low body mass compared to that of the mother, the longer-term consequences

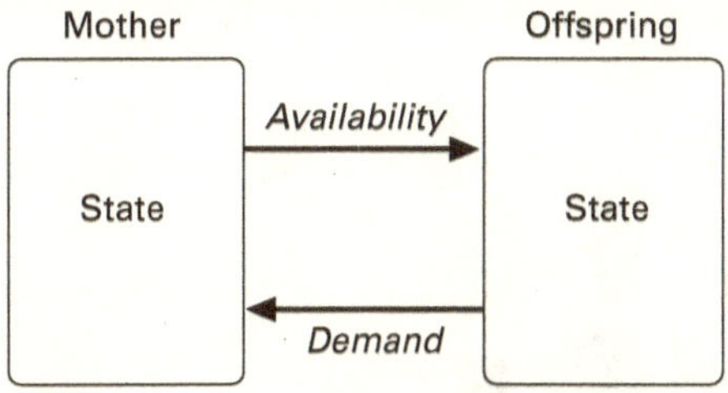

Fig. 10.2 The mother's availability to her offspring is influenced by her own state and the behaviour of the offspring. The demands of the offspring are affected by its state and its mother's behaviour. The mother's state is influenced by her previous availability and how she then responded to her offspring's demands, as well as on environmental conditions and whether or not she is pregnant. The offspring's state is dependent on its stage of development and on how successful it was in securing milk from its mother in the past.

for post-weaning care of being demanding are not heavy. As the offspring grows, however, these delayed effects of being demanding start to rise and, at the same time, the chances of the young surviving without maternal milk begin to improve. By the time the offspring has reached the late pre-weaning stage, its optimum demands have dropped to low values.

The optimal weaning ages for offspring depend greatly on how much care is given after weaning. If a little is characteristically given by the species, optimum demand by the offspring remains high until the demands of switching to primarily solid food become paramount. The greater the amount of post-weaning care the mother gives, the earlier the age relative to weaning when her offspring's demanding behaviour should start to decline. The general point is that an offspring benefits from reducing its demanding behaviour as it gets older and also benefits from monitoring maternal availability which is a measure of her state.

Each mother should be sensitive to the condition of her offspring so that, if it is still in need of care but reasonably well developed, she may forego a breeding opportunity in order to nurture it through to independence. Young should be sensitive to the condition of their mothers and adjust their pattern of development accordingly since their mothers respond not only to the state of the young but also to their own condition. The interplay between mother and offspring is summarized in Fig. 10.2.

Evidence for a two-way process comes from an experiment with

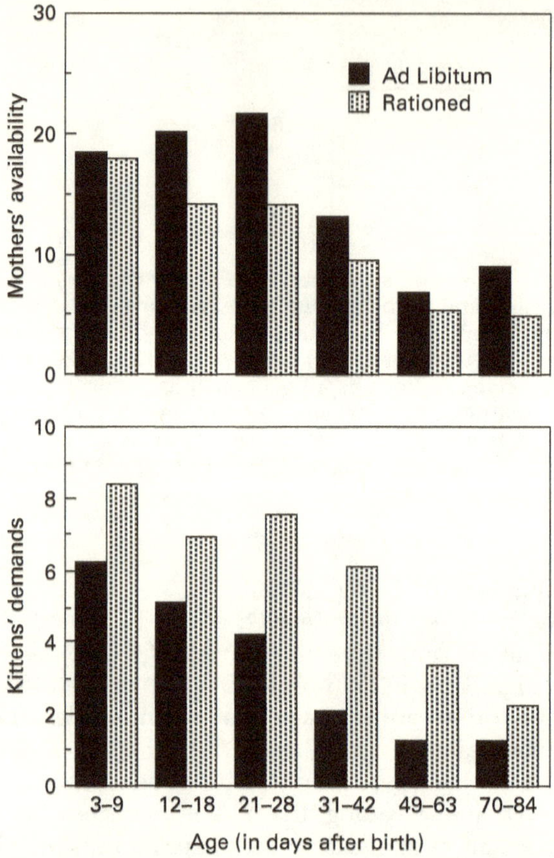

Fig. 10.3 Changes in the relationships of mother cats and their kittens when given *ad libitum* food and when rationed. The mother's availability (expressed as the percentage number of observations in which the kittens were in a suckling position) is shown in the top panel. The kittens' demands (expressed in terms of the percentage number of observations in which the kittens nuzzled against the flank of the mother) are shown in the lower panel. (From Bateson *et al.*, 1990.)

domestic cats in which mothers were given 80% of an *ad libitum* diet (Bateson *et al.*, 1990). Unsurprisingly, the rationed mothers were marginally less available to their offspring than those on an *ad libitum* diet but the offspring evidently felt this and demanded significantly more by nuzzling her flanks (see Fig. 10.3). The net effect was that the kittens of the rationed mothers put on weight at the same rate as the kittens of mothers given *ad libitum* food. Other studies suggest that the mothers would certainly have been unable to sustain the same growth rate in their kittens if rationing had been more severe or if the litters had been larger. The proposal is that maternal availability could be used to predict the timing of weaning. Up to a threshold, the harder the offspring has to work in order to get onto its mother's nipple, the later the predicted time of weaning. Above that threshold which might be marked by maternal aggression as well as lack of availability, the offspring should anticipate weaning occurring earlier than normal.

The offspring may also need to prepare for the probable world in which they have to grow up. Members of the same species, the same sex and the same age sometimes differ dramatically from each other. 'Alternative tactics' within a species commonly arise because an individual has the capacity to respond in more than one way according to environmental conditions or its own body state. Such conditional responses during development are well known in the social insects, in which one sister might be adapted for producing thousand of eggs, another has massive jaws used in defence of the nest and another is equipped with foraging skills never expressed by the other two. Similar environmentally induced differences occur more frequently in mammals than had been realized. Young mammals may pick up crucial information from their mothers about when to wean themselves and how to develop afterwards on the basis of cues that they pick up from their nursing mothers. For instance, in the experiment on domestic cats, which I have already mentioned, kittens of rationed mothers developed quite differently from those of mothers given *ad libitum* food, playing much more in the weeks after weaning as if they were preparing for an earlier break-up of the family group than the kittens growing up in a nutritionally rich environment.

The process of weaning in mammals is not happily explained in terms of conflicts of interest that inevitably lead to squabbling. From a behavioural standpoint, the interplay between parent and offspring is much more dynamic than was conceived by the sociobiologists. The mother has to balance the maintenance of her body condition, easily debilitated by energetically costly lactation, against responding sensitively to the needs of current offspring. If the current offspring lag behind in development, the mother may increase her reproductive success if she extends parental care.

For its part, each offspring has to balance demanding maximum resources and attention from its mother up to the last moment that she is prepared to feed it against being sensitive to its mother's state. The young may have to pay attention to the condition of the mother because of the need to take into account both the immediate effects of maternal care on survival but also the post-weaning contributions of the mother. Moreover, to adopt a phenotype that is appropriate to the environment into which they will have to fend for themselves, the young may need to respond to information provided by the mother.

The mother and her offspring are unlikely to have perfect knowledge of each other either initially or during development. Therefore, each needs to monitor its own and the other's often rapidly changing states.

Conclusion

In this chapter I have tried to sketch the pendulum swings of biologists' thinking about behavioural development and communication over the last twenty years. Despite the swings backwards and forwards, the issues are starting to be resolved. A satisfying aspect of the modern systems approaches to behavioural development is that relatively simple conditional rules are able to generate the behavioural diversity observed in practice. Many features of such systems are necessarily intrinsic, in the sense that they have to be present if an appropriate response to variable external conditions is to be made. This is not to deny that such features have to develop. No integrated component of the nervous system springs fully armed out of the genes and, it must be remembered, the development of such components may be severely disrupted by departures from the conditions that were present in the environment of evolutionary adaptedness.

Intrinsic rules for communication, like everything else, may themselves be changed by higher-order rules. This feature of ontogeny has important implications for the way we think. No simple or even sensible correspondence can be found between the behaviour of a complex system and the conditions that started off the developmental process. The processes of change should not be likened to the placing of one brick upon another.

The work on behavioural development in animals is relevant to the interplay between the human child and its parents because it challenges us to look at the dynamics of ontogeny. What are the consequences when the relationship is abnormal? The non-linearities in the processes may generate discontinuities. As a result, the effects of events at one stage may have a profound influence on those at the next, even though the dynamics may be such that little or no correlation is found between what an individual does at one stage and what it does later in its life (Hinde and Bateson, 1984).

A central part of my argument is that, commonly, animal signals are reliable. The modern position on the biology of communication is helpful in as much as it buttresses the view that frequently the exchanges are cooperative rather than manipulative. That is important when looking for the connections between the work on animals and that on the reciprocity between parent and child in humans. The close monitoring of the other by parent and offspring in the pre-weaning period in mammals also has important implications for the study of our own species. Biology has a useful contribution to make in suggesting that the child's subsequent developmental path may be induced by parental behaviour. On this view, we should not treat individual differences as variation around a typical pattern of human development. Nor should we treat deviations as being necessarily pathological. Rather, the differences represent the most appropriate pathway for that individual and information about which pathway to take comes from the parents.

Acknowledgements
I am grateful to Stein Bråten for bringing together such an interesting group of scientists at the original meeting in Oslo. Colwyn Trevarthen very kindly read an earlier version of my chapter; we did not always agree but he was invariably stimulating.

CHAPTER 11

Social-experiential contributions to imitation and emotion in chimpanzees

Kim A. Bard

Introduction

This chapter concerns the communicative competence of newborn chimpanzees. It was with the knowledge garnered from studies of intersubjectivity (e.g. Trevarthen, 1979a) and early preverbal communication (e.g. Bullowa, 1979) that I began my investigations of newborn chimpanzees. I wondered if the type of emotional communication so elegantly described in these studies existed between newborn chimpanzees and adults. If so, it would highlight the broad importance of emotional communication in evolution and de-emphasize the exclusive nature of the link between intersubjectivity and human language. Emotional communicative exchanges have been observed between newborn chimpanzees and their mothers (Bard, 1994a, 1995; Plooij, 1984). I designed studies to compare the extent of similarities and differences in chimpanzee and human emotional communication and intersubjectivity.

The comparative perspective

The investigation of chimpanzee infants is important to further our knowledge of the evolutionary and developmental foundations of brain and behaviour relations. Can the cross-species study of similar capacities at birth reveal significant comparative relations between behavioural flexibility and plasticity in cortical development? Are similar developmental mechanisms responsible for changes in behaviour across primate species? Many questions remain unanswered with respect to the extent of similarity in behavioural and brain capacities. Chimpanzees, in particular among primate species, are comparable to humans in the realms of extended pre-adult development (e.g. Bruner, 1972; van Lawick-Goodall, 1968a, b), communication and language skills (e.g. Gardner and Gardner, 1989; Hayes and

Hayes, 1951; Plooij, 1979; Premack, 1972; Savage-Rumbaugh *et al.*, 1978), cognitive skills (e.g. Mathieu and Bergeron, 1981), and behavioural performance (e.g. Boesch and Boesch, 1989; Gallup, 1970; Plooij, 1984; Rijt-Plooij and Plooij, 1987). Although caution is advised in over-generalizations based on parallels in performance, there is no doubt that chimpanzees and humans are close evolutionary relatives (e.g. King and Wilson, 1975).

Newborn chimpanzees, in many respects, are indistinguishable from newborn humans; both are unable to support their own weight by clinging (Bard, 1995; van Lawick-Goodall, 1968a, b; Jacobsen *et al.*, 1932; Plooij, 1984); both are equally helpless to survive without active cradling and nurturing by competent adults (Bard, 1994a; Rijt-Plooij and Plooij, 1987); both exhibit similar levels of neurobehavioural integrity as measured by the same tests (Bard *et al.*, 1992; Bard, 1994b; Hallock *et al.*, 1989; Redshaw, 1989); and both exhibit an ability to engage on an emotional communicative level with a social companion. Infancy research has revealed the social competence of the human newborn, reflecting an innate intersubjectivity (Trevarthen, 1979a, this volume). Infancy research with chimpanzees since the middle of the 1980s has provided a foundation for concluding that there are significant commonalities, in the ability of newborns to engage in face-to-face communication, to engage in social interactions, and to express emotions.

The human newborn is an active participant in even early face-to-face interactions which are the context in which both social skills and communication skills develop. The competence of the human newborn in the face-to-face context is evident when the infant alerts and brightens in the eyes and face (Brazelton, 1979), follows faces and voices, moves the body in synchrony with speech rhythms (Condon and Sander, 1974), imitates facial expressions, and even turns away and self-consoles when stimulation is excessive (Brazelton, 1973; Sammons, 1989; Tronick, 1989). Chimpanzee mothers spend some time engaged in face-to-face interactions with their infants, and moreover spend lots of time in communicative tactile games which typically are not accompanied by mutual eye gaze (Bard, 1994a; Rijt-Plooij and Plooij, 1987). Adult chimpanzees have abilities which include taking turns (de Waal, 1989), gestural and intentional communication (Fouts *et al.*, 1982; Gardner and Gardner, 1989; Leavens *et al.*, 1996), and use of natural and artificial symbol systems (Premack, 1972; Savage-Rumbaugh *et al.*, 1978). It is reasonable to look for the developmental foundation of these capacities and to expect to find commonalities between species.

Emotional expression

We know very little about emotional development in chimpanzees. We do know that *adult* chimpanzees exhibit a wide range of emotional expressions: they laugh when playing, scream with excitement, and convey distress with unmistakable facial and vocal expressions. According to Goodall (1986; van Lawick-Goodall 1968a, b), communicative expressions exist in 1-year-old chimpanzee infants but we know very little about the ontogeny of emotional expression in chimpanzees. In order to enter into a communicative system, it is required that an individual have behaviours that can assume communicative meanings. This applies whether the individual is a human newborn, a two-word-speaking toddler or a chimpanzee newborn. Meaningful behaviours can develop from the most basic elements of neonatal behaviour, such as crying and alert attention.

With human-based assessments as a tool, I began to study the capacity of newborn chimpanzees to engage in meaningful behavioural exchanges. I have conducted normative studies of chimpanzee development and documented the performance of over fifty newborns on the Brazelton Neonatal Behavioral Assessment Scale NBAS (e.g. Bard *et al.*, 1992). The NBAS is perhaps the most widely used evaluative technique for human newborns and, because we use the exact same procedures, we can compare the behavioural performance of newborn chimpanzees to that of newborn humans. The NBAS has provided information on the capacities of newborn chimpanzees and their emotional expressions, and in fact provided the impetus for investigating neonatal imitation. During administration of the NBAS, we found newborn chimpanzees exhibited a variety of species-typical facial and vocal expressions that carried emotional meaning easily interpretable to human examiners.

From infancy research, we know that human neonates express interest, pleasure, surprise, disgust, sadness and crying (e.g. Field *et al.*, 1984; Oster and Ekman, 1978). Moreover, we know the types of stimuli that facilitate the expression of each of these emotions. Similar descriptions of emotional expression for neonatal chimpanzees, and the contexts in which they occur, are the primary goals of this chapter.

Approach

Subjects

Between January 1987 and July 1993, forty-six chimpanzee neonates (*Pan troglodytes*) were placed in the nursery of the Yerkes Regional

Primate Research Center of Emory University. Chimpanzee infants at the Yerkes Center remain with their biological mother provided that her care is adequate. Although most chimpanzees exhibit competent social and reproductive behaviours, some adult females are not competent mothers (Bard, 1994a, 1995; Rogers and Davenport, 1970). Specifically, they lack sufficient behavioural skills to care for their infants, such as picking up the infant, providing support and allowing for adequate nursing. Additional skills evident in mothers with good maternal competence include enjoyment, responsiveness and mutual eye gaze (Bard, 1994a). It is only in those cases when the mother does *not* have sufficient maternal skills that newborn chimpanzees are placed in the nursery. Many of these mothers do not touch the baby or handle the baby in any way. The assessments of these infants after they are placed in the nursery reveal that they are healthy and normal as evaluated by veterinarians and behavioural scientists specializing in newborn chimpanzees.

Thirty-four of the neonates that were placed in the nursery at birth are the subjects of this study. The other twelve neonates, from the initial group of forty-six, remained with their biological mothers as their mothers initially exhibited adequate maternal care. However, with time, the mothers began to show less and less competency in caring for their infants, so these infants were placed in the nursery days or weeks after birth (Bard, 1994a). Data from these twelve neonates may not accurately reflect age of onset due to time spent with mother, so they are not included in these analyses.

Settings

Standard care: Twenty-one neonates (eleven males and ten females) were given standard nursery care which consisted of exposure to humans as caregivers with minimal nurturing of communicative interactions. The philosophy was that species-typical behaviours would develop through exposure to conspecific peers. The chimpanzee neonates remained in an incubator except for the scheduled times when a bottle was given and their nappies changed. During these times, the human caretaker wore a blue face mask and clean uniform of a solid white colour. The infants might remain swaddled during feedings (i.e., not allowed to cling to the caretaker). The caretaker monitored the amount that the infant drank and the health status as reflected in muscle tone, infant behavioural state, etc. but did not necessarily interact with the infant. In fact, the infant was often laid on the back looking at the ceiling while drinking from a bottle, minimizing the amount of time the infant and the caretaker were in a face-to-face position. Note that infants are placed in contact with other chimpanzee infants as soon as possible, as early as 30 days of age. These are not isolation-raised chimpanzees but rather peer-raised chimpanzees.

Responsive care: Sixteen neonates (eight males and eight females) were given responsive care which consisted of moderate exposure to humans as caregivers but the humans nurtured species-typical chimpanzee behaviour. In the enriched chimpanzee social communicative experimental setting, the chimpanzees were given physical contact with a human research assistant specifically trained in chimpanzee-style parenting. Responsive care was given for four hours per day, five days per week. The protocol was designed for an adult human to provide the emotional and physical needs of a chimpanzee infant with the goal to nurture species-typical chimpanzee development (Bard and Gardner, 1996; Veira and Bard, 1994). The caregiver's face was visible and responsive emotional expressions were given in chimpanzee communicative style (as described in van Lawick-Goodall, 1968). The newborns were exposed to sights, sounds and smells of chimpanzees of all ages. Physical contact with other chimpanzees, however, was limited to other infants and juveniles, those considered safe for newborn chimpanzees (i.e. no contact with adolescent or adult chimpanzees, owing to safety considerations for human and newborn). The infant was supported while in a vertical position, encouraged to cling and encouraged to look at others rather than the chimpanzee-style parent. Note that this setting was part of a research project designed to enhance competence, well-being and the development of species-typical chimpanzee behaviour in chimpanzees raised in a nursery setting (for more details see Bard, 1996).

Procedures

All subjects were assessed with the Brazelton Neonatal Behavioral Assessment Scale (NBAS: Brazelton, 1984) beginning as early as 36 hours after placement in the nursery and continuing every other day through the neonatal period (Bard *et al.*, 1992; Bard, 1994b). During the NBAS assessments descriptive notes were taken, documenting the sequence of items and behavioural responses including facial expressions and vocalizations. In addition, four assessments were videotaped, the first test, usually day 2, day 14, day 29, and the last test at week 12. The NBAS test is semi-structured so that many items are given in a fixed order although some are given when the infant is in the appropriate behavioural state (especially for Orientation items). The typical recommended order is habituation, uncover, reflexes of the feet and hands, inanimate orientation, pull-to-sit, stand, reflexive

Table 11.1 *Facial and vocal expressions emitted by young chimpanzees: age of onset (number of subjects)*

Expressions	Standard care (21)	Responsive care (16)	Total (37)
Smile	10.9 (21)	8.7 (16)	11.0 (37)
Greeting	5.5 (14)	8.5 (15)	7.0 (29)
Pout	17.0 (14)	16.9 (10)	17.0 (24)
Fuss	3.3 (21)	3.6 (16)	3.5 (37)
Scream face	15.0 (16)	13.0 (13)	14.1 (29)
Cry	5.3 (21)	5.4 (16)	5.3 (37)
Anger*	24.0 (3)	20.3 (14)	21.0 (17)
Threat bark	27.8 (6)	43.8 (6)	35.8 (12)
Alarm call	14.5 (2)	20.8 (6)	19.3 (8)
Effort grunt*	16.1 (16)	11.3 (16)	13.7 (32)
Laughter	37.8 (18)	34.7 (12)	36.6 (30)
Tongue click**	14.6 (13)	22.3 (7)	17.3 (20)
First Test Day	2.6	3.0	

Note: * Group difference in number of subjects
** Group difference in age of onset

walk, place, incurvation, prone, crawl, glabella, tonic deviation of the head and eyes (i.e. spin), animate orientation items, defensive reaction, tonic neck reflex (TNR), and Moro reflex (Brazelton, 1984).

The age of onset for each expression was recorded for each chimpanzee. T-tests were conducted to compare the mean age of onset for each group. Chi-square tests were conducted to determine whether the distributions of individuals who emitted an expression differed between groups. Prototypic contexts were defined in terms of the most frequently occurring cluster of NBAS behaviour associated with the first occurrence of each expression.

Results

Three expressions were found to occur in every infant chimpanzee: smile, fuss and cry. Four additional expressions occurred in most of the subjects: greeting, scream face with no vocalization, effort grunts and laughter. Three expressions were used by more than half the chimpanzees in appropriate contexts: pout face with no vocalization, mad face and tongue clicks. The remaining vocalizations of threat bark and alarm, although present in a small proportion of subjects, did not occur in an appropriate context. The remainder of this section is devoted to presentation of comparisons between rearing groups (Table 11.1).

Fig. 11.1 Julie, a 1-year-old infant chimpanzee, smiles while playing with Arthur, who is 4 years old, as part of the responsive care program.

All chimpanzees smiled. The average age of onset was 10 days; some individuals smiled on the first test, at 2 or 3 days of age, whereas some chimpanzees smiled, during the NBAS, for the first time at 17 days of age. Fig. 11.1 illustrates a prototypic chimpanzee smile. In addition, we found that chimpanzees smiled during the part of the NBAS exam concerned with orientation (Fig. 11.2). Smiles also occurred frequently with the pull-to-sit item as the infants attained a vertical posture for the first time in the NBAS exam and during play throughout the test.

Rearing environment influenced the frequency of smiling. The number of smiles during the NBAS exam is plotted separately for males and females, and for standard care compared with responsive care at 2 and 30 days of age (Fig. 11.3: significant rearing environment by gender interaction, $F(1,30) = 7.33$, $p < .01$). In standard care, females smiled significantly more often than males. But under responsive care, males and females smiled equally often, and the level was intermediate between the standard care levels. Providing care that was responsive to each individual's needs, in this case, negated the sex difference in smiling.

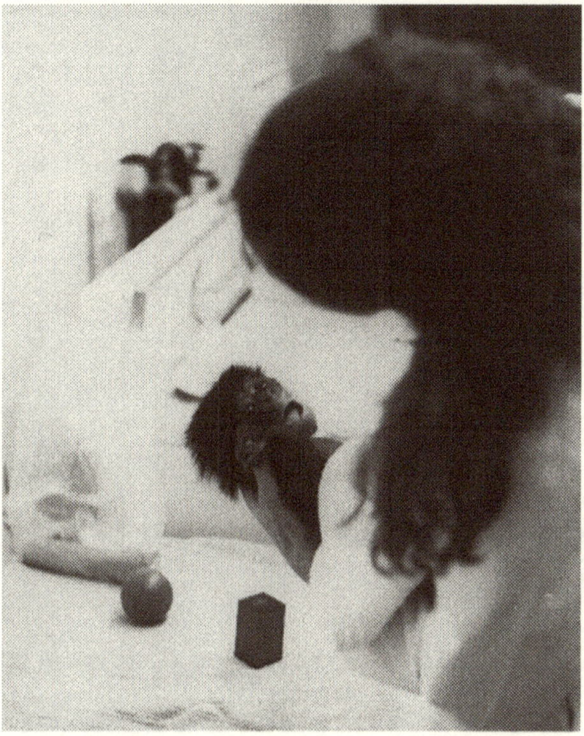

Fig. 11.2 Carole, a standard care infant, smiled when she was 15 days of age, as she followed the examiner's animated and talking face during orientation

A greeting is a friendly vocalization, typically given by chimpanzees when they meet each other after a period of time apart (Goodall, 1986). In other words, a greeting is the equivalent of saying 'hello'. Twenty-nine out of the thirty-seven of chimpanzee subjects expressed a greeting, typically before the end of the first week of life (range 2 to 22 days).

Greetings, even in the neonatal period, occurred in the appropriate context of social interactions. Neonates in both groups first greeted with orientation items (particularly human animate auditory), pull-to-sit (which brings the neonate to a sitting position facing the examiner), and at the camera or camera person when being filmed. Chimpanzees given responsive care, which emphasizes species-typical caregiving, were more likely to emit greeting vocalizations and standard care infants were less likely to emit greetings in the first 30 days of life

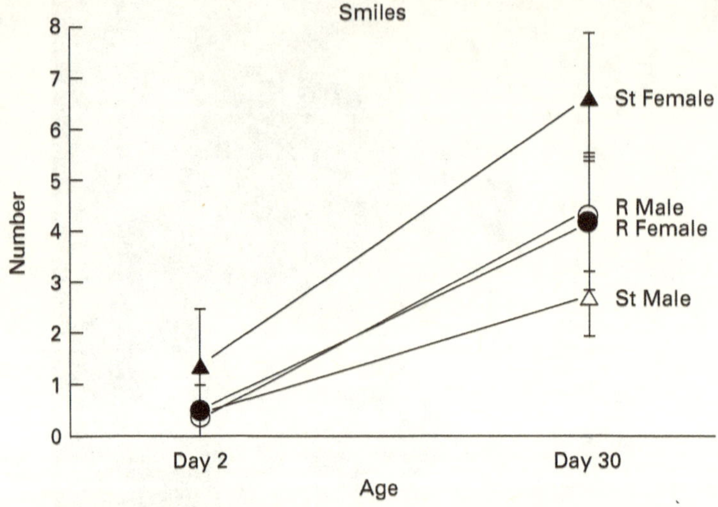

Fig. 11.3 Number of smiles in newborn female and male chimpanzees reared in two environments

compared to the number expected by chance ($Chi^2(1) = 5.17$, $p < .05$; Fisher's exact probability = .048).

Mild distress or fussiness was evident in all chimpanzee neonates. Fig. 11.4 illustrates a chimpanzee's pout, which is the facial expression associated with mild distress. Twenty-four of the thirty-seven subjects exhibited mild distress, with the facial expression of a pout without vocal fussiness. Pout was observed to occur at 17 days of age, on the average, in subjects of both rearing groups (range 2 to 56 days). Neonates in both groups showed a pout face for the first time with the aversive reflexive items of the Brazelton (i.e. spin and Moro), and sometimes during orientation items when the infants were not grasping the examiner. Some of the standard care neonates initially showed this expression during the pull-to-sit and defensive reaction as well, while some of the responsive care neonates made a pout face when they were repositioned. In contrast, fussiness consisted of a pout face with vocalized hoos and whimpers. Fussiness, in human and chimpanzee neonates, is often accompanied by considerable motor activity.

There were no rearing effects on the age of onset or number of subjects expressing fussiness. Fussiness was exhibited in the first NBAS test, when the chimpanzees were 2 or 3 days of age (range 1 to 11 days). Fussiness occurred predictably and most often when chimpanzee neonates were laid down on their back. Distress vocalizations

Fig. 11.4 Newborn chimpanzees exhibit mild distress with a pout and no vocalization

occurred with repositioning of the neonate and during the aversive items.

Moderate to extreme distress in neonates is expressed by crying. Fig. 11.5 illustrates the facial and motoric components of a crying chimpanzee.

A scream face without a vocalization occurred in twenty-nine of the thirty-seven subjects at 14 days of age, on the average (range 2 to 64 days). The responsive care neonates exhibited scream faces for the first time during some of the aversive items, e.g. spin, prone, Moro, but most often with tonic neck reflex (TNR). The standard care neonates also exhibited scream faces for the first time during aversive items, particularly spin, TNR and defensive reaction, but most often during Moro. A cry was defined as a scream face with vocalizations. Chimpanzee cries are more piercing than the typical human cry. Nursery-reared chimpanzees cry less often, and for shorter durations, than do human neonates during the NBAS exam (Bard, 1994b). On the average, chimpanzees cry on the second test, that is, 5 days of age. There are individual differences, of course, as in the case of one individual who did not cry during a NBAS exam until she was 21 days of age.

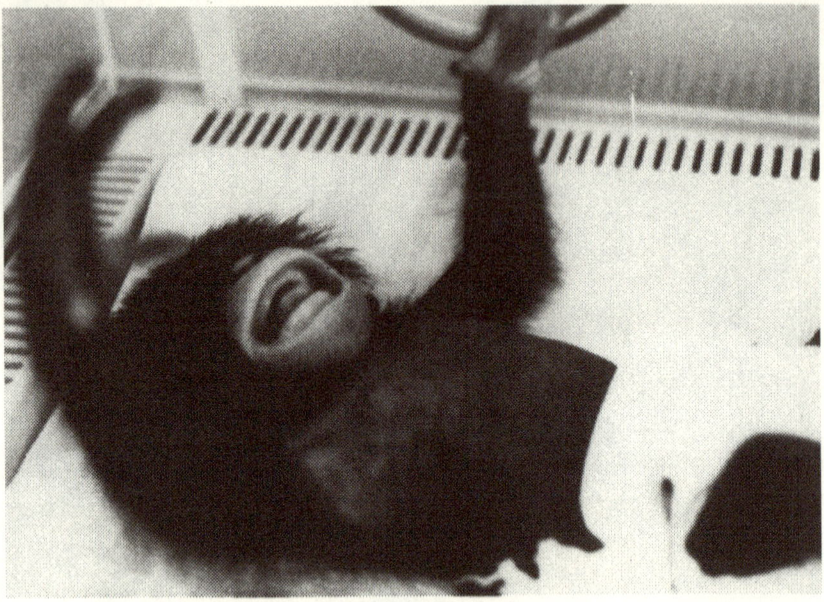

Fig. 11.5 Newborn chimpanzees exhibit crying with facial, vocal and motoric components

Chimpanzees cry when they are laid down on their back, or during the most intrusive assessment of reflexes (the tonic neck reflex, defensive reaction, or the Moro) which occur at the end of the NBAS exam and sometimes owing to repositioning of the infant while in the examiner's arms. The Moro is elicited by a sudden lack of support to the head. Human newborns almost always cry when these reflexes are elicited either by the paediatrician or during the NBAS exam. There were no rearing effects on the age of onset or number of subjects who cried or exhibited a scream face without distress vocalization.

On occasion, neonates may show anger, with what is called a mad face. The neonatal version of a mad face is similar to the facial expression of anger in adults. Anger is most evident in the bulged upper and bulged lower lips, nicely illustrated by Rosemary, a responsive care infant (Fig. 11.6).

We observed anger in only three of the twenty-one standard care chimpanzees, but in fourteen of the sixteen behavioural intervention chimpanzees ($Chi^2(1) = 19.3$, $p < .01$). We believe that this difference reflects the expectation formed as early as the first weeks of life: that

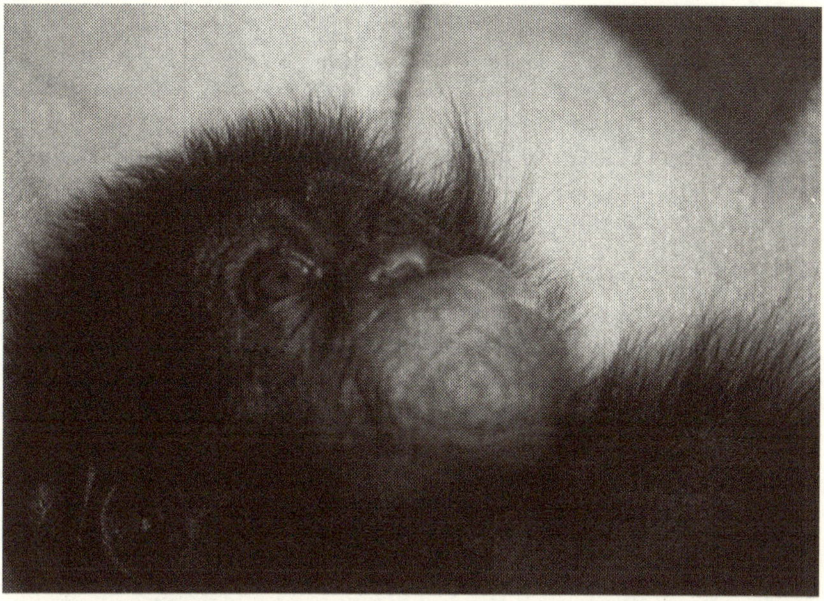

Fig. 11.6 Rosemary, a responsive care newborn chimpanzee, exhibits anger with a mad face

standard care infants must cope by themselves whereas responsive care infants expect others, especially when they are present, to facilitate.

When motor performance is being assessed, chimpanzees typically fuss. But responsive care infants express anger, evident in the mad-face facial expression and in the jerky muscle movements of the arms and legs. Anger was expressed during different contexts of NBAS (i.e. orientation, defensive reaction, asymmetric tonic neck reflex), but what was common to the contexts in which expression of anger was observed was that the infant was out of physical contact with the examiner but in imminent distress, and the examiner was not yet engaged in active consoling efforts.

With expenditure of physical energy, thirty-two of the thirty-seven chimpanzees exhibited 'effort grunts'. Effort grunts are given on the items which involved physical exertion. On the defensive reaction, when a cloth is placed lightly covering the face, the infant typically swipes and attempts to grasp at the cloth trying to remove it. Other items of the motor cluster of the NBAS exam, such as assessment of muscle tone in the prone position or assessment of range of movement while on the back and assessments of reflexes such as passive tone, tonic neck reflex, crawl, or Moro were often accompanied by sounds of physical effort. Three-quarters of the standard care infants emitted effort grunts compared with 100% of the responsive care infants (Fisher's exact probability = .047). Increasing the physical activity of neonates, part of responsive care, may begin a positive feedback loop of increasing their physical energy and thereby increasing their likelihood of emitting effort grunts.

Tongue clicks were recorded, not really as emotional expressions, but either as early indications of grooming vocalizations or as potentially imitative responses. They were almost always first exhibited in response to chimpanzee grooming sounds made by the experimenter during orientation. They also occurred for the first time with less frequency during the human auditory items. A significant group difference was found in age of onset ($t = 2.56$, $p < .02$): standard care infants exhibited tongue clicks at an earlier age than did responsive care infants. There was no rearing group difference in number of subjects: approximately 50% of the subjects in each rearing group emitted tongue clicks.

Threat and alarm are two vocal expressions which are exhibited by some infant chimpanzees. A threat bark sounds like a cough, whereas an alarm call is a high-pitched sound. In very young chimpanzees, they are emitted in an inappropriate context, or in an inappropriate combination with other emotional expressions. On occasion, we hear a neonatal chimpanzee emit a single alarm call or a threat bark when really a greeting would have been more appropriate. Only twelve chimpanzees emitted a threat bark, at 36 days of age on the average, and only eight chimpanzees emitted an alarm, at 19 days of age on the average. Threat barks were emitted most often for the first time when the neonate was being repositioned. However, some responsive care neonates first threat barked to a rattle or a chimp vocalization, while some standard care neonates first threat barked to a ball or during assessment of passive tone. Alarm calls were exhibited for the first time by both groups in response to sounds, either sounds that the experimenter made or manipulated (i.e. a rattle) during orientation, or in response to an external noise. There were no rearing effects and no gender differences in onset of threat or alarm, or in the number of subjects who emitted a threat bark or alarm call.

Chimpanzees laugh, when tickled, when playing and during games. Laughter of infants is *very* soft and very *breathy*. During the NBAS assessments, we were surprised to find chimpanzees smiling. We certainly did not expect to hear them laugh. But, we found that thirty of thirty-seven chimpanzees laughed, typically when they were

37 days old (range 10 to 77 days). Laughter occurred during social interactions, typically in the context of assessing orientation. Chimpanzees all tended to laugh for the first time in response to an orientation item in which the neonate sees and hears the experimenter making chimpanzee grooming sounds. Tactile stimulation such as tickles or incidental touches elicited laughter in many cases. During social interactions when infant chimpanzees were 12 weeks of age, the examiner and the infant interact, and then the examiner is ready to move on. Many times, the infant prolongs the social interaction by reaching a hand to the examiner while smiling. Clearly, young chimpanzees engage socially with the examiners, and clearly the interactions are enjoyable as the infants smile and laugh.

Discussion of results

In summary, a variety of facial and vocal expressions are exhibited by neonatal chimps during administration of the NBAS. Four different facial expressions and eight different vocalizations were exhibited by at least some of the neonates in both the standard care and responsive care groups. For both groups, positive emotional expressions (greeting, laughter, tongue click and smile) were most often exhibited for the first time by the neonates during administration of orientation items, touch or play, and the motor item of pull-to-sit. Negative emotional expressions for both groups (threat bark, mad face, pout face, scream, scream face and distress vocalizations) were most often exhibited for the first time during repositioning of the neonate and administration of aversive items. Differences with regard to the first day in which the expression was exhibited, how many of the neonates exhibited an expression, or the context under which an expression was exhibited occurred between groups with some, but not all, of the expressions. Differences, where they occurred, were sporadic, and did not seem to indicate overall that neonates from either group were more or less advanced with regard to emotional expression.

There are three conclusions we can make about emotions. Neonatal chimpanzees express the emotions of happiness, distress, fear and anger. Positive emotions of happiness are expressed by the behaviours of smiling and laughter, as well as by vocal greetings. Neonatal chimpanzees express the emotions of sadness and distress, as seen in pouts, fussiness and crying.

All of the emotional expressions that occur in nursery-reared chimpanzees also occur in chimpanzee infants raised by their biological mothers (Bard, 1994a, b, c; Plooij, 1984; van Lawick-Goodall,

Fig. 11.7 Mother-reared chimpanzee infants smile when they are tickled

1968a, b). For instance, mother-reared chimpanzee infants smile when they are tickled (Fig. 11.7). In infants raised by their mother, these emotional expressions are more difficult to see.

We have not yet documented the first occurrence of emotional expressions in mother-reared neonatal chimpanzees, but we have the data comparing emotional development of two groups of nursery-reared chimpanzees. There were some differences in emotional expression which appeared to be associated with differences in the two environments. Both rearing environments are considered to be within the range of acceptable rearing environments. Additionally, the early rearing environment appears to affect males and females differently. At this point we are unable to conclude that there are any long-term consequences in emotional development associated with differential rearing. Preliminary data, however, from another study in my laboratory, indicate that if the early rearing environment is extremely stressful, then there are long-term and negative consequences in terms of emotional reactivity and coping (Bard and Gardner, 1996).

Our second conclusion is that the emotional expressions that we found in neonatal chimpanzees are similar, both in form and in emotional tone, to those found in adult chimpanzees. In addition, most emotions are expressed in the same context and in response to the same type of stimuli for both neonates and adults. It seems, however, that further learning and experience are required in order for infant chimpanzees to use alarm calls and threats in the appropriate situations.

Finally, the emotional tone, or quality of expression in neonatal chimpanzees is strikingly similar to the emotional tone of expressions found in human neonates. In fact, many of the same NBAS items were responded to with the same emotional expression by both chimpanzee and human newborns (e.g. Field *et al.*, 1982).

Discussion

Is primary intersubjectivity part of our primate heritage or is it a capacity unique to the human species? Is a communicative environment required for primary intersubjectivity? Newborn behavioural capacities within the social communicative realms are comparable in human and chimpanzee. Infants engage with primary caregivers to express emotion, to communicate during social interactions and to engage socially with another individual.

Neonatal imitation may provide the opportunity to engage in primary intersubjectivity. A recent study suggests that some chimpanzee newborns are able to imitate human facial models of tongue protrusions, mouth openings and a series of three tongue clicks (Bard and Russell, in press). Although face-to-face interactions do occur between neonatal chimpanzees and their biological mothers, these events are not actively encouraged or prolonged by the chimpanzee mother as they are by human caregivers (Bard, 1994b).

Emotional expression and the interpersonal communication of emotion are essential components of primary intersubjectivity. The evidence presented in this chapter suggests that chimpanzee newborns are responding emotionally in a very similar manner to human newborns, demonstrating positive vocal greetings and smiles in response to familiar faces and voices, and even expressing anger when social-emotional expectations are violated. That the chimpanzee emotional system develops in interaction with the social environment is evident even within the neonatal period, but the evidence is more compelling as development proceeds. In another study from my lab (Bard and Gardner, 1996), following up the current subjects later in the first year of life, we found emotional expressiveness was highly influenced by the emotional responsiveness of the environment. Chimpanzees that were raised under the most emotionally responsive conditions expressed the highest levels of positive emotions (e.g. happiness), and expressed the least fearfulness and tension. These group differences were evident beginning at 6 months for fearfulness and at 7 months for happiness, suggesting that there may be two different developmental mechanisms at play (i.e. approach and avoidance; see Davidson, 1993 for additional physiological and neuroanatomical evidence). Early socialization processes may directly influence the neuroanatomical bases of emotion and emotion regulation (e.g. Dawson, 1994b). An early exposure to an environment in which emotional responsivity is maximized seemed greatly to facilitate the development of an emotionally responsive temperament whereas early exposure to a stressful and unresponsive environment seemed to facilitate the development of a tense and fearful temperament.

Primary intersubjectivity develops through social and emotional communicative exchanges prior to the development of secondary intersubjectivity. A recent study provides evidence that the current chimpanzees, when they were between 1 and 3 years of age, engaged in social referencing as one form of secondary intersubjectivity (Russell *et al.*, 1997). Young chimpanzees seek information about novel objects from their caregivers through referential glances (gaze shifts between a novel object and the primary caregiver), and the emotional message that they receive influences their interaction with the objects (negative messages increase their avoidance of the object and positive messages influence their visual attention towards the object).

Early reports of imitation in human infants less than 3 days of age surprised developmental psychologists. The initial report documented the ability of neonates to match facial actions of tongue protrusion, mouth opening and lip protrusion (Meltzoff and Moore, 1977). Subsequently neonatal imitation was replicated in other laboratories (e.g. Maratos, 1982) and the phenomenon was extended to include facial expressions (Field *et al.*, 1982), head movements (e.g. Meltzoff and Moore, 1989) and some vocalizations (Kugiumutzakis, 1992b). Furthermore, neonatal imitation has been found to occur in many testing conditions (e.g. Maratos, 1982; Kaitz *et al.*, 1988; Kugiumutzakis, 1992a) which vary from those with rigid, standardized and non-interactive methodologies (e.g. Meltzoff and Moore, 1977) to those that emphasize the communicative context of parent–infant interactions (e.g. Kugiumutzakis, 1992a).

In contrast to early theories which attributed imitation solely to cognitive abilities (e.g. Piaget, 1945/1962), current emphasis places imitation within the social communicative framework (e.g. Bullowa, 1979; Kugiumutzakis, 1983; Meltzoff and Moore, 1992). Kugiumutzakis (this volume) advocates that neonatal imitation is the earliest form of communicative expression (e.g. Trevarthen, 1982a). The videotaped findings of the imitation of vocalizations in human infants 10 to 45 minutes after birth attest to the communicative effort that they are willing to invest in order to imitate (Kugiumutzakis, 1992a). Thus, Kugiumutzakis presents strong evidence that neonatal imitation is a result of an innate intersubjectivity. Intersubjectivity provides the innate basis of the intention to communicate which these researchers suggest is the function served by imitation (Trevarthen and Hubley, 1978:213).

In parallel with the shift in interpretation of imitation in human literature, there is a renewed consideration of social-communicative variables in demonstrations of imitation in non-human primates (e.g. Bard and Russell, in press). It has long been the contention of primatologists that chimpanzee intellect excels in its social application (e.g. Byrne and Whiten, 1988; de Waal, 1982; Jolly, 1976; Humphrey, 1976; van Lawick-Goodall, 1968a, b). In fact, the discovery of 'theory of mind' in chimpanzees by Premack and Woodruff (1978) sparked a new research area in child psychology (e.g. Baron-Cohen *et al.*, 1985; Whiten, 1991). Social-communicative experiences do not necessarily coincide with developing cognition, especially in laboratory chimpanzees; thus comparative investigations of the development of imitation and emotional communicative development are particularly important.

Some neonatal chimpanzees imitated facial actions of tongue protrusion, mouth opening and sound production, e.g. tongue clicks (Bard and Russell, in press). The presence of neonatal imitation in chimpanzees highlights the evolutionary origins of imitation. The presence of imitation in the neonatal period has been assumed to be indicative of an innate predisposition (Meltzoff and Moore, 1977; Trevarthen, 1979a). Evidence of imitation in neonatal chimpanzees, therefore, must be considered indicative of a predisposition for imitative learning in this species.

Currently, there is controversy concerning the influence of the human cultural environment on imitative learning in non-human primates (e.g. Bard, 1993; Boesch, 1993; Tomasello *et al.*, 1993). The argument follows that tutorials in a human-type communicative system are necessary for imitation, especially for the more sophisticated imitative performances evident in deferred imitation or imitation of tool use.

Some chimpanzee newborns seemed to imitate facial actions while attending to the examiner's animated face during the NBAS (Bard *et al.*, 1992). The facial act often matched both the adult's facial act and the examiner's emotional tone. During assessment of attention to sounds, both human and chimpanzee species-typical sounds, some infants produced sounds seemingly in imitation of the species-typical sound. The infants' sound production seemed to occur shortly after they had heard the species-typical sounds. Finally, after a new NBAS examiner conducted sessions in which she animated her face by protruding her tongue rather than opening her mouth which is what I did, the chimpanzee neonates began to emit tongue protrusions seemingly in response to the examiner's model.

Imitation of facial expressions by chimpanzee neonates represents a chimpanzee capacity to imitate that is similar to that of humans. Chimpanzees appeared more capable of imitating when tested in a communicative paradigm rather than a rigid format, which suggests that imitation serves a communicative function for chimpanzees as well. How this predisposition relates to later imitative capacity in chimpanzees is unknown. The evidence presented here suggests that social environment is important in the nurturing of imitative capacity in the child and the chimpanzee.

Social learning begins to exert an influence on development even within the newborn period (Bard, 1994c; Bard and Russell, in press). Differences in rearing environment relate to differences in emotional expressions and to differences in emotionally reactive interpretations of standard environmental events. Inborn temperamental characteristics interact with environmental consequences in the expression of both imitative and emotional responses.

We are still very unsure about how these early proclivities relate to later imitative capacity. Does imitation atrophy, like muscle tissue, if not regularly exercised? Does neonatal imitation need to be actively nurtured, through a social communication system, in order to develop further? Are *human* social communication systems the *only* type that supports the development of imitation? These are not the only questions about imitation that remain unanswered. Further experimental research will bring us closer to understanding imitation, and the functional mechanisms that underlie and support imitation, in human and non-human primates and in other animals.

Often the search for characteristics that are unique to the human species provides as much valuable information on commonalities as on differences. The demonstration of neonatal imitation in chimpanzees further challenges notions of unique human propensities. Future research efforts can explore the mechanisms which support the development of imitative capacity. There continues to be debate as to whether the same mechanism is responsible throughout development.

Chimpanzees can be productively utilized to investigate social communicative foundations for imitation and emotion.

Acknowledgements

Research supported in part by MH grants RR-00165, RR-03591, and RR-01658. Grateful appreciation is extended to Kathy Gardner, Kelly McDonald, Patricia Hebert and Connie Russell.

CHAPTER 12

Imitation: the contributions of priming and program-level copying

Richard W. Byrne

Until recent years, psychologists studying animals have generally regarded imitation as a low-effort mechanism for acquiring behaviours that might otherwise be laborious to acquire by trial-and-error learning. Imitation was assumed to be widespread in the animal kingdom, and to require no understanding, insight or reasoning abilities to practise. The 1980s and 1990s have seen a radical change in this view. It is now suspected that imitation is a difficult skill for animals, in the sense that it necessarily involves elaborate mental representations or complex transformation of information in the brain; further, reviewers have seriously doubted whether any non-humans can imitate (Byrne, 1994; Galef, 1988; Tomasello *et al.*, 1993; Visalberghi and Fragaszy, 1990; Whiten and Ham, 1992). Most of the traditionally accepted cases of animal imitation have proved vulnerable to re-interpretation in terms that do not involve imitation. Instead, the traditional associative learning mechanisms of behaviourist psychology, classical and operant conditioning, are seen as the means of learning, influenced by various social effects. Most direct experimental tests of animal imitation, designed to exclude associative learning, have produced failure. It has begun to seem a possibility that true imitation may be restricted to humans, and that perhaps the ability to imitate is a cognitive 'Rubicon' between human and non-human. In this climate, only a few experimental studies argue for animal imitation (Custance *et al.*, 1995; Hayes and Hayes, 1952; Heyes *et al.*, 1992; Palameta, 1989; Whiten *et al.*, 1996).

Both the theoretical reformulation and the new data have brought the views of comparative psychologists closer to the analysis normal in developmental psychology. Developmentalists have seldom doubted that imitation is a complex skill, and one that is important in the child's growing understanding of the world and how to operate with it (Piaget, 1945/1962). From this perspective, it is unsurprising that animals should often fail to imitate. Even the operational definitions – the patterns of behaviour treated as diagnostic of imitation in experimental tests – have converged. In both fields, imitation has recently been identified by a significant divergence between two groups of subjects, following the opportunity to observe one of two possible actions exhibited by another individual, but in the absence of any reward contingent on the behaviour's performance (Galef, 1988; Heyes, 1993, for comparative psychology; Meltzoff and Moore, 1977 and this volume, Heimann, and Kugiumutzakis, both this volume, for developmental psychology). Each group watches a model do an action, and actions are different; if the groups diverge, with actions more frequently matching those of the model each one saw, imitation is claimed.

In this chapter I shall argue that the appearance of harmony between these disciplines is illusory, and that in fact similar-sounding definitions have captured radically different kinds of behaviour. I offer a theoretical synthesis in which the data, recently offered as evidence of imitation in non-humans, are treated as no more than the result of a cognitively simple process reliant on conditioning. In this view, what is 'special' about neonatal imitation in humans, and lacking in the superficially similar non-human results, is the computational complexity of the perspective transformation involved. However, there is another sort of imitation that is distinct in mechanism and function from what happens in neonatal imitation, or in most animal social learning. This behaviour, which for a convenient label I call 'program-level imitation', is closer to the everyday sense of imitation, and is a mechanism that seems to have evolved to enable rapid acquisition of complex novel skills. With the elaborate skills that mountain gorillas use for dealing with herbaceous plant foods as an example, I discuss what evidence is needed to detect program-level imitation in behaviour, and whether gorilla food preparation provides any.

A model of social learning as priming

Comparative psychology has apparently made more progress on what imitation is not than what it is. As can be seen in the reviews mentioned above, there is now a whole catalogue of mechanisms to 'explain away' animal actions that superficially look like imitation: local enhancement, stimulus enhancement, goal emulation, social facilitation, contagion, response facilitation and so on. In every case, genuine new learning occurs only by conditioning, just as in conventional animal learning, not as a direct result of observation. There seems to be a surplus of explanatory mechanisms that all serve the same purpose: that is, to bootstrap individual learning under social circumstances, producing results that casual observers are prone to interpret as imitation. In reality, I believe that all the important effects can be subsumed under a single idea, that of *priming* (Byrne, 1994). Moreover, priming proves to be powerful enough to incorporate some data currently claimed to imply imitation.

Consider an imaginary animal whose behaviour is governed by its *brain records*, each record representing an event in its world. There are three types of brain record, corresponding to *stimuli* (that is, environmental configurations that, by learning, can come to signal other stimuli or trigger responses), *responses* (that is, unitary actions in the animal's repertoire) and *goals*. These three categories of brain record, of course, deliberately reflect the theoretical entities of traditional animal learning theory, since the priming account is designed to complement this theory. However, I should stress that in doing so I do not wish to imply that every tenet of behaviourism is correct; indeed, the very idea of a 'brain record', an unobservable entity, is anathema to most behaviourists.

Now suppose that each brain record has an individual activity level[1] and that the relative activity of each affects the animal's actions. Stimuli with high activity levels are noticed more readily; responses with high activity levels are performed more frequently; goals with high activity levels tend to take precedence over others. Additionally, the animal is constructed such that, other things being equal, when it notices a conspecific gaining something valuable for survival, corresponding brain records will be 'primed' by having their activity levels increased.

First, consider how the priming affects brain records of the *stimuli* that surround the noticed event. These stimuli would include the location, any other things nearby, and the conspecific that has just gained the item. Automatically, the observer's attention will afterwards tend to be concentrated on these things, since their brain records are now primed. Most important for helping it learn, the animal will focus on the site of the reward and any associated objects. Once that happens, trial-and-error learning will automatically be much more efficient, and the animal will thus be more likely to learn the actions necessary for the reward than one that has not had the chance of observation. This will produce the phenomenon known as *stimulus enhancement* (Spence, 1937), believed to underlie much social learning in animals. The acid test to distinguish between stimulus enhancement and imitation is that the latter necessarily requires the observer to see the actions of the other animal. One example of the application of this test will illustrate the recent experimental approach to claims of animal imitation. In the 1940s and 1950s, the habit of tearing off the card caps of milk bottles spread among various species of birds in Britain, especially tits, *Paridae;* later, birds learnt to peck through the foil bottle tops that replaced the card ones. Careful collation of records showed that the habit spread from centres of dissemination (Fisher and Hinde, 1949), and it was presumed for many years that the birds learnt by imitation. However, Sherry and Galef (1984) showed in experiments that tits learnt just as quickly without ever seeing another bird dealing with the caps: finding opened milk bottles was sufficient to facilitate learning of the necessary trick, and so cause the habit to spread. This is now taken as a classic case of stimulus enhancement acting to channel attention onto the crucial location, the bottle top; once the bird is there, trial and error exploration with its natural repertoire of pecking and tearing actions is sufficient to allow efficient learning. Much social learning in animals is probably dependent on stimulus enhancement for its efficiency.

Different consequences would be expected when the sight of a conspecific achieving some result primes the brain record of that result, as a *goal*. Automatically, the observer would then be more likely to work towards that particular goal. This effect, another part of comparative psychology's repertoire of alternative mechanisms to true imitation, has been called *emulation*[2] (Tomasello, 1990; Whiten and Ham, 1992). The acid test between imitation and emulation is that the actions of the observed model are not matched by those of the observer, only the result achieved is the same. Emulation is perhaps most strikingly shown in the vocal 'imitation' of parrots and myna birds. The sounds copied by a bird are more or less physically identical in form to the source. This applies even in cases where, as with a myna bird's imitation of the exact formant structure of human speech, the mechanism of production is completely different (bird syrinx *versus* human supralaryngeal tract). Vocal imitation by birds has more similarities with a tape recorder than with imitation as practised by humans: it achieves the same result, but in a way utterly different from the original actions. Emulation has also been suggested to underlie chimpanzees' learning to use an object as a tool (Tomasello *et al.*, 1987), but this is controversial (Byrne and Russon, in press).

Finally, consider the effect of priming the brain record corresponding to the specific *response* that the observed animal was using. Automatically, the observer will be more likely to perform behaviour of the same type – and once the appropriate behaviour is made probable in this way, trial and error learning will be speeded (Byrne, 1994). Necessarily, this can only apply to actions already in the repertoire, since actions novel to it will not have brain records: the acid test between this *response facilitation* and imitation is whether new action patterns can be learnt by observation alone. A related tendency was suggested to exist by Thorpe under the name *contagion* (Thorpe, 1963). He wished to account for the strikingly synchronized responses of some animals, for instance the sudden flight and subsequent sharp wheeling of a flock of shore birds disturbed by a predator, as an adapted response inborn in individuals. Thorpe envisaged that animals are equipped by evolution with certain fixed connections between eliciting stimuli and fixed action patterns. In some cases, the eliciting stimulus and the action pattern may happen to be the same; for instance, the hard-wired response to seeing a conspecific suddenly take flight is to take flight. The response appears contagious, but the linkage is an adaptation resulting from natural selection and not a product of individual experience. In principle, contagion might account for the infant's tendency to copy facial expressions, 'neonatal imitation'. This is thought to function as a social mechanism, allowing the infant to identify the mother as 'like me' (Meltzoff and Gopnik, 1993), and increasing the concordance of mother and infant's behaviour may be a precursor to later conversation (see Trevarthen, this volume). If these social effects are important in development, contagious copying of a few maternal facial gestures may plausibly have evolved by natural selection. Since in contagion the linkage between eliciting stimuli and action patterns is hard-wired not computed, there would be no need for the infant to realize (as adults do) that the facial gestures look the same to others. However, this is only plausible as an explanation for a small number of actions, whose copying would routinely be beneficial for the individual's survival. Thus the range of gestures or sounds that the neonate can copy is crucial to the continuing debate on the mechanism of neonatal imitation: as the set of actions shown to be copied increases, the plausibility of contagion decreases (Anisfeld, 1991; Meltzoff, 1996; Kugiumutzakis, this volume). If neonatal imitation is not explicable by contagion, then it must involve a dramatic transformation from (another's) visual appearance to (the self's) muscle movements, a cognitively complex performance.

If stimulus enhancement, goal emulation and response facilitation all occurred together, the result would look impressively like imitation. An animal, seeing a conspecific doing a certain action at a certain place and so gaining a reward, would go to the same location and perform the same action, for the same reward. It should therefore be clear why it is that comparative psychologists believe that conditioning, channelled by social effects, is a powerful null hypothesis – against which they must pit any apparent evidence for imitation in animals. In certain circumstances, especially social ones, these mechanisms can undoubtedly cause patterns of behaviour that look very like imitation. The fact that these effects can all be unified under the single explanatory device of primed brain records demonstrates forcibly that all are 'simple', to be preferred as explanations (by Lloyd Morgan's canon) to claims of conceptually complex imitation.

Consequences for an understanding of imitation

Accepting the priming theory of social learning changes the criteria for identifying imitation, and brings into question the experimental evidence for imitation in animals. Consider what is the most obvious diagnostic test between response facilitation and imitation. Only responses in the existing repertoire can be primed, whereas imitation can enable *novel* behaviours to be learnt, without the contingent rewards necessary to condition trial-and-error learning. Novelty of action is necessary, though not sufficient, to identify imitation. However, as we have seen, the operational definition of imitation recently adopted in comparative psychology does not include any requirement of novelty. Instead, it looks for significant changes in frequency of responses already present or latent in the repertoire, after opportunities for observation but not conditioning.

Response facilitation can only operate on actions that look very much the same to actor and observer. However, the visual appearance of an action is often similar, whether an individual performs an action itself or watches another do it. For instance, Palameta found that pigeons shown another pigeon dealing with a covered food source in one of two ways were likely to use the same way themselves in a subsequent test. Birds that watched pecking through the paper cover tended to peck covers, whereas those that saw the cover torn off tended to tear covers off (Palameta, 1989; Palameta and Lefebvre, 1985). Pecking and tearing are normal pigeon behaviours, and appear similar in visual form whether done by the self or another, so response facilitation can account for these data. In addition to pigeons, this applies also to data from budgerigars (Dawson and Foss, 1965; Galef *et al.*, 1986) and chimpanzees (Whiten and Custance, 1996; Whiten *et al.*, 1996). Only in the recent experiments of Heyes is a significant perspective transformation incorporated, albeit a simple one, left for right (Heyes *et al.*, 1992). Rats watched a demonstrator rat push a hanging bar repeatedly either to left or right for food reward. They viewed from behind the bar, so their left was the demonstrator's right; nevertheless, when placed into the cage, they tended to push the bar in the 'correct' direction immediately (in fact, pushing in either direction was rewarded, so a positive result could not be caused by conditioning). Since this might have been a result of stimulus enhancement, towards the part of the cage to which the bar was swung, the swinging bar was then moved through a right angle before the observer rat was placed in the cage. This had no effect on the rat's tendency to push the bar in the same direction (left or right) as it had watched, apparently showing imitation. However, an alternative explanation emerges from asking how the rats might have oriented themselves when placed in the experimental compartment (Byrne and Tomasello, 1995). Presumably the hanging bar was a prominent landmark, especially given the stimulus enhancement towards the bar to be expected from the rats' prior observations. But if this was the rats' major landmark, they would have been disoriented when placed into the test cage: to be precise, disoriented by 90°. The rotated bar would thus seem to the rats to be in the same place (although the food tray appears moved), and only we as external observers realize that the rats are now pushing towards a different point in the cage. Observation of the rats' behaviour in the apparatus might help to resolve these dilemmas, but this was not made.

In sum, then, I suggest that the behaviours lumped as 'imitation' in recent comparative and developmental work are not the same. Social learning in animals has a utilitarian function, not a social one: to acquire novel adaptive responses to problems in the environment with minimal effort. None of the experimental evidence currently available is sufficient to demonstrate animal imitation. The problem is that recent experimental work has not insisted on novel behaviours. The behaviour observed can be accounted for by a cognitively simple mechanism, priming of responses already in the repertoire, in conjunction with individual learning by conditioning. Neonatal imitation is social in function, and cognitively complex (unless it is simply a matter of contagion). I shall go on to consider whether there is another sort of imitation, included in common-sense ideas of what imitation is and potentially useful in social learning, using the complex feeding behaviour of gorillas to illustrate the possibility.

Mountain gorilla food-processing

The behaviour of some animal species may indeed resemble that of the imaginary animals of learning theory, in which individuals respond to observable stimuli with unitary actions from their repertoire in pursuit of straightforward goals. With such species, identification of genuine imitation, as opposed to the results of socially primed individual learning, will be very difficult. Great apes, however, respond to problems with actions that are sometimes complex and certainly not unitary. Even defining the units of behaviour and cataloguing the complete repertoire is apparently very difficult in apes, to judge by the infrequency with which it is done. Paradoxically, the very complexity of great ape behaviour may make it easier to recognize imitation. Unfortunately, experimental work on animal imitation, even in great apes, has up to now used tasks for which simple actions are appropriate. To illustrate my point, then, I shall instead use observational data: the sophisticated food preparation skills of mountain gorillas.

Mountain gorillas inhabiting the Virunga mountains of Rwanda spend the greater part of each day feeding on herbaceous vegetation in lush meadows among montane forests. Their need for some special feeding techniques in dealing with these herbs can be seen from considering mountain gorilla ecology. Like humans, gorillas have simple stomachs. They cannot digest the large amounts of cellulose and lignin that a true leaf-eater, like a cow or a colobus monkey, can live on; nor can they neutralize the poisonous secondary compounds that protect many tropical leaves. Most populations of gorillas therefore, over the rest of the species' wide range, eat ripe fruit. Fruit contains abundant energy in the form of simple sugars, but it is low in protein and vitamins. Fruit-specialist great apes make up the nutrient deficiencies with a wide range of diet supplements, like insects, leaf tips, bark, flowers and fungi. In the Virungas, there are no ripe fruit, but the lush herbaceous vegetation contains several plants which, like salads, are rich in protein and other nutrients and lacking poisonous secondary compounds. The problem for the gorillas is that, unlike salads, these herbs are adapted to deter consumers; they are physically defended from being eaten. Nettle, *Laportea alatipes*, has painful stings, especially on stems, petioles and leaf-edges; celery, *Peucedanum linderi*, has a hard and woody outer case around the soft, pithy stem interior favoured by gorillas; thistle, *Carduus nyassanus*, is armed with strong spines; and even bedstraw, *Galium ruwenzoriense*, is densely covered in tiny hooks, primarily helping the plant to clamber over other vegetation but also making it very difficult to eat. Most mammals simply cannot deal with these problems except by the bacterial processes of the gut, so Virunga herbs are mainly eaten by antelopes, buffalo and elephant, whose specialized (or simply very large) guts can digest the whole plants. Gorillas, on the other hand, deal with the problems rather as humans might: by using skilled and complex manual processing to remove or neutralize the plant defences. Those four species of plants in fact make up 85% of mountain gorilla diet (Watts, 1984).

Complexity of technique can be illustrated by nettle-processing. Minimizing contact between the hands and the most sting-covered parts of the nettle, a skilled gorilla carries out the following sequence (Byrne and Byrne, 1993): (i) pulls a plant into range by the soft leaves at the spike tip; (ii) strips off the leaves with cone-shaped cupped hand, so that only leaf undersides contact the skin; (iii) tears off the protruding leaf petioles with rocking or twisting motion against the other hand; (iv) deftly extracts any dead leaf remains from the leaf-blade bundle; (v) folds the bundle over the thumb and holds it folded, so that leaf-edges are enclosed; and (vi) pops it into the mouth, avoiding lip contact; in addition, some parts of this sequence may be repeated on occasion. To graph the organization of manual actions for an animal using this sort of process, we devised a notation based on flow charts (see Fig. 12.1a). As inspection of this readily shows, multiple stages must be sequenced correctly; several stages require bimanual coordination; some parts of the process can be repeated till a criterion is reached (roughly speaking, 'enough food for a handful'); this means that portions of the process are treated as sub-routines, and these sub-routines can be either single actions, or quite long sequences. This level of complexity was found for all adult and juvenile animals when eating nettle, and indeed the techniques of all individuals are very similar (except that the whole process was mirror-reversed in about half the population).

Many species of animal are known to have some particularly remarkable skill, an adaptation developing under tight genetic channelling. This explanation is unlikely to apply in this case, for two reasons. The Virunga population of gorillas is the only one known to use the nettle technique – indeed, it would make no sense for most gorillas to be able to process nettle. Nettle is a temperate plant which gorillas only encounter above 3000m in Central African mountains. Secondly, the techniques mountain gorillas use for other plants are quite different. For instance, using the same flow-chart notation to represent bedstraw-processing (Fig. 12.1b) shows that most of the manual operations are quite different, as is the overall organization. Also, although both techniques are highly lateralized, precisely which hand is the 'dominant' one is here more obvious, since more of the process is unimanual and more of the fine-finger operations are carried out by the same hand. Nevertheless, the bedstraw technique is also a complex process showing organizational complexity, sub-routine structure and deftness. Rarer foods that are *not* defended tend to be processed in a much simpler way, but the processes for celery stem, thistle stem and thistle leaves are similarly individual but complex (Byrne and Byrne, 1991).

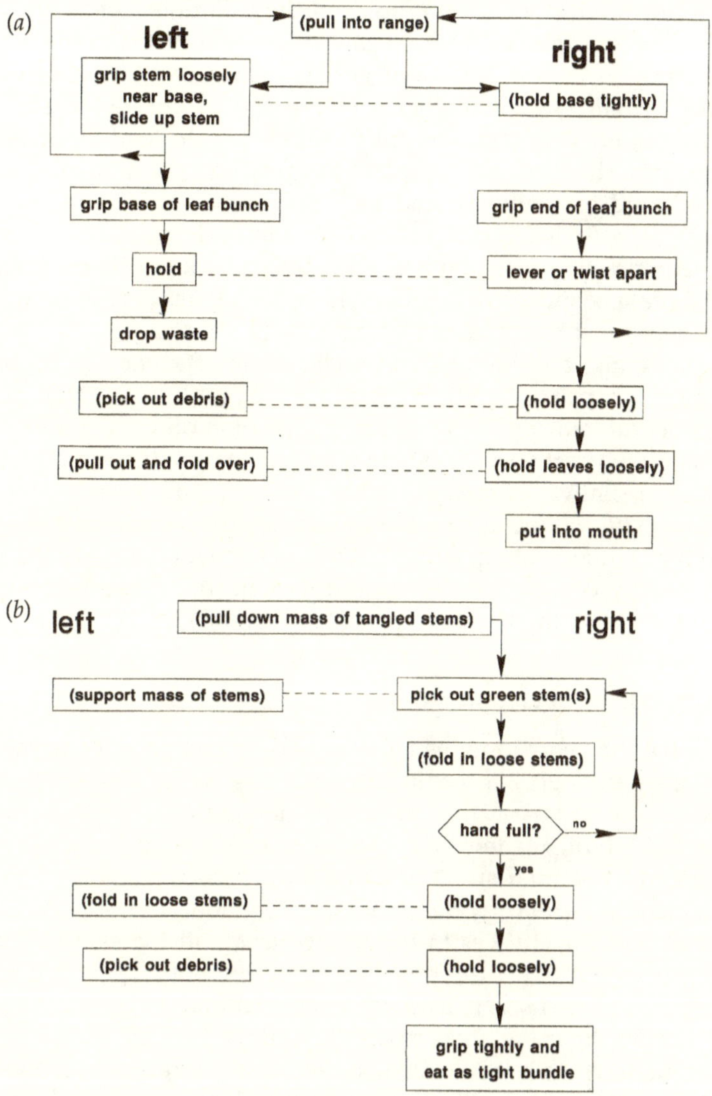

Fig. 12.1 Flow charts to describe the preparation of two plants to eat, as it is done by a mountain gorilla: (*a*) nettle *Laportea alatipes*; (*b*) bedstraw *Galium ruwenzoriense*. The process starts at the top and ends when a handful is put into the mouth; actions are shown in square boxes; most actions are highly lateralized, and left and right sides of the figure show where there are significant hand preferences; horizontal dotted lines show when the actions of the two hands must be accurately coordinated.

How might the more complex of the techniques used by mountain gorillas be acquired? There seems little doubt that learning what to eat is straightforward for infant gorillas, since they are showered with food remains by the mother from the first day of life. In addition, the priming effect of stimulus enhancement would tend to focus a young gorilla's attention on the plant-as-growing as a potential source of food, and emulation would help define the final goal – for nettle, a neat little folded bundle, with only the undersides of leaves visible. The interesting question becomes, how does a gorilla first acquire the elaborate sequence of coordinated actions that come in between? The answer must be consistent with two facts. After 3 years of age, the age of weaning, there is no further change in efficiency as measured by time to prepare a handful of food (Byrne and Byrne, 1991): techniques are learnt quickly. Second, for an infant mountain gorilla the only potential direct social influences on feeding are the mother, whom an infant usually accompanies when foraging, and the silverback leader male, who – alone among the rest of the group – tolerates infants close to him while feeding. Other individuals are intolerant of the presence of nearby conspecifics when feeding, and the dense herb vegetation means that animals are out of sight when only a few metres apart.

Acquisition of complex skills

Unlike the behaviours usually studied by comparative psychologists, when a new gorilla feeding technique is learnt it is not a matter of adding a unitary action to a limited repertoire. Instead, many acts must be built up into one particular logical structure, out of a vast range of potential structures (the term 'structure' is used to include sequential regularity, bimanual coordination, and sub-routine structure). The novelty lies in the *arrangement*, and the skill is as much to organize and structure some basic repertoire of actions into novel and complex patterns as to learn new basic actions.

Further, there is good reason to believe that the techniques learnt are hierarchically organized, rather than simple associative chains, because of their sub-routine structure (Byrne and Russon, in press). Portions of the processing sequence can be repeated until a criterion is reached, at which point the normal sequence is resumed; these portions can be of various lengths. This fluid resumption of an interrupted sequence shows that higher-level organization is present, enabling the gorilla to keep track of the point at which the (accumulative) sub-routine was entered and return to it (see Fig. 12.2). Other interruptions can be handled, in addition: if a piece of debris is noticed in the half-prepared bundle at any stage, it is removed with

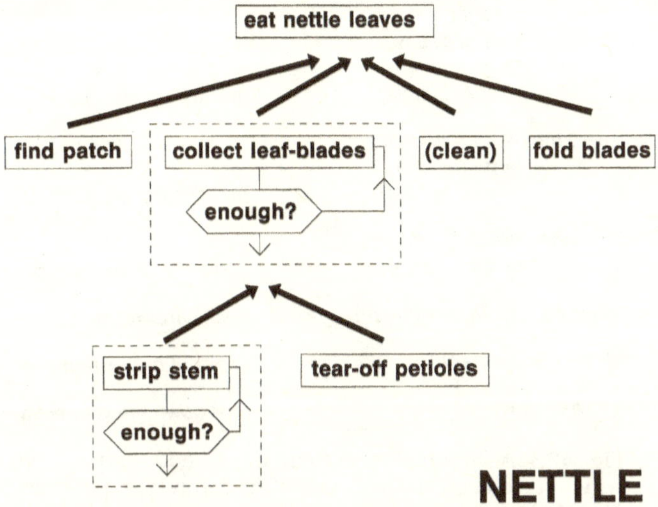

Fig. 12.2 Control diagram of a food preparation technique with hierarchical structure and two embedded feedback loops; this produces the process of nettle preparation shown in Fig. 12.1a

deft mouth-hand co-ordination, a sub-routine which is common to other leaf-processing programs (Fig. 12.2 shows only the point at which this operation is usually performed). If a gorilla is distracted by some social interaction, it will afterwards resume processing of the same bundle of food without losing track. 'Hierarchical organization' should not be understood to imply an organization in which control is necessarily always imposed from above (a rigidly top-down organization). It is highly likely that many decisions about manual actions are local ones, dependent on the precise detail of plant encountered. All that is meant is that the organization of goals and sub-goals is hierarchical. The sub-process working towards each sub-goal may well have considerable autonomy – there may be periods of 'heterarchical' control. Nor is it intended to mean that the organization of action is inflexible in structure, as might be expected from a conventional computer program or phrase-structure grammar. Instead, it is highly likely that gorilla processing techniques are so responsive to differences among food types that different hierarchical structures result on different occasions. Representation of the technique as a production system (see Fig. 12.3) captures this sensitivity nicely: as in the example mentioned of debris-cleaning, if a stage is unnecessary, the sub-process is never triggered.

With this background, we can return to the question of how several

1	*(bedstraw bundle tight free of debris, large enough, in neat bundle)*	=>	*(eat with shear bites)*
2	*(bedstraw bundle free of debris, large enough, in neat bundle)*	=>	*(roll against chin)*
3	*(bedstraw handful large enough, in neat bundle)*	=>	*(loosen grip and pick out debris)*
4	*(bedstraw handful large enough)*	=>	*(fold in trailing stems)*
5	*(bedstraw in easy reach)*	=>	*(pick out green stem, add to handful)*
6	*(bedstraw in view)*	=>	*(pull down mass of stems)*

Fig. 12.3 A production system for a food preparation technique which produces the process of bedstraw preparation shown in Fig. 12.1b

techniques of such complexity are acquired so rapidly. In particular, is acquisition aided by seeing the action-sequence used by another animal (the mother or silverback), or are these techniques learnt entirely individually? With hierarchically structured behaviour, there exists a range of possibilities between the dichotomy of 'imitation' or 'no imitation'. A process may be imitated at several different levels. The lowest level in the hierarchy must consist of the smallest possible elements of action which can be independently controlled by the individual (their size will depend on the precision of neural control of action in the species). In a great ape, extensive neural representation of the hands allows rather precise control, and this set of basic elements may be very large. Groups of these basic elements, assembled together during the animal's interactions with the world, form higher-level units of behaviour, and this process of hierarchical grouping can continue to arbitrary complexity. The *repertoire* of the individual (a term which is often left undefined) consists therefore of all the lowest-level elements plus the already-assembled higher-level groups of elements, because each of these behaves as 'an action' once it has been learnt. *Novel* actions are those sequences of actions (including basic elements and already-existing groups of elements) which are assembled for the first time.

Imitation allows the assembly of novel sequences of these units by observation; but imitation may occur at many different levels, with radically different consequences for what we would observe. With imitation at the lowest level in the hierarchy, details of manual style, hand preference and idiosyncratic movements will match in the behaviour of model and observer; with all details of style matching, experimental psychologists would presumably be confident that imitation was occurring throughout, since the opposite is used to reject imitation (Tomasello, 1990). (Experimental psychologists' emphasis on rather exact duplication of the detail of behaviour is an inevitable result of their use of simple, non-hierarchical actions in their experiments.) At higher levels, however, it is possible that the overall form might be imitated, but the fine detail acquired by trial and error. This would cause a striking match of behaviour at *coarse* levels of description, i.e. higher hierarchical levels, contrasting with non-matching actions at *fine* levels of detail. Thus, imitation at different hierarchical levels will produce distinctively different patterns of behavioural similarity and difference at different levels of analysis. What pattern do gorillas show?

There are two reasons to think that the fine grain of manual actions is learnt without imitation. When we adopted a very detailed level of analysis, looking at the exact hand-configurations and movements used to achieve each of the 6–10 sub-processes in a technique, we found that every animal uses several functionally equivalent variants for each sub-process, and that each animal has a different preferred set (Byrne and Byrne, 1993). This striking idiosyncrasy is a hallmark of trial-and-error acquisition. Moving to a slightly coarser level, at which minor style differences are ignored but left- and right-handed forms remain distinct, we used the pattern of hand-preferences to trace imitation. Since only the mother or the male leader is a potential model, if this level of detail is learnt by imitation, hand-preferences (which are very strong in every animal) would strongly tend to run 'in families': the hand-preference of an offspring would correlate either positively or negatively with that of the mother, or that of the silverback male. Gorillas have two statistically independent hand-preferences, those for leaf- and stem-processing, and the Virunga animals' genealogies are known, so there was quite sufficient data to detect any such effect. In fact, there was none: the distribution was precisely what one would expect by chance (Byrne and Byrne, 1991). At this level, too, there seems no need to invoke imitation as an explanation.

A very different pattern emerged when we moved to the level of *overall form* of the process. Instead of idiosyncrasy, great standardization was found (Byrne and Byrne, 1993). In every animal, the organization of each technique is essentially the same. Given the very large number of possible sequences in which 6–10 different elements could be combined, this standardization was remarkable, and contrasts strikingly with the variability of element repertoires. It is very implausible that the constraints of the environment should be so tight that every animal would end up with the same hierarchical structure. Instead, it seems what may be happening is imitation of the sequence and coordination of elements and their organization as sub-routines.

Program-level imitation

To distinguish this sense of 'imitation' from how the term is used in describing the data from neonatal humans, a new term is needed. I have called it *program-level imitation* (Byrne, 1993, 1994; Byrne and Russon, in press), and provisionally defined this as *copying the structural organization of a complex process (including the sequence of stages, subroutine structure and bimanual coordination), by observation of the behaviour of another individual, while perhaps furnishing the exact details of actions by individual trial-and-error learning*. Whereas neonatal imitation affects actions already in the individual's repertoire, and probably has a social function in the relationships between infant and adults, program-level imitation can allow novel arrangements of actions to be learnt by observation alone, potentially facilitating skill learning. However, if experimental psychology's definitions of 'true' imitation focus on the elicitation of behaviours already in the individual's repertoire, as recognized by physical similarity to actions observed in others, or tested with the two-group procedure invented by Dawson and Foss, then this important behaviour will remain unidentifiable in animals. Despite the neologism, program-level imitation is not something foreign to developmental psychology. Consider, for instance, the sort of 'imitation' described by Bauer and Mandler (1989) when they studied 16-month-old children's copies of adults' sequences of action. They found that the children required less observation and were more accurate if the sequences were of actions that were causally related, such as the steps in bathing a teddy-bear. Any actions unrelated to the job in hand tended to be missed out in the children's imitations; nevertheless, the authors refer to the copying as imitation. Imitation of this kind is clearly sensitive to task organization, and corresponds exactly to program-level imitation. A new word is useful, however, to distinguish it from the sort of imitation found in neonate humans; this, in turn, might be termed *action-level imitation*.

Imitation at program-level implies an ability to operate with task structure and behavioural organization. However, the process by which this is achieved is not necessarily a mysterious or complicated one. For instance, the crucial sub-goals of many complex physical tasks are 'visible' by their observable results in the sequence of action. The intermediate product that each component process achieves is essential to the next stage, and so these particular states necessarily recur in every effective sequence. In contrast, the exact sequence of steps leading to and from each of these crucial states can vary between occasions without affecting efficiency. These different 'pathways' reflect matters of style and detail irrelevant to success, and would typically vary randomly from time to time, and more systematically with the initial state of the raw material, the animal's locomotor state and so on. This gives an observable way of identifying intermediate sub-goals in another individual's spontaneous behaviour, provided that performing the task produces continual changes in the physical world, as in the case of gorilla food preparation or hominid tool manufacture. In this way, an individual observing a skilled practitioner would in principle be in a position to 'see' the sub-goals as well as the final 'goal' at which the model is aiming. The details of how each sub-goal is met can then be picked up by individual trial and error – a process that may indeed be more efficient than acquisition by imitative copying of the movements themselves.

The important point is that to *organize* these observations into a goal structure for itself, the individual also needs some sort of mental apparatus with *workspace* storage capacity; a system restricted merely to reacting to stimuli in the environment would not do. Similarly, the individual must be able to retain in long-term memory the *program structure* once it is constructed, to use in the future; a memory consisting of simple associations would not do.

Concluding speculations

The contention of this chapter has been that the trend towards sceptically discounting evidence of imitation in animals should be extended somewhat further. The experimental data currently offered in support of animal imitation are vulnerable to reinterpretation as response facilitation or other forms of socially mediated priming, augmenting individual learning association. The problem is that, in recent work on imitation, no insistence has been made that novel behaviour patterns are learnt. In turn, this is probably a consequence of the use of experimental tasks for which single-action solutions are appropriate, making the definition of 'novel' highly problematic (Heyes, 1996; Zentall, 1996). Novelty can be more easily identified in more complex behaviour, as novel rearrangements of actions already in the repertoire, building up recursively into hierarchically organized behaviour (Byrne and Russon, in press). It remains to be seen whether experimentalists can design tasks with the logical complexity needed to circumvent this difficulty (Whiten and Custance, 1996).

At present, only certain spontaneous animal behaviour allows analysis at more than one level in a complex hierarchy. These analyses are incomplete (in particular, a longitudinal study of development is needed to trace changes in organization during acquisition), but already they point strongly towards the existence of 'program-level' imitation in gorillas, and no doubt other great apes. In this, the overall organization of a complex routine is acquired by observation, but the detail of precise actions is picked up by individual experimentation. The consequent differences in the final product, at differing levels in the hierarchy, enable program-level imitation to be identified in spontaneous behaviour, without experimentation. To bring this capacity of apes under full experimental control, very different tasks will be needed than have so far been used in studies of animal imitation.

It may be worth considering whether program-level imitation *is* normal, human-type imitation, and asking if humans make much use of mimicking single actions. Program-level imitation appears well adapted for the acquisition of elaborate mechanical skills, whereas action-level imitation seems clumsy and inefficient for this purpose, liable to enshrine inefficient trivia in a 'superstitious' manner. There is no doubt that humans do both, but perhaps action-level imitation (including neonatal imitation) evolved to serve social functions, and is only recruited for learning new problem-solving techniques in some desperation, when the logical structure of what the observed model is doing remains opaque.

The cognitive apparatus implied by program-level imitation – memory for program organization rather than simple associations, and workspace for assembling novel goal-structures – is closely related to other human capacities: forward planning, natural language and propositional thought. The tentative suggestion from our data that gorillas share these cognitive underpinnings has clear implications for the antiquity of some important elements of human cognition.

Notes

1 Cognitive psychologists will note the debt this account owes to Morton's 'Logogen theory' of word recognition (Morton, 1970).

2 However, Tomasello now treats emulation as a way in which an observer can learn the 'affordances' or potential uses of an object by watching the results of another individual's actions, without learning the actions themselves (Tomasello and Call, 1994). On this interpretation, emulation is a more powerful mechanism than priming of an existing goal, perhaps representationally as complex as imitation.

CHAPTER 13

Do concepts of intersubjectivity apply to non-human primates?

Juan Carlos Gómez

A common sense definition of 'intersubjectivity'

In this chapter I shall address the question of to what extent intersubjectivity can be found in primates other than humans and what we can learn about it from adopting a comparative and evolutionary perspective on this issue. Let me start by trying to define the concept of intersubjectivity. This is not a term commonly found in dictionaries, but we can undertake a definition relying upon its components – *inter* and *subjectivity*. According to the Collins English Dictionary, 'subjective' is anything 'belonging to, proceeding from, or relating to the mind of the thinking subject and not the nature of the object being considered', or anything 'relating to or emanating from a person's emotions, prejudices, etc.'. Our subjectivity is, therefore, the way we perceive, think about and feel about the world. I become intersubjective when my subjectivity is capable of taking the subjectivity of others as its object, i.e. when my mind thinks about the minds of other subjects, or when I feel about the minds or the feelings of others. For example, if I am merely looking at an object you are handling and my mind thinks about or, simply, perceives this object, I am not being intersubjective. However, if I think about what you might be thinking or feeling about that object, then I am intersubjective (Fig. 13.1). For intersubjectivity to exist, therefore, it is not enough that the same object is the target of two different subjectivities. Rather it is necessary that my subjectivity is addressed at how your subjectivity takes that object.

However, this approach captures only a part of what is implied by the prefix 'inter'. Indeed, as illustrated in Fig. 13.1 left, a person A can be said to be intersubjective if he takes into account what another person B has in her mind. But this is a *one-way intersubjectivity*, in that only A is aware of B's thoughts. A more complex kind of intersubjectivity is that in which both subjects are reciprocally aware of each other's awareness (Fig. 13.1 right). This can be called *two-way intersubjectivity*.[1]

Another interesting dualism is apparent in the dictionary definition

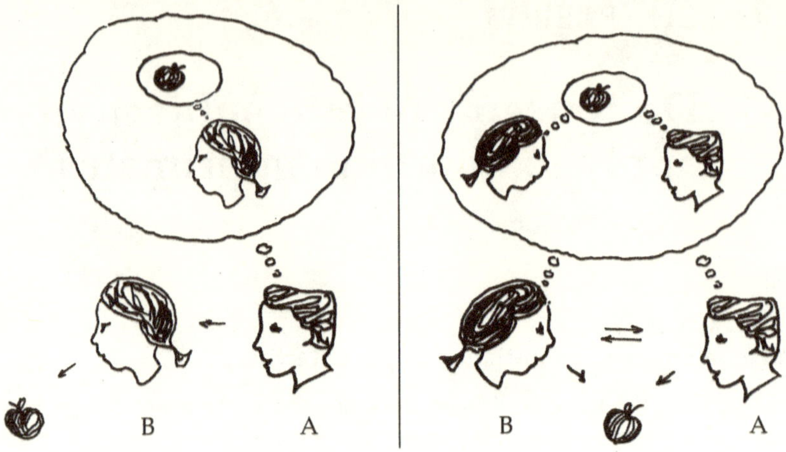

Fig. 13.1 Two kinds of intersubjectivity. See text for explanation.

of subjectivity quoted before. One of the entries refers to 'the mind of the thinking subject', whereas the other refers to the 'person's emotions'. Feeling and thinking seem to single out themselves as two sides of subjectivity. This dualism, as we shall see, has important consequences in the psychological study of intersubjectivity.

Two psychological approaches to the study of intersubjectivity

In recent years the problem of intersubjectivity has been approached by developmental psychology in two different ways, reflecting these two sides of subjectivity – thinking and feeling – and to some extent also reflecting the distinction between one-way and two-way intersubjectivity. The first approach has been heralded under the banner of 'theory of mind' (Astington *et al.*, 1988; Baron-Cohen *et al.*, 1993; Carruthers and Smith, 1996; Lewis and Mitchell, 1994; Whiten, 1991). This label reflects the view that any appraisal of another's subjectivity must be based upon some sort of theoretical knowledge – as opposed to direct perception or primary representation – of the other person's mind. According to the extreme versions of this view, our knowledge of other minds is due to the operation of specialized mechanisms that build up a corpus of knowledge and presuppositions about subjectivity similar in many respects to scientific theories (Gopnik, 1993).

Other authors working under this heading of 'theory of mind' (TOM for short) do not defend a strict 'theory theory' view and use the expression merely as a convenient label. However, they tend to share the idea that knowledge of other minds must be based upon some kind of abstract representations, usually referred to as 'metarepresentations'. Although there are discrepancies between authors as to the exact meaning of the term (Leslie and Roth, 1993; Perner, 1993), a 'metarepresentation' can be roughly defined as the representation of a representation attributed to a subject – a representation being something unobservable, a 'theoretical' or 'imaginary' entity. A person's subjectivity is equated to the internal representations this person entertains about the world. Intersubjectivity, therefore, can be achieved only if one is capable of representing the internal representations of the other person.

This approach to intersubjectivity focuses upon the 'thinking' side of people. Its object of research is mainly the understanding of epistemic states such as belief or ignorance. Although TOM researchers have also studied how children understand volitional states, such as desire, they approach them as internal mental states. It is also common that the TOM approach focuses upon one-way intersubjectivity, since the experimental situations used to study theory of mind usually involve the understanding of what a third person knows or believes about something.

However, in psychology the term 'intersubjectivity' was originally linked to a different approach focused upon the perception and feeling of emotions, rather than upon the construction of theories of the mind. Its advocate was Colwyn Trevarthen (1979a, 1980, this volume). He defended that, from very early on, human infants can achieve intersubjectivity through emotional interactions. The subjectivity of others is *felt* by infants, who are capable of attuning themselves to it, in the same way as they display their own subjectivity by means of emotional behaviours to which adults adjust themselves. In Trevarthen's view and according to other recent advocates of similar theories (notably Hobson, 1991a, 1993a, b, this volume; and Bråten, 1993, this volume), an emotional intersubjectivity precedes and is inseparable from the 'intellectual' intersubjectivity studied by authors working under the label of 'theory of mind'. This emotional intersubjectivity is usually displayed in dialogical situations and corresponds roughly to what I identified earlier as 'two-way' or 'second-person' intersubjectivity. A typical example of this is the interaction between a mother and a baby exchanging looks and facial expressions in a structured pattern of interaction.

A summary of the relations between these two approaches to intersubjectivity appears in Fig. 13.2. The TOM approach started with the study of how children understand epistemic mental states such as belief. However, it soon extended back its inquiries, looking for earlier manifestations of TOM abilities. Desire understanding is found at

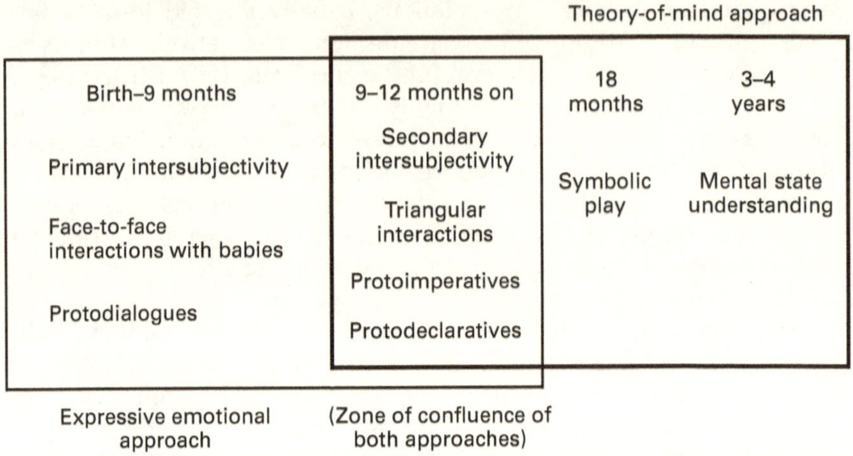

Fig. 13.2 Two approaches to the study of intersubjectivity. See text.

around 3 years of age; pretence and fiction, whose close connection to false-belief understanding is argued by Leslie (1987), are both produced and understood as early as 18–24 months. But the earliest manifestation of theory of mind is usually taken to occur at around 9–12 months, when infants start pointing out things to people and engaging in a number of behaviours that are identified under the label of 'Joint Attention' (Adamson and Bakeman, 1991). These behaviours are studied by TOM authors from the intellectual point of view, in so far as they seem to reflect some understanding of other people's minds. For example, in so-called 'protodeclarative' pointing, infants seem to be striving to make other people *notice* things (e.g. a balloon in the air), i.e. to affect other people's mental states about the world (Baron-Cohen, 1989; Leslie and Happé, 1989). For TOM theorists, what matters is the kind of abstract representation infants must use to achieve this understanding of other people's subjectivity.

On the other hand, the emotional intersubjectivity tradition starts its inquiries almost from the very beginning of infants' lives. A *primary* intersubjectivity is said to exist already in 3- to 4-month-olds, capable of interrelating their emotions with adults' in protodialogic exchanges (Trevarthen, 1979a, this volume). The 9–12 months period is seen as a culmination phase in which previous advances in both object and people knowledge are integrated into complex patterns that constitute a phase of *secondary* intersubjectivity. One-year-old infants are motivated to include their manipulations and perceptions of objects in their interactions with people, and vice versa. At that age infants actively *share* their activities, perceptions and emotions about the world with other people.

It is then at the 9–12 months period that the two research traditions in intersubjectivity seem to meet. But this is a paradoxical meeting. For one tradition, this period represents the blossoming of an advanced form of intersubjectivity appearing as the culmination of previous developments; for the other, it is the very beginning of intersubjectivity and one of its simplest manifestations. Let's have a closer look at this period.

Intersubjectivity in 1-year-olds

The intersubjectivity of 9- to 12-month-old infants is characterized by a number of abilities, among them pointing and reaching to objects, following the gaze of others, making eye contact in interactions, using other people's emotional expressions as a reference to guide their own behaviour, etc. (see Schaffer, 1984, and Adamson, 1996, for reviews, as well as other chapters in this book). All these behaviours have in common that they involve what is known as 'joint-attention abilities', i.e. the coordination of the attention of two or more people around a common focus of interest. For example, an infant pointing to an object strives to make the person look at the object the infant is already looking at. Conversely, an infant following the gaze of an adult is discovering and sharing this person's focus of attention.

The TOM approach has mainly emphasized how sharing the focus of visual attention with others provides the infant with a sort of window into the mind of the other person. Through this window infants start forming 'triadic' representations that allow them to adjust to other persons' view of the situation (see Baron-Cohen, 1995, for a quintessentially representationalist account). The emotional approaches to intersubjectivity, however, emphasize the expressive and affective components of those triadic interactions of infants. For example, Hubley and Trevarthen (1979) analysed the interactive behaviours of 1-year-old infants not only in terms of 'reaching', 'pointing' or 'looking to the face', but also in terms of 'complying with instructions', 'accepting assistance', 'acquiescing', 'resisting' or 'making facial expressions'. More recently, Hobson (1993a) has emphasized how these triangular behaviours are an expression of 'relatedness' which is not based upon the infant's 'representation of the caregivers' representations of the situation', but upon a perception of the caregiver's behaviour both as emotionally expressive and as directed to the external world (p. 141).

This contrast is again a reflection of the emphasis upon one-way, intellectual or third-person intersubjectivity by the TOM approach versus the emphasis upon two-way, expressive or second-person intersubjectivity by Trevarthen, Hobson and other advocates of the expressive/emotional approach. Underlying this conflict, there is a more general confrontation between approaches trying to understand subjectivity as representational structures and computations and approaches that believe that subjectivity is based upon phenomena other than internal representations.

In this paper I shall try to offer some reflections about these conflicting approaches from a comparative evolutionary perspective. To do this I shall concentrate upon the repertoire of joint-attention and expressive behaviours that Trevarthen called 'secondary intersubjectivity'. These constitute an ideal arena to launch an inquiry into non-human intersubjectivity because in humans they appear before the onset of productive language, and are therefore amenable to being investigated in other animals.

Are non-human primates intersubjective (in Trevarthen's sense)?

The question of Trevarthenian intersubjectivity in primates other than humans has been explicitly addressed in only two studies – by Perinat and Dalmáu (1989), and Gómez, (1989, 1990a, 1992) – both working with hand-reared gorilla babies and both focused on secondary intersubjectivity. Perinat and Dalmáu (1989) failed to find any sign of secondary intersubjectivity in two baby gorillas. Indeed they failed to find even traces of intrinsically motivated object manipulations, which they considered to be a prerequisite for secondary intersubjectivity. Their conclusion was that secondary intersubjectivity was probably an exclusively human achievement. In my study (Gómez, 1989), however, I found the prerequisite object manipulations in a young female gorilla and described a number of gorilla–human interactions that could constitute evidence of secondary intersubjectivity in the gorilla. To check this interpretation I carried out a more formal analysis of the gorilla's interactions with people and objects using the categories and definitions Hubley and Trevarthen (1979) used with human infants.

Fig. 13.3 shows that the gorilla did engage in almost all the interactive categories identified by Hubley and Trevarthen: she would follow instructions in her manipulations, accept or resist the assistance of humans in getting goals, follow their actions upon an object, and take, offer or give objects to the humans. The gorilla coordinated these 'praxic acts' with 'interpersonal acts' – vocalizing, making facial expressions, looking at the face of the other person or touching him/

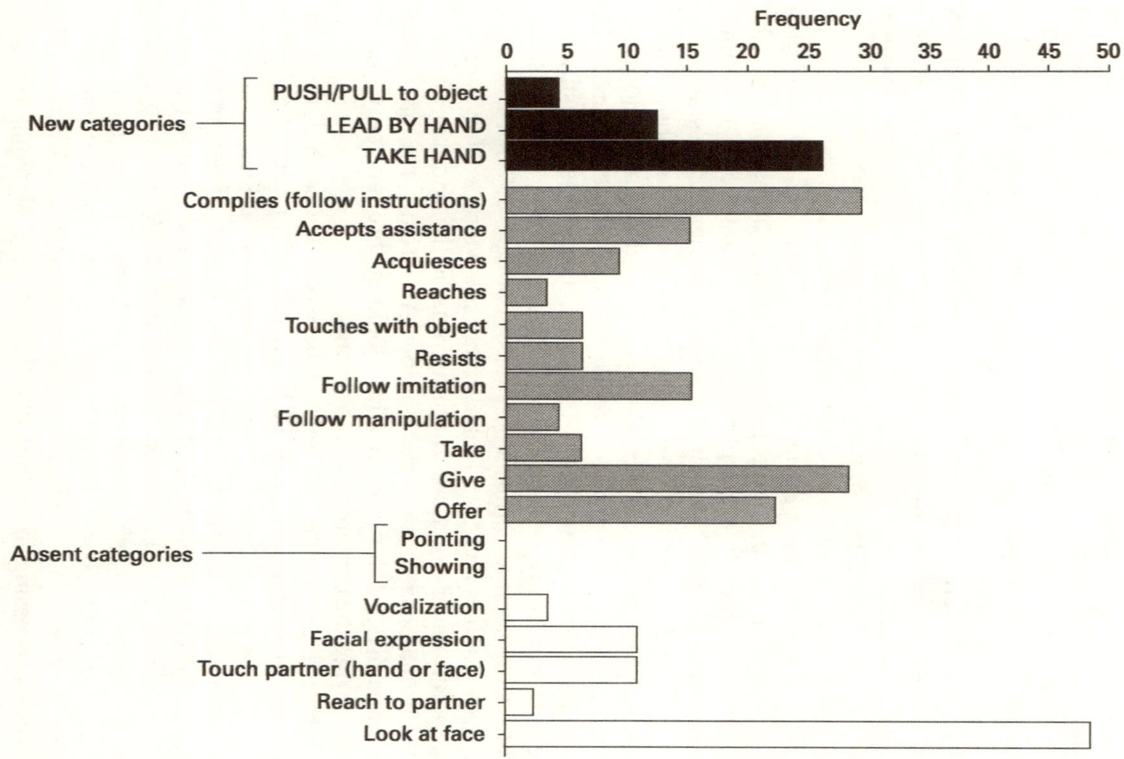

Fig. 13.3 Frequency of secondary intersubjective behaviours, as defined by Hubley and Trevarthen (1979) in a hand-reared gorilla (adapted from Gómez *et al.*, 1993).

her. Since, according to Hubley and Trevarthen (1979), the coordination of praxic and interpersonal acts is the crucial identifying feature of secondary intersubjectivity, the above results show that this kind of intersubjective interaction is present in hand-reared gorillas.

However, as Gómez (1992; see also Gómez *et al.*, 1993) points out, there are at least two interesting differences between his gorilla and the human infants studied by Hubley and Trevarthen. First, to analyse the gorilla's interactions, three new categories had to be added to the original list – those identified as 'contact gestures'. Taking the hand of the human towards objects and leading the human by the hand were very frequent actions within the gestural repertoire of the gorilla. A second difference had to do with the absence of two of Trevarthen's categories (collapsed into a single one in Fig. 13.3) in the gorilla's repertoire – showing things to people and pointing.

One possibility is that these differences compensate for each other. The gorilla could be using contact gestures to perform the interactive functions served by pointing gestures in the human infant, the difference being merely a morphological one. However, the simultaneous absence of other 'showing' gestures in the gorilla suggests a deeper difference. She never used her contact gestures to show things to other people (e.g. she did not take people to a thing with the aim of showing them that thing, but to make them do something with it). Even in her most 'showing-like' gestures, there was a distinctive difference from the typical protodeclarative gesturing of infants. For example, a repeated action by this subject (Gómez, 1992) was to take people to a window and then look through the window. However, the gorilla would never point out anything outside the window or check back the human gaze once at the window. Apparently, her aim was to be accompanied by the human while looking through the window, but not sharing the contemplation of things.

Therefore, an important difference between the secondary intersubjectivity of gorillas and that of human infants is that the former seem to communicate mainly to make people do things – things as varied as mending a broken toy, making it work, opening a lock, playing with a ball, or sitting down in front of a window; not just requesting food, as sometimes (Seidenberg, 1986; Seidenberg and Petitto, 1979) apes have been portrayed as doing. Human infants also use their gestures to 'show' things to other people, without intending, apparently, to provoke any action apart from their looking at the objects and expressing something about them. This 'showing' function of preverbal gestures has been called 'protodeclarative' gesturing (Bates *et al.*, 1975).

How can we explain the absence of protodeclarative gestures in the great apes? The TOM approach to intersubjectivity may provide a basis for an explanation of this difference.

Are great apes intersubjective (in the theory-of-mind sense)?

This explanation is based upon an important finding in human developmental psychology: children with autism, who are supposed to suffer from a deficit in their TOM abilities, typically lack protodeclarative gestures (Baron-Cohen, 1989; Curcio, 1978). This correlation between having a deficit in TOM and not being able to produce protodeclaratives is one of the main reasons why the proponents of the TOM approach consider joint attention abilities to be linked to the same abstract, metarepresentational mechanism as other TOM abilities. Protodeclaring infants would be trying to affect the mental states of other people with their pointing gestures: for example, making them *know* that there is a balloon in the window. To do this, the infant should be capable of entertaining some representation of the other person's knowledge or the other person's mental experience of noticing the balloon. The argument goes that this ability is not needed to make requesting gestures (also known as 'protoimperatives', after Bates *et al*, 1975), because the goal of requesting gestures is to make people do things – give an object, start a toy, open a door, etc. These are concrete aims that can be represented with ordinary, first-order representations (see Gómez *et al.*, 1993, for a detailed analysis of this argument).

A possible explanation of why apes do not make protodeclarative gestures is, therefore, that these might require the cognitive mechanism of metarepresentation, and apes would be devoid of it. The TOM mechanism would be as uniquely human as language itself. As a consequence, non-human primates would not be properly intersubjective in the TOM sense. They would be unable to represent other people's mental states, and would be restricted to taking into account their behaviours; whereas human infants would be truly intersubjective because they would possess the requisite cognitive mechanism of metarepresentation. Children with autism would have severe problems with being intersubjective because they have this mechanism seriously damaged.

This interpretation about the lack of TOM competence in non-human primates has been reinforced in recent years by a number of authors who have tried to assess the TOM abilities of apes with non-verbal analogues of the tests carried out with children. The results of these tests have been negative or are subject to methodological criticisms (see Heyes, in press, for a recent critical review). Povinelli

(1996) argues that even in the relatively simple domain of understanding visual attention, there is evidence that chimpanzees do not understand the internal mental state of *seeing* underlying the behaviour of *looking*.[2] According to this author, chimpanzees only learn (in accordance with the predictions of learning theory) 'the observable contingencies between eyes, eye direction, and subsequent behaviours'. He specifically denies that his chimpanzee subjects were able to appreciate that an attentive experimenter 'was connected to them in a subjective manner' (p. 317). According to this view, therefore, non-human primates are not intersubjective in the TOM sense.

A similar sceptical view has recently been advanced in relation to human infants. Corkum and Moore (1995) suggest that genuine joint-attention abilities do not appear in babies until after the first year of life. They suggest that general learning mechanisms could explain how younger infants may get 'involved in joint attention without the infant's understanding the nature of attention' (p. 81). According to this, therefore, human infants may not be intersubjective in the TOM sense, either; at least not as early as assumed by the Trevarthenian approach.

In conclusion, infants' communicative behaviours at the end of the first year of life are certainly the meeting point of the TOM and the emotional approaches to intersubjectivity, but they also constitute a 'divergence point' where the conflicting theoretical interpretations of both views are most clearly shown. The main conflict revolves around the issue of whether complex intellectual abilities – based upon the understanding of mental states as internal representations – are or are not needed to engage in what Trevarthen and Hubley (1978) identified as 'secondary intersubjectivity'. Is it possible to find a way of integrating both approaches? I shall address this issue, turning back to the problem of non-human primate intersubjectivity.

Calling and checking attention in the great apes

If the difference between ape and human infant intersubjectivity is a cognitive one – an inability to represent attention as a mental state – apes should be as incompetent in their handling of attention for executive purposes as they seem to be in producing protodeclarative behaviours. The apparently intersubjective behaviours of apes should be reducible to mere trial-and-error associations or perhaps intelligent, instrumental manipulations of other people merely focused upon their 'efficiency' in providing them with rewards. Interpersonal actions such as looking to the faces of others (see Fig. 13.3) would not be truly intersubjective. These behaviours should be fully explainable as mere instrumental actions in terms of learning theory. I have argued (Gómez, 1990b, 1991, 1992; Gómez *et al.*, 1993) that this is not the case: those behaviours are neither mere trial-and-error learnings nor a simple extension of the apes' tool-using and manipulative skills. The apes instead seem to be relying *specifically* upon some intersubjective understanding of attention that is qualitatively different from their understanding of the physical world or other aspects of the social world.

My argument goes as follows. Take a typical displacement request (where the gorilla asks the person to move to a particular location): it is not that the gorilla simply takes the person by the hand in a particular direction. Typically, the gorilla would first of all *call the attention* of the human to whom she was going to address her request. The way to call the attention of the person would consist typically of touching him and waiting until the person looked down to the gorilla, whereby the person's and the animal's eyes would meet. Only then, would the gorilla take the human's hand and carry out the request (usually making further eye contacts during the request itself). This and the other gorillas studied by Gómez (1992) developed a repertoire of gestures specialized in calling the attention of people before making a request: pulling the clothes, patting the leg, touching a hand, holding out the hand towards the person, turning the human's head towards their eyes, throwing straw to the human, and, at least in the case of a young female, using the gorilla vocalization known as 'pig grunt'. In every case, the gorilla would first make eye contact with the human and then make the request.

The use of these attention-calling and attention-checking behaviours cannot be explained as the result of a mere association process based upon an increase in the probability of obtaining the reward when requests are accompanied by eye contact. The appearance of attention-checking behaviours in the above gorilla implied no change in the success rate of her demands (always under 50%). New behavioural elements – attention-calling and checking behaviours – were incorporated into an existing procedure, rendering it more complex and elaborate, but without increasing the efficiency of the procedure in terms of the number of times the gorilla was eventually rewarded. Moreover, calling the attention of the human had sometimes the paradoxical effect of rendering the goal more difficult to attain by alternative means. For example, a door might be more firmly secured after the gorilla's interest in having it opened was demonstrated or a 'forbidden' object might be moved to a more remote place. The joint attention behaviours displayed by the gorilla could be understood only in terms of the intersubjective exchanges (eye contact, facial expressions, vocalizations) they provoked, not in terms of their problem-solving efficiency.

The existence of elaborate procedures adapted to deal with the attention of others suggests, therefore, that apes do have some specific understanding of attention, even if this understanding is only used for executive purposes. However, this need not be an understanding of attention as an internal mental state or representation separable from perceivable 'body states' (cf. Hobson, 1993a, and this volume; and Mundy *et al.*, 1993, for similar accounts). Let me elaborate upon this idea.

Understanding attention: the bodily ways of mentalism

Attention is not a mere physical property of organisms (like having hands, legs or, for that matter, eyes). Attention is an *attitude* an organism can adopt towards the external world, a way in which it can use its eyes, legs, etc., establishing a special connection between itself and a target in the environment. Then, when an organism perceives attention in others, it perceives something that physically is not there. This need not mean, however, that the perceiver carries out inferences about the mental attitudes underlying the other's behaviour. Long ago, Gestalt researchers established that the apprehension of Gestalt qualities – such as apparent movement – could be interpreted as a primary perceptual phenomenon, not as the product of inferences (Wertheimer, 1912). In the same sense, an infant need not infer that the eyes of the person are guided by a mental state (his interest in object X) to see his behaviour as attention to X. For example, the proto-declaring infant may be trying to provoke the attitude of attending to X in the other, this attitude being expressive rather than mental, i.e. more akin to a bodily posture – perceived in a Gestalt way – than to a mental attitude. The infant tries to affect how the other relates to an object, not how the other thinks about the object; in other words, the infant's actions are addressed at changing not the adult's *re-presentation* of the object but the adult's *presentation* to the object. This leads us back to the conflict between intellectual and emotional/expressive conceptions of intersubjectivity.

As we have seen before, some authors think that a truly inter-subjective understanding of attention should imply the ability to represent 'attention' as an internal and unobservable mental state, and that anything short of this should be considered as not intersubjective. However, a hypothesis like the one I have just discussed opens the possibility of there being something like a practical conceptualization of different bodily attitudes as 'attentive' without a corresponding,

Cartesian conceptualization of a separable mental state of 'attention'. It is as if apes and young children would be capable of categorizing bodily attitudes with the qualifying adjective 'attentive', but are not able to develop the substantive, abstract concept of 'attention' that could be used in the absence of any material support. This opens the possibility of there being a mentalistic perception and categorization of behaviour in the absence of abstract, independent concepts of mind and mental states. Denying that this is possible (i.e. defending the view that the perception of 'attentiveness' in behaviour should be based upon a previous concept of attention) would be equivalent to denying that one can perceive red or yellow objects in the absence of a previous, abstract concept of 'redness' or 'yellowness'. Furthermore, I defend the hypothesis that apes and human infants not only are capable of discriminating 'attentive' from 'non-attentive subjects', but also can perceive and represent subjects *as attentive* or *as inattentive* without having an abstract concept of *attention*.

In summary, I propose that there is a way of perceiving and representing mental states as emergent properties of bodily states. Apes, probably, understand mental states not as propositional attitudes but as 'positional attitudes'. They do not represent other organisms' representations; they represent other organisms' 'presentations' in relation to external targets. These, however, are not reducible to the particular bodily positions or movements that instantiate them, as the red colour is not reducible to a list of red objects.

This alternative conceptualization of intersubjectivity provides a unifying arena for the two conceptions at issue. But it is not devoid of problems. It is, as yet, a vague formulation in need of conceptual clarification and elaboration (as are the similar attempts by Hobson (1993a, this volume), Whiten (1993a), or Trevarthen himself). And it has to demonstrate its ability to deal with problematic empirical evidence, like the problem of why apes do not engage in protodeclarative behaviours. If great apes' intersubjectivity includes an understanding of attention, why is it subordinated to executive goals, whereas from very early on human infants are also capable of pursuing 'declarative' goals with their gestures?

Gómez *et al.* (1993) suggest that perhaps we are dealing with a difference that should be labelled 'motivational' rather than cognitive. The *motives* of apes for engaging in joint attention would be partially different from those of human infants. Apes can intersubjectively show and hide things from others; but always as part of a wider plan to make or prevent others from doing things. Humans do the same, but they also seem to be able to show things with a motive of 'shared contemplation' (cf. Werner and Kaplan, 1963/1984).

An important part of Trevarthen's conception of intersubjectivity involves the idea that human psychological growth is regulated by 'motives' for interaction (Trevarthen, 1982b). Perhaps the difference between ape and human infant secondary intersubjectivity lies not so much in the cognitive structures underlying their interactions with others as in the 'motives' that activate these structures and, therefore, may affect their subsequent developmental pathways, eventually leading to different cognitive systems subserving intersubjectivity. Early ape and human intersubjectivity would mainly differ not in its 'thinking', intellectual side, but in its emotional, motivational one. If Trevarthen's conception of motives as regulators of psychological growth is right, then this initial difference may lead later to important 'intellectual' differences in the intersubjectivities of apes and humans.

Secondary intersubjectivity could originally have emerged in evolution as a set of abilities to regulate and understand conspecifics' executive behaviours. These abilities would include skills to understand the attentional and expressive behaviours of others. Although these skills were originally subordinated to executive goals, organisms like human infants developed the ability – the 'motives' – to exercise these intersubjective skills by themselves. This could have involved, among other things, a change in the motivational system regulating the use of joint-attention skills.

According to this view, the mechanisms involved in preverbal intersubjectivity are different from the metarepresentational ones involved in later TOM abilities. It is not that in development the mechanisms of TOM intersubjectivity take over the functions carried out by a more primitive emotional/expressive intersubjectivity. TOM mechanisms may have emerged in evolution as an improvement in the way certain intersubjective functions are carried out and perhaps also as a way of creating new intersubjective functions. However, my proposal is that there are intersubjective functions for which TOM mechanisms are radically inadequate. These intersubjective functions continue to be subserved by the more 'primitive', non-metarepresentational mechanisms (Gómez, 1994, 1996).

Summary and conclusion

In summary, concepts of intersubjectivity – both those of Trevarthenian origin and those rooted in the TOM perspective – can be fruitfully applied to non-human primates. Furthermore, their investigation in non-human animals provides an opportunity for reflection about their underlying assumptions and about the possibility of integrating them, recognizing the many faces of the phenomenon of intersubjectivity: one-way and two-way, third-person and second-person, intellectual and emotional, etc. Evidence from non-human primates suggests that there seem to be some pre-metarepresentational ways of interlinking subjectivities about objects. This evidence also suggests that concepts akin to the Trevarthenian 'motives for interaction' could be useful in explaining the differences between human infant and non-human primate intersubjectivity. The precise nature of the mechanisms involved remains, however, to be elucidated.

Acknowledgements

Initial drafts of this chapter were written with the help of a grant of the 'Subprograma General en el Extranjero. MEC'. The final version was completed under DGICYT Grant PB95–0377.

Notes

1 These two different kinds of intersubjectivity can also be labelled 'third-person' and 'second-person' intersubjectivity. (See Gómez, 1996, for further elaboration of this idea.)

2 The discouraging experimental evidence about chimpanzee intersubjectivity found by Povinelli and his team in a series of training studies (Povinelli, 1996) contrasts with the results found by other researchers using different experimental methods. For example, in a study with chimpanzees using a setting that did not require previous training, I found that those subjects who had had more extensive contact with humans were capable of understanding the role of joint visual attention in requests (see Gómez, 1996, for a partial, preliminary report). There is even some initial evidence of understanding of covert mental states (Gómez, 1996). But what I want to discuss here is not the methodology or the experimental evidence available about non-human primate understanding of minds *à la* TOM (for this see Heyes, in press and Gómez, in press), but the conceptual problem of what should count as intersubjectivity

CHAPTER 14

Imitation and the reading of other minds: perspectives from the study of autism, normal children and non-human primates

Andrew Whiten and Julie D. Brown

Introduction

At the core of this chapter are new studies of the imitative repertoires associated with autism, compared with those of normal children and non-autistic people with mild learning difficulties. Research on this subject is important with respect to the prospects for practical remediation in autism, as we shall discuss later (see also Nadel, this volume). Given the context of this book we shall also be concerned with the implications of this research for understanding certain fundamentals of human development, particularly links between imitation and capacities discussed elsewhere in the volume under the headings of intersubjectivity, theory of mind and mindreading. Thus we pick up discussion of themes initiated in Part I of the volume.

An even wider framework for this examination includes social cognition in our evolutionary kin, the non-human primates. In recent years a new wave of empirical and theoretical analysis has drawn out potential links between the ways in which some of the psychological phenomena at the heart of this book form similar patterns in both their ontogenetic and evolutionary growth, as revealed by study of human children and non-human primates. Thus, we begin our analysis with a brief history of the recent key developments in our own and others' research with monkeys and apes; we then draw out the links with recent studies of imitation and mindreading in child studies, which sets the scene for our own findings on autism.

Evolutionary and ontogenetic parallels in links between imitation and mindreading?

Primate mindreading?

Premack and Woodruff's classic paper 'Does the chimpanzee have a theory of mind?' (1978) was the springboard for the now massive body of work charting the development of a theory of mind in children (for overviews see Carruthers and Smith, 1996; Lewis and Mitchell, 1994; Whiten, 1991). Strangely however, and despite some brilliant ethological theorizing about why and where we might expect the evolution of an ability to read others' minds (Humphrey 1980; Krebs and Dawkins, 1984), no further work was forthcoming on mindreading in primates for over a decade. Particularly odd, in retrospect, was that no contribution was made by primatologists studying their subjects in natural social groups, the 'Machiavellian' character of which was being charted (Byrne and Whiten, 1988; de Waal, 1982).

It was in this climate that Byrne and Whiten (1985) documented cases of deception being utilized tactically in wild baboons. This led us to prepare a catalogue of such behaviour in primates, with contributors from the international community of primate researchers (Whiten and Byrne, 1988a). In this our primary goal was a *functional classification* of what was achieved by the deception concerned (*concealing* things, *distracting* others, and so on). But we also noted that these functions could in principle be achieved, plausibly with more finesse, if the protagonists were discriminating relevant states of mind in others. In a certain minority of the records we collected we suggested there was evidence favouring a mindreading, rather than a mere behaviour-reading, interpretation.[1]

In the light of recent emphasis on joint visual attention as a likely foundational stage in the ontogeny of the human mindreading system (Baron-Cohen, 1995), it is of particular interest that we discovered that the majority of records concerned primates' *monitoring and manipulation of attention*[2] (Whiten and Byrne, 1988b). Other episodes, particularly those concerning counter-deception, suggested that some subjects were sensitive to the intentional state of their protagonists, in particular discriminating between their apparent and deceptive intent. The subjects offering the most impressive evidence of this were chimpanzees.

A second round of our collation exercise produced an enlarged corpus of records (Byrne and Whiten, 1990) which suggested that other great apes, in addition to chimpanzees, were able to discriminate such states of mind in others. Species of monkey for which we have even more numerous records of deception did not generate similar evidence, but did offer signs of being able to compute something of the visual perspective of others, as in hiding objects or parts of themselves from them (Byrne and Whiten, 1991, 1992).

Mindreading and pretence

At the same time that these signs of monkey/ape differences began to emerge, Leslie (1987) urged that cognitive parallels between mindreading and pretending suggested that pretend play might be a developmental precursor of a theory of mind. In evidence, he cited correlations between pretend play and the early signs of mentalism in young normal children, and a correlated *deficit* in both pretence and mentalism in autism.

Turning Leslie's hypothesis towards primates, Whiten (1988) and Whiten and Byrne (1991) noted that, where comparable studies for chimpanzees and certain monkeys exist, it appears to be only in the chimpanzee that we find evidence both for mindreading – as noted above – and for the kind of thematic pretend play predicted by the theory. In both mindreading and pretend play, the subject goes beyond a *primary*, literal representation of the world as directly perceived (the very job of primary perception, as Leslie noted), to construct a *secondary*, non-literal representation (either a pretend world, or the world from the mental perspective of another individual).

Mindreading and imitation

Whiten and Byrne (1991) suggested that other abilities might be correlated with mindreading and pretence in apes, including innovatory tool-making, and the ability to use remote representations of self, like mirrors. But another apparently correlated factor picked out was *imitation*. Evidence was beginning to suggest that, contrary to common assumptions, monkeys are not proficient in imitating novel actions, whereas chimpanzees and possibly other apes are (Whiten, 1989). In recent years, driven by an onslaught of critiques (e.g. Galef, 1992; Heyes, 1993; Tomasello, 1994; Whiten and Ham, 1992), more rigorously designed methods have produced more convincing evidence of imitation in apes (Russon, 1997, for a review). Work in our own research group has utilized two main approaches (Whiten and Custance, 1996). One has involved a more systematic version of that first applied by Hayes and Hayes (1952), in which the subject is taught to imitate on the command 'do this!' (the Do-As-I-Do, or DAID test). Then, a battery of novel actions can be tested. Using this technique,

Table 14.1 *Matching acts identified in the Do-As-I-Do experiment with two chimpanzees (after Whiten and Custance 1996)*

TOUCH	SHOULDER	**	SINGLE	OPEN HAND	**
IN	ELBOW	**	HAND	WIGGLE FINGERS	**
SIGHT	STOMACH	***		WAVE STIFFLY	**
	THIGH	*		ARCH FINGERS	**
	FOOT	**	FACIAL	PROTRUDE LIPS	*
TOUCH	BACK OF HEAD	***		LIP SMACK	***
OUT OF	TOP OF HEAD	**		TEETH CHATTER	**
SIGHT	NOSE	***		PUFF CHEEKS	*
	EAR	*	FACE -	MOUTH POP	**
SYMM.	CLAP	**	HEAD	LIP WOBBLE	**
HAND	ALL DIGIT TOUCH	***		PULL MOUTH SIDES	*
	INTERLINK FINGERS	***		LOOK UP	**
	ROLL FISTS	**		LOOK RIGHT	*
	PEEKABOO	**	WHOLE	JUMP	**
ASYMM.	CLAP BACK OF HAND	***	BODY	FLAP ARMS	**
HAND	CLAP TWO DIGITS	*		HUG SELF	***
	GRAB THUMB	***		FOOT TO FOOT	**

Notes: Table includes all actions identified at least once:
*** Identifed for both subjects by at least one coder.
** Identified for one subject by at least one coder.
* Identified for at least one subject, on coder's second guess.
Descriptions given here are intended to convey the range of actions presented; comprehensive descriptions are offered in Custance *et al.* (1995).

Custance *et al.* (1995) found imitation of a range of actions (Table 14.1). Of particular interest with respect to questions of intersubjectivity and 'mapping' of actions between the perspectives of self and other (see Meltzoff and Moore, this volume, and Bråten, this volume), these subjects found it no harder to imitate actions involving out-of-sight body parts (e.g. facial imitation, touching parts of the body out of sight) than those done under visual guidance (Custance *et al.*, 1994).

A second, complementary approach has examined more naturalistic functional tasks, involving analogues of food-processing problems like those faced in the wild (Whiten *et al.*, 1996). Opening of an artificial fruit was demonstrated to chimpanzees and young children using one of two alternative methods ('morphs') to remove each of three parts of the 'shell'. When subjects were given access to the fruit, the question was whether imitation would be evident in a tendency to perform the previously observed morph more than the alternative. Children showed this for two of the three main elements of the shell, and chimpanzees for one element (Fig. 14.1): thus, chimpanzees

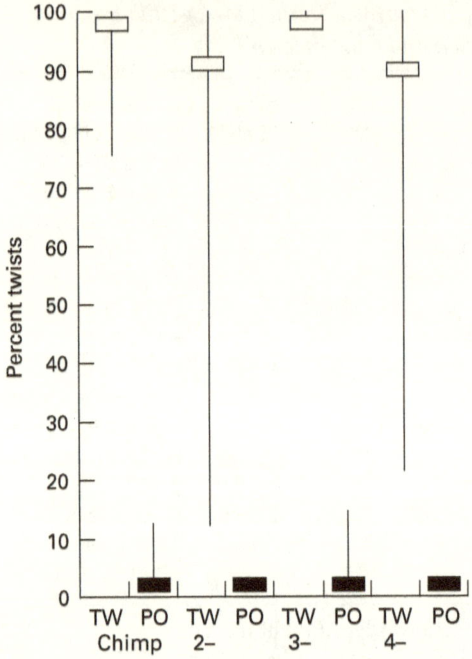

Fig. 14.1 Percentage of morph 'twist' shown by chimpanzees and 2-year-old, 3-year-old and 4-year-old children who had previously witnessed 'twist' (TW: light bar) or 'poke' (PO: dark bar) actions on an 'artificial fruit'. Medians and interquartile ranges. After Whiten and Custance, 1996.

showed statistically significant imitation, but children revealed themselves the more thorough-going cultural species.

It might make sense that such imitative ability in apes would be linked with mindreading, for imitation requires a perspective translation between one individual's action program and the matching one the imitator constructs (see Whiten and Ham, 1992 and Whiten, 1996a, in press b, for fuller treatment of the nature of such linkages). On these empirical and theoretical bases, Whiten and Byrne (1991) made the prediction that deficits in imitation might therefore also be linked to those in mindreading and pretence in the case of autism.

Imitation-mindreading links in ontogeny and primatology

Coincidentally in press at the same time as this primatologically inspired speculation was a review by Rogers and Pennington (1991), which surveyed the small and scattered literature on imitation tests with autistic subjects and proposed that there exists an important developmental linkage between imitation in infancy and the later development of a theory of mind (see also Part I of this volume). Thus, the correlation between mindreading, pretence and imitation explored by Whiten and Byrne (1991) in the case of apes compared with monkeys finds echoes in the pattern of difficulties reported to be experienced by autistic subjects, suggesting that some rather fundamental cognitive linkages, or cognitive substrate, may underly such general patterns (see also Byrne, 1995; Gallup, 1982; Whiten, 1996a).

The possible existence of such patterns is an exciting framework for further research in the disciplines represented in this book. However, the tentative nature of the current evidence must be emphasized. Although more evidence has accumulated in favour of elements of theory of mind in apes (see Whiten, 1993a, 1996a, 1997, in press a and Byrne, 1995, for reviews), recent work with young chimpanzees has found evidence inconsistent with such a conclusion (Povinelli and Eddy, 1996). Tomasello and Call (1997) and Heyes (in press) argue that the existence of a theory of mind in primates is not supported by the evidence. It is therefore appropriate to think of the correlations outlined above cautiously, as a working hypothesis, and still quite a young one at that: but one which we would be foolish to ignore in the design of the next generation of experiments and observations.

Autism and imitation

The studies reviewed by Rogers and Pennington pointed in a fairly consistent way to deficits in imitative capacity in autism. Some of these would be predicted rather directly from the deficits already described in pretence and theory of mind (i.e. imitating 'pretend' acts), but there were also difficulties in imitating basic body movements and actions on objects (DeMyer *et al.*, 1972; Herzig *et al.*, 1989; Ohta, 1987; Jones and Prior, 1985; Sigman and Ungerer, 1984). Rogers and Pennington concluded that their review showed 'specific deficits (i.e. worse than mentally retarded MA and CA matched comparison groups) in imitation of simple motor movements and affect expressions, as well as in higher-level symbolic imitations in autistic persons' (1991:141).

Rogers and Pennington went on to suggest for the first time that *imitation* is a key early foundation in the normal development of a theory of mind and that 'early capacities involving imitation, emotion-sharing, and theory of mind are primarily and specifically deficient in autism. Further, these three capacities involve forming

Table 14.2 *Studies of imitation in autism*

Study	Body/ gestures	Actions with objects	Symbolic actions
DeMyer *et al.* 1972	X	o	–
Thatcher 1977	o	–	–
Curcio and Piserchia 1978	o	–	X
Hammes and Langdell 1981	–	o	X
Sigman and Ungerer 1984	X	–	–
Jones and Prior 1985	X	–	–
Ohta 1987	X	–	–
Morgan *et al.* 1989	o	–	–
Herzig *et al.* 1989	X	–	X
Abrahamsen and Mitchell 1990	X	–	–
Stone *et al.* 1990	X	X	–
Heimann *et al.* 1992	X	o	X
Rogers and McEvoy 1993	X	o	–
Charman and Baron-Cohen 1994	o	o	–

Key:
X some deficits found for autistic subjects
o no deficits found
– not tested

and coordinating social representations of self and other at increasingly complex levels via representational processes that extract patterns of similarity between self and other' (p. 137). Meltzoff and Gopnik (1993) have also argued for an important linkage between imitation and the development of theory of mind, but in an interestingly different way, as described and extended by Meltzoff and Moore (this volume).

All this argues for more attention to be paid to questions of imitation in autism. Table 14.2 lists the main studies (and see also Smith and Bryson, 1994). Since Rogers and Pennington's review, the picture appears to have become a little less clear. Some studies have produced results consistent with the earlier ones suggesting a rather general deficit, but others have found difficulties only with symbolic imitation. Charman and Baron-Cohen (1994) found no differences between autistic children and controls matched for mental age on gestural or object-directed imitation. However, they used tests used previously with normal 9-month-olds, and it remains possible that difficulties would have been experienced with more advanced tasks. Surveying the whole range of studies summarized in Table 14.2, it is unfortunate that most have focused on only one or two limited areas of imitation from the potential spectrum of body/gesture/vocal/object-related/symbolic. Modelled actions vary in complexity, as does the extent to which other samples were tested to control for mental age. Accordingly we decided that a comprehensive examination of imitation in autism and its hypothesized links with intersubjective capacities was needed, and below we summarize some key results from the study. Brown (1996) should be consulted for further details.

A study of achievements and difficulties with imitation in autism

Samples

Table 14.3 describes the study samples. The sample of older autistic subjects was included to investigate possible later development in imitative capacity: few such samples have been described in the literature to date. The sample of young autistic subjects was tested to extend the developmental range similarly, in this case to the younger chronological and mental ages at which processes emphasized by Rogers and Pennington, and Meltzoff and colleagues, might be more likely to be operative. Samples of 3- to 4- and 5- to 6-year-old normal children were included for comparison purposes, covering a key period of theory of mind development. The sample of children with mild learning difficulties (MLD) was included to permit comparisons influenced more by mental than chronological age. Additional comparisons were made between sub-groups of these samples matched more exactly on chronological age and mental age respectively.

Classical tests of false-belief attribution were failed by 80% of the autistic children, consistent with the sample originally studied by Baron-Cohen *et al.* (1985). Of the adult autistic sample, half failed such tests.

Table 14.3 *Samples in a study of imitation efforts*

Group	CA means	MA means	Number of subjects
Autistic children	12;1	4;9	11
Autistic adults	24;8	6;9	10
Young autistic children	5;8	n/a	6
MLD	11;8	6;2	11
5- to 6-year-olds	5;4	5;7	12
3- to 4-year-olds	3;4	3;6	11

Table 14.4 *Categories and examples of actions in Do-As-I-Do test*

Category of actions	Number of actions	Example and description
Verbal speech	3	'Oh Dear!' – Doll is pushed off chair (or step) until falls on face. Model looks at child and says 'Oh, Dear!'.
Verbal non-speech	8	Yawn – Loud yawn noise with hand over mouth.
Facial	5	Puff out cheeks – Lips together and cheeks filled with air until they bulge (cf. Table 14.1).
One-handed	7	Lip wobble – Bottom lip is protruded, the right hand forms a fist with the index finger extended and placed sideways on bottom lip. Fingers are then moved up and down causing lip to flap and make a noise (cf. Table 14.1).
Two-handed	12	Grasp thumb – Left hand is held in a fist with thumb extended sideways (palm away from body). The right hand then forms a fist around the extended thumb (palm away from body before hand is curled) (cf. Table 14.1).
Whole body	9	Sit and rock – With hands placed on knees, model rocks back and forward.
Meaningful actions	6	Brush teeth – Right hand is raised to mouth as if holding toothbrush and moved as if cleaning teeth.
Non-symbolic actions with objects	19	Play xylophone – A coloured xylophone is beaten (six notes in a descending rhythm).
Symbolic actions with objects	9	Saw board (no saw) – Cork board is held on edge with the left hand and then the right hand is closed to an 'open' fist, as if holding a saw, then a sawing action is performed over board.

Elicited imitation

An important distinction should be drawn in any context (including experiments) between the question of whether a subject *can* imitate and whether it *does* imitate a model (Whiten and Custance, 1996). For the first of these, a powerful method is the 'Do-As-I-Do (DAID) approach (Custance *et al.*, 1995). In this, the subject is encouraged to

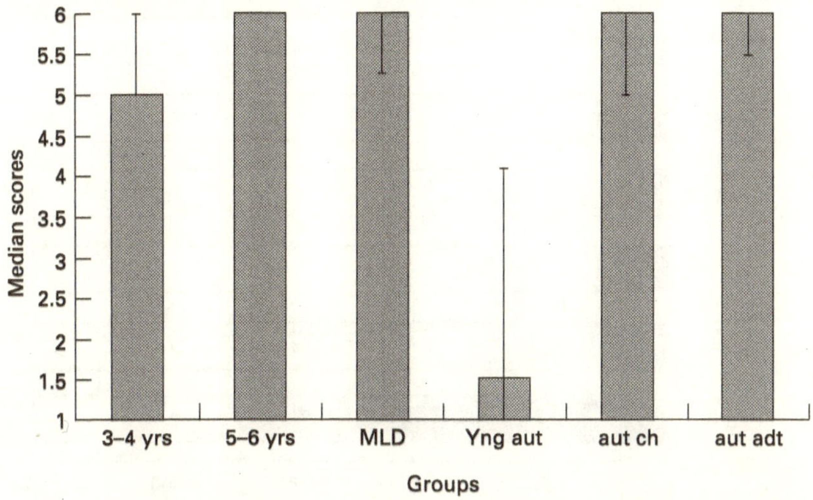

Fig. 14.2 Imitation scores across seventy-eight actions used in the Do-As-I-Do test with 3- to 4-year-old, 5- to 6-year-old, mild learning difficulties (MLD), young autistic, autistic child and autistic adult samples.

grasp the rule 'Do what I did', through a series of prompts. Once the rule has been clearly assimilated the prompts can largely be dropped, and testing can proceed over a large number of actions of different types.

Here we report results using seventy-eight actions covering nine different categories (Table 14.4). Tests were made with the subject sitting opposite (face-to-face with) the experimenter. Subjects' responses were later independently coded using a scale from 6 (accurate imitation) down to 2 (any manual action) or 1 (no response). Scores of 3–5 coded increasing degrees of accuracy. Interobserver reliabilities computed as correlations for such scores on twenty of the actions averaged 0.67.

The first result to note is that a general deficit in imitation in autism was not supported. To the contrary, as Fig. 14.2 shows, the autistic children and adults performed well. The only significant difference lay in the low scores of the young autistic children when compared with other groups (Kruskall-Wallis test: $p = 0.0004$). In fact scores of 5 or 6 predominated for the autistic adults and children, and on this measure they fell between the MLD and 3- to 4-year-old children (Fig. 14.3). The young autistic children clearly performed poorly, but even so about half their responses were judged to involve some attempt to imitate, and some of these efforts were judged accurate enough to score 6.

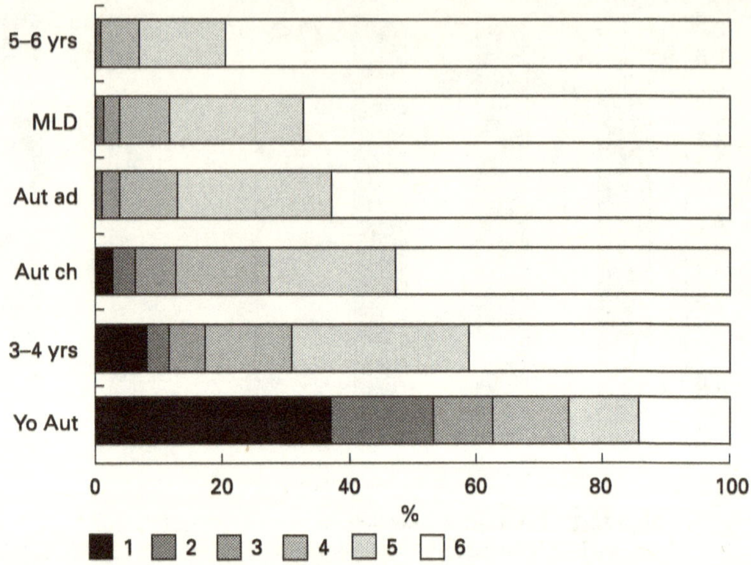

Fig. 14.3 Relative frequencies of scores from 6 (accurate imitation) to 1 (no attempt) on Do-As-I-Do test.

These results do not show the predicted general deficit in imitation the Rogers and Pennington theory implies: some imitative competence appears largely intact in all except the young autistic sample. On the other hand, the poor performance of this young autistic sample is consistent with the theory. When imitation *was* attempted by these children it was not well formed compared to the performance of other groups, as illustrated in Fig. 14.2. It was not possible to assess the mental age of these young children on the same scale as the other samples (BPVS and TROG). However, the fact that at chronological age 5 they had such difficulties with imitation suggests that in early phases of development there could well be the type of imitative barrier that Rogers and Pennington propose as fundamental in the cascade of deficits characterizing autism.

Other results to highlight as relevant to the Rogers and Pennington theory, as well as those described in earlier chapters (see especially Bråten's discussion of the implications of companion space theorems for autism), are those where difficulties in self–other translation are evidenced by responses in which the imitating subject creates an action which to him will look similar to what he saw when he watched the demonstrator, instead of what the demonstrator would see. He fails to translate appropriately, or 'invert' the action to his own perspective as actor. An example is 'peekaboo', performed by the demonstrator with palms towards her own face, and sometimes inaccurately imitated such that the palms are orientated away from the imitator's face (i.e. the actor sees the backs of the hands both when the demonstrator performs the act, and when he himself attempts it). Other actions suffering this type of mistranslation involve one hand acting on the other, such as grasping the thumb, or making a T-shape of one hand against the other. For grasp thumb (see Fig. 14.4), the autistic children scored significantly worse than the 5- to 6-year-old children (median 3.4 versus 6: Kruskall-Wallis test, $p = 0.01$), although we should also note that all groups made *some* of these reversal errors. The autistic children's difficulty with grasp thumb remained in a comparison of samples matched for mental age on BPVS.

Spontaneous imitation on a functional task

The previous experiments examined the question, 'can these subjects imitate?', by encouraging or eliciting imitation. In a further experiment, subjects merely observed another person performing a task which was functional in gaining them a reward, and whether they then spontaneously imitated the technique observed was examined.

The task used was the 'artificial fruit' opening described earlier. This was already known to stimulate imitation in 2- to 4-year-old normal children (Whiten *et al.* 1996). One important change in the experiment with the present samples, however, was that the 'whole fruit' was presented, with all the barriers in place. (The fruit was originally designed to test for imitation of the whole action sequence required, but in the chimpanzee study each of the two sets of barriers was presented separately because of the scepticism then current about primate imitative propensity!) It was therefore possible to assess imitation separately for each of the three elements required to open the 'fruit' and also with respect to the overall configuration, or sequence of these acts ('sequence imitation' (Whiten and Custance, 1996); cf. 'program imitation' (see Byrne, this volume)).

Evidence of imitation was obtained for young normal children's actions on two of the three main components of the task (Table 14.5). The autistic and MLD groups, by contrast, did not produce significant evidence of imitation on any item. Fig. 14.5 illustrates the results for the 'bolts' component, as an example.

There is thus an interesting contrast with the results of the DAID test reported earlier. Imitation can be *elicited* from autistic subjects (with the exception of the young sample) at levels often similar to those of control subjects such as those used here: yet the same subjects tend not

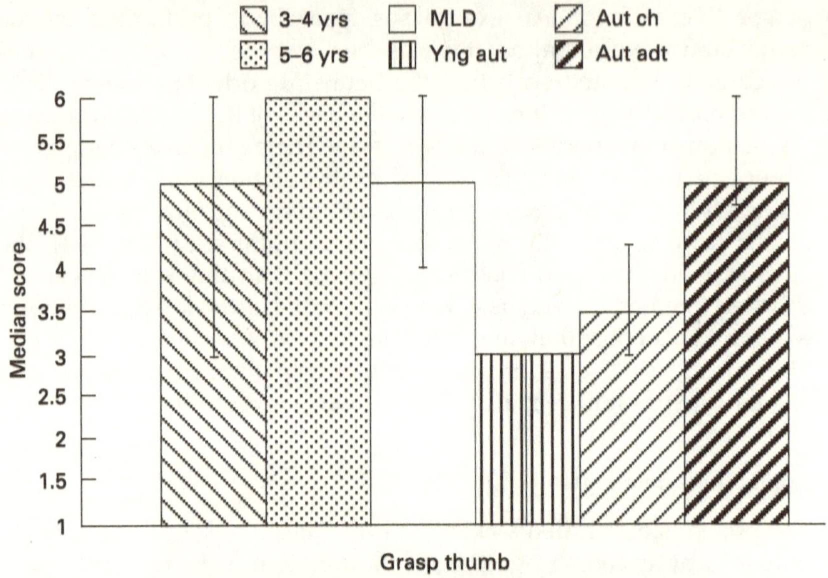

(*a*)

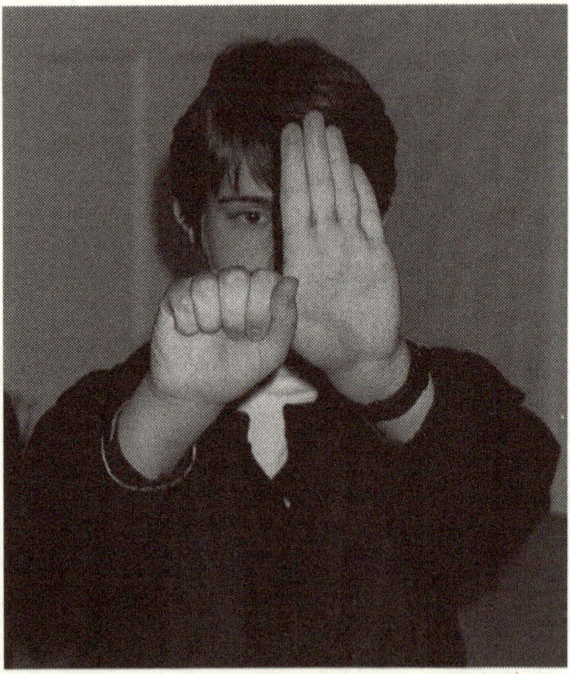

Fig. 14.4 Imitation of grasp thumb – scores and illustrations: (*a*) Demonstrated action 'grasp thumb';

(*b*)

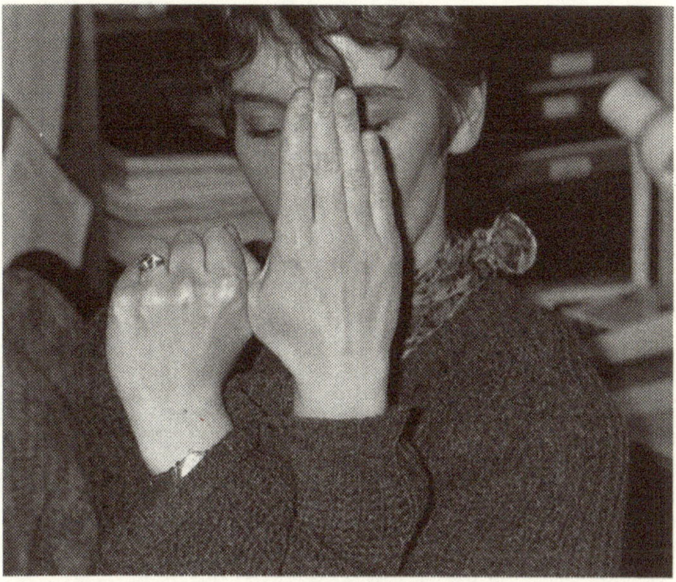

(*c*)

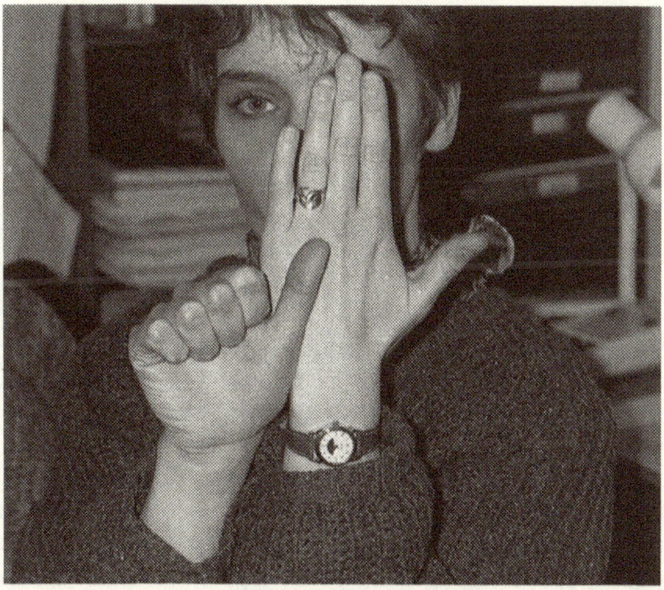

Fig. 14.4 (*cont.*) (*b*) imitation of grasp thumb with two-handed reversal; (*c*) imitation of grasp thumb with one-handed reversal.

Table 14.5 *Summary of imitation effects by group*

Group	Handle		Bolts	
Autistic adults	n.s.	n=11	n.s.	n=10
Autistic children	n.s.	n=12	n.s.	n=11
MLD	n.s.	n=9	n.s.	n=9
5- to 6-year-olds	***	n=12	*	n=12
3- to 4-year-olds	**	n=12	*	n=12

Notes: *** $p < 0.001$
** $p < 0.01$
* $p < 0.05$

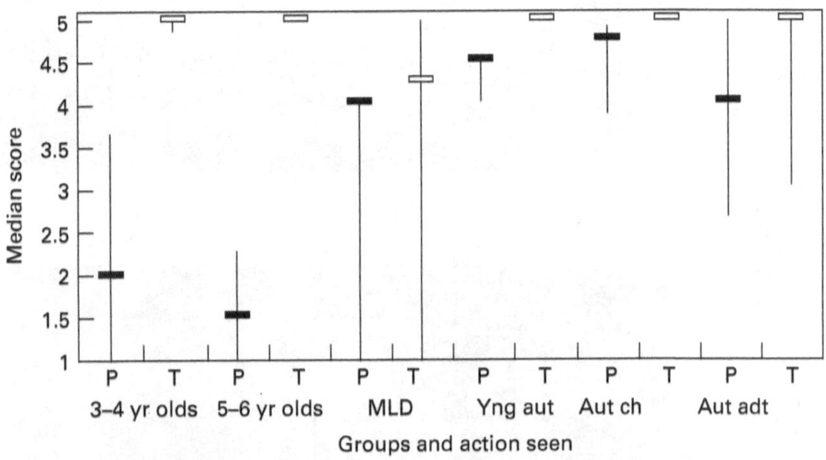

Fig. 14.5 Score on tendency to display morph 'twist' (5 = twist; 1 = poke) for subjects who had witnessed 'twist" (T: open bar) or 'poke' (P: dark bar) on artificial fruit.

to imitate *spontaneously*, while the normal children do. Whether this is a characteristic of autism *per se*, however, is not so clear, since the MLD sample also did not show a significant imitative tendency.

Looking at the data in a different way suggests that the contrast between groups is not as absolute as these statistics imply. Fig. 14.6 shows combined scores for all three elements of the task, transformed in such a way as to provide an index of overall imitative tendency (15 would mean a subject clearly performed all the actions they had witnessed, rather than the alternative, on all three components; a score of 9 would be achieved if they were equally likely to perform the one not witnessed as the one witnessed). Scores are shown for a first, and a second, attempt (each preceded by a demonstration). Although there is

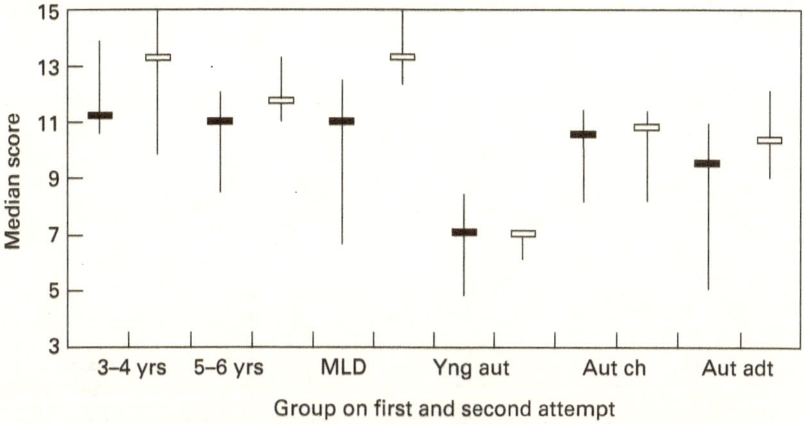

Fig. 14.6 Imitation score across all three component actions for opening artificial fruit, first and second attempts.

a trend for the autistic samples to have lower imitative scores than the non-autistic samples (as we would expect from Table 14.5), the autistic child and adult median imitation indices are all positive, and the scores for the autistic children are not significantly lower than for the non-autistic samples. There are thus some signs of imitation in these autistic samples, even on this task. Note, however, that there is a suggestion in Fig. 14.6 that each of the non-autistic groups is more imitative on the second attempt: there is no hint of this for any of the autistic groups.

Deferred imitation

Deferred imitation appears not to have been tested with any of the autistic samples listed in Table 14.2, despite the fact that it imposes additional cognitive demands in comparison to the DAID and spontaneous, immediate imitation contexts covered. Deferred imitation was tested with essentially the same groups referred to above, using a task similar to those described in the previous section in that it could be done by two different methods. The apparatus consisted of a box-like case which could be held in one hand. In the case was a sliding drawer, removal of which was demonstrated using either a 'wiggle and pull' method orientated in one direction, or an alternative 'push to side' method which took the drawer out in a direction at right angles to the pull method. Inside the drawer was a treat. Twenty-four hours later, subjects were given the object and asked if they would like to play with it.

Differences between scores which provided significant evidence of

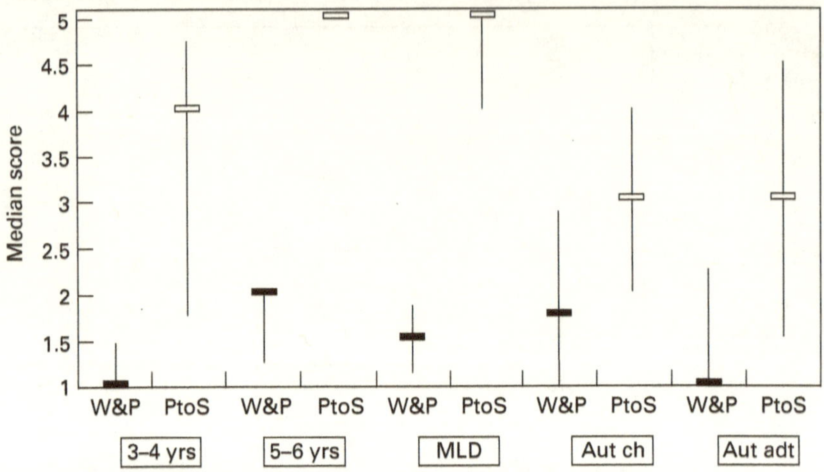

Fig. 14.7 Score on tendency to display morph 'push to side' for subjects who had witnessed 'push to side' or 'wiggle and pull'.

imitation were found only for the 5- to 6-year-old children and MLD sample (Fig. 14.7). Trends are in the same direction for all samples, suggesting that a weak imitative tendency may be present even where the contrasts are not significant, but note that this effect is most evident for the 3- to 4-year-olds, who have mental ages lower than those of the autistic children and adults. Thus again there appears to be a deficit in the imitative tendency of the autistic samples: unlike the case of the spontaneous imitation analysed in the previous section, however, here there is a difference between the MLD and autistic samples.

Discussion

Imitation and mindreading

What are the implications of these results for theoretical formulations about imitative and intersubjective processes developed by Whiten and Byrne (1991), Rogers and Pennington (1991) and authors in Part I of this volume? The most general conclusion to be emphasized, given the negative tenor of previous research as summarized in Table 14.2, is that there is no absolute deficit in imitation in the autistic older child and adult samples tested here. The DAID experiment showed that they could handle the concept of imitation, as embodied in the request to 'Do what I did'; and the predominance of scores in the 5–6 range (6 being a judgement of accurate imitation) shows they have an ability to copy a range of acts. Thus, the classic failure to succeed in theory-of-mind (false-belief attribution) tests shown by the majority of the autistic subjects did not prevent them expressing this basic imitative ability. The notion of an all-pervading imitative deficit coupled to autism and mindreading deficits, suggested by most of the studies reviewed by Rogers and Pennington and others in Table 14.2, is not supported.

An immediate question this raises is why so many earlier studies have produced those negative results, in comparison to the present ones. One answer is suggested by the contrast of these positive DAID results with more negative ones obtained in the functional and deferred imitation tasks, which relied on spontaneous imitation. It appears that the DAID approach is one which can elicit imitation when autistic subjects would not normally show it (whereas non-autistic controls might show imitation equally in elicited and spontaneous contexts). It is difficult to assess how well this explains the variance in findings, because several of the papers supply little information about the degree of encouragement given, but it appears that great variation exists. DeMyer *et al.* (1972), for example, just attracted the subjects' attention by calling 'look!' and their name, and offered five trials in which a response might be given. Mental age of subjects tested also varies across studies. Clearly, these variables need investigating systematically in future studies. The final point to make about these comparisons is that the present study is not the only one to find few or no differences in imitation compared to control samples, as Table 14.2 also shows.

However, the overall positive character of the autistic responses has to be qualified in several ways which speak to the proposed linkages with mindreading or intersubjectivity. First, there is the performance of the younger sample of autistic children, which stands out so dramatically in Fig. 14.2. It is of course difficult to identify and test very young autistic subjects and this was a small sample, not part of the main part of this study; moreover we have neither systematic estimates of mental age nor mental age controls, so we cannot be sure if the lack of imitation is unusual given the mental level of these children. The imitative tendencies of normal 9-month-olds (Meltzoff, 1988) suggest it may well be, such findings then being more consistent with the Rogers and Pennington model in which a deficit in imitation occurs in early mental development, with negative sequelae for aspects of mindreading at later stages, even if at those later ages an imitative capacity does itself become operative. Whiten (1996a) makes a parallel point with respect to phylogenetic as opposed to ontogenetic patterns in the order of emergence of these phenomena: if mindreading evolves 'on the back' of an intersubjective process of imitation, mindreading species would be expected to be good imitators, whereas those capable of simple imitation would not necessarily show any well-developed mindreading.

Another qualification is that the battery of actions we used incorporated mostly quite simple actions (principally to permit comparison with other studies in the literature): most could be regarded as 'single step' actions rather than incorporating a complex sequence. Consistent with this would be the relative lack of imitation produced with respect to the 'artificial fruit', which could be regarded as more complex. However, an analysis of the extent to which autistic subjects followed the sequence or program of actions they had seen used to open the box, irrespective of any (lack of) copying of the specific 'morph' used at each step, showed that two thirds of them followed the three steps in the same order (cf. Byrne, this volume, on program-level imitation). That many DAID test actions were more like single steps thus seems unlikely as an explanation of why so many successes occurred, in so far as most subjects appeared able to recreate the sequence of fruit shell removal.

The final qualification is that autistic subjects did show lack of imitation in the spontaneous and deferred tasks, in contrast to normal and MLD controls: and within the DAID test itself they showed difficulties on reversal (Fig. 14.4), as well as others described more fully in Brown (1996), notably those concerning meaningful/symbolic actions, consistent with previous findings summarized in Table 14.1. Two broad classes of explanation have been offered for why a deficit in imitation might be associated with lack of mindreading and it is worth considering each as a potential reason for these results.

One conjecture is that a link might exist because imitation involves effectively translating from an action done by another individual from their perspective, into what it is to do it from one's own perspective: put this way, it appears an inherently intersubjective phenomenon (Bråten, 1994a, b and this volume; Byrne, 1994; Mitchell, 1993; Whiten and Byrne, 1991; Whiten and Ham, 1992; cf. Heyes, 1993 and in press). The reversal errors found here are consistent with this 'mental perspective change' conjecture, as are the similar errors recorded in the study by Ohta (1987). Many of the actions used in the DAID test appeared to involve little complex perspective change, but those that did, significantly that illustrated in Fig. 14.4, created difficulties. It is also possible that the lack of imitation in the spontaneous and deferred tasks reflects the same difficulty in so far as these tasks were geometrically complicated compared to those of most of the DAID acts.

The second, alternative conjecture is that imitation failures are due to a lack of facility in recognizing what others are *trying to do* – i.e. a lack of intentional interpretation of the actions of the model (see

Tomasello *et al.*, 1993). This could plausibly explain the lesser imitation in the spontaneous conditions because if the observer does not see the demonstrator as trying to do something (get the fruit open), he may be unlikely to attend to *what* the demonstrator is doing to that end. Such an 'intention reading' difficulty applies less to the DAID test because it is so explicitly structured as to make it clear to the subject what his task is (to try to copy what the other does).

At present, it is not possible to determine more clearly whether either or both of these two classes of explanation – 'mental perspective change' or 'intention-reading' – are on the right lines, but future experiments explicitly directed at this distinction should be able to do so.

Implications for intervention

Somewhat paradoxically at first sight, given the immediately preceding discussion, it may be the case that imitation can offer a useful remedial route[3] in autism (see also Dawson and Galpert, 1990; Nadel and Pezé, 1992; Tryon and Keane, 1986). As we have shown above, autistic subjects like those studied here are far from devoid of imitative ability, whatever the deficits in particular aspects of imitation. If Rogers and Pennington and/or Meltzoff and colleagues are right in their hypotheses about the role of imitation in the early ontogeny of mindreading, it could be important to build on this later-emerging imitative ability. Of particular relevance here is what appears to be a quite significant discrepancy between a capacity for imitation when actively elicited, and relative lack of a spontaneous imitative tendency. This pattern seems to suggest that these autistic individuals have a certain imitative competence, but lack the motivation or attentional processes which guide normal individuals into spontaneous imitation of certain acts they witness.

That it might be possible to nurture and encourage this imitative competence is suggested by the fact that the experimenter (JB) found that of all the series of experiments conducted with these subjects (including many others on, for example, emotion recognition and visual perspective-taking, reported in Brown, 1996), the DAID series was the one which generated the most active enjoyment and engagement of the autistic subjects. The adults did particularly well in this context, which is interesting given that they performed less imitation in the spontaneous conditions than did the autistic children. It seems plausible that as such autistic individuals mature they may well appear never to imitate spontaneously, yet a certain ability is there, dormant as it were, to be elicited by appropriately structured social interactions (taking note of the specific difficulties in complex inversions, perhaps): then it could possibly play an important part in stimulating a further cascade of intersubjective engagement.

Notes

1 It is worth emphasizing that cases that suggested some kind of mindreading were a minority in the corpus: the study is too frequently misinterpreted as claiming that all tactical deception is intentional. There was never any such implication, as a careful reading of our clearly stated definitions will show.

There is not the space in this chapter to dwell on the quite deep and complex subject of what will really count as mindreading (or theory of mind, or intersubjectivity), particularly in non-verbal creatures like apes and human infants: where does mindreading become different from behaviour-reading? What, for example, would count as evidence of an infant's reading its father's emotion, rather than just his emotional expression? This topic is addressed fully in Whiten (1994, 1996b). In the first of these papers, it is argued that the best answer to the question – mind- or behaviour-reading? – is to distinguish grades of mindreading rather than a yes/no distinction. In the second, the idea is expounded that to recognize a mental state is to recognize an intervening variable which sits at the explanatory juncture between many different situations, and many different, but importantly predictable, behavioural outcomes.

2 One of us (AW) has recently explored the intersubjective basis of joint attention in chimpanzees, following a study by Baldwin (1994) which showed that human infants at 18 months of age require only that a parent gaze at an object and name it for the infant to adopt that name appropriately. Baldwin suggests that this is evidence of the beginnings of mindreading in that the infant seems to read the parent as directing a 'psychological spotlight' onto objects in the environment, which is what their utterances are *about*. The chimpanzee test was performed with signing apes who can name an object typically touched or held up to them; in the experiment, however, they had a new experience: the human experimenter simply looked up at an object and said, 'Austin (or Sherman) what's that?' Both chimpanzees' first few responses were correct, and thus offered highly significant evidence that they see others' attention in the same way as the 18-month old infants (Whiten, in press b).

For discussion of primate emotion literature relating to concerns in this volume, see Whiten 1993b.

3 As the idea of a mindreading deficit/delay in autism has become accepted, so in recent years efforts have begun to be made to create appropriate remediation programmes. These have mostly been directed at rather directly creating the conditions in which autistic individuals might learn about 'other minds', through intensive experiences or explicit teaching (McGregor *et al.*, 1998, cite studies to date). But none of these comes close to the idea of intervening in early development, or targeting early proposed foundations for theory of mind, like imitation.

PART IV

Intersubjective attunement and emotion in language learning and use

CHAPTER 15

The intersubjective foundations of thought

R. Peter Hobson

Introduction

How do human beings acquire the capacity to think? The answer to this question depends, of course, on what is to count as 'thinking'. In this chapter, I shall focus upon the capacity to think *about* (not merely of) the world, and about alternative courses of action that one may take, or attitudes one may hold, within that world. My thesis is that the kind of 'distancing' one needs to achieve from one's own immediate engagement with the surroundings in order to reflect upon and think *about* things and events is a distancing effected through intersubjective communication with others. Moreover, it is in the context of communication that a child comes to discover what it means to anchor meanings in symbolic vehicles of thought. If this account is correct, then we may discern how typically human forms of abstract and creative symbolic thought develop on the basis of infants' experiences of affectively patterned intersubjective engagement with other people.

The course of the chapter will be as follows. I shall begin by reflecting on the nature of thinking and its relation to self-reflective awareness. The discussion will raise epistemological issues to do with the underpinnings for our concept of persons. I shall move on to trace an outline account of infant development, mapping what seem to be the major staging-posts *en route* to the child's acquiring new powers of reflective thinking in the middle of the second year of life. I shall also dwell on one specific facet of early language acquisition, the comprehension and use of the personal pronouns 'I' and 'you'. Finally, I shall turn to developmental psychopathology in order to see whether here we might find some evidence to justify the rather abstract arguments I have been pursuing.

The nature of thinking

The philosopher David Hamlyn (1978:76) writes as follows: 'For a thought to be a genuine thought it must be about something, and something else must be thought about that something; so that there is in that thought something corresponding to the distinction between subject and predicate that becomes explicit in language itself.' Although one might wonder how much hangs on the notion of a 'genuine' thought, I think it is important to observe how to have a thought *about* something; one somehow has to fix in the mind (by another thought) that which is to be thought-about. We might depict the situation as follows:

Thought 2 ^{about} [Object of thought 1]

This is, of course, a highly abstract characterization of what thought is. A thought cannot exist without a thinker who thinks it; a predicate cannot be made except by a language-user who chooses to make some comment about a selected subject. This said, it may be worth dwelling on certain features of this scheme, and especially on the notion of 'aboutness'.

Before plunging in to pluck the concept of mental aboutness from swirling philosophical waters, let me draw strength from the ever-friendly Shorter Oxford English Dictionary. Here are some definitions of the word 'about', which (importantly, I think) has both adverbial and prepositional uses.

First, as an adverb without an object:

I. Position. Around the outside; on or towards every side; all around. As in: 'He looks about to see what has happened', or more evocatively, from the 'Rime of the Ancient Mariner' by Samuel Taylor Coleridge:

> About, about in reel and rout
> The death-fires danced at night.

II. Motion. Round, in revolution; in succession. As in: 'He brings it about that . . .'

Secondly, as a preposition with an object:

I. Position. On the outside of; on or towards every side of; somewhere near. As in: 'The meadows about Oxford'.
Connection: Attached to as an attribute or circumstance. As in: 'This is about an important topic' or 'You may wonder what I am going on about'.

II. Motion. Round, as in beating about the bush.

I find it especially interesting how the word 'about' is linked to thoughts of someone moving around some focal point, a point that is separate from but also near to the person in motion. There is also a meaning related to the idea of successive events, as in 'to bring about: to cause to revolve'. At the same time, we have the aspect of aboutness to do with connectedness, or being concerned with, as in the philosophically intriguing example of *Much Ado About Nothing*.

I am not simply labouring the point that 'aboutness' implies both connectedness and differentiation between something (be it a thought, an action, a linguistic term, or whatever) and what that something is about. I am also trying to capture, through our language, how 'aboutness' is not as static a notion as one might think – not merely a matter of a thought or whatever 'having direction' towards something – but it also encompasses a sense of bodily movement as a person adopts alternative positions or stances *round about* an object, situation or event. My intent is to conjure an image of how one can move in thought from one stance to another in relation to a particular object of thought, by moving to the psychological position of another person who is related to that same object of thought in a different way. In the case of transitions that take place solely within an individual's mind, the 'other person' term might appear to be redundant, for surely one simply passes from thought to thought. Quite so, but we also need to explain how it is possible to develop the capacity to move from discrete thought to discrete thought, as well as to communicate thought from person to person. My thesis is that we shall need to begin with infants' interpersonal communication and their ability (so to speak) to move across persons psychologically, if we are to discover the origins of their own, individual abilities to think.

Let me anticipate what is to come, by providing a frame for the picture I shall be offering. Consider how an infant may experience adjustments in attitude during interpersonal transactions. Suppose we imagine a 12-month-old perceiving another person to have a particular attitude towards some object on which the child's attention is focused, or the infant perceiving a person performing an action on something. Note we have two senses of aboutness here: the infant and the other person are situated 'about' the object in question (a fact that relates to the physical embodiment of infant, other person and object), and the participants' mental states or actions are directed towards and thus connected with ('about') the object-as-experienced. Now suppose the infant identifies with the attitude or action manifest in the other person's bodily expressions or movements, so that the infant comes to assume the other's psychological stance. If it were the case that the infant understood her new psychological orientation to *be* a new and separate psychological orientation, and moreover one that was 'about' something other than itself, such movement to another person's mental stance would constitute a movement in thought. My claim will be that this configuration of interpersonal events is indeed the cradle of thought.

Enough of playing with language and imagery. What about the serious philosophy of intentionality? In attempting to distinguish the mental from the physical, Brentano (1874/1973) drew attention to the fact that a mental state has directedness towards something else as its object, but this something else that a mental state is 'about' need not exist. We can fear the devil, whether or not the devil exists. We can believe that psychology is an advanced science, but we may be deluded. Moreover, we may misrepresent something as something else, as when a shadow is taken to be the devil. Even in the normal case, we represent things in such-and-such a manner, or according to a certain description-for-me, when other characterizations could equally apply. The person whom I think about as a subject for one of my experiments, someone else thinks about as a much-loved son.

In order to pinpoint what is critical for the developmental psychology of thinking, and specifically to highlight the need to explain the 'aboutness' of representational mental states, I shall refer to the currently popular terminology of propositional attitudes introduced by Bertrand Russell (1940). The canonical format is: A person believes (or hopes, or fears, or intends, or . . .) *that* such-and-such is the case. A person can have the same attitude towards different propositions (e.g. can believe X, or Y, or . . .), or take different attitudes towards the same proposition (e.g. can believe, or hope, or fear, that X).

We must be wary of a hazard in framing the matter this way. The hazard is exemplified by my statement about taking attitudes towards the same proposition, as if it were the proposition (or representation) itself that one believed, hoped or feared. This is true of beliefs only to the extent that the proposition believed is taken to characterize *reality*. In other words, the belief concerns reality characterized in a certain way, that is, in a way captured by the proposition. I believe the proposition 'It is raining' only in so far as I take this to be a correct statement about reality. So, too, a 'proposition' is hoped for or feared only to the extent that the proposition is a way of describing a reality or potential reality that is hoped for or feared. If I fear that the devil will get me, what I fear is not my representation of the devil getting me, but rather the actual devil actually getting me – a potential reality that I need to represent if I am to fear it, but a potential reality nonetheless.

I believe that, from a developmental perspective, there are disastrous consequences if we allow the elegance of the propositional attitude format to introduce a kind of conceptual apartheid into our theory. We should not begin by allowing mental representations or propositions to fall on one side of a divide, and attitudes on the other. One consequence would be that we could not explain how 'representations' have meaning or aboutness. They would sit in the mind as so many entries in Searle's (1980) Chinese Room. Faced with this impending disaster, the representation theorist's only option would appear to be an abject retreat into methodological solipsism (Fodor, 1980).

What, then, *is* the appropriate starting point for a developmental theory of thinking? How might one explain the origins of creative symbolic functioning and the emergent properties of representational thought, with all the flexibility and power that comes with having propositional attitudes? How *do* mental representations represent? And how do children acquire understanding that people relate to the world-as-represented?

I think we need to begin with the fact that infants (not representations or even schemes) start out by relating to the world and to other people through attitude and action. As Martin Buber (1958:18) wrote: 'In the beginning is relation.' The reason that representations are connected to that which they represent is that representations are the cognitive distillate of human beings' attitudes towards and psychological engagement with the world. As Vygotsky (1962/1986:8) stated: 'every idea contains a transmuted affective attitude toward the bit of reality to which it refers'. By the very nature of people's attitudes, the world is subsumed under qualitatively distinct 'descriptions' for the person whose attitudes they are. If I am afraid of something, then that something falls under the description of 'something frightening'. The characterization of the object-in-the-world accords with the ways in which the object becomes the focus of attitudes and actions. It is in this relation between the infant-as-experiencer and the world-as-experienced that we shall find the sources of representation and representational 'aboutness'.

Let me lead up to my own account of the early development of thought, by noting how some Greats of developmental psychology laid the groundwork for my approach. Piaget (1936/1977) provided an impressive if incomplete account of how, in infancy, objects are initially assimilated to (and defined by) separate schemes of action, but are eventually emancipated to become objects in their own right in so far as the infant abstracts objects from immediate actions on the objects, and coordinates which schemes are together applicable to this object and which to that. An apple is that kind of roundish object which can be held, sucked, eaten, etc., but not bounced; a ball is that kind of object which can be held, sucked, bounced, etc., but not eaten. Werner (1948) added an important emphasis on the affective as well as sensorimotor dimensions of meaning-conferring schemes. So, for example, a person is (amongst other things) that kind of object towards which one tends to have certain kinds of feeling. These points are important because they bring home how infants move from dealing with what we adults might call 'abstractions' like holdability, suckability and interpersonal relatability, to the ability to identify particulars through combinations of qualities. The qualities in question have to do with what objects and events afford in relation to the infants' meaning-conferring actions and feelings. Therefore the content of concepts is constituted in accordance with an individual's propensities to relate to the world in particular ways. As we shall see, for example, one would have precious little concept of persons, if one was unable to relate to people with appropriate kinds of feeling.

When we move on in development to the matter of capturing things-as-related-to in symbolic thought, Werner and Kaplan (1963/1984) began to explore how the kind of psychological distancing needed for an infant to distinguish between symbols and referents was somehow bound up with psychological distancing between infant and caregiver. These authors, however, were unable to explain how there occurred the 'emergence of symbols from an interpersonal matrix' (Werner and Kaplan, 1963/1984:71). Vygotsky (1978:57) insisted that the higher cognitive functions originated as 'actual relations between human individuals', but he too left much unexplained about how this happened. My suggestion will be that it is through experience of interpersonally coordinated *attitudes* towards things-as-related-to that children come to recognize the distinction between attitudes and the objects of those attitudes, or between thoughts and things, and that it is in conjunction with this insight that infants acquire symbolic representational thought.

A theory of development (in four pages)

I shall now offer an account which attempts to integrate what has gone before. I shall condense what I say to an absolute minimum, having written on this topic at greater length elsewhere (e.g. Hobson, 1993a, b, 1994a).

The argument goes roughly like this. Early in infancy, babies experience the environment as a kind of given which engages their feelings, affords opportunities for action, and meets or frustrates their needs. Here we need to supplement the accounts of Piaget and Werner cited above. What we need to add is that certain 'things' within the environment, what we adults call persons, allow unique modes of mutual and reciprocal exchange. Infants must experience (as another non-inferred given) what Trevarthen (1979a) has insisted is an *intersubjective* connectedness with, and at times disconnectedness from, other persons. Here biologically provided capacities for interpersonal affective coordination are critical. The reason that feelings are so important is that it is only through patterned interpersonal affective coordination, and the infant's capacity to register in her own feelings the emotional attitudes of others (especially, when another person is relating to herself), that the infant comes to understand what it means to share experiences, and ultimately what it means to be a person who *has* subjective mental life. It is only through being connected with others in feeling that the infant subsequently comes to distinguish among 'persons' who have their own psychological states that are both similar to yet distinct from the infant's own.

Then towards the end of the first year of life, and before understanding much about persons, infants register and react to the directedness of other people's attitudes and actions towards a shared world. This is attested by the many manifestations of secondary intersubjectivity and social referencing, for example requesting people to act on objects, showing objects to others, or evaluating objects according to other people's emotional reactions to the objects in question (e.g. Bretherton *et al.*, 1981; Trevarthen and Hubley, 1978). Moreover, infants have a propensity to adopt the attitudes and intentions of others. This level of interpersonal identification and imitation does not so much result from but rather contributes to the child's understanding of self and other.

I believe the infant's perception of, emotional reactions to and appropriation of other people's attitudes both towards the world and towards her own attitudes, are critical for disembedding the infant from an immediate, unreflective, 'concrete' apprehension of the environment; that is, they are critical for the development of thinking. The reason is that they constitute the route by which the infant comes to adopt, and in due course to recognize, multiple attitudes to the same things and events. If the same things can be the objects of different attitudes, then things are different from thoughts. With insight into this, the child can knowingly confer novel attitudes (thoughts) onto familiar things in symbolic play, and can appreciate how she herself as well as others can capture and intentionally convey attitudes and thoughts in language.

Let me consider this from the point of view of aboutness. In the paradigmatic case of secondary intersubjectivity, we have what I have called the 'relatedness triangle' (Hobson, 1993a, 1994a), in which the infant relates to an object or event, an adult relates to the same object or event, and the infant relates to the adult's way of relating to that object or event. Note how we have two people situated 'about' an object, and how the infant takes the adult's attitude to be 'about' the object. If the infant now assumes the adult's attitude *and* maintains awareness of the physical-cum-psychological separateness between herself and the person from whom the new attitude has been adopted, then it is as if the infant has moved about the object psychologically, assuming one and then another attitude. Or again, the infant who tries to engage the adult with some object is attempting to bring round or 'bring about' the adult's focus of attention, often physically as well as psychologically causing the adult to revolve into a new orientation.

I am not claiming that at this point, around the end of the first year, the infant *understands* much about the way in which an object may mean different things to different people, that is, the way in which a given object may fall under a different description-for-me and description-for-her. On the contrary, I am suggesting that the business of perceiving and registering the directedness of someone else's attitude, and the movement towards assuming that attitude or attempting to bring another person's attitude in line with one's own, are accomplished without such understanding. This configuration of interpersonal events is itself what makes the growth in understanding possible over the coming months of life. In other words, it is through an infant's experiences of her own attitudes, alongside and with other people's attitudes to a visually specified world, that she *comes* to appreciate two complementary facts of psychological life: objects can have multiple meanings-for-persons, and persons can hold multiple attitudes to given objects. Or to put this differently, objects can fall under different descriptions for people, and different descriptions can be applied in a way that is a function of the person whose descriptions they are.

It is, of course, much easier to state that a certain kind of understanding develops than to state how it develops. I shall restrict myself to remarking on two amongst several factors that probably play an important role in the transition towards the infant's enhanced self-reflective awareness and understanding of persons-with-minds around the middle of the second year. Until now, I have been concerned with the basis for an infant's awareness of subjective mental life, and so I have focused on the significance of interpersonal attitudes rather than actions. The interpersonal coordination of actions is also important, however. After all, the 12-month-old infant perceives, relates to and often imitates another person's actions, and this surely contributes to as well as stems from the infant's awareness of self–other correspondences and distinctiveness (Meltzoff, 1990; Russell, 1994). I believe that there are somewhat separable components to an infant's ability to recognize and identify with a person's attitudes on the one hand, and with a person's actions on the other (Hobson, 1994b). For example, there may be ways of imitating goal-directed actions which do not implicate an awareness of the other as a person who has intentions to achieve the goal. Whatever the case here, interpersonal negotiation through action, perhaps especially through modes of action that either are expressive or are intended to effect communication, is going to play a role in promoting self–other awareness.

The second factor I shall mention has to do with an infant's capacity to adopt others' attitudes towards its own attitudes and actions (Hobson, 1993c; Mead, 1934; Tomasello, 1993). As G. H. Mead (1934) described, significant symbols arise in conjunction with self-reflective awareness when the child takes the role of the other *vis-à-vis* itself. The child recognizes that the gestures used by others to communicate to the self are also gestures that can be used by the self to communicate similar messages to others. It is worth pausing to examine this intriguing relationship between self-reflective awareness and symbolic functioning.

Consider the case of symbolic play, which is in some ways more straightforward than symbolizing in language. As Leslie (1987) describes, symbolic play may involve making one thing stand for another, or attributing pretend properties to objects, or inventing imaginary objects. For this to be 'true' symbolizing, the child needs to be aware of what she is doing in designating one thing by another, attributing properties, and so on: it is not enough merely to treat one thing as if it were another (Huttenlocher and Higgins, 1978). If symbolizing entails that the child knowingly introduces and applies to the symbolic vehicle descriptions-for-persons decontextualized from their usual contexts of application, then we might say that the child who symbolizes is aware of playfully applying a pretend description-for-me to an object that is recognized to have a distinct for-serious description. Moreover, the child's playful knowing looks, as well as her ability to tune into the play of others, appear to demonstrate her awareness that a pretend description-for-me may differ from a pretend description-for-other. Thus it would seem that a certain degree of self-reflective awareness is a prerequisite for creative symbolic functioning. If this is so, it is probably no coincidence that new levels of empathy and interpersonal role-taking (Hoffman, 1975), as well as new expressions of self-consciousness (Kagan, 1982), emerge in concert with creative symbolic play at around 18 months of age.

According to this account, therefore, it is the interpersonal (I–Thou) developmental pathway that leads to the cognitive revolution that eventuates in the 18-month-old's awareness that the world is not simply given – things can also be *taken* to mean this, that or the other in symbolic play. Or again, language-users can make sounds express or communicate particular attitudes. This discovery of the joys of symbolizing requires that the child grasps the difference between selves (including the child's own self) who have attitudes and intentions, and a world towards which those attitudes and intentions are directed. It is this insight that enables the child to decontextualize and transpose attitudes on to novel objects and, with this, to anchor meanings in the materials of symbolic play. It is the same insight that yields acts of predication, in that the child expresses an attitude as 'comment' upon a target that already exists in the mind under some alternative characterization. The theoretical proposal, then, is that the $1\frac{1}{2}$-year-old child acquires a profoundly enriched cognitive repertoire by coming to *understand* something about persons with their own subjectively grounded representations of the world. It is this understanding that enables the child to exploit her own capacity for applying multiple meanings to objects in play, simply because now she understands that this is something she (as a person) can do!

Perhaps I might conclude this section of the chapter by bringing together the issues of self-development and symbolizing, this time in language, by considering a development that occurs soon after the period with which we have been concerned. This development involves the child's comprehension and use of the personal pronouns 'I' and 'you', as well as such related terms as 'my' and 'mine', towards the end of the second year of life. The interest here is that, in order to produce a word like 'mine' in an appropriate context, a child must have witnessed someone saying 'Mine!' when the word expressed that *other* person's attitude of possessiveness and/or appropriation. That is, the child must have recognized that when the other person said 'Mine!', the anchorage of the word was in the speaker's own attitude-cum-action. It is only by identifying with that attitude, and then adopting the term 'Mine!' as expressive of that attitude, that the child could come to express her own possessive attitude with this same term. It is interesting that Charney (1980) reports how in nearly all of the young children she studied, the earliest uses of 'my' were produced while a child was acting on an object – searching for, grabbing, acting upon, or claiming it, usually when the object was *not* the child's – rather than expressing more permanent ownership. The pronouns 'I' and 'me' also appeared in contexts such as those of searching for, requesting, claiming or noticing an object, rather than describing the child's own body. I mention the case of personal pronouns in order to highlight the movement in psychological stance and attitude that is so central to intellectual as well as social development. The business of identifying with the attitudes of others occurs with increasing cognitive elaboration over the first two years, but it remains rooted in more-than-cognitive modes of interpersonal relatedness.

Developmental psychopathology: the case of autism

There has been more than a little speculative content to what I have been saying. Why should anyone believe this rather than competing accounts of the origins of symbolic representation and thought? Of course it is insufficient merely to note coincidences in development, and cleverly to suggest that this emergent function depends on that. We need evidence. The problem is that, in considering the normal case, it is often difficult to analyse the causal relationship (if any) among correlated psychological functions, a matter that is especially difficult when a cluster of rather diverse abilities (self-awareness, social role-taking, creative symbolic play, aspects of language) are being related one to another.

One avenue of investigation is to study the associations and dissociations among psychological abilities that occur both synchronously and diachronically across development in children who are abnormal. For arguments about the interconnectedness among self-awareness, interpersonal understanding, symbolic play and language, the case of childhood autism has become something of a *cause célèbre* (e.g. contributions to Baron-Cohen *et al.*, 1993; Hobson, 1993a; Leslie, 1987). Not surprisingly, there is more agreement over the nature of autistic children's impairments than over the appropriate way to explain their co-occurrence, and even in the former respect there are substantial divergences in interpretation (for example, concerning autistic children's deficits in symbolic play; Lewis and Boucher, 1988). My thesis is that the roots of autistic children's *characteristic* abnormalities in thinking are to be found in their deficient capacity for interpersonal engagement, with the accompanying impoverishment in their experiences of primary and secondary intersubjectivity. For now, I shall simply point out the plausibility of such an account by offering a cursory review of the kinds of communicative and cognitive deficit one finds in autism.

I shall catalogue just some of the suggestive evidence. First, in the domain of non-verbal communication, autistic children appear to be specifically impaired in emotional expressiveness, emotion recognition and affective responsiveness to others (e.g. Dawson *et al.*, 1990; Hobson, 1991b; Kasari, Sigman, Mundy and Yirmiya, 1990; Ricks, 1975; Sigman *et al.*, 1992). They have a specific abnormality in sharing experiences of things with other people in 'protodeclarative acts' (e.g. Loveland and Landry, 1986; Mundy *et al.*, 1986; Wetherby and Prutting, 1984), and they relatively rarely engage in social referencing (e.g. Sigman *et al.*, 1992). They appear to be deficient in their ability and/or propensity to imitate others (e.g. Curcio, 1978; Dawson and

Adams, 1984), although it remains to specify the scope of this abnormality.

When it comes to considering language, there are a substantial number of autistic people who never talk at all, and one is prompted to wonder whether these profoundly handicapped individuals ever grasp what linguistic communication *is* (which is perhaps of little wonder, if they do not grasp what it means to share or have other kinds of coordinated experience with others). In linguistic as in 'prelinguistic' functioning, autistic children seem less inclined or able to share experiences or information, and markedly less able to assume the attitudes of others or to orientate others in attitude (as opposed to action) through linguistic means. The manifestations of such difficulties range through pragmatic language problems in adjusting speech forms according to what is being conveyed to whom and with what attitude (e.g. Baltaxe, 1977; Loveland *et al*., 1989; Tager-Flusberg and Anderson, 1991), to limitations in the understanding of words (especially metaphors) that require a kind of meta-attitude to the speech act itself (e.g. Happé, in press). They often appear to have specific difficulties in comprehending and using personal pronouns (e.g. Bosch, 1970; Jordan, 1989; Kanner, 1943; Lee *et al*., 1994).

Along with the above deficits in non-verbal and verbal communication, autistic children display limited signs of self-reflective awareness, for instance rarely appearing coy before their own mirror-images (e.g. Dawson and McKissick, 1984; Spiker and Ricks, 1984), and rarely showing self-conscious emotions such as pride or shame (e.g. Bosch, 1970). So, too, they have marked deficits in the exuberant forms of creative symbolic play seen in normal young children (e.g. Baron-Cohen, 1987; Sigman and Ungerer, 1984; Wing and Gould, 1979; Wulff, 1985). Even in the relatively uncommon instances of autistic children playing at attributing new meanings to objects, there is almost never the imaginative productivity that suffuses non-autistic children's play. They also have specific limitations in understanding both their own and other people's minds (Baron-Cohen *et al*., 1993; Hobson, 1993a).

Obviously, the abnormalities in language and symbolic play also count as reflections of abnormalities in thinking. Both in their performance on standard IQ tests such as the WISC (e.g. Bartak *et al*., 1975; Lockyer and Rutter, 1970; Tymchuk *et al*., 1977), and in their spontaneous language in natural contexts (e.g. Bosch, 1970; Ricks and Wing, 1975; Wing, 1981), autistic individuals manifest a difficulty in distancing themselves from a given, fixed, 'concrete' mode of apprehending the world in order to think flexibly about it. A typical example, mentioned by Wing (1981), is that of the autistic child who when asked to put something down, always had to put it on the floor; another is of the autistic savant described by Scheerer *et al.* (1945), who responded to a doctor's 'Goodbye, my son' with 'I am not your son.' Such examples from the linguistic domain are especially striking, but the autistic person's one-track thinking is also apparent in his or her stereotyped preoccupations and perseverative tendencies, and a lack of flexibility in planning (Ozonoff *et al.*, 1991; Hughes and Russell, 1993).

In the introduction to this chapter, I made a connection between thinking about the world and considering alternative courses of action one might take, or attitudes one might hold, within that world. In reviewing these observations on autistic children, one is struck by their difficulty in achieving the kind of distance from their own engagement with the world, in their case a mode of engagement that usually involves *doing* things, in order to reflect on the 'multiple-meanings' potential both of objects and of language. It is possible that certain of autistic individuals' tendencies to one-track, concrete, literal, perseverative thinking and lack of planning may be a direct manifestation of impairments in frontal lobe functioning (Ozonoff *et al.*, 1991; Rogers and Pennington, 1991). When one takes into account autistic people's deficits in self-awareness, communication and interpersonal understanding, however, it would seem equally plausible that primary deficits in intersubjective engagement are at the developmental roots of their limited capacities for thinking. Suppose it is the case that the ability to think 'about' things arises out of the ability to perceive and assume other people's psychological orientations 'about' given objects and events. Suppose also that one requirement for such co-orientation towards the world is a propensity to become psychologically engaged with others through biologically prepared patterns of intersubjective relatedness. If it is the case that the essence of autism is a profound impairment in intersubjectivity (Hobson, 1991c, 1993a; Rogers and Pennington, 1991), then one might expect that autistic children would present with a syndrome of characteristic deficits in the realms of language and thinking, deficits that bear a specific relation to abnormalities in the realms of interpersonal relatedness and affect-related non-verbal communication. Such indeed is the picture of autism.

Conclusions

In this contribution I have followed the intellectual leads of Vygotsky (1962/1986) and Werner and Kaplan (1963/1984) in analysing how the early emergence of self-reflective awareness and symbolic thought is to be understood as a process of distancing the infant from her immediate engagement with the world, through specific forms of social experience. To put it rather unsubtly, I have suggested that early forms of interpersonal responsiveness, identification and imitation are what disengage an infant from a one-track relation with the environment, and enable her to acquire self-consciousness, to distinguish attitudes from the objects of those attitudes, to apply new meanings or descriptions-for-persons to the materials of symbolic play, and to gain insight into the nature of predication and naming. If the account is correct, it exemplifies Vygotsky's thesis that sophisticated mental capacities arise through the interiorization of interpersonal processes.

I have attempted to flesh out this perspective, by examining how certain of the cognitive and linguistic impairments of autistic individuals appear to reflect developmental sequelae to primary deficits in intersubjective communication. At the very least, the phenomena of autism should prompt us to re-evaluate our theories about the nature and development of thinking.

I have set my developmental scheme against the backcloth of considerations about the nature of thought. Thoughts (or in modern parlance, 'representations') have 'aboutness'. The format of propositional attitudes highlights how, in the course of development, 'propositions' (or in my terms, descriptions-for-persons) can become partly emancipated from particular attitudes, in so far as objects or events characterized in a certain way may be feared, wished-for, believed, and so on. I have attempted to explain how symbolic representations of the world have aboutness and transposability in virtue of the fact that they are the cognitive distillate of a person's attitudes, abstracted through intersubjective transactions with others. As Langer (1957) pointed out, symbols are vehicles for the conception of objects, and our conceptions of objects have much to do with attitudes and actions (or potential attitudes and actions) that the objects in question afford. Moreover, symbolic communication is a matter of one person using symbols to re-orientate other people's minds in accordance with the attitudes evoked by the symbols. Hence we can observe how there is continuity in the kinds of intra- and interpersonal psychological process that lead to the emergence of symbolism, and the kinds of intra- and interpersonal process that underpin the functioning of symbolic thought and communication once it develops. In my view, these are the intersubjective foundations of thought.

Acknowledgements
I am indebted to the writings of David Hamlyn, and thank him for his personal help. I have also gained much from lively discussions with Mike Tomasello.

CHAPTER 16

Language, culture and intersubjectivity: the creation of shared perception

Patricia K. Kuhl

Sharing an emotion or idea with another person is fundamental to being human. The shared perception we seek when we communicate is part of the fabric of our daily lives. As adults, we use language to help us convey to others the emotions and thoughts we experience, but infants are unable to communicate with language. Can infants share perception without language? Is there some understanding of other people, some primitive form of intersubjectivity, prior to language?

An early vehicle in infants' development of understanding other people may be the experience of shared perception. It would assist in producing shared states of mind, helping infants mentally align themselves with adults of the culture. We can thus pose more fundamental questions. Do infants share our perceptions? If they do, is it because perception is largely biologically determined? Does experience play a role in shaping a shared perception with other human beings?

Recent work on the effects of experience on perception show that experience plays an important role. I study language, in particular the effects of ambient language on infants. I have shown that early auditory experience profoundly alters perception (Kuhl, 1994a). The research indicates that listening to ambient language causes infants to form culturally specific 'perceptual maps' for human speech. These maps serve as *filters* through which language is perceived. The study of the formation of culturally specific filters is one of the focuses of this chapter.

My work indicates that mental maps for speech are brought about through linguistic experience, that they develop unconsciously, do not require reinforcement, and, once in place, are very difficult to undo. I have described experience as 'warping' perception because the brain maps physical information in a way that distorts reality. Fortunately, the mental maps that result are shared among those whose experience is similar and this, in turn, facilitates linguistic communication.

What the research offers to the debate on the development of intersubjectivity is a detailed example of how experience shapes perception. These findings suggest a mechanism by which certain aspects of culture and language may be transferred from adults to infants, and how common experience may assist in producing a common 'perceptual filter' through which the world can be viewed. This, in turn, would be expected to result in mental states that can be more easily understood and shared.

Linguistic subjectivity

I travel to foreign countries to examine the results of nature's experiments on language: the linguistic abilities of people whose perceptual experiences vary greatly by virtue of the fact that they were born and raised in different language environments. On one of my recent trips, I was reminded of the vast difference between perception in people of different cultures. I was in Japan, setting up an experiment with infants in collaboration with my Japanese colleagues. The experiment had to do with elementary units of speech, phonetic units, specifically the consonants /r/ and /l/. Our experiment was designed to test American and Japanese infants on the perception of these sounds. The Japanese language does not distinguish between the two and the experiment was designed to test whether young infants from the two cultures could hear the difference between them.

My colleagues and I had set up the laboratory, with its loudspeakers and computers, and began to play the /r/ and /l/ stimuli that I had recorded in America and carried on computer disk to Japan. As the program was launched and the sounds began to play, I was relieved. The disk was unscathed; the stimuli were intact. The design called for repetitions of one of the two sounds as a kind of background sound ('/ra/, /ra/, /ra/'), which would, at some point, switch to repetitions of the second sound ('/la/, /la/, /la/'). The infant's task was to listen to the sounds and produce a head-turn response for a visual reinforcer when the sound changed. We have shown in numerous experiments that infants are quite good at this.

At the first sound switch, I looked at my colleagues and smiled. The program worked. The sounds had changed at the appropriate moment. Everything was set. I then realized that only I and my research assistant (who had joined me on the trip) were smiling. My Japanese colleagues were straining, listening as hard as they could to the sounds emanating from the loudspeaker. There was no recognition among the Japanese that the sound had changed from /ra/ to /la/. They listened again and again as I indicated when the switch occurred. There was still no recognition of a change in the sound. The test separated those in the room into two groups, Americans and Japanese, people whose perceptual systems were obviously very different.

As this experience shows, in adulthood our perception of speech involves a kind of subjectivity. Perception is not equivalent across cultures. Rather than reflecting the objective properties of the stimulus, perception reflects properties of the mind. Speakers of a given language discriminate the critical differences in phonetic units contained in their own native language, but have difficulty discerning differences between phonetic contrasts that are not used in their native language. Japanese adults have notorious difficulty discriminating /r/ from /l/ (Miyawaki *et. al.*, 1975); Americans have equal difficulty discriminating Spanish /b/ and /p/ (Abramson and Lisker, 1970).

The effects of language experience extend beyond perception. Learned actions that are reflected in speech production in the form of our native-language 'dialects' also develop in response to language experience. Dialects develop early in life (by the end of the second year), are similar within social groups, and tend to remain with us for life, and cause us to produce foreign languages with an 'accent'.

The perceptual and perceptual-motor systems underlying language are not easily retrained. Once established, they resist change. We listen to speech with a highly subjective 'native-language ear'; we speak with an equally distinct 'native-language tongue'. How are these rather indelible effects brought about in people? How is it that perception and action within social groups are brought into line with one another while remaining distinct from those of other groups?

Studies on infants demonstrate that developmental speech perception and production show an interesting transition. A universal, or language-general pattern, is exhibited early in life (Kuhl, 1994b). In the first few months, infants discern differences between all the phonetic units used in the world's languages and produce a set of language-universal sounds (Ferguson *et al.*, 1992). In contrast to the culture-bound patterns shown by their parents, infants can be described as 'citizens of the world' in the initial state.

Within a very short time, however, there is evidence to suggest that infants' abilities become language-specific. By 12 months, infants across cultures fail to discriminate foreign-language contrasts they once discriminated (Werker and Polka, 1993; Werker and Tees, 1984). Prior to one year, their speech production abilities change and begin to reflect those of the ambient language community (de Boysson-Bardies, 1993). What brings about the divergence seen in infants after only a short period of listening to ambient language?

The cause of linguistic subjectivity and transition: a new view

The thesis presented here is that linguistic experience results in an interesting kind of learning (Kuhl, 1993, 1994a). Given linguistic input, the perceptual and perceptual-motor systems underlying speech show self-organization accompanied by a loss in flexibility. The vehicle for change is argued to be *representations* stored in memory that capture the regularities of a specific language. Infants' speech representations alter infants' abilities. They result in 'perceptual maps' that specify perceived distances. These maps differ critically in speakers of different languages.

An important point for theory is that the regularities of language encoded by infants as they listen to speech include more than their auditory properties (Kuhl and Meltzoff, 1982). As I will shortly explain, the visual properties of speech are encoded as well. Moreover, infants' perceptual representations, reflecting the voices and faces of talking people, cause infants to attempt to mimic these patterns, as seen in studies in our laboratory on vocal imitation (Kuhl and Meltzoff, 1996). Motor information is thus added to infants' speech representations. In short, infants' store 'polymodal' aspects of speech – the auditory and visual speech they experience, and the motor patterns they themselves produce.

To explain these theoretical claims, a number of laboratory studies will be reviewed in some detail. Some of this work is highly technical, but cannot be omitted without sacrificing important aspects of the findings.

The 'perceptual magnet effect' and mental maps for speech

Work in my laboratory has produced an effect that helps explain how language experience affects speech perception. The effect shows that linguistic experience alters perception by warping the underlying acoustic space; this changes the perceived distances between speech stimuli (Iverson and Kuhl, 1995; Kuhl, 1991a, 1993, 1994a).

Our first behavioural assay supporting these claims was a phenomenon uncovered in the laboratory that I refer to as the *perceptual magnet effect* (PME). PME was observed in studies using phonetic prototypes, the best or most representative instances of phonetic categories. Our studies showed that phonetic prototypes appeared to

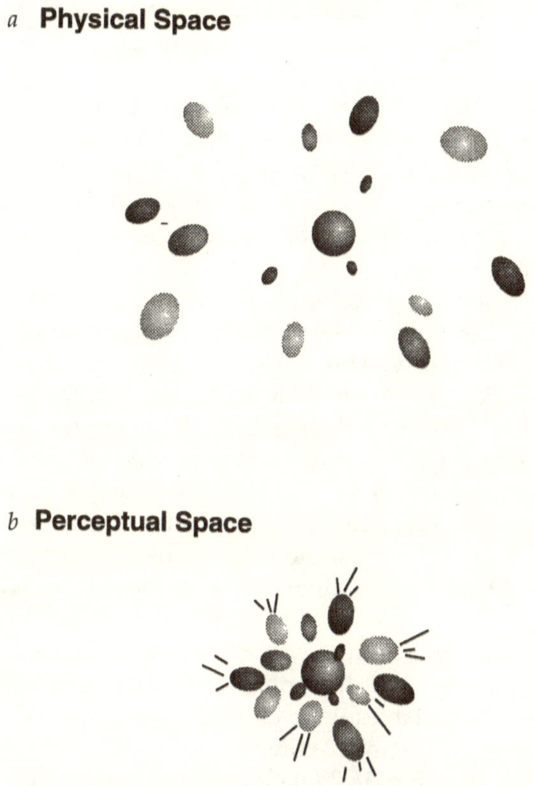

Fig. 16.1 The perceptual magnet effect, when (*a*) a variety of sounds in a category surround the category prototype, (*b*) they are perceptually drawn towards the prototype.

function like 'perceptual magnets' for other sounds in the category (Kuhl, 1991a; Kuhl and Iverson, 1995). As illustrated in Fig. 16.1, when listeners heard a phonetic prototype and attempted to discriminate it from sounds that surround it in acoustic space (*a*), the prototype displayed an attractor effect on the surrounding sounds. It perceptually pulled other members of the category towards it, making it difficult to hear differences between the prototype and surrounding stimuli (*b*). Poor instances from the category (non-prototypes) did not function in this way.

Phonetic prototypes and magnet effects were shown to be language specific. Vowel prototypes, for example, differ across languages. They occur in the same acoustic space, but languages differ in the number and location of vowel categories within the acoustic space. In tests on speakers of many different languages on a set of sixty computer-generated vowel stimuli, speakers of different languages reported hearing different numbers of vowels, and identified different 'hot-spots', locations of the best or most representation instances of particular vowels (Willerman and Kuhl, 1996). For example, in the set of sixty vowels, Swedes heard six types, while Americans heard only two. What was perceived as a particularly good /i/ vowel (as in the word 'beet') to an American, was not perceived as a good instance of any Swedish vowel, according to the Swedes (Kuhl, 1992a).

Differences in phonetic prototypes and magnet effects are most dramatically seen, however, in experiments on consonants (Iverson and Kuhl, 1996; Kuhl and Iverson, 1995). These studies show that the PME alters perception of the entire acoustic space underlying phonetic categories by creating a 'perceptual map' of the underlying space. In the example I shall describe, the consonants /r/ and /l/ were used. These sounds differ greatly in languages that contain both sounds, such as American English, German and Finnish; in Japanese, where only /r/ exists, the sound produced crosses many categories and is perceived by Americans as a poor instance of either /r/, /l/ or /d/.

American and Japanese adults were tested with computer-generated syllables beginning with /r/ and /l/ (Iverson and Kuhl, 1996; Kuhl *et al.*, 1995). The syllables were created by varying their critical acoustic components to create a 2-dimensional grid. A physical map of the stimuli is shownin Fig. 16.2 (*a*). Stimuli in the grid were equally distant from one another from a physical standpoint. The question was, when listeners' perception of these sounds is tested, what do their perceptual maps look like? Do they mirror the physical map – that is, is the perception of distance a direct complement of real physical distance?

American and Japanese listeners identified each syllable, rated its category goodness, and estimated the perceived similarity for all possible pairs of stimuli using a scale from '1' (very dissimilar) to '7' (very similar). Similarity ratings were scaled using MDS techniques. These techniques map similarity on to distance. Pairs of stimuli that are perceived as very similar are placed close to one another in the space while those perceived as very dissimilar are placed far apart. The resulting picture provides a mental map of perceived distance that can be contrasted with the map of physical distance.

The mental maps of American and Japanese listeners were very different. In both cases, perceived distance differed from real physical distance. The physical (acoustic) differences between pairs of stimuli were equal (Fig. 16.2*a*); however, perceived distance was warped for

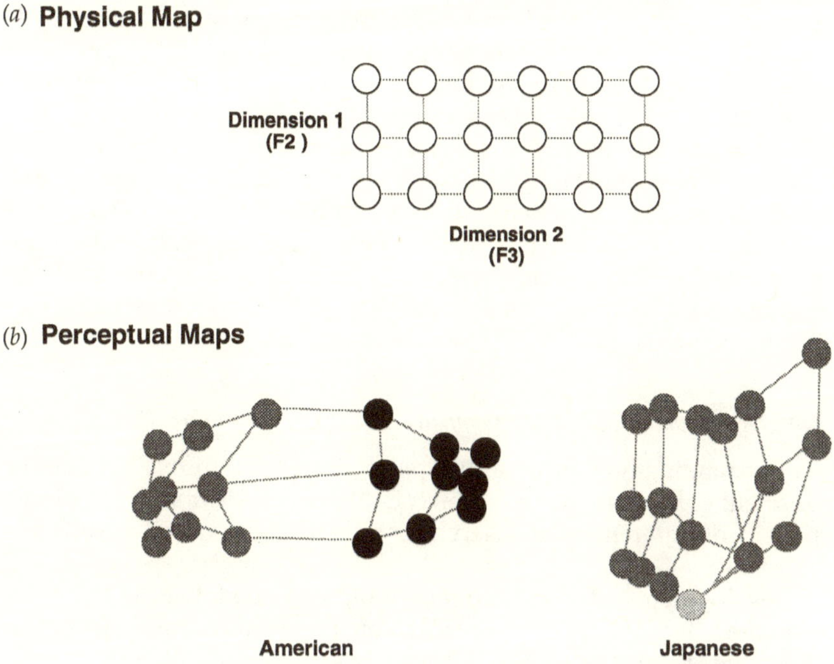

Fig. 16.2 Physical (acoustic) versus perceptual maps. (*a*) Consonant tokens of /r/ and /l/ were generated to be equally distant from one another in acoustic space. (*b*) When listeners from two different cultures (American and Japanese) perceive them, distance is distorted.

both groups of subjects (Fig. 16.2*b*). Moreover, the perceptual space was differentially warped for people from the two cultures.

Examining the Americans' mental map, there are two areas where stimuli are clustered, one in the region of the best /r/ and the other in the region of the best /l/. In these areas, discrimination is difficult because the stimuli are perceived as very similar Here, perceptual space is described as *shrunk*, representing the predicted magnet effects surrounding the /r/ and /l/ prototypes. Perceptual space was greatly reduced as surrounding stimuli were perceptually drawn to the prototype. Interestingly, perceptual space near the boundary that separates the two categories was expanded – *stretched*. It is as though the two magnet attractors repel one another, making the two categories easier to distinguish.

In contrast, examine the perceptual map for Japanese adults. It is very different. As predicted, there was no evidence of any magnet effects – there were no perceptual clusters showing a shrinking of the perceptual space around prototypes (because none of these sounds matches very closely Japanese speakers' phonetic prototypes), and there was no stretching of the perceptual space at the boundary between two categories (because no boundary is perceived).

The results show quite clearly that linguistic experience results in distinct mental maps. These maps specify relative perceptual distances as well as the dimensions to which listeners attend. The critical point for theory is the fact that, in both cases, perception does not mirror reality. Perception is shaped by linguistic experience to create mental maps that are configured very differently for speakers of different languages.

Language experience and developmental change in perception

Understanding how profoundly speech perception differs in adults of different cultures made us curious about infants. How early could this pattern of differences be observed in infants being raised in different cultures?

Developmental studies on 6-month-olds revealed that the PME was exhibited by 6-month-old infants for the sounds of their native language (Kuhl, 1991a). When tested with American English vowels, infants at 6 months showed far greater generalization around a prototype of the vowel /i/ than they did around a non-prototype of the same category. In other words, infants in America were, by 6 months of age, already behaving like adult speakers of the language. Their perceptual systems were already tuned to match those of adults in the culture.

The next question, of course, was whether this is the product of linguistic experience. This question was answered by a cross-cultural study on 6-month-old infants conducted in the United States and Sweden (Kuhl *et al.*, 1992). Infants from both countries were tested with two vowel prototypes, an American English vowel prototype, /i/ (as in 'peep'), and a Swedish vowel prototype, /y/ (as in 'fye'). If the PME was produced by language experience, infants ought to exhibit the magnet effect only for the native-language vowel they had been listening to; on the other hand, if the PME was part of infants' universal language abilities, infants in both cultures might exhibit the effect for the prototypes of both languages.

The results demonstrated that the PME in 6-month-old infants was affected by linguistic experience. American infants demonstrated the magnet effect only for the American English /i/; they treated the Swedish /y/ like a non-prototype. Swedish infants showed the opposite pattern, demonstrating the magnet effect for the Swedish

/y/ and treating the American English /i/ as a non-prototype. This is the earliest age at which language experience has been shown to alter phonetic perception in infants.

Prenatal auditory experience

Infants' exposure and response to sound do not begin at birth. In the womb the foetus is exposed to sound which it appears to respond to (Lecanuet and Granier-Deferre, 1993). Studies on the acoustics of speech and the intrauterine environment suggest that intense (above 80 dB), low-frequency sounds (particularly below 300 Hz, but as high as 1000 Hz with some attenuation) penetrate the womb. This means that the prosodic patterns of speech, including voice pitch and the stress and intonation characteristics of a particular language and speaker, are transmitted to the foetus, while the sound patterns that allow phonetic units and words to be identified are greatly attenuated. (This can be compared to listening to speech through the wall of a room – a human voice can be identified, but words cannot be made out.)

Apparently, infants learn from their intrauterine exposure to sound. Prenatal learning occurs for the more global, prosodic aspects of language. By the time infants are born, exposure to sound *in utero* has resulted in a preference for native-language over foreign-language utterances (Mehler *et al.*, 1988; Moon *et al.*, 1993). The mother's voice (DeCasper and Fifer, 1980) and simple stories she read during the last trimester (DeCasper and Spence, 1986) are also recognized by infants at birth. Interestingly, the low-frequency sound that penetrates the womb has an amplitude envelope that reflects the opening and closing of the mouth as alternate consonant-vowel sequences are produced. This sound pattern is quite simple and would mirror the human mouth while speaking. At birth, when infants first see a human talking, the sound pattern would, for the first time, be matched up with the sound source that produced it. This is likely to occur soon after birth when the infant catches sight of the mother's face articulating, in synchrony with her voice, the sound that penetrated the womb. It is possible that an infant's first notion of 'another' occurs when the familiar sound of the mother's voice is initially linked to her face.

Shared perception generates shared action: experience and the development of speech-motor movements

Thus far, the discussion has focused on shared perception. Yet, language involves more than perception. We speak, and as adults our speech motor patterns are imbued with acoustic markers that identify the cultural and linguistic group to which we belong.

Adult speech patterns are heavily coloured by a native-language dialect which encompasses the pronunciation pattern, rhythm, timing, stress and intonation typical of a specific language. Dialects are very noticeable, and once established are notoriously difficult to alter. Speakers of the same language, such as English, produce it distinctly. One needs only to compare American, English, Australian and Scottish speakers to realize how different it sounds. Even within the same country, dialects are sufficiently distinct to allow experts to identify the specific locale in which the speaker resides – New Yorkers from the Bronx as opposed to Brooklyn, for example, can be identified by their dialects.

How and when do we acquire the indelible speech patterns that match those of our social group? The thesis presented here is that infants' acquisition of life-long dialects rests on two things: innate links between perception and action, and infants' acquired representations of speech that are stored in memory. Perception-action links that exist in infants at birth extend the influence of linguistic experience beyond perception to the motor patterns acquired in speech. The end result is that social groups who speak the same language share linguistic perception and speech-motor acts.

Support for this claim is derived from two sources. First, studies of vocal imitation show that young infants are capable of matching the speech patterns they hear. Second, evidence of developmental change in infants' productions from 12 to 20 weeks of age show that, over time, infants' vocalizations converge on targets specified by native-language input. These findings support the view that stored representations of speech alter not only perception, but action as well.

The first indication of young infants' abilities to imitate in a carefully controlled laboratory setting came from an early study on 18- to 20-week-old infants' abilities to detect correspondences between auditory and *visual* presentations of speech. The study was an infant version of a 'lipreading' study (Kuhl and Meltzoff, 1982). In the study, infants were shown two faces, side-by-side (Fig. 16.3). Each face silently articulated a single vowel, one /a/ and the other /i/. While watching the two faces, infants were presented one of the vowels auditorially from a loudspeaker located midway between the two faces. While infants listened to the sound and watched the two faces, we measured their visual fixations. The results indicated that infants looked significantly longer at the face of the woman silently articulating the vowel that matched the one they heard, as opposed to the mismatched face.

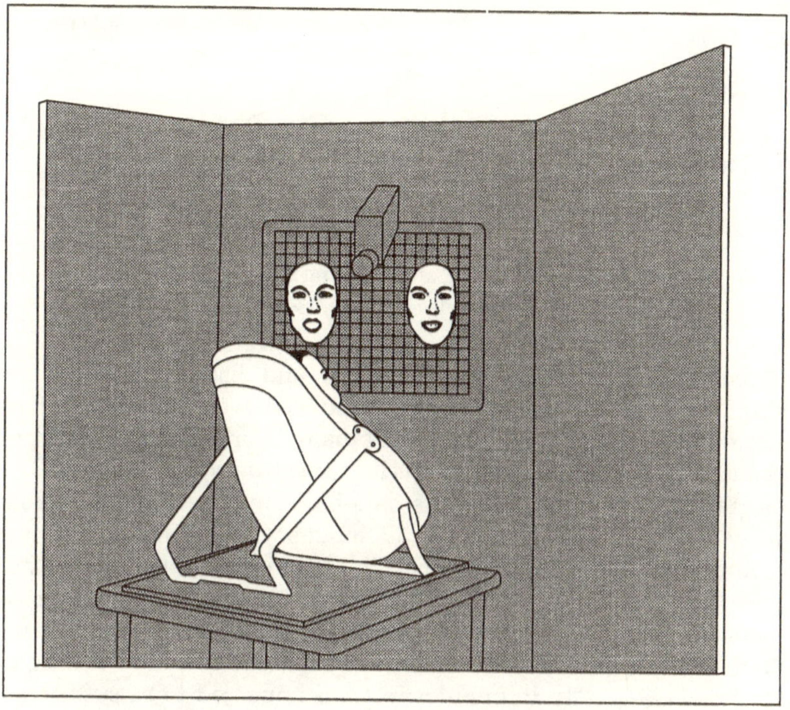

Fig. 16.3 The bimodal perception of speech. Infants watched two faces, side-by-side, pronouncing silently the vowels /a/ (*left*) and /i/ (*right*).

Infants' auditory-visual abilities were themselves interesting and important (as described below), but infants in the study taught us something else: while listening and watching the video, they tended to imitate the vowel they heard as well as the pitch contour on which it was carried (Fig. 16.4). When doing so, they alternated their productions with the adult speaker, taking turns with the face on the video. They did not produce speech when the same faces were presented with non-speech tones matching the amplitude envelope (the loudness curve over time), indicating that infants at this age were aware of the fact that human mouths produce sounds, not tones. This suggested that infants at 18 weeks were already aware of sounds they themselves could produce.

This initial finding led us to conduct further studies on vocal imitation in even younger infants (Kuhl and Meltzoff, 1996). In these studies, 12-, 16- and 20-week-old infants watched a video of a woman articulating either /i/, /a/ or /u/ for 5 minutes on each of three

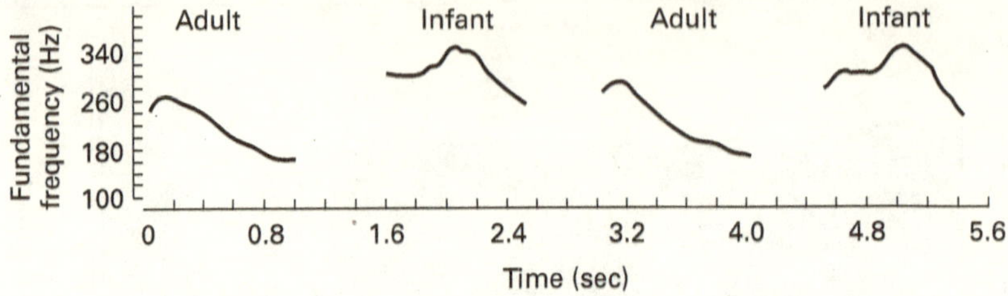

Fig. 16.4 While watching and listening to a video of an adult's talking face, infants vocally imitated the pitch pattern produced by the adult.

consecutive days. While they watched and listened to the video presentation, every utterance they produced was recorded. Infants' utterances were analysed both perceptually (using phonetic transcription) and instrumentally (computerized spectrographic analysis).

Regarding vocal imitation, the data indicated that infants imitated the vowels they heard. Across all infants, more /a/ vowels were produced in response to /a/ than in response to either /i/ or /u/; more /i/ vowels were produced in response to /i/ than to either /a/ or /u/; more /u/ vowels were produced in response to /u/ than to either /a/ or /i/. The total amount of exposure to sound during the experiment was only 15 minutes; yet this appeared to be sufficient to alter infants' productions. If 15 minutes of laboratory exposure to a vowel is sufficient to influence infants' vocalizations, then listening to ambient language for weeks would be expected to provide a powerful influence on infants' production of speech.

We in fact found evidence of such long-term developmental change in infants' vowel productions between 12- and 20-weeks of age (Fig. 16.5). The areas of vowel space occupied by infants' /a/, /i/ and /u/ vowels become progressively more tightly clustered at each age, mirroring in vowel space the arrangement of /a/, /i/ and /u/ vowels seen in adult speakers of the language.

Both findings suggest that infants store perceptual representations of speech that subsequently alter speech production. The long-term change seen in infants' vocalizations over the 8-week period between 12- and 20-weeks of age indicates that infants' utterances are converging on the targets produced by adult speakers of English. The effects of short-term exposure to speech indicate that infants are capable of vocally imitating the speech patterns they hear, and that a relatively short amount of exposure (15 minutes) induces them to do so in the laboratory.

Infants' capacities to act on stored representations have been amply demonstrated in studies of gestural imitation (Kuhl and Meltzoff,

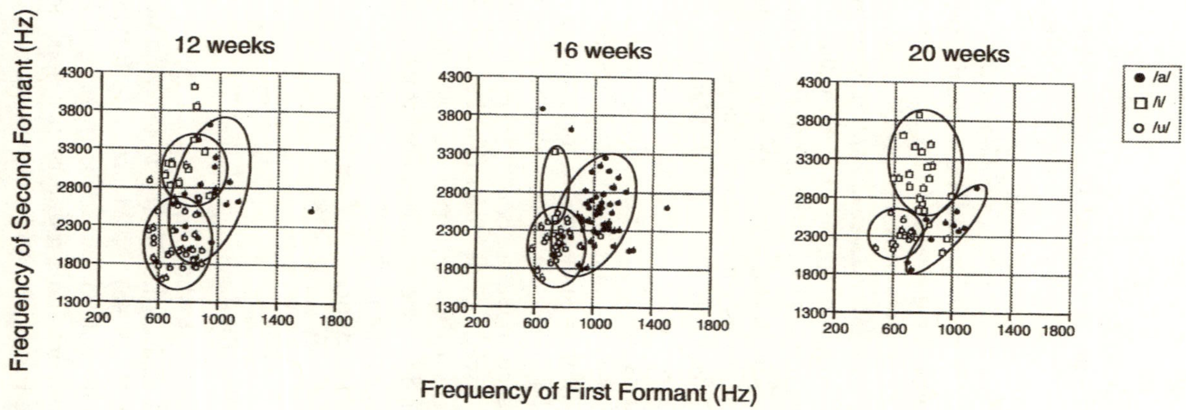

Fig. 16.5 The locations of /a/, /i/ and /u/ vowels produced by 12-, 16- and 20-week-old infants.

1995; Meltzoff, this volume; Meltzoff and Kuhl, 1994). What is additionally shown here is that relatively long-term exposure to a stimulus in a natural setting – speech spoken by multiple talkers over multiple occasions – is organized and stored, so that action over an equally long time can be guided by those target representations. If this view is correct, it explains how infants being reared by speakers of a given language develop speech-motor patterns that gradually converge on the 'mother tongue'. Thus, both infants' perceptual systems and their speech-motor systems are altered by language input. Speech experience shapes the perceptual system (by establishing mental maps that filter infants' perception of speech), and perceptual-motor links for speech extend the influence of experience to the speech-motor system. Infants' stored memory representations for speech are thus viewed as the common cause for perceptual and sensory-motor learning.

Studies on auditory-visual perception of speech also indicate that speech representations include information about the gestures seen on the face of the talker. Data from studies of infants indicate they perceive auditory-visual correspondences for speech (Bahrick and Pickens, 1988; Kuhl and Meltzoff, 1982: fig. 3; MacKain *et al.*, 1983). Second, adults and children who view mismatched auditory-visual syllables perceive 'illusions' that fuse the auditory and visual inputs (e.g. Green *et al.*, 1991; McGurk and MacDonald, 1976). New cross-cultural studies on auditory-visual speech perception extend this work by showing that while people of all cultures experience auditory-visual illusions, speech movements are perceived differently by people whose language backgrounds differ (Kuhl *et al.*, 1994). Seeing lips come together means different things to speakers of different languages. This provides evidence that we store information about the visual concomitants of speech and that they too influence perception. Apparently, given infants' auditory-visual abilities, visual information regarding speech is stored very early in life.

A theory of speech development

These data and ideas have led to the formation of a three-phase theory of speech development called the *Native Language Magnet* (NLM) theory (Kuhl, 1992a, 1993, 1994a). NLM accounts for the fact that infants change from universal language listeners and speakers to highly constrained perceivers and producers of a specific language, and that evidence of the transition can be measured in the laboratory before the end of the first year of life. The model explains how infants' developing native-language speech representations alter both speech perception and production.

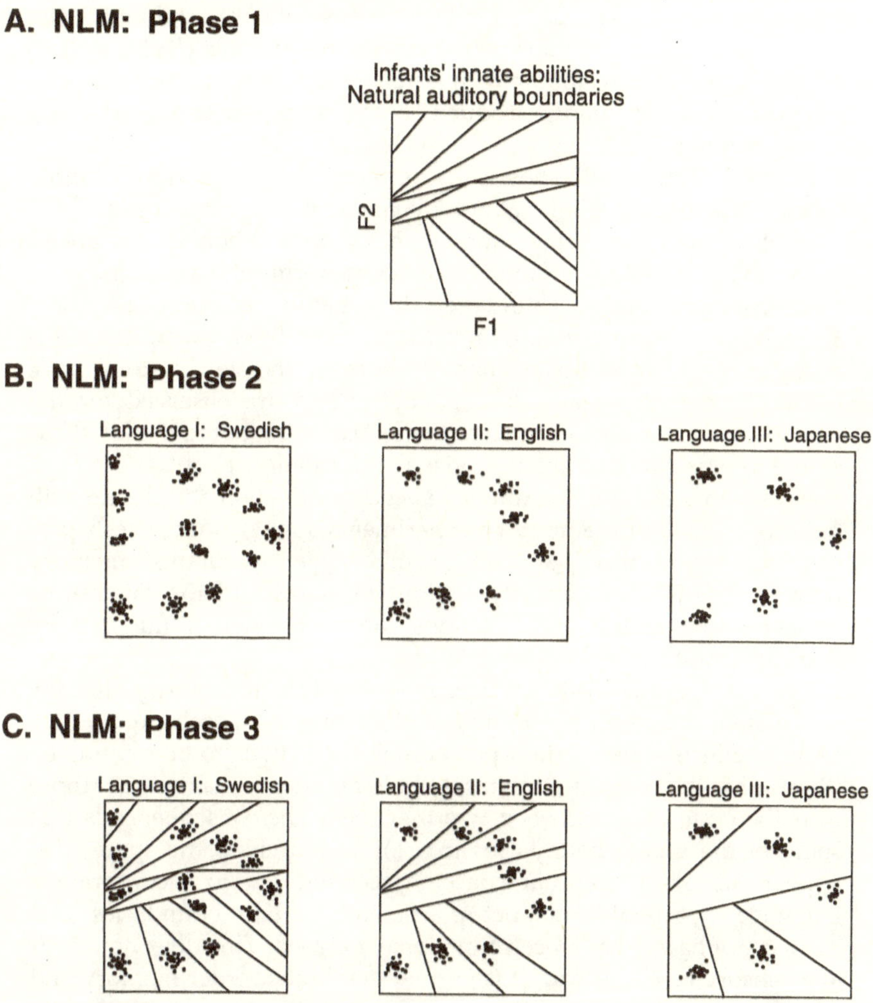

Fig. 16.6 Kuhl's Native Language Magnet model of speech development.

Phase 1 describes the initial state of infants' speech perception abilities. At birth, infants show a universal tendency to discriminate the sounds of all languages, as shown by the hypothetical 'boundaries' separating all the vowels of all languages in Fig. 16.6A. According to NLM, the perceptual boundaries in Phase 1 are inherent in auditory processing. They are due not to a 'language module' or other language-specific device, but to more basic auditory perceptual processing mechanisms. The notion that innate boundaries are attributable to basic auditory perceptual processing is buttressed by the fact that these same perceptual boundary phenomena are exhibited in the same places in acoustic space by non-human animals (Kuhl, 1991b). At this stage in development, infants' production abilities are also language general; infants produce cooing sounds that are universal across cultures.

Phase 2 (Fig. 16.6B) shows that a short time later a substantial change has been brought about by ambient language input. By 6 months of age, something more than the innate boundaries are in place. At this stage, infants have some form of stored memory representations of the sounds of their native language. Swedish, English and Japanese infants' representations differ, owing to differences in the distributional characteristics of the vowels they have heard. It is at this stage that magnet effects are observed for the prototypes of vowels in each language. According to the model, these stored representations include visual information about speech. At this stage in development, infants' speech production abilities are still quite primitive, but laboratory experiments suggest that speech production is also being shaped at this stage by infants' memory representations. The capacity to imitate, shown in the laboratory, indicates that infants' vocalizations can be strongly influenced by auditory input.

Phase 3 (Fig. 16.6C) shows how magnet effects recursively alter the initial state of speech perception, and eventually speech production. Magnet effects cause certain perceptual distinctions to be minimized (those near the magnet attractors) while others are maximized (those near the boundaries between two magnets). The consequence is that some of the innate boundaries that initially divided the space 'disappear' as the perceptual space is reconfigured to incorporate a language's particular magnet placement. Certain boundaries that existed in Phase 1 have been functionally erased. This does not occur at a sensory level; instead, it is argued that higher-order memory and representational systems have altered infants' perceptual abilities. By Phase 3, a perceptual space once characterized by simple boundaries has been replaced by a warped space dominated by magnet effects.

In Phase 3, infants' productions of speech begin to show the effects of language experience. Infants from different cultures produce sounds that are measurably different at this stage, in each case mirroring the ambient language. Thus, both the observed perceptual clustering (the magnet effect) and the convergence of utterances on a specified target (vocal imitation) can be linked to infants' speech representations that are stored in memory. Speech representations are thus seen as the common cause of changes observed in the perceptual and sensory-motor systems of infants exposed to a particular language (Fig. 16.7).

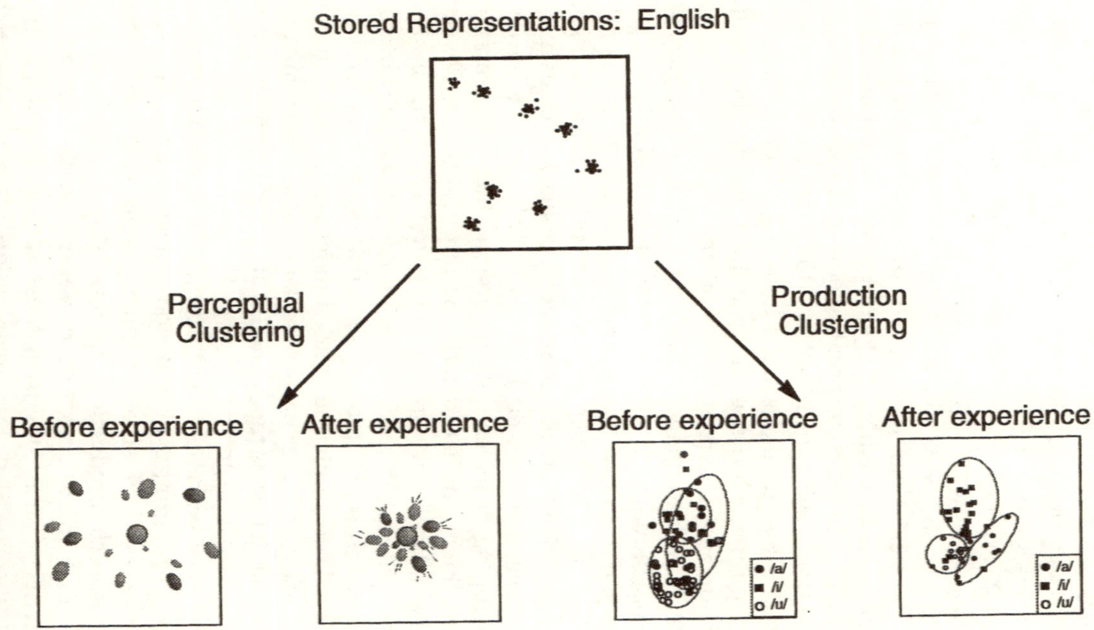

Fig. 16.7 Stored representations of native-language speech are the common cause of both the change in infants' speech perception (tighter perceptual clustering as seen in the magnet effect) and speech production (tighter clustering of the vowels they themselves produce).

Shared perception as an initial precondition for intersubjectivity

I have argued that experience exerts a strong influence on perception. Infants' experience with ambient language altered their perceptual systems in a way that was conducive to the development of a particular language. This occurred at an early stage in development, prior to the comprehension or production of first words. In answer to one of the initial questions posed, we have shown that infants can and do share perception with adults of the culture, and show that shared perception precedes language. In fact, the perceptual filters I have described would greatly assist infants at higher levels of language, particularly at the next stage in language development when they acquire words and master the phonology of the language. Outside the domain of language, shared perceptual filters would be expected to assist infants in the development of an understanding of others. Shared perception between infants and adults of a culture contributes to a shared view of the world and this may be a precondition to the achievement of humans' understanding of others.

The kind of learning and memory implicated in these studies is not the usual kind of stimulus-response learning described by psychologists in which some form of external reinforcement is necessary. The learning described here, in which speech perception becomes highly restricted, appears to be unconscious and implicit; it takes place without reinforcement; it is difficult to undo. This form of learning results in a mapping between information in the world and its representation in the brain that distorts the physical world. Physical differences and similarities are not directly perceived on the basis of their real characteristics. Instead, perception is biased, distorted; I refer to it as warped. It is a memory system that organizes experience to highlight only those similarities and differences in the incoming input that are relevant to a particular language. These memory systems, and the mental maps they contain, are presumably shared by speakers of the same language.

Basic links between perception and action extend the influence of experience one step further. Information encoded from language experience in the form of stored memory representations subsequently affects speech production. Infants' stored representations serve as targets that infants seek to achieve. As infants converge on the sound patterns of their language, these sensory-motor patterns themselves are incorporated into their representations of speech. Speech production develops into a set of fairly indelible motor patterns, equal, in their resistance to change, to the perceptual patterns that gave rise to them during their formation.

The work reviewed here thus shows that infants perceive and store in memory aspects of the auditory, visual and motor information in speech and that this subsequently alters both speech perception and production. A hypothesis presented for discussion and debate is that the memory systems implicated in language learning, as described by NLM, may underlie certain other aspects of cultural learning, wherein experience with people of a particular culture results in both the perception and action of behaviours that are typical and appropriate for the cultural milieu in which the infant is being raised. Infants mentally capture the regularities of language in the voice and the face, and perhaps the regularities of a culture in the behaviour patterns and habits evidenced by people. Infants are subsequently altered by that experience, both perceptually and by their own developing actions. In the process, they become behaviourally and perceptually inducted as members of a particular society. Shared perception and action may play an important role in this process. The shared perceptual framework and the communication it allows may constitute a first step, perhaps, in the development of intersubjectivity.

Acknowledgements

Preparation of this chapter was supported by grants from NIH (DC 00520, HD 18286 and HD 22514). The author thanks Andy Meltzoff for inspiration on the topic of intersubjectivity and for comments on an earlier draft of the chapter, and gratefully acknowledges the assistance of Erica Stevens and Charmaine Morton in the preparation of the manuscript.

CHAPTER 17

Intersubjectivity in early language learning and use

Nameera Akhtar and Michael Tomasello

Studies of intersubjectivity in early language development have focused almost exclusively on the semantic *content* of children's early utterances, especially on their use of words such as *want* and *think* to refer to internal or mental states in the third year of life (e.g. Bretherton and Beeghly, 1982; Dunn *et al.*, 1987). However, if we consider the *processes* by which young children learn and use their early language, it is clear that intersubjectivity plays a crucial role in language development well before any such mental state words are acquired.

Beginning in the prelinguistic period, Trevarthen and Hubley (1978) described in detail a number of processes of 'secondary intersubjectivity' in which an adult and child take turns acting on an object of mutual interest, much as they might take turns in a linguistic conversation about a topic of mutual interest. Bruner (1983) emphasized that prelinguistic interactions of this type involve the intersubjective process of 'joint attention', and thus lay the foundation for the child's initial comprehension and production of acts of linguistic reference. Tomasello and Todd (1983) and Tomasello and Farrar (1986) have demonstrated empirically that the quantity and quality of joint attentional interactions in which young children participate are directly related to the rate and style of their early linguistic development. These lines of work all demonstrate quite clearly that children's earliest linguistic interactions depend crucially on more basic processes of social interaction involving secondary intersubjectivity between adult and child.

In this chapter, we explore systematically the central role of intersubjectivity in the process of language development, both from the point of view of language learning and from the point of view of language use. In language learning, intersubjective processes are apparent as children attempt to determine an adult's focus of attention in using a new piece of language, sometimes in fairly complex interactive situations. In language use, intersubjective processes are manifest as children perform acts of reference and predication and converse with others; in all of these communicative situations they show clear evidence of understanding something of the listener's understanding. The key social-cognitive skill that underlies children's meaningful participation in all such linguistic interactions is an understanding that the behaviour of others is intentional, and that the attention and intentions of others can be manipulated and shared.

Language learning

We take it as axiomatic that to learn a new piece of language the child must in some sense enter into an intersubjective (joint attentional) state with a mature language user (Tomasello, 1988, 1992). Perhaps the major impediment to an appreciation of this fact is the implicit assumption of most researchers that the prototypical case of lexical acquisition is the child's learning the name of a concrete object by means of an adult's ostensive labelling. While it is true that in Western middle-class culture adults often stop what they are doing and name objects for their language-learning children, in many other cultures adults do not provide their children with mini-linguistics lessons of this type (Lieven, 1994; Scheiffelin and Ochs, 1986). In many cultures, if the child is to learn a new word she must do so in the natural flow of everyday social action and interaction – often with siblings and other children (Barton and Tomasello, 1994). Moreover, even in Western middle-class culture, the mini-linguistics lessons that children experience involve almost exclusively the naming of objects; to learn words for properties, relationships and actions the child must determine the adult's intended referent from within the flow of ongoing social interactions (Tomasello, 1995a).

We would argue that, even in the ostensive naming context, word learning is constituted by very basic processes of intersubjectivity in which the child must determine the adult's focus of attention by means of cues involving gestures, eye gaze and the like. In non-ostensive contexts, in which children must learn words in the natural flow of social interaction, however, intersubjective processes appear more prominent because the cues children must use are more subtle and complex. Let us begin with these more complex cases.

Verbs

Tomasello and Kruger (1992) found that when American middle-class mothers interact with their language-learning children they use verbs most often to regulate their children's behaviour, not to label ongoing activities. Most common are cases in which the adult directs or anticipates the child's behaviour ('Throw it' or 'Are you going to roll it?'), or checks on the child's intention to do something ('Do you want to bounce it?') – all cases in which the child hears the word before the intended action occurs, if indeed it occurs at all. In a sample of twenty-four mother–child dyads, these instances of what Tomasello and Kruger called the Impending Action context comprised over 60% of all maternal verb uses. Ostensive labelling of ongoing actions was much less frequent (less than 20% of verb uses). Tomasello and Kruger also found in a lexical training study that children learned a novel verb better in the impending action context than in an ostensive labelling context in which the action was labelled as it was occurring.

In standard theories of word learning, the child is said to make word-to-world 'mappings'; however, it is difficult to imagine how children could perform such a mapping in this training study, given that the referent action was not perceptually available at the time the new word was heard. But from within the social-pragmatic view of language acquisition we may hypothesize that children learned the new word in this context by attempting to understand the intentions of the adult as she geared up for action. Tomasello and Barton (1994, Study 3) tested this hypothesis directly. In this study 24-month-old children were taught two novel verbs, one in each of two experimental conditions (both involving an impending action). In the Target-First condition an adult experimenter used a novel verb to announce her intention to perform a novel action, for example, 'I'm going to PLUNK Big Bird!' She then performed the target action intentionally, saying 'There!', followed by another action performed 'accidentally', in an awkward fashion, saying 'Whoops!'. In the Target-Last condition, the accidental action was performed first and the intentional action was performed only afterwards. The outcome was that children quite readily associated the novel word with the intentional action, regardless of whether it occurred immediately after the novel word or later, after an intervening accidental action. Children in this study thus demonstrated their ability to enter into a joint attentional (intersubjective) state with the adult by determining her intended action, and by applying their knowledge that adults use new pieces of language to indicate intended, not accidental, actions.

Another possibility for how children might learn verbs for impending actions is that they might use prior event knowledge to determine an adult's referential intent. After repeated interactions in a given situation, children may form a script or event representation (Nelson, 1986) which allows them to anticipate or predict what is likely to happen next in a given situation. If they then hear someone announce an intention to perform a specific action in this same context, they may be able to associate their anticipation of the up-coming action with the new verb they hear. If children are indeed able to do this, then they may not need to perceive the referent action at all after hearing the novel verb to attach an appropriate meaning to it.

Akhtar and Tomasello (1996, Study 2) examined this hypothesis by creating a scripted situation in which 24-month-old children were able to predict which of a number of novel actions was impending. All children received the same pretraining in which four different toy characters were reliably associated with four novel actions, so that they would learn which character performed which action. Children were then randomly assigned to one of two experimental groups in which they were exposed to a novel verb in one of two ways. For the Referent group, the experimenter set out the target action prop and announced her intention to perform an action: 'Let's MEEK Big Bird!' She then proceeded to meek Big Bird. For subjects in the Absent Referent group, the experimenter also set out the target action prop and said the same thing but, after searching, told the child she was unable to find Big Bird. Consequently, she could not perform the target action (*meeking*), and children in this group never saw the referent action after hearing the novel verb. The outcome was that children in both experimental groups were able to learn the new verb, and learning was equivalent in these two groups. Thus, children in the Absent Referent group were able to establish intersubjectivity with an adult in this scripted situation without ever seeing the referent action paired with the novel verb. To do this they had to understand that the adult intended to perform the target action, and that the novel verb was meant to refer to that intended action, even though it was never actually performed.

Finally, Tomasello and Akhtar (1995, Study 2) attempted to see whether children in this same age range could learn a new verb in a scripted situation when a novel object was present as a potentially competing referent. First, children saw an adult perform a novel and nameless action (target action) with a novel and nameless object (target object). Then the adult simply said '*Widget!*' as she handed the child the target object. What differed among groups of children was the adult's behaviour just before and during the use of this novel word. Children in the Action-Highlighted group watched the adult prepare for the target action to be performed by the child (by orientating the prop correctly to him) before she produced the novel word; she then used the novel word as if requesting that the child preform the action while alternating her gaze between the child and the action prop. Children in the Object-Highlighted group saw no prior preparation of the prop, but heard the word *Widget* used as label, while the adult alternated her gaze between the child and the object. The outcome was that children in the Action-Highlighted condition learned the new word for the target action, whereas children in the Object-Highlighted condition learned the new word for the target object. To learn the new verb in this situation children had to understand from the adult's non-verbal behaviours that she was requesting an action of them (not labelling an object).

Together, what these studies demonstrate is that young children can learn new verbs in situations in which an adult is using language not to teach them words but to regulate or anticipate the ongoing social interaction. They learn novel verbs for impending actions, intentional actions, intended but not performed actions, and actions requested of them by adults. Their ability to learn in this wide variety of pragmatic contexts suggests that children are not simply associating word and perceived world, nor are they even associating words with the next action the speaker performs. Rather, they are engaged in an active and flexible process in which they are monitoring the actions of adults, discriminating between unintentional and intentional actions, and discerning what adults intended for them to do. These results demonstrate quite clearly that 24-month-old children are able to establish intersubjectivity with an adult in fairly complex interactive situations and to make use of their knowledge of past interactions to determine what an adult might have in mind when uttering a novel word.

Object labels

It is possible that the word-learning processes we have just outlined are peculiar to verbs. Perhaps to learn an object label children have to have their attention explicitly drawn to the object before or as the new word is said. Indeed, there are some studies that seem to support this interpretation, since they have shown that it is easiest for young children to learn a new object label when they are already attending to the referent object at the time it is labelled (Dunham *et al.*, 1993; Tomasello and Farrar, 1986). However, although such ostensive labelling may in some cases facilitate children's acquisition of object labels, recent research suggests that it is not a necessary condition.

Tomasello and Barton (1994, Study 4) presented 24-month-old children with a situation in which an adult announced that she was going to find a 'toma' in one of five buckets. There were two experimental conditions. In the Target-First condition, the adult went immediately to a bucket and excitedly found an object and handed it to the child. In the Target-Last condition, the adult first found and rejected (by scowling at and replacing) two objects before excitedly finding and handing the child a third object. The outcome was that children learned the new word equally well in the two conditions. Note that in the Target-Last condition if children associated the novel word with the next object the adult looked at, they would think that the first (rejected) object was the 'toma'. Only one of fifteen children chose this object in the comprehension test, however, whereas eight children learned the novel word for a third (target) object (see Baldwin, 1993a, for a similar finding). Thus, as in the verb-learning studies, in order to establish the intersubjectivity necessary for word learning, children in this noun-learning study had to monitor the adult's intentional states (using various pragmatic cues) and associate the new word only with the object she intended to find.

Children of this age can also learn a word in a finding game even when the adult's finding intention is not fulfilled. In a design analogous to that used to explore the role of event knowledge in verb learning (see Verbs section above). Akhtar and Tomasello (1996, Study 1) had 24-month-old children participate in a script in which an adult experimenter consistently found four nameless objects in three buckets and a toy barn. The object in the barn served as the target object, and the locations of all objects remained constant for a given child, enabling subjects to form expectations of which object would be found in each location. In the language modelling rounds, the experimenter announced her intention to find a specific object: 'Now let's find the TOMA!' In the Referent condition, she proceeded to find and extract the target object from the barn. In the Absent Referent condition, she attempted to open the barn but told the child that it was locked; thus, children in this group never saw the target object after hearing the novel word. Results indicated that children were able to learn the object label even if they had not seen the object perceptually paired with the new word. To do this they had to rely on their event knowledge of what was likely to happen next and on their knowledge of how (for what purposes) adults use novel words.

Another cue that children of this age might be using is discourse novelty. Children (as well as adults) attend to what is most salient in a given situation and, as their attentional systems are attracted to novelty, perhaps the most novel element in the situation may be taken as the referent of a new word (Baker and Greenfield, 1988). Akhtar *et al.* (1996) examined the role that discourse novelty might play in the learning of object labels. Twenty-four-month-old children first played with three nameless objects with two experimenters and a parent; no language models were given. One experimenter and the parent then left the room while the child and the other experimenter played with a fourth object (the target) for an equal amount of time. The adults then returned to give the language model. Upon entering the room the adults looked at the group of objects (being careful not to single out any one object with eye gaze) and said: 'Look, I see a GAZZER in there! A GAZZER!' Thus, from the child's point of view the only thing different about the target object was that it was new to the discourse context for the adults. The outcome was that children learned the new word for the object that was new for the adults. To do this they had to understand that adults tend to label things that are new to the discourse context and, moreover, that discourse novelty is determined from the speaker's point of view.

Finally, results of another recent study (Tomasello and Akhtar, 1995, Study 1) indicate that 2-year-olds' attention to novelty may also help them determine to which ontological category a given word may belong. There were two experimental groups. In both groups, children heard a new word modelled as a one-word utterance ('Modi!') just as a nameless target object was performing a nameless target action. What differed between these groups was the behaviour leading up to the model. In the Action-Novel condition, children performed multiple actions on the target object so that when the language model was presented the target action was the novel element in the discourse context. In the Object-Novel condition, children performed the target action on multiple objects so that when the language model was presented the target object was the novel element in the discourse context. Results indicated that the children associated the word with the element that was new to the discourse context at the time of the model; most children in the Action-Novel condition associated the word with the target action and most children in the Object-Novel condition associated the word with the target object. Thus, discourse novelty can also be used by young 2-year-olds to determine a novel word's ontological status.

Overall, then, in a fashion very similar to the studies of verb learning, these studies of noun learning demonstrate that 24-month-old children can learn object labels in a variety of complex interactive situations. Although there is a tendency to think of the ostensive labelling paradigm as prototypical for learning object labels, it may not be for all children, especially those outside of the Western middle class. In any case, what these studies show is that young children are able to learn object labels in many different contexts, and that they do so by tuning in to a wide variety of pragmatic cues to adult referential intentions. From this theoretical perspective, it is also important to recognize that even the ostensive labelling of objects is best described in this way: children must determine the adult's referential intention by determining her focus of attention. It is just that in this case they do so with relatively straightforward cues such as gaze direction and pointing so that the sophisticated processes of social cognition the child engages in tend to be taken for granted.

Younger children

All of the findings we have so far reported are for children at around their second birthdays. Because many children have been active word learners for some months prior to this time, it is possible that what we are observing is a set of learned strategies that build on a somewhat simpler process that characterizes earlier development; for example, younger children may simply associate words they hear with things they are currently perceiving. A series of recent studies indicate that this is not the case.

Baldwin (1991, 1993b) has employed what she calls a 'discrepant labelling paradigm' to demonstrate that children as young as 18 months of age do not simply passively associate object labels with the things they are looking at. In this paradigm, an adult utters a label for an object while the child is visually focused on *another* object. In these studies children as young as 14 months tend to look up to check the direction of the adult's gaze while she is uttering the novel label, suggesting that they may understand that adults tend to label things they (the adults) are looking at (Baldwin, 1995). It is not until 18 months, however, that there is clear evidence (from comprehension measures) that children are able to use this understanding effectively, to attach the label to the object the adult was looking at. Thus, by the middle of the second year of life, children can use an adult's gaze direction as a cue to her referential intent.

This fact, however, does not establish that 18-month-olds possess a truly intersubjective appreciation of referential intent. Rather, it may be that they have simply learned to use gaze direction as a discriminative cue (Moore and Corkum, 1994); that is, they may have learned from past experiences that following an adult's gaze leads to interesting sights. Following the adult's line-of-regard would lead children to the target toy and perhaps enhance its salience. Thus, the children in Baldwin's study may have linked the label with the target object only because of its increased salience and not because they understood something about the adult's referential intent (Baldwin and Moses, 1994). Although a subsequent control study (Baldwin, 1993a, Study 2) showed that enhancing the salience of the target object without looking at it did not lead to word learning, the possibility remains that when children do use line-of-regard, they do so automatically and without intersubjective understanding.

Results of two recent studies suggest that this is not the case. Tomasello *et al.* (1996) replicated two of the object label studies reported above with 18-month-old children. As in Tomasello and Barton (1994, Study 4), children were presented with a situation in which an adult announced that she was going to find a *toma* in one of several buckets. She then proceeded to find and reject one object before excitedly finding the target object. Because the children were so young (18 months) more models were given than to the 24-month-olds in the original study. As with the older children, most of these younger subjects chose the intended object in the comprehension test, and their performance was equivalent to the performance of a control group of subjects who saw the target object immediately after the language model.

The second study was a replication of Akhtar and Tomasello (1996, Study 1) with 18-month-old children. As in that study, a script was established in which an adult experimenter consistently found four nameless objects in three buckets and a toy barn. In the language modelling rounds, the experimenter announced her intention to find a specific object. In the Referent group, she proceeded to find and extract the target object from the barn, whereas in the Absent Referent group she attempted to open the ban but told the child that it was locked. The results indicated that the 18-month-old children were able to learn the object label even if they had not seen the object perceptually paired with the label.

Young children with small vocabularies are frequently faced with situations in which there are multiple potential referents present when they hear a new word modelled. As such, they must have some means of determining which of several objects an adult intends to label. As Baldwin's studies have shown, line-of-regard may be an important cue in such situations. But there are situations in which line-of-regard and pointing may not be diagnostic of an adult's referential intent. In these situations, children must rely on some other cue as to what the adult intends. Children as young as 18 months of age are able to do this by relying on their event knowledge and their understanding of various cues to adults' referential intentions.

Discussion

We believe that these findings indicate that from the very beginning word learning may be a thoroughly intersubjective process.

The results of these lexical training studies demonstrate quite clearly that early lexical acquisition does not depend on simple associations between words and perceived referents. Rather, children as young as 18 months of age are already adept at using cues to establish intersubjectivity in a wide variety of word-learning situations in which the intended referent is not perceptually available at the time the new word is said. The situations simulated in these studies – situations with multiple potential referents – are presumably common in the lives of children just beginning to learn language. Children's remarkable ability to determine accurately the referents of new words in these situations shows that they can use an adult's line-of-regard, affective and behavioural cues indicating the fulfilling or thwarting of an intention, event knowledge and discourse novelty (from another's perspective) to understand speakers' referential intentions and thus to learn words in a wide range of action and discourse contexts.

To acquire a new word – to learn to comprehend and produce it in conventionally appropriate contexts (one instance of what Tomasello *et al.*, 1993, call 'cultural learning') – the child must enter into a state of joint attentional focus (intersubjectivity) with a mature language user.

Language use

It is useful to consider language use from the point of view of a basic theoretical dichotomy in the study of the pragmatics of conversation: topic and comment. In this view each turn of a mature linguistic dialogue must make reference to (i) the topic the speaker wishes the participants to focus on and (ii) the comment (or predication) the speaker wishes to make about that topic. Briefly, the ontogeny of children's ability to control topic-comment structure is as follows (see Table 17.1; Tomasello, 1988). Children's earliest forays in communication are the face-to-face 'protoconversations' characteristic of primary intersubjectivity during early infancy. These direct emotional exchanges have no topic-comment structure. At around 9–12 months of age children begin to engage in communicative interactions aimed at drawing an adult's attention to some topic, either with a non-linguistic gesture or with a piece of language proper. These early attempts have topic but not comment structure. At around 18 months of age children first begin to predicate. They do this by first establishing a topic non-linguistically, for example by holding up an object for the adult to see, and then adding a comment or predication linguistically (e.g. 'Wet'). Finally, sometime before their second birthdays children gain purely linguistic control of topic-comment structure, using conventional

Table 17.1. *Processes of communication and predication in early human development*

Age	**Process of communication**	**Topic**	**Comment**
0–6 months	Primary intersubjectivity	–	–
6–12 months	Secondary intersubjectivity	non-linguistic	–
12–18 months	First words	linguistic	–
18–24 months	First predication	non-linguistic	linguistic
24+ months	Conversation	linguistic	linguistic

linguistic forms both to direct a communicative partner to a topic and to comment on that topic (e.g. 'Shirt wet' or 'It's wet').

We would like to focus more closely on three steps in this process to illustrate children's early skills of intersubjectivity as manifest in their productions of: early linguistic symbols, early predications and early conversations.

Linguistic symbols

Human language differs from other forms of communication in that it involves the use of symbols to represent different meanings or intents. One crucial difference between linguistic symbols and communicative signals is that symbols are decontextualized communicative acts that are used to stand for or represent a given communicative intention (Bates, 1979; Premack, 1990; Werner and Kaplan, 1963/1984). This is clearly an important aspect of communicative symbols. Recently, however, Tomasello (1996) has drawn attention to another unique characteristic of linguistic symbols that highlights their intersubjective character more clearly, that is, their *reciprocal* nature (the bi-directionality of the sign in Saussurean terminology). Indeed the very definition of a conventional communicative symbol is that both the speaker and the listener simultaneously appreciate its communicative significance from the other's perspective; that is, one who produces such a symbol in a communicative act comprehends it (from the listener's perspective) as she produces it (Mead, 1934; Savage-Rumbaugh, 1990). Linguistic symbols are thus inherently intersubjective in that they are communicative acts that people both understand and understand that others understand.

Not all communicative behaviours are reciprocal in this way.

Pre-linguistic infants use a number of intentional gestures that are often ritualized from non-communicative behaviours; for example, the 'hands-up' gesture as a request to be picked up may be a ritualization of the infant trying to pull its way up to the parent's arms. There is no evidence that pre-linguistic infants comprehend these early gestures when produced by another, so they cannot be viewed as true symbols. The same may also be said of some of children's earliest attempts at language. Some proportion of children's early 'words' may be learned through ritualization as well, that is, ritualization in which the child mimics an adult sound ('word') and then the adult responds in some predictable and interesting way. These so-called pre-symbolic forms are often characterized as being simply a part of an activity, not a symbol standing for anything else in the activity (Bates, 1979). They are also not reciprocal – the child does not understand the adult's understanding of them – and thus we may call them vocal signals.

It is difficult to determine precisely which of children's early words are true symbols. But Tomasello (1996) argues that the intersubjective reciprocity characteristic of linguistic symbols is a natural outcome of the cultural learning process – the implication being that any communicative behaviour learned through ritualization or blind mimicking will not be inherently reciprocal. The reasoning is this. Cultural learning – in the form of imitative learning (Tomasello *et al.*, 1993) – requires that the child understand not only the adult's communicative intention in using a novel piece of language, but also the fact that she, the child, may use this same piece of language when she has the same communicative intention. That is to say, in comprehending a new word the child comes to understand that the adult is using the word to encourage her to focus her attention on one specific aspect of the current situation. To learn to produce the word herself, the child must in some sense identify with the adult's intention so that she can make the transition to cases in which she has the same communicative intention, that is, the intention to encourage another person to focus on the same aspect of the situation. A graphic depiction of this process, and how it contrasts to a model of word learning in which symbols are not recognized as explicitly reciprocal, is presented in Fig. 17.1.

Children's early linguistic symbols that are learned via cultural learning are thus reciprocal and intersubjective by their very nature. Learning to use conventional symbols in the way that others use them relies both on children's ability to perceive and understand the behaviour of others intentionally and on their tendency to identify with others so that they may be able to express similar intentions in similar circumstances in the future. Understanding other individuals

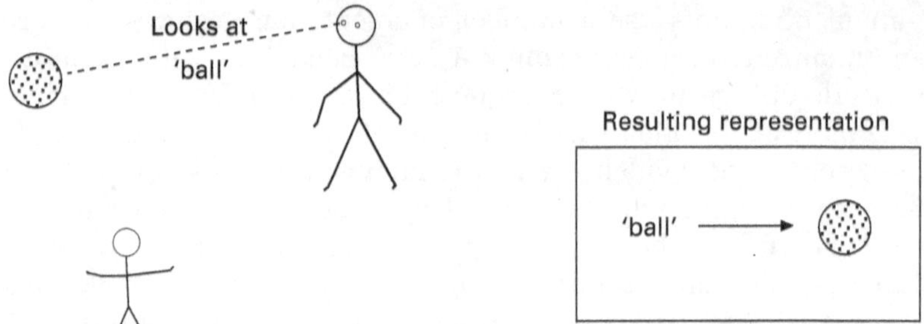

Version 1: The mapping metaphor

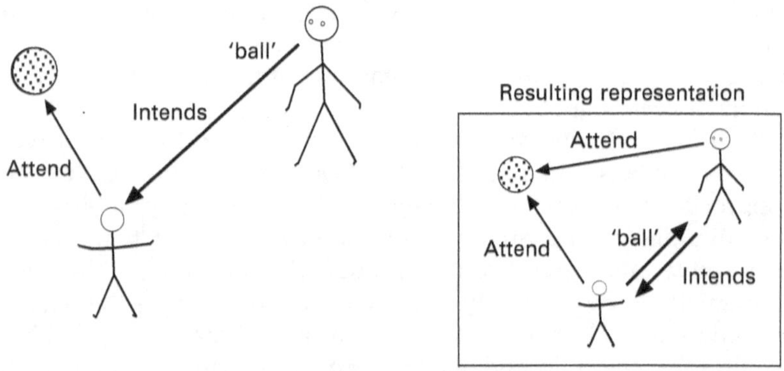

Version 2: The cultural learning metaphor

Figure 17.1 Two hypotheses about the intersubjective process in word learning: (*top*) Version 1, the mapping metaphor; (*bottom*) Version 2, the cultural learning metaphor.

as intentional agents, and the intersubjectivity that this presupposes, is thus the key social-cognitive skill necessary for children's early abilities to communicate with others.

Predication

An act of linguistic reference involves one individual directing the attention of another individual to some aspect of their shared environment. Acts of predication are those acts in which one individual first establishes joint attention with another on some topic (linguistic or non-linguistic), and then linguistically expresses a comment on that topic, for example the child holds up a toy for another to see and then says 'Mine'. Thus, both of these types of linguistic acts – reference and predication – clearly require at least two individuals engaged in intersubjectivity. What is crucial in predication is, first, that the child knows already that she and the adult are jointly attending to the same event, and, second, that the child has a choice of which aspect of the event to talk about or comment upon: object, activity, property, location or whatever. What the child is doing in such cases is choosing a particular psychological orientation or attitude, from among other possible orientations and attitudes, that she wishes the adult to take towards some entity to which they already share attention.

There are thus two aspects to predication: the establishing of topic and the predication itself. Let us look at each in turn. First, young children are able to establish topics for purposes of predication, or at least recognize that they have been established, from before the middle of the second year of life. Before an act of predication children of this age first secure the adult's attention to that topic through non-linguistic or linguistic means, for example, by holding up a toy car and saying 'Car' until the adult responds affirmatively, only then saying 'Broken' (Atkinson, 1979). Similarly, Scollon's (1979) analysis of 'vertical constructions' indicates that children who are at the one-word stage in language production often let the adult establish a topic in their conversational turn (e.g. the adult says 'Look at the clown') and then the child makes a comment on that topic (e.g. 'Dancing'). The adult's turn in this type of vertical construction may establish the topic and the child's part may provide the comment or new information. Thus, from almost the beginning stages of language use, the child appears to understand that the listener's attention must first be focused on a given topic before additional (new) information can be effectively given.

The second element of a predication is the predication or comment itself, and here we would like to stress the role of choice. If the child has one and only one symbol for talking about a given situation, there can be no predication – no matter the word's status in adult language. For example, if the child always says 'Hot', and can only say 'Hot', to a cup of steaming coffee, then it is odd to say that the child is predicating because predication is an intentional act that implies a choice of means. We prefer to identify an act of predication only when it is the case that the child has at her disposal other symbols to designate other aspects of the situation if she so chooses. The important point for current purposes is that children's use of predication in this precise sense demonstrates a very sophisticated level of social cognition to 18- to 24-month-old children. When the child holds up a ball and says 'Wet' or 'Blue' or 'Mine' or 'Roll', she is asking the

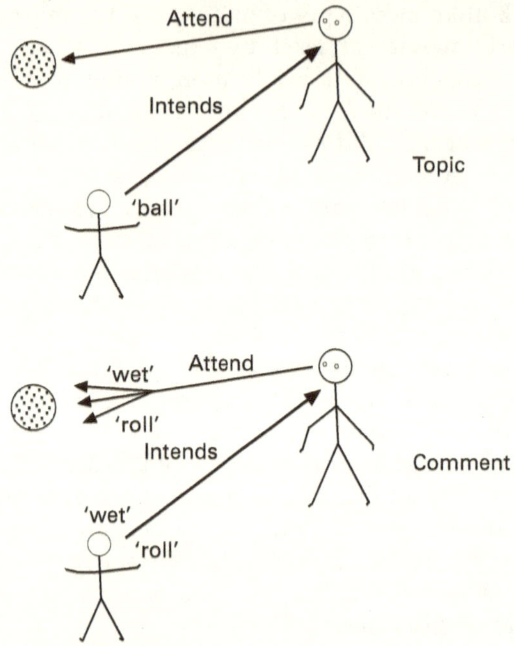

Figure 17.2 Process of predication in early language development; (*top*) topic; (*bottom*) comment.

listener to attend to some specific aspect – out of other possible aspects – of that ball. Predication thus requires some notion that other persons can intentionally modulate their attention in response to linguistic and non-linguistic means of communication, often while not changing their visual orientation at all (see Fig. 17.2).

It is also important that once the child has a choice of linguistic elements to use in a situation, children at the one-word stage of language production tend to verbalize the element that is new to the situation. For example, if a child has just been watching a sibling place blocks in a box, and the sibling suddenly places a ball in the box, the child is likely to verbalize 'ball' at that point in the interaction (Greenfield, 1979, 1982; Greenfield *et al.*, 1985). Greenfield and Zukow (1978) and Baker and Greenfield (1988) have provided experimental confirmation for this finding by manipulating elements in scripted situations and demonstrating that young children tend to talk about what is new in the current discourse context. This is true at both the one-word and two-word stages of language production (Baker and Greenfield, 1988; Weisenburger, 1976) and there is additional evidence that, in their two-word utterances, children place more stress on the information that is new (Wieman, 1976).

Greenfield has argued from these findings that, from the very beginning of language development, young children operate with a 'principle of informativeness' in that the new or variable components of a situation are generally the most informative. Talking about what is most informative seems to imply that children understand what is new from the perspective of the listener. However, Greenfield does not claim that children are necessarily talking about what is new or most informative from the *listener's* perspective. Indeed, she maintains that early use of the principle of informativeness may simply reflect the fact that children speak about what is new or informative from their *own* perspective (Greenfield, 1982); that is, they may egocentrically talk about whatever new thing captures their attention. Her data do not directly address this issue, however, as the experimental studies have involved situations in which the critical elements were new to both speaker and listener. What is needed is an experimental situation in which what is new to the listener is not new to the child. If children are more likely to talk about what is new to the other person in this situation than in a situation in which the information is equally new/old to both speaker and listener, then one could claim that they are sensitive to the listener's perspective.

O'Neill (1996, Study 1) presented 2-year-olds with these two types of situations to investigate whether they are capable of assessing their mothers' knowledge states. She presented children ranging in age from 2;6 to 2;10 with a task in which they had to ask their mothers for help in retrieving a toy from a shelf. On each of four trials the child subjects witnessed a new toy being hidden in one of two distinct containers on the shelf. On two of these trials, their mothers also witnessed the hiding of the toy. On the other two trials, mothers did not witness the hiding and therefore were not aware of the correct location. As expected, in asking for help, children were more likely to name the toy and name its location on the trials when their mothers had *not* witnessed the hiding. In a second study with somewhat younger 2-year-olds (2;3 to 2;4), children's use of pointing gestures demonstrated that they too differentiated between trials on which their mothers had witnessed the hiding event and trials on which they had not. These results indicate that 2-year-olds are indeed sensitive to what is new information to another, and that their communication with others reflects this understanding.

Predication is thus a type of communicative act that requires intersubjectivity and, interestingly, is not seen in non-linguistic forms of communication. Bees do not predicate anything of the flowers they locate for their hivemates, nor do monkeys predicate anything of the predators to whom they alert their groupmates. Predication is a thoroughly intersubjective process that involves an unprecedented kind of specificity and detail: there is joint attention both in terms of a general establishment of topic and in terms of the more specific establishment of some new aspect of that topic that seems worthy of sharing with a communicative partner.

Conversation

Intersubjective skills are also apparent when we examine young children's conversational abilities, especially their behaviour when intersubjectivity breaks down. Recent studies indicate not only that young children are aware when communication breaks down, but that they possess a number of strategies for repairing a given breakdown based on their understanding of its cause. For example, when an adult signals non-comprehension or makes a request for clarification, children between 11 and 19 months of age may repeat their original communicative attempt, augment it with gestures and/or emphasis, or substitute another word or gesture (Golinkoff, 1986, 1993). One- to two-year-old children adjust the type of repair they use in different communicative situations (e.g. Gallagher, 1977, 1981; Marcos, 1991; Marcos and Kornhaber-le-Chanu, 1992). As a particularly revealing example, Tomasello *et al.* (1984) found that 2-year-olds were more likely to repeat their initial utterance when queried by their mothers, and were more likely to reformulate when queried by an adult stranger. This differential responding suggests that they may be sensitive to the fact that strangers are less likely to understand them whereas their mothers may have only misheard.

Further evidence that toddlers were sensitive to adults' misunderstandings comes from studies in which an adult experimenter signals non-comprehension in distinct ways (Wilcox and Webster, 1980). For example, Anselmi *et al.* (1986) showed that children tend to provide repetitions of their entire utterance in response to a general query such as 'What?' or 'Huh?', but respond with only the required information after a specific query such as 'You want what?' Even though exact repetitions would form appropriate responses to specific queries, the children most often repeated only the asked-for information. This suggests not only that they have understood the adult's query, but also that they know that they should provide only that information of which the listener is not aware.

Furrow and Lewis (1987) extended this finding in an experiment demonstrating that the initial utterance in a contingent query sequence – that is, the child's utterance that is being queried – also influences the child's response to a request for clarification. Twenty times during the play session an experimenter feigned non-comprehension of a preschool child's comprehensible utterance by asking 'What?' The social context of the child's original utterance, a rough indicator of the child's original intent, was shown to influence the child's response to the query. There were fewer repetition responses (and more non-responses, or ignoring) when the child's initial utterance was a case of 'private speech'. This makes perfect sense because if the original intent was not to communicate, then there would be no need to repeat or reformulate one's utterance. Thus, children not only provide information of which adults are unaware, but they provide only information of which the listener needs to be aware.

The results of these studies indicate quite clearly that young children recognize when communication has broken down, and that they have a variety of means for repairing breakdowns. It is important, however, to explore their motivations for making such repairs, as the nature of their motivations has implications for whether they should be credited with any intersubjective understanding at all. Shatz and O'Reilly (1990), for example, argue that, rather than demonstrating an understanding of others' communicative needs, children's responses to requests for clarification may simply reflect their desire to achieve material goals through others.

The basis for this conclusion was one finding from a study of sixteen $2\frac{1}{2}$-year-olds in conversation with their parents. This finding was that children responded more frequently (and successfully) to requests for clarification of their requests than they did to requests for clarification of their assertions; that is, the children were more motivated to repair a misunderstanding when they wanted some action or object from the parent and did not get it, than when they were simply telling the parent about something. However, as Golinkoff (1993) has pointed out, this statistically significant difference may not be *conceptually* significant when one examines the actual numbers; children responded to 84% of requests for clarification made of their assertions and to 94% of requests for clarification made of their requests. One could just as well focus on the fact that children responded to over 80% of requests for clarification when there were no material goals to speak of; this result in itself implies that children are often motivated solely by the goal of providing information or communicating effectively. This conclusion is further strengthened by the finding that overall the children in Shatz and O'Reilly's study made about three times as many assertions as they did requests. As assertions do not involve any material goals – the child is communicating purely for 'sharing' his/her thoughts and feelings – it appears that young children's use of language is motivated more by a desire to express themselves and establish intersubjectivity than by a desire to accomplish behaviour goals (Bloom and Beckwith, 1989).

Conclusion

In this brief review we have attempted to highlight the central role of intersubjective processes in early language learning and language use. The studies of word learning demonstrate that children as young as 18 months of age are skilled at using a variety of pragmatic cues to establish intersubjectivity with adults and, in this way, learn new words from them. The studies of language use show that young children use linguistic symbols reciprocally and predicatively. From soon after their first birthdays they use language with a reciprocal understanding of its communicative significance for others, they predicate particular aspects of a situation in manipulating the attention of others (establishing a joint topic before doing so), and they comment on what is new in a given situation. In situations of communicative breakdown, they also show a remarkable ability to determine the cause of the breakdown and then effectively reformulate their previous (misunderstood) utterance. They do not do so indiscriminately, however; whether and how they reformulate their utterance depends on characteristics of the misunderstood utterance, their interlocutor and the specific type of query made. All of these types of language use depend in a fundamental way on the process by which children establish and maintain intersubjectivity with adults. Moreover, as in the case of language learning, we believe that these intersubjective processes depend crucially on young children's basic understanding of persons as intentional agents whose attention may be followed, manipulated and shared.

The more we think about processes of linguistic communication, the less we like saying such things as intersubjectivity 'facilitates' or 'plays a role' in early language. Instead, we believe it is more accurate to say simply that language is an inherently intersubjective phenomenon through and through. Conventional linguistic symbols are nothing more or less than tools that human beings have collaboratively invented for establishing, regulating and maintaining intersubjective interactions with fellow human beings.

Throughout this chapter we have alluded to the central role played by children's emerging understanding of the intentions and intentional states of others. It may be true that from birth human infants can engage in affectively meaningful interactions with others

(Trevarthen, this volume), and it is possible that they possess a 'virtual other' as a part of their neonatal psychological equipment (Bråten, 1993; this volume). Nevertheless, a fundamental change in how infants relate to and understand others takes place during their second year of life. It is at this age that they begin to share attention with adults to outside entities, as evidenced by the emergence of such things as social referencing, gaze following, imitative learning of actions on objects, and prelinguistic gestural communication. This sharing of attention depends on infants' understanding that other persons can intentionally direct their perception and behaviour to different aspects of the environment. It is no accident, we would argue, that the earliest language emerges at around the same time as these developments, and that it is in language that we see many of the most sophisticated expressions of the understanding and manipulation of the intentional states of others. This is because, as an almost purely conventional system, language is an almost purely intersubjective phenomenon.

CHAPTER 18

Fictional absorption: emotional responses to make-believe

Paul L. Harris

Developmental psychologists have often emphasized cognitive discontinuities between infants and adults. In this chapter, I discuss one domain where there is continuity. Children are similar to adults in their capacity for being absorbed in fictional materials such as stories or dramas. I argue that such absorption comes about when a point-of-view is taken up within the make-believe framework alongside one or other of the main characters. Events within the make-believe framework, rather than real events, are then appraised from that perspective, and thereby arouse emotion. Emotional reactions to fictional events do not reflect any confusion about their ontological status but a temporary recalibration of the appraisal system.

The emergence of pretence

An obvious early index of children's preoccupation with make-believe is their capacity for pretend play. The pioneering observations of pretend play by Piaget (1945/1962) led investigators to focus on the lone child's production of pretend play. More recent research has emphasized the way that children engage in joint pretence. For example, in the course of the third and fourth year, children begin to engage in collaborative role play: a pair of children will adopt complementary roles such as mother and baby or doctor and patient (Dunn and Dale, 1984). Joint pretence is especially interesting for my purposes because it illustrates the way that children understand pretence, even when it is produced by someone other than themselves. Here, in embryonic form, we see the child's engagement in a fiction or drama even when it is created, in part, by someone else.

Below, I emphasize two important aspects of joint pretence. First, when attempting to make sense of a pretend episode, children deploy their causal understanding of events in the real world. Second, despite this transfer of knowledge from reality to fiction, there is little indication that young children confuse the two.

The transfer of causal knowledge

In our research, we have shown that 2-year-olds can work out the imaginary consequences of a play partner's make-believe actions. For example, 2-year-olds watched while a Duck puppet (manipulated by the experimenter) carried out a two-step piece of mischief (Harris *et al.*, 1994, Experiments 1 and 2). To interpret what the Duck had done, children needed to infer the causal links between her successive actions. For example, in one episode, the Duck picked up an empty milk carton and with a tipping movement pretended to pour some liquid into the tray of a matchbox. Next, the Duck picked up the matchbox tray, and turning it upside down, pretended to pour its contents over a toy horse. Children were very good at describing the outcome. They realized that *milk* had been tipped over the horse. To do this, they must have imagined the pretend milk going into the matchbox tray, being carried in it towards the horse, and then being tipped over the horse. Notice that the final action of inverting the tray of the matchbox could not be interpreted without reference to the preceding action in which it had been filled with milk.

Despite the pedestrian nature of these pretend episodes, they illustrate an important point. Objectively speaking, the children saw only empty containers being picked up, tilted or inverted. Thus, children must have used their knowledge of naive physics to figure out what was happening in the make-believe episodes: they realized that a liquid would tip out of a tilted carton, and fall down into a container directly below; they also realized that a substance or liquid would be transported in the container if it was moved in an upright position; and finally, they realized that if this container was inverted, its contents would douse the animal victim. Effectively, children must have deployed their understanding of containers, motion and gravity to imagine what the Duck was doing because none of these causal outcomes was visibly realized.

Children also readily saw the Duck as carrying out these mischievous actions. They invested her with independent agency, although they could see that the real source of these actions was the experimenter rather than the puppet. Children's attribution of agency emerged even more plainly in a follow-up study (Harris and Surman, 1994). Children watched while the experimenter made a toy animal move across the table in a characteristic fashion. For example, a rabbit was made to 'hop' across, and a fish to 'swim' across. When asked to say what the animals were doing, children readily described them in terms of their characteristic pattern of locomotion, ignoring the fact that the experimenter was visibly propelling the animals.

A minor addition to the scene led children to make more complex attributions. When a second animal, similar in appearance to the first, was placed at the terminus of the movement of the first animal, children incorporated this into their accounts. They described this second animal as the goal of the journey made by the first. For example, children said that the rabbit 'wanted to see his friend' or that the fish 'was going to say hello'. Not surprisingly, the pattern of attributions shifted again, if the second animal was placed at the starting-point rather than the terminus. Now the moving animal was variously described as 'frightened of' or 'wanting to run away from' the stationary animal. Thus, faced with the experimenter's displacement of one inanimate toy in relation to another, 2-year-olds spontaneously glossed it as an intentional agent deliberately moving towards or away from a goal. Just as they did with the movements of the containers in the experiments described earlier, children brought their causal understanding to bear in interpreting the pretend scenario. In the present case, however, it was their understanding of animate agency rather than naive physics.

We often think of the world of make-believe as a realm where children ignore the constraints of the real world. Indeed, children sometimes act out situations in their pretend play that they would like to happen but which are forbidden or unlikely. In this respect, fantasy allows children to escape from the constraints of the real world (Piaget, 1945/1962). Yet the structure of the child's imagination is also guided by reality. The above findings show that children deploy their understanding of causal regularities in the real world to make sense of events in the pretend world.

Recent research has revealed a similar process when adults read fiction. Admittedly, pretend play uses the symbolism of props and gesture whereas stories use the symbolism of language. Notwithstanding the difference in symbolic medium, pretend play and stories are both made up of discrete but causally linked episodes. Yet such causal links may not be made explicit. Hence, it is often up to the audience to supply those causal links themselves. The importance of such constructive causal processing in story comprehension has been established with various techniques (Graesser *et al.*, 1994). Reaction time experiments are especially revealing because they show that readers make inferences on-line – as they move from one phrase to the next. Suppose that readers are presented with the following pair of sentences: 'Dorothy poured the bucket of water on the bonfire. The fire went out.' Although the causal connection is not explicitly stated, readers are likely to connect the two sentences mentally into an antecedent–consequent pairing by drawing the inference that it was the water in the bucket that caused the fire to go out. Consistent with this assumption, readers who have just encountered these two sentences are quick to answer a test question that coincides with that activated inference, for example: 'Does water extinguish fire?' By contrast, readers who are presented with a control pair of sentences ('Dorothy placed the bucket of water by the fire. The fire went out.') answer the test question more slowly (Singer *et al.*, 1992).

When children read stories, they display the same type of constructive effort after meaning. In particular, their reading speed is affected by the ease with which a given segment of text can be causally connected to what has gone before. For example, we gave children stories that included the following sentence: 'He saw his hair getting shorter.' The speed with which children read this sentence and moved on to the next depended on the preceding context. Children who had read about a boy waiting for his turn at the hairdresser read this sentence more rapidly than children who had read about a boy waiting for his turn at the dentist (Harris *et al.*, 1981).

In sum, whether we focus on the make-believe world created by children in the course of pretend play, or on the fictive world entered into by a reader, the construction of those worlds depends on the active importation of real-world causal knowledge.

The distinction between make-believe and reality

Granted that young children transpose their understanding of the real world to the pretend world, one might argue that this is because they conflate the two worlds. Although this argument is unlikely to apply to older children and adults when they read stories, it may be applicable to young children engaged in pretence.

It is not easy to question 2-year-olds about the status of imaginary episodes or creatures, but this is feasible with slightly older children. For example, Wellman and his colleagues (Estes *et al.*, 1989; Wellman and Estes, 1986) asked 3- and 4-year-olds about two different types of entity – imagined entities and real entities. Children were asked to imagine a pair of scissors, and also shown an actual pair of scissors. They were then questioned about the properties of each. The children were quite systematic in their ability to differentiate between the two: they realized, for example, that the real pair of scissors was a publicly visible entity that could be seen by other people whereas the imagined pair of scissors was invisible to others; they also understood that the imagined pair of scissors – unlike the real pair of scissors – could be transformed by thought alone. For example, they realized that one could imagine the pair of scissors opening and closing, whereas thinking would have no effect on the real pair of scissors.

However, one may doubt that children apply this ontological distinction to all imaginary entities. Consider two well-known developmental phenomena. About 40% of young children adopt an imaginary companion. Having invented such companions, children often insist on their presence: they ask that a special place be reserved for them at dinner, and become upset if the companion is somehow 'lost' or 'separated'. Children's emotional reactions in these cases can be quite intense, and assuaged only when the companion is duly acknowledged or reinstated. Children also display 'imaginary fears'. They claim to be frightened of monsters or ghosts and exhibit the pattern of behaviour characteristic of genuine fear: they avoid places likely to harbour monsters, they seek the proximity of an adult, or they adopt various precautionary strategies such as carrying a shield (Harris *et al.*, 1991; Jersild, 1947).

Given their emotional reactions towards such imaginary creatures, it is tempting to conclude that children think of them as real. With this possibility in mind, we asked children to make judgements not just about relatively prosaic entities, but also about extraordinary creatures such as ghosts, witches or monsters (Harris *et al.*, 1991). In fact, children were questioned about three different types of item: real items that were quite ordinary (e.g. a pair of scissors), imagined items that were also quite ordinary (e.g. an imagined pair of scissors) and imagined items that were extraordinary (e.g. an imagined monster). For each type of item, children made two different judgements: they said whether it was real or not, and they said whether the experimenter could see it or not. Fig. 18.1 shows the results. Children distinguished sharply between the real and imagined ordinary items, just as Wellman and his colleagues had found. The key experimental issue was how children would respond concerning the imagined extraordinary items. Would they think of them as being like the real items or the imagined ordinary items? Fig. 18.1 offers no indication that children misconstrued the ontological status of the imagined monsters, ghosts and witches. The imagined extraordinary items were judged as being like the imagined ordinary items.

Although these results were persuasive, we wondered whether children might show signs of ontological confusion if the imagined creatures were more vivid and potentially frightening. So, in a follow-up experiment children were asked not just to imagine a creature such as a monster or ghost, but to imagine the creature chasing after them. Children seemed to comply with this instruction in that several children subsequently reported that they found the experience

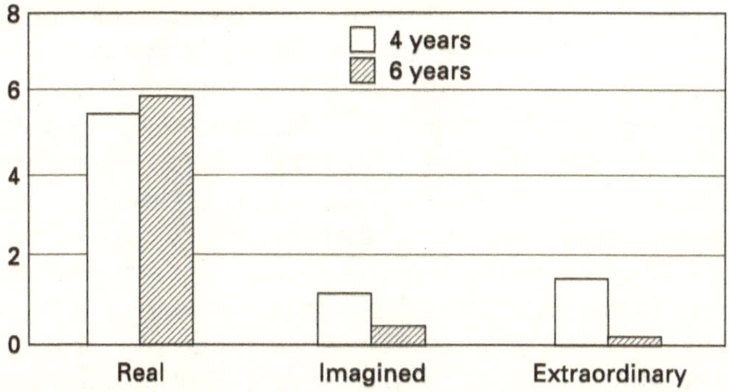

Fig. 18.1 Mean number of realist responses by age and type of item.

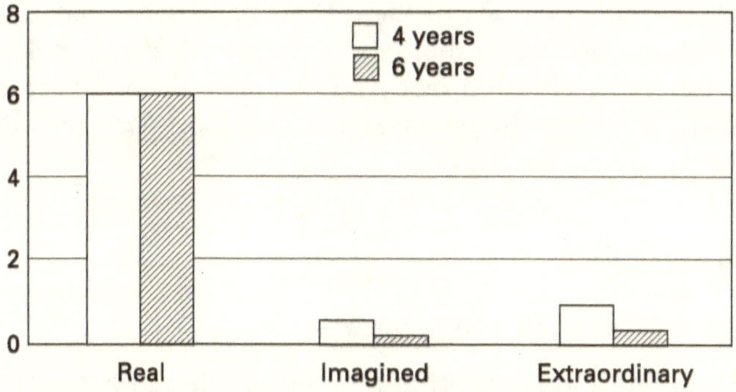

Fig. 18.2 Mean number of realist responses by age and type of item in follow-up experiment in which the children were asked to image the creature chasing after them.

somewhat frightening. Nevertheless, they continued to make the same judgements as they had in the first study: the imagined extraordinary items were judged in the same way as the imagined ordinary items as shown in Fig. 18.2.

In one further study of this issue, Goy (1990) looked at children's judgements about imaginary friends. She located a sample of 4-year-olds who, according to their parents' report, had invented an imaginary companion. The children were questioned about the status of this imaginary friend as compared to their best friend at preschool. In particular, they were asked to say which friend they could really hear and which friend they could only pretend to hear. Only one child out of a group of sixteen children with an imaginary companion made any mistakes on these questions.

All these findings suggest that young children are not confused about the ontological status of imaginary creatures. More generally, they highlight an interesting paradox. How is it that children display emotional reactions to the products of their imagination? Why do they fear monsters whom they themselves have invented, or become upset at the loss of a companion whom they have lost only in their imagination?

A moment's reflection reveals that the paradox is more pervasive than I have suggested. It is not just young children who show such emotional reactions. Adults also become emotionally involved in make-believe. Horror films do horrify; pornography provokes erotic feelings; and thrillers thrill. Yet if children's emotional involvement in make-believe cannot plausibly be attributed to ontological confusion, this line of argument is still more implausible for adults who presumably are quite lucid about the difference between fact and make-believe. The implication is that emotional responses to make-believe, whether by young children or by adults, should not be attributed to conceptual confusion. In the next section, I propose an alternative explanation, making three plausible assumptions.

Fictional absorption

A point-of-view within the make-believe world

The first assumption is that children and adults can enter into a state of 'fictional absorption'. A hallmark of that state is that they temporarily adopt a point-of-view situated inside the make-believe world rather than the real world. To be more precise, they adopt – in their imagination – a particular point-of-view relative to the geography and the temporal sequence of events within the narrative. Frequently, that point-of-view is situated alongside one or the other of the main characters. Thus, fictional absorption is characterized by a state of 'altercentric participation' to use Bråten's terminology (cf. this volume, chapters 5 and 20). Once someone is in this state, it is the narrative – rather than the real world – that specifies what events are about to happen, and what objects are close at hand. What counts as *here* versus *there*, and *now* versus *then*, is specified within the make-believe world. We are all familiar with this state and can recognize it easily when we become involved in a story or film. Normal inputs from everyday reality are temporarily held in abeyance while attention is focused on the incoming make-believe inputs. Once we are absorbed into the world of the story, film or play, the question of whether those fictional events are make-believe is side-lined. A consideration of that question presupposes a point-of-view outside of the fictional frame. In short, the process of fictional absorption suspends any epistemic reflection on the status of the fictive world.

Our point-of-view within a fictional world will typically correspond to a greater or lesser extent with that of the central characters. We imagine ourselves in the same place as them, with the same time-frame as them. The extent to which our perspective precisely coincides with theirs will depend on the particular genre and its conventions. Sometimes, a narrator or director will allow us to share a character's private perspective on the events of the narrative. For example, an internal monologue or the angle of the camera will reveal how the world appears to that character. In such cases, our perspective and his or hers are virtually coincident. Often, however, our perspective is similar but not coincident. We must infer hidden thoughts and emotions from what the character says and does. Finally, we may be given a privileged perspective in which we learn about events pertinent to a particular character, but as yet unknown to him or her. Note, however, that despite the richness of these structural devices for shifting our point-of-view, none of them takes us outside of the make-believe frame, or places us at an insuperable distance from the central characters. Rather, they govern our point-of-view within the space occupied by those characters.

Engaging the appraisal system

The second assumption is that the state of fictional absorption temporarily engages our appraisal system – the system by which we assess the emotional significance of events. Events that take place within the make-believe frame are appraised for their emotional significance from our point-of-view within that frame. The appraisal system is disengaged from its standard mode of operation, namely the appraisal of real-world events, and is directed instead at events within the story frame. Events that befall the make-believe protagonists will be evaluated just as if they were really happening. For example, an event that threatens a central character is appraised in much the same way as a threat to a real-life companion or enemy. Feelings of fear or panic will be attributed to the character.

The control of emotional responses

The third assumption is that unless a child engaged in pretence or a reader of fiction deliberately inhibits the appraisal system, emotionally charged make-believe events are likely to evoke an emotional response on their part. Thus, players and readers not only attribute emotions to fictional characters, they feel emotions themselves, either directly in response to events that befall those characters, or in response to the emotions attributed to those characters.

The intensity of such emotional reactions can, however, be modulated. In particular, in the course of development, children begin to exploit their appreciation of the distinction between make-believe and reality to select their point-of-view, and thereby regulate their emotional reactions to fiction. They can magnify their response by deliberately moving their point-of-view to particular loci within the make-believe frame. For example, they can allow themselves to identify closely with the perspective of a given protagonist, and vicariously suffer or enjoy his or her fate. Alternatively, they can move their point-of-view out of the make-believe frame and distance themselves from a fictional episode by dismissing it as 'just a story'. In this latter case, their emotional response to the fictional events is likely to be attenuated.

Evidence for fictional absorption

Although we are all familiar with fictional absorption first-hand, there has been little direct investigation of the process. Nonetheless, several studies lend support to each of the three assumptions described above.

Adopting a point-of-view

I relied heavily on the notion of a perspective or point-of-view. Research on text-processing indicates that this is not just a loose metaphor. In comprehending a text, readers do indeed adopt a point-of-view, mentally locating themselves within the scene that is being described. Typically that locus is coincident with or close to the locus of a central character. Moreover, consistent with Bråten's concept of altercentric participation, it shifts when that character moves to a new location. Once adopted, such a perspective operates as a kind of cognitive spotlight illuminating certain objects while leaving others in darkness.

To illustrate, readers were presented with the following sentence: 'Bill was sitting in the living room reading the evening paper.' If readers situate themselves in that same room near the central character, they should find it easier to process sentences that describe subsequent events as if they happened in relation to that locus. Consistent with that assumption, Black *et al.* (1979) found that subjects subsequently read sentence (a) faster than sentence (b):

(a) Before Bill had finished the paper, John came into the room.
(b) Before Bill had finished the paper, John went into the room.

As noted, readers not only adopt a point-of-view that is similar to that of a central character, they also move their point-of-view along with that character, and selectively highlight certain objects. For example, Morrow *et al.* (1987) found that when subjects read that a central character was moving from one room to another, they were slower at answering questions about items in the room that had been left as compared with the room to be entered; and they were even slower to answer questions about rooms that had not been entered at all. It was as if readers' cognitive spotlight was aimed in the direction of travel adopted by the central character. Similar results emerged in an experiment by Glenberg *et al.* (1987). Subjects read a text about a runner who either put on or removed his sweatshirt and then went jogging round the lake. If then asked whether the word 'sweatshirt' had occurred in the story subjects answered more quickly if the runner had put on his sweatshirt rather than removed it. Again, the implication is that readers move their spotlight along with the main character so that information about the sweatshirt is retrieved faster if it falls within that spotlight rather than outside its arc. More generally, this research shows that it is meaningful to suppose that readers adopt a point-of-view that specifies their current location and attentional focus within the make-believe spatiotemporal framework of a story (Bower and Morrow, 1990).

Engaging the appraisal system

Does fictional absorption engage the appraisal system? More specifically, do subjects work out the emotional implications of events that are not actually taking place but which they are invited to imagine. Although this issue has been less thoroughly investigated, Gernsbacher, Goldsmith and Robertson (1992) provide supportive evidence. Subjects read a simple story about a sequence of events likely to elicit emotion in a central character. For example, in one story the main character stole money from a shop where his best friend worked and subsequently learnt that his friend had been fired. Subjects were then asked to read a test sentence containing an emotion word that matched the emotion implied by the story (e.g. guilt) or mismatched that emotional state (e.g. proud). They read the former sentence quicker than the latter, implying – to borrow the metaphor of the cognitive spotlight once more – that the emotional implications of the main character's actions had been inferred and highlighted.

These results are intriguing but one might argue that readers use their appraisal processes in a relatively unemotional fashion. They can work out what the protagonist is feeling but they experience no concurrent emotion themselves. Is there evidence, therefore, that pretend inputs can drive the emotional system itself? One way to explore this question is to monitor activity in the autonomic nervous system when subjects are engaged in looking not at a real scene but at a painting or photo. Damasio and his colleagues asked adults to view a series of slides (Damasio *et al.*, 1991). Most of the slides depicted bland scenes but a minority depicted disturbing, emotionally charged scenes. Normal adults produced large skin conductance responses on seeing the disturbing images but not on seeing the banal ones. Thus, although they were seated comfortably in a chair looking at slides, and not actually witnessing the scenes depicted, they did not respond in a cold-blooded fashion.

Similar findings have emerged from studies using textual rather than photographic materials. Vrana and Lang (1990) asked adults to study and remember two different types of sentence. One type described a frightening situation, for example: 'I tense as the nurse slowly injects the sharp needle into my upper arm and beads of sweat cover my forehead.' The other type described a relatively pleasant situation, for example: 'I am relaxing on my living room couch looking out of the window on a sunny autumn day.' Subjects were then prompted to recall either one or the other type of sentence. As they did so, they were sometimes startled by a loud click. Subjects displayed a stronger startle reaction – typically associated with a negative emotional state – when they were concurrently in the process of recalling a frightening as compared with a pleasant, relaxing situation. Moreover, the size of this increase depended on how subjects recalled the sentences. Startle reactions were especially marked if subjects were instructed to imagine being in the situation described; they were less marked if subjects were asked to repeat the sentence silently to themselves or simply to ignore the sentence and relax.

In summary, several lines of evidence show that when subjects process stories or pictures they appraise the emotional significance of the material, and not simply in a cold-blooded, cognitive fashion. Psycho-physiological changes associated with actual emotion rather than the attribution of emotion are also apparent.

The control of emotion

Fictional absorption not only leads to the attribution of emotion to characters within the story, it also arouses relevant emotion in the

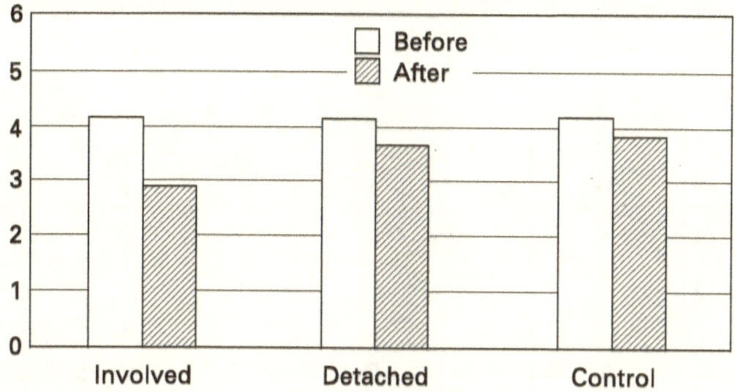

Fig. 18.3 Mean level of mood before and after story as a function of group.

reader. Nonetheless, that emotion can be regulated. We have obtained evidence for these effects in a study of young children. We asked 6-year-olds to listen to a sad story which described how a family was about to move to a new city, obliging the main character to say goodbye to a close friend (Meerum Terwogt *et al.*, 1986). Children were allocated to one of three groups, each group receiving a different set of orientating instructions. One group was given instructions likely to heighten absorption: they were asked to try to involve themselves in the story and to feel sad like the main character. A second group was given instructions likely to reduce absorption: they were asked to remain detached – to listen to the story such 'that you won't become sad yourself'. Finally, a third group was given no instructions, except to 'listen carefully' to the story.

The effects of these instructions were assessed in three different ways. First, children were asked to report on their mood before and after the story. As might be expected, all three groups reported that they felt quite cheerful before the story. After the story, each group reported a drop in their mood, but for children in the involved group this decline was especially marked. The results are illustrated in Fig. 18.3.

Children were asked to retell the story in their own words, and we looked for evidence that they had encoded the emotional elements of the story differently depending on the orientating instructions. In all three groups, children tended to focus on the key elements of the story, and the length of their narrative was approximately the same. Nevertheless, children in the involved group were more likely to describe sad elements of the story. They used more words for emotion (e.g. 'sad', 'shocked') and more phrases connoting emotion (e.g. 'he

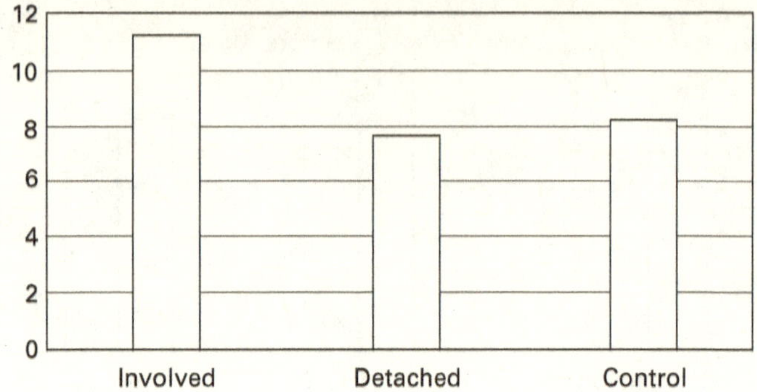

Fig. 18.4 Mean emotion scores for story recall as a function of group.

fell down on the bed crying'). Hence, as can be seen in Fig. 18.4, the three groups differed in the number of references to emotion. There was also a link between mood and recall. Children who reported feeling sad after the story were more likely to include such emotional words and phrases in their recall.

Finally, although a sad mood was associated with greater recall of sad elements in the story, this was not because it led to a generalized improvement in memory. Children who reported that they felt sad after the story did less well on a picture memory task unrelated to the story content.

Thus, consistent with the assumption that fictional material affects the emotional mood of a reader, children in all three groups reported being affected by the sad story. Nonetheless, the orientating instructions moderated that influence. When asked to involve themselves in the story, children reported a greater decline in their mood, mentioned more sad elements in their recall, and performed worse on a standard memory test. By contrast, children asked to adopt a detached orientation to the story or left to their own devices showed only a slight drop in mood, rarely mentioned the explicitly emotional aspects of the story, and performed normally on a standard memory task. Thus, the involved group displayed the hypothetical state of absorption to a more marked degree: they entered into the feelings experienced by the main character in the story.

How did children follow the experimenter's instructions? Children in the involved and detached groups were interviewed at the end of the experiment about the strategies they had adopted. Many children had difficulty in reporting what they had done. Alternatively – and these replies were common in the involved group – children said that they did not need to do anything special because being involved in the story was a natural attitude. Nonetheless, a minority were able to provide some informative reports of particular strategies. Children in the involved group mentioned a family of techniques likely to increase their engagement in the fate of the story character: they mentioned pretending that the events in the story were actually happening to them, or to someone close to them, or they tried to link the events in the story with a similar experience of their own. By contrast, children in the detached group cited strategies that would be likely to disengage them from the fate of the story character. In particular, they mentioned reminding themselves that it was 'just a story' or 'not real'. Again these results fit the analysis given earlier. Involved children adopted strategies likely to maintain their point-of-view within the story frame close to that of the central character; they side-lined their knowledge of the fact that they were reading a mere story. In contrast, detached children deliberately moved their point-of-view outside of the story frame by reminding themselves of its fictional status.

The strategies that the children described echoed to an uncanny extent the strategies that adults reported in a much earlier study reported by Koriat *et al.* (1972). In that study, adults repeatedly watched a film about industrial safety. Some scenes in the film were disturbing because they portrayed accidents such as finger laceration or amputation. Prior to later screenings, subjects were given different instructions regarding the emotional stance that they should adopt. Some were asked to remain detached and uninvolved whereas others were asked to let themselves go – to become emotionally involved; finally, a control group was given no specific instructions except to watch the film attentively. Thus, these three orientations were similar to those described in the study of children described above.

Physiological indices showed that subjects were successful in complying with these instructions: the detached group were less aroused during the film than the involved group. Moreover, in a subsequent interview about the strategies that had been used to comply with the instructions, the detached and involved groups emphasized different techniques. Identification with the events and people in the film (e.g. 'I tried to imagine that it is happening to me') was the strategy mentioned most often in connection with the instructions calling for involvement. Subjects aiming at detachment, on the other hand, claimed that they reminded themselves of the status or creation of the film. For example, they reminded themselves that 'it was a film rather than a real occurrence' or they focused 'on the technical aspects involved in its production'.

Putting these two studies together, there is a striking continuity in the way that children and adults approach stories and films. If they allow themselves to be involved, to hold their point-of-view within the story frame, close to that of the central characters, such materials elicit an emotional reaction equivalent to real input. Conversely, both children and adults can deliberately remain detached. This detachment is achieved primarily through the use of an ontological override. Subjects remind themselves that they are confronted not by a real event, but by a manufactured, non-real input. Effectively, they move their point-of-view to a point outside of the make-believe frame so that the frame itself is salient rather than the events that take place within it.

The basis for fictional absorption

Absorption in fiction is pervasive: it is exhibited in the context of a huge variety of cultural media – children's fairy stories, comics, short stories, novels, television soap operas, costume dramas, video nasties, Hollywood blockbusters and so on. Granted this heterogeneity, it seems unlikely that a single psychological impulse underpins such absorption. Instead, it seems more plausible that there are a variety of fictional impulses, each cultivated or even created by a particular genre. Those who repeatedly expose themselves to a given genre will gain a taste for the fictional world that it offers. According to this account, the taste for detective stories or horror movies is a bit like the taste for whisky or tobacco: steady consumption of either may be habit-forming but there is no single universal impulse underpinning all such dependencies.

I suspect that this argument, and analogy, are flawed and that there is a human impulse towards fictional absorption notwithstanding the huge variety of sustenance available for its satisfaction. In particular, there appear to be certain individuals who show a pathological indifference towards fiction. An analysis of that indifference will bring certain features of our normal response to fiction into relief.

Autistic children display a puzzling triad of symptoms: they are poor at forming social relationships; they are deficient in language, notably the conversational or pragmatic aspects of language; and their pretend play is repetitive or non-existent. Although early research hinted that autism might be triggered by unresponsive parents, subsequent studies indicate a genetic basis for the disorder. Rather than consider the entire spectrum of difficulties displayed by autistic children, I will focus on their limited imagination.

As noted earlier, normal children start to produce pretend play in the second year of life. Kanner (1943), the first clinician to identify the syndrome of autism, commented on the impoverished play of autistic children. Subsequent investigations have borne out his astute observations. In a large epidemiological survey of children with autistic-like difficulties in establishing social relationships, Wing (1978) noted that almost all such children either exhibited no pretend play at all, or engaged in simple, repetitive pretend routines. The normal pattern of increasing complexity and elaboration was almost entirely absent in this sample. More recently, Baron-Cohen *et al.* (1992) have reported an epidemiological survey of toddlers that includes parental reports on the emergence of pointing and pretend play during the second year of life. A tiny minority of children failed to exhibit both of these behaviours. Follow-up diagnoses of these children have confirmed that almost all of them are autistic, or exhibit many of the classic features of autism, pending a firm diagnosis. In short, the failure to produce pretend play is now known to be an important early indicator of autism.

What is the exact nature of the deficiency shown by autistic children in their pretend play? One possible suggestion is that they do not grasp the special logic of pretence in which imaginary creatures (a companion or monster) or substances (tea in a cup) are called into being or in which one object (a piece of playdoh) may substitute for another (a sausage). This proposal is ruled out by the fact that under certain circumstances autistic children do exhibit an understanding of pretence. When given some toys or everyday objects and asked to pretend with them, autistic children will comply (Lewis and Boucher, 1988). Moreover, if they watch an adult experimenter act out various pretend transformations (e.g. pretending to pour tea from a teapot over a toy pig) they can identify the pretend outcome correctly (e.g. by pointing to a picture of a pig covered in tea) (Kavanaugh and Harris, in press). Thus, autistic children show the same transposition of causal reasoning from the real world to the pretend world that is displayed by normal children. Finally, if asked to think of, and act out, various pretend actions, autistic children can comply with the instruction satisfactorily (Jarrold *et al.*, 1994).

An alternative proposal is that autistic children have the cognitive competence to pretend but have difficulty in generating pretend themes, especially when left to their own devices (Harris, 1993). In everyday parlance, they 'lack imagination'. Considerable support has emerged for this proposal. For example, autistic children rarely generate any pretend actions when they are given a set of toys and left to their own devices (Baron-Cohen, 1987; Lewis and Boucher, 1988). In addition, if they are asked to produce pretend actions, they do so with much less fluency than control groups matched for mental age (Jarrold *et al.*, 1994).

If the generative disposition to pretend provides a psychological foundation for becoming absorbed in a fictional world, we should expect autistic children to be disinclined to take that step. This is consistent with descriptions of autistic children's pattern of interests. Case studies suggest that in early childhood they fail to show the fascination of the normal child at being told a story. Moreover, when autistic people develop interests in later life, these are rarely directed at fictional material. They become interested in domains that are complex but factual and predictable: railway timetables, calendars and dates.

Still, we need to carry our analysis further. Why is the generative disposition to pretend important for fiction? How does it tempt the normal child to spend hours curled up with a book, while the autistic child remains indifferent? Earlier, I presented experimental evidence for the familiar fact that fictional material induces emotion. Make-believe events are appraised as if they were real events. In my view, this is the key to the difficulty faced by autistic children. Specifically, the hypothesis is as follows: when reading a book or listening to a story, we imagine the scenes and events depicted. More generally, a piece of fiction is an extended series of props for our imagination: it prompts us to conjure up a landscape, a set of characters and a series of episodes. In particular, we mentally locate our phenomenal point-of-view alongside that of the central characters. To the extent that we engage in this imaginative transposition – and our success will depend on our own generative capacity – we become absorbed. In particular, if we allow ourselves to engage with the make-believe characters, so that their fate is temporarily our fate, then emotion will ensue.

The implication is that autistic children cannot get this process underway. Lacking the generative disposition to pretend, they fail to meet the makers of fiction half-way: they do not deliver on their part of the bargain which is to position themselves mentally alongside the story protagonists within the fictional frame. Granted that this transposition does not properly get underway, there is little to feed into their emotional system. It is as if they naturally adopted the 'detached' stance that was included in the two experiments described earlier. Note, however, that this analogy is only partially correct. In the case of normal children and adults, the detached stance can be knowingly adopted to block the emotion-inducing effects of absorption. In the case of autistic children, by contrast, my hypothesis is not that they knowingly adopt this detached stance, but rather that they lack the resources to do otherwise.

Summary and conclusions

To sum up the argument, there is an early-emerging disposition to become absorbed in a fictional world. Granted that state of absorption, events that befall the characters in that fictional world generate emotion in the absorbed subject. This process requires a natural disposition, a disposition that may be weak or absent in the case of a developmental psychopathology such as autism. Admittedly, that disposition can be shaped in many ways. Children will be exposed to particular types of material, identify to a greater or lesser extent with the protagonists, and cultivate particular tastes in the course of development. Still, the fact that children's sensibility can be cultivated does not undermine my basic claim: for fiction to do its work, it needs to build on an imaginative involvement by the child. Finally, the imaginative involvement of early childhood is continuous with the imaginative involvement of adulthood. This continuity thesis conflicts with the standard notion of cognitive development in psychology. On that view, cognitive development involves the gradual construction of a quasi-scientific theory of the real world. Children are characterized as increasingly sophisticated theorists in the domains of physics, biology and psychology. A problem with this account is that it portrays the child in terms of a metaphor that is of limited applicability to adults, let alone children. Scientific theorizing is an extremely rare and late-emerging enterprise in the context of cultural history. By contrast, the creation and consumption of fictional worlds is a pervasive human enterprise. If my argument is correct, it implies two important conclusions. First, contrary to the standard view, a central mode of human cognitive functioning is in place even in early childhood, and undergoes no major transformation. Second, the construction of theories of the real world is, and is likely to remain, a minority preoccupation, notwithstanding its pre-eminence as a metaphor in contemporary theories of cognitive development, whereas children and adults are natural experts at exploring the world of fiction.

CHAPTER 19

Intersubjective attunement and linguistically mediated meaning in discourse

Ragnar Rommetveit

Introduction

In his essay 'What is Man?' Martin Buber (1962) gives a thought provoking account of the development of Western philosophy. The very question 'What is Man?' is in Buber's opinion the basic philosophical question raised by Kant and the point of departure for all 'serious anthropological thought'. Such thought, Buber argues, is suppressed during periods of 'normal' tradition-bound scientific research and 'epochs of habitation' within philosophy. Its core question – 'What is Man?' – is at such times considered futile or even nonsensical because some preliminary and partial answer to it is embedded in the prevailing mode of thought and tacitly taken for granted as *the* (final) answer.

With Buber's question in mind, my aim for this chapter is to explore potential implications of the convergent evidence on the ontogeny of human intersubjectivity for our understanding of language acquisition and linguistically mediated meaning in adult discourse. Such evidence, I shall argue, challenges us to re-examine the architecture of 'mature' human intersubjectivity and to engage in novel 'serious anthropological thought' about the inherent dialogicity of Man and the individual mind's boundaries towards and embeddedness in a cultural collectivity.

On infant intersubjectivity and elementary social responsivity in adult discourse

Let me first comment upon some of the terms employed in discussion on infant intersubjectivity by other contributors to this book. Stein Bråten (1988a, 1992, this volume) refers to early infant–adult communication as an activity taking place in the mode of felt immediacy (as opposed to re-presentational mediacy). Lynne Murray (1991, this volume) describes infant intersubjectivity as a rudimentary capacity on the part of the infant to apprehend the emotional and interpersonal significance of adult behaviours and to regulate their own responses accordingly. Giannis Kugiumutzakis (this volume) posits these two inter-coordinated levels of activity in neonatal imitation: one unconscious level of conceptlessly perceiving and effortlessly communicating with the core of the other's mind, and another level of conscious, intentional and effortful imitation. And introducing the concept of primary intersubjectivity, Colwyn Trevarthen (1974a, 1992, this volume) maintains that the inner motivation for protoconversation is the intermental activity itself with its expressions of interest and pleasure.

What I want to explore are some potential implications of the above insights into infant intersubjectivity for our understanding of language acquisition, linguistically mediated meaning, and the embeddedness of the individual mind in a cultural collectivity, or as Trevarthen (this volume) expresses it, how 'the natal fabric of human minds contains specified in it the mutual responsiveness persons require to create a community of meaning'.

Nelson Goodman (1978:8) maintains that 'feeling without understanding is blind, and understanding without feeling is empty'. The infant's rudimentary hermeneutic activity is, in view of the contributions to this volume, neither blind nor empty. Affective perspective-taking constitutes a prerequisite for and inextricable aspect of the small child's 'learning how to mean' (Halliday, 1975), and continues, as Bråten (1992; this volume) argues, to be available throughout adult life. We just learn to restrain it as we grow older.

The infant's early communicative efforts are apparently an *intrinsically* rewarding activity in the sense that they are aimed at nothing else than *understanding* and *sharedness,* i.e. at dyadic states of intersubjectivity. And this, according to Jürgen Habermas, is not only true of preverbal communication. His main objection against 'intentional semantics' is that it seems to conceive of linguistically mediated understanding as a subordinate, merely instrumental, feature of communicative acts. Understanding is intrinsically motivated, Habermas maintains, and sharedness and aim are built into the essence of human language. In German: *Verständigung wohnt als Telos der menschlichen Sprache inne* (Habermas, 1981, I:387).

The Swedish social psychologist Johan Asplund claims that this intrinsically motivated responsiveness – in his terms, an elementary social responsivity (Asplund, 1987) – is not merely a transient component of the embryonic human self, transforming a biological organism into a genuinely social and potentially moral human being. Elementary social responsivity, he argues, remains throughout life an essential, even though most of the time heavily restrained and harnessed, component of our transaction with others in face-to-face encounters. And one reason why we know so little about the interface between the individual human mind and its cultural habitat is, in Asplund's view, that mainstream individualistic and cognitivist models of man in psychology and sociology tend to bypass that interface. Such models have very little to offer of insights into the kind of cognitive-emotive expansion and transcendence of the individual mind students of infant intersubjectivity are concerned with.

An expression such as 'expansion of the mind' is, of course, metaphorical. It is indeed nearly impossible to talk of the mind in a terminology devoid of spatial metaphors. When referring to the mind in the following, however, I have 'in' (my) mind something that by definition refuses simple location, for example, in terms of neurological 'hardware' within the skin. And let me on this issue, instead of engaging in extensive philosophical argumentation, quote Hacker, a student of Wittgenstein. He maintains: 'What may grow in the brain, e.g., a tumor, cannot grow in the mind, and what may grow in the mind, e.g., suspicion, cannot grow in the brain' (Hacker, 1990:135). This is a response to Chomsky's (1988:7) claim that when we speak of the mind we are speaking at some level of abstraction of yet unknown mechanisms of the brain.

To speak about the localization of the mind, Hacker argues, is to make a categorical mistake, as absurd as to ask for measurement of the extension of the colour red. My concern is definitely not with unknown mechanisms of the brain, but with the mind as 'transcending the skin'.

Language – a tool kit, a computational system or a prosthetic device?

Language has, by philosophers and psychologists adopting a broad phylogenetic-historical perspective, been conceived of as an *instrument* or a *tool kit*, and by cognitivists as 'a computational system of some kind that provides structural descriptions of linguistic expressions that determine their sound and meaning' (Chomsky, 1988:60). Recently, however, scholars who are concerned with the ontogenesis of human intersubjectivity and intrigued by the inherent dialogicity of mind have argued that such metaphors should be abandoned and replaced by a conception of language as a *prosthetic device*. One of them is Jerome Bruner, who in his book *Acts of meaning* also makes the bold claim that 'culture is constitutive of the mind' (Bruner, 1990:33). The expansion of individual 'mental space' attained by language acquisition and literacy resembles in important respects the expansion of bodily experienced space of locomotion attained by a blind man's use of his stick. And prosthetic mediational means differ markedly from instruments such as, for instance, petrol gauges of cars. The latter remain outside of us. The former, once thoroughly appropriated, become embodied and part of ourselves, yet in such a way that we come to 'dwell in them' (Shotter, 1990:100–1).

The stick employed by the blind man, however, is his personal property and serves to reduce his dependence upon fellow human beings. His word, on the other hand, is 'a two-sided act. . . determined equally by *whose* word it is and *for whom* it is meant' (Volosinov, 1986:86). And even the most casual exchange of words between conversation partners involves them in the long-term history via which their words are formed and, simultaneously, in the continuing reproduction of their language (Giddens, 1982:11). Language must hence from an ontogenetic and sociocultural perspective be conceived of as a prosthetic device by which individual mental activity is expanded and transformed into genuinely communicative activity.

On intersubjective attunement in the mode of felt immediacy

A prerequisite also for adult linguistic mediation of meaning?

Let me at this stage briefly comment upon a case which may provoke us to ponder what happens when our capacity for immediate attunement to conversation partners fails. A schizophrenic patient is telling his doctor about a dancing party (a ball). 'I too was invited', he says,

> 'I went to the ball – and *it rolled away*'.

And we may wonder: must not also *adult, linguistically mediated intersubjectivity* – like states of primary intersubjectivity observed in infant–mother interaction – *be taken for granted by both conversation partners in order to be achieved?* Does not the bewilderment and alienation experienced by the schizophrenic patient when listening to his own utterance of the homonymous word 'ball' suggest that word meaning somehow has lost its mooring to its ontogenetic foundation?

Consider, next, how in normal, everyday discourse words are imbued with meaning from temporarily shared social realities established within the mode of felt immediacy. The hero is in this case Mr Smith, who repeatedly occurs in my recent attempts to convey the gist and common-sense plausibility of a dialogically based approach to intersubjectivity. He was first brought to my attention by the sociologist Herbert Menzel (1978) and is, in my somewhat extended version of Menzel's story, a fireman living in a suburb. His service to proponents of hermeneutic-dialogical communication theory is simply to be seen in his garden pushing a machine around on the grass early one Saturday morning.

What is going on in Mr Smith's garden may under different dialogically established background conditions be made sense of in a variety of different ways. Different expressions, such as MOW THE LAWN, WORK, or ENGAGE IN LEISURE-TIME ACTIVITY can give rise to different meanings of the not-yet-verbalized state of affairs.

A neighbour prying into the miserable marital relations of the Smiths may for instance tell us that she 'sees' Mr Smith 'avoid the company of his wife'. Perhaps this also captures the feelings of Mrs Smith when left alone at the kitchen table with the morning coffee in front of her. But when the phone rings and her friend Betty asks her: 'That lazy husband of yours, is he still in bed?', Mrs Smith answers: 'No,–

> Mr Smith is WORKING this morning; he is mowing the lawn.'

A short time afterwards, Mrs Smith receives another phone call, this time from Mr Johnson, who, she tacitly takes for granted, rings to find out as he usually does whether her husband is free to go fishing with him. So, when he asks, 'Is your husband working this morning?', Mrs Smith answers: 'No,–

> Mr Smith is NOT WORKING this morning; he is mowing the lawn.'

On both occasions, Mrs Smith is telling the truth, even though she states that Mr Smith is WORKING in the first phone conversation, and NOT WORKING in the second. What is made known about one and the same 'external' state of affairs is inextricably fused with different, yet in each case intersubjectivity endorsed concerns. In her conversation with Mr Johnson, Mrs Smith adopts a position attuned to his concern about going fishing, i.e. a position from which the LEISURE-TIME ACTIVITY rather than other potential aspects of her husband's activity acquires salience. A state of intersubjectivity is thus attained by reciprocal perspective setting and perspective-taking (Rommetveit, 1992).

Mrs Smith's 'attunement to the attunement of the other' (Barwise and Perry, 1983) is not an act of will but *immediate*, rather than reflectively monitored 'computation' involving choice among alternative 'mental representations' or lexical entries of WORK. It has the character of an I–Thou transaction (Buber, 1958) with an inherent dialogicity rooted in protoconversation, and hence in an experiential world which is 'from the outset . . . not private . . . but an intersubjective world' (Schutz, 1945:534). Mrs Smith's replies are clearly immediate and spontaneous. I shall thus argue that such attunement to the attunement of the other in the mode of felt immediacy (Bråten, 1992, this volume) is available throughout life.

Ten theses

The developing individual mind within a cultural-linguistic collectivity

As Barwise and Perry (1983) claim, the prototypical discourse situation is in some important sense circular. Its inherent circularity consists in a peculiar 'attunement to the attunement of the other'. This appears to pervade the infant's transactions with the adult caretaker from birth on, as documented by extensive investigations of human infants (Neisser, 1985:41–3; Trevarthen, 1974a, 1992; Trevarthen and Hubley, 1978; Trevarthen and Logotheti, 1987), and in many of the chapters by other seminal authors in this book. And let me now, joining Bråten in his efforts to explicate potentially axiomatic features of these novel insights into the ontogenesis of human intersubjectivity, try to follow up his propositions (Bråten, 1984, 1988a) in a set of theses about the embeddedness of the individual mind in a cultural-linguistic collectivity (Rommetveit, 1992):

(1) The human infant is, as far as mental development is concerned, dyadically embedded and dialogically operative.
(2) The developing human mind is hence dialogically constituted.
(3) Adult verbal communication develops out of preverbal interaction between infant and adult caretaker as a dyadically structured and, in some important sense, circular activity.
(4) Hence, knowledge mediated by ordinary language represents situated, contextual and dialogically established understanding of our lifeworld (*Lebenswelt*) from within.
(5) Different potential aspects of our 'external' world (i.e. of objects, events, actions and other *not-yet-verbally described* states of affairs) are generated when states of affairs are made sense of and 'brought into language' from different positions.
(6) Aspects of that 'external' world generated on the basis of firmly shared ecological-cultural background conditions tend to become objectified and acquire status of shared social realities.
(7) Such firmly shared background conditions constrain the range of possible human perspectives on states of affairs in everyday

communication, yet remain as a rule unacknowledged as long as they stay fixed.

(8) Human cognition and communication are, within limits set by such constraints, characterized by perspectival relativity.

(9) Options with respect to perspectives on states of affairs entering human discourse reflect the range of possible human interests, commitments and concerns pertaining to those states of affairs.

(10) A distinctive and pervasive feature of the prototypical human discourse situation is a peculiar 'attunement to the attunement of the other' in the mode of felt immediacy.

In his letter conversations with Lady Wilby, Peirce (1977:197) discusses the general issue of shared social reality in terms of 'that mind into which the minds of the utterer and the interpreter have to be fused'. The ways in which conversational minds 'fuse' are indeed so far only very fragmentarily known. Yet, in view of phenomenological inquiries, such 'fusion' of minds in conversation would have to be contingent upon whether the discourse situation is characterized by *immediate I–Thou – or mediated I–It* – transactions. Aspects of states of affairs other than those jointly attended to by conversation partners are invisible to them under I–Thou conditions of immediate 'attunement to the attunement of the other'. Such reciprocally adjusted perspective setting and taking is in principle *cognitively penetrable* in the sense that it is accessible to inspection and voluntary control, yet actually *cognitively penetrated* and reflectively monitored only under (I–It) conditions of alienation on the part of conversation partners.

Language acquisition

*A prosthetic, yet cognitively **and** emotionally penetrated expansion of the developing individual mind?*

The expression 'cognitive penetrability' is borrowed from a cognitive scientist, Zenon Pylyshyn. He distinguishes between our *cognitively penetrable mental functions* on the one hand and our *functional architecture* on the other. The former are influenced by purely cognitive factors such as beliefs and goals (Pylyshyn, 1980:111) and correspond to what another cognitive scientist, David Andler (1988:207), calls 'personal processes', i.e. processes that concern and have significance for a human being as a whole. The latter, our functional architecture, is cognitively impenetrable and, when conceived of in dynamic terms, a pattern of processes instantiating causal physical or biological laws as opposed to human agency and reason (Pylyshyn, 1980:123). Such processes are by Andler called 'subpersonal processes'. They elude any attempts (as simple human beings) at recognition, monitoring and instruction and are 'as radically inaccessible to inspection and volition as the release of hormones or the constriction of capillaries' (Andler, 1988:208). And the issue I now want to explore is what happens when we apply Pylyshyn's dichotomy to adult language use. Have we then to do with cognitively penetrable functions, or has language – once thoroughly appropriated – become part of our functional architecture?

The conception of language as a prosthetic device invites us to scrutinize its mooring to preverbal infant–adult intersubjectivity and, as a consequence, also to question Pylyshyn's rationalist dichotomy. Language is replete with concepts, categorizations and modes of understanding developed by generations before us and, therefore, definitely *cognitively penetrated*. My spontaneous use and immediate understanding of an expression such as 'Platonic love', for instance, may indeed be interpreted as instantiating a prosthetic expansion of my individual mind into the spiritual realm of Plato. But is such an expansion a purely cognitive affair, completely devoid of emotional and moral content? And is not my immediate understanding of such an expression – even though admittedly *cognitively penetrated* – in some important respects actually *cognitively impenetrable* and nearly as 'radically inaccessible to inspection and volition as the release of hormones and the constriction of capillaries'?

Such questions may sound absurd to psycholinguists whose outlook on language and mind has been strongly affected by metaphors and models introduced by the pioneers of the cognitive revolution in linguistics and psychology. And the very conceptions of the human mind as 'something extending beyond the skin' and of language as a cognitively *and* emotionally penetrated prosthetic device are indeed by Bruner (1990) and Wertsch (1991) introduced in an attempt to elaborate a 'dialogical alternative' (Wold, 1992) to mainstream rationalist cognitive psychology about the individual organism.

A word can never, not even when thoroughly appropriated, become a personal property on a par with the blind man's stick. As the Russian scholar Mikhail Bakhtin, one of the most eloquent and persuasive advocates of a dialogical paradigm, puts it (1981:239): 'The word in language is half someone else's.' And, Bakhtin maintains, 'The life of a word is contained in its transfer from one mouth to another, from one context to another, from one generation to another. In this process the word does not forget its own path and cannot completely free itself from these concrete contexts into which it has entered' (1984:202). The young child 'appropriates' the word with its inherent and culturally transmitted content, Bakhtin says, by adapting it to her or his own semantic and expressive intentions. Such appropriation depends crucially, as Akhtar and Tomasello (this volume) have shown, on young children's skills in establishing intersubjectivity with adults. And let me at this stage, in order to illuminate genuinely prosthetic aspects of children's appropriation of novel words, engage in a brief literary excursion.

In a fascinating book about his own childhood in an upper-middle-class family, the Norwegian journalist and novelist Johan Borgen (1965) recounts how the word 'shameful' (in Norwegian: 'skammelig') entered his own, 'private', vocabulary. It happened during a family excursion to a small island in the Oslo fiord. Sitting behind him on the cliff was an old, very properly dressed, man. Some drunkards were leaving the island in a very shabby boat, full of holes in its sail. Watching them leave, the old man put his hat on his head and said: '*Shameful!*'

When he afterwards on various occasions himself uttered that word, Borgen suggests, it was on each occasion imbued with meaning from the facial expression of that man on that cliff. '*Shameful*!' the young Johan would say when an alien dog had entered the garden and shat in the flower-bed – and with the very same moral indignation towards that event as the old man had revealed towards the departing drunkards in the shabby boat.

Borgen's account of how the word 'shameful' entered his active childhood vocabulary may in my view be read as a carefully conducted case study of how words – *when appropriated with the mode of felt immediacy* – may serve to expand *and* embed a developing individual mind into a cultural collectivity. His use of the word in response to the alien dog in the flower-bed is spontaneous, yet very appropriate, and for that reason in Borgen's retrospective account at the same time a ritual act and circumstantial evidence of his own premature initiation into the realm of bourgeois adulthood.

Hilary Putnam maintains: 'Using any word – whether the word be "good", or "conscious", or "red", or "magnetic" – involves one in a history, a tradition of observation, generalization, practice and theory. It also involves one in the activity of *interpreting* that tradition and of adopting it to new contexts, extending and criticizing it' (Putnam, 1981:203). He also argues that the fact/value distinction is hopelessly fuzzy in everyday discourse. A word such as 'inconsiderate', for instance, is (in his colleague Nelson Goodman's terms) 'blind' if completely deprived of referential content and 'empty' if entirely devoid of feeling and evaluation (Putnam, 1981:139).

Emotive word meaning was a perfectly legitimate theme in psychology of language prior to the cognitive revolution, and the central theme in Charles Osgood's extensive studies of 'the affective meaning systems' (Osgood, 1962). A number of studies of children's acquisition of word meaning, moreover, indicate that the characteristic emotive-evaluative flavour of an abstract and presumably primarily descriptive word seems indeed to be captured and appropriated *prior to* its cognitive-referential content. Thus, Ervin and Foster (1960) report, in a study of American first- and sixth-graders' use of a set of adjectives, that the younger children tended to use words with different cognitive-referential contents but essentially the same emotive-evaluative flavour synonymously. The difference between age groups was particularly striking when the children were asked to use the adjectives 'happy', 'good' and 'pretty' to describe drawings of faces. The three words are very similar as far as emotive meaning is concerned, whereas at least 'happy' and 'pretty' in adult language use have distinctively different referential functions. However, a majority of the first-graders used all three adjectives synonymously in their descriptions. And Ervin and Foster (1960:275) suggest that 'what remains as a connotative, metaphorical relationship in adults, may in many cases start as a denotative nondifferentiation'.

The findings of Ervin and Foster were later corroborated in a developmental study of Norwegian children's sorting and prompted recall of words. The study was conducted by Karsten Hundeide and me (Rommetveit and Hundeide, 1967) and our conclusions were unequivocal: children are indeed at a surprisingly early age capable of 'feeling' the emotive-evaluative flavour of even highly abstract, but strongly emotionally loaded words. They know that words such as 'sincerity' and 'democracy' are nice whereas 'corruption' and 'crime' are bad words. The culturally appropriate emotive meaning of such words is revealed to the child in emotional display and prosodic features of speech in adult discourse and – to use Stein Bråten's terminology – understood within the mode of felt immediacy. Intonation is in Bakhtin's view 'the sound that value makes' (Clark and Holquist, 1984:10). And *prosody,* it seems, is a particularly 'prosthetic' feature of our language use, i.e. closer to our 'guts', to a greater extent 'embodied', and less accessible to reflective monitoring than *lexical choice.* By careful attention to a conversation partner's emotional engagement and intonation we may hence, it seems, capture the distinctive emotive-evaluative flavours of even totally novel and cognitively unintelligible words and expressions.

From response-ability to responsibility

On infant intersubjectivity, moral development and discourse-internal ethics

Protoconversation between infant and adult caretaker within the mode of felt immediacy has no topic outside the interaction itself. The infant's response-ability is reflected in attunement to the behaviour of the adult. The very immediacy of the attunement to mother's smile, however, implies that it is not optional and under voluntary control. The infant is thus *response-able*, i.e. able to respond, but not (morally) *responsible* for its contributions to the interaction. We cannot demand of neonates that they shall reciprocate Giannis Kugiumutzakis' (this volume) *morally* founded attitude of asking for permission to engage in conversation with them. However, the spontaneous, not reflectively monitored, transcendence of the infant's embryonic self into the feelings and intentions of the adult caretaker, Trevarthen (this volume) argues, is a prerequisite not only for entrance into a community of meaning, but also for the development of moral agency.

Child–adult interaction during early language acquisition is necessarily asymmetric in the sense that it is the adult – not the child – who is supposed to know what words mean. A 1-year-old boy, for instance, may eagerly watch his mother's face while talking to her and pay close attention to her reaction to his utterance in order to explore what is being meant by it. And the community of meaning a child is entering by appropriating novel words and adapting them to her or his semantic and expressive intentions is a community pervaded by individual human concerns and shared, culturally transmitted social realities, prejudices and values. Appropriation of expressions and words such as 'Platonic love', 'inconsiderate' and 'shameful', I have suggested, lends a genuinely moral aspect or dimension to the developing mind (within a particular Western subculture). 'Learning how to mean' within the cultural-moral habitat into which one is born, it seems, is thus a prerequisite for moral development: since the child's learning how to mean is contingent upon her or his inborn capacity to establish intersubjectivity in early, preverbal interaction with adult caretakers, so is her or his prosthetic and to a considerable extent linguistically mediated mental expansion into the sphere of morality.

It is only by *being held accountable* for what we do and for what we mean by what we say, however, that we develop into persons with moral stances of our own. And accountability presupposes choices among options and foresight into consequences of choice, i.e. reflective consciousness and self-control. Protoconversation between infant and adult within the mode of felt immediacy is therefore, as far as the infant's contribution is concerned, even though a prerequisite for subsequent development of human moral agency, a kind of *premoral* rather than *proto-moral* human interaction. But what, then, about early manifestations of turn-taking resulting in convergence of attention onto some 'topic' introduced by the adult caretaker? What, for instance, about a 9-month-old girl's contribution to the interaction when she willingly abandons the activity she at that moment is engaged in and eagerly attends to the object towards which her mother is directing her attention?

Emile Benveniste (1977:75) maintains: 'It is in and through language that man constitutes himself as a *subject*.' The transcendence of the little girl's immediately experienced life world in the above case, however, entails a subordination of her *'I'* to a dyadically and temporarily established *'we'* resembling the *'we'* of a collectivity endowed with moral authority. Voluntary subordination, however, is in my view a proto-moral feature of human interaction and a *sine qua non* in dialogical 'fusion' of individual minds. Let me hence, provokingly, add a thesis about the development of moral agency to Benveniste's claim about the linguistically constituted human subject: *It is in and through dialogue that man constitutes himself as a moral agent.*

Consider, once more, Mrs Smith's two telephone conversations. She is sitting in her kitchen and – like the little girl prior to her mother's intervention – imprisoned within her own private life world. The only way *she* can make sense of her husband's mowing the lawn at such an early hour is by supposing that he is evading her company. What she tells about his activity in the garden, however, is in the first conversation attuned to her friend Betty's concern about Mr Smith's laziness and in the second conversation to Mr Johnson's prospect of going fishing with him. Her reply is on each occasion devoid of information about her own self-centred outlook on Mr Smith's lawn mowing and hence a genuine and proto-moral answer, i.e. it entails a voluntary subordination of her subjectivity to an intersubjective perspective introduced by, respectively, her friend Betty and Mr Johnson.

But have I not argued that her attunement to the attunement of the other is immediate and not at all reflectively monitored? Suppose that Mrs Smith, being angry with her husband and unwilling to let him go fishing, had told Mr Johnson (as she told Betty) that he was 'working', but *deliberately withheld the information that the work he was engaged in was actually lawn-mowing, i.e. leisure-time activity.* This is, in retrospect, indeed one of Mrs Smith's options in her chat with Mr Johnson. Her adult mastery of language as 'a computational system' and of the meaning potentials of the word 'work' endows her with the option to use it for manipulative purposes by telling lies disguised as 'literal truths'. The fact that she did not reflect upon nor even envision that option at all, however, suggests in my view that what once started as a premoral transcendence of her embryonic self into the feelings and intentions of her adult caretaker has developed into a mature and deep-seated form of proto-morality in her dialogical encounters with fellow human beings.

Communication within the mode of felt immediacy is hence an issue discussed not by students of infant intersubjectivity only, but also by researchers inquiring into adult discourse and by philosophers dealing with discourse-internal ethics. Even Ervin Goffman, who in his studies of human interaction is almost exclusively concerned with its routinized and ritualized features, maintains that the interactional order differs from other kinds of social orders in a not only tolerated but actually demanded 'component of non-rational impulsiveness' (Goffman, 1972:115). And immediacy, authenticity and openness towards the other person are by Hans Georg Gadamer and Martin Buber conceived of as proto-moral virtues, not only ontogenetically, as essential for development of moral agency, but also as prerequisites for optimal – and ethically praiseworthy – dialogues between mature minds.

A basic openness towards one another is thus by Gadamer (1975:342–3) considered a prerequisite for genuine human attachment, and reflectively attained detachment from the mode of felt immediacy destroys in his view the moral commitment inherent in proto-moral dialogical encounters. Reflective detachment may be mutual or unilateral, i.e. both partners in a dialogue or only one of them may adopt an attitude of alienation and inferentially based or prefabricated understanding of the other. The latter case – unilateral detachment – may in Buberian terms be described as a situation in which person A adopts an *I–it* orientation towards another person B whereas the latter throughout their encounter remains open and responsive towards A in an *I–Thou* manner. B's openness towards A entails in the latter case the tacit but false assumption that A is equally immediate and responsive towards B. This particular asymmetry with respect to mode of transaction makes it therefore possible for the reflectively detached person to exploit his conversation partner's immediate self-exposure for manipulative purposes.

Such a reflective detachment would by Buber and Gadamer be conceived of as *immoral*. The ideal dialogue is in their view a transaction between two persons exposing their innermost feelings and thoughts while remaining maximally open and sensitive to one another.

On sequential, hidden and simultaneous dialogicity and the multi-voicedness of the modern mind

The 'fusion of minds' in human conversation and discourse (Peirce, 1977:197) is a recurrent theme in Mikhail Bakhtin's writing and further explicated by James Wertsch (1991, 1992) in terms of *sequential* and *simultaneous dialogicity*. Sequential dialogicity is, I think, very well documented already in studies of protoconversation in infancy, for instance in Lynne Murray's studies (this volume) of child's and mother's reactions to *live versus replay* communicative activity. Every *live* sequence is jointly produced by mother and child. You cannot understand one without understanding the other. And notice that the same holds true for Mrs Smith's and her conversation partners' contributions to the contextually appropriate meaning of her expressions 'working' and 'not working' in the two telephone conversations. We cannot understand what is meant by the word 'working' in her reply without understanding the question triggering her answer. Sequential dialogicity is thus cogently revealed in semantic analysis of so-called adjacency pairs of conversational turns. Each single turn has to be interpreted from a dual perspective: as potentially context-bound, attuned to preceding turn(s); and as potentially context-constitutive, constraining and/or governing subsequent contributions. The elementary units in a consistently dialogically based analysis of discourse are therefore, as Linell and Markova (1993) maintain, not individually produced monological speech acts, but jointly produced *dialogical inter-acts*.

This is also Bakhtin's and Volosinov's stance towards words 'alive', towards words imbued with meaning from mutually responsive conversation partners. A word, we remember, Volosinov (1986:82) claims, 'is a two-sided act . . . determined equally by *whose* word it is and *for whom* it is meant'. And this, it seems, is also true of written discourse, for instance of Hacker's cited response to Chomsky's remarks about the mind and unknown physical mechanisms of the brain. What Hacker means when writing about tumours in the brain and suspicions in the mind can hardly be fully understood unless we know that it is meant for Chomsky. And the conception of the word as *a two-sided act* or an *inter-act* is in my view fully congruent with that of language as a prosthetic device expanding our mental activity by increasing our dependency upon fellow human beings. A dialogical encounter between an enlightened layman and an expert endowed with a knowledge and terminology transcending lay knowledge and ordinary language may be nearly as asymmetric as the conversation in which a 1-year-old boy is watching his mother's face and attending to her reaction to his utterance in order to explore what is being meant by it. The words I use when talking to a car mechanic about what is wrong with the engine, for instance, are hardly determined *equally* by me and the car mechanic. They are hopefully more intelligible to the expert *for whom* they are meant than they are to me, *whose* words they are.

The canonical human utterance within the monological and cognitivist 'conduit paradigm' (Reddy, 1979) of communication *qua* information transmission is *the assertion* with its postulated, exclusively speaker-determined 'propositional content'. And recent attempts at computer simulation of cognition and communication may, as suggested by Winograd (1985), be interpreted as scientific-technological extensions of an analytic-rationalist philosophical tradition concerned with pure, decontextualized human reason. A definite exception is Stein Bråten's (this volume; in press) attempt at neurocomputational simulation of the infant's engagement with the adult caretaker and re-enactment (with the virtual other) of what the infant previously has felt to co-enact with the adult in virtue of altercentric participation. Vygotsky, however, maintains: 'Thought is not merely expressed in words, it comes into existence through them' (Vygotsky, 1962/1986:128). And since a word is a 'two-sided act', partially determined by *for whom* it is meant, so, according to Vygotsky, Volosinov and Bakhtin, also is *the thought that comes to existence through it*. Even the thoughts coming into existence through overtly assertive contributions to a dialogue (such as, for instance, Hacker's response to Chomsky) are in subtle ways deeply affected by *for whom* they are meant. The canonical utterance within a dialogical approach to language and mind is therefore not the autonomous assertion, but the dialogically embedded *answer*.

Ideas emerge, according to Bakhtin, when 'voices and consciousnesses' come into contact. Even the innermost thoughts of Raskolnikov and other characters of Dostoevsky are, in Bakhtin's view, dialogical. Not-yet-verbalized experiences are made sense of and – to use Gadamer's (1975) expression – 'brought into language' by one mind addressing another in attempts, e.g. to blame or justify her- or himself. A characteristic feature of such socially embedded mental activity, moreover, is *'the loophole of the consciousness and the word'*, i.e. 'the retention for oneself of the possibility for altering the ultimate, final meaning of one's own words' (Bakhtin, 1984:313). The meaning of one's own words may under optimal dialogical conditions be expanded and deepened by one's conversation partner's interpretation of them. What exists as a merely vaguely felt and wordless insight, moreover, may be transformed into reflectively accessible self-knowledge by our very efforts to mediate that vaguely felt insight to a fellow human being.

Some of the monologues in Dostoevsky's novels, Bakhtin maintains, are actually dialogues in disguise. A character considering suicide, for instance, betrays by his choice of words at the beginning of his soliloquy that he is indeed engaged in argumentation with his mother. Later on, his choice of words and modes of reasoning echo previous dialogical encounters with a rival. The sequential dialogicity of the monologue is thus revealed in subtle shifts of terminology and modes of argumentation, i.e. in an attunement of the solitary hero's words and thoughts to particular significant others for whom they are meant. What remains invariant across varieties of human communication ranging all the way from an infant's protoconversation with the adult caretaker to a sophisticated adult's monologically disguised dialogue with significant others about existential problems is thus, it seems, an attunement of one individual mind to the attunement of another. And in order to unveil hidden sequential dialogicity in overtly monological language and thought, Bakhtin invites us to engage in the following thought experiment:

> Imagine a dialogue of two persons in which the statements of the second speaker are omitted, but in such a way that the general sense is not violated. The second speaker is present invisibly, his words are not there, but deep traces left by these words have a determining influence on all the present and visible words of the first speaker. We sense that this is a conversation, although only one person is speaking, and it is a conversation of the most intense kind, for each present, uttered word responds and reacts with its every fiber to the invisible speaker, points to something outside itself, beyond its own limits, to the unspoken words of another person. (Bakhtin, 1984:197)

Simultaneous dialogicity or 'multi-voicedness' is perhaps most cogently instantiated in parody, when one voice transmits what another voice has said before, but with 'a shift of accent' (Bakhtin, 1984:199). The overtones of irony and sarcasm that emerge in parody are due to the simultaneous presence of two voices in the utterance, that of the speaker and that of the person whose words he quotes. The notion of voice for Bakhtin, however, cannot be reduced to vocal-auditory signals. 'It applies to written as well as spoken communication, and it is concerned with the broader issues of a speaking subject's perspective, conceptual horizon, intention, and world view' (Wertsch, 1991:51). It is also concerned with culturally inherited world views and conceptual horizons, i.e. with *'voices from the past' which the developing young mind is bound to encounter in dialogues with significant others.* Its own voice may hence, as Harris (this volume) suggests in his discussion of fiction and emotional response to make-believe, come to appropriate, echo and/or parody the voices of fictional characters, glorious mythological warriors and pious saints.

Our *embeddedness* within a cultural collectivity may indeed be assessed in terms of *lack of awareness* of the intrusion of such voices from our shared cultural history in our own. A presumably secularized Norwegian family, for instance, would be genuinely surprised when made aware of how often metaphors from the Bible and paraphrases of fragments of biblical texts enter their family conversations. And so probably also would lay people in Paris when made aware of the fact that many of the words they spontaneously use in conversations about mental illness echo Sigmund Freud's voice. This is what Serge Moscovici (1961) demonstrates in his study of intertextual relations between their everyday discourse and texts written by Freud during the first decades of this century. And such explorations can indeed be expanded backwards into intertextual connections between Freud's writings and Greek mythology.

The modern Western mind is thus, as Charles Taylor (1989) maintains in his historical account of the making of modern identity, *multivoiced*. The genesis of personal identity, he claims, is from an ontogenetic as well as from a historical perspective genuinely and profoundly dialogical, and 'our identity is deeper and more many-sided than any of our possible articulations of it' (Taylor, 1989:29). Hidden dialogicity in our 'inner' and overtly monological deliberations over moral issues may hence, Taylor suggests, echo conflicting moral voices from the past: 'We sympathize with both hero and anti-hero; and we dream of a world in which one could be in the same act both' (Talyor, 1989:24). The insights into infant intersubjectivity and early child–adult communication reflected in the contributions to this volume, I have argued, challenge us to re-examine the architecture of mature, linguistically mediated intersubjectivity and, in particular, the individual mind's boundaries towards and embeddedness in a cultural-linguistic collectivity. The hidden dialogicity and multi-voicedness of our adult, 'inner' and overtly monological deliberations over moral issues, I have suggested, may be interpreted as a prosthetic expansion of the individual mind, starting as a transcendence of the infant's embryonic self into the intentions and feelings of the adult caretaker (cf. Part I, this volume). The community of linguistically mediated meaning the child enters is a community imbued with human concerns, emotions and culturally transmitted morality. The emotive-evaluative meaning of words, it seems, is appropriated within the mode of felt immediacy, and *at a very early age*. Responsitivity to moral stances adopted by adult conversation partners, moreover, lends a moral dimension to the developing individual mind. Development of *responsibility*, i.e. moral agency, it seems, is thus contingent upon *response-ability* in dialogical encounters with morally engaged significant others.

How, then, can these exploratory excursions into the intersection between the developing individual mind and its cultural-linguistic habitat contribute to novel 'serious anthropological thought'?

The partial and tacitly taken for granted answer to Martin Buber's question 'What is Man?' within mainstream individual cognitive psychology and cognitive science entails in my view a puritan evasion of issues having to do with the human mind's 'extension beyond the skin' and embeddedness in a cultural-linguistic collectivity. Accumulated evidence from studies of infant intersubjectivity and early infant–adult communication over the last two decades encourages us to pursue such fascinating and extremely complex issues in our scientific research and hence, hopefully, to deepen our understanding of Man as a dialogically constituted and thoroughly culturally embedded creature.

CHAPTER 20

Intersubjective communion and understanding: development and perturbation

Stein Bråten

This book has offered an examination of the foundations, development and impairment of intersubjective attunement and communicative understanding. From laboratory and field studies of children within and across families and cultures, and with comparative views on autism and animal learning and parent–offspring relations, explanatory principles and systems models have been proposed. They vary with the domains focused upon. Four domains may be distinguished in terms of these characteristics: (I) mutual bodily subject–subject attendance and attunement in dyadic systems, evolving into (II) triangular subject–subject–object systems involving objects of joint attention, and supporting self–other reflective systems of communication and understanding that are mediated by (III.1) first-order symbolic re-presentations and (III.2) second-order simulation of mind. Without such mediational characteristics, and in virtue of their consensual characteristics of felt immediacy, the primary and secondary domains may properly be defined to be domains of *interpersonal communion*. They emerge, as we have seen, in the first year of childhood and persist throughout normal life. This will be further exemplified in this conclusion.

Foundational domains endure to support higher-order domains

Scientific narratives of child development differ according to whether or not the operating characteristics of lower-level domains are considered to continue to be operational in later normal development. In Freud's theory, for example, the infantile stage closed off from social reality and dominated by the pleasure principle re-emerges only in pathological cases of 'infantile regression'. No such regressive logic is implied by the levels or domains distinguished in this volume (cf. also Stern, 1985), simply because they entail sociality from the outset. The operating characteristics of each lower-level domain normally endure to support or interact with operations in higher-level domains. This is symbolized by the staircase, not a ladder, in Fig. 20.1.

From first weeks	*From about 6–9 months*	*From about 18–24 months*	*From about 3–6 years of age*

III.2. Symbolic communication involving *second-order* mental understanding of thoughts and emotions in self and other in virtue of recursive mental simulation of mental processes – beginning with discovery of deceit and attribution of false beliefs, and with co-narrative fictional constructions with peers, and evoked when lower-order processes break down

III.1. Symbolic communication involving *first-order* mental understanding of self's and other's activities in virtue of mental co-enactment of activity intended or pretended – beginning with symbolic conversation, joint pretence, and imagination of unrealized movements, and continuing in adult discourse unless distortion evokes second-order process

II. (Secondary) Interpersonal communion in a *triangular* subject-subject–object format involving shared attention and participation in the object-oriented movements of one another – beginning with cooperative use of objects of joint emotional referencing and imitative learning from altercentric participation in object-handling movements, affording e-motional memory which continues to be supportive of higher-order processes

I. (Primary) Interpersonal communion in *dyadic* systems of participants in a reciprocal subject–subject format in which they attend and attune to one another's emotive expressions and gesture- and sound-producing movements, inviting semblant re-enactment and affect attunement – beginning, when conditions permit, with neonatal imitation and protoconversation in the mode of felt immediacy, which continues throughout normal life as a potential for dialogic closure with others and to underlie higher-order modes of engagements in symbolic and conceptual mediacy.

→ *(life)time*

Fig. 20.1 Levels or domains of intersubjective attunement and understanding in childhood. Examples of capabilities at the primary (I) and secondary (II) levels of interpersonal communion and socio-emotive bodily attunement, and at the first-order (III.1) and second-order (III.2) levels of symbolic communication and mental understanding. The indication of age, which continues to be pushed back in time by new findings, serves merely as a heuristic ordering device. Each lower level endures throughout life as an evolving operating domain supportive of higher level domains.

Thus, the *primary* processes (I) of interpersonal bodily attunement, already at play when circumstances permit in the first weeks after birth, continue to be evoked throughout life, for example manifested by teenagers in intimate symbolic conversation (III.1) who mutually tune in to one another's movements, states and expressions.

In the second quarter of the first year, such bodily attunement begins to involve the baby's participation in the caregiver's attention-inviting moves towards objects brought into play. This prepares for the *secondary* characteristics (II) of triangular relatedness involving joint attention to objects of social-emotional referencing (Hobson, this volume; Trevarthen, this volume), and for altercentric participation in the caregiver's handling of objects, for example when being spoon-fed (Bråten, this volume). Again, the caregiver's unwitting opening of mouth (cf. Fig. 5.1) attests to how consensual bodily attunement can accompany deliberate activity in higher-level domains.

In the *tertiary* domain of symbolic communication and first-order reflective self–other understanding (III.1), the capability to imagine virtual movements and other's moves appears to be demonstrated by the 18-month-olds described by Meltzoff and Moore (this volume). Such processes of imagining unrealized or aborted object-handling are also evoked in infants engaged with adults in collaborative teasing. For example, the infant may offer something to the adult and then – as the adult reaches for it – withdraw the food or object with a big smile (Chevalier-Skolnikoff, 1982: 324; Reddy, 1991:146). In order to find the aborted move funny, the infant must somehow virtually complete (in the infant's companion space) the adult's complementary response of taking the bait or food.

Imagination of others' moves is a form of mental simulation of bodily movements, perhaps precursory of *second-order* mental simulation (III.2) of others' thoughts and emotions. Attempts at perspective-taking by mental construction and simulation would be inefficient if not nurtured by primary social-emotive connectivity, and unnecessary when the other's perspective is felt 'from the inside' (Bråten, 1993; this volume).

Domains of intersubjective attunement and communion

In an outside self-centred observer's stance, one is by definition excluded from interpersonal communion. Yet, artificially induced or natural breakdown of this elusive phenomenon evokes awareness of its absence (Buber, 1958; Grandin, 1995; Murray, this volume; Stern, 1985).

The primary domain of intersubjective attunement (I)

This primary domain is here defined to involve mutual interpersonal attunement by which the participants, in the pre-reflective mode of felt immediacy, consensually attend and bodily attune to one another's emotive expressions and gesture- and sound-producing movements. As we have seen, when circumstances permit, such intersubjective attunement is exhibited already in neonatal imitation and early protoconversation, and has been examined *inter alia* in these terms: motivational or emotive connectivity (e.g. Trevarthen, this volume; Kugiumutzakis, this volume); identity-probing bodily similarity (Meltzoff and Moore, this volume); pruning of the infant's perceptual space (Kuhl, this volume); and altercentric participation (Bråten, this volume). Such participatory altercentric perception of the other's movements has been described in terms of a virtual-other mechanism which complements the infant's bodily self-feeling. This enables the embodied developing mind to re-create and transform itself as a self-organizing dyad in these two primary forms of engagement: (i) (proto)dialogic closure in interpersonal communion with actual others; (ii) self-dialogue (with the virtual other) in dis-engagement from actual others. Both kinds of engagement conform to the same operational format. Hence, no operational jump is entailed by the baby's pleasant alternation between mutually attuned interplay in (i) and self-engagement in (ii). When dis-engaging in contentment, for example, when having been put to bed after a protodialogic 'dance' or 'duet' at the nursing table, this may come to nurture circular re-enactment with the baby's virtual other.

Transition from (i) to (ii) is manifested also in less pleasant circumstances, for example when the baby is suddenly faced with a 'still face' mother in perturbation experiments. Such a transition, evoked by a replay of a live and lively mother, appears even to be demonstrated in Murray's double-video design (this volume Fig. 6.1, Fig. 20.2), even though these 2-month-olds were deprived of mother's smell and touch during the preceding video-mediated live interchange. After 'happy' engagement with the live mother on the monitor, they exhibited symptoms of let-down and dis-engagement during exposure to the replay mother (Murray and Trevarthen, 1985).

The state transition diagram in Fig. 20.2 (bottom) applies to such reported cases, provided experimental release from the initial state (i). If these distancing conditions prevent the baby and live mother from realizing that state, this model predicts no discernible difference in the baby's behaviour during experimental live and replay sequences. In such cases, babies will have to self-engage, while looking for an opening for reunion with the mother precluded from the presentational immediacy of their companion space. This may explain the failure to replicate Murray's and Trevarthen's results by Marian *et al.* (1996), who question whether 2-month-olds can discriminate in these conditions. They point out, however, that they may not have allowed mother and child sufficient time to adjust to these depriving circumstances and reach a happy 'peak' interplay before replication began. This is a pertinent example of open-ended issues that await further replications and investigations.

The domain of triangular subject–subject–object communion (II)

In the secondary domain, objects of shared attention are brought into play in the consensual world in which the interacting companions coexist. Such intersubjective phenomena of shared reference to objects, states and events evoke a triangular subject–subject–object sense of aboutness (Hobson, this volume).

As we have seen in Part I, participatory perception of others' object-handling invites circular re-enactments. This is illustrated by 9-month-olds who exhibit deferred imitation, and by 11-month-olds who reciprocate the caregiver's spoon-feeding. When objects and events of shared attention and joint emotional referencing are involved, conditions are provided for the beginning of language meaning, also in a social-cognitive referential sense (Akhtar and Tomasello, this volume).

Communal relatedness in the consensual sense of felt immediacy facilitates such cultural learning and is again revealed by perturbation; abortion of affect attunement evokes the baby's awareness of its absence. This is illustrated by the mother–infant dyads in Stern's (1985) perturbation experiment. First, the mother voices her naturally attuned accompaniment to the child's playing with some toy on the floor. When she then compels herself to get out of tune by overplaying or underplaying her comments, the infant invariably stops playing and turns around to look at the mother. When she again resumes and expresses a state of natural affect attunement, the infant resumes playing.

Domains of symbolic communication and mental understanding

Some of the mothers in Stern's perturbation experiments actually found it difficult to get out of tune with their children, that is, to simulate inauthentic voicing of comments. This indicates how

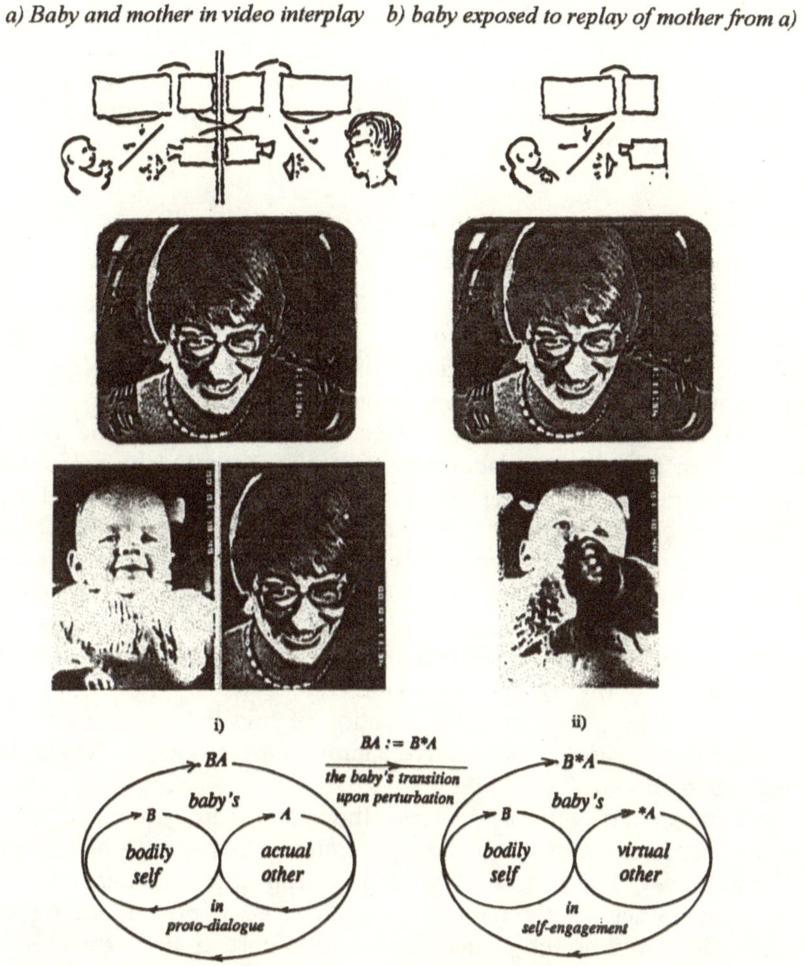

Fig. 20.2 (*Left, Top*) Mother and 2-month-old in the unperturbed interplay in Murray's double video experiment (cf. Fig. 6.1).
(*Photos have been supplied by Murray and Trevarthen, 1985*).

(*Left, Below*) State diagram of the baby's protodialogic closure with the mother, in contrast to the reaction upon perturbation.

(*Reproduced from Bråten, 1996c*)

(*Right, Top*) Baby exposed to replay of the mother from the happy interplay with the baby's actual (m)other in a).
(*Right, Below*) State diagram of the baby's withdrawal and transition to self-comforting engagement (with the baby's virtual other) – unlike the mothers who, when they were faced with a replay baby, continued to address their represented baby trying to reactivate the broken protoconversation.

affective processes evoked in the above foundational domains can interact with processes in higher-level domains of re-presentational and simulational mediacy, and invite processes at the conscious level to be in harmony with processes of felt immediacy (cf. Damasio, 1994; Kugiumutzakis, this volume).

The first-order level of symbolic communication and reflective understanding (III.1)

First-order interpersonal communication mediated by concepts and symbols begins to be operative with predication (Akhtar and Tomasello, this volume) and evolves with the capability of perspective-taking in conceptual and re-presentational mediacy.

Two-year-olds manifest intersubjective understanding and reflectiveness in joint and collaborative pretence mediated by self–other representation and meta-representations ('I a Daddy' (Dunn and Dale, 1984); 'this banana a phone'). We find a precursory announcement of this creative capability already in the first year of human infancy, when the baby transforms a dummy, a piece of wool or some other 'transitional object' (Winnicott, 1953) into an actualized companion for self-engaging activity, sometimes involving circular re-enactment, conforming to (ii), of interpersonal engagements. The same self-dialogical format applies to the creation of invisible companions by older children, and to self-conversation in preschoolers (Vygotsky, 1962/1986; Bråten, 1995, 1998).

In their shared cultural lifeworld, they engage in symbolic conversation mediated by symbolic and generalized conceptions of self and others (Mead, 1934), and show anticipation and understanding of self's and other's activities as being intended or pretended. Again, this is facilitated by the primary capacity to participate in the other's gestural and sound-producing movements. Successful compliance with invitations mediated by 1.person and 2.person references ('You do as I do') depends on consensual processes, which appear to be partly impaired in autism (Whiten and Brown, this volume). And such participant perception probably supports first-order reading and mental simulation of others' intended movements. As demonstrated by Meltzoff and Moore (this volume), 18-month-olds are capable of realizing and enacting a successful novel performance from watching a model's failure, for example, to pull a dumbbell apart. Their imagining or simulating that performance brought to a successful end may announce rudiments of an emerging capability for mental simulation of others' mental processes (Bråten, this volume).

The second-order level of symbolic communication and recursive understanding (III.2)

Even though consensual processes of interpersonal attunement escape awareness, unless perturbed, they are concurrent with smoothly running, first-order symbolic communication (cf. Buck, 1984, 1993), while probably incompatible with characteristics operating in a dis-engaging sense at the *second-order* level of intersubjective understanding. Understanding of other minds in virtue of recursive mental simulation of mental processes may be accompanied by self-comments in a more or less valid mental state languaging about others' thoughts and feelings. In a dis-engaging sense, such second-order characteristics probably begin to emerge with the discovery of deceit and by discerning deception in others. One of their manifestations is the attribution of false beliefs. In the co-engaging sense this level opens for communicative participants and peers who creatively and narratively engage in co-constructed actual and fictional worlds, bringing to bear also consensual characteristics.

Second-order mechanisms, whether studied from the viewpoints of mindreading, theory of mind, or simulation of mind, have been predicted to be activated by voluntary or involuntary perturbation of processes in the lower-level domains. Two illustrative cases will be referred to here, one experimental (Murray and Trevarthen, 1986) and one narrative (Grandin, 1995).

First, when mothers in a parallel version of Murray's double-video experiment were unwittingly exposed to a replay of the baby from the previous live interplay, the mothers shifted to a more imperative or questioning mode of addressing the replay baby, punctuated by self-comments. Irrespective of whether a qualitative transition has been evoked in the mother, her impression of the baby's behaviour, evaluated by mental simulation against her generalized expectations from previous interplays, may account for this self- and other-addressing shift.

Second, reporting from her life with autism, Temple Grandin (1995) indirectly supports Bråten's (1974) proposal that mental simulation of processes in and between minds is evoked upon breakdown of communicative understanding. Grandin recounts how she was at a loss to understand other people in intimate communication, and how it took years for her to realize that most social interactions were regulated by emotions: 'I was a scientist trying to figure out the ways of the natives. I wanted to participate, but I did not know how' (Grandin, 1995:132). Facilitated by Grandin's peculiar capacity for concrete imagery (discussed by Sacks, 1995:271n), her way of adjusting has *inter alia* been to rehearse from mental 'play back' – like running a video in her mind – previous encounters with other people and to anticipate by mental simulation how interpersonal encounters may evolve: 'I run [mental] video simulations of all the different things the other person might ask' (Grandin, 1995:135).

Baron-Cohen (1995:141) regards Grandin's description as giving us 'a clue as to how successfully adapted individuals with autism may have managed to circumvent their mindblindedness'. True, but it may also give us a clue as to why other individuals normally do *not* behave like scientists, having to construct or evoke a theory of mind.

Conclusion: some further open-ended issues

This book has drawn attention to the social-emotional and intersubjective roots of communicative competence and reflective consciousness. Affectionate engagements between adults and infants, and later between peers, appear to be essential to the development of the mind's dialogical and self-reflective consciousness. Reflected in the dyadic organization of the developing mind and in the regulation of normal brain development (Bråten and Trevarthen, 1994), emotions evoked in affectionate interpersonal communion support self–other organizing systems development, transcending the boundaries of subjects who defy definition in the sense of monadic in-dividuals (Mead, 1934; Rommetveit, this volume).

Between emotion and reason

The interrelation between interaffective consensual capacity and conscious, dialogical competence manifests itself in the various domains defined above – from the confluence of affect in primary and secondary intersubjective communion to the symbolic and second-order levels of self–other mental simulation and construction mediated by symbolic and second-order re-presentations.

Kugiumutzakis (this volume) suggests that processes of communion with the core of the other's mind are operating in harmony with processes of deliberation at the conscious level. Oatley (1992:89) suggests that emotion has a consciousness-raising function by changing goal priorities and loading into readiness a small suite of plans for action. Damasio (1994) offers evidence that emotional experiences affect decisions via a non-conscious route by loading alternatives with evaluative biases. One of the implications of the present book is this: rather than being regarded as mere subjective phenomena, *feelings and emotions invite consideration as interpersonal and intersubjective phenomena* (cf. also Bråten, 1992, 1998; Dawson, 1994a, b; Tucker, 1992). This dialogical systems perspective has implications for connectionist modelling and simulation, indicating that the time is ripe for attempting *inter*-connectionist simulations – with a view to exploring how the social-emotive and altercentric nature of the interacting brain interacts with processes driven by intellect in attempts to take a distancing stance.

From bodily to mental simulation?

One unresolved issue concerns the precise nature of the inter-relations between the characteristics of intersubjective communion and second-order mechanisms of recursive intersubjective understanding of other minds. There may be a tutorial path, as suggested by Meltzoff and Moore (this volume), from experience of bodily resemblance to discovering familiarity of minds. In studies of neonatal imitation, the experimenter may be seen to invite the newborn to bodily simulation of the adult's movements. We have asked: is this a precursor of mental simulation of others' movements, and is there an ontogenetic path to simulation of other minds from bodily simulation of others' movements? While some replies have been offered in this volume, we are still far from understanding the qualitative jump from infant intersubjectivity to children's second-order understanding of other's thoughts and emotions. Whatever the replies may be to these questions in the future, the nurtural and developmental foundations of communal bodily connectivity in early ontogeny cannot be bypassed.

Between evolution of culture and communication

In sociology, Tönnies (1912) identifies the historic transition from communal *Gemeinschaft* to formal societal *Gesellschaft*. In *Origins of the modern mind*, Donald (1991) distinguishes cultural stages of episodic immediacy and *Mimesis* from symbolic stages of *mythos* and *logos*. They invite comparison with the ontological domains distinguished above. However, even though auto-organizational inventiveness plays a part in phylogeny, sociogenesis and ontogeny, they differ, in this critical respect: while societal evolution from phylogeny has involved the generation of new cultural life worlds in new domains never before entertained, the child is born into the peculiar rhythms and musical sounds of a language culture that already exists, nurturing the self-creative transitions from consensual communion to symbolic, narrative communication. In spite of such pitfalls of comparison, there are also promises in drawing parallels between phylogeny and ontogeny, as demonstrated a century ago by Baldwin (1895).

The ontogenetic path of nurtured transitions to higher-order domains has been a natural concern throughout the present book. Several contributors have emphasized the persistence of the primary and secondary domains. For example, Harris (this volume) points to the affective accompaniment of fictional engagement, and Rommetveit (this volume) emphasizes how primary attunement to the attunement of the other in felt immediacy underlies normal adult discourse. The book's common theme of social and emotional responsiveness in domains of intersubjective attunement and understanding in ontogeny has implications for social and ecological responsibility. An understanding of the issues raised here has consequences also for the deep ethical questions of our time.

We are only at the beginning of a crucial quest that takes us into the next century.

References

Abbott, S. (1992). Holding on and pushing away: comparative perspectives on an Eastern Kentucky child-rearing practice. *Ethos* 20: 33–65.

Abrahamsen, E. P., and Mitchell, J. R. (1990). Communication and sensori-motor functioning in children with autism. *Journal of Autism and Developmental Disorders* 2: 75–85.

Abramson, A. S., and Lisker, L. (1970). Discriminability along the voicing continuum: cross-language tests. In *Proceedings of the Sixth International Congress of Phonetic Sciences Prague 1967*, pp. 569–73. Prague: Academia.

Abramson, L. T., Seligman, M. E. P., and Teasdale, J. D. (1978). Learned helplessness in humans: critique and reformulation. *Journal of Abnormal Psychology* 87: 49–74.

Abravanel, E., and DeYong, N. G. (1991). Does object modeling elicit imitative-like gestures from young infants? *Journal of Experimental Child Psychology* 52: 22–40.

Abravanel, E., and Sigafoos, A. D. (1984). Exploring the presence of imitation during early infancy. *Child Development* 55: 381–92.

Adamson, L. B. (1996). *Communication development during infancy.* Boulder: Westview.

Adamson, L. B., and Bakeman, R. (1991). The development of shared attention during infancy. In *Annals of child development*, vol. VIII, ed. R. Vasta, pp. 1–41. London: Jessica Kinsley Publishers.

Adkins, A. W. H. (1970). *From many to one.* New York: Cornell University Press.

Aggleton, J. P. (ed.) (1992). *The amygdala: neurobiological aspects of emotion, memory, and mental disfunction.* New York: Wiley-Liss.

Aitken, K. J., and Trevarthen, C. (1997). Self-other organization in human psychological development. *Development and Psychopathology.* (in press).

Akhtar, N., Carpenter, M., and Tomasello, M. (1996). The role of discourse novelty in early word learning. *Child Development* 67: 635–45.

Akhtar, N., and Tomasello, M. (1996). Twenty-four-month-old children learn words for absent objects and actions. *British Journal of Developmental Psychology* 14: 79–93.

Allman, J., and Brothers, L. (1994). Faces, fear and the amygdala. *Nature* 372: 613–14.

Altmann, J. (1974). Observational study of behavior. *Behavior* 49: 227–264.

(1980). *Baboon mothers and infants.* Cambridge, MA: Harvard University Press.

Andler, D. (1988). Studying cognition today. In *Artificial intelligence and language*, ed. H. Sinding-Larson. Oslo: Tano.

Anisfeld, M. (1991). Neonatal imitation. *Developmental Review* 11: 60–97.

Anselmi, D., Tomasello, M., and Acunzo, M. (1986). Young children's responses to neutral and specific contingent queries. *Journal of Child Language* 13: 135–44.

Apostle, H. G. (1981). *Aristotle on the soul.* Crinnell, Iowa: The Peripatetic Press.

Aristotle (1936). *Peri poietikis* (About poetics). Athens: Estia.

(1963). Logic. In *The philosophy of Aristotle,* ed. R. Bambrough. New York: New American Library.

(1964). *Rhitoriki* (Rhetorics). Athens: Zacharopoulos.

(1975). *Peri psychis* (De anima). Athens: Zacharopoulos.

(1980). *The Nicomachean ethics.* Oxford: Oxford University Press.

Asplund, H. (1987). *Det sociala livets elementära former.* Gøteborg: Bokförlaget Korpen.

Astington, J. W., and Gopnik, A. (1991). Theoretical explanations of children's understanding of the mind. *British Journal of Developmental Psychology* 9: 7–31.

Astington, J., Harris, P., and Olson, D. (eds.) (1988). *Developing theories of mind.* Cambridge: Cambridge University Press.

Atkinson, M. (1979). Prerequisites for reference. In *Developmental pragmatics,* ed. E. Ochs and B. B. Schieffelin, pp. 229–49. New York: Academic Press.

Attkinson, J., and Braddick, O. (1982). Sensory and perceptual capacities of the neonate. In *Psychobiology of the human newborn,* ed. P. Stratton, pp. 191–220. New York: Wiley.

Axelos, K. (1974). *O Heraclitos kai i philosophia* (Heraclitus and philosophy). Athens: Exantas.

Bagionas, A. (1992). *Historia tis Archaias Hellenikis Ethikis* (History of the Ancient Greek Ethics). Thessaloniki: Thessaloniki University Press.

Bahrick, L. E., and Pickens, J. N. (1988). Classification of bimodal English and Spanish language passages by infants. *Infant Behavior and Development* 11: 277–96.

Baillargeon, R., Spelke, E. S., and Wasserman, S. (1985). Object permanence in five-month-old infants. *Cognition* 20: 191–208.

Baker, N. D., and Greenfield, P. M. (1988). The development of new and old information in young children's early language. *Language Sciences* 10: 3–34.

Bakhtin, M. M. (1981). *The dialogical imagination.* Austin: University of Texas Press.

(1984). *Problems of Dostoevsky's poetics.* Minneapolis: University of Minnesota Press.

Baldwin, D. (1991). Infants' contribution to the achievement of joint reference. *Child Development* 62: 875–90.

(1993a). Early referential understanding: infants' ability to recognize referential acts for what they are. *Developmental Psychology* 29: 832–43.

(1993b). Infants' ability to consult the speaker for clues to word reference. *Journal of Child Language* 20: 395–418.

(1995). Understanding the link between joint attention and language. In *Joint attention,* ed. C. Moore and P. Dunham, pp. 131–58. Hillsdale, NJ: Erlbaum.

Baldwin, D. A., and Moses, L. J. (1994). Early understanding of referential intent and attentional focus: evidence from language and emotion. In *Children's early understanding of mind,* ed. C. Lewis and P. Mitchell, pp. 133–56. Hillsdale, NJ: Erlbaum.

(1996). The ontogeny of social information gathering. *Child Development* 67: 1915–39.

Baldwin, J. M. (1891). Suggestion in infancy. *Science* 17: 113–17.

(1895). *Mental development in the child and the race*. New York: Macmillan.

Ball, W. A., and Vurpillot, E. (1981). Action and perception of displacement in infancy. In *Infancy and epistemology*, ed. G. Butterworth, pp. 115–36. Brighton: The Harvester Press.

Baltaxe, C. A. M. (1977). Pragmatic deficits in the language of autistic adolescents. *Journal of Paediatric Psychology* 2: 176–80.

Bandura, A. (1977). *Social learning theory*. Englewood Cliffs, NJ: Prentice-Hall.

Bard, K. A. (1993). A developmental theory requires developmental data. *Behavioral and Brain Sciences* 16: 511–12.

(1994a). Evolutionary roots of intuitive parenting: maternal competence in chimpanzees. *Early Development and Parenting* 3: 19–28.

(1994b). Similarities and differences in neonatal behavior of chimpanzee and human infants. In *The role of chimpanzees in research*, ed. G. Eder, E. Kaiser and F. King, pp. 43–55. Basle: Karger.

(1994c). Very early social learning: the effect of neonatal environment on chimpanzees' social responsiveness. In *Current primatology*, vol. III, ed. J. J. Roeder, B. Thierry, J. R. Anderson and N. Herrenschmidt, pp. 339–46. Strasburg: Université Louis Pasteur.

(1994d). Social-experiental contributions to imitation and emotional expression in chimpanzees. Paper presented at the Symposium on 'Intersubjective communication and emotion in ontogeny: between nature, nurture and culture' in the Norwegian Academy of Science and Letters, Oslo, 25–30 August.

(1995). Parenting in primates. In *Handbook of parenting*, vol. II, ed. M. Bornstein, pp. 27–58. Mahwah, NJ: Erlbaum.

(1996). Responsive care: behavioral interventions for nursery-reared chimpanzees. Paper presented to the 1996 ChimpanZoo Conference. Tuscon, AZ.

Bard, K. A., and Gardner, K. H. (1996). Influences on development in infant chimpanzees: enculturation, temperament, and cognition. In *Reaching into thought: the minds of the great apes*, ed. A. Russon, K. A. Bard and S. T. Parker, pp. 235–56. Cambridge: Cambridge University Press.

Bard, K. A., and Russell, C. L. (in press). Evolutionary foundations of imitation: social, cognitive, and developmental aspects of imitative process in non-human primates. In *Imitation in infancy*, ed. J. Nadel and G. Butterworth. Cambridge: Cambridge University Press.

Bard, K. A., Hopkins, W. D., and Fort, C. L. (1990). Lateral bias in infant chimpanzees (*Pan troglodytes*). *Journal of Comparative Psychology* 104: 309–21.

Bard, K. A., Platzman, K. A., Lester, B. M., and Suomi, S. J. (1992). Orientation to social and nonsocial stimuli in neonatal chimpanzees and humans. *Infant Behavior and Development* 15: 43–56.

Barnard, P. J., Scott, S. K., and Murray, L. (1997). Depression, early experience and the development of schematic models of the self. Manuscript submitted for publication.

Barnes, B. (1995). *The elements of social theory*. London: UCL Press, University College, London.

Baron-Cohen, S. (1987). Autism and symbolic play. *British Journal of Developmental Psychology* 5: 139–48.

(1989). Joint-attention deficits in autism: towards a cognitive analysis. *Development and Psychopathology* 1(3): 185–9.

(1990). Autism: a specific cognitive disorder of 'mind-blindness'. *International Review of Psychiatry* 2: 79–88.

(1995). *Mindblindness: an essay on autism and theory of mind*. Cambridge, MA: MIT Press.

Baron-Cohen, S., Allen, J., and Gillberg, C. (1992). Can autism be detected at 18 months? *The British Journal of Psychiatry* 161: 839–43.

Baron-Cohen, S., Leslie, A. M., and Frith, U. (1985). Does the autistic child have a theory of mind? *Cognition* 21: 37–46.

Baron-Cohen, S., Tager-Flusberg, H., and Cohen, D. J. (eds.) (1993). *Understanding other minds: perspectives from autism*. Oxford: Oxford University Press.

Barresi, J., and Moore, C. (1996). Intentional relations and social understanding. *Behavioral and Brain Sciences*, 19: 107–54.

Barrett, K., and Campos, J. J. (1987). Perspectives on emotional development. In *Handbook of infant development* (2nd edn), ed. J. D. Osofsky, pp. 555–78. New York: Wiley.

Bartak, L., Rutter, M., and Cox, A. (1975). A comparative study of infantile autism and specific developmental receptive language disorder. *British Journal of Psychiatry* 126: 127–45.

Barton, M. E., and Tomasello, M. (1994). The rest of the family: the role of fathers and siblings in early language development. In *Input and interaction in language acquisition*, ed. C. Gallaway and B. J. Richards, pp. 109–34. Cambridge: Cambridge University Press.

Bartsch, K., and Wellman, H. M. (1989). Young children's attribution of action to beliefs and desires. *Child Development* 60: 946–64.

Barwise, J., and Perry, J. (1983). *Situations and attitudes*. Cambridge, MA: MIT Press.

Bates, E. (1979). *The emergence of symbols*, New York: Academic Press.

Bates, E., Camaioni, L., and Volterra, V. (1975). The acquisition of performatives prior to speech. *Merrill-Palmer Quarterly* 21: 205–26.

Bateson, G. (1955). Expressive behavior among the Balinese – learning behavior in Bali. Appendix in C. Darwin, *The expression of the emotions in man and animals*. New York: Philosophical Library.

Bateson, M. C. (1971). The interpersonal context of infant vocalization. *Quarterly Progress Report of the Research Laboratory of Electronics* 100: 170–6.

(1975). Mother–infant exchanges: the epigenesis of conversational interaction. In *Developmental Psycholinguistics and Communication Disorders; Annals of the New York Academy of Sciences*, vol. CCLXIII, ed. D. Aaronson and R. W. Rieber, pp. 101–13. New York: New York Academy of Sciences.

(1979). 'The epigenesis of conversational interaction': a personal account of research development. In *Before speech*, ed. M. Bullowa, pp. 63–77. Cambridge: Cambridge University Press.

Bateson, P. (1990). Animal communication. In *Ways of communicating*, ed. D. H. Mellor, pp. 35–55. Cambridge: Cambridge University Press.

(1991). Are there principles of behavioural development? In *The development and integration of behaviour: essays in honour of Robert Hinde*, ed. P. Bateson, pp. 19–40. Cambridge: Cambridge University Press.

(1994). The dynamics of parent–offspring relationships in mammals. *Trends in Ecology and Evolution* 9: 399–403.

(1995). Design for a life. In *Individual development over the lifespan*, ed. D. Magnusson, pp. 1–20. Cambridge: Cambridge University Press.

Bateson, P., and Gomendio, M. (1992). *Behavioural mechanisms in evolutionary perspective*. Madrid: Instituto Juan March.

Bateson, P., and Horn, G. (1994). Imprinting and recognition memory: a neural net model. *Animal Behaviour* 48: 695–715.

Bateson, P., Mendl, M., and Feaver, J. (1990). Play in the domestic cat is enhanced by rationing the mother during lactation. *Animal Behaviour* 40: 514–25.

Bateson, P. P. G., and Reese, E. P. (1969). The reinforcing properties of conspicuous stimuli in the imprinting situation. *Animal Behaviour* 17: 692–9.

Bauer, P., and Mandler, J. (1989). One thing follows another: effects of temporal structure on 1- and 2-year-olds' recall of events. *Developmental Psychology* 25: 197–206.

Bayley, N. (1969). *Bayley scales of infant development*. New York: Psychological Corporation.

Beardsley, M. C. (1982). *Aesthetics*. Alabama: The University of Alabama Press.

Bechara, A., Damasio, H., Tranel, D., and Damasio, A. R. (1997). Deciding advantageously before knowing the advantageous strategy. *Science* 275: 1293–94.

Beebe, B. (1982). Micro-timing in mother–infant communication. In *Non-verbal communication today: current research*, ed. M. Key, pp. 169–95. New York: Mouton.

Beebe, B., Jaffe, J., Feldstein, S., Mays, K., and Alson, D. (1985). Inter-personal timing: the application of an adult dialogue model to mother–infant vocal and kinesic interactions. In *Social perception in infants*, ed. F. M. Field and N. Fox, pp. 249–68. Norwood, NJ: Ablex.

Beebe, B., and Lachmann, F. M. (1988). The contribution of mother–infant mutual influence to the origins of self- and object-representations. *Psychoanalytic Psychology* 5(4): 305–37.

Beebe, B., Stern, D., and Jaffe, J. (1979). The kinesic rhythm of mother–infant interactions. In *Of speech and time*, ed. A. W. Siegman and S. Feldstein. Hillsdale, NJ: Erlbaum.

Beilin, H. (1992). Piaget's enduring contribution to developmental psychology. *Developmental Psychology* 28(2): 191–204.

Benjamin, J. (1988). *The bonds of love: psychoanalysis, feminism, and the problems of domination*. New York: Pantheon.

Benveniste, E. (1977). Subjectivity in language. In *Language as a way of knowing*, ed. M. Nystrand. Toronto: The Ontario Institute for Studies in Education.

Bernstein, N. (1967). *Coordination and regulation of movements*. New York: Pergamon.

Berridge, K. C. (1994). The development of action patterns. In *Causal mechanisms of behavioural development*, ed. J. A. Hogan and J. J. Bolhuis, pp. 147–80. Cambridge: Cambridge University Press.

Berthoz, A. (1996). Neural basis of decision in perception and in the control of movement. In *Neurobiology of decision-making*, ed. A. R. Damasio, H. Damasio and Y. Christen, pp. 83–100. Berlin: Springer.

Bion, W. R. (1962). The psychoanalytic study of thinking. *International Journal of Psychoanalysis* 43: 306–10.

Black, J. B., Turner, T. J., and Bower, G. H. (1979). Point of view in narrative comprehension, memory, and production. *Journal of Verbal Learning and Verbal Behavior* 18: 187–98.

Bloom, L., and Beckwith, R. (1989). Talking with feeling: integrating affective and linguistic expression in early language development. *Cognition and Emotion* 3: 313–42.

Boesch, C. (1993). Towards a new image of culture in wild chimpanzees? *Behavioral and Brain Sciences* 16: 514–15.

Boesch, C., and Boesch, H. (1989). Hunting behavior of wild chimpanzees in the Tai National Park. *American Journal of Physical Anthropology* 78: 547–73.

Bolhuis, J. J. (1991). Mechanisms of avian imprinting: a review. *Biological Reviews* 66: 303–45.

Bolhuis, J. J., Johnson, M. H., and Horn, G. (1985). Effects of early experience on the development of filial preferences in the domestic chick. *Developmental Psychobiology* 18: 299–308.

Bond, A. M. (1989). Toward a resolution of the paradox of aggressive displays: Optimal deceit in the communication of fighting ability. *Ethology* 81: 29–46.

Borgen, J. (1965). *I barndommens rike* (In the realm of childhood). Oslo: Gyldendal.

Bornstein, M. H. (1991). *Cultural approaches to parenting*. Hillsdale, NJ: Erlbaum.

Bornstein, M. H., and Lamb, M. E. (1992). *Development in infancy* (3rd edn). New York: McGraw-Hill.

Bosch, G. (1970). *Infantile autism*. New York: Springer-Verlag.

Bower, G. H., and Morrow, D. G. (1990). Mental models in narrative comprehension. *Science* 247: 44–8.

Bower, T. G. R. (1974/1982). *Development in infancy.* San Francisco: W. H. Freeman.

Bowlby, J. (1984). *Attachment and loss*, vol. I. Reading: Pelican Books.

Bråten, S. (1973). *Tegnbehandling og meningsutveksling* (Symbol and meaning processing in interaction). Oslo: Scandinavian University Press.

(1974). Coding simulation circuits during symbolic interaction. *Proceedings on the 7th International Congress on Cybernetics*, pp. 327–36. Namur: Association Internationale de Cybernétique.

(1982). Simulation and self-organization of mind. *Contemporary philosophy*, vol. II, ed. G. Floistad, pp. 189–218. The Hague: Martinus Nijhoff.

(1984). The third position – beyond artificial and autopoietic reduction. *Kybernetes* 13: 157–63.

(1986). Consent and dissent: postulating the virtual other. Paper presented at the Gordon Research Conference on Cybernetics of Cognition, Wolfeboro, June 1986 (published revised in *Between rationality and cognition*, ed. M. Campanella, pp. 205–35. Torino: Meynier, 1988).

(1988a). Dialogic mind: the infant and the adult in protoconversation. In *Nature, cognition and system*, vol. I, ed. M. Carvallo, pp. 187–205. Dordrecht: Kluwer Academic Publishers.

(1988b). Between dialogic mind and monologic reason: postulating the virtual other. In *Between rationality and cognition*, ed. M. Campanella, pp. 205–35. Torino: Meynier.

(1989). G. H. Meads filosofi som grunnlag for dialogisk forståelse (G. H. Mead's philosophy as foundation of dialogical understanding). In *Oppdragelse til det moderne*, ed. H. Thuen and S. Vaage, pp. 95–118. Oslo: Universitetsforlaget.

(1992). The virtual other in infants' minds and social feelings. In *The*

Dialogical alternative, ed. A. H. Wold, pp. 77–97. Oslo: Scandinavian University Press.

(1993). Social-emotional and auto-operational roots of cultural (peer) learning. Commentary. *Behavioral and Brain Sciences*, 16: 515.

(1994a). The companion space theorem. Paper presented at the ISIS Pre-Conference on Imitation. Paris, 1 June 1994. Published in *Intersubjective communication and emotion in ontogeny: between nature, nurture and culture. Symposium Pre-proceedings*, ed. S. Bråten, pp. 15–16. Oslo: The Norwegian Academy of Science and Letters, 25–30 August.

(1994b). Self–other connections in the imitating infant and in the dyad: the companion space theorem. Paper presented at the Symposium on Intersubjective Communication and Emotion in Ontogeny: Between Nature, Nurture and Culture, in the Norwegian Academy of Science and Letters, Oslo, 25–30 August.

(1995). The creative self-dialogue in children. In *Problem solving and cognitive processes*, ed. G. Kaufmann, T. Helstrup, and K. H. Teigen, pp. 283–313. Bergen: Fagbokforlaget.

(1996a). When toddlers provide care: infants' companion space. *Childhood* 3(4): 449–65.

(1996b). Infants demonstrate that care-giving is reciprocal. *Centre for Advanced Study Newsletter* 2 (November 1996): 2.

(1996c). Videoanalyse av spedbarn i samspill bidrar til å oppheve et modellmonopol. In *Kvalitative metoder i samfunnsforskning*, ed. H. Holter and R. Kalleberg, pp. 165–91. Oslo: Universitetsforlaget.

(1997a). Altercentriskt deltagande som förklaring til att spädbarn kan ge omsorg. In *Seendets pendel*, ed. B. Isenberg and F. Oddner, pp. 181–200. Stockholm: Bokförlag Symposium 1997.

(1997b). Egocentric and altercentric perception in infant imitative learning. Keynote address at the Sixth European Workshop on Imagery and Cognition, Oslo 9–13 August 1997. In *EWIC Proceedings*, ed. T. Helstrup and R. H. Logie, pp. 1–2. Oslo: The Norwegian Academy of Science and Letters.

(1997c). From communion to communication – transitions in the child and in the culture. Public lecture on the occasion of the opening of the project 'Die Kultur im sozialen Wandeln', organized by G. Dux, Zentrum für interdisziplinäre Forschung, Bielefeld, 15–18 October 1997.

(1998). *Kommunikasjon og samspill – fra födsel til alderdom* (Communication and interplay – from birth to old age). Oslo: Tano Aschehoug.

(in press). *Modellmakt og altersentriske spedbarn. Essays on Dialogue in Infant & Adult*. Bergen: Sigma.

Bråten, S., and Espelid, R. (1990). Visual ambiguity: simulation of neural networks in competition. *BSC 90/4*. Bergen: Bergen Scientific Centre IBM.

Bråten, S., and Trevarthen, C. (1994). Beginnings of cultural learning. Paper presented at the ZiF symposium on the Formative Process of Society, Bielefeld, 17–19 November.

Brazelton, T. B. (1973). Neonatal behavioral assessment scale. *Clinics in Developmental Medicine* 50. Philadelphia: Lippincott.

(1979). Evidence of communication in neonatal behavioral assessment. In *Before speech*, ed. M. Bullowa, pp. 79–88. New York: Cambridge University Press.

(1984). *Neonatal behavioral assessment scale* (2nd edn). Spastics International Medical Publications. Philadelphia: Lippincott.

Brazelton, T. B., Koslowski, B., and Main, M. (1974). The origins of reciprocity: the early mother–infant interaction. In *The effect of the infant on its caregiver*, vol. I, ed. M. Lewis and L. A. Rosenblum, pp. 49–76. New York: Wiley.

Brazelton, T. B., and Tronick, E. (1980). Preverbal communication between mothers and infants. In *The social foundations of language and thought*, ed. D. R. Olson, pp. 299–315. New York: Norton.

Brazelton, T. B., Tronick, E. Z., Adamson, L., Als, H., and Wise, S. (1975). Early mother–infant reciprocity. In *Parent–infant interaction*, ed. M. Hofer. Amsterdam: Elsevier.

Brazelton, T. B., and Young, C. C. (1964). An example of imitative behavior in a nine-week-old infant. *Journal of the American Academy of Child Psychiatry* 3: 53–67.

Brehmer, B. (1980). In one word: not from experience. *Acta Psychologica* 45: 223–41.

Brentano, F. (1874/1973). *Psychology from an empirical standpoint*. London: Routledge and Kegan Paul.

Bretherton, I., and Beeghly, M. (1982). Talking about internal states: the acquisition of an explicit theory of mind. *Developmental Psychology* 18: 906–21.

Bretherton, I., McNew, S., and Beeghly-Smith, M. (1981). Early person knowledge as expressed in gestural and verbal communication: when do infants acquire a 'theory of mind'? In *Infant social cognition*, ed. M. E. Lamb and L. R. Sherrod, pp. 333–73. Hillsdale, NJ: Erlbaum.

Brother, L. (1990). The social brain: a project for integrating primate behavior and neurophysiology in a new domain. *Concepts of Neuroscience* 1: 27–51.

Brown, J. D. (1996). Imitation, play and theory of mind in autism: an observational and experimental study. PhD thesis, University of St Andrews.

Brown, J. R., and Dunn, J. (1991). 'You can cry, mum': the social and developmental implications of talk about internal states. In *Perspective on the child's theory of mind*, ed. G. E. Butterworth, P. Harris, A. Leslie and H. Wellman, pp. 237–56. Oxford: Oxford University Press.

(1992). Talk to your mother or your sibling? Developmental changes in early family conversations about feelings. *Child Development* 63: 336–49.

(1996). Continuities in emotion understanding from 3 to 6 years. *Child Development* 67: 789–802.

Brown, J. R., Donelan-McCall, N., and Dunn, J. (1996). Why talk about mental states? *Child Development* 67: 836–49.

Bruner, J. S. (1968). *Processes of cognitive growth: infancy.* (Heinz Werner Lectures, 1968), Worcester, MA: Clark University Press.

(1972). Nature and uses of immaturity. *American Psychologist* 27: 687–708.

(1976). From communication to language – a psychological perspective. *Cognition* 3: 255–87.

(1983). *Child's talk: learning to use language*. New York: Norton.

(1990). *Acts of meaning*. Cambridge, MA: Harvard University Press.

(1996). *The culture of education*. Cambridge, MA: Harvard University Press.

Bruner, J. S., and Sherwood, V. (1975). Early rule structure: the case of peekaboo. In *Play*, ed. J. S. Bruner, A. Jolly and K. Sylva. Harmondsworth: Penguin Books.

Buber, M. (1958). *I and thou* (R. G. Smith trans., 2nd edn). Edinburgh: T. Clark and T. Clark.

(1962). What is Man? In *Philosophy in the twentieth century*, vol. IV, ed. W. Barrett and H. D. Diken, pp. 688–719. New York: Random House.

Buck, R. (1984). *The communication of emotion.* New York: The Guilford Press.

(1993). Spontaneous communication and the foundation of the interpersonal self. In *The perceived self,* ed. U. Neisser, pp. 216–36. Cambridge: Cambridge University Press.

Bullowa, M. (1979). *Before speech,* New York: Cambridge University Press.

Burlingham, D. (1967). Empathy between infant and mother. *Journal of the American Psychoanalytic Association* 15: 764–80.

Bushnell, I. W. R., Sai, F., and Mullin, J. T. (1989). Neonatal recognition of the mother's face. *British Journal of Developmental Psychology* 7: 3–15.

Butterworth, G. (1981). Object permanence and identity in Piaget's theory of infant cognition. In *Infancy and epistemology,* ed. G. Butterworth, pp. 137–69. Brighton: The Harvester Press.

(1991). Origins of self-perception in infancy. *Psychological Inquiry* 3: 103–111.

Butterworth, G., and Cochran, E. (1980). Towards a mechanism of joint visual attention in human infancy. *International Journal of Behavioral Development* 3: 253–72.

Butterworth, G., Harris, P., Leslie, A., and Wellman, H. (eds.) (1991). *Perspectives on the child's theory of mind.* Oxford: Oxford University Press.

Butterworth G. E., and Jarret, N. L. M. (1991). What minds have in common is space: spatial mechanisms serving joint visual attention in infancy. *British Journal of Developmental Psychology* 9: 55–72.

Byrne, R. W. (1993). Hierarchical levels of imitation. Commentary. *Behavioural and Brain Sciences* 16: 516–17.

(1994). The evolution of intelligence. In *Behaviour and evolution,* ed. P. J. B. Slater and T. R. Halliday, pp. 223–65. Cambridge: Cambridge University Press.

(1995). *The thinking ape.* Oxford: Oxford University Press.

Byrne, R. W., and Byrne, J. M. E. (1991). Hand preferences in the skilled gathering tasks of mountain gorillas (*Gorilla g. beringei*). *Cortex* 27: 521–46.

(1993). Complex leaf-gathering skills of mountain gorillas (*Gorilla g. beringei*): variability and standardization. *American Journal of Primatology* 31: 241–61.

Byrne, R. W., and Russon, A. (in press). Learning by imitation: a hierarchical approach. *Behavioral and Brain Sciences.*

Byrne, R. W., and Tomasello, M. (1995). Do rats ape? *Animal Behaviour* 50: 1417–20.

Byrne, R. W., and Whiten, A. (1985). Tactical deception of familiar individuals in baboons. *Animal Behaviour* 33: 669–73.

(1990). Tactical deception in primates: the 1990 database. *Primate Report* 27: 1–101.

(1991). Computation and mindreading in primate tactical deception. In *Natural theories of mind,* ed. A. Whiten, pp. 127–42. Oxford: Basil Blackwell.

(1992). Cognitive evolution in primates: evidence from tactical deception. *Man* 27: 609–27.

Byrne, R. W., and Whiten, A. (eds.) (1988). *Machiavellian intelligence.* Oxford: Oxford University Press.

Campos, J. J., and Stenberg, C. R. (1981). Perception, appraisal and emotion: the onset of social referencing. In *Infant social cognition,* ed. M. E. Lamb and L. R. Sherrod, pp. 273–314. Hillsdale, NJ: Erlbaum.

Campos, J. J., Campos, R. G., and Barrett, K. C. (1989). Emergent themes in the study of emotional development and emotional regulation. *Developmental Psychology* 25: 394–402.

Carruthers, P., and Smith, P. K. (eds.) (1996). *Theories of theories of mind.* Cambridge: Cambridge University Press.

Caryl, P. G. (1979). Communication by agonistic displays: what can games theory contribute to ethology? *Behaviour* 68: 135–44.

Cassidy, J., Parke, R. D., Butkovsky, L., and Braungart, J. (1992). Family–peer connections: the roles of emotional expressiveness within the family and children's understanding of emotions. *Child Development* 63: 603–18.

Cernoch, J. M., and Porter, R. H. (1985). Recognition of maternal axillary odours by infants. *Child Development* 56: 1593–8.

Chantrey, D. F. (1974). Stimulus preexposure and discrimination learning by domestic chicks: effect of varying interstimulus time. *Journal of Comparative and Physiological Psychology* 87: 517–25.

Charman, T., and Baron-Cohen, S. (1994). Another look at imitation in autism. *Development and Psychopathology* 6: 403–13.

Charney, R. (1980). Speech roles and the development of personal pronouns. *Journal of Child Language* 7: 509–28.

Chevalier-Skolnikoff, S. (1982). A cognitive analysis of facial behaviour in Old World monkeys, apes, and human beings. In *Primate communication,* ed. C. T. Snowdon, C. H. Brown and M. R. Peterson, pp. 303–68. Cambridge: Cambridge University Press.

Chisolm, J. S. (1981). Residence patterns and the environment of mother–infant interaction among the Navaho. In *Culture and early interactions,* eds. T. M. Field, A. M. Sostek, P. Vietze and P. H. Leiderman, pp. 3–20. Hillsdale, NJ: Erlbaum.

(1989). Biology, culture, and the development of temperament: a Navaho example. In *The cultural context of infancy,* vol. I, ed. J. K. Nugent, B. M. Lester and T. B. Brazelton, pp. 341–66. Norwood, NJ: Ablex.

Chomsky, N. 1988. *Language and problems of knowledge.* Cambridge, MA: MIT Press.

Cicchetti, D., and Pogge-Hesse, P. (1981). The relation between emotion and cognition in infant development. In *Infant social cognition,* ed. M. E. Lamb and L. R. Sherrod, pp. 205–72. Hillsdale, NJ: Erlbaum.

Cioni, G., and Castellaci, A. M. (1990). Development of fetal and neonatal motor activity: implications for neurology. In *Sensory-motor organization and development in infancy and early childhood,* ed. H. Block and B. Bertenthal. Dordrecht: Kluwer.

Clark, K., and Holquist. M. (1984). *Mikhael Bakhtin.* Cambridge, MA: Harvard University Press.

Clutton-Brock, T. H., and Albon, S. D. (1979). The roaring of red deer and the evolution of honest advertisement. *Behaviour* 69: 135–44.

Cohn, J. F., and Tronick, E. Z. (1983). Three-month-old infants' reaction to simulated maternal depression. *Child Development* 54: 185–93.

(1989). Specificity of infants' response to mothers' affective behaviour. *Journal of the American Academy of Child and Adolescent Psychiatry* 28: 242–8.

Condon, W. S., and Sander, L. W. (1974). Synchrony demonstrated between movements of the neonate and adult speech. *Child Development* 45: 456–62.

Cooper, J. M. (1993). Rhetoric, dialectic, and the passions. In *Oxford studies in ancient philosophy,* vol. XI, ed. C. C. W. Taylor, pp. 175–98. Oxford: Clarendon Press.

Copleston, F. S. J. (1962). *A history of philosophy,* vol. I. New York: Image Books.

Corkum, V., and Moore, C. (1995). Development of joint visual attention in infants. In *Joint attention: its origins and role in development,* ed. C. Moore and P. J. Dunham, pp. 61–83. Hillsdale, NJ: LEA.

Cressini, B. (1987). How to know what infants know: historical notes on an ever-present problem. In *Perceptual development in early infancy,* ed. B. E. McKenzie and R. H. Day. Hillsdale, NJ: Erlbaum.

Crisp, R. (1992). White on Aristotelian happiness. In *Oxford studies in ancient philosophy,* vol. X, ed. J. Annas, pp. 233–40. Oxford: Clarendon Press.

Cummings, E. M., and Davies, P. (1994). *Children and marital conflict.* New York: Guilford.

Curcio, F. (1978). Sensorimotor functioning and communication in mute autistic children. *Journal of Autism and Childhood Schizophrenia* 8: 281–92.

Curcio, F., and Piserchia, E. A. (1978). Pantomimic representation in psychotic children. *Journal of Autism and Childhood Schizophrenia* 8: 181–9.

Custance, D. M., and Bard, K. A. (1994). The comparative and developmental study of self-recognition and imitation: the importance of social factors. In *Self-awareness in animals and humans,* ed. S. T. Parker, M. Boccia and R. W. Mitchell. Cambridge: Cambridge University Press.

Custance, D. M., Whiten, A., and Bard, K. (1994). The development of gestural imitation and self-recognition in chimpanzees and young children. In *Current primatology,* vol. II, eds. J. J. Roeder *et al.* Strasburg: Université Louis Pasteur.

(1995). Can young chimpanzees (*Pan troglodytes*) imitate arbitrary actions? Hayes and Hayes (1952) revisited. *Behaviour* 132: 839–58.

Dahlgren, S. O., and Gillberg, C. (1989). Symptoms in the first two years of life: a preliminary population study of infantile autism. *European Archives of Psychiatry and Neurological Sciences* 238: 169–74.

Damasio, A. R. (1994). *Descartes' error: emotion, reason and the human brain.* New York: C. P. Putman's Sons.

Damasio, A. R., Tranel, D., and Damasio, H. (1991). Somatic markers and the guidance of behavior: theory and preliminary testing. In *Frontal lobe function and dysfunction,* ed. H. S. Levin, H. M. Eisenberg and A. L. Benton, pp. 217–29. New York: Oxford University Press.

Darwin, C. (1871/1981). *The descent of man and selection in relation to sex.* Princeton, NJ: Princeton University Press.

(1872/1955). *The expression of the emotions in man and animals.* New York: Philosophical Library.

Davidson, R. (1993). Cerebral asymmetry and emotion: conceptual and methodological conundrums. *Cognition and Emotion* 7: 115–38.

Davies, P., and Cummings, E. M. (1994). Marital conflict and child adjustment: an emotional security hypothesis. *Psychological Bulletin* 116: 387–411.

Dawkins, R. (1976). *The selfish gene.* Oxford: Oxford University Press.

Dawkins, R., and Krebs, J. R. (1979a). Animal signals: information or manipulation. In *Behavioural ecology,* ed. J. R. Krebs and N. B. Davies, pp. 282–309. Oxford: Blackwell.

(1979b). Arms races between and within species. *Proceedings of the Royal Society of London,* B, 205: 489–511.

Dawson, B. V., and Foss, B. M. (1965). Observational learning in budgerigars. *Animal Behaviour* 13: 470–4.

Dawson, G. (1994a). Development of emotional expression and emotion regulation in infancy. In *Human behavior and the developing brain,* ed. G. Dawson and K. W. Fisher, pp. 346–79. New York: The Guilford Press.

(1994b). Frontal EEG correlates of individual differences in emotion expression in infants: a brain systems perspective on emotion. *Monographs of the Society for Research in Child Development* 59: 135–51.

Dawson, G., and Adams, A. (1984). Imitation and social responsiveness in autistic children. *Journal of Abnormal Child Psychology* 12: 209–26.

Dawson, G., and Galpert, L. (1990). Mothers' use of imitative play for facilitating social responsiveness and toy play in young autistic children. *Development and Psychopathology* 2: 151–62.

Dawson, G., Grofer Klinger, L., Panagiotides, H., Hill, D., and Spieker, S. (1992). Frontal lobe activity and affective behavior of infants of mothers with depressive symptoms. *Child Development* 63: 725–37.

Dawson, G., Hill, D., Spencer, A., Galpert, L., and Watson, L. (1990). Affective exchanges between young autistic children and their mothers. *Journal of Abnormal Child Psychology* 18: 335–45.

Dawson, G., and McKissick, F. C. (1984). Self-recognition in autistic children. *Journal of Autism and Developmental Disorders* 14: 383–94.

de Boysson-Bardies, B. (1993). Ontogeny of language-specific syllabic productions. In *Developmental neurocognition*, ed. B. de Boysson-Bardies *et al.*, pp. 353–63. Dordrecht: Kluwer.

de Boysson-Bardies, B., Schonen, S. de, Jusczyk, P., MacNeilage, P., and Morton, J. (1993). *Developmental neurocognition*. Dordrecht: Kluwer.

De Romily, J. (1992). *Vasta kardia mou* (Endure my heart). Athens: Asty.

de Vries, M., and Super, C. M. (1978). Contextual influences on the neonatal behavioral assessment scale and implications for its cross-cultural use. *Monographs of the Society for Research in Child Development* 43: 92–101.

de Waal, F. (1982). *Chimpanzee Politics*. New York: Harper and Row.

(1989). *Peacemaking among primates*. Cambridge, MA: Harvard University Press.

Deag, J. M., Lawrence, C. E., and Manning, A. (1987). The consequences of differences in litter size for the nursing cat and her kittens. *Journal of Zoology* 213: 153–79.

DeCasper, A. J., and Carstens, A. A. (1981). Contingencies of stimulation: effects on learning and emotion in neonates. *Infant Behavior and Development* 4: 19–35.

DeCasper, A. J., and Fifer, W. P. (1980). Of human bonding: newborns prefer their mothers' voices. *Science* 208: 1174–6.

DeCasper, A. J., and Spence, M. J. (1986). Prenatal maternal speech influences newborns' perception of speech sounds. *Infant Behavior and Development* 9: 133–50.

DeMyer, M. K., Alpern, G. D., Barton, S., DeMyer, W. E., Churchill, D. W., Hingtgen, J. N., Bryson, C. Q., Pontius, W., and Kimberlin, C. (1972). Imitation in autistic, early schizophrenic and non-psychotic subnormal children. *Journal of Autism and Childhood Schizophrenia* 2: 264–87.

Denham, S. A. (1986). Social cognition, prosocial behavior, and emotion in preschoolers: contextual validation. *Child Development* 57: 194–201.

Denham, S. A., McKinley, M. J., Couchoud, E. A., and Hold, R. (1990). Emotional and behavioral predictors of preschool peer ratings. *Child Development* 61: 1145–52.

Descartes, R. (1637/1976). *Logos peri methodou* (Discourse on method). Athens: Papazisi.

Deutsch, F., and Madle, R. A. (1975). Empathy: historic and current conceptualizations, measurement, and a cognitive theoretical perspective. *Human Development* 18: 267–87.

Di Pellegrino, G., Fadiga, L., Fogassi, L., Gallese, V., and Rizzolatti, G. (1992). Understanding motor events: a neurophysiological study. *Experimental Brain Research* 91: 176–80.

Dienstbier, R. A. (1979). Emotion-attribution theory. In *Nebraska Symposium on Motivation 1978*, vol. XXVI, pp. 237–306. Lincoln and London: University of Nebraska Press.

Donald, M. (1991). *Origins of the modern mind.* Cambridge, MA and London: Harvard University Press.

Dore, J. (1983). Feeling, form and intention in the baby's transition to language. In *The transition from pre-linguistic communication*, ed. R. Golinkoff. Hillsdale, NJ: Erlbaum.

Dunham, P. J., Dunham, F. S., and Curwin, A. (1993). Joint attentional states and lexical acquisition at 18 months. *Developmental Psychology* 29: 827–31.

Dunham, P., Dunham, F., Hurshman, A., and Alexander, T. (1989). Social contingency effects of subsequent perceptual-cognitive tasks in young infants. *Child Development* 60: 1486–96.

Dunkeld, J. (1978). *The function of imitation in infancy.* Doctoral dissertation, University of Edinburgh, Department of Psychology.

Dunn, J. (1988). *The beginnings of social understanding*. Oxford: Basil Blackwell.

(1993). Young children's close relationship beyond attachment. *Individual differences and development series*, vol. IV. Newbury Park, CA: Sage Publications.

(1994). Changing minds and changing relationships. In *Children's early understanding of mind*, ed. C. Lewis and P. Mitchell, pp. 297–310. Hillsdale, NJ: Erlbaum.

(1995). Children as psychologists: the later correlates of individual differences in understanding of emotions and other minds. *Cognition and Emotion* 9: 187–201.

Dunn, J., Bretherton, I., and Munn, P. (1987). Conversations about feeling states between mothers and their young children. *Developmental Psychology* 23: 132–9.

Dunn, J., Brown, J., and Beardsall, L. (1991). Family talk about emotions, and children's later understanding of others' emotions. *Developmental Psychology* 27: 448–55.

Dunn, J., Brown, J., and Maguire, M. (1995). The development of children's moral sensibility: individual differences and emotion understanding. *Developmental Psychology* 31: 649–59.

Dunn, J., Brown, J., Slomkowski, C., Tesla, C., and Youngblade, L. (1991). Young children's understanding of other people's feelings and beliefs: individual differences and their antecedents. *Child Development* 62: 1352–66.

Dunn, J., and Dale, N. (1984). I a daddy: 2-year-olds' collaboration in joint pretend with sibling and with mother. In *Symbolic play*, ed. I. Bretherton, pp. 3–41. New York: Academic Press.

Dunn, J., and Kendrick, C. (1982). *Siblings*. Cambridge, MA: Harvard University Press.

Dunn, J., and Munn, P. (1985). Becoming a family member: family conflict and the development of social understanding in the second year. *Child Development* 56: 764–74.

Dunn, J., and Shatz, M. (1989). Becoming a conversationalist despite (or because of) having an older sibling. *Child Development* 60: 399–410.

Eckerman, C. O. (1993). Imitation and toddlers' achievement of co-ordinated action with others. In *New perspectives in early communicative development*, ed. J. Nadel and L. Camaioni, pp. 116–38. London: Routledge.

Edwards, C. P. (1992). Cross-cultural perspectives on family-peer relations. In *Family-peer relationships:* ed. R. D. Parke and G. W. Ladd, pp. 285–316. Hillsdale, NJ: Erlbaum.

(1993). Behavioral sex differences in children of diverse cultures: the case of nurturance to infants. In *Juvenile primates*, ed. M. E. Pereira and L. A. Fairbanks, pp. 327–38. New York: Oxford University Press.

Edwards, C. P., and Gandini, L. (1989). Teachers' expectations about the timing of developmental skills: a cross-cultural study. *Young Children* 44(4): 15–19.

Edwards, C., Gandini, L., and Giovannini, D. (1996). The contrasting developmental expectations of parents and early childhood teachers in two cultural communities. In *Parents' cultural belief systems*, ed. S. Harkness and C. Super, pp. 270–88. New York: Guilford.

Edwards, C. P., and Whiting, B. B. (1993). 'Mother, older sibling, and me': The overlapping roles of caregivers and companions in the social world of two- to three-year-olds in Ngeca, Kenya. In *Parent–child play: descriptions and implications*, ed. K. MacDonald, pp. 305–30. Albany: State University of New York Press.

Eibl-Eibesfeldt, I. (1979). Human ethology: concepts and implications for the sciences of man. *Behavioral and Brain Sciences* 2: 1–57.

(1989). *Human ethology.* New York: Aldine de Gruyter.

Eisenberg, R. B. (1975). *Auditory competence in early life.* Baltimore: University Park Press.

Elman, J., Bates, E. A, Johnson, M. H., Karmiloff-Smith, A., Parisis, D., and Plunkett, K. (1996). *Rethinking innateness*, Cambridge, MA: MIT Press.

Engle, P. L., Zeitlin, M., Medrano, Y., and Lino, G. M. (1996). Growth consequences of low-income Nicaraguan mothers' theories about feeding 1-year-olds. In *Parents' cultural belief systems*, ed. S. Harkness and C. M. Super, pp. 428–46. New York: Guilford Press.

Ervin, S. M., and Foster, G. (1960). The development of meaning in children's descriptive forms. *Journal of Abnormal and Social Psychology* 61: 271–5.

Eslinger, P., and Damasio, A. (1985). Severe disturbance of higher cognition after bilateral frontal lobe ablation: patient EVR. *Neurology* 35: 1731–41.

Estes, D., Wellman, H. M., and Woolley, J. D. (1989). Children's understanding of mental phenomena. In *Advances in child development and behavior*, ed. H. W. Reese, pp. 41–87. San Diego: Academic Press.

Fairbanks, L. A. (1993). Juvenile vervet monkeys: establishing relationships and practicing skills for the future. In *Juvenile primates*, ed. M. E. Pereira and L. A. Fairbanks, pp. 211–27. New York: Oxford University Press.

Fairbanks, L. A., and Pereira, M. E. (1993). Juvenile primates: dimensions for future research. In *Juvenile primates*, ed. M. E. Pereira and L. A. Fairbanks, pp. 359–66. New York: Oxford University Press.

Fantz, R. L. (1963). Pattern vision in newborn infants. *Science* 140: 296–7.

Ferguson, C. A. (1978). Learning to pronounce: the earliest stages of phonological development in the child. In *Communicative and cognitive abilities*, ed. F. D. Minifie and L. L. Lloyd, pp. 273–97. Baltimore: University Park Press.

Ferguson, C. A., Menn, L., and Stoel-Gammon, C. (eds.) (1992). *Phonological development*. Timonium, MD: York Press.

Fernald, A. (1989). Intonation and communicative interest in mother's speech to infants: Is the melody the message? *Child Development* 60: 1497–1510.

(1992). Human maternal vocalizations to infants as biologically relevant signals: an evolutionary perspective. In *The adapted mind*, ed. J. H. Barlow, L. Cosmides and J. Toody, pp. 391–428. Oxford: Oxford University Press.

Fernald, A., Taeschner, T., Dunn, J., Papousek, M., Boysson-Bardies, B. de., and Fukui, I. (1989). A cross-language study of prosodic modifications in mothers' and fathers' speech to preverbal infants. *Journal of Child Language* 16: 477–501.

Fiamenghi, G. A. (1997). Intersubjectivity and infant–infant interaction: imitation as a way of making contact. *Annual Report, Research and Clinical Center for Child Development*, Hokkaido University, no. 19: 15–21.

Field, T. M. (1977). Effects of early separation, interaction deficits and experimental manipulation on infant mother face-to-face interaction. *Child Development* 48: 763–71.

(1985). Neonatal perception of people: motivational and individual differences. In *Social perception in infants*, ed. T. M. Field and N. A. Fox. Norwood, NJ: Ablex.

(1992). Infants of depressed mothers. *Development and Psychopathology* 4: 49–66.

Field, T. M., Cohen, D., Garcia, R., and Greenberg, R. (1984). Mother–stranger face discrimination by the newborn. *Infant Behavior and Development* 7: 19–25.

Field, T., Goldstein, S., Vaga-Lahr, N., and Porter, K. (1986). Changes in imitative behavior during early infancy. *Infant Behavior and Development* 9: 415–21.

Field, T., Greenberg, R., Woodson, R., Cohen, D., and Garcia, R. (1984). A descriptive study of facial expressions during Brazelton neonatal behavior assessments. *Infant Mental Health Journal* 5: 61–71.

Field, T. M., Woodson, R., Greenberg, R., and Cohen, D. (1982). Discrimination and imitation of facial expressions by neonates. *Science* 218: 179–81.

Fischer, K. W., Shaver, P. R., and Carnochan, P. (1990). How emotions develop and how they organise development. *Cognition and Emotion* 4: 81–127.

Fisher, J., and Hinde, R. A. (1949). The opening of milk bottles by birds. *British Birds* 42: 347–57.

Flavell, J. H. (1988). The development of children's knowledge about the mind: from cognitive connections to mental representations. In *Developing theories of mind*, ed. J. W. Astington, P. L. Harris and D. R. Olson, pp. 244–67. New York: Cambridge University Press.

Fodor, J. (1980). Methodological solipsism considered as a research strategy in cognitive science. *Behavioral and Brain Sciences* 3: 63–109.

Fogel, A. (1993). *Developing through relationships*. Chicago: University of Chicago Press.

Fogel, A., and Thelen, E. (1987). Development of early expressive action from a dynamic systems approach. *Developmental Psychology* 23: 747–61.

Fontaine, R. (1984). Imitative skills between birth and six months. *Infant Behavior and Development* 7: 323–33.

Fouts, R. S., Hirsch, A. D., and Fouts, D. H. (1982). Cultural transmission of a human language in a chimpanzee mother–infant relationship. In *Psychobiological perspectives*, ed. H. E. Fitzgerald, J. A. Mullins and P. Gage, pp. 159–93. Child Nurturance Series 3. New York: Plenum Press.

Freud, A., and Burlingham, D. (1973). Infants without families. Reports on the Hampstead Nurseries 1939–1945. In *The writings of Anna Freud*, vol. III, pp. 574–5. New York: International Universities Press.

Freud, S. (1911). Formulations on the two principles of mental functioning.

Yearbook, vol. III, no. 1. In *Standard edition of Freud's psychological writings*, 12: 215–26. London: Hogarth Press.

(1921/1986). *Group psychology and the analysis of the ego*. London: Penguin Books, vol. XII.

Friedlander, B. (1970). Receptive language development in infancy. *Merrill Palmer Quarterly* 16: 7–51.

Frijda, N. H. (1986). *The emotions*. Cambridge: Cambridge University Press.

Frith, C. D. (1992). *The cognitive neuropsychology of schizophrenia*. Hillsdale, NJ: Erlbaum.

Frykholm, G. (1983a). *Perceived identity I: recognition of others by their kinematic patterns*. Uppsala Psychological Reports (serial no. 352).

(1983b). *Perceived identity II: learning to recognize others by their kinematic patterns*. Uppsala Psychological Reports (serial no. 351).

Fukushima, K. (1988). Neocognitron: a hierachical neural network capable of visual pattern recognition. *Neural Networks* 1: 119–30.

Furrow, D., and Lewis, S. (1987). The role of the initial utterance in contingent query sequences: its influence on responses to requests for clarification. *Journal of Child Language* 14 : 467–79.

Fuster, J. M. (1995). *Memory in the cerebral cortex*. Cambridge, MA: MIT Press.

Gadamer, H. G. (1975). *Wahrheit und Methode*. Tübingen: J. C. B. Mohr.

Galef, B. G., Jr. (1988). Imitation in animals: history, definitions, and interpretation of data from the psychological laboratory. In *Social learning*, ed. T. Zentall and B. G. Galef, Jr, pp. 3–28. Hillsdale, NJ: Erlbaum.

(1992). The question of animal culture. *Human Nature* 3: 157–78.

Galef, B. G., Manzig, L. A., and Field, R. M. (1986). Imitation learning in budgerigars: Dawson and Foss (1965) revisited. *Behavioural Processes* 13: 191–202.

Gallagher, T. (1977). Revision behaviors in the speech of normal children developing language. *Journal of Speech and Hearing Research* 20: 303–18.

(1981). Contingent query sequences within adult–child discourse. *Journal of Child Language* 8: 51–62.

Gallimore, R., Goldenberg, C. N., and Weisner, T. S. (1993). The social construction and subjective reality of activity settings: implications for community psychology. *American Journal of Community Psychology* 21(4): 537–59.

Gallup, G. G., Jr. (1970). Chimpanzees: self-recognition. *Science* 167: 86–7.

(1982). Self-awareness and the emergence of mind in primates. *American Journal of Primatology* 2: 237–48.

Gardner, B. T., and Gardner, R. A. (1989). Prelinguistic development of children and chimpanzees. *Human Evolution* 4: 433–60.

Gardner, J., and Gardner, H. (1970). A note on selective imitation by a six-week-old infant. *Child Development* 41: 1209–13.

George, C., and Main, M. (1979). Social interaction of young abused children: approach, avoidance, and aggression. *Developmental Psychology* 23: 114–23.

Gernsbacher, M. A., Goldsmith, H. H., and Robertson, R. R. W. (1992). Do readers mentally represent characters' emotional states? *Cognition and Emotion* 6: 89–111.

Gibson, J. J. (1979). *The ecological approach to visual perception*. Boston: Houghton-Mifflin.

Giddens, A. (1982). *Profiles and critiques in social theory*. London: Macmillan.

Gillberg, C. (1991). The Emanuel Miller Memorial Lecture: Autism and autistic-like conditions: subclasses among disorders of empathy. *Journal of Child Psychology and Psychiatry* 33: 813–42.

Gilligan, C. (1982). *In a different voice*. Cambridge MA: Harvard University Press.

Glenberg, A., Meyer, M., and Lindem, K. (1987). Mental models contribute to foregrounding during text comprehension. *Journal of Memory and Language* 26: 69–83.

Godfray, H. C. J. (1991). Signalling of need by offspring to their parents. *Nature* 352: 328–30.

Goffman, E. (1972). *Interaction ritual*. Harmondsworth: Penguin Books.

Goldman, A. I. (1989). Interpretation psychologized. *Mind and Language*, 4(3) (reprinted in *Folk psychology*, ed. M. Davies and T. Stone, pp. 74–99. Oxford: Blackwell).

Goldman-Rakic, P. S. (1985). Toward a neurobiology of cognitive development. In *Neonate cognition*, ed. J. Meehler and R. Fox. Hillsdale, NJ: Erlbaum.

Golinkoff, R. M. (1986). I beg your pardon? The preverbal negotiation of failed messages. *Journal of Child Language* 13: 455–76.

(1993). When is communication a 'meeting of minds'? *Journal of Child Language* 20: 199–207.

Gomendio, M. (1991). Mother–offspring relationships and consequences for fertility in rhesus macaques. *Animal Behaviour* 42: 993–1005.

Gómez, J. C. (1989). La comunicación y la manipulación de objetos en crías de gorila. *Estudios de Psicología*, 38: 111–28.

(1990a). The development of secondary intersubjectivity in infant gorillas. Paper presented to 13th Annual Meeting of the American Society of Primatologists, Davis, CA.

(1990b). The emergence of intentional communication as a problem-solving strategy in the gorilla. In *'Language' and intelligence in monkeys and apes*, ed. S. T. Parker and K. R. Gibson, pp. 333–55. Cambridge: Cambridge University Press.

(1991). Visual behavior as a window for reading the minds of others in primates. In *Natural theories of mind*, ed. A. Whiten, pp. 195–207. Oxford: Basil Blackwell.

(1992). El desarrollo de la comunicación intencional en el gorila. PhD dissertation, Universidad Autónoma de Madrid.

(1993). The comparative study of early communication and theories of mind: ontogeny, phylogeny, and pathology. In *Understanding other minds*, ed. S. Baron-Cohen, H. Tager-Flusberg and D. J. Cohen, pp. 397–426. Oxford: Oxford University Press.

(1994). Shared attention in ontogeny and phylogeny: SAM, TOM, Grice, and the great apes. *Cahiers de Psychologie Cognitive/Current Psychology of Cognition* 13(5): 590–8.

(1996). Ostensive behavior in the great apes: the role of eye contact. In *Reaching into thought*, ed. A. Russon, S. Parker and K. Bard. Cambridge: Cambridge University Press.

(in press). Assessing theory of mind with nonverbal procedures: problems with training methods and an alternative 'key' procedure. *Behavioral and Brain Sciences*.

Gómez, J. C., Sarriá, E., and Tamarit, J. (1993). The comparative study of early communication and theories of mind: ontogeny, phylogeny and pathology. In *Understanding other minds*, ed. S. Baron-Cohen, H. Tager-Flusberg and D. Cohen, pp. 397–426. Oxford: Oxford University Press.

Goodall, J. (1986). *The chimpanzees of Gombe*. Cambridge, MA: The Belknap Press of Harvard University Press.

Goodman, N. (1978). *Ways of worldmaking*. Hassocks: Harvester Press.

(1984). *Of mind and other matters*. Cambridge, MA: Harvard University Press.

Gopnik, A. (1993). How we know our minds: the illusion of first-person knowledge of intentionality. *Behavioral and Brain Sciences* 16: 1–14.

Gopnik, A., and Meltzoff, A. (1993). Imitation, cultural learning and the origins of 'theory of mind'. Commentary. *Behavioral and Brain Sciences*, 16: 521–3.

(1997). *Words, thoughts, and theories*. Cambridge, MA: MIT Press.

Gopnik, A., and Wellman, H. M. (1995). Why the child's theory of mind really *is* a theory. In *Folk psychology*, ed. M. Davies and T. Stone, pp. 232–58. Oxford: Blackwell.

Gordis, F. W., Rosen, A. B., and Grand, S. (1989). Young children's understanding of simultaneous conflicting emotions. Presentation at the Biennial meetings of the Society for Research in Child Development, Kansas City, MO.

Gordon, R. M. (1986). Folk psychology as simulation. *Mind and Language* 1(2) (reprinted in *Folk psychology*, ed. M. Davies and T. Stone, pp. 60–73. Oxford: Blackwell).

Goren, C. G., Sarty, M., and Wu, P. Y. K. (1975). Visual following and pattern discrimination of face-like stimuli by newborn infants. *Paediatrics* 56: 544–9.

Goy, C. (1990). The status of children's imaginary companions. Unpublished research project, Department of Experimental Psychology, University of Oxford.

Graesser, A. C., Singer, M., and Trabasso, T. (1994). Constructing inferences during narrative text comprehension. *Psychological Review* 101: 371–95.

Grafen, A. (1990). Biological signals as handicaps. *Journal of Theoretical Biology* 144: 517–46.

Grandin, T. (1995). *Thinking pictures and other reports from my life with autism*. New York: Doubleday.

Green, K. P., Kuhl, P. K., Meltzoff, A. N., and Stevens, E. B. (1991). Integrating speech information across talkers, gender, and sensory modality: female faces and male voices in the McGurk effect. *Perception and Psychophysics* 50: 524–36.

Greenfield, P. M. (1979). Informativeness, presupposition, and semantic choice in single-word utterances. In *Developmental pragmatics*, ed. E. Ochs and B. B. Schieffelin, pp. 159–66. New York: Academic Press.

(1982). The role of perceived variability in the transition to language. *Journal of Child Language* 9: 1–12.

Greenfield, P. M., Reilly, J., Leaper, C., and Baker, N. (1985). The structural and functional status of single-word utterances and their relationship to early multi-word speech. In *Children's single-word speech*, ed. M. D. Barrett, pp. 233–67. London: John Wiley.

Greenfield, P. M., and Zukow, P. (1978). Why do children say what they say when they say it? An experimental approach to the psychogenesis of presupposition. In *Children's language*, vol. I, ed. K. E. Nelson. New York: Gardner Press.

Greenspan, S. I. (1982). *Psychopathology and adaption in infancy and early childhood*. Clinical Infant Reports 1. New York: International Universities Press.

Grice, H. P. (1957). Meaning. *Philosophical Review* 66: 377–88.

(1975). Logic and conversation. In *Syntax and semantics: speech acts,* ed. R. Cole and J. Morgan. New York: Academic Press.

Grieser, D. L., and Kuhl, P. K. (1988). Maternal speech to infants in a tonal language: support for universal prosodic features in motherese. *Developmental Psychology* 24: 14–20.

Groenewegen, H. J., Wright, C. I., and Beijer, A. V. J. (1996). The nucleus accumbens: gateway for limbic structures to reach the motor system. In *The emotional motor system,* ed. G. Holstege, R. Bandler, and C. B. Saper. Amsterdam: Elsevier.

Gruber, H. E. (1974). *Darwin on man.* London: Wildwood.

Guillaume, P. (1925/1971). *Imitation in children.* Chicago: The University of Chicago Press.

Guthrie, W. K. (1967). *The Greek philosophers.* London: Methuen.

Habermas, J. (1970). Towards a theory of communicative competence. In *Recent sociology,* vol. XII, ed. H. P. Dreitzel, pp. 115–48. London: Macmillan.

(1981). *Theorie des kommunikativen Handelns.* Frankfurt a. M.: Suhrkampf Verlag.

Hacker, P. M. S. (1990). Chomsky's problems. *Language and Communication* 10: 127–48.

Hagekull, B. (1985). Individual stability in dimensions of infant behavior. *Infant Behavior and Development* 4: 97–108.

Hagekull, B., Lindhagen, K., and Bohlin, G. (1980). Behavioral dimensions in one-year-olds and dimensional stability in infancy. *International Journal of Behavioral Development* 3: 351–64.

Halliday, M. A. K. (1975). *Learning how to mean.* London: Edward Arnold.

(1979). One child's protolanguage. In *Before speech,* ed. M. Bullowa, pp. 171–90. Cambridge: Cambridge University Press.

Hallock, M. B., Worobey, J., and Self, P. S. (1989). Behavioral development in chimpanzee (*Pan troglodytes*) and human newborns across the first month of life. *International Journal of Behavioral Development* 12: 527–40.

Hamlyn, D. W. (1978). *Experience and the growth of understanding.* London: Routledge and Kegan Paul.

Hammes, J. G. W., and Langdell, T. (1981). Precursors of symbol formation and childhood autism. *Journal of Autism and Developmental Disorders* 11: 331–46.

Happé, F. G. E. (in press). Communicative competence and theory of mind in autism: a test of relevance theory. *Cognition.*

Harris, P. L. (1989). *Children and emotion.* Oxford: Basil Blackwell.

(1991). The work of the imagination. In *Natural theories of the mind,* ed. A. Whiten, pp. 283–304. Oxford: Blackwell.

(1993). Pretending and planning. In *Understanding other minds,* ed. S. Baron-Cohen, H. Tager-Flusberg and D. J. Cohen, pp. 228–46. Oxford: Oxford University Press.

(1994a). The child's understanding of emotion: developmental change and the family environment. *Journal of Child Psychology and Psychiatry* 35: 3–28.

(1994b). Understanding pretence. In *Children's early understanding of mind,* ed. C. Lewis and P. Mitchell, pp. 235–60. Hillsdale, NJ: Erlbaum.

(1995). Imagining and pretending. In *Mental simulation,* ed. M. Davies and T. Stone, pp. 170–84. Oxford: Blackwel.

Harris, P. L., Brown, E., Marriott, C., Whittall, S., and Harmer, S. (1991). Monsters, ghosts and witches: testing the limits of the fantasy–reality distinction in young children. *British Journal of Developmental Psychology* 9: 105–23.

Harris, P. L., and Gross, D. (1988). Children's understanding of real and apparent emotion. In *Developing theories of mind*, ed. J. W. Astington, P. L. Harris and D. R. Olson, pp. 295–314. Cambridge: Cambridge University Press.

Harris, P. L., and Kavanaugh, R. D. (1993). Young children's understanding of pretense. *Monographs of the Society for Research in Child Development* 58: 1, serial no. 231.

Harris, P. L., Kavanaugh, R. D., and Meredith, M. (1994). Young children's comprehension of pretend episodes: the integration of successive actions. *Child Development* 65: 16–30.

Harris, P. L., Kruithof, A., Meerum Terwogt, M., and Visser, T. (1981). Children's detection and awareness of textual anomaly. *Journal of Experimental Child Psychology* 31: 212–30.

Harris, P. L., and Surman, G. (1994). Children's attribution of agency. Unpublished manuscript, Department of Experimental Psychology, University of Oxford.

Harter, S. (1986). Cognitive-developmental processes in the integration of concepts about emotions and the self. *Social Cognition* 4: 119–51.

Harter, S., and Buddin, B. J. (1987). Children's understanding of the simultaneity of two emotions: a five-stage developmental acquisition sequence. *Developmental Psychology* 23: 388–99.

Hartup, W. W. (1983). Peer relations. In *Handbook of child psychology*, vol. IV: *Socialization, personality, and social development*, ed. P. H. Mussen, pp. 103–96. New York: Wiley.

Hayes, K. J., and Hayes, C. (1951). The intellectual development of a home-raised chimpanzee. *Proceedings of the American Philosophical Society* 95: 105–9.

(1952). Imitation in a home-raised chimpanzee. *Journal of Comparative and Physiological Psychology* 45: 450–9.

Hayes, L. A., and Watson, J. S. (1981). Neonatal imitation: fact or artifact? *Developmental Psychology* 17: 655–60.

Heimann, M. (1989). Neonatal imitation, gaze aversion, and mother–infant interaction. *Infant Behavior and Development* 12: 495–505.

(1991). Neonatal imitation: a social and biological phenomenon. In *Behavioral biology*, ed. T. Archer and S. Hansen. Hillsdale, NJ: Erlbaum.

(1992). Neonatal imitation: integrating findings from three Swedish studies. *Göteborg Psychological Reports* 22(4).

(1994). Neonatal imitation – a fuzzy phenomenon? In C. v. Hofsten, F. Lacerda and M. Heimann (Chairs), Early development of perceptual, cognitive, and sensory-motor skills in young infants. International symposium, Grangärde, Sweden.

(1997). The never ending story of neonatal imitation. Poster presented at the VIIIth European Conference on Developmental Psychology, Rennes, France.

Heimann, M., Nelson, K. E., and Schaller, J. (1989). Neonatal imitation of tongue protrusion and mouth opening: methodological aspects and evidence of early individual differences. *Scandinavian Journal of Psychology* 30: 90–101.

Heimann, M., and Schaller, J. (1985). Imitative reactions among 14–21 day old infants. *Infant Mental Health Journal* 6: 31–9.

Heimann, M., and Ullstadius, E. (1997). Neonatal imitation and imitation among children with autism and Down syndrome. In *Imitation in infancy*, ed. J. Nadel and George Butterworth. Cambridge: Cambridge University Press.

Heimann, M., Ullstadius, E., Dahlgren, S.-O., and Gillberg, C. (1992). Imitation in autism – a preliminary research note. *Behavioural Neurology* 5: 219–27.

Heimann, M., Ullstadius, E., and Swerlander, A. (1997). *Imitation in eight young infants with Down syndrome*. Department of Psychology, Göteborg University, Sweden. Submitted for publication.

Hepper, P. G., Scott, D., and Shahidullah, S. (1993). Newborn and fetal response to maternal voice. *Journal of Reproductive and Infant Psychology* 11: 3, 147–53.

Herzig, M. E., Snow, M. E., and Sherman, M. (1989). Affect and cognition in autism. *Journal of the American Academy of Child and Adolescent Psychiatry* 28: 195–9.

Heyes, C. M. (1993). Imitation, culture and cognition. *Animal Behaviour* 46: 999–1010.

(1996). Genuine imitation. In *Social learning in animals: the roots of culture*, ed. C. M. Heyes and B. G. Galef, pp. 371–89. New York: Academic Press.

(in press). Theory of mind in nonhuman primates. *Behavioral and Brain Sciences*.

Heyes, C. M., Dawson, G. R., and Nokes, T. (1992). Imitation in rats: initial responding and transfer evidence. *Quarterly Journal of Experimental Psychology* 45B: 229–40.

Hinde, R. A. (1977). Mother–infant separation and the nature of inter-individual relationships: experiments with rhesus monkeys. *Proceedings of the Royal Society of London*, B, 196: 29–50.

(1981). Animal signals: ethological and games-theory approaches are not incompatible. *Animal Behaviour* 29: 535–42.

Hinde, R. A., and Bateson, P. (1984). Discontinuities versus continuities in behavioural development and the neglect of process. *International Journal of Behavioral Development* 7: 129–43.

Hobson, R. P. (1991a). Against the theory of 'theory of mind'. *British Journal of Developmental Psychology* 9: 33–51.

(1991b). Methodological issues for experiments on autistic individuals' perception and understanding of emotion. *Journal of Child Psychology and Psychiatry and Allied Disciplines* 32: 1135–58.

(1991c). What is autism? In *Psychiatric clinics of North America 14*, ed. M. Konstantareas and J. Beitchman, pp. 1–17.

(1993a). *Autism and the development of mind*. Hove, Sussex: Erlbaum.

(1993b). The emotional origins of interpersonal understanding. *Philosophical Psychology* 6: 227–49.

(1993c). Understanding persons: the rôle of affect. In *Understanding other minds: perspectives from autism*, ed. S. Baron-Cohen, H. Tager-Flusberg and D. Cohen, pp. 204–27. Oxford: Oxford University Press.

(1993d). Through feeling and sight to self and symbol. In *The perceived self*, ed. U. Neisser, pp. 254–79. Cambridge: Cambridge University Press.

(1994a). Perceiving attitudes, conceiving minds. In *Children's early understanding of mind*, ed. C. Lewis and P. Mitchell, pp. 71–93. Hillsdale, NJ: Erlbaum.

(1994b). Apprehending attitudes and actions: separable abilities in early development? *Development and Psychopathology* (in press).
Hoffman, M. L. (1975). Developmental synthesis of affect and cognition and its implications for altruistic motivation. *Developmental Psychology* 11: 607–22.
(1977). Empathy, its development and prosocial implications. In *Nebraska Symposium on Motivation*, vol. XXV, ed. C. B. Keasey, pp. 169–217. Lincoln: University of Nebraska Press.
(1981). Is altruism part of human nature? *Journal of Personality and Social Psychology* 40: 121–37.
(1982). Development of prosocial motivation: empathy and guilt. In *The development of prosocial behavior*, ed. N. Eisenberg, pp. 281–313. New York: Academic Press.
Holmlund, C. (1995). Development of turntakings as a sensorimotor process in the first 3 months: a sequential analysis. In *Children's language*, vol. VIII, ed. K. E. Nelson and Z. Réger, pp. 41–64. Hillsdale, NJ: Erlbaum.
Holstege, G., Bandler, R. and Saper, C. B. (eds.) (1997). *The emotional motor system*. Amsterdam: Elsevier.
Homer (1983). *Odysseia* (The Odyssey). Athens: OEDV.
Honey, R. C., Horn, G., and Bateson, P. (1993). Perceptual learning during filial imprinting: evidence from transfer of training studies. *Quarterly Journal of Experimental Psychology* 46B: 253–69.
Honey, R. C., Horn, G., Bateson, P., and Walpole, M. (1995). Functionally distinct memories for imprinting stimuli: behavioral and neural dissociations. *Behavioral Neuroscience* 109: 689–98.
Horn, G. (1985). *Memory, imprinting, and the brain*. Oxford: Clarendon Press.
(1991). Cerebral function and behaviour investigated through a study of filial imprinting. In *The development and integration of behaviour*, ed. P. Bateson, pp. 121–48. Cambridge: Cambridge University Press.
Horn, G., and McCabe, B. J. (1984). Predispositions and preferences. Effects on imprinting of lesions to the chick brain. *Animal Behaviour* 32: 288–92.
Howe, N., and Ross, H. (1990). Socialization, perspective-taking, and the sibling relationship. *Developmental Psychology* 26: 160–5.
Hubley, P., and Trevarthen, C. (1979). Sharing a task in infancy. In *Social interaction and communication during infancy*, ed. I. C. Uzgiris, pp. 57–80. San Francisco: Jossey Bass.
Hughes, C., and Russell, J. (1993). Autistic children's difficulty with mental disengagement from an object: its implications for theories of autism. *Developmental Psychology* 29: 498–510.
Humphrey, N. K. (1976). The social function of intellect. In *Growing points in ethology*, ed. P. P. G. Bateson and R. A. Hinde, pp. 303–17. Cambridge: Cambridge University Press.
(1980). Nature's psychologists. In *Consciousness and the physical world*, ed. B. Josephson and V. Ramachandran, pp. 57–80. London: Pergamon.
(1984). *Consciousness regained*. Oxford: Oxford University Press.
Hunt, M. (1993). *The story of psychology*. New York: Doubleday.
Hutcheson, F. (1755). *A system of moral philosophy*. Glasgow.
Huttenlocher, J., and Higgins, E. T. (1978). Issues in the study of symbolic development. In *Minnesota symposia on child development*, vol. XI, ed. W. A. Collins, pp. 98–140. Hillsdale, NJ: Erlbaum.
Inwood, B. (1984). Hierocles: theory and argument in the second century AD. In *Oxford studies in ancient philosophy*, vol. II, ed. J. Annas, pp. 151–83. Oxford: Clarendon Press.

Iverson, P., and Kuhl, P. (1995). Mapping the perceptual magnet effect for speech using signal detection theory and multidimensional scaling. *Journal of the Acoustical Society of America* 97: 553–62.

(1996). Influences of phonetic identification and category goodness on American listeners' perception of /r/ and /l/. *Journal of the Acoustical Society of America*, 99: 1130–40.

Izard, C. E. (1979). Emotions as motivations: an evolutionary-developmental perspective. In *Nebraska symposium on motivation 1978*, vol. XXVI, pp. 163–200. Lincoln and London: University of Nebraska Press.

(1992). Basic emotions, relations among emotions and emotion–cognition relations. *Psychological Review* 99: 561–5.

Izard, C. E., and Buechler, S. (1980). Aspects of consciousness and personality in terms of differential emotions theory. In *Emotion*, ed. R. Plutchik and H. Kellerman, pp. 165–87. New York: Academic Press.

Jacobsen, C. F., Jacobsen, M. M., and Yoshioka, J. G. (1932). Development of an infant chimpanzee during her first year. *Comparative Psychology Monographs* 9: 1094.

Jacobson, S. W. (1979). Matching behavior in the young infant. *Child Development* 50: 425–30.

Jaffe, J., Stern, D. N., and Peery, J. C. (1973). Conversational coupling of gaze behavior in prelinguistic human development. *Journal of Psycholinguistic Research* 2: 321–30.

James, W. (1884). What is an emotion? *Mind* 9: 188–205.

Jarrold, C., Boucher, J., and Smith, P. K. (1994). Generativity deficits in pretend play in autism. Unpublished manuscript, Department of Psychology, University of Sheffield.

Jeannerod, M. (1994). The representing brain: neural correlates of motor intention and imagery. *Behavioral and Brain Sciences* 17: 187–245.

Jersild, A. T. (1947). Emotional development. In *Manual of child psychology* (2nd edn), ed. L. Carmichael, pp. 833–917. New York: John Wiley.

Johnson, M. H., and Horn, G. (1986). Dissociation between recognition memory and associative learning by a restricted lesion to the chick forebrain. *Neuropsychologia* 24: 329–40.

(1988). Development of filial preferences in dark-reared chicks. *Animal Behaviour* 36: 675–83.

Johnson, M. H., and Morton, J. (1991). *Biology and cognitive development*. Oxford: Basil Blackwell.

Jolly, A. (1976). Lemur social behavior and primate intelligence. *Science* 153: 501–6.

Jones, V., and Prior, M. (1985). Motor imitation abilities and neurological signs in autistic children. *Journal of Autism and Developmental Disorders* 15: 37–46.

Jopling, D. (1993). Cognitive science, other minds and the philosophy of dialogue. In *The perceived self*, ed. U. Neisser, pp. 290–309. New York: Cambridge University Press.

Jordan, R. R. (1989). An experimental comparison of the understanding and use of speaker-addressee personal pronouns in autistic children. *British Journal of Disorders of Communication* 24: 169–79.

Josselson, R. (1996). *The space between us*. Thousand Oaks, CA: Sage (originally published San Francisco: Jossey Bass, 1992).

Kagan, J. (1982). The emergence of self. *Journal of Child Psychology and Psychiatry and Allied Disciplines* 23: 363–81.

Kaitz, M., Meschulach-Sarfaty, O., Auerbach, J., and Eidelman, A. (1988). A reexamination of newborns' ability to imitate facial expressions. *Developmental Psychology* 24: 3–7.

Kanner, L. (1943). Autistic disturbance of affective contact. *The Nervous Child* 2: 217–50.

Kaplan, L. J. (1977). The basic dialogue and the capacity for empathy. In *Communicative structures and psychic structures*, eds. N. Freedman and S. Grand, pp. 87–107. New York: Plenum.

Kasari, C., Sigman, M., Mundy, P., and Yirmiya, N. (1990). Affective sharing in the context of joint attention interactions of normal, autistic and mentally retarded children. *Journal of Autism and Developmental Disorders* 20: 87–100.

Kavanaugh, R. D., and Harris, P. L. (in press). Understanding the outcome of pretend transformations. *Developmental Psychology*.

Keller, H., and Gauda, G. (1987). Eye contact in the first month of life and its developmental consequences. In *Psychobiology and early development*, ed. H. Rauh and H.-Ch. Steinhausen, pp. 129–43. Amsterdam: Elsevier.

King, M. C., and Wilson, A. C. (1975). Evolution at two levels in humans and chimpanzees. *Science* 188: 107–16.

Kirk, G. S., Raven, J. E., and Schofield, M. (1983). *The presocratic philosophers*. Cambridge: Cambridge University Press.

Klaus, M. and Kennell, J. (1982). *Parent–infant bonding*. St Louis: Mosby.

Klein, M. (1957). *Envy and gratitude*. London: Tavistock; New York: Basic Books.

Klimes-Dogan, B., and Kistner, J. (1990). Physically abused preschoolers' responses to peers' distress. *Developmental Psychology* 26: 599–602.

Klinnert, M. D., Campos, J. J., Sorce, J. F., Emde, R. N., and Svejda, M. (1983). Emotions as behavior regulators: social referencing in infancy. In *Emotion*, vol. II: *Emotions in early development*, ed. R. Plutchik and H. Kellerman, pp. 57–86. New York: Academic Press.

Kochanska, G., and Thompson, R. A. (1997). The emergence and development of conscience in toddlerhood and early childhood. In *Parenting strategies and children's internalization of values*, ed. J. E. Grusec and L. Kuczynski, pp. 53–77. New York: Wiley.

Koepke, J. E., Hamm, M., Legerstee, M., and Russel, M. (1983). Neonatal imitation: two failures to replicate. *Infant Behavior and Development* 6: 97–102.

Kohut, H. (1977). *The restoration of the self*. New York: International Universities Press.

Kokkinaki, N. (1998). The contribution of imitation in infant–father and infant–mother interaction in two cultures. PhD thesis, Department of Psychology, University of Edinburgh (in preparation).

Koriat, A., Melkman, R., Averill, J. R., and Lazarus, R. S. (1972). The self-control of emotional reactions to a stressful film. *Journal of Personality* 40: 601–19.

Korner, A. F., and Thoman, E. B. (1972). The relative efficacy of contact and vestibular-proprioceptive stimulation in soothing neonates. *Child Development* 43: 443–53.

Kraemer, G. K. (1997). Psychobiology of early social attachment in rhesus monkeys. Clinical applications. *Annals of New York Academy of Sciences* 807: 401–18.

Kraut, M. (1982). Social presence, facial feedback, and emotion. *Journal of Personality and Social Psychology* 42: 853–63.

Krebs, J. R., and Dawkins, R. (1984). Animal signals: mind reading and manipulation. In *Behavioural ecology*, ed. J. R. Krebs and N. B. Davies. Oxford: Blackwell.

Kugiumutzakis, G. (1983). *Imitative phenomena*. MA thesis, Department of Psychology, University of Uppsala.

(1985a). The origin, development and function of the early infant imitation. PhD thesis, Department of Psychology, University of Uppsala.

(1985b). Development of imitation during the first six months of life (*Uppsala Psychological Reports* 377). Uppsala: Uppsala University.

(1988). I genesis tis anthropinis mimesis. (The origin of human imitation). *Psychologica Themata* 1(1): 5–21.

(1992a). Self-recognition as pre-condition of the infant imitative communication. Paper presented at the XIVth Congess of the International Primatological Society, Strasburg, 15–21 August.

(1992b). Phonitikes mimiseis stin epikinonia miteras–vrephous (Vocal imitations in mother–infant communication). In *Proodos stin anaptyxiaki psychologia ton proton chronon* (Progress in developmental psychology of the first years), ed. G. Kugiumutzakis, pp. 93–137. Heraklion: Crete University Press.

(1993). Intersubjective vocal imitation in early mother–infant interaction. In *New perspectives in early communicative development*, ed. J. Nadel and L. Camaioni, pp. 23–47. London: Routledge.

(1994). Is early human imitation an emotional phenomenon? Paper presented at the Symposium on 'Intersubjective Communication and Emotion in Ontogeny' in the Norwegian Academy of Science and Letters, Oslo, 25–30 August.

(1996). Psychologia ke o fthonos tis fysikis (Psychology and physics envy). In *I psychologia stin Hellada simera* (Psychology in Greece today), ed. F. Tsalikoglou, pp. 39–68. Athens: Plethron.

(in press). Origins and genesis of early infant mimesis to facial and vocal models. To appear in *Imitation in infancy*, ed. J. Nadel and G. Butterworth. Cambridge: Cambridge University Press.

Kuhl, P. K. (1991a). Human adults and human infants show a 'perceptual magnet effect' for the prototypes of speech categories, monkeys do not. *Perception and Psychophysics* 50: 93–107.

(1991b). Perception, cognition, and the ontogenetic and phylogenetic emergence of human speech. In *Plasticity of development*, ed. S. E. Brauth, W. S. Hall and R. J. Dooling, pp. 73–106. Cambridge, MA: MIT Press.

(1992a). Infants' perception and representation of speech: development of a new theory. In *Proceedings of the International Conference on Spoken Language Processing*, ed. J. J. Ohala, T. M. Nearey, B. L. Derwing, M. M. Hodge and G. E. Wiebe, pp. 449–56. Edmonton: University of Alberta.

(1992b). Psychoacoustics and speech perception: internal standards, perceptual anchors, and prototypes. In *Developmental psychoacoustics*, ed. L. A. Werner and E. W. Rubel, pp. 293–332. Washington, DC: American Psychological Association.

(1993). Innate predispositions and the effects of experience in speech perception: the native language magnet theory. In *Developmental neurocognition*, ed. B. de Boysson-Bardies *et al.*, pp. 259–74. Dordrecht: Kluwer.

(1994a). Learning and representation in speech and language. *Current Opinion in Neurobiology* 4: 812–22

(1994b). Speech perception. In *Introduction to communication sciences and disorders*, ed. F. D. Minifie, pp. 77–148. San Diego: Singular.

Kuhl, P. K., and Iverson, P. (1995). Linguistic experience and the 'perceptual magnet effect'. In *Speech perception and linguistic experience*, ed. W. Strange. Timonium, MD: York Press.

Kuhl, P. K., and Meltzoff, A. N. (1982). The bimodal perception of speech in infancy. *Science* 218: 1138–41.

(1995). Vocal learning in infants: development of perceptual-motor links for speech. *Proceedings of the XIIIth International Congress on Phonetic Sciences* 1: 146–9.

(1996). Infant vocalizations in response to speech: vocal imitation and developmental change. *Journal of the Acoustical Society of America* 100: 2425–38.

Kuhl, P. K., Tsuzaki, M., Tohkura, Y., and Meltzoff, A. N. (1994). Human processing of auditory-visual information in speech perception: potential for multimodal human–machine interfaces. In *Proceedings of the International Conference on Spoken Language Processing*, pp. 539–542. Tokyo: Acoustical Society of Japan.

Kuhl, P. K., Williams, K. A., Lacerda, F., Stevens, K. N., and Lindblom, B. (1992). Linguistic experience alters phonetic perception in infants by 6 months of age. *Science* 255: 606–8.

Kuhl, P. K., Yamada, R., Tohkura, Y., Iverson, P., Stevens, E. B., and Adachi, T. (1995). Language experience alters adults' 'perceptual maps' for speech. Under review.

Lacan, J. (1979). *The four fundamental concepts of psychoanalysis*. Harmondsworth: Penguin Books.

Lane, H. (1977). *The wild boy of Aveyron*. London: Granada.

Langer, S. K. (1957). *Philosophy in a new key* (3rd edn). Cambridge, MA: Harvard University Press.

Lazarus, R. (1991). Cognition and motivation in emotion. *American Psychologist* 46(4): 352–67.

Leahey, T. H. (1987). *A history of psychogy* (2nd edn). Englewood Cliffs, NJ: Prentice Hall.

Leavens, D. A., Hopkins, W. D., and Bard, K. A. (1996). Indexical and referential pointing in chimpanzees (*Pan troglodytes*). *Journal of Comparative Psychology* 110: 346–53.

Lecanuet, J.-P., Fifer, W. P., Krasnegor, N. A., and Smotherman, W. P. (eds.) (1995). *Fetal development*. Hillsdale, NJ: Erlbaum.

Lecanuet, J. P., and Granier-Deferre, C. (1993). Speech stimuli in the fetal environment. In *Developmental neurocognition*, ed. B. de Boysson-Bardies *et al.*, pp. 237–48. Dordrecht: Kluwer.

LeDoux, J. E. (1986). Sensory systems and emotion: a model of affective processing. *Integrative Psychiatry* 4: 237–48.

(1989). Cognitive-emotional interactions in the brain. *Cognition and Emotion* 3: 267–89.

(1993). Emotional systems in the brain. *Behavior and Brain Research* 58: 69–79.

(1994). Emotional memory: in search of systems and synapses. In *Brain Mechanisms*, ed. F. M. Crinella and J. Yu. New York: Annals of New York Academy of Sciences 702: 149–58.

Lee, A., Hobson, R. P., and Chiat, S. (1994). I, you, me and autism: an experimental study. *Journal of Autism and Developmental Disorders* 24: 155–76.

Lee, D. N., Craig, C. M. and Grealy, M. A. (1998). Coordinating movement using an intrinsic tau-guide (forthcoming).

Lee, P. C., Majluf, P., and Gordon, I. J. (1991). Growth, weaning and maternal investment from a comparative perspective. *Journal of Zoology* 225: 99–114.

Legerstee, M. (1991). The role of person and object in eliciting early imitation. *Journal of Experimental Child Psychology* 51: 423–33.

Leiderman, P. H., and Leiderman, G. (1977). Economic change and infant care in an East African agricultural community. In *Culture and infancy,* ed. P. Leiderman, S. Tulkin and A. Rosenfeld, pp. 405–38. New York: Academic Press.

Leiderman, P. H., Tulkin, S., and Rosenfeld, A. (1977). *Culture and infancy.* New York: Academic Press.

Lenneberg, E. H. (1967). *Biological foundations of language.* New York: Wiley.

Leslie, A. M. (1984). Infant perception of a manual pick up event. *British Journal of Developmental Psychology* 2: 19–32.

(1987). Pretense and representation: the origins of 'theory of mind'. *Psychological Review* 94: 412–26.

(1988). Some implications of pretence for mechanisms underlying the child's theory of mind. In *Developing theories of mind,* ed. J. W. Astington, P. L. Harris, and D. R. Olson, pp. 19–44. Cambridge: Cambridge University Press.

Leslie, A. M., and Happé, F. (1989). Autism and ostensive communication: the relevance of metarepresentation. *Development and Psychopathology* 1: 205–12.

Leslie, A. M., and Roth, D. (1993). What autism teaches us about metarepresentation. In *Understanding other minds: perspectives from autism,* ed. S. Baron-Cohen, H. Tager-Flusberg and D. Cohen. Oxford: Oxford University Press.

LeVine, R. A., Dixon, S., LeVine, S., Richman, A., Leiderman, P. H., Keefer, C. H., and Brazelton, T. B. (1994). *Child care and culture.* New York: Cambridge University Press.

LeVine, R. A., and LeVine, S. (1988). Mother–child interaction in diverse cultures. Guest lecture, University of Oslo, 22 August.

Lewis, C., and Mitchell, P. (eds.) (1994). *Children's early understanding of mind.* Hove: Erlbaum.

Lewis, V., and Boucher, J. (1988). Spontaneous, instructed and elicited play in relatively able autistic children. *British Journal of Developmental Psychology* 6: 325–39.

Lieven, E. V. M. (1994). Crosslinguistic and crosscultural aspects of language addressed to children. In *Input and interaction in language acquisition,* ed. C. Gallaway and B. J. Richards, pp. 56–73. Cambridge: Cambridge University Press.

Linell, P., and Markova, J. (1993). Acts in discourse: from monological speech acts to dialogical inter-acts. *Journal for the Theory of Social Behaviours* 23: 174–95.

Lock, A. (1980). *The guided reinvention of language.* London: Academic Press.

Lock, A. (ed.) (1978). *Action, gesture and symbol.* New York: Academic Press.

Locke, J. L. (1993). *The child'spath to spoken language.* Cambridge MA and London: Harvard University Press.

Lockyer, L., and Rutter, M. (1970). A five to fifteen year follow-up study of infantile psychosis: IV Patterns of cognitive ability. *British Journal of Social and Clinical Psychology* 9: 152–63.

Long, A. A., and Sedley, D. N. (1987). *The Hellinistic philosophers*, 2 vols. Cambridge: Cambridge University Press.

Lorenz, K. (1971). *Studies in animal and human behaviour*, vol. I. Cambridge, MA: Harvard University Press.

Loveland, K. A., and Landry, S. H. (1986). Joint attention and language in autism and developmental language delay. *Journal of Autism and Developmental Disorders* 16: 335–49.

Loveland, K. A., Tunali, B., Kelley, M. L., and McEvoy, R. E. (1989). Referential communication and response adequacy in autism and Down's syndrome. *Applied Psycholinguistics* 10: 301–13.

Luria, A. R., and Vygotsky, L. S. (1992). *Ape, primitive man and child*. New York: Harvester-Wheatsheaf.

Maccoby, E. E. 1988. Gender as a social category. *Developmental Psychology* 24: 755–65.

McFarlane, J. (1975). Olfaction in the development of social preferences in the human neonate. In *Parent–infant interaction*, ed. M. Hofer, Amsterdam: Elsevier.

McGregor, E., Whiten, A., and Blackburn, P. (1998). Teaching theory of mind by highlighting intention and illustrating thoughts: a comparison of their effectiveness with three-year-olds and autistic subjects. *British Journal of Developmental Psychology* (in press).

McGurk, H., and MacDonald, J. (1976). Hearing lips and seeing voices. *Nature* 264: 746–8.

MacKain, K., Studdert-Kennedy, M., Spieker, S., and Stern, D. (1983). Infant intermodal speech perception is a left-hemisphere function. *Science* 219: 1347–9.

McKenzie, B., and Over, R. (1983). Young infants fail to imitate facial and manual gestures. *Infant Behavior and Development* 6: 85–95.

MacLean, P. D. (1970). The triune brain, emotion, and scientific bias. In *The Neuroscience second study program*, ed. F. O. Schmitt, pp. 336–49. New York: The Rockefeller University Press.

Macmurray, J. (1961). *Persons in relation* (vol. II of *The form of the personal*). London: Faber and Faber.

Mahler, M. S., Pine, F., and Bergman, A. (1975). *The psychological birth of the human infant*. New York: Basic Books.

Main, M., and George, C. (1985). Responses of abused and disadvantaged children to distress in agemates. *Developmental Psychology* 21: 407–12.

Malatesta, C. Z., Culver, C., Tesman, J. R., and Shepard, B. (1989). The development of emotion expression during the first two years of life. *Monographs of the Society for Research in Child Development* 54 (serial no. 219).

Malatesta, C. Z., Grigoryev, P., Lamb, C., Albin, M., and Gulver, C. (1986). Emotion socialization and expressive development in preterm and full-term infants. *Child Development* 57: 316–30.

Malatesta, C. Z., and Haviland, J. M. (1982). Learning display rules: the socialization of emotional expression in infancy. *Child Development* 53: 991–1003.

Malloch, S. N., Sharp, D., Campbell, A. M., and Trevarthen, C. (1997). Measuring the human voice: analysing pitch, timing and loudness quality in mother/infant communication. (Proceedings of the International Symposium on Musical Acoustics, Edinburgh, 19–22 August 1997), *Proceedings of the Institute of Acoustics* 19.

Maratos, O. (1973). The origin and development of imitation in the first six months of life. PhD thesis, Department of Psychology, Geneva University. (Also as paper presented at the Annual Meeting of the British Psychological Society, Liverpool).

(1982). Trends in the development of imitation in early infancy. In *Regressions in mental development*, ed. T. G. Bever, pp. 81–101. Hillsdale, NJ: Erlbaum.

(1996). Newborn and infant imitation: a case of intersubjective communication. Paper presented at the Second European Research Conference on The Development of Sensory, Motor and Cognitive Abilities in Early Infancy, Barcelona, Spain, April.

Marcel, G. (1950). *Mystery of being*, vol. I. London: The Harvill Press.

Marcos, H. (1991). Reformulating requests at 18 months: gestures, vocalizations, and first words. *First Language* 11: 361–75.

Marcos, H., and Kornhaber-le Chanu, M. (1992). Learning how to insist and clarify in the second year: reformulation of requests in different contexts. *International Journal of Behavioral Development* 15: 359–76.

Marian, V., Neisser, U., and Rochat, P. (1996). Infants' sensitivity to interpersonal contingency: an attempt to replicate Murray and Trevarthen. Paper presented at the International Conference of Infant Studies, Providence, April.

Marler, P. (1980). Primate vocalization: affective or symbolic? In *Speaking of apes*, ed. T. Sebeok and J. Umiker-Sebeok, pp. 221–9. New York: Plenum Press.

(1991). Differences in behavioural development in closely related species: birdsong. In *The development and integration of behaviour*, ed. P. Bateson, pp. 41–70. Cambridge: Cambridge University Press.

Martin, G. B., and Clark, R. D. (1982). Distress crying in neonates: species and peer specificity. *Developmental Psychology* 18: 3–9.

Martini, M., and Kirkpatrick, J. (1981). Early interactions in the Marquesas Islands. In *Culture and early interactions*, ed. T. M. Field, A. M. Sostek, P. Vietze and P. H. Leiderman, pp. 189–214. Hillsdale, NJ: Erlbaum.

Masters, J. C. (1979). Interpreting 'imitative' response in early infancy. *Science* 205: 215.

Mathieu, M., and Bergeron, G. (1981). Piagetian assessment of cognitive development in chimpanzees (*Pan troglodytes*). In *Primate behavior and sociobiology*, ed. A. B. Chiarelli and R. S. Corruccini. New York: Springer-Verlag.

Maurer, D., and Maurer, C. (1988). *The world of the newborn*. New York: Basic Books.

Maynard Smith, J. (1994). Must reliable signals always be costly? *Animal Behaviour* 47: 1115–20.

Mead, G. H. (1934). *Mind, self, and society*. Chicago: University of Chicago Press.

Meerum Terwogt, M., Schene, J., and Harris, P. L. (1986). Self-control of emotional reactions by young children. *Journal of Child Psychology and Psychiatry* 27: 357–66.

Mehler, J., Jusczyk, P., Lambertz, G., Halsted, N., Bertoncini, J., and Amiel-Tison, C. (1988). A precursor of language acquisition in young infants. *Cognition* 29: 143–78.

Meltzoff, A. N. (1981). Imitation, intermodal coordination, and representation in early infancy. In *Infancy and epistemology*, ed. G. Butterworth, pp. 85–114. Brighton: Harvester Press.

(1985). The roots of social and cognitive development: models of man's original nature. In *Social perception in infants*, ed. T. M. Field and N. Fox, pp. 1–30. Norwood, NJ: Albex.

(1988). Infant imitation and memory: nine-month-olds in immediate and deferred tests. *Child Development* 59: 217–25.

(1990). Foundations for developing a concept of self: the role of imitation in relating self to other and the value of social mirroring, social modeling, and self practice in infancy. In *The self in transition*, ed. D. Cicchetti and M. Beeghly, pp. 139–64. Chicago: University of Chicago Press.

(1995). Understanding the intentions of others: re-enactment of intended acts by 18-month-old children. *Developmental Psychology* 31: 838–50.

(1996). The human infant as imitative generalist: a 20-year progress report on infant imitation with implications for comparative psychology. In *Social learning in animals*, ed. B. G. Galef and C. M. Heyes, pp. 347–70. New York: Academic Press.

Meltzoff, A. N., and Borton, W. (1979). Intermodal matching in human neonates. *Nature* 282: 403–4.

Meltzoff, A. N., and Gopnik, A. (1993). The role of imitation in understanding persons and developing a theory of mind. In *Understanding other minds*, ed. S. Baron-Cohen, H. Tager-Flusberg and D. J. Cohen, pp. 335–66. Oxford: Oxford University Press.

Meltzoff, A. N., and Kuhl, P. K. (1994). Faces and speech: Intermodal processing of biologically relevant signals in infants and adults. In *The development of intersensory perception*, ed. D. J. Lewkowicz and R. Lickliter, pp. 335–69. Hillsdale, NJ: Erlbaum.

Meltzoff, A. N., and Moore, M. K. (1977). Imitation of facial and manual gestures by human neonates. *Science* 198: 75–8.

(1983a). Newborn infants imitate adult facial gestures. *Child Development* 54: 702–9.

(1983b). The origins of imitation in infancy: paradigm, phenomena and theories. In *Advances in infancy research*, vol. II, ed. L. P. Lipsitt, pp. 266–301. Norwood, NJ: Albex.

(1989). Imitation in newborn infants: exploring the range of gestures imitated and the underlying mechanisms. *Developmental Psychology* 25: 954–62.

(1992). Early imitation within a functional framework: the importance of person identity, movement, and development. *Infant Behavior and Development* 15: 479–505.

(1994). Imitation, memory, and the representation of persons. *Infant Behavior and Development* 17: 83–99.

(1995). Infants' understanding of people and things: from body imitation to folk psychology. In *The body and the self*, ed. J. Bermúdez, A. J. Marcel and N. Eilan, pp. 43–69. Cambridge, MA: MIT Press.

(1997). Explaining facial imitation: a theoretical model. *Early development and parenting* 6:179-92.

(1998). Object representation, identity, and the paradox of early permanence. *Infant Behavior and Development* 21: 200–36.

Merlean-Ponty, M. (1962). *Phenomenology of perception*. London: Routledge.

Michotte, A. (1946/1963). *The perception of causality.* London: Methuen.

Miller, N. E., and Dollard, J. (1941). *Social learning and imitation.* New Haven: Yale University Press.

Mitchell, R. W. (1993). Mental models of mirror-self-recognition: two theories. *New Ideas in Psychology* 11: 295–325.

Miyawaki, K., Strange, W., Verbrugge, R., Liberman, A. M., Jenkins, J. J., and Fujimura, O. (1975). An effect of linguistic experience: the discrimination of [r] and [l] by native speakers of Japanese and English. *Perception and Psychophysics* 18: 331–40.

Mock, D. W., and Forbes, L. S. (1992). Parent–offspring conflict: a case of arrested development. *Trends in Ecology and Evolution* 7: 409–13.

Moon, C., Cooper, R. P., and Fifer, W. P. (1993). Two-day-olds prefer their native language. *Infant Behavior and Development,* 16: 495–500.

Moore, C., and Corkum, V. (1994). Social understanding at the end of the first year of life. *Developmental Review* 14: 349–72.

Moore, C., and Dunham, P. (eds.) (1995). *Joint attention.* Hillsdale, NJ: Erlbaum.

Moore, M. K. (1990). Foundations for developing a concept of self. In *The self in transition,* ed. D. Cicchetti and M. Beeghly, pp. 139–64. Chicago: University of Chicago Press.

Moore, M. K., Borton, R., and Darby, B. L. (1978). Visual tracking in young infants: evidence for object identity or object permanence? *Journal of Experimental Child Psychology* 25: 183–98.

Moore, M. K., and Meltzoff, A. N. (1978). Object permanence, imitation, and language development in infancy: toward a neo-Piagetian perspective on communicative and cognitive development. In *Communicative and cognitive abilities,* ed. F. D. Minifie and L. L. Lloyd, pp. 151–84. Baltimore: University Park Press.

Morelli, G. A., and Tronick, E. Z. (1991). Parenting and child development in the Efe foragers and Lese farmers of Zaire. In *Cultural approaches to parenting,* ed. M. H. Bornstein, pp. 91–113. Hillsdale, NJ: Erlbaum.

Morgan, S. B., Cutrer, P. S., Coplin, J. W., and Rodrigue, J. R. (1989). Do autistic children differ from retarded and normal children in Piagetian sensorimotor functioning? *Journal of Child Psychology and Psychiatry* 30: 857–64.

Morrow, D. G., Greenspan, S., and Bower, G. (1987). Accessibility and situation models in narrative comprehension. *Journal of Memory and Language* 26: 165–87.

Morton, J. (1970). A functional model for memory. In *Models of human memory,* ed. D. A. Norman, pp. 203–54. New York: Academic Press.

Morton, J., and Johnson, M. H. (1991). CONSPEC and CONLERN: a two-process theory of infant face recognition. *Psychological Review* 98: 164–81.

Moscovici, S. (1961). *La psychoanalyse.* Paris: PVF.

Muir, D. W., and Hains, S. M. J. (1993). Infant sensitivity to perturbations in adult facial, vocal, tactile, and contingent stimulation during face-to-face interactions. In *Developmental neurocognition,* ed. B. de Boysson-Bardies *et al.,* pp. 171–85. Dordrecht: Kluwer.

Mundy, P., Sigman, M., and Kasari, C. (1993). Theory of mind and joint attention deficits in autism. In *Understanding other minds,* ed. S. Baron-Cohen, H. Tager-Flusberg and D. Cohen. Oxford: Oxford University Press.

Mundy, P., Sigman, M., Ungerer, J., and Sherman, T. (1986). Defining the social deficits of autism: the contribution of non-verbal communication measures. *Journal of Child Psychology and Psychiatry and Allied Disciplines* 27: 657–69.

Munroe, R. H., and Munroe, R. L. (1971). Household density and infant care in an East African society. *Journal of Social Psychology* 83: 3–13.

Munroe, R. H., Munroe, R. L., and Shimmin, H. S. (1984). Children's work in

four cultures: determinants and consequences. *American Anthropologist* 86: 369–79.
Murphy, L. B. (1937). *Social behavior and personality.* New York: Columbia University Press.
Murray, L. (1980). The sensitivities and expressive capacities of young infants in communication with their mothers. PhD thesis, University of Edinburgh.
(1988). Effects of post-natal depression on infant development: direct studies of early mother–infant interactions. In *Motherhood and mental illness*, vol. II, ed. I. Brockington and R. Kumar. Bristol: John Wright.
(1991). Intersubjectivity, Object Relations Theory, and empirical evidences from mother–infant interactions. *Infant Mental Health Journal* 12: 219–32.
(1992). The impact of postnatal depression on infant development. *Journal of Child Psychology and Psychiatry* 33: 543–561.
(1994). The development of the 5 year old children of postnatally depressed and well mothers. Paper presented at the Marce Society Conference, Cambridge, September 1994.
Murray, L., and Cooper, P. J. (eds.) (1997). *Postpartum depression and child development*. New York: Guilford Press.
Murray, L., Fiori-Cowley, A., Hooper, R., and Cooper, P. J. (1996). The impact of postnatal depression and associated adversity on early mother infant interactions and later infant outcome. *Child Development* 67: 2512–26.
Murray, L., Hipwell, A., Hooper, R., Stein, A., and Cooper, P. (1996). The cognitive development of 5-year-old children of postnatally depressed mothers. *Journal of Child Psychology and Psychiatry* 37: 927–35.
Murray, L., Kempton, C., Woolgar, M., and Hooper, R. (1993). Depressed mothers' speech to their infants and its relation to infant gender and cognitive development. *Journal of Child Psychology and Psychiatry* 34: 1083–01.
Murray, L., and Trevarthen, C. (1985). Emotional regulation of interactions between two-month-olds and their mothers. In *Social perception in infants*, ed. T. M. Field and N. A. Fox, pp. 177–97. Norwood, NJ: Ablex.
(1986). The infant's role in mother–infant communication. *Journal of Child Language* 13: 15–29.
Nadel, J. (1980). The functional role of imitation in personality development: Wallon's contribution. *French-Language Psychology* 1: 169–77.
Nadel, J., and Pezé, A. (1993). What makes immmediate imitation communicative in toddlers and autistic children. In *New perspectives in early communicative development*, ed. J. Nadel and L. Camaioni, pp. 139–56. London: Routledge.
Naess, A. (1953). *Interpretation and preciseness.* Oslo: The Norwegian Academy of Science.
Nagy, E., and Molnár, P. (1994). *Homo imitans* or *Homo provocans*? Abstract, *International Journal of Psychophysiology* 18(2): 128.
(1997). Imprinting and stress in early development. Poster, International Congress of Stress, Budapest, 1–5 July 1997.
Nakano, S. (1994). Developmental changes in young children's understanding of their mothers' play intentions during playful teasing. Paper presented at the 13th Biennial Meeting of the International Society for the Study of Behavioral Development, 28 June–2 July, 1994, Amsterdam.
Nakano, S. and Kanaya, Y. (1993). The effects of mothers' teasing: Do Japanese

infants read their mothers' play intention in teasing? *Early Development and Parenting* 2(1): 7–17.

Neisser, U. (1988). Five kinds of self-knowledge. *Philosophical Psychology* 1: 35–59.

(1993). The self perceived. In *The perceived self,* ed. U. Neisser, pp. 3–21. Cambridge: Cambridge University Press.

Nelson, K. (1986). *Event knowledge.* Hillsdale, NJ: Erlbaum.

Newson, J. (1977). An intersubjective approach to the systematic description of mother–infant interaction. In *Studies in mother–infant interaction,* ed. H. R. Schaffer, pp. 47–61. London: Academic Press.

(1979). The growth of shared understandings between infant and caregiver. In *Before speech,* ed. M. Bullowa, pp. 207–22. Cambridge: Cambridge University Press.

Newton, P. (1994). Preschool prevarication: an investigation of the cognitive prerequisites for deception. PhD thesis, University of Portsmouth.

Nicoll, C. S., and Meites, J. (1959). Prolongation of lactation in the rat by litter replacement. *Proceedings of the Society of Experimental Biology and Medicine* 10: 81–2.

Nieuwenhuys, R. (1996). The greater limbic system, the emotional motor system and the brain. In *The emotional motor system,* ed. G. Holstege, R. Bandler and C. B. Saper. Amsterdam: Elsevier.

Nussbaum, M. C. (1992). Tragedy and self-sufficiency: Plato and Aristotle on fear and pity. In *Oxford studies in ancient philosophy,* vol. X, ed. J. Annas, pp. 107–59. Oxford: Clarendon Press.

Nussbaum, M. C., and Rorty, A. O. (eds.) (1992). *Essays on Aristotle's De anima.* Oxford: Clarendon Press.

Oatley, K. (1992). *Best laid schemes.* Cambridge: Cambridge University Press.

Ohta, M. (1987). Cognitive disorders of infantile autism: a study employing the WISC, spatial relationship conceptualization, and gesture imitation. *Journal of Autism and Developmental Disorders* 17: 45–62.

O'Keefe, J. (1985). Is consciousness the gateway to the hippocampal cognitive map? In *Brain and mind,* ed. D. A. Oakley, pp. 59–98. London: Methuen.

(1992). Self consciousness and allocentric maps. Paper presented at the King's College Research Centre, Workshop on Perception of Subjects and Objects, Cambridge, 17–22 September.

O'Neill, D. K. (1996). Two-year-old children's sensitivity to a parent's knowledge state when making requests. *Child Development* 67: 659–77.

O'Rahilly, R. and Müller, F. (1994). *The embryonic human brain.* New York: Wiley-Liss.

Osgood, C. E. (1962). Study on the generality of affective meaning systems. *American Psychologists* 7: 10–28.

Oster, H., and Ekman, P. (1978). Facial behavior in child development. In *Minnesota Symposium on Child Psychology,* vol. II, ed. W. A. Collins, pp. 231–76. Hillsdale, NJ: Erlbaum.

Osterling, J., and Dawson, G. (1994). Early recognition of children with autism: a study of first birthday home videotapes. *Journal of Autism and Developmental Disorders* 24: 247–57.

Ozonoff, S., Pennington, B. F., and Rogers, S. J. (1991). Executive function deficits in high-functioning autistic individuals: relationship to theory of mind. *Journal of Child Psychology and Psychiatry and Allied Disciplines* 32: 1081–1105.

Paillard, J. (1960). The patterning of skilled movements. *Handbook of Physiology; Section I: Neurophysiology,* vol. III: pp. 1679–1707. Washington, DC: American Physiological Society.

Palameta, B. (1989). The importance of socially transmitted information in the acquisition of novel foraging skills by pigeons and canaries. PhD thesis, University of Cambridge.

Palameta, B., and Lefebvre, L. (1985). The social transmission of a food technique in pigeons: what is learned. *Animal Behaviour* 33: 892–6.

Panksepp, J. (1992). A critical role for 'affective neuroscience' in resolving what is basic about basic emotions. *Psychological Review* 99(3): 554–60.

Papadopoulos, T. (1979). *Democritos.* Athens: Athanasopoulos.

Papousek, H. (1967). Experimental studies of appetitional behavior in human newborns and infants. In *Early behavior,* ed. H. W. Stevenson, E. H. Hess and H. L. Rheingold. New York: Wiley.

Papousek, H., and Bornstein, M. H. (1992). Didactic interactions: intuitive parental support of vocal and verbal development in human infants. In *Nonverbal vocal communication: comparative and developmental aspects.* ed. H. Papousek, U. Jurgens and M. Papousek, pp. 209–29. Cambridge: Cambridge University Press/Paris: Editions de la Maison des Sciences de l'Homme.

Papousek, H., and Papousek, M. (1975). Cognitive aspects of preverbal social interaction between human infants and adults. In *Parent–infant interaction,* ed. E. Hofer, pp. 241–69. Amsterdam: Elsevier.

(1977). Mothering and the cognitive head-start: psychobiological considerations. In *Studies in mother–infant interaction,* ed. H. R. Schaffer, pp. 63–85. London: Academic Press.

(1987). Intuitive parenting: a dialectic counterpart to the infant's integrative competence. In *Handbook of infant development* (2nd edn), pp. 669–720, ed. J. D. Osofsky. New York: Wiley.

(1997). Fragile aspects of early social interaction. In *Postpartum depression and child development,* ed. L. Murray and P. J. Cooper, pp. 35–53. New York: Guilford Press.

Papousek, M. (1994). Melodies in caregivers' speech: a species specific guidance towards language. *Early Development and Parenting* 3: 5–17.

Papousek, M., and Papousek, H. (1989). Forms and functions of vocal matching in interactions between mothers and their precanonical infants. *First Language* 9: 137–58.

Papousek, M., Papousek, H., and Symmes, D. (1991). The meanings and melodies in motherese in tone and stress languages. *Infant Behavior and Development* 14: 415–40.

Parton, D. A. (1976). Learning to imitate in infancy. *Child Development* 47: 14–31.

Pawlby, S. J. (1977). Imitative interactions. In *Studies in mother–infant interaction,* ed. H. R. Schaffer, pp. 203–24. London: Academic Press.

Peirce, C. S. (1977). *Semiotics and signifiers: the correpondence between Charles S. Peirce and Lady Wilby.* Indianapolis: Indiana University Press.

Peng, M., Johnson, C., Pollock, J., Glasspool, R., and Harris, P. L. (1992). Training young children to acknowledge mixed emotions. *Cognition and Emotion* 6: 387–401.

Pereira, M. E. (1988). Effects of age and sex on intragroup spacing behavior in juvenile savanna baboons (*Papio cynocephalus cynocephalus*). *Animal Behavior* 36: 184–204.

Pereira, M. E., and Fairbanks, L. A. (eds.) (1993). *Juvenile primates*. New York: Oxford University Press.

Perinat, A., and Dalmáu, A. (1989). La comunicación entre pequeños gorilas criados en cautividad y sus cuidadoras. *Estudios de Psicología* 32–4: 11–29.

Perner, J. (1991). *Understanding the representational mind*. Cambridge, MA: MIT Press.

(1993). The theory of mind deficit in autism: rethinking the metarepresentational theory. In *Understanding other minds*, ed. S. Baron-Cohen, H. Tager-Flusberg and D. Cohen. Oxford: Oxford University Press.

Pettit, G. S., and Bates, J. E. (1989). Family interaction patterns and children's behavior problems from infancy to 4 years. *Developmental Psychology* 25: 413–20.

Piaget, J. (1926/1959). *The language and thought of the child*. London: Routledge.

(1932/1977). *The moral judgement of the child*. London: Routledge and Kegan Paul.

(1935). Les théories de l'imitation. *Cahiers de Pédagogie Expérimentale et de Psychologie de l'Enfant* 6: 1–13.

(1936/1977). *The origin of intelligence in the child*. Harmondsworth: Penguin.

(1945/1962). *Play, dreams, and imitation in childhood*. New York: Norton.

(1954). *The construction of reality in the child*. New York: Basic Books.

(1968). *Six psychological studies*. New York: Vintage Books.

Piaget, J., and Inhelder, B. (1969). *The psychology of the child*. New York: Basic Books.

Pinker, S. (1994). *The language instinct*. London and New York: Penguin Books.

Plato (1963). *Kratylos* (Cratylus), vol. XIII; *Kritias* (Critias), vol. III; *Nomoi* (Laws), vol. XIV; *Menon* (Meno), vol. V; *Phaidon* (Phaedo), vol. II; *Phaidros* (Phaedrus), vol. XIII; *Politikos* (Politicus), vol. IX; *Politeia* (Republic), vols. V–VIII; *Sophistis* (Sophist), vol. XII; *Timaios* (Timaeus), vol. XI. Athens: Etaireia Hellinikon Ekdoseon.

(1975). *Laws*. Harmondsworth: Penguin Books.

(1980). *The Republic*. Harmondsworth: Penguin Books.

Ploog, D. (1992). The evolution of vocal communication. In Papousek, H., Jurgens, U. and Papousek, M., *Nonverbal vocal communication*. Cambridge: Cambridge University Press.

Plooij, F. X. (1979). How wild chimpanzee babies trigger the onset of mother–infant play and what the mother makes of it. In *Before speech*, ed. M. Bullowa, pp. 223–43. Cambridge: Cambridge University Press.

(1984). The behavioral development of free-living chimpanzee babies and infants. *Monographs on infancy*, vol. III. Norwood, NJ: Ablex.

Plutchik, R. (1987). Evolutionary bases of empathy. In *Empathy and its development*, ed. N. Eisenberg and J. Strayer, pp. 38–46. Cambridge: Cambridge University Press.

Pöppel, E. (1994). Temporal mechanisms in perception. *International Review of Neurobiology* 37: 185–202.

Povinelli, D. J. (1996). Chimpanzee theory of mind? The long road to strong inference. In *Theories of theories of mind*, ed. P. Carruthers and P. K. Smith, pp. 293–329. Cambridge: Cambridge University Press.

Povinelli, D. J., and Eddy, T. J. (1996). What young chimpanzees know about seeing. *Monographs of the Society for Research in Child Development*, vol. LXI, no. 2, serial no. 247.

Prechtl, H. F. R. (1982). Assessment methods for the newborn infant: a critical evaluation. In *Psychobiology of the human newborn*, ed. P. Stratton, pp. 21–52. New York: Wiley.

Prechtl, H. F. R., and O' Brien, M. J. (1982). Behavioral states of the fullterm newborn: The emergence of a concept. In *Psychobiology of the human newborn*, ed. P. Stratton, pp. 53–73. New York: Wiley.

Premack, D. (1972). Teaching language to an ape. *Scientific American* 227: 921–99.

(1990). Words: what are they, and do animals have them? *Cognition* 37: 197–212.

Premack, D., and Woodruff, G. (1978). Does the chimpanzee have a theory of mind? *Behavioral and Brain Sciences* 1: 515–26.

Price, J. L., Carmichael, S. T., and Drevets, W. C. (1996). Networks related to the orbital and medial prefrontal cortex; a substrate for emotional behavior? In *The emotional motor system*, ed. G. Holstege, R. Bandler and C. B. Saper, pp. 523–36. Amsterdam: Elsevier Science BV.

Putnam, H. (1981). *Reason, truth, and history.* Cambridge: Cambridge University Press.

Pylyshyn, Z. W. (1980). Computation and cognition: issues in the foundations of cognitive science. *Behavioral and Brain Sciences* 3: 111–69.

Ratner, N., and Bruner, J. S. (1978). Games, social exchange and the acquisition of language. *Journal of Child Language* 5: 391–400.

Reddy, M. (1979). The conduit matephor – a case of frame conflict in our language about language. In *Metaphor and thought*, ed. A. Certoney, pp. 284–324. Cambridge: Cambridge University Press.

Reddy, V. (1991). Playing with others' expectations: teasing and mucking about in the first year. In *Natural theories of mind*, ed. A. Whiten, pp. 143–58. Oxford: Basil Blackwell.

Reddy, V., Hay, D., Murray, L. and Trevarthen, C. (1997). Communication in infancy: mutual regulation of affect and attention. In *Infant development*, ed. G. Bremner, A. Slater and G. Butterworth, pp. 247–74. Hove: Psychology Press.

Redshaw, M. E. (1989). A comparison of neonatal behavior and reflexes in the great apes. *Journal of Human Evolution* 18: 191–200.

Reisenzein, R., and Schönpflug, W. (1992). Stumpf's cognitive-evaluative theory of emotion. *American Psychologist* 47: 34–45.

Reissland, N. (1988). Neonatal imitation in the first hour of life: Observations in rural Nepal. *Developmental Psychology* 24: 464–9.

Richman, A. L., LeVine, R. A., New, R. S., Howrigan, G. A., Wells-Nystrom, B., and LeVine, S. E. (1988). Maternal behavior to infants in five cultures. In *Parental behavior in diverse societies*, ed. R. A. LeVine, P. M. Miller and M. M. West, pp. 81–98. San Francisco: Jossey Bass.

Ricks, D. M. (1975). Vocal communication in pre-verbal normal and autistic children. In *Language, cognitive deficits, and retardation*, ed. N. O'Connor, pp. 75–80. London: Butterworths.

Ricks, D. M., and Wing, L. (1975). Language, communication and the use of symbols in normal and autistic children. *Journal of Autism and Childhood Schizophrenia* 5: 191–221.

Rijt-Plooij, H. van de, and Plooij, F. X. (1987). Growing independence, conflict, and learning in mother–infant relations in free-ranging chimpanzees. *Behavior* 101: 1–86.

(1993). Distinct periods of mother–infant conflict in normal development:

sources of progress and germs of pathology. *Journal of Child Psychology and Psychiatry* 34: 229–45.

Rinn, W. E. (1984). The neuropsychology of facial expression: a review of the neurological and psychological mechanisms for producing facial expressions. *Psychological Bulletin* 1: 52–77.

Ritvo, S., and Provence, S. (1953). Form perception and imitation in some autistic children: diagnostic findings and their contextual interpretation. *The Psychoanalytic Study of the Child* 8: 155–61.

Rizzolati, G., Camarda, R., Fogassi, M., Gentilucci, M., Luppino, G., and Matelli, M. (1988). Functional organization of interior area 6 in the macaque monkey. *Experimental Brain Research* 71: 491–507.

Rogers, C. M., and Davenport, R. K. (1970). Chimpanzee maternal behavior. *The chimpanzee* 3: 361–8. New York: Karger, Basel.

Rogers, S. J., and McEvoy, R. E. (1992). *Praxis in high functioning persons with autism*. Unpublished manuscript, University of Colorado.

Rogers, S. J., and Pennington, B. F. (1991). A theoretical approach to the deficits in infantile autism. *Development and Psychopathology* 3: 137–62.

Rogoff, B., Mistry, J., Goncu, A., and Mosier, C. (1993). Guided participation in cultural activity by toddlers and caregivers. *Monographs of the Society for Research in Child Development* 58(8), series no. 236.

Rolls, E. T. (1992). Neurophysiological mechanisms underlying face processing within and beyond the temporal visual cortical areas. *Philosophical Transactions of the Royal Society of London*, Series B, 335: 11–21.

Rommetveit, R. (1968). *Words, meanings and messages*. New York and London: Academic Press.

(1974). *On message structure*. New York: Wiley.

(1990). On axiomatic features of a dialogical approach to language and mind. In *The dynamics of dialogue*, ed. I. Markova and K. Foppa, pp. 83–104. New York: Harvester Wheatsheaf.

(1992). Outlines of a dialogically based social-cognitive approach to human cognition and communication. In *The dialogical alternative*, ed. A. H. Wold, pp. 19–44. Oslo: Scandinavian University Press.

Rommetveit, R., and Hundeide, K. (1967). Emotive and representational components of meaning in word sorting and recall. *Pedagogisk Forskning* 11: 47–59.

Ronnqvist, L. (1993). Arm and hand movements in neonates and young infants. PhD thesis, University of Umea.

Ross, E. D. (1996). Hemispheric specialization for emotions, affective aspects of language and communication and the cognitive control of display behaviors in humans. In *The emotional motor system*, eds. G. Holstege, R. Bandler and C. B. Saper, pp. 583–94. Amsterdam: Elsevier.

Rothenberg, B. (1970). Children's social sensitivity and the relationship to interpersonal competence, intrapersonal comfort, and intellectual level. *Developmental Psychology* 2: 335–50.

Runeson, S. (1977). On the possibility of 'smart' perceptual mechanisms. *Scandinavian Journal of Psychology* 18: 172–9.

(1983). On visual perception of dynamic events (originally published 1977). *Acta Universitatis Upsaliensis: Studia Psychologica Upsaliensia* (serial no. 9).

Runeson, S., and Frykholm, G. (1981). Visual perception in lifted weight. *Journal of Experimental Psychology: Human Perception and Performance* 7: 733–40.

(1983). Kinematic specification of dynamics as an information basis for person and action perception: Expectation, gender, recognition, and deceptive intention. *Journal of Experimental Psychology: General* 4: 585–615.

Russell, B. (1940). *An inquiry into meaning and truth*. London: Allen and Unwin.

Russell, C. L., Bard, K. A., and Adamson, L. A. (1997). Social referencing by young chimpanzees (*Pan troglodytes*). *Journal of Comparative Psychology* 111: 185–93.

Russell, J. (1994). Agency and early mental development. In *The body and the self*, ed. J. Bermudez, A. J. Marcel and N. Eilan. Cambridge, MA: MIT Press.

Russon, A. E. (1997). Exploiting the expertise of others. In *Machiavellian intelligence II*. ed. A. Whiten and R. W. Byrne. Cambridge: Cambridge University Press.

Ryan, J. (1974). Early language development: towards a communicational analysis. In *The integration of a child into a social world*, ed. M. P. M. Richards, pp. 185–213. Cambridge: Cambridge University Press.

Saarni, C., and Harris, P. L. (1989). *Children's understanding of emotion*. New York: Cambridge University Press.

Sacks, O. (1995). *An anthropologist on Mars*. London: Picador.

Sagi, A., and Hoffman, M. L. (1976). Empathic distress in the newborn. *Developmental Psychology* 12: 175–6.

Sammons, W. A. H. (1989). *The self-calmed baby*. Boston: Little, Brown, and Co.

Saper, B. C. (1996). Role of the cerebral cortex and striatum in emotional motor response. In *The emotional motor system*, eds. G. Holstege, R. Bandler and C. B. Saper, pp. 537–50. Amsterdam: Elsevier.

Savage-Rumbaugh, E. S., Rumbaugh, D. M., and Boysen, S. T. (1978). Symbolic communication between two chimpanzees (*Pan troglodytes*). *Science* 201: 641–4.

Savage-Rumbaugh, S. (1990). Language as a cause-effect communication system. *Philosophical Psychology* 3: 55–76.

Scarr, S., and McCartney, K. (1983). How people make their own environments: a theory of genotype → environment effects. *Child Development* 54: 424–35.

Schaffer, H. R. (ed.) (1977). *Studies in mother–infant interaction*, London: Academic Press.

(1984). *The child's entry into a social world*. London: Academic Press.

Schanberg, S. M., and Field, T. N. (1987). Sensory deprivation, stress and supplemental stimulation in the rat pupu and preterm neonate. *Child Development* 58: 1431–47.

Scheerer, M., Rothmann, E., and Goldstein, K. (1945). A case of 'idiot savant': an experimental study of personality organisation. *Psychological Monographs* 58 (269): 1–63.

Schieffelin, B., and Ochs, E. (1986). *Language socialization across cultures*. Cambridge: Cambridge University Press.

Schore, A. N. (1994). *Affect regulation and the origin of the self*. Hillsdale, NJ: Erlbaum.

Schutz, A. (1945). On multiple realities. *Philosophical and Phenomenological Research* 5: 533–76.

Scollon, R. (1979). An unzippered condensation of a dissertation on child language. In *Developmental pragmatics*, ed. E. Ochs and B. B. Schieffelin, pp. 215–27. New York: Academic Press.

Searle, J. R. (1969). *Speech acts*. Cambridge and New York: Cambridge University Press.

(1980). Minds, brains, and programs. *Behavioral and Brain Sciences* 3: 417–57.

Seidenberg, M. S. (1986). Evidence from great apes concerning the biological basis of language. In *Language learning and concept acquisition*, ed. W. Demopoulos and A. Marras, pp. 29–53. Norwood, NJ: Ablex.

Seidenberg, M. S., and Petitto, L. A. (1979). Signing behavior in apes: a critical review. *Cognition* 7: 177–215.

Shantz, C. U. (1975). Social cognition. In *Handbook of child psychology*, vol. III. *Cognitive development*, ed. J. H. Flavell and E. M. Markman, pp. 495–555. New York: Wiley.

Shatz, M., and O'Reilly, A. (1990). Conversational or communicative skill? A reassessment of two-year-olds' behaviour in miscommunication episodes. *Journal of Child Language* 17: 131–46.

Sherrington, C. S. (1906). *The integrative action of the nervous system*. New Haven: Yale University Press.

Sherry, D. F., and Galef, B. G., Jr (1984). Cultural transmission without imitation: milk bottle opening by birds. *Animal Behaviour* 32: 937.

Shotter, J. (1974). The development of personal powers. In *The integration of a child into a social world*, ed. M. P. M. Richards, pp. 215–44. Cambridge: Cambridge University Press.

(1990). *Knowing of the third kind*. Utrecht: ISOR/University of Utrecht.

Sigman, M., Kasari, C., Kwon, J.-H., and Yirmiya, N. (1992). Responses to the negative emotions of others by autistic, mentally retarded, and normal children. *Child Development* 63: 796–807.

Sigman, M., and Ungerer, J. (1981). Sensorimotor skills and language comprehension in autistic children. *Journal of Abnormal Child Psychology* 9: 149–65.

(1984). Attachment behaviors in autistic children. *Journal of Autism and Developmental Disorders* 14: 231–43.

(1984). Cognitive and language skills in autistic, mentally retarded, and normal children. *Developmental Psychology* 20: 293–302.

Simion, F., Valenza, E., Umiltà, C., Mori, S., and Dalla Barba, B. (1996). Face preference at birth is subcortically mediated. Poster presented at the Biennial International Conference on Infant Studies, Providence, USA, April.

Simner, M. L. (1971). Newborn's response to the cry of another infant. *Developmental Psychology* 5: 136–50.

Simpson, M. J. A., Simpson, A. E., Hooley, J., and Zunz, M. (1981). Infant-related influences on birth intervals in rhesus monkeys. *Nature* 290: 49–51.

Singer, M., Haldorson, M., Lear, J. C., and Andrusiak, P. (1992). Validation of causal bridging inferences in discourse understanding. *Journal of Memory and Language* 31: 507–24.

Skinner, B. F. (1953). *Science and human behavior*. New York: Macmillan.

Slater, A. (1995). Individual differences in infancy and later IQ. *Journal of Child Psychology and Psychiatry* 36: 69–112.

Slomkowski, C. L., and Dunn, J. (1992). Arguments and relationships within the family: differences in children's disputes with mother and sibling. *Developmental Psychology* 28: 919–24.

Smith, A. (1759). *The theory of moral sentiments*. Glasgow (6th edn 1790). Oxford: Clarendon, 1976 (reprint, Indianapolis: Liberty Fund, 1984).

Smith, I. M. (1995). Imitation and gestural representation in autism. Poster presented at Society for Research in Child Development, Indianapolis, March 30–April 2.
Smith, I. M., and Bryson, S. E. (1994). Imitation and action in autism: a critical review. *Psychological Bulletin* 116: 259–73.
Sorce, J. F., Emde, R. N., Campos, J. J., and Klinnert, M. D. (1985). Maternal emotional signaling: its effect on the visual cliff behavior of 1-year-olds. *Developmental Psychology* 21: 195–200.
Sostek, A. M., Vietze, P., Zaslow, M., Kreiss, L., van der Waals, F., and Rubinstein, D. (1981). Social context in caregiver–infant interaction: A film study of Fais and the United States. In *Culture and early interactions*, eds. T. M. Field, A. M. Sostek, P. Vietze and P. H. Leiderman, pp. 21–40. Hillsdale, NJ: Erlbaum.
Spence, K. W. (1937). Experimental studies of learning and higher mental processes in infra-human primates. *Psychological Bulletin* 34: 806–50.
Sperry, R. W. (1950). The neural basis of the spontaneous optokinetic response produced by visual inversion. *Journal of Comparative and Physiological Psychology* 43: 482–9.
(1952). Neurology and the mind-brain problem. *American Scientist* 40: 291–312.
Spiker, D., and Ricks, M. (1984). Visual self-recognition in autistic children: Developmental relationships. *Child Development* 55: 214–25.
Spitz, R. A. (1965). *The first year of life*. New York: International Universities Press.
Sroufe, L. A. (1996). *Emotional development*. Cambridge: Cambridge University Press.
Stein, B. E., and Meredith, M. A. (1993). *The merging of the senses*. Cambridge, MA: MIT Press.
Stein, B. E., Meredith, M., and Wallace, M. T. (1994). Development and neural basis of multisensory integration. In *The development of intersensory perception*, ed. D. J. Lewkowicz and R. Lickliter, pp. 81–105. Hillsdale, NJ: Erlbaum.
Stern, D. N. (1971). A micro-analysis of mother–infant interaction: behaviors regulating social contact between a mother and her three-and-a-half-month-old twins. *Journal of American Academy of Child Psychiatry* 10: 501–17.
(1974). The goal and structure of mother–infant play. *Journal of the American Academy of Child Psychiatry* 13: 402–21.
(1984). Affect atttunement. In *Frontiers of infant psychiatry*, vol. II, ed. J. D. Call, E. Galenson and R. L. Tyson, pp. 3–14. New York: Basic Books.
(1985). *The interpersonal world of the infant*. New York: Basic Books.
(1990). Joy and satisfaction in infancy. In *Pleasure beyond the pleasure principle*, ed. R. A. Glick and S. Bone, pp. 13–25. Newhaven, CT: Yale University Press.
(1993). The role of feelings for an interpersonal self. In *The perceived self*, ed. U. Neisser, pp. 205–15. New York: Cambridge University Press.
(1996). *The motherhood constellation*. New York: Basic Books.
Stern, D. N., Beebe, B., Jaffe, J., and Bennett, S. L. (1977). The infant's stimulus world during social interaction: a study of caregiver behaviors with particular reference to repetition and timing. In *Studies in mother–infant interaction*, ed. H. R. Schaffer, pp. 177–202 . New York: Academic Press.
Stern, D. N., and Gibbon, J. (1980). Temporal expectancies of social behaviours

in mother–infant play. In *Origins of infant social responsiveness*, ed. E. Thoman, pp. 409–29. Hillsdale, NJ: Erlbaum.

Stern, D. N., Hofer, L., Haft, W., and Dore, J. (1985). Affect attunement: the sharing of feeling states between mother and infant by means of intermodal fluency. In *Social perception in infants*, ed. T. M. Field and N. A. Fox, pp. 249–68. Norwood, NJ: Ablex.

Stern, D. N., Jaffe, J., Beebe, B., and Bennett, S. L. (1974). Vocalization in unison and alternation: two modes of communication within the mother–infant dyad. *Annals of the New York Academy of Science* 263: 89–100.

Stern, D. N., Spieker, S., and MacKain, K. (1982). Intonation contours as signals in maternal speech to prelinguistic infants. *Developmental Psychology* 18: 727–35.

Still, A., and Costall, A. (1991). *Against cognitivism*. New York: Harvester and Wheatsheaf.

Stolerow, R. D., Brandhoft, B., and Attwood, G. E. (1983). Intersubjectivity on psychoanalytic treatment. *Bulletin of the Menninger Clinic* 47(2): 117–28.

Stone, W. L., Lemanek, K. L., Fishel, P. T., Fernandez, M. C., and Altemeier, W. A. (1990). Play and imitation skills in the diagnosis of autism in young children. *Pediatrics* 86: 267–72.

Stout, G. F. (1903/1915). *The groundwork of psychology*. London: New Tutorial Press.

Strack, E., Martin, L. L., and Stepper, S. (1988). Inhibiting and facilitating conditions of the human smile: a non-obstrusive test of the facial feedback hypothesis. *Journal of Personality and Social Psychology* 54: 768–77.

Stratton, P. (1982). Rhythmic functions in the newborn. In *Psychobiology of the Human Newborn*, ed. P. Stratton, pp. 119–45. New York: Wiley.

Strawson, P. F. (1959). *Individuals: an essay in descriptive metaphysics*. London: Methuen.

Sullivan, H. S. (1953). *The interpersonal theory of psychiatry*. New York: Norton.

Sullivan, M. W., Lewis, M., and Alessandri, S. M. (1992). Cross-age stability in emotional expressions during learning and extinction. *Developmental Psychology* 28(1): 58–63.

Super, C. M., and Harkness, S. (1986). The developmental niche: a conceptualization at the interface of child and culture. *International Journal of Behavioral Development* 9: 545–69.

Super, C. M., Harkness, S., van Tijen, N., van der Vlugt, E., Fintelman, M., and Dikstra, J. (1996). The three R's of Dutch childrearing and the socialization of infant arousal. In *Parents' cultural belief systems*, ed. S. Harkness and C. M. Super, pp. 447–66. New York: Guilford Press.

Sykoutris, I. (1936). *Aristotelous peri poietikis* (Aristotle's Poetics). Athens: Estia.

Tager-Flusberg, H., and Anderson, M. (1991). The development of contingent discourse ability in autistic children. *Journal of Child Psychology and Psychiatry and Allied Disciplines* 32: 1123.

Tatam, J. (1974). The effects of an inappropriate partner on infant sociability. MA thesis, University of Edinburgh.

Taylor, C. (1989). *Sources of the self*. Cambridge, MA: Harvard University Press.

ten Cate, C. (1994). Perceptual mechanisms in imprinting and song learning. In *Causal mechanisms of behavioural development*, ed. J. A. Hogan and J. J. Bolhuis, pp. 116–46. Cambridge: Cambridge University Press.

Thatcher, M. (1977). An application of Piaget's theory to autistic children. Doctoral dissertation, California Institute of Asian Studies. *Dissertation Abstracts International* 38: 919B.

Thelen, E., and Smith, L. B. (1994). *A dynamic systems approach to the development of cognition and action.* Cambridge, MA: MIT Press.

Thiels, E., Cramer, C. P., and Alberts, J. R. (1988). Behavioral interactions rather than milk availability determine decline in milk intake of weanling rats. *Physiology and Behavior* 42: 507– 15.

Thompson, R. A. (1987). Empathy and emotional understanding: the early development of empathy. In *Empathy and its development*, ed. N. Eisenberg and J. Strayer, pp. 119–45. New York: Cambridge University Press.

(1993). Socioemotional development: enduring issues and new challenges. *Developmental Review* 13: 372–402.

(1998). *Early brain development and early intervention.* Lincoln: University of Nebraska Press.

(1998). Early sociopersonality development. In *Handbook of child psychology* (5th edn), vol. III, *Social, emotional, and personality development*, ed. N. Eisenberg, pp. 25–104. New York: Wiley.

Thorpe, W. H. (1963). *Learning and instinct in animals.* London: Methuen.

Tönnies, F. (1912). *Gemeinschaft und Gesellschaft.* Berlin: Karl Curtius.

Tomasello, M. (1988). The role of joint attention in early language development. *Language Sciences* 11: 69–88.

(1990). Cultural transmission in the tool use and communicatory signaling of chimpanzees? In *'Language' and intelligence in monkeys and apes*, ed. S. T. Parker and K. R. Gibson, pp. 274–311. Cambridge: Cambridge University Press.

(1992). The social bases of language acquisition. *Social Development* 1: 67–87.

(1993). On the interpersonal origins of self-concept. In *The perceived self*, ed. U. Neisser, pp. 174–84. Cambridge: Cambridge University Press.

(1994). The question of chimpanzee culture. In *Chimpanzee cultures*, ed. R. W. Wrangham, W. C. McGrew, F. B. M. de Waal and P. G. Heltne, pp. 301–17. Cambridge, MA: Harvard University Press.

(1995a). Pragmatic contexts for early verb learning. In *Beyond names for things*, ed. M. Tomasello and W. E. Merriman, pp. 115–46. Hillsdale, NJ: Erlbaum.

(1995b). Joint attention as social cognition. In *Joint attention*, ed. C. Moore and P. Dunham, pp. 103–30. Hillsdale, NJ: Erlbaum.

(1996). The cultural roots of language. In *Communicating meaning*, ed. B. M. Velichkovsky and D. M. Rumbaugh, pp. 275–307. Mahwah, NJ: Erlbaum.

Tomasello, M., and Akhtar, N. (1995). Two-year-olds use pragmatic cues to differentiate reference to objects and actions. *Cognitive Development* 10: 201–24.

Tomasello, M., and Barton, M. (1994). Acquiring words in non-ostensive contexts. *Developmental Psychology* 30: 639–50.

Tomasello, M., and Call, J. (1994). Social cognition of monkeys and apes. *Yearbook of Physical Anthropology* 37: 273–305.

(1997). *Primate cognition.* Oxford: Oxford University Press.

Tomasello, M., Davis-Dasilva, M., Camak, L., and Bard, K. (1987). Observational learning of tool-use by young chimpanzees. *Human Evolution* 2: 175–83.

Tomasello, M., and Farrar, J. (1986). Joint attention and early language. *Child Development* 57: 1454–63.

Tomasello, M., Farrar, M. J., and Dines, J. (1984). Children's speech revisions for a familiar and an unfamiliar adult. *Journal of Speech and Hearing Research* 27: 359–63.

Tomasello, M., and Kruger, A. C. (1992). Acquiring verbs in ostensive and nonostensive contexts. *Journal of Child Language* 19: 311–33.

Tomasello, M., Kruger, A. C., and Ratner, H. H. (1993). Cultural learning. *Behavioral and Brain Sciences* 16: 495–552.

Tomasello, M., Strosberg, R., and Akhtar, N. (1996). Eighteen-month-old children learn words in non-ostensive contexts. *Journal of Child Language* 23: 157–76.

Tomasello, M., and Todd, J. (1983). Joint attention and lexical acquisition style. *First Language* 4: 197–212.

Tomkins, S. S. (1962). *Affect, imagery, consciousness: the positive affects,* vol. I. New York: Springer.

(1979). Script theory: differential magnification of affects. In *Nebraska Symposium on Motivation 1978,* vol. XXVI, pp. 201–36. Lincoln and London: University of Nebraska Press.

(1980). Affect as amplification: some modifications in theory. In *Emotion,* ed. R. Plutchik and H. Kellerman, pp. 141–64. New York: Academic Press.

Trehub, S. E. (1990). The perception of musical patterns by human infants: the provision of similar patterns by their parents. In *Comparative perception,* vol. I, ed. M. A. Berkley and W. C. Stebbins, pp. 429–59. New York: Wiley.

Trehub, S. E., Trainor, L. J., and Unyk, A. M. (1993). Music and speech processing in the first year of life. *Advances in Child Development and Behaviour* 24: 1–35.

Trevarthen, C. (1974a). Conversations with a two-month-old. *New Scientist* 2: 230–5.

(1974b). The psychobiology of speech development. In *Language and brain,* ed. E. H. Lenneberg, pp. 570–85. Boston: Neurosciences Research Program.

(1977). Descriptive analyses of infant communicative behavior. In *Studies in mother–infant interaction,* ed. H. R. Schaffer, pp. 227–70. London: Academic Press.

(1978). Modes of perceiving and modes of acting. In *Psychological modes of perceiving and processing information,* ed. J. H. Pick, pp. 99–136. Hillsdale, NJ: Erlbaum.

(1979a). Communication and cooperation in early infancy: a description of primary intersubjectivity. In *Before speech,* ed. M. Bullowa, pp. 321–47. New York: Cambridge University Press.

(1979b). Instincts for human understanding and for cultural cooperation: their development in infancy. In *Human ethology,* ed. M. von Cranach, K. Foppa, W. Lepenies and D. Ploog, pp. 530–71. Cambridge: Cambridge University Press.

(1980). The foundations of intersubjectivity: development of interpersonal and cooperative understanding in infants. In *The social foundations of language and thought: essays in honor of J. S. Bruner,* ed. D. Olson, pp. 316–42. New York: Norton.

(1982a). Basic patterns of psychogenetic change in infancy. In *Regressions in mental development,* ed. T. Bever, pp. 7–46. Hillsdale, NJ: Erlbaum.

(1982b). The primary motives for cooperative understanding. In *Social cognition,* ed. G. Butterworth and P. Light, pp. 77–103. London: Harvester Press.

(1983). Interpersonal abilities of infants as generators for transmission of language and culture. In *The behavior of human infants,* ed. A. Oliverio and M. Zappella, pp. 145–76. New York: Plenum.

(1984a). Biodynamic structures, cognitive correlates of motive sets and development of motives in infants. In *Cognition and motor processes*, ed. W. Prinz and A. F. Saunders, pp. 327–50. Berlin, Heidelberg and New York: Springer Verlag.

(1984b). Emotions in infancy: regulators of contacts and relationships with persons. In *Approaches to emotion*, ed. K. Scherer and P. Ekman, pp. 129–57. Hillsdale, NJ: Erlbaum.

(1985a). Facial expressions of emotion in mother–infant interaction. *Human Neurobiology* 4: 21–32.

(1985b). Neuroembryology and the development of perceptual mechanisms. In *Human growth* (2nd edn), ed. F. Falkner and J. M. Tanner, pp. 301–83. New York: Plenum.

(1986a). Development of intersubjective motor control in infants. In *Motor development in children*, ed. M. G. Wade and H. T. A. Whiting, pp. 209–61. Dordrecht: Marthinus Nijhof.

(1986b). Form, significance and psychological potential of hand gestures of infants. In *The Biological foundation of gestures*, ed. J.-L. Nespoulous, P. Perron and A. R. Lecours, pp. 149–202. Hillsdale, NJ: Erlbaum.

(1987a). Infancy, mind in. In *Oxford companion to the mind*, ed. R. Gregory, pp. 362–8. Oxford: Oxford University Press.

(1987b). Sharing makes sense: intersubjectivity and the making of an infant's meaning. In *Language topics: essays in honour of Michael Halliday*, ed. R. Steele and T. Threadgold. Amsterdam and Philadelphia: John Benjamins.

(1988). Universal cooperative motives: how infants begin to know the language and skills of the culture of their parents. In *Acquiring culture*, ed. G. Jahoda and I. M. Lewis, pp. 37–90. Beckenham, Kent: Croom Helm.

(1989). Les relations entre autisme et développement socioculturel normal. In *Autisme et troubles du développement global de l'enfant*, ed. G. Lelord, J. P. Muh, M. Petit and D. Sauvage. Paris: Expansion Scientifique Française.

(1990a). Growth and education in the hemispheres. In *Brain circuits and functions of the mind: essays in honour of Roger Sperry*, ed. C. Trevarthen, pp. 334–57. New York: Cambridge University Press.

(1990b). Signs before speech. In *The semiotic web*, ed. T. A. Sebeok and J. Umiker-Sebeok, pp. 689–755. Berlin and New York: Mouton de Gruyter.

(1992). An infant's motive for speaking and thinking in the culture. In *The dialogical alternative*, ed. A. H. Wold, pp. 99–138. Oslo: Scandinavian University Press.

(1993a). The function of emotions in early infant communication and development. In *New perspectives in early communicative development*, ed. J. Nadel and L. Camaioni, pp. 48–81. London: Routledge.

(1993b). The self born in intersubjectivity: an infant communicating. In *The perceived self*, ed. U. Neisser, pp. 121–73. New York: Cambridge University Press.

(1993c). Predispositions to cultural learning in young infants. Commentary. *Behavioral and Brain Sciences* 16: 534–5.

(1994). Infant semiosis. In *Origins of semiosis*, ed. W. Nöth, pp. 219–52. Berlin: Mouton de Gruyter.

(1996). Lateral asymmetries in infancy: implications for the development of the hemispheres. *Neuroscience and Biobehavioral Reviews* 20: 571–86.

(1997a). Foetal and neonatal psychology: intrinsic motives and learning behaviour. In *Advances in perinatal medicine*, ed. F. Cockburn. (Proceedings of the XVth European Congress of Perinatal Medicine, Glasgow 10–13 September 1996.)

(1997b). Macmurray's 'mother and child': defining the infant's natural place in the field of the personal. In *The primacy of persons as agents in relationships*, ed. H. A. Carson. Humanities Press International.

(1998a). The nature of motives for human consciousness. *Psychology: The Journal of the Hellenic Psychological Society* (Special issue *The place of psychology in contemporary sciences*, Part 2, ed. T. Velli) 4(3): 187–221.

(1998b). Language development: mechanisms in the brain. In *Encyclopedia of neuroscience* (2nd edn, with CD-ROM), ed. G. Adelman and B. H. Smith. Amsterdam: Elsevier Science.

Trevarthen, C., and Aitken, K. J. (1994). Brain development, infant communication, and empathy disorders: intrinsic factors in child mental health. *Development and Psychopathology* 6: 597–633.

Trevarthen, C., Aitken, K. J., Papoudi, D., and Robarts, J. Z. (1998). *Children with autism*. London: Jessica Kingsley.

Trevarthen, C., and Hubley, P. (1978). Secondary intersubjectivity: confidence, confiding, and acts of meaning in the first year. In *Action, gesture, and symbol*, ed. A. Lock, pp. 183–229. London: Academic Press.

Trevarthen, C., Kokkinaki, T., and Fiamenghi, G. A. Jr. (1998). What infants' imitations communicate: With mothers, with fathers and with peers. In *Imitation in infancy*, ed. J. Nadel and G. Butterworth. Cambridge: Cambridge University Press.

Trevarthen, C., and Logotheti, K. (1987). First symbols and the nature of human knowledge. In *Symbolisme et connaissance/symbolism and knowledge*, ed. J. Montangero, A. Tryphon and S. Dionnet, pp. 65–92. Cahier no. 8, Jean Piaget Archives Fondation. Geneva: Jean Piaget Archives Fondation.

Trevarthen, C., Murray, L., and Hubley, P. A. (1981). Psychology of infants. In *Scientific foundations of clinical paediatrics* (2nd edn), ed. J. Davis and J. Dobbing, pp. 211–74. London: Heinemann Medical.

Trillmich, F. (1990). The behavioural ecology of maternal effort in fur seals and sea lions. *Behaviour* 114: 3–20.

Trivers, R. L. (1974). Parent–offspring conflict. *American Zoologist* 14: 249–64.

Tronick, E. Z. (1989). Emotions and emotional communication in infants. *American Psychologist* 44: 112–19.

Tronick, E. Z., Als, H., and Adamson, L. (1979). Structure of early face-to-face communicative interactions. In *Before speech*, ed. M. Bullowa, pp. 349–72. Cambridge: Cambridge University Press.

Tronick, E., Als, H., Adamson, L., Wise, S., and Brazelton, T. B. (1978). The infant's response to entrapment between contradictory messages in face-to-face interaction. *Journal of the American Academy of Child and Adolescent Psychiatry* 17: 1–13.

Tronick, E. Z., Als H., and Brazelton T. B. (1980). Monadic phases: a structural description analysis of infant–mother face-to-face interaction. *Merrill-Palmer Quarterly* 26: 3–24.

Tronick, E. Z., and Cohn, J. F. (1989). Infant–mother face-to-face interaction: Age and gender differences in coordination and occurrence of miscoordination. *Child Development* 60: 85–92.

Tronick, E. Z., and Field, T. (eds.) (1986). *Maternal depression and infant disturbance*. San Francisco: Jossey Bass.

Tronick, E. Z., Morelli, G. A., and Winn, S. (1987). Multiple caretaking of Efe (Pygmy) infants. *American Anthropologist* 89: 96–106.

Tronick, E. Z., and Weinberg, M. K. (1997). Depressed mothers and infants: failure to form dyadic states of consciousness. In *Postpartum depression and child development*, ed. L. Murray and P. J. Cooper, pp. 54–81. New York: Guilford Press.

Tryon, A. S., and Keane, S. P. (1986). Promoting imitative play through generalised observational learning in autistic-like children. *Journal of Abnormal Child Psychology* 14: 537–49.

Tucker, D. M. (1992). Developing emotions and cortical networks. In *Minnesota symposium on child psychology*, vol. XXIV, *Developmental behavioral neuroscience*, ed. M. R. Gunnar and C. A. Nelson, pp. 75–128. Hillsdale NJ: Erlbaum.

Turner, F., and Pöppel, E. (1983). The neural lyre: poetic meter, the brain and time. *Poetry*, August 1983, 277 (reprinted in Turner, F. (1985) *Natural classicism: essays on literature and science*. New York: Paragon House).

Turner, V. (1982). *From ritual to theatre*. New York: Performing Arts Journal Publications.

Turney, T. H. (1978). Human neonatal and infant behavioral assessment scales being applied to chimpanzees. *Laboratory Primate Newsletter* 17: 14–15.

Tymchuk, A. J., Simmons, J. Q., and Neafsey, S. (1977). Intellectual characteristics of adolescent childhood psychotics with high verbal ability. *Journal of Mental Deficiency Research* 21: 133–8.

Uzgiris, I. C. (1981). Two functions of imitation during infancy. *International Journal of Behavioral Development* 4: 1–12.

Valentine, C. W. (1930). The psychology of imitation with special reference to early childhood. *British Journal of Psychology* 21(2): 8–132.

van Hooff, J. A. R. A. M. (1972). A comparative approach to the phylogeny of laughter and smiling. In *Nonverbal communication*, ed. R. A. Hinde, pp. 209–41. Cambridge: Cambridge University Press.

(1973). A structural analysis of the social behavior of a semi-captive group of chimpanzees. In *Social communication and movement*, ed. M. V. Cranach and I. Vine, pp. 75–162. New York: Academic Press.

van Lawick-Goodall, J. (1968a). A preliminary report on expressive movements and communication in the Gombe Stream chimpanzees. In *Primate studies in adaptation and variability*, ed. P. Jay, pp. 313–74. New York: Holt, Rinehart, and Winston.

(1968b). Behaviour of free-living chimpanzees of the Gombe Stream area. *Animal Behavior Monographs* 1: 163–311.

Vedeler, D. (1991). Infant intentionality as object directedness: an alternative to representationalism. *Journal for the Theory of Social Behaviour* 21(2): 431–48.

Veikos, T. (1988). *Oi Prosokratikoi* (Pre-Socratics). Athens: Zacharopoulos.

Veira, Y., and Bard, K. A. (1994). Developmental milestones for chimpanzees raised in a responsive care nursery. *American Journal of Primatology* 33: 246.

Vieth, W., Curio, E., and Ernst, U. (1980). The adaptive significance of avian mobbing. III Cultural transmission of enemy recognition in blackbirds: cross-species tutoring and properties of learning. *Animal Behaviour* 28: 1217–29.

Vinter, A. (1986). The role of movement in eliciting early imitations. *Child Development* 57: 66–71.

Visalberghi, E., and Fragaszy, D. M. (1990). Do monkeys ape? In *'Language' and intelligence in monkeys and apes*, ed. S. T. Parker and K. R. Gibson, pp. 247–73. Cambridge: Cambridge University Press.

Volosinov, V. N. (1986). *Marxism and the philosophy of language*. Cambridge, MA: Harvard University Press.

von Frisch, K. (1967). *The dance language and orientation of bees*. Cambridge, MA: Harvard University Press.

von Holst, E. and Mittelstaedt, H. (1950). Das Reafferenzprinzip. *Naturwissenschaften* 37: 256–72.

Vrana, S. R., and Lang, P. J. (1990). Fear imagery and the startle probe reflex. *Journal of Abnormal Psychology* 97: 487–91.

Vygotsky, L. S. (1934/1986). *Thought and language* (rev. trans. by A. Kozulin). Cambridge, MA: MIT Press.

(1978). Internalization of higher psychological functions. In *Mind in society*, ed. M. Cole, V. John-Steiner, S. Scribner and E. Souberman, pp. 52–67. Cambridge, MA: Harvard University Press.

Wallis, G., and Rolls, E. T. (1996). A model of invariant object recognition in the visual system. Pre-publication paper, Department of Experimental Psychology, University of Oxford.

Wallon, H. (1928). La maladresse. *Journal de Psychologie* 25: 61–78 (reprinted in *Enfance*, Special Issue on Henri Wallon, vol. VII, pp. 72–84, 1985).

Walton, G. E., Bower, N. J. A., and Bower, T. G. R. (1992). Recognition of familiar faces by newborns. *Infant Behavior and Development* 15: 265–9.

Watson J. S. (1972). Smiling, cooing and the game. *Merrill-Palmer Quarterly* 18: 323–39.

Watts, D. P. (1984). Composition and variability of mountain gorilla diets in the central Virungas. *American Journal of Primatology* 7: 323–56.

Weinberg, M. K., and Tronick, E. Z. (1994). Beyond the face: an empirical study of infant affective configurations of facial, vocal, gestural and regulatory behaviors. *Child Development* 65: 1503–15.

(1996). Infant affective reactions to the resumption of maternal interaction after the still-face. *Child Development* 67: 905–14.

Weisenburger, J. L. (1976). A choice of words: two-year-old speech from a situational point of view. *Journal of Child Language* 3: 275–81.

Weisner, T. S. (1984). Ecocultural niches of middle childhood: a cross-cultural perspective. In *Development during middle childhood*, ed. W. A. Collins, pp. 335–69. Washington, DC: National Academy Press.

(1987). Socialization for parenthood in sibling caretaking societies. In *Parenting across the lifespan: biosocial dimensions*, eds. J. B. Lancaster, J. Altmann, A. S. Rossi and L. R. Sherrod, pp. 237–70. New York: Aldine de Gruyter.

Wellman, H. M. (1990). *The child's theory of mind*. Cambridge, MA: MIT Press.

Wellman, H. M., and Estes, D. (1986). Early understanding of mental entities: A reexamination of childhood realism. *Child Development* 57: 910–23.

Werker, J. F., and Polka, L. (1993). The ontogeny and developmental significance of language-specific phonetic perception. In *Developmental neurocognition*, ed. B. de Boysson-Bardies *et al.*, pp. 275–88. Dordrecht: Kluwer.

Werker, J. F., and Tees, R. C. (1984). Cross-language speech perception: evidence for perceptual reorganization during the first year of life. *Infant Behavior and Development* 7: 49–63.

Werner, H. (1948). *Comparative psychology of mental development*. Chicago: Follett.

Werner, H., and Kaplan, B. (1963/1984). *Symbol formation*. Hillsdale, NJ: Erlbaum.

Wertheimer, M. (1912). Experimentelle Studien über das Sehen von Bewegung. *Zeitschrift für Psychologie* 61: 161–265.

Wertsch, J. V. (1991). *Voices of the mind: a sociocultural approach to mediated action*. Cambridge, MA: Harvard University Press.

(1992). A dialogue on message structure: Rommetveit and Bakhtin. In *The dialogical alternative,* ed. A. H. Wold, pp. 65–76. Oslo: Scandinavian University Press.

Wetherby, A. M., and Prutting, C. A. (1984). Profiles of communicative and cognitive-social abilities in autistic children. *Journal of Speech and Hearing Research* 27: 364–77.

White, S. H. (1992). G. Stanley Hall: from philosophy to developmental psychology. *Developmental Psychology* 28(1): 25–34.

Whiten, A. (1988). From literal to non-literal social knowledge in human ontogeny and primate phylogeny. Paper presented at Primate Society of Great Britain meeting on Social Knowledge in Primates.

(1989). Transmission mechanisms in primate cultural evolution. *Trends in Ecology and Evolution* 4: 61–2.

(1991). *Natural theories of mind.* Oxford: Basil Blackwell.

(1993a). Evolving a theory of mind: the nature of non-verbal mentalism in other primates. In *Understanding other minds,* eds. S. Baron-Cohen, H. Tager-Flusberg and D. J. Cohen, pp. 367–96. Oxford: Oxford University Press.

(1993b). The evolution and development of emotional states, emotional expressions and emotion-reading in human and non-human primates. Unpublished manuscript, University of St Andrews. Presented at Mellon Symposium on Emotions, a Bio-Cultural Perspective, Emory University.

(1994). Grades of mindreading. In *Children's early understanding of mind,* ed. C. Lewis and P. Mitchell, pp. 47–70. Hillsdale, NJ: Erlbaum.

(1996a). Imitation, pretence and mindreading: secondary representation in comparative primatology and developmental psychology. In *Reaching into thought,* ed. A. Russon, K. A. Bard, and S. T. Parker. Cambridge: Cambridge University Press.

(1996b). When does smart behaviour reading become mindreading? In *Theories of theories of mind,* ed. P. Carruthers and P. K. Smith. Cambridge: Cambridge University Press.

(1997). The Machiavellian mindreader. In *Machiavellian intelligence II,* ed. A. Whiten and R. W. Byrne. Cambridge: Cambridge University Press.

(in press, a). Evolutionary and developmental origins of the mindreading system. In *Piaget, evolution and development,* ed. J. Langer and M. Killen. Hove: Erlbaum.

(in press, b). Chimpanzee cognition and the question of mental re-representation. In *Metarepresentation,* ed. D. Sperber. Oxford: Oxford University Press.

Whiten, A. (ed.) (1991). *Natural theories of mind.* Oxford: Basil Blackwell.

Whiten, A., and Byrne, R. W. (1988a). Tactical deception in primates. *Behavioral and Brain Sciences* 11: 233–73.

(1988b). The manipulation of attention in primate tactical deception. In *Machiavellian intelligence,* eds. R. W. Byrne and A. Whiten, pp. 211–23. Oxford: Oxford University Press.

(1991). The emergence of metarepresentation in human ontogeny and primate phylogeny. In *Natural theories of mind,* ed. A. Whiten, pp. 267–81. Oxford: Basil Blackwell.

Whiten, A., and Custance, D. (1996). Studies of imitation in chimpanzees and children. In *Social learning in animals,* ed. C. M. Heyes and B. G. Galef, pp. 291–318. San Diego: Academic Press.

Whiten, A., Custance, D. M., Gomez, J.-C., Teixidor, P., and Bard, K. A. (1996). Imitative learning of artificial fruit processing in children (*Homo sapiens*) and chimpanzees (*Pan troglodytes*). *Journal of Comparative Psychology* 110: 3–14.

Whiten, A., and Ham, R. (1992). On the nature and evolution of imitation in the animal kingdom: reappraisal of a century of research. In *Advances in the study of behavior*, ed. P. J. B. Slater, J. S. Rosenblatt, C. Beer and M. Milinski, pp. 239–83. San Diego: Academic Press.

Whiten, A., Irving, K., and MacIntyre, K. (1993). Can three year olds and people with autism learn to predict the consequences of false belief? Paper presented at the British Psychological Society Developmental Psychology Section Annual Conference, Birmingham.

Whiten, A., and Perner, J. (1991). Fundamental Issues in the Multidisciplinairy Study of Mindreading. In *Natural theories of mind*, ed. A. Whiten, pp. 1–18. Oxford: Basil Blackwell.

Whiting, B. B. (1980). Culture and social behavior: a model for the development of social behavior. *Ethos* 8: 95–116.

Whiting, B. B., and Edwards, C. P. (1988). *Children of different worlds*. Cambridge, MA: Harvard University Press.

Whiting, B. B., and Whiting, J. W. M. (1975). *Children of six cultures*. Cambridge, MA: Harvard University Press.

Whiting, J. W. M. (1981). Environmental constraints on infant care practices. In *Handbook of cross cultural human development*, ed. R. H. Munroe, R. L. Munroe and B. B. Whiting. New York: Garland STPM Press.

Wieman, L. A. (1976). Stress patterns of early child language. *Journal of Child Language* 3: 283–6.

Wilcox, M. J., and Webster, E. J. (1980). Early discourse behavior: an analysis of children's responses to listener feedback. *Child Development* 51: 1120–5.

Willerman, R., and Kuhl, P. K. (1996). Cross-language speech perception: Swedish, English, and Spanish speakers' perception of front rounded vowels. *Proceedings of the 1996 International Conference on Spoken Language Processing* 1: 442–5.

Wilson, E. O. (1975). *Sociobiology:*. Cambridge, MA: Harvard University Press.

(1976). Author's reply to multiple review of 'Sociobiology'. *Animal Behaviour* 24: 716–18.

Wing, L. (1978). Social, behavioural and cognitive characteristics: an epidemiological approach. In *Autism*, ed. M. Rutter and E. Schopler, pp. 27–45. London: Plenum.

(1981). Language, social and cognitive impairments in autism and severe mental retardation. *Journal of Autism and Developmental Disorders* 11: 31–44.

Wing, L., and Gould, J. (1979). Severe impairments of social interaction and associated abnormalities in children: epidemiology and classification. *Journal of Autism and Developmental Disorders* 9: 11–29.

Winnicott, D. W. (1953). Transitional objects and transitional phenomena: a study of the first not-me possession. *International Journal of Psycho-Analysis*, 59: 89–97.

(1956/1992). Primary maternal preoccupation. In *Through paediatrics to psychoanalysis*, ed. M. Masud and R. Khan, pp. 300–5. London: Hogarth Press.

(1960/1985). The theory of the parent–infant relationship. In *The maturational process and the facilitating environment*, ed. J. D. Sutherland, pp. 37–55. London: Hogarth Press.

(1962/1985). Ego integration in child development. In *The maturational process and the facilitating environment*, ed. J. D. Sutherland, pp. 56–63. London: Hogarth Press.

Winograd, T. (1985). Moving the semantic fulcrum. *Linguistics and Philosophy* 8: 91–104.

Wittgenstein, L. (1972). *Philosophical investigations*, trans. G. E. M. Anscombe. Oxford: Basil Blackwell and Mott.

Wold, A. H. (ed.) (1992). *The dialogical alternative.* Oslo: Scandinavian University Press.

Wolf, A. W., Lozoff, B., Latz, S., and Paludetto, R. (1996). Parental theories in the management of young children's sleep in Japan, Italy, and the United States. In *Parents' cultural belief systems*, ed. S. Harkness and C. M. Super, pp. 364–84. New York: Guilford Press.

Wolff, P. H. (1963). Observations on the early development of smiling. In *The determinants of infant behavior*, vol. II, ed. B. M. Foss, pp. 113–38. London: Methuen.

(1968). Serial organization of sucking in the young infant. *Pediatrics* 42: 943–56.

(1987). *Behavioral states and expression of emotions in early infancy.* Chicago: University of Chicago Press.

Wulff, S. B. (1985). The symbolic and object play of children with autism: a review. *Journal of Autism and Developmental Disorders* 15: 139–48.

Wundt, W. (1896/1969). *Outlines of psychology.* St. Clair Shores, MI: Scholarly Press.

Xu, F., and Carey, S. (1996). Infants' metaphysics: the case of numerical identity. *Cognitive Psychology* 30: 111–53.

Yerkes, R. M. (1943). *Chimpanzees.* New Haven: Yale University Press.

Youngblade, L. M., and Dunn, J. (1995). Individual differences in young children's pretend play with mother and sibling: links to relationships and understanding of other people's feelings and beliefs. *Child Development* 66: 1472–92.

Zahavi, A. (1975). Mate selection – a selection for a handicap. *Journal of Theoretical Biology* 53: 205–14.

Zahn-Waxler, C., and Kochanska, G. (1990). The origins of guilt. In *Socioemotional development*, vol. XXXVI, ed. R. Thompson, pp. 183–258. Lincoln: University of Nebraska Press.

Zahn-Waxler, C., and Radke-Yarrow, M. (1982). The development of altruism: alternative research strategies. In *The development of prosocial behavior*, ed. N. Eisenberg, pp. 109–37. New York: Academic Press.

(1990). The origins of empathic concern. *Motivation and Emotion* 14: 107–30.

Zahn-Waxler, C., Radke-Yarrow, M., Wagner, E., and Chapman, M. (1992). Development of concern for others. *Developmental Psychology* 28: 126–36.

Zahn-Waxler, C., Robinson, J. L., and Emde, R. N. (1992). The development of empathy in twins. *Developmental Psychology* 28: 1038–47.

Zajonc, R. B. (1980). Feeling and thinking. Preferences need no inferences. *American Psychologist* 35: 151–75.

(1984). On the primacy of affect. *American Psychologist* 41: 862–7.

Zazzo, R. (1957). Le problème de l'imitation chez le nouveau-né. *Enfance* 10: 135–42.

Zeitlin, M. (1996). My child is my crown: Yoruba parental theories and practices in early childhood. In *Parents' cultural belief,* ed. S. Harkness and C. M. Super, pp. 407–27. New York: Guilford Press.

Zeller, E., and Nestle, W. (1883/1980). *Historia tis Hellinikis philosophias* (History of Greek philosophy). Athens: Estia.

Zentall, T. R. (1996). An analysis of imitative learning in animals. In *Social learning in animals,* ed. C. M. Heyes and B. G. Galef, pp. 221–43. San Diego: Academic Press.

Author index

Subject index

Studies in Emotion and Social Interaction

First Series
Editors: Paul Ekman and Klaus R. Scherer

Handbook of Methods in Nonverbal Behavioral Research
Edited by Klaus R. Scherer and Paul Ekman

Structures of Social Action: Studies in Conversational Analysis
Edited by Max Atkinson and John Heritage

Interaction Structure and Strategy
Starkey Duncan, Jr., and Donald W. Fiske

Body Movement and Speech in Medical Interaction
Christian Heath

The Emotions
Nico Frijda

Conversations of Friends: Speculations on Affective Development
Edited by John M. Gottman and Jeffrey G. Parker

Judgment Studies: Design, Analysis, and Meta-analysis
Robert Rosenthal

The Individual, Communication, and Society: Essays in Memory of Gregory Bateson
Edited by Robert W. Rieber

Language and the Politics of Emotion
Edited by Catherine Lutz and Lila Abu-Lughod

Fundamentals in Nonverbal Behavior
Edited by Robert Feldman and Bernard Rimé

Gestures and Speech
Pierre J. M. Feyereisen and Jacques-Dominique de Lannoy

Landscapes of Emotion: Mapping Three Cultures of Emotion in Indonesia
Karl G. Heider

Contexts of Accommodation: Developments in Applied Sociolinguistics
Howard Giles, Justine Coupland, and Nikolas Coupland

Best Laid Schemes: The Psychology of Emotions
Keith Oatley

Interpersonal Expectations: Theory, Research, and Applications
Edited by Peter David Blanck

Emotional Contagion
Elaine Hatfield, John T. Cacioppo, and Richard L. Rapson

Exploring Affect: The Selected Writings of Silvan S. Tomkins
Edited by E. Virginia Demos

www.ingramcontent.com/pod-product-compliance
Lightning Source LLC
LaVergne TN
LVHW090257210926
848480LV00001B/54
9780521029896